MW01493756

THE PROJECT-STATE
AND ITS RIVALS

The Project-State and Its Rivals

A New History of
the Twentieth
and Twenty-First
Centuries

Charles S. Maier

HARVARD UNIVERSITY PRESS

Cambridge, Massachusetts
London, England
2023

Copyright © 2023 by the President and Fellows of Harvard College
All rights reserved
Printed in the United States of America

First printing

Library of Congress Cataloging-in-Publication Data

Names: Maier, Charles S., author.
Title: The project-state and its rivals : a new history of the twentieth
and twenty-first centuries / Charles S. Maier.
Description: Cambridge, Massachusetts : Harvard University Press, 2023. |
Includes index.
Identifiers: LCCN 2022038056 | ISBN 9780674290143 (cloth)
Subjects: LCSH: Twentieth century. | Twenty-first century. | Political
sociology. | Politics and culture—History—20th century. | Politics and
culture—History—21st century. | Politics, Practical—Social aspects.
Classification: LCC JA76 .M32528 2023 | DDC 306.209—dc23/eng/20221101
LC record available at https://lccn.loc.gov/2022038056

For Anne

Contents

Preface

This work arose as an effort to make sense of the political and economic transformations of our time. This can be a treacherous ambition: the historian's present is always changing and at times drastically. I was born a half year before World War II began in Europe. As a young but politically aware observer, I lived through episodes of the Cold War, then forty years later witnessed what seemed to be its sudden and surprising conclusion. Leave aside the digital revolution or the changes in medical science that have transformed all our lives, my adult lifetime has seen the vigorous postwar recovery of Germany and Japan, the peak of US economic and international primacy, and the legal (if not socioeconomic) dismantling of its racial hierarchies; in recent decades, the stupendous rise of Chinese national power; and, even as I send this manuscript to press in my eighties, the Russian effort to reconstitute the imperial hold it formerly exercised in Eastern Europe.

This book, however, focuses on developments that do not always spring to mind as constitutive of our times. I believe nation and territory and cultural specificities provide important coordinates for structuring historical narrative, but this book does not emphasize these markers. It is not a general survey of world history, nor a history of the nation-state system and its conflicts, nor a story of celebrated and infamous leaders, important though they have been. It bypasses the military history of the great wars, the genocides, and the development of regimes that brought early death to perhaps 200 million people of the 11 billion or so who lived during a part or all of the twentieth century. Instead, I have tried to illuminate other conflicts and forces that have successively shaped or, perhaps more precisely, allowed the evolving political outcomes of the twentieth century and the first quarter of the twenty-first.

To this end, I propose collective protagonists that are different from the heroes and villains many histories follow. I focus first on "project-states," both democratic and totalitarian, with ambitious agendas for transforming political institutions, civil society, and even mentalities. Second, I examine "resource empires," lingering formally until the 1960s and thereafter bequeathing international legacies of racial and economic inequality that still remain powerful. Third and fourth, the book discusses the transnational domains of "capital" and of the organizations supposedly devoted to disinterested "governance." My account of the last hundred-some years thus seeks to follow the evolution and changing weight of these four collective agents, sometimes working against each other, sometimes in tandem. This does not mean that our older historical categories such as democracies and dictatorships are invalid or obsolete. This is hardly the case. But reframing long-term categories of historical analysis can provide a more comprehensive sense of the changes under way for a century or more. I have felt challenged, I must confess, by Montesquieu, who argued in the mid-eighteenth century that the laws— by which he also meant institutions—had to be consistent with each other; that when one changed all must change; and that their underlying relationship was what he called "the spirit of the laws."[1] I have tried to account for our new spirit of the laws.

Are there lessons to be learned from this history? Can it be "applied" or provide us guidance for the present? My view of a historical work is that besides conveying information about the past, it should most importantly enlarge the world of the reader, somewhat as listening to a fine musical performance enhances the listener. It should provide an awareness of connectedness and difference, analogy, complexity, regularity, and contingency. Perhaps it makes readers better able to confront the policy decisions they must face; perhaps it instructively illuminates past shortsightedness, but it cannot predict which alternatives will yield success. As John Stuart Mill recognized in *A System of Logic*, it takes only one altered variable among many to make the present differ fundamentally from the past.

Still, I do think there is a lesson that this perspective on the past can provide. It is that an active project-state, an innovative economy, and disinterested governance need to remain in some balance: Without alternate sources of political agency, the project-state alone can become abusive; excessive rewards to capital will corrupt; and the prescriptions of rational governance alone remain feeble and often unaware of self-interest that may have motivated their prescriptions. The remnants of empire and the decay of republics suggest,

I believe, that societies cannot sustain good government if inequality exceeds certain boundaries; but that belief is admittedly a political one, and what those boundaries are is difficult to say. I tend to believe that institutions of governance play a generally beneficial role and deserve the authority they claim particularly in view of the climate change that challenges us all. Nonetheless, as my last chapter suggests, the claims of governance and expertise can produce their own backlash, and accommodating them in a democracy is a difficult task. In any case, if a reader wants guidance from the past outlined in this book as well as an interpretation, these rather commonplace suggestions would be my offering.

This work does not aspire to be an encompassing narrative of global developments since 1900 or even 1914. My own long-term research has centered on Western Europe and to a degree the United States, and I have focused on these areas at the expense, most likely, of doing justice to significant currents of thought and political aspirations that emanated from Latin America, Asia, and Africa. Moreover, while this book draws on my own historical reading and teaching for more than half a century, it does not claim to rest on direct immersion in the archives that exist for the countries and institutions discussed even when I have the language capacity. It does cite primary sources at points where I have undertaken previous research (findings that went into specialized articles and essays), but it rests more on the monographic investigations of other scholars. To turn around the old statement about standing on the shoulders of giants: I for one see further because I stand on the shoulders of my graduate students, past and present, and other young researchers. In my citations, I have tried to privilege recent scholarship, which often productively revises and amplifies older classic accounts. Of course, I have read and can cite only a selection of all the works that have been produced on the developments under study. By and large, I do not cite general historical works that have provided narrative background even though some are very valuable.

I realize as I end this book that I am completing a series of works that have focused on the development of modern states. I never intended a trilogy, nor would I describe them as such. The earlier books, *Leviathan 2.0: Inventing Modern Statehood* (2005) and *Once Within Borders: Territories of Power, Wealth, and Belonging since 1500* (2015), focused on the links between territory and statehood while this current book attempts to analyze the state as one actor among other collective agents that shape political and economic developments. This should not imply that I have abandoned geopolitical concerns, but they are not the path to historical reconstruction chosen here. Still, many of the themes link up to my statement "Consigning the Twentieth Century to History" of the year 2000 and my first book, *Recasting Bourgeois Europe*, of almost half a century back. Perhaps like an old dog, I have dug up and gnawed on bones I forgot that I had buried.

Still, in other ways this book revises my earlier work. Implicitly it subordinates many of my long-standing concerns with the legacies of Nazism, Italian fascism, and Communism. I certainly do not want the concept of the project-state to be read as erasing the difference between lawful democratic regimes and repressive governments, or the distinctions between left and right regimes from each other, as usually understood. Project-states have served as a force for good and for evil; some have aspired primarily to make their society more equitable, and others have sought to make their national power more fearsome. No one who has grown up in the twentieth century or after can really confront them devoid of their moral character. But social scientists and historians can still seek typologies that include experiences we find odious and those from which we draw inspiration.

The spectrum of political outcomes suggested here also differs from what I envisaged at the end of *Leviathan 2.0* seven years ago. But it would be a stubborn scholar who felt no need to revise his or her concepts over the course of time. And I have been enough of a nonscholar to want to explore new themes and subjects, perhaps at the cost of deepening my knowledge of previous ones. No doubt were I to be in a position to revisit this work in, say, ten or twenty years, I would think differently again. But that task will have to be left to younger readers, including those students, colleagues, friends, and family to whom I am so indebted.

Let me acknowledge just a few of those debts here: most immediately to my editor at Harvard University Press, Andrew Kinney; then at the Minda de Gunzburg Center for European Studies: Peter Hall, Arthur Goldhammer, and Hans-Helmut Kotz, with whom I taught a course on the European Union for several years, all of whom read or listened to portions of the manuscript. Other companions at the center, some still present—Grzegorz Ekiert, Peter Gordon, Patrice Higonnet (my colleague of longest standing), Maya Jasanoff, Alison Frank Johnson, Mary Lewis, Derek Penslar, and Daniel Ziblatt—and others now elsewhere, David Blackbourn and Niall Ferguson, have made it a wonderful intellectual home for decades. The Harvard History Department has been my alternate mooring for most of my career; I've been continually inspired by its commitment to teaching and innovative research. Let me cite close intellectual and career-long colleagues in Europe, Patrick Fridenson and Jürgen Kocka. Commentators on chapters or supporters of this project for years have included recent students Tim Barker and Ian Kumekawa, earlier students Steven Press and Jamie Martin, now teaching at Stanford and Harvard, respectively, and well-established former students Daniel Sargent and John Connelly now at Berkeley; also participants in the Weatherhead Initiative for Global History that I have codirected for almost a decade with Sven Beckert. Paul Schmelzing, currently of the Economics Department at Boston College, crafted the colonial balance sheets in Chapter 2. Most recently, Bruno Settis reviewed material on Italy in Chapter 5. I cannot name all those who have provided sustaining intellectual companionship. Teaching first with Niall and then Sven over the years has continued to renew mental energies. The students in our seminars as well as my undergraduate classes have been an ongoing stimulus to question and rethink the past whose relevance and urgency we strive to convey. I started the writing as a guest at the utopian Wissenschaftskolleg in Berlin in 2018 and was able to carry on while teaching at Sapienza University of Rome in 2019 thanks to an invitation from Andrea Guiso. I apologize for failing to cite many more of the friends and colleagues who have been continually supportive and, as I look back, have provided so many of this career's rewards.

Closer to home, my grown children, Andrea, Nicholas, and Jessica, their spouses, and the older tranche of my grandchildren have listened sympathetically as I laconically reported, "I've been working on my book," even as they unsuccessfully prodded me to explain what I was writing. Pauline's memory and example continues to inspire my efforts. But gratitude most of all this time to Anne Sa'adah, professor emerita of government at Dartmouth College, who consented to be my partner and wife in late life and has given me love, care, affection, and superbly intelligent companionship far beyond my merits. This, at last, is her book; she has believed in it.

THE PROJECT-STATE
AND ITS RIVALS

Introduction

History's Protagonists

HISTORIANS STUDY CHANGE, but earlier histories of the last hundred years did not prepare us for the transformations around the world that have overtaken our politics and societies during the late twentieth and early twenty-first century. Until recently, historical accounts centered on Europe and America focused on the long struggle between democratic ideologies and their authoritarian or totalitarian competitors—fascism and nazism, conventionally classified on the right, and communism on the left. These developments seemed to climax with democratic victories in 1945 or the remarkable collapse of the European communist regimes in 1989–1991, depending on the conflicts under scrutiny, whether World War II or the Cold War. For historians concerned with the populations that lived in Asia and Africa, the passage from colonial domination to independent statehood played a similar role in organizing a narrative of events that culminated between 1945 and the 1960s. Certainly, the second half of the twentieth century was marked by brutal postcolonial and civil wars, a dangerous nuclear stalemate, and many dismaying reversions into dictatorship. Nonetheless, by the 1990s repressive racial legal institutions in South Africa and the United States were dismantled, and many of the authoritarian regimes in Asia and Latin America and Europe had been democratized. Uphill battles but an upbeat story.

History, of course, did not end in 1989. The 1990s brought the destructive wars of Yugoslav secession and severe economic depression in Russia. The current century has been characterized by the most severe international economic crisis since the world depression of the 1930s, by the rise of ethnic nationalist and racist movements revealing traits familiar from interwar fascism, the murderous tenacity of religious zealots, the rise of would-be autocrats, and the plight of millions of unwanted refugees. Add to that the threat of trade wars, cyber disruptions, and renewed great-power confrontation, a global epidemic, premonitions of environmental catastrophe, and just as this book goes to press, the cruel atavistic war in Ukraine. Among many of the laments in the last few years, several among many have stuck with me, first the verdict of the respected British economic columnist Martin Wolf, who wrote somberly in late 2017 about the "great recession": "The West let its financial system run aground in a huge financial crisis. It has permanently underinvested in its future. In important cases, notably the US, it has allowed a yawning gulf to emerge between economic winners and the losers. Not least, it has let lies and hatred consume its politics."[1] The daughter of a distinguished Italian political family caught up in the earlier great conflicts of the mid-twentieth century wrote toward 2020, "The history not only of Italy, but of all Europe and the entire world seems to have turned down a completely new road, different from those that have opened to us in the postwar decades. I do not know where this road will lead; there are numerous signs of danger and degradation. . . . We have the sensation that catastrophe can emerge from within us, annulling humanity's consciousness of the need to respect others . . . and of the will to imagine a future and to construct it."[2] More recently, David Brooks, the conservatively inclined commentator for the *New York Times,* sought an explanation for why "history is reverting toward barbarism," and he asked, "What is the key factor that has made the 21st century so dark, regressive and dangerous?"[3]

The question that has engaged me in this book is related but different: how to write a history of the twentieth century and the years to date of the twenty-first that can account both for the successes of liberal democracy some three decades ago and the "dark, regressive and dangerous" developments since then?[4] Major syntheses have wrestled with the legacy of a dark and violent path, the vicissitudes of postwar recovery beset by traumatic collective memory, and the tensions of overarching ideological conflict.[5] Others have stressed the long road toward welfare, prosperity, and emancipation. I do not believe that "history" is necessarily a story of progress toward liberal democracy or greater equality. We cannot know whether the next decades will take us further into the dark or reverse course again. But can we narrate the story until now as more than an unending contest between democrats and authoritarians with successive rounds going toward one contender or another? And if those obvious ideological opponents are not our main focus, which protagonists should be? My answer is set out below.

How Did We Get Here? A History for Our Era

Two approaches to the history of the past century have predominated until recently. For writers who have remained focused on 1933, 1945, or 1989, dominant inquiries have usually sought to explain the conditions under which democracy thrives or decays, or conversely when authoritarian regimes arise or collapse. Eric Hobsbawm's celebrated *Age of Extremes* followed these vicissitudes from the left. Samuel Huntington and Francis Fukuyama drew political typologies from a conservative perspective.[6] Given the great ideological struggles of the twentieth century, most historians have seen the era since the eighteenth-century revolutions as an epic contest between democratic and authoritarian, even totalitarian, regimes. For historians on the left, progress has entailed overcoming accumulated hierarchy based on wealth, race, and gender, on privilege based on birth, and unjustified authority. Conservatives, in contrast, have argued that the underlying peril arose from democratic overreach. They warn that societies have heedlessly destroyed institutions that may have accommodated inequalities but provided organic social roots and shelter.[7]

I have earlier termed these historical accounts *moral narratives*; they were organized or at least justified in terms of the great principles at stake.[8] That term was not meant to diminish their significance. The contests at their center were indeed fundamental as all the great intellectuals of the era recognized. They claimed the passions, liberties, and lives of participants. We still rightly worry about dangers to liberal democracy, at home and abroad. But there are other ways to think about the history of the last hundred years than as a contest between democracies and dictatorships, emancipation and oppression, fascists and communists, or even just between liberals and conservatives, left and right, or moderates and the ideologically obsessed.

Many historians, mostly of a younger generation and on the left, who have sought to explain developments since 1989 have in fact shifted focus from the confrontation of democracy and authoritarianism. They are transfixed by the power of capital, the advance of globalization (at least until the past decade), and the success of neoliberalism, that is by trends that reduce the role of states as the preeminent agents of world history in favor of the economically powerful. Such a focus helps make sense for the years since 1989 and, as I argued twenty years ago, since the changes of the 1970s. That decade marked a point of inflection between a century-long global regime (from the 1860s into the 1970s) that seemed clearly organized around territorial states—their commerce, conflicts, and ideologies—and the era in which we have found ourselves since. Although we still divide the world into nation-states, contemporary developmental forces seem increasingly to cross their boundaries and leave territorial orientations behind. The state is not disappearing, but it functions in a far denser milieu of influences. The process has been far from uniform, however. How can we best comprehend both the order of states and the transnational developments that sweep the globe?

The approach in this work is to identify and follow basic historical protagonists that have operated over the course of the past century, both when states loomed as decisive actors and when they appeared overshadowed by other agents. My protagonists are collective actors who possess different sources of power and public influence and seek to maximize their historical roles. Four such agents of transformation have seemed particularly important to me. Two are based on the potential for exploiting territorially organized political authority, the *project-state* and the *resource empire*. Two draw upon sources of influence that cut across territorial jurisdictions: what I term the *realm or community of governance* based on normative aspirations and the *web* or *domain of capital* consisting of individuals and firms working to secure and increase economic returns. These four agents are not the only possible protagonists, but together they carry the weight of a lot of history.

Critics may well object that the different and sometimes opposed actors within each of these historical "forces"—ambitious leaders, political parties, business enterprises, foundations, nongovernmental organizations (NGOs), and so forth—outweigh whatever abstract unity they might have possessed or unified influence they exerted. Whether they do or not must remain a subjective determination in each case, but I try to take account of internal distinctions. Conversely, readers who are interested in the history of political economy, as I myself have been, usually take as a working premise that capital and the state cannot really be disentangled. But although they are usually found in interdependent relationships, they can be distinguished analytically like threads in a tapestry, and I believe it is fruitful to do so. Let me emphasize that none of the four collective agents deployed here has operated in isolation; each has joined forces with one or more of the others. But they vary in their impact, and their changing power and importance determine, or at least reveal, many of the developments and events of history as experienced. The history that follows is thus based on the evolving interactions between varieties of territorial rule and forms of nonterritorial power. It does not wager on any particular future for confirmation but tries to provide a framework that makes progressive as well as regressive outcomes plausible. Its aim, moreover, is not just to write a history of current crises and conflicts, although it hopes to illuminate them. Primarily, it seeks to explain the longer-term stresses inherent in earlier institutional arrangements, like the structural flaws in a bridge or building that suddenly collapses after we were convinced it was totally robust. History constantly surprises, but the job of the historian is to make it seem less surprising.

The Project-State and the Resource Empire

With respect to the territorial protagonists, two major themes occupy this history. The first is the rise and eclipse—final or not no one can say; this history must remain unresolved—of what I term the activist *project-state*. The project-state was a political unit that consciously aspired to inflect the course of history. If large enough, it wanted to play a leading and perhaps hegemonic role in international society. No matter what its size and power, it aspired to change social and economic relations in a profound way and not just to prolong administrative continuity. Project-states had a transformative agenda; they were based on authoritarian and even totalitarian as well as liberal and democratic coalitions seeking to reform sclerotic institutions or societies that seemed unacceptably unequal. In addressing the societies they proposed to reform, they organized their recruitment of personnel and legitimation of rule around ideologies: grand historical narratives that served project-state maintenance. By and large, the diagnoses and projects envisioned one of two approaches; call them left and right. Either they beheld a society flawed by historic legal and material inequalities that needed to be rectified, whether by revolution or redistribution, or they perceived a national community deficient in family, ethnic, or other organic bonds—"invertebrate," to cite José Ortega de Gasset's phrase for Spain—which had in one way or another to be disciplined.[9]

The project-state as used in this book differs from other regimes that political scientists have often evoked, such as the developmental-state and earlier the administrative-state. The developmental-state stood out by its active guidance of economic modernization.[10] The administrative-state was an older concept designed to emphasize the functional specialization of governing agencies. It often suggested a suffocating bureaucratization, such as conveyed by Max Weber's metaphor of the "iron cage." How to control it democratically seemed the major problem.[11] The project-state, in contrast, supposedly sought to energize the citizenry, even if its leaders often settled for mere acclamation.

The project-state was often just a phase of longer-term government since the fervor demanded could rarely be sustained beyond a few years or a decade at most. Leaders, however, would occasionally try to whip up enthusiasm for a renewed phase of civic mobilization, sometimes with a search for enemies or mere slackers.

No hard-and-fast line sets the project-state apart, but it entails a degree of self-aware ambition. Its leaders set an agenda they understand as going far beyond ordinary administration, whether in terms of social change or state authority. They sense a historical calling. The "projects" are described at greater length below, but they included significant extension of social services and welfare, raising the level of national education, and mobilizing a civic or revolutionary and national consciousness. Reflect briefly on the idea of the project itself. "An individual or collaborative enterprise that is carefully planned to achieve a particular aim," according to the *Oxford English Dictionary*: a word derived from the Greek "to look forward." Wikipedia gives the Manhattan Project, the Apollo program, the Human Genome Project, and the Great Pyramid of ancient Egypt as examples. This history associates the project with a public, communal effort, but in the twentieth and twenty-first centuries, private enterprises assumed public dimensions and can excite the public imagination: Henry Ford's River Rouge auto plant early in the last century; today, perhaps Elon Musk's SpaceX. Certainly, state projects have an ambiguous historical record. They have mobilized societies or those speaking in their name to construct the Tennessee Valley Authority on one hand and Auschwitz on the other hand.

Social theorists on the left have argued that this peril is inherent in the nature of capitalist modernity. *Economist* magazine editors and many far more doctrinaire commentators tend to believe that the danger arises from the nature of the state and believe that when anchored in a market society, the project remains benevolent. American projects have usually been associated with either the visionary entrepreneur or the analogy of war: for example, the war on poverty, the war on terror, the war on cancer. Results are mixed. Our public health projects—mass vaccination campaigns for polio and today COVID-19, for instance—have been technologically impressive but have faced difficulties arising from poverty, our racial history, and a polarized polity.

Achieving transcendent security at home and sometimes abroad could become a project in its own right, above all because the project-state often saw itself as embattled and indeed often was. At recurrent moments, its architects felt themselves standing at Armageddon. Some of the opposed forces were impersonal legacies of poverty and dependence. But for pathological rulers and parties, opposition took the form of alleged mortal conspiracies of class, race, or faith. Project-states were sometimes founded by ambitious politicians but also emanated from military cadres who seized power in the conviction that civilian rulers were decadent, corrupt, or leftist and that only patriotic and selfless armed forces could regenerate the nation.

The idea of a project-state raises analytical and ethical problems and I want to recognize their difficulties. When project-states were powerful international units, they tended to define their aspirations in universalist terms. They aspired to make a world hospitable for their values, whether expressed in terms of a superior civilization, race, or ideological merit. National projects easily became imperial projects, and project-states have often been in a situation of conflict with each other, of cold if not hot war. The inverse relationship also holds. War makes states and it makes project-states in particular. If this book is read in a time of war, the state will seem a more important protagonist than if it is read in an interval of peace.

The concept of a project-state raises another difficulty as an analytical tool—to me the weightiest. Should activist regimes that do not systematically violate human rights really be seen as akin in any way to those that practice political violence and coercion as a major technique for molding society? Should not the distinction between regimes that seek to preserve individual liberty and dignity (even if riddled with pockets of injustice) and those that trample on them, whether at home or abroad, remain the fundamental distinction in making sense of our epoch's political history? Can the historian justifiably suspend this moral categorization in trying to make the past intelligible? Most public commentators have doubled down on the fundamental difference between authoritarian and liberal states. Does it not remain the primal distinction of our time and is it not just sophistry to obscure it?

I would certainly not erase the distinction as a guide to political action. Most historians of the United States, whether yea-saying or critical, would also have resisted. So too would some of the great European historical thinkers such as Jules Michelet and Karl Marx as would in particular historians of Nazism and Stalinism and a theorist such as Hannah Arendt. History for them remained a moral drama. Niccolò Machiavelli and Max Weber, on the other hand, derived important insights from such a suspension of moral criteria. More recently, Charles Tilly notably insisted that the sine qua non of force lay behind government as it did behind gangs.[12] Some, such as Alexis de Tocqueville, could retain their moral commitment but still perceive the institutional similarities. This work proposes a pragmatic response. It is not intended to equate project-states, but it argues that looking beyond the distinction between liberal-democratic and authoritarian, even totalitarian regimes, helps reveal the dynamics of recent history. And it can also compel us to think more clearly about the defects of our own political systems.

Project-states were usually creatures of war, revolution, or profound national crisis. For some countries—China, Turkey, and Mexico—their transformative regimes emerged from the revolutions that had shaken their societies in the decade before World War I. Russia had undergone a wave of revolution and counterrevolution after 1905. These significant upheavals were compressed and at times armed efforts to shatter semifeudal rural hierarchies and clientelist politics, which had also provided for an outsize role for foreign interests. But even in nonrevolutionary situations, advocates of the project-state envisaged the creation of a new society that transcended traditionalist loyalties oriented toward the family, church, or military but were rather to be based on enhanced civic consciousness. The great interwar depression of the 1930s prompted the reemergence of an American project-state (albeit bitterly contested) with the New Deal. Democratically oriented projects were resumed with the defeat of fascism in World War II and continued into the 1960s.

Most of these struggles were carried on by the institutional form that dominated the history of the last 200 years, the organized political party, either a new one or one of long standing energized by domestic crisis. Organized parties, with professional staffs and subsisting between elections, justifiably drew the attention of political theorists and sociologists throughout the twentieth century. Whether single or many, they dominated the history of regimes the world over, though often to atrophy in energy and vitality. The party in turn sometimes emerged from a political movement—a mix of spontaneous upheaval and carefully cultivated enthusiasm and anger, not yet institutionalized into the governmental apparatus. Movements might erupt during moments of economic discontent or resentment at political exclusion, volcanoes of history that broke through the crust of routine sometimes to generate project states, often ultimately to congeal anew within a ritualized arrangement for exercising power. My major interest has been the states they helped transform more than the movements themselves, but as in the most recent eruption, labeled as populism (discussed in chapter 10), regime and movement can be hard to disentangle.

Thinkers as diverse as Michel Foucault and James Scott have suggested that in effect all states must be project-states; they want to enumerate, make "legible," and rationalize their subjects. Examining religious as well as political institutions from the late Middle Ages, Foucault introduced the ideas of "governmentality" and "biopolitics" to describe a state agenda for molding populations.[13] But there are different degrees of intervention and states can vary in their activism, asserting a role in war and crisis that becomes routine over time. The difference in intensity, I believe, justifies the special category, even when historians dispute whether the label is usefully applied to one or another case. In fact, all the major belligerents in the world wars had to become project-states temporarily to the degree that they intervened to harness their populations to the overriding objective of national survival. The wars compelled participants to coordinate economies and societies to an unprecedented and ever more pervasive degree. But although many of the belligerents undertook this effort for the duration, they also dismantled controls once peace was secured. We are examining the regimes that undertook or attempted major intervention in peacetime.

Not all states, of course, were project-states; many were content to penetrate less deeply if too much unrest did not threaten the political regime. Project-states often involved an unleashing of violence that could exhaust populations and was hard to sustain beyond a decade or two. Some societies (usually thought of as liberal) resisted this recourse, at least at home and in their national politics, though allowing it in colonies or the enforcement of segregation or ethnic cleansing in unofficial capacities. Other states governed through layers of familiar elites especially when they had the additional task of ruling a far-flung and ethnically diverse empire. Finally, the project-state itself seemed to lose its momentum by the 1970s. Other less collective objectives took over, and the great historical moment of the project-state, at least in the West, faltered in disillusion. Until yesterday, at least European and American societies were living through a phase of its abandonment and rejection. Whether it is reviving at the present moment is yet to be determined.

The other territorially defined form of rule this book follows is a variant of imperial control I term the *resource empire*, which is discussed in Chapter 2. Empires are forms of state, but the idea of a state or a nation-state implies formally equality with other sovereign polities, often as signified by membership in international associations. Empires claim superiority of one sort or another over other peoples or political units who do not yet have sovereignty. The resource empires were certainly not the only form of imperial control, but they represented the effort to enjoy the fruits of overseas colonies that had already been conquered before World War I or were gained as a prize of victory in 1918–1919 from other colonial powers. Resource empires were less structures of restless territorial acquisition (interwar Japan and Italy's efforts excepted) than of extraction—hopefully, though rarely in fact, cash cows for beneficiaries in the metropole or settlers in place. The League of Nations helped inscribe a new, largely racially or ethnically based status quo that envisaged indefinite tutelage through the mandate system. The elusive standards of "civilization," or "readiness for self-rule," remained powerful normative justifications.

The winding up of the resource empires followed during the quarter century after World War II. But if the formal empires ended, the one-time colonies often continued to furnish material resources and labor power for their former rulers. The resource empire demands our attention not only for its history as such but as a source of ongoing relationships of economic inequality—privilege and power of the global north and continuing disadvantage for the global south. There were many reasons: the stigmas of racial difference did not bleach out; the cultural resources of the old metropole continued to exert their magnetism over postcolonial elites. Metropolitan firms relied on their plantation products—fruits, vegetable oils, and fibers—and on the minerals that local laborers dug out of their mines, and most important in an age of expanding energy needs, on their petroleum resources. The contests over what might be called petro-empires (see Chapters 6 and 7) remained important through the third quarter of the twentieth century. More generally, the economic fortunes among nations and regions in a globalized world have remained significantly unequal as the descriptors "third world" or "global south" imply. Inequalities of wealth and economic autonomy have prolonged a twilight afterlife for the resource empire.

Domains of Governance and Capital

Operating alongside (and often within) states and resource empires were organizations and networks that aspired not to sovereign power but to moral and political influence and/or to material gain. They might have headquarters based within territorial states, but they increasingly functioned within international or transnational domains defined here as the domains of *governance* and of *capital*, both discussed in Chapter 3. We can use varying terms: "domain," "realm," "community," "space," "field," "web"; they all refer metaphorically to networks of decentralized participants that mobilized public opinion and finance often across national lines. Think of them as creating something like a gravitational or magnetic field in physics, filling international space with invisible lines of energy or influence.[14]

The term "governance" has surged in popularity since the 1980s. (See the n-gram in Chapter 7.) Today, it often means just the procedures and usages according to which nonpolitical organizations are managed, rules "governing" behavior where the coercive capacity that states possess does not apply. But it can carry more specific implications, which are those relevant for this account. The realm of governance I refer to here includes the nonstate or interstate organizations that proposed to intervene in society by invoking ethical, normative, or "expert" considerations, whether supported by laws and governments or not. The dense development of international law and courts constitutes a major part. Transnational health provision provides another.[15] (In the eighteenth century, the Republic of Letters might have been seen as having an analogous role. In the nineteenth and early twentieth centuries, the idea of "public opinion" summoned up some of the same ideas.) These organizations operated both within state borders and in international "space." Historians used to regard the international domain as the passive arena for contending national foreign-policy ambitions, but many today increasingly argue that the international (or transnational) arena is a space that in effect shapes its own normative practices.[16] To resort to another metaphor from physics, if the life of states was bound together by the strong forces of alliances and interests, the realm of governance constituted the weak force of transnational opinion.

Whereas the rules that states imposed might be decreed by a single actor whether individual or cohesive party, the norms of governance usually emerged from a collective deliberation. Participants in that process sought to discern and enact public goods that politics or markets do not always provide: an end to civil violence, human rights, honest government, access to education, better medical care, and environmental preservation. But by promoting reforms for states and firms, actors in the realm of governance also prolonged the continuity of resource empires and sometimes the hegemony of powerful states. The champions of governance claimed the self-evidence of norms just as American colonists once declared the self-evidence of rights. The claim of governance had a long history well before the term became widely used in the 1980s. Combatting global inequality would eventually became a major goal of United Nations agencies and NGOs, but advocates of international governance long sought to negotiate compromises between the reformist ideas championed by pre-1914 international liberalism and the aspirations of conservatives to uphold—or even restore—what they believed to be the status quo of a peacefully accepted inequality of peoples and races.[17]

The world depression of the 1930s undermined the conditions that allowed these reformist projects to prosper. Instead, it increased the assertiveness of project-states, weakened the authority of resource empires, and ripped apart the international realm of governance by the end of the decade. The realm of governance was reconstituted after 1945 and seemed to increase in vigor—but its success depended on its partnerships with the web of capital and ambitious states.[18] After World War II, as Chapters 4 and 7 discuss, the role of organizations claiming to advance governance became increasingly problematic. Some clung to humanitarian ends; others seconded (and even aspired to form) their own government's political and economic goals, convinced that they were advancing objectively humane values even as they required the resources of their home nations and economic systems to prevail. The line between norms and interests became very wobbly as interests were advanced as rights. The phenomenon of "think tanks" revealed that party and economic interests could adopt the prestigious form of the foundation to sponsor a partisan agenda. The analyst of global politics is left to ask whether claims of "governance" did not really become just a discursive strategy for a new would-be elite, unable or unwilling to see the interests they were serving, whether others' or their own.[19] The concluding chapter suggests in fact that ambitious leaders and many voters in the twenty-first century have mobilized against the pretensions of governance communities.

The web of capital has included the individuals and organizations—firms, banks, trade associations—that participated in markets, where they reciprocally exchanged goods, labor, real property, and promises of future payments in a framework supposedly free of legal or extralegal compulsion. Capitalism as an institution, however, involves more than the role of markets for organizing economic life.[20] It is a system of production and of exchange dependent on money equivalents—that is, upon a common and preferably stable measurement of value (a *numéraire*) to allow exchanges of all sorts of commodities, labor, and natural resources beyond direct barter.[21] Nonstate owners retain the ownership of much, if not all, property. Its production model usually entails small groups of managers or employers directing a larger number of workers and receiving a higher income for doing so. Although it is often taken for granted, capitalism incorporates a role for time and duration in establishing how much goods and labor are worth. It presupposes that at the end of cycles of production and exchange, the values attributed to the economy should normally be greater than at the beginning.[22] Something marketable has been *added* whether by dint of physical labor or mental effort, extraction from nature, technological change, or heightened desirability. How that precisely occurs has often been puzzling; Marx believed that ultimately it must derive from labor, but how it was put into the stream of capital was part of the reproduction problem with which he continually wrestled. If attributed to firms, the additional value is designated profit; if attributed to society as a whole, we talk about economic growth. Marxists in particular use the term "accumulation," in part to signal their ideological affiliation with each other.

Of course, how this increase (or in some cases, decrease) should be distributed is a question of politics. For capitalism is also characterized by a particular relationship to political systems. It frequently relies on the state for investing in technological innovation. It certainly relies on the state to protect those who control economic assets from theft, abusive practices, and sometimes disastrous losses. It relies on the state again to set essential parameters, such as key interest rates and a budget for public expenditures, assuming it does so in the interests of capital and growth. And at the same time, capitalism needs a state that allows firms and individuals to accumulate assets with monetary value and regulates the legal framework for the economic process. Thus, although there are many exceptions, twentieth-century capitalism evolved toward what was called a mixed economy in which private ownership, contracts, and profit remained critical.[23]

Despite many historians' treatment of capitalism as an all-encompassing causal framework, my own view is that the political system, based on the resources of power, whether accumulated by force or consent, remains conceptually independent. Thus, this book is not a history of capitalism, though it includes the agents in that system as key actors in historical change as a whole. These agents include very different forms of activity: on the one hand, entrepreneurs and firms who produce and sell manufactures or commodities, on the other hand, those who extend the credit, insurance, and legal services that facilitate their activity. Their respective policy interests have often been in opposition to each other, but they remain entangled in the process of wealth creation in market societies.

Characteristic of the interaction of state and the agents of capital in the modern era and the twentieth and twenty-first centuries, in particular, was the "decision" vastly to increase the money claims available in any current time period against promises of future redemption. The demands of war constituted one motive. Social conflict and welfare commitments also led to this expedient.

So, too, did the central insight of financial firms that promising future gains could generate private wealth in the present. No society can truly tap wealth that has not yet been created any more than it can recruit labor or soldiers from the yet unborn. But it can encourage mobilization of innovations, resources, techniques, and potential that lie fallow in the present, a process we describe as economic growth. In so doing, it multiplies claims on future payments that have present value and can produce massive transfers of wealth, whether intended or not. Sorting out these claims has constituted an agonizing theme of recent history.

The great wars in particular contributed to this outcome. National debts multiplied and were increased too by the claims enforced by the victors in peace settlements or from national credits extended in aid programs. As a result, the high-level participants in the web of capital became important through the 1920s both as leaders of profit-seeking firms and experts in allegedly restoring an international financial order. As such, they were also participants in the web of governance. The custodians of capital failed, however, to assure continued global prosperity between the wars for multiple reasons—above all, as they tried to reconcile the overhanging burden of international debt (and reparations) with their single-minded focus on international currency stability. They also seemed powerless to maintain the income of the world's agricultural producers and protect them against widespread poverty.

Following World War II, these actors constructed a more stable fabric within the U.S.-led Bretton Woods order. Experts and firms pursued different roles. Multinational firms claimed a larger role. By the 1970s, they captured a lot of alarmed attention, and today they hover as superficially decentralized entities, sited in an economic space where their global reach often evades the regulation states can deploy. In the contemporary digital era, moreover, the technologies that they provide for an almost universal consumer public—notably the social media and increasingly nonstate money—have provided incentives to free themselves from political control and even from the weaker reins of governance. The very nature of capital, moreover, continually evolves and becomes increasingly immaterial, liberated from its traditional sources of natural endowments, control of labor, and accumulation of savings—arising finally from the belief in its own continued increase (see Chapters 8 and 9).

This confluence of efforts indicates the fact that each of the collective actors presented here—project-state, resource empire, realm of governance, and web of capital—could hardly subsist on its own. They were discernable forces contending for power, norms, and wealth but not independently effective. The agents for each required the cooperative efforts of the others even when they were rivals for influence and power. Their personnel often overlapped. In wartime above all, the state sought step by step to incorporate economic actors into its acknowledged scope for setting goals and priorities. As studies of war production show, it met less outright resistance than inertia and its own internal bureaucratic rivalries. The networks of governance often served state purposes and often aspired to serve states. They lent states the respectability of "soft power," to borrow Joseph Nye's felicitous term; but their agendas transcended raison d'état. They also increasingly required the collaboration of economic and financial institutions. States, on their part, required economic viability; there was no firm line in the twentieth century between capital and resource empire; nor did the leaders associated with the realm of governance really divorce themselves from the objectives of capital. It remains an open question whether many important institutions should be classified as within only domain or another, say, capital or governance.[24] Yet for all the braiding together of objectives, programs, and personnel, we can usefully understand the circumstances of recent history by trying to trace each strand on its own, understanding, however, that as if in some spreadsheet of history, any change in one of these variables produced changes in the others.

Other historians might suggest different protagonists as fundamental. What about the domain of religion, it needs to be asked—whether faith or institutional practice? Certainly, it continues to play a critical role in the world of states and popular movements, whether in the Islamic mobilization so crucial to history in the Middle East or in Evangelical movements that have come to weigh so heavily on politics in the Americas. Readers may object to my subordination of religion as the prejudice of a secular intellectual, but insofar as religious commitments motivate political action, whether in Iran, Israel, Poland, the United States, Myanmar, or so many other places, I have considered them as a motivation for a variant of project-state. I do not mean to disparage the religious convictions that motivate these currents, but their activism in this world seems keyed to making state projects prevail. What, too, about the working classes, the proletariat so crucial for Marxists? My scheme envisages labor as a component of the realm of capital when it does not exercise decisive political power and as a force behind the project-state when it does. Alternative histories are possible, but given the desire to understand our current conditions, the collective agents I will work with seem promising. The reader can decide whether they help sort out the developments of the last hundred years.

To anticipate the developments narrated here, project-states outside Asia reveal an ambiguous trajectory after the 1960s. From one perspective, they failed to generate convincing public agendas. They seemed increasingly just to serve the classes that had access to the skills of a digital economy, mass entertainment, or political office itself. Their leaders increasingly retreated from political management of society and turned to markets to achieve social results. But from an alternate point of view, this "great transformation" amounted to an alternative state project in its own right. Margaret Thatcher and Ronald Reagan, to take the most salient leaders, deployed tremendous political energy to transform the states they ruled and to liberate the market economy. By the 1990s, even the leaders of the opposition left parties became cheerleaders for largely untethered capital under the slogan of "market democracy."

Resource empires were to disappear as major actors, but the opportunities for neo-imperial transfers of wealth hardly disappeared. Instead, they were transmuted not into some enduring postimperial commonwealth but into capital assets. These were sometimes independent but often ventures such as jointly held oil firms still controlled by former imperial rulers or by the new postcolonial states. In the successive phases of rapid technological change after the two world wars—first the modernization of industry and agriculture and then the digital revolution—capitalist firms seized the opportunity to metastasize into the domains of national politics and transnational governance. Chapters 5 and 6 will wrestle with these changes.

It is the realm of governance that is perhaps the hardest to describe or to populate in ordinary terms. Its international role was apparent from before World War I and grew between the wars. Emerging within late-communist regimes under the rubric of "civil society" or elsewhere as international and nonprofit organizations, it could stand up to state power, but it withstood less effectively the transformed technologies and financial possibilities of the 1990s and after. The collapse of the Communist Party regimes also contributed to this result, as private firms or new post-Soviet oligarchs captured once-socialized assets. With states hollowed, the energies of governance largely neutralized or even arousing a populist resistance of their own, and capital largely amenable to whatever government allows it to prosper, the personalist regimes we have encountered in recent years—whether in the United States from 2017 until 2021 and still today in Brazil, Turkey, India, Hungary, and elsewhere—captured the blighted institutional landscape, both territorial and transnational.

To be clear, I am not trying to personify these abstractions. Men and women manage states, exploit imperial acquisitions, accumulate wealth, and try to discern and shape community values. These protagonists are not even "ideal types" intended to clarify real existing phenomena. They are not institutions in the sense of bounded organizations.[25] Historians often take refuge in the notion of "deeper" or "underlying" causes. But that is not really what is at stake either; I am not claiming causal primacy for interests or ideals or ingrained allegiances. Rather, this history tries to follow some dominant efforts to secure collective aspirations, whether for national communities, economic organizations, or selected public goods.

The contemporary historian's present is always a cloud of possibilities. How are the agents of history traced in this work likely to develop? Will capital remain the dominant transnational force as structures of governance focus their energies on limiting state abuses, climate change, or fighting medical and social catastrophes? Great corporations depend on territorial states even as they seek to emancipate themselves from the constraints and levies of state control. But the state is hardly finished. In dozens or hundreds of contexts, it is fighting back, seeking to capture revenues generated by international firms, trying to bridle or nationalize the new information channels that are curated by global information providers. States are strengthened in times of international conflict. At the same time, however, the state is also symbiotically entwined with the providers of capital and technology, and the outcome may be, as it has often before, a condominium of the powerful, private and public. The chapters that follow document the unfolding of these developments.

For the moment, therefore, the new spirit of the laws in Western Europe and America—to take Montesquieu's concept of the institutional gestalt that I cited earlier—has produced an institutional result far from what so many Europeans and Americans aspired to in 1989.[26] The "order" that has emerged is puzzling in many ways. It is not simply "counterrevolutionary" in the way that we might describe the suppression of the Arab Spring. It followed from the triumph of many of the principles and aspirations of 1989. It has not been the result of a simple increase in global inequality, for whereas inequality has increased within Western societies, many of the poorer world societies have become wealthier, above all China. It is in fact not "order" in the way theorists such as Samuel Huntington or Francis Fukuyama or Henry Kissinger would have used the word but a potentially explosive impasse of conflicting privileges and resentments.[27]

Order, of course, is the pervasive trope of conservatives who fear that the accustomed hierarchies of the world are losing their legitimacy. Those who tend to invoke it usually want to defend political arrangements that favor and reassure those already enjoying influence or wealth. But if it does not mean uncontested hierarchies within societies and the absence of war between them, it is not easy to specify wherein it consists. Disorder is a more palpable condition. As we confront the turmoil of the refugee crisis in the Mediterranean, the toll taken by Mexican and Latin American drug gangs, the partisan rage and disregard of fact in US politics, the uncertain state of the European Union, the mushrooming of a transnational billionaire elite and of untethered corporations, the viral spread of social media, the intensity of religious militancy, the enthusiasm for authoritarian leaders appealing to ethnic identities at the expense of state institutions, much of the globe seems to be undergoing a surge of hostility to the "order" that seemed to prevail until the current century. China presents the major exception, but whether it too might fall into "disorder," as it has periodically over the last three millennia, is impossible to predict.

Must a history, however, that sees a transformation of a global system dating from the 1970s view the earlier postwar years in a rosy hue as a period of sociopolitical equilibrium or "order"? I would reject this implication—the postwar balance of forces contained many repressive elements, in politics, the workplace, family and emotional life, organized religion, aesthetic possibilities, and of course in terms of race and gender. Is any period, even one of apparent stability, it can be asked more fundamentally, ever really an era of equilibrium or order?[28] The term can lead us astray. Political equilibrium is not a condition of repose but rather one of countervailing tensions that is rarely prolonged in time.

What follows is a history of the changing balance among the protagonists of the twentieth century and the first decades of the twenty-first, each one embodied in an institutional arrangement. The long-term prospects seem up for grabs, especially at the current moment. Written histories have an end point; for this one, it is the present. But history as the life and struggles of humanity goes on through time. Perhaps in retrospect, this will seem a history that could have been conceived only in a moment of democratic disillusion. Perhaps it will be read as testament to a brief interval when the distinction between liberal and authoritarian states gave the misleading illusion of weakening. Perhaps if we are fortunate, it will seem an alarmist account negated by later events. Every contemporary written history is a provisional stocktaking, and lived history is defined by its surprises. No doubt there will be further surprises and new understandings.

PART ONE

The Era of World Wars

I

Paths to the Project-State

ONE OF THE GREAT monuments constructed in the wake of World War I does not rise above the battlefields of the western front or in fact above any of the far-flung sites of combat. Neither does it shelter the remains of a soldier "known only to God" in a marble sarcophagus or beneath an eternal flame in a national capital. It is a series of about one hundred volumes on the *Economic and Social History of the World War* commissioned by the Carnegie Endowment for International Peace and comprising studies by national teams of historians. Published during the two decades after the war, the investigations examine the organization of increasingly militant factory workers, the evolution of hospitals and medicine, the impact of economic blockade, the changing age profiles of populations after so many males from ages twenty to forty-five had perished, the production of munitions, the allocation of scarce shipping and food and textiles, the shock to state finances, the mortality of children and of the aged in the face of food shortages and disease, the relaxation of sexual inhibitions, and the growing sense that despite all the efforts of state planning, life was becoming a lottery. Some of the monographs still stand as landmark studies by notable social scientists: G. D. H. Cole's report on British works councils, Luigi Einaudi's summary of Italian wartime finance, David Mitrany's study of the quasi-feudal subjection of the Romanian peasant, and Albrecht Mendelssohn-Bartholdy's reflections on the mentality of wartime Germany from his 1930s Yale refuge, among others.[1] Significant studies also followed the second war, but no equivalent, internationally coordinated series of investigations emerged. The Carnegie Endowment's history remains a testimony to the project-state whose emergence it was intended to record.

What It Was . . . and Was Not

The authors who got to work after 1918 understood that state and society had become intertwined in an unprecedented effort during the huge struggle just ended. State agencies had allocated raw materials, rationed food, organized producer cartels, coordinated shipping, given official representation to labor delegates in factories, and established prenatal care, among other interventions. They endeavored to sustain the morale needed to accept the continuing conscription of hundreds of thousands young men every year, many of whom were mangled or swiftly perished. Wartime governments in sum had to organize society to help it survive the most arduous of ordeals. The Great War lay at the most recent origin of the twentieth-century project-state—a term I use to specify a regime that seeks not merely to govern day to day but to transform the nonpolitical institutions of society—economic outcomes, public health, religious commitments and secular loyalties, landscapes and cityscapes. It allowed fantasies of radical malleability. President Woodrow Wilson and his supporters, entering the world war in 1917 promised a war to transcend war, institute democracy, and establish an organization for perpetual peace. The German Supreme Command envisaged the virtual conscription of industrial labor at home under the Hindenburg plan, and by 1917–1918, the British and French were not far behind. At the same time, the General Staff command fighting a war deep into Russian imperial territories entertained proposals for transformation of the Polish, Baltic, and White Russian provinces that would subjugate the allegedly backward indigenous Slavic peasantry, clear out what they beheld as parasitic Jewish traders and their dirty shtetls, settle German farmers and guarantee agrarian independence. Defeat in 1918 drove these plans underground, but they and some of their advocates remained to energize a new National Socialist leadership.[2]

So, too, defeat in the war frustrated the Young Turks' ambitions for military and political and economic modernization of the Ottoman Empire, if not their genocidal population policies. But it also left a remnant of military reformers under Mustafa Kemal (later Atatürk) to institute a state project in Anatolia that would reclaim Turkey from Greek and British occupying forces by 1922. The war, too, gave the Bolshevik leadership their chance to seize a decisive foothold during 1917 as the imperial Russian armies wearied and decomposed on the front while political leaders in revolutionary Saint Petersburg proved unable to control popular aspirations for peace and land. The ending of the war thus fused hopes for military organization with utopian notions of reclaiming a purified society. Societal transformation was a project too daunting and too divisive to be left to civilians alone. The project-state would always retain a military and competitive component.[3]

The demands of the world war were not the only stimulus for the twentieth-century project-state. Revolutionary movements outside Europe had set about constructing new regimes that aspired to profound transformation. A half century earlier, the most ambitious rulers of Japan's territorial domains set out to renovate their country and preempt subjection by Western powers. They lay the foundation for an East Asian project-state. The first decades of the twentieth century brought a wave of revolutionary upheavals that shook Russia, Mexico, China, Iran, and the Ottoman Empire—all large societies, still preponderantly agrarian but deeply impacted by the industrial and imperialist powers.[4] Some began as limited middle-class efforts to transfer power from a ruling clique to a parliament or to military reformers. But they could not always control activist peasant and urban labor movements mobilized by intellectuals who aspired to create modern regimes that would oust a governing elite allegedly corrupted by foreign wealth.

The project-states that revolutions brought to power usually depended on the role of a single party that could exploit political collapse. As a party that resolutely aggravated social dislocation and crises in Russia from 1905 to 1914, then after 1917 and through the upheaval of collectivization after 1928, the Bolsheviks provided the most spectacular example. Elsewhere, military cadres, imbued with a sense that they must redeem their nation from foreign exploitation or civilian corruption, could also provide the nucleus of a project-state. Mustafa Kemal's Turkey, Chiang Kai-shek's nationalist movement based in Nanjing and certainly its Communist Party rival and successor after 1949, Egypt's Free Officers who removed King Farouk in 1952 and the "old regime" associated with him, or the clerics who unseated the shah in 1978 and subdued their initial leftist allies are important examples. In most of these cases, whether based on party or soldiers, transformative authority tended to concentrate increasingly on a personal leader to whom heroic capacities could be attributed. The results were and remain ambiguous. As was the case in Republican China after 1911, the new regimes could become afflicted by corruption, warlord rivalries, and foreign invasion. Their policies could also impose disastrous costs on their population, as in the Soviet Union, or the rhetoric of transformation might outrun the accomplishments, as was the case in fascist Italy.

Ideological programs can be traced to fervent beginnings in the decades before World War I. Radical parties in Europe, whether conventionally labeled as left or right, had elaborated fundamental critiques of liberal politics. Vladimir Lenin's 1902 pamphlet "What Is to Be Done?" made the case for a dedicated revolutionary cadre that must ruthlessly guide the large and exploited but unfocused proletariat. Nationalist and authoritarian thinkers, among them Action française ideologue Charles Maurras and the spokesman for syndicalist militancy Georges Sorel, were contemptuous of parliamentary debate and praised violence as regenerative. Maurras's young adherents took to splashy and aggressive demonstrations. The reality of war a few years later suggested to many more participants that the role of unquestioned command and the exercise of violence were recourses for survival.

The level of commitment to political activity required by the project-state—whether forged in war or revolution—would remain hard to sustain. Sometimes when ideological energies seemed to flag, organizers doubled down on the cathartic value of radical violence. Joseph Goebbels would call for "total war" in 1943; Mao Tse-tung would unleash cultural revolution in 1966–1967. More benign transformative experiments—the German revolution of 1918–1919, the American New Deal, the French Popular Front, the British Labour government of 1945—also envisioned project-states, but they aroused a hostile and debilitating opposition. The radical energies of the project-state surged and then abated, sometimes achieving significant institutional change but also leaving stagnation, disappointment, and melancholy. The episodes remain, however, as the most dramatic feature of the past century's vicissitudes, the Himalayas of twentieth-century history.

Readers are entitled to pose some hard questions. In what sense might it be said that the project-state was anything new? After all, the seventeenth-century Puritan "saints," certainly the French Jacobins, and most new regimes and groups of rulers who had taken power in revolutionary times possessed the same fervor for political transformation—do they count? Yes, along with other revolutionary upheavals including Haiti, they kindled transformative hopes, but they usually aimed at overturning old repressive legal institutions rather than building a more encompassing state even if they ended by imposing even greater degrees of constraint.[5] Arguably, the Napoleonic regime in France and the wartime organization of the US federal government during the Civil War could be described as project-states, and both bequeathed precedents and institutions for more "stateness." All historical phenomena can be shown to have precedents. As a continuing and nonexceptional form of polity, however, the project-state came into its own in the twentieth century.

It still remained difficult in the nineteenth century to harness the indigenous resources to institute what might count as a project-state. Many charismatic and talented leaders in Africa, Latin America, and South Asia might organize formidable military polities that subjugated neighboring lands for a decade or two but could not institutionalize the fiscal and bureaucratic institutions to construct durable states. Some leaders attempted to launch a thoroughgoing reform program but collided with the persistent realities of clientelist politics and insufficient material resources. The Middle East and Latin America proved to be a graveyard for project-states. Sometimes outside imperial powers aborted local programs lest they lose their own domination of a region. Mohammed Ali, who possessed the skill and ambition to build a project-state in Egypt during the early nineteenth century, collided with the British and French protectors of an Ottoman empire they deemed more compliant and serviceable for their own ambitions. Iranian reformers in the late nineteenth century remained squeezed between rival British and Russian desires to preserve a feeble monarchy as buffer for their respective neighboring empires. In East Asia, as noted, the Japanese successfully created a project-state but clearly limited democratic dimensions for the sake of military, industrial, and bureaucratic modernization. The would-be modernizers of the Qing Empire in the late nineteenth century ran up against not merely the conservatives of a faction-ridden imperial court but countervailing European and Japanese programs for imperial domination of their woefully armed and industrialized society. Would-be revolutionaries in Cuba and the Philippines collided with American policies, which remained in favor of their achieving independence from their Spanish rulers but not autonomy from their US patrons.

One reason was that the American proconsuls in the overseas territories that had been occupied since 1898 believed that they should be preparing new project-states themselves—not in their own continental territory but in the transoceanic periphery. As elsewhere, military planners would remain enthusiasts for societal intervention, an early version of nation-building. Denying simple imperialist objectives, Americans—the most celebrated perhaps, physician and colonel Leonard Wood—envisaged combinations of liberation, hygiene, and institution-building (such as police) in areas that had languished under Spanish plantation rule.[6] The causes of progressive reform at home, then of liberating Europe from German militarism from 1914 to 1918, then later, overcoming the Great Depression would bring this crusading impulse home to the North American continent. The Japanese, who accumulated their own transoceanic periphery in Taiwan, Korea, and the outposts in Shandong and the Liaodong peninsula (Dalien/Dairen) entertained analogous imperialist projects although under more ruthless military auspices.

Why, to address a further issue, should not the results of national unification and territorial centralization in the mid-nineteenth century count as project-states? The statesmen who unified Italy and Germany in the preceding century had taken on a strenuous political mission. But creating a state as a project is not the same as constructing a project-state. For a Cavour or Bismarck, the effort was to magnify the states they steered, Savoy and Prussia as armatures of larger national structures. For the intellectuals, the political mission presupposed that a national people already existed with some degree of self-awareness, and it sought to provide them with viable institutions, in a competitive world or to overcome civil strife: "We the people . . . to form a more perfect union." The project-state, on the other hand, was the work of leaders who often felt that they had to form or reinspire a people. The society they took in hand, so they believed, had not yet really come into being as a cohesive whole; or it had once existed and then fallen into corruption or banality; or it had become demoralized or had been taken over by evil agents. The project-state was redemptive. Not all eventual leaders of project-states started out by conceiving so ambitious a mission. Many, including civilians such as Franklin Roosevelt, had participated in military or administrative service during the world war. Some wanted only to hold office, solve a temporary crisis, get people back to work, or eliminate corruption and foreign influence; but to resolve the defects, they found their agenda inexorably grew more encompassing.

Finally consider the question that the author has asked himself throughout: whether project-states can be clearly distinguished as a subset of states in general. A major strand of contemporary social science claims that to "see like a state," to think in terms of "governability," or to make societies "legible" through classification and statistics makes all states effectively into project-states, potentially repressive if not totalitarian.[7] I disagree; the borders of the concept may be fuzzy, but the project-state strives to reshape society and not just to control it. Admittedly, the ambition to acquire or retain power can itself become an objective that requires, as eighteenth- and nineteenth-century liberals understood, subverting "intermediate bodies" or the forces of "civil society." It could also lead to expansion abroad: statehood in the international area might entail the assertion of dominance over other states or over peoples presumed to lack states and history.

Political scientists have used concepts similar to the project-state for analysis of diverse regimes, but distinctions are important. The project-state, as pointed out in the Introduction, refers to a governing enterprise that was different from what some have called the developmental state. Development, or what social scientists a half century ago liked to term modernization, was of course one sort of project. Leaders such as Chiang Kai-shek or Mustafa Kemal Atatürk wanted their countries to be "modern" in the sense that Europe or America was supposedly modern—that is possessing industry, programs for public hygiene, and secular education, but project-states could already have achieved a high level of economic and institutional development, as indeed many of those in interwar Europe had already done. [8] The project-state was not just a large state as measured say by the share of national income it collected, redistributed in social spending, or devoted to public works and the military. In Western Europe, the public sector share of national income distributed through the state (largely to military expenses, interest payments on the public debt, education, and infrastructure) surged in World Wars I and II then fell back, but it has grown from roughly 8–15 percent before 1914 to 40–55 percent today. Almost all governments in today's developed world have taken charge of programs for public health and transport, advanced education, and the like. Most of these programs have become familiar and expected. Neither is the project-state necessarily what political scientists have termed a strong state.[9] That designation usually is meant to suggest that the state can successfully make extensive demands on society, that it can "penetrate" preexisting institutions, whether political, familial, or religious, and can collect revenues and mobilize citizens in public causes. Certainly, the project-state aspired to these capacities, but it did not necessarily achieve them. It is a term used here to suggest ambition and program but not always accomplishment. Benito Mussolini's "fascist man" or Sun Yat-sen and Chiang Kai-shek's "New Life" remained rhetorical aspirations.

Case Histories and General Patterns

Some project-states have appeared as relatively brief phenomenon—they were historical stages of ongoing polities, the solar flares of regimes that burst into heated activity during crises and then burned out or settled back into ordinary historical continuity when leadership changed. Others renewed their energy over several decades and successive waves of upheaval. Mexico's initial uprising of diverse political leaders and clienteles against long-time strongman Porfirio Díaz soon dissolved into civil war between regionally based militias with varying ambitions and programs. General Álvaro Obregón managed to impose a stable regime in 1920 (before being assassinated in 1928 like several of his predecessors), but it took another decade or so to firm up the new regime under the aptly named Institutional Revolutionary Party (PRI). Even then by the 1930s, there would follow violent clashes with the Cristeros, a movement of armed protest against anticlerical policies, and a renewed conflict with the British owners of the nationalized petroleum industry until finally by the late 1930s, President Lázaro Cárdenas consolidated a one-party democratic settlement. Acceptance of state discipline by a revolutionary peasantry that was now benefiting from extensive communalization of land (the *ejido*) was critical to the outcome.[10]

Along with the Bolshevik experiment in Russia but a far more scattered and diverse set of activists, China provided the hugest arena for reformers and revolutionaries seeking to construct a project-state. As armed revolts against the dynasty broke out in many cities in the fall of 1911, the common theme was despair with the court whose emperor and advisers were seeking to roll back the reforms that more enlightened officials had started to launch in the last decade. The last-ditch effort by the Manchu court and officials triggered an ethnic as well as political upheaval. Out of the Manchu disintegration, two centers of republican institutions emerged: the National Assembly in Beijing and the military revolutionary party that would become the Kuomintang (KMT) in Nanjing and seize control between 1927 and 1931. From the perspective of the post–World War II Communist triumph, the accomplishments of the Republic (1911–1949) have often seemed feckless, condemned by corruption and by Chiang Kai-shek's authoritarianism, but the agenda was ambitious. The republican parliamentary regime based in Beijing witnessed the mass demonstrations of the May 4th (1919) movement, then settled into a succession of short-lived rivals, overshadowed by provincial warlords nearby. In the south, under the tutelage of the Third International's agent, Michael Borodin, Sun Yat-sen and then Chiang articulated their own state vision and modeled their KMT party-state on the Bolshevik example. Joseph Stalin miscalculated, however, in urging the local Communist Party to continue collaboration with Chiang's KMT. Once KMT loyalists had seized Nanjing in 1927, the party turned ruthlessly on its Communist adherents in a mass purge dramatically memorialized in André Malraux's novel *Man's Fate*. Establishing a capital in Nanjing was the founding act of a decade of transformation that would culminate in the northern expedition to take Beijing by 1931; it also opened the party to a process of *trasformismo* in which opportunist warlords, bureaucrats intent on securing a future as officials and favored private businessmen, rushed to join. Young radicals and intellectuals produced blueprints supposedly based on the broad principles that the ideological patriarch Sun Yat-sen had enunciated in exile. As, however, a recent author has argued, "Suppression of political activism accompanied careful choreographed expressions of civic enthusiasm. Deploying the political machinery of a radical revolutionary party, the GMD [Guomindang / KMT] embraced revolutionary capitalism, but rejected Western materialism and imperialism. It sought an ethno-communal solution to China's semi-colonial status."[11]

In light of Chiang's devastating defeat in the civil war (1945–1949) and the far more radical transformations that followed the victory of Mao Tse-tung's People's Republic, it was easy to denigrate the Nationalist achievement. The Cold War stakes of the debate for American politics with the McCarthyite attack on US advisers for undercutting Chiang influenced the effort to show how Chiang's vanity and stubbornness bore responsibility for his collapse.[12] The wartime and post-1945 calculations appeared comparable to how later rueful American critics viewed the sad final act of the South Vietnamese government (1973–1975) or the recent collapse of the Afghan regime once Washington removed its forces (2021). In that light, can the Nanjing Republic really be counted, therefore, as a project-state? Indeed, according to Chiang himself and other qualified observers, "the revolution" had "failed" by the early 1930s. KMT goals along with politics in Beijing remained most intent on checking potential rivals for leadership. But it also faced extraordinary challenges. It sought to claim a nation geographically fragmented, beset by inundations, global depression, and Japanese invasion. Agricultural prices declined by about half between the late 1920s and mid-1930s. From 1929 to 1931 / 1932, China's adherence to a soft-money silver standard favored investment and peasant debtors, but once Britain and the United States left the gold standard, that advantage was erased and foreign investment dried up as well. The US Silver Purchase Act, passed at the behest of western mining states, resulted in silver being drained from China's reserves; and the foreign capital that was made available had to be devoted to recovery from the serious flooding of the Yangtze River in 1931 that displaced over 25 million people.[13]

Perhaps it would be most accurate to say that the Chinese national regime that established its capital in Nanjing until the Japanese invasion of 1937 sought to control a turbulent mobilization of projects to build an effective and modern state. The effort partook of the same energies and aspirations as other project-states. There was no single model of national strengthening, but rival domestic programs marked many of the activist governments of the 1930s—whether the New Deal, the Soviet Union, or the Third Reich. Chiang worked for a militarized national state, and affinities of his program to European fascist movements has remained at the center of historical debate: its nationalism, authoritarianism, and in its depiction of the Chinese nation as a victimized collective proletariat echoed themes redolent in Italian and postwar German nationalism. Productivist ideology also was influential. Song Ziwen, who had family connections with Chiang, came the closest to a financial technocrat and business spokesman within the regime and lasted the longest. He worked the hardest to treat finances and the economy as an autonomous force and pressed for the organization of a National Economic Council influenced by corporatist ideas. Chiang, preeminently concerned with military unification of the remaining warlord territories, managed to clip the wings of the new council that debuted in 1931, placing it under the executive department he headed. Funding depended on American loans destined for recovery from the disastrous 1931 floods. Given the Japanese pressure after 1931, including the attacks on Shanghai, the council managed to emerge as a critical agency and collaborate with the other strand of nationalist reformism, the peasant-based corporatist project proposed by Wang Jingwei and his collaborators who entered the KMT government in the mid-1930s after earlier left-wing flirtation. Increasing the productive powers of the countryside and increasing its purchasing power, Wang held, would facilitate national industrialization. He sought to combine earlier reformist ideas for an autarkic peasant-based economy, inspired by Sun Yat-sen, with Italian corporativist ideas. Wang originally followed Chiang to the KMT wartime capital in inland Chungking but returned to head a collaborationist Republic of China in Nanjing under Japanese occupation. Only his death in Japan in 1944 spared him a postwar treason trial and probable execution. Wang's trajectory parallels that of the French labor corporatists who threw in their lot with Vichy and he was labeled a Chinese Vidkun Quisling.[14] The reality is that under conditions of foreign occupation, no program of state-organized labor organization could be evaluated in the abstract without taking into consideration its role in the great and cruel wartime struggle, and none could be imposed without repression.

In Europe by the spring of 1919, the European states that had entered the war or undertaken mass revolution seemed to be on the verge of durable transformation. Some were strengthened, some shattered; many were in the grip of revolution and civil war or bloody struggles over boundaries. The sprawling czarist empire had decomposed and was stripped of its western possessions by its adversaries in early 1918, then by emerging national units. Successor claimants to East Central European territory continued to wage brutal ragtag warfare for several years in an effort to determine which inter-mingled ethnic group would belong to which new political unit.[15] Inside the Russian heartland, Bolsheviks asserted precarious control but were assailed on all sides by counterrevolutionary and Western coalitions. The Hapsburg possessions were seized by national claimants who embarked on brave efforts at democratic statehood but were mistrustful of each other while their economic exchanges withered. The German Reich, which had counted on its military and industrial organization to prevail, faced humiliating defeat and a continuing blockade as radicalized soldiers and workers claimed revolutionary authority in its largest cities. Demonstrations, suppressed by right-wing veterans' units, seethed in Berlin, the Ruhr, and Munich. The new republican regime soon had to assent to territorial losses and an undefined stream of payments to the victors. The countries that had prevailed—Britain, France, even Italy, all supported by the United States, unscathed across the ocean—could celebrate victory but had fought out bitter disputes over war aims and had lost up to 10 percent of their young men. Even as the toughened leaders who had led the Allies to victory had asserted a new social and economic discipline, the potential for industrial discontent grew and was to be asserted through 1919 in massive strikes and demonstrations. The victors' colonial subjects were also restive and demanded the self-government and democracy that they believed had been promised by Woodrow Wilson's visionary addresses. Claimants for self-rule or the militant advocates of a new socialist international sparked agitation in the cities of South Asia, Africa, and the Middle East, only to learn that the promises might be granted at best in a distant future. Their delegations would return disappointed from the great peace conference in Paris. Nonetheless, many in the metropoles as well as in the colonies believed that a new social and political order was to emerge from the war—a new beginning and the chance for a league of peace. Returning veterans, politically aroused intellectuals, the hard-bitten revolutionaries, and those merely trying to take up the severed ends of family life all made their claims on what briefly seemed an open and malleable future.[16]

The project-state emerged from crisis, but not all crises yielded successful project-states. Some countries soldiered onward with politics as usual; others

responded unsuccessfully. Not all the states and political elites that improvised interventionist regimes during the war wished to maintain a high
degree of state involvement in the economy and society once peace returned.
The war separated those who wished to preserve the exaltation, heroism, and
collective bonding they derived or remembered from the war from the mass
of workers, businessmen, women and families, and a new generation who
wanted to move on with family and occupational life. In some cases, through
the 1920s, regimes remained divided between parties that had social-
democratic agendas (as in Weimar Germany and republican Austria) and
their long-term political adversaries who wished to establish citizenship based
on traditionalist structures (church or military).

US leaders called for a "return to normalcy." Let business and families resume their familiar lives. Others—we cannot quantify them, but their clamor
compensated for their probably small numbers—could not demobilize psy-
chologically. If soldiers, they missed the remembered camaraderie of army
life. If civilians, they may have missed the sense of collective purpose and dedication the war could evoke. Some felt committed to the level of central regulation and state authority that the wartime project had entailed. They
emerged addicted to transformative agendas, whether socialist on the left or
nationalist on the right. The state should continue to serve, not merely as
an administrative entity or a historical given but as an instrument by which
bureaucratic reformers or zealous partisans could mold a plastic national
society. Revolutionary upheaval or economic crisis or even the paralysis of
parliamentary decision making could unleash this energy needed to prevent
a relapse into prewar politics.

Over the postwar decade, however, national societies constructed a set of
institutions, some democratic, others authoritarian, that seemed to promise
an accepted and relatively stable result. By the mid-1920s, workaday electoral
politics brought conservatives and centrists to power in Britain, France, Germany, the Low Countries, Scandinavia, and North America. Behind the unrest, stability in Western Europe was achieved less through electoral politics
than by implicit social compact, as industrial leaders and those longtime
working-class representatives who shied from radical action reached consensus on centrist policies that provided advances in social policy and a free
hand for entrepreneurs and property. Industrial leaders negotiated cartel
agreements across national borders to stabilize markets within the prospect
of moderate growth. But this convergence of the political centers still left some
older cleavages to fester, such as those of religion and education. Neither

could they conclusively remove the grievances left by the peace settlements of 1918–1919, whether the overhanging reparations issues or the new, contested boundaries of East Central Europe. Here were continuing opportunities for demagogues.

National economies seemed to recover after bankers confirmed—willingly or not, by means of radical currency depreciation on the European continent—that perhaps half the European household savings accumulated as of 1914 had been liquidated in the Great War. Inflation could be good for business and tolerable for organized workers even as it operated as a confiscatory tax on the middle classes' bank accounts, war bonds, and life insurance policies. States and firms could shed the debts they owed at home. But critical to the business recovery was the fact that private American loans through the mid- and late 1920s promised to make the Europeans' debts across borders (including projected German reparations) and across the ocean to US taxpayers and investors far less of an impediment to renewing commerce and industry. Stabilization of postwar capitalism meant the future was less plastic than it had appeared.[17]

For many, this meant relief and progress—democratic regimes had been achieved in much of Central Europe; but for others, whether Western or colonial revolutionaries, setback and defeat, even as they preserved party and labor organizations to keep their aspirations alive. Many of the latter were to be imprisoned, beaten, or killed; and in some of European societies, new authoritarian regimes would treat their liberal opponents at home with a violence that the powers victorious in the Great War applied only to their colonial subjects (or in the United States to racial minorities). Liberal democracy (and a hard-core Bolshevik effort to seize power) in postwar Hungary had been the first to succumb to authoritarian military and civilians. It would collapse in stages in Italy before an innovative unleashing of a movement based on nationalism and violence tolerated by bourgeois elites who wanted to roll back working-class assertiveness. The king of Spain installed a military dictator, and the officer corps in Poland decided that the new republic had to be placed under their control. The example encouraged generals in Argentina and elsewhere in Latin America to seize power anew. Admirals and generals played a continuing and constitutionally inscribed role in governing Japan, although they seemed prepared to let civilian politicians play at running the country.

Other signs of trouble included the staging of political conflict in the streets whether in Paris over the collapse of the franc in 1926, the British General

Strike of 1926, or the acquittal of violent right-wing political demonstrators in Vienna in 1927, which led angry Socialist protesters to torch the Austrian supreme court. As the advent of fascism had demonstrated in Italy from 1919 to 1922 (reprising nineteenth-century revolutionary demonstrations and the 1915 rallies by those pressing to enter the world war), the public staging of politics with the violence it easily generated always had the potential to escape the restraints of constitutional procedures. Politics as theater—that is, rowdy demonstrations—had become endemic in the decade before 1914 and was an even more tempting recourse after the world war. Indeed, what seemed to matter across the urban centers of the world was often less everyday politics than performative, akin to the new edgy cultural developments prefigured in the creative decade before 1914 but becoming a frequent recourse in postwar streets and factories.

The really profound innovations in science and music and painting had burst upon the world, it seemed, in a few years around 1905; but their mass resonance followed in the postwar—through the cinema, the new jazz coming from America, the modern styles, whether for austere housing blocks or opulent art deco buildings, the bolder gendered behavior of young women and men, the mass athletics, daring airplane flights, and the growing pervasiveness of automobile traffic. Urban society, whether in New York, Paris, Berlin, Moscow, Shanghai, or Tokyo, seemed to detach itself even more than before the war from its rural hinterlands.[18] Those left to stagnate or even perhaps to thrive in the provinces resented the metropolitan centers of supposed decadence. They could demonstrate that they would not let customary status or values, patriarchal, religious, or racial, be dismissed without a backlash. In the United States, the crusade for prohibition, the revival of the Ku Klux Klan, the shutdown of mass immigration, and the reluctance to allow the teaching of evolution in school curricula testified to the fractures of a society that had briefly engaged with the wider world of international politics and felt betrayed by the experience.[19]

By the early 1930s, global economic crisis threw all the recently renegotiated socioeconomic settlements into question. Depressed agricultural prices and growing unemployment, which soon overwhelmed new and underfunded unemployment insurance funds, radicalized the electorates of Central Europe where voting still mattered. Mass migrations from the afflicted regions to the Americas, formerly so important a valve for development and social stability, was no longer an option once the United States established national quotas for immigrants in 1924. Peasants and farmers around the world had suffered through five years or more of stagnation, poverty, and growing indebtedness. Agricultural distress proved the most persistent and pervasive problem whether in economies that had substantially reduced farming (e.g., Britain and Belgium) to less than 10 percent of its labor force, those that kept a substantial agricultural sector in being (the United States, Canada, and Germany at about 25 percent), and those where it engaged from a third to half the families of the country (France, Scandinavia, and the less developed world).[20] Farm prices had crashed in the Depression and in some cases weakened significantly before.

Global politics was still hostage to the hardships faced by peasants and farmers the world over. The anguish of farmers and peasants was like a huge millstone dragging on the global economy between the wars. Farmers could not be fired, but they could be foreclosed. Prices for their commodities could fall far more proportionally than those of industrial goods. Growing single crops for markets, they and their families could suffer malnutrition and subsist in a countryside only partially electrified and, as in the case of the dust bowl, ecologically degraded. In China, devastating floods in 1931 worsened their misery. In the Soviet Union, the confrontation with a regime that fundamentally distrusted the rural masses who had taken over landlord and village holdings after 1917 produced divergent policy recommendations from the mid-1920s on. Stalin exploited the disagreements within the Communist Party to ally with and then denounce their respective advocates. By the end of the 1920s, he opted for a fierce policy to collectivize peasant holdings, enforced by trials and deportations of those farmers who resisted and the denial of food imports into a Ukraine in the throes of famine. (How many millions of country folks' lives have been sacrificed by remote elites under the spell of doctrine—whether collectivist convictions in the case of Communist Russia and China from the late 1920s to the end of the 1950s, or dogmas of market rationality in the case of British administrators in Ireland a century before and in India in 1943!) Soviet advocates of a less drastic agricultural policy in the 1920s, such as Nikolai Bukharin, paid with their lives during the purges of the next decade.[21]

The world economic and financial crisis of the 1930s spread distress to industry as well and now compelled the would-be architects of global stabilization to address economic arrangements alongside the political ones (see Chapter 3). The prevailing orthodoxy of global austerity—cutting wages and government expenditures—only aggravated the distress. The resource empires enjoyed some cushion to allow feckless deflationary policies to continue at home, although even they were forced into some unprecedented monetary devaluation of their currencies in terms of external standards: the pound against gold (and the dollar) in 1931, the dollar (against gold in 1933), the French franc, repeatedly from the mid-1930s, the Japanese yen from the mid-1930s.[22] Advocates of these adjustments had to argue against those who resisted, and their policies tended to fight real contraction less through the hoped-for revival of exports than the accompanying fall of interest rates at home, which allowed an uptick in business investment or new housing. Ultimately, so Keynesians maintained, it took fiscal, not monetary policies including deficit spending if need be, to get beyond the painful years of depression, and it took preparations for war to justify much of the new spending.[23] (The result was a decade of needless misery on a global scale for those afflicted—to be matched in individual countries only with the collapse of the Soviet Union in the 1990s or briefer crises in "emerging" market economies around the turn of the current century or in the southern periphery of the European Union from 2008 for another wasted decade!) Amid the economic wreckage of the 1930s, political innovation beckoned urgently. Church and local welfare no longer sufficed to cushion poverty; states would have to prop up agricultural markets with national marketing boards to stabilize supply and prices. Neither was it enough to combat family misery with direct aid; capitalism was in disrepair and called out for new institutions for structuring competition. Canada, Australia, Sweden, and ultimately the United States and France sought salvation with new coalitions among economic interventionists. In the shadow of Germany's new Nazi government, Central Europe turned toward militarist and authoritarian governments.

The project-state that reemerged in this agitated period would characterize regimes otherwise bitterly opposed to each other over the next half century. Its advocates believed that political institutions should and could decisively reshape civil society—civil-society associations, economies, aesthetic expression, the family, and the physical environment—and even individual mentalities. Its leaders and civil servants were confident that politics should not just preserve ways of life but also transform them. To govern was not merely a question of winning mass support, holding office and applying the rule of party and / or the rule of law, although the capacity to decisively exercise power was a prerequisite. To rule was a redemptive vocation. Some forms of redemption sounded more threatening than others: creating the fascist man who would live as a lion and not as a jackal was a different project than raising out of poverty "one third of a nation ill-housed, ill-clad, ill-nourished." Mussolini called for the former, Franklin Roosevelt strived for the latter, even as Roosevelt's project exalted democracy's mission in quasi-religious tones.[24]

Leaders and Labor

The project-state—whether on the left or the right—required and nurtured a special relationship between its leaders and a mass public. "Leader" became a highly charged term—obviously for fascism where Il Duce and the Führer became the ordinary and, in Germany, the legal title—but also in the Soviet Union, where the early debate over whether the term *vozhd* should be attributed to the party or to an individual was resolved in favor of the latter as Stalin consolidated his power from 1924 to 1929.[25] By the 1930s, there were many *nachal'niki* or "heads," in factories, departments, and so forth but only one *vozhd* or leader. Contemporary American usage with all its books on "leadership" in business and other activities has made the term a relatively functional attribute devoid of mystique. But through the earlier twentieth century, the leader and leadership retained an almost mystical aura of authority. The leader's lieutenants took satisfaction in being led. As necessary as the rapport felt between the leader and the individual—though that was important—was the performative appeal that the leader had to exert over a crowd assembled to listen, sometimes in a stadium or square, sometimes over the new medium of radio.

Even for democratic leaders, acclamation by the crowd or what commentators called—with approval on the left and concern on the right—the masses remained a resource for governing. In the prewar decades, conservative commentators described the masses as a dangerous encroaching mob, responding to instinctual collective impulses. Vilfredo Pareto, Gustave Le Bon, and many others envisaged these dark crowds much as Francisco Goya had depicted their superstitious village predecessors in his nightmarish paintings of *romeros* or pilgrimages a century earlier. The "masses" emerged as a term in Social Democratic and Socialist discourse before World War I, as these parties planned to mobilize the political resources of collective action, including the "mass strike" to force political change. Educated observers beheld this rapport ambiguously. Did it not awaken archaic collective impulses? Critical liberals tended to ascribe the enthusiasm of mass crowds to a dangerous preconscious response, as did Thomas Mann in his 1930 allegory of fascism, "Mario and the Magician."

From the end of the nineteenth century on, these impulses were rediscovered as a challenging problem but potentially a political resource. As Francisco

Campos, an adviser to Brazilian dictator Getúlio Vargas and admirer of fascism declared, "The masses are fascinated by charismatic personalities. This is what is at the heart of political integration. The larger and more active the masses, the more political integration becomes possible only through the dictatorship of a personal will. Dictatorship is the political regime of the masses. The only natural expression of the will of the masses is the plebiscite: that is to say, of acclamation and appeal before choice."[26] Democratic leaders of project regimes, whether the New Deal or the Popular Fronts, also drew on the crowds to define and to support their political rallies. The project-state could not really do without the electricity of the assembled audience; it depended on more than rational argumentation alone.

The proletariat presented the same ambiguous valence as did the "masses" or allegedly backward colonial subjects. The working class like the amorphous "masses" presented twentieth-century politics with its unprecedented challenge. The project-state worked hard to reorient it into a component of national consensus. For the dictatorships, organizing leisure-time activities became a necessary effort and the Dopolavoro and Kraft durch Freude became major party bureaucracies.[27] The proletarian was not necessarily hostile to modern industrial society but supposedly was unable to comprehend the intricate organization of factory work. By the 1930s, American manuals and journals of business management, which had exalted technological and engineering skills through the 1920s, now presented running a firm as a task for a boss with the psychological capacity to harmonize personal relations. Elton Mayo and Fritz Roethlisberger emphasized these new imperatives in their management treatises. Scientific management by the 1930s meant less the application of assembly-line organization than overseeing the factory as a mini-society whose population had to be manipulated by wise executives.[28]

The idea of representation also changed accordingly. The autonomous citizen of 1789 was to be supplemented or replaced by representatives nominated by the "organic" sectors that the across class lines—mining, agriculture, heavy industry, artisanal production, hospitality, health care, and so on—a structure called corporatism or corporativism, already outlined in legal theory and Catholic social doctrines and elaborated by Mihail Manoilescu, the Romanian writer who found readers throughout the Latin world.[29] The term became identified most closely with fascist Italy, where after a few years of ideological indecision, Mussolini's regime sought to displace the representation of individual citizens by delegates of functional or economic interests. Although fascist Blackshirts had helped put him into power in late 1922 with years of violence against worker organizations, Mussolini initially clamed to celebrate independent industrialists and a liberal economy. In 1923, however, he compelled industry leaders to sign an encompassing bargaining agreement with the official fascist labor unions. With the clampdown on the press and opinion in 1925, the thoroughgoing authoritarian concepts of Minister of Justice Alfredo Rocco gained ascendancy. Expansion of police powers and a political tribunal was accompanied by a swing in economic policy toward corporativism and autarky. Following a surprising steel strike by obstreperous fascist labor leaders in Brescia in 1925, which seemed to challenge Fascist Party supremacy, Rocco's 1926 law on syndical representation stipulated that the government would recognize only one workers' and one employers' *sindacato*—the preexisting fascist union, not the socialist or communist organization—for twenty-two branches of the economy. Lockouts and strikes were prohibited. Even so, the activism of fascist labor leaders (some with Syndicalist, even Industrial Workers of the World [IWW] origins) remained too strong within the organization to be tolerated by Mussolini, and in 1928, the hitherto unified fascist syndical bloc was broken up (*il sbloccamento*) into weaker components essentially subordinated to the managerial components. An elaborate corporativist structure emerged, including a Ministry of Corporations (1926), then a National Council of Corporations (1930), a Labor Magistrate to settle disputes, and a Charter of Labor setting out workers' rights and obligations, and finally in 1939 the transformation of the parliament into a Chamber of Fasces and Corporations. Alessio Gagliardi's recent account claims that the workers' voice got a hearing in welfare and other legislation, but the most significant result may have been the international "bragging rights" that Mussolini could claim for having found a third way between capitalism and communism.[30] Whatever that achievement might have amounted to would be swept away by the disastrous results of war and civil war and occupation.

Militant labor activity was not incompatible with fascist or Nazi enthusiasms. In Italy, the Genoan dockworkers and return migrants who had been active in the IWW maintained syndicalist loyalties, deeply resented the official socialist unions and formed the basis of the fascist union movement. In Germany, the factory-floor shop-steward movement, also resentful of the official Social Democratic General Trade Union Confederation, gravitated toward the Nazis. Across the Atlantic, Juan and Evita Perón built a direct rapport with Buenos Aires's working classes, more plebiscitary than corporatist. But Getúlio Vargas's revolt against the Brazilian parliamentary state in 1930 evolved into a semicorporatist regime with the constitution of 1934 and reaffirmed his trajectory with the New State of 1937. Vargas, however, dropped Campos, who was too tainted by outright fascism, when he returned to power in 1942, favoring instead the technocratic and corporatist proposals of Oliveira Viana, and eventually making gestures toward parliamentary revival as he moved toward the anti-Axis side in the world war. The conflicting authoritarian, military, and liberal pressures may have contributed to his suicide in 1954.[31]

The Third Reich dissolved the Socialist, Communist, and Catholic trade unions and incorporated labor into the Deutsche Arbeitsfront. Despite the compulsory structure, labor remained a crucial actor within so industrial a country, and the organization a bureaucratic prize whose leaders needed to maintain some credibility as tending to working-class interests. Once production for war accelerated, the heightened demand for labor meant that de facto tendencies toward collective bargaining on working conditions and wages might even creep back in.[32]

For leaders of the American New Deal, which faced real competitive elections, the alliance with independent labor leaders was crucial. But the administration initially turned to an encompassing National Recovery Act (NRA), which in an effort to end the ruinous collapse of prices allowed corporations to override antitrust restraints and write their own guidelines for competition. Section 7a of that omnibus signature measure of the "hundred days" provided for legally sanctioned labor unions on a national scale, overruling the many state impediments that still existed. The NRA, however, would be struck down by the Supreme Court in 1935, and the economy would take a renewed plunge in 1936–1937 as government spending slowed. In response, during its second term the Roosevelt administration supported the Wagner Act of 1937 that established a National Labor Relations Board and guaranteed union organizing rights. The flirtation with corporatism ended, but the alliance with a powerful labor movement—now itself reenergized with the emergence of the Congress of Industrial Organizations to challenge the American Federation of Labor—remained fundamental.

A moment's reflection as well as the historical record makes it clear that project-states that sought to enfold the organizations of civil society within governmental and party organizations must lead to intense internal bureaucratic conflicts. Although the project-state was often in the hands of a single party, bitter and sometimes lethal divisions were endemic. Mussolini and Adolf Hitler each faced zealots who wanted to push radical party control of administration and military organization further than the leaders would accept. The two dictators sought to exert discipline over potentially "radical" dissidents early on—Hitler in the infamous Blood Purge of June 30, 1934, Mussolini with the labor legislation of 1926—and managed to repress insurrectionary tendencies. Nonetheless, authoritarian parties, even when they were based on "revolutionary vanguards," or comrades who had taken great risks together to seize power, divided into bitter factions and sometimes murderous purges once they had a regime in place. Chiang's "right" KMT loyalists liquidated their "left" party members and then the party's Communist allies in 1927. In 1927, Kemal had tried and executed some of the Unionist (Young Turk) leaders who had come to criticize his hold on power. Stalin's purges provided the most spectacular and lethal demonstration of the leader's determination to crush any possible challenge as well as to take revenge for earlier dissent. The dictator's wave of show trials in the 1930s, just the tip of the iceberg of the convulsion, disgraced, imprisoned, and murdered his former Bolshevik comrades, all in the name of the party they had served.

No matter how apparently united their regimes might seem or how great a sense of purpose they conveyed, project-states were thus not the cohesive instruments that commentators often deduced from their demanding agendas and, in the case of the dictatorships, their brutal politics. Rather, they were riddled with rivalries, overlapping offices, and sometimes paralyzing infighting. Ad hoc agencies were created to tackle new interventions in markets, as they had been in World War I. Parties talked about eliminating bureaucracy, but in the pursuit of rapid action, they created contending bureaucracies. The Bolsheviks, hardly in power for a decade, found the new commissariats they had created so entrenched that they organized another organization, Rabkrin, just to check the agencies recently instituted.[33] The New Deal inherited the Civil Works Administration to construct infrastructure; then it created the Public Works Administration to vastly expand its projects. When these seemed to take too long to get men to work, Harry Hopkins used the Federal Employment Relief Authority to carve out the Works Project Administration (WPA). Hitler entrusted the emerging autobahns to the energetic construction agency under Fritz Todt, known simply as Organisation Todt. Shortly after, Hermann Goering, the buccaneering air minister, managed to aggregate power as head of the 1936 Four Year Plan designed to prepare Germany for war. He succeeded in consolidating control of the low-grade iron ore holdings in central Germany so he could stand up to the more traditional Ruhr coal and steel magnates. His crash expansion of armaments, which required ramping up imports, led to a face-off with the more economically orthodox Hjalmar Schacht who worried about the pressures on the German balance of payments.[34] Ambitious men who were appointed to lead the agencies were jealous of their authority: they defended their new powers and claimed to be truer executors of their leader's objectives than their rivals. Discussing the Nazi project of exterminating the Jews through the early 1940s, Hitler's biographer Ian Kershaw has stressed the apt formula of one eager mid-level careerist that the good Nazi had to "work toward the Führer," that is anticipate his genocidal intentions even if he preferred not to make them literally explicit.[35] But in democratic systems where progressive reform and not murder was at stake, loyal staff also wanted to work toward "the boss," as Harry Hopkins envisaged his service for Roosevelt, and certainly most difficult of all, in the Soviet Union to work toward Stalin—a chancy calculation that often drastically shortened one's adult life.

As historians later unraveled these tangled and hastily assembled governing machines after they either collapsed or became more routinized, some were led to describe them as a sort of "pluralism," and even "weak" dictatorships, descriptions that were easily though misleadingly criticized as apologetic.[36] Dictatorships and democracies both had to overcome internal friction. Hitler and Roosevelt—one hesitates to bracket the German leader whose inner life was constructed around contempt, rancor, and hatred with the buoyant and generous (if at times devious) American president—were both reluctant to decide among their contending subordinates with their diverse policies until they absolutely had to. Understandably so, since fundamental priorities in peace and war were at stake. Nor did the welter of conflicts derive only from the styles of the respective leaders. The German regime had to balance and eventually subordinate a venerated military, a tradition-laden bureaucracy, and powerful economic organizations along with its ruthless SS administrators of political terror.[37] The American New Deal was subject to the conservatives entrenched in regional strongholds and a powerful national legislature along with a Supreme Court that did not hesitate to strike down important policy initiatives.[38] But the infighting, confusion, and overlap of functions should not confuse the observer. It did not indicate weakness but testified to the new tasks taken on, to the willingness to experiment with diverse approaches to prosperity and power, and to the zeal of those who had attained their moment of influence and authority. States that retained private ownership of the economy—which was the case outside the Soviet Union—became powerful by delegating to business experts the productive processes they needed to centralize. When the system creaked and groaned, the economists could blame the state, which indeed was one of the impulses that motivated the German Ordoliberals during and after the war. They wanted to restore a supposedly purer economic order; the previous world struggle showed that it could not have functioned under conditions of wartime.

Transforming Bodies and the Landscape

The project-state never released its hold on bodies as well as minds, and its citizens' bodies were connected with its other physical resources, including the landscape. It followed what Michel Foucault has labeled a biopolitics agenda. Its populations were viewed as a collective resource to be shaped by eugenic and hygienic, and, in the case of Nazism, by genocidal policies. Indeed, the primacy of these policies remained central to wartime planning, which meant that the SS was always an actor that had to be included. Certainly, the differences were crucial: the Rockefeller Foundation's plans to "eliminate" diseases were different from the SS's ideas of eliminating people.[39] Nonetheless, the project-state envisaged a hygienic component. Concepts of public health became integral. Some writers used the term *social engineering* to refer to the general idea of shaping the environment to produce a well-integrated citizenry that functioned harmoniously in factory or city.[40] All these goals had long been present. Clean public housing as in Weimar Germany, "Red Vienna," and Sweden had been integral to the effort. Although contested by many supporters of tradition, "modern" architecture in general with its allegedly "functional" design was an indicator of the overriding mentality. Economic and social "planning," urban sociology, and eugenics all belonged to this admittedly vague constellation of approaches, which included the ideas of Taylorism and Fordism from the 1920s.

The project-state celebrated conservation and set aside parkland.[41] It encouraged collective gymnastics and displayed massed bodies in athletic exercises. It required physical prowess not only on the part of individual heroes but also collective teams. The male gendered body in particular, sometimes longed for by those who celebrated it, had become an icon of the age of imperialism, along with the revival of the Olympic Games in 1896 and foundation of the Rhodes Scholarship, the heroic sojourn in the American West, the airplane flight over first the English Channel, later the Atlantic (Italo Balbo's 1936 flight to Chicago) or the Arctic.

Between the wars, the project-state sought to inculcate enthusiasm and not merely consent. It exploited the resources of high modernism—the bold geometries of public murals, often infused with critiques of capitalism or war, and sometimes painted over, as at the LaGuardia Airport maritime terminal, once a Cold War sensibility set in. Accessibility to a mass audience was crucial, and what the Soviets celebrated as socialist realism found its analogues in the United States.[42] Public buildings ended up as neoclassic compromises between modernism and tradition. Washington's architects retained their love of Ionic columns. Stalin's architects, like the later set designers of Batman's Gotham, borrowed from the New York skyscrapers of the 1920s. Modernity could find its place in fascist construction: Goering's Air Ministry and Italian rationalist architecture in the new towns of the cleared Pontine marshes, and finally the buildings planned for EUR, the great exposition on the outskirts of Rome to commemorate the anniversary of the regime and constructed in time for its ending.

As Patrizia Dogliani observes, the shaping of leisure and landscape went together. The New Deal showed the way with WPA projects, the US Forest Service and Soil Conservations Service, Resettlement Administration, and best known, the Civilian Conservation Corps, employing more than 1.5 million youth in 3,000 camps. The United States had pioneered in national parks; now it sent observers to report on the European effort, often rather uncritically: "The very foundation stones of the Nazi, Fascist, and Communistic movements are the children and the young people.... American public recreation institutions and organizations are not the mediums of propaganda for any particular political idea of the state except the general idea of love, devotion, loyalty to the nation. This is exactly the same idea embodied in those countries where the nation, the state, the party are considered as identical."[43] The state had not originated the almost mystical bonding of body and landscape in Central Europe, but it understood how to exploit it. By 1935, the Third Reich established a compulsory six-month labor service to inculcate the organic connection between "blood and land." Italy followed suit with the proliferation of seaside and Alpine camps and the creation in 1937 of the Italian Youth of the Littorio (Gioventù Italiana del Littorio) named for the fascist symbol of the lictor's rods, increasingly prominent as the militarized GIL.

Physical activity accompanied mastery of the landscape. The project-state envisaged the national territory and its colonies as a central target of transformation. Territory assumed an almost organismic role: highways would bind it together as the railroads had done in the previous century; national highway systems both encouraged mobility but simultaneously canalized it into purposive activity that demonstrated mastery of space as well as citizens. Foreign tourism revived in Italy after the Depression, and the state coordinated the agencies. Auto touring was not yet a working-class activity but did make its way among bourgeois and functionary families. Autobahns, American parkways, and French *routes nationales* became engraved in the national imaginary. The Mexican regime embarked on a clear program of aesthetics and development, although its national imprint soon yielded to commercial considerations.[44] Reality usually lagged behind the hype, and as always, bureaucratic agencies and ministries quarreled over the authority for projects. But nothing conveyed the need for the project-state like the cinematic representations of endangered landscapes such as Pare Lorentz's celebrated films *The Plow That Broke the Plains* and *The River*.

Under totalitarian auspices, people and places could be steam-shoveled simultaneously. Karl Schlögel has described the construction of the White Sea Canal:

> At stake was not simply a building project but the "transformation," the "reforging" (perekovka) of human beings through work—or, more to the point, the use of forced labour to transform hundreds of thousands of prisoners.... In October 1932, 125,000 prisoners were engaged there. Working in unspeakable conditions, they built a canal of 227 kilometers, together with its locks, ports and bridges, smashing and excavating their way through the rocky and swampy terrain of Karelia. The mortality rate in 1933, for example was 10.56 per cent—8,870 people in all.... In many respects the second canal was a straightforward appeal to the first ... plundered for its barracks and working implements ... key personnel assumed management roles in the second ... prisoners from Karelia sent to the new site.... The number of prisoners at Dimitlag grew as follows: 1932, 10,400; 1933, 51,502; 1934, 156,314; 1935, 188,792; 1936, 192,034; 1937, 146,920; 1938, 16,068.... [So too] the Moscow-Volga canal finished in the summer of 1937 was a project full of superlatives ... 3.8million cubic meters of concrete ..."an authentic work of art of our great heroic Stalinist epoch."[45]

Colonies became a privileged site of developmental plans. Despite the complex and layered societies that they contained, whether in Africa, Bali, Korea, and elsewhere, their new masters could treat them as tabula rasa.

What emerged combined concepts of so-called modernist development and public hygiene. "Rational architecture" under fascism characterized new towns—some in the cleared marshes south of Rome, such as Sabauda, others in Libya and Eritrea.[46] The Japanese were particularly active in Taiwan (Formosa), which they controlled since wresting it from China and the indigenous Taiwanese in 1895. Higgledy-piggledy neighborhoods oriented around Chinese temples were replaced by grid plans in which state Shinto shrines took a coordinating role.[47] Modernizing the colonial city meant also the construction of water and drainage systems, endowing Taipei with a public waterworks from 1913 on. The great Tokyo earthquake of 1923 was a catalyst for modern architecture in Tokyo and in Taiwan. In 1935, the Japanese celebrated the fortieth anniversary of colonization with a great exposition, four years after the Colonial Exposition in Paris and the 1933 Chicago Century of Progress Exposition.[48]

Enthusiasm, however, is an elusive quality and potentially misleading as an index of the transformative capacity. It also runs down. By the late 1930s, despite all the crowds and the strutting, the new construction, the historian can detect symptoms of a flagging—or at least an institutionalization of the project-state: a transition toward bureaucracy, staged rituals, familiar patterns of art and aesthetics. Radical projects became harder to sustain in the democratic states such as France and the United States and even Mexico; they were buttressed by commemorative programs and ceremony. Although the energies of these regimes seemed at a height, without continuing radicalization it was not clear how they would be sustained. The New Deal's congressional majority evaporated in the 1938 and 1940 elections. The Nazis turned toward a sharpening of their anti-Semitic measures, including the violence of Kristallnacht and preparation for war. Stalin and the Communist Party of the Soviet Union could attempt to continue their revolution through the purges. And war and then the Cold War would not allow the project-state's public energies to surrender its grip.

This raises an important issue: did / does the project-state have a propensity for military involvement, an elective affinity for war? After all, war not only helped nurture the project-state but remained endemic in the years when project-states were vigorous. Thinkers from Immanuel Kant on have argued that states where public opinion and liberal governments prevailed were less likely to go to war, at least with each other—a correlation political scientists call "democratic peace theory."[49] The finding may be robust for pairs of democratic states but still inconsequential since democratic states have found themselves frequently at war with nondemocratic states. Reverse, moreover, the question to ask about pairs of states that do not go to war with each other; many are nondemocratic. Sadly, however, a far more meaningful correlation exists between project-states and military involvement. The energies of project-states can be a source of regional turmoil; their programs call for an international milieu hospitable to their domestic values that can provoke their own interventions abroad or the incursions of foreign powers. If domestic resistance limits their plans for restructuring, leaders may seek foreign opponents. Obviously, some of the authoritarian ones—fascist Italy, National Socialist Germany, Hirohito's Japan—glorified military success and envisaged military prowess and conquest as central to their project. Soviet Russia and the United States ended up repeatedly in war even as they professed peace. The issue is not whether their wars were justified or "aggressive" but whether programs of national renewal were likely to churn up the international milieu enough to make armed conflict more likely, and if so, what policy implications might arise. Should we beware the international ramifications of the project-state?

Impulses from World War II

World War II compelled governments to develop their instruments for economic planning as it had in World War I. The overriding project was a given: national victory or at least survival. But the imperative of war did not necessarily yield a more efficient state. Wartime means chronic scarcity—of manpower, raw materials, and transportation. Conscription imposes labor scarcity; production of weaponry cuts into the civilian economy. Military planners seek to arrogate economic functions with mixed success. The relative advanced status of the American, British, and German economies did not really resolve the problems since individual firms, government agencies, and the armed forces all sought to claim as many resources as they could and control the administration needed. The Japanese faced the challenge of maintaining a large land army in China and Southeast Asia while fighting on a major ocean theater against an enemy with far greater industrial capacity. With heightened wartime discipline reinforcing patriotic calculations, it was hardly likely that labor could or would press a left agenda before catastrophic defeat. At that point, however, Allied occupation forces would assure social order.[50]

Yet even in countries facing defeat, the software capabilities of the project-state advanced. Control of the information needed to coordinate the war economy was critical and every national economy had theoretically to yield to state control while state agencies had to learn how to get a statistical handle on available resources and urgent requirements. The talented Fritz Todt went from the autobahns to armaments, and after his mysterious death in a plane crash, Albert Speer took over, working with the so-called committees and rings of relevant industrialists. Adam Tooze's study of German statistical agencies emphasizes the role of both Hans Kehrl at the Economic Ministry—a textile industrialist and "passionate Nazi" recruited in stages for ever more important functions—and Rolf Wagenführ, the chief organizer of German statistical agencies. "Amid the ruins of the German state a new relationship flourished between expertise and politics."[51] The struggle for statistical mastery did not eliminate rival political concepts. As the prospect of a lost war became ever more real—if always undiscussable in official circles— two concepts for the relationship of the postwar state and the German economy were discernable. Kehrl and Wagenführ anticipated ever tighter planning with a collaboration between industrialists and state planners, not for management of the factories themselves but for their coordination: a technocratic state supervising a national private economy. The same desperate struggle for production convinced the Ordoliberal economists centered on Freiburg that the autonomy of the market economy must be reaffirmed, albeit scaffolded by state legislation that would preserve competition and ensure social welfare, to limit any lurch to the left. Within government circles, the "Ordo" concept influenced Ludwig Erhard, who would become the economic administrator of the postwar bizonal occupation authority and ultimately Konrad Adenauer's successor in the 1960s.[52]

The challenge for statistical summation of the economy was not only the gathering of data—although it took an effort to get firms to report the relevant quantities—but making useful and comparable categories of data, then applying them for wartime purposes. Pervading all the efforts was the unavoidable fact of relative scarcity—resources available to the wartime state were never enough for all the claims that would be made on them. Even the wealthy and protected US "Arsenal for Democracy" had to meet contending priorities of the European and Pacific theaters and the needs of its allies as well as its own forces. Manpower had to be allocated both for combat and for industry, shipyard capacity for freighters and for warships, and the latter had to be prioritized among landing craft, submarines, and surface vessels. Albert Speer would later opine that had the Allies concentrated on taking out German ball-bearing factories, the Nazi war effort would have ground to a halt; however, he did not say that the costs in terms of Allied aircraft and crews had been devastating and unacceptable.[53]

New techniques emerged—the operational research in Britain that sought to calculate the efficiency of bombing tactics or shipping safety, or the relatively crude but difficult-to-gather tables of wartime outputs and their needed inputs that Wagenführ assembled, or the efforts that the Soviets had made to quantify all national products and their components into a ninety-row horizontal and vertical table, which Russian émigré Vassily Leontief developed in America as input-output analysis and its related branch of data management, linear programming. Wartime urgently compelled optimization—that is, maximizing changing goals under conditions of constraint. Britain perhaps had the easier task for this sort of planning: manpower and shipping were the overwhelmingly scarce resources that claimed priority in the calculations.[54] But for all wartime participants clarifying the data, developing the matrices, and soon the bulky early computers needed to solve them was critical for the growth of state capacity. The postwar period with all their shortages— at least for countries other than an America wealthier than ever—would prolong the mentality. The Marshall Plan of the late 1940s would also be conceived as a program to overcome the critical postwar bottleneck of American imports needed for European recovery. The rhetoric of the project-state was all about aggregate quantities achieved—gross national product was enshrined as the aggregate of aggregates—but the motivation behind the index always remained the quantities still needed.

Road and traffic planning remained important into the 1950s and after but more to satisfy a middle-class public that could acquire autos and take less ideologically laden vacations. German traffic engineers in the 1950s debated about what roads and rails integrated a national territory.[55] Meanwhile, the major infrastructure project of the Eisenhower administration was the laying down of the Interstate Highway System so that America caught up with and surpassed the autobahns. From the 1920s on, auto highways had become folkloric like the railroads before them: fabled US Route 66 roughly paralleled the legendary Atchison, Topeka, and the Santa Fe. But ultimately, a road would be just a road, increasingly choked by the vehicles hauling private goods and family travelers.

Nonetheless, as World War II transitioned into the Cold War, rival alliances, and the Korean War (or for Britain, France, and the Netherlands into colonial conflicts), the connection of the project-state and male military virtue remained. This historian's boy scout troop in the early 1950s would have its junior high and high school adolescents devoting half their weekly meeting time to practicing how to march for the village Memorial Day parade. The poet Stephen Vincent Benet was no longer around to ask us, as he had queried the dead in the 1930s, why we were marching; we would not have had the awareness to answer that we were being marched for the sake of a concept of citizenship that would largely dissolve by the 1960s. The project-state still imposed memories and set a cadence, but the urgency of its causes was weakening.

2

The Promise of Resource Empires

1919: THE PARIS PEACE CONFERENCE that convened, at least in Woodrow
Wilson's eyes, to confirm the rights of nations and peoples, was still to leave
about a quarter of the world's almost 2 billion inhabitants as colonial or imperial subjects. Huge swathes of territory with populations mostly of color were
governed by remote states they had never chosen as rulers and over whose
regime they had no voice. Nonetheless, whether as a reservoir for conscripts,
contract labor, or traditional military units, the colonies had made significant
contributions to their metropole's military campaigns and had suffered heavy
losses. Colonial domains remained a significant component of state power
and resources and would continue as such until after mid-century.

World War I, however, compelled the colonial powers to reassert the legitimacy of their rule given the emphasis on self-determination that President Wilson's framing of the conflict entailed. Empire had to be rethought
and repurposed, fitted out with even a loftier purpose than the prewar concepts of civilizational superiority. As a form of rule, it needed to be integrated
as a component of what the colonial powers conceived as global order and,
not least, reinforced as an economic asset, profitable for "settler colonists" in
the territories, investors in the metropole, and hopefully for state budgets as
well. Could the resources of empire be made fungible—that is, transformed
from direct control to economic capital and to political and cultural influence? In historical perspective, we can answer yes, but not if the traditional
form of direct dominion was insisted on. The viceroys and the durbars, the
governors general, the command of white soldiers and police over local con-
stabularies of color would eventually have to go, as would the ministries for
the colonies, and finally even this historian's favorite artifact: the store selling
vêtements pour les pays chauds replete with its pith helmets and Sahara whites
on the Boulevard de Saint-Germain in Paris.

Empire naturally had its critics in the metropole. For many of them, most notably Vladimir Lenin, the recent Great War seemed an outgrowth of imperialist competition. Nonetheless, to attribute a direct causal relationship between World War I and colonial rivalries is difficult. Conflicts over some colonial arenas—Manchuria and Korea, the remnant of the Ottoman domains in the Balkans—led to appallingly sanguinary wars for the twenty years before 1914. But other crises, in Africa and the Middle East, were patched up, at least provisionally. The British and Germans reached agreement on development of the Ottoman (Berlin to Baghdad) railways. German truculence in the second Moroccan crisis was bought off by transferring a slice from French Congo to German Togo and Cameroon. Properly managed, colonial empire might be a joint white man's (and Japanese) enterprise. International confrontations, however, still flared in the heart of Europe; and after earlier conflicts had been defused (each, however, at the cost of exacerbating reciprocal resentments and suspicions), the threats and counterthreats arising from the Austrian declaration of war on Serbia in the summer of 1914 following the assassination of Archduke Francis Ferdinand drew the great powers into the first large-scale European conflict since the wars of Italian and German unification.

Imperial powers became arrayed on both sides of the conflict. Some were countries that possessed overseas *colonial* empires—France, Britain, Germany, even small Belgium, largely occupied by the German army, then Italy, Japan, and the United States as recently acquisitive powers. Others were nations that were themselves organized as empires over their multiethnic landed domains—Austria-Hungary, Ottoman Turkey, and Russia.[1] Their fate diverged sharply with the results of the war. German colonies overseas and the Arab possessions of the Ottomans were prizes for redistribution; landed empires in Europe were ripe for dissolution and reconstitution as nation-states. Wilson's idea of self-determination, which came to loom so large as American military intervention proved decisive in ending the military stalemate by 1918, potentially undermined empire in general. For the victorious Allies, the challenge was how to deflect it from undermining their own possessions. They were largely successful. The world between the wars remained a world of empires, although in theory all aspiring to a goal of eventual comity of nations—albeit one safely remote in time. The mandate system of the League of Nations as well as the League itself was designed to reconcile the conflicting aspirations of retaining empires and creating a global society of nations.

By some measures, the interwar period represented the refulgent climax of empire. Empire, of course, is a capacious category that covered a large variety of hierarchical institutions, ideologies, and practices negotiated locally on the ground as well as organized from distant capitals. The British still envisaged their empire as embracing the self-governing dominions of Great Britain such as Canada and the Maritimes, Australia, and New Zealand; but imperial rule is more precisely applied to territories where final decision power rested with the delegates or the government of the metropole. It included territories where dominion was real if contested, such as the Indian Raj, the African settler colonies, and the Middle East (Palestine, Jordan, Oman, as well as the many island centers from Hong Kong and Singapore to Bermuda and the West Indies. Iraq and Egypt were protectorates, in effect client kingdoms allowed internal party politics but hardly any control of foreign policy or their key resources, oil and the Suez waterway, respectively. According to important recent studies, imperial rule was about the management of differences among the diverse peoples governed under an overarching state. But it was equally devoted to managing inequality, thus preserving privilege, often according to putatively racial categories. And managing inequality meant that coercion and violence were always held in reserve even when not actively deployed.[2]

The Economic Calculus

This chapter, concerned as it is with the economic promise of colonial possessions, focuses on the extensive and long-established British, French, and Dutch domains. The British and French acquired effective control of German territory in Africa and the Ottoman domains outside Anatolia (Anatolia itself they were compelled to evacuate by Mustafa Kemal) in 1919. Once their effort to control the Turkish littoral along with their Greek allies collapsed catastrophically in 1922, the two treaty powers no longer envisaged military expansion; along with the Dutch, they were satiated in terms of territory. Their efforts were devoted to suppressing indigenous discontent and, as mandatory powers confirmed by the new League of Nations, firming up their control and advancing profitable development. Mastery of their vast domains in Asia and Africa still relied on soldiers, but the purpose evolved. One of the French bards of empire would sum up the mission of the past on the occasion of the great colonial exposition of 1931, "French West Africa is in some ways an army establishment. Every post has at least one military tomb."

The colonial cities were precarious implantations. The railroads were characterized by "their strategic origins and their imperial design. It was a matter above all of rapidly transporting troops and being able to repress efforts at insurrection. It was a matter finally of struggling against the enormous distances . . . of once and for all sounding the depths of the land."[3] The rhetoric evoked a mission achieved, not the task ahead. Yet the celebrant had a point: even as their rulers sought to make them spaces for capital and commerce, empires remained cages of conquest, constrained compromises with market rationality.

Both Lenin and Joseph Schumpeter writing in the middle of the ongoing world war had valid, though opposed, insights: imperialism had a hand-and-glove relationship with competitive capitalism, indeed signaled its final state, according to the former. But it rested in fact, according to the latter, on "precapitalist" and supposedly "atavistic" drives for territorial acquisition and domination.[4] From before 1914 to the end of formal empires after World War II, it would be hard to disentangle the two motivations. And geostrategic rivalry among the imperial great powers was perhaps regrettable but not devoid of its own rationality. Easier to distinguish were the relatively satiated older empires and the hungrier regimes that would coalesce as the Axis powers by the late 1930s. Their urge to dominate was closer to the surface and in line with their domestic authoritarian procedures. This does not mean that empires associated with fascism or overturning the new status quo reached by the mid-1920s followed no economic logic. To the contrary, the dynamic of conquest, with its momentum toward ever-wider war, meant that ambitious states with limited raw materials or industrial capacity would have to acquire the resources to engage in more extensive conquests. Hence the vicious logic of expansion for Italy, Germany, and Japan: they needed to make war to be ready for war. This was certainly the case when these imperial powers confronted not weak native populations but large abutting states or other large powers that would oppose their ambitions. In that case, the economic calculus of empire entailed not just profits but acquisition of coal, metals, and oil.

The case of Italy needs be mentioned only briefly. Between 1911 and the loss of the colonies in 1943, occupation was too brief and tenuous to allow for coherent economic development. The country remained economically most active in the Balkans. Early champions had cited the need to find an outlet for surplus population, but the sandy shores on the other side of the Mediterranean were hardly a propitious arena. Italian nationalists, however, felt aggrieved by their European neighbors' acquisition of colonies. Italy's prewar liberal prime minister, Giovanni Giolitti, had sought to appease their growing influence at home by seizing Libya in 1911 from an Ottoman sovereignty weakened by Turkey's post-1908 revolutionary turmoil. During the world war and the peace conference, the country's then-conservative leadership sought to secure the Dalmatian Coast. Once Mussolini was in power, he truculently pressed for Adriatic gains in the 1920s and then a decade later, a military extension of East African territory at the expense of one of the continent's two remaining independent Black polities (along with Liberia), Ethiopia.[5]

Japan's vigorous expansion, on the other hand, was always imbued with a plausible economic calculus alongside a search for regional hegemony. In a brief decade and a half (1895–1910), Japan had acquired Taiwan from China, northern Sakhalin island along with a foothold (and railroad concessions) in the Manchurian provinces, and control and then annexation of independent Korea. By 1912, when the Taisho emperor succeeded the Meiji emperor, its ruling groups were tugged at by different impulses. Civilian leaders and liberal military officers (some of whom served as prime ministers) envisaged a great-power vocation by joining the Western club, absorbing Euro-American science and legal culture, and participating in the dividends of empire left by the world war. They also tolerated the growth of a parliamentary and political party institutions and even labor unions so long as they did not become too militant. Until the onset of the world depression, the Japanese liberals retained a dominant voice; the foreign office, parliament, and the parties seemed to control policy; Tokyo signed the Washington treaties in 1922, accepting (over significant military dissent) naval arms limitations in the Pacific and a pledge to respect the territorial integrity of China. Its diplomats played an active role first at Versailles and then in the new international court of arbitration. Others, concentrated in the military, resented Europe's intervention to limit their earlier imperial gains and believed they had a vocation to wrest East Asia from British or Russian threats and Chinese decadence.

But the political balance changed by the end of the decade. The young Showa emperor Hirohito had come to the throne in 1926, evidently fascinated by military and imperial trappings. The military units based in the city of Dalien / Dairen and the Liaodong peninsula—the so-called Kwantung Army—became a hotbed of impatient military expansionists. Using the pretext of protecting the South Manchurian Railway, the spine of Japanese industrial and coal mining interests in the northern provinces, they moved to establish control throughout Manchuria in 1931. Tokyo dared not disavow the action, and in stages from 1932 to 1934, the Kwantung Army leadership set up a supposedly independent Manchurian Empire, Manchukuo, and placed "the last emperor," "Henry" Puyi, deposed in Beijing in 1911, on its throne as its compliant sovereign. Underlying the conquest was an economic plan, developed by the staff officer Ishiwara Kanji, exponent of a Japanese fascism and future war with the West, for exploiting Manchurian resources under Japanese control as a springboard for industrial and strategic capacity in the war he saw likely to follow. Although there were tensions, Japanese Manchukuo proved perhaps the most integrated global arena for capitalist and military cooperation.[6] League condemnation led to Tokyo's exit from Geneva; over the course of the 1930s, military control progressively tightened over the regime in general. Young military officers resorted to a politics of assassination to intimidate older moderates. Their conviction grew that Japan must dominate China whether through intimidation or conquest.

A similar logic underlay Nazi projects for creation of a European imperial redoubt that would control agrarian and mineral resources up the Urals.[7] The architects of Axis empires understood they had to control a resource-rich heartland that could withstand the hostility of Great Britain and eventual American resistance. They had to conquer to be able to conquer; but in so doing, so it was erroneously calculated, they could make their vast dominions unassailable. After the onset of the world depression in the 1930s, however, such thinking in terms of territorial zones of economic exploitation was not limited to the aggressive powers. Shorn of the military component, it became a more general vision and seemed the prerequisite just for a peaceful enjoyment of imperial fruits. Peaceful, that is, with respect to the relationship among the colonial powers. The relationship of the empires to their subjects rested if not always on overt violence, still on a preponderance of coercive capacity. Needless to say, hopes for a resource empire did not always correspond with the results achieved.

Empires and Project-States

The relationship of the interwar empires (most of which would in fact endure into the decade or more after World War II) to project-states needs a word of explanation. Colonial empires were certainly national projects but not simply the equivalent of project-states that aimed at social renovation at home. As suggested above, for authoritarian regimes at home, empire remained an integral ideological component of nationalist authoritarian rule. Adolf Hitler remained focused on subjugation of adjacent countries rather than recovering African possessions, although that prospect enticed some of the Nazi Party and members of the older conservative collaborators such as Hjalmar Schacht. Even in the increasingly authoritarian Polish Republic a cohort of enthusiasts agitated for acquisition of some African territory.[8] Certainly for liberal societies, too, empires remained important for national prestige and international status. Their administrators often envisaged projects of colonial development—social and economic, including reform of agrarian relations, sometimes educational and even political within a safe framework of co-optation. But self-government was far away. Extensive administrative tasks had to be delegated to indigenous chiefs and elites and promising native intellectuals who might acquire their masters' culture and become auxiliaries in rule. For the primary and astonishing fact of colonial rule was the minuscule number of Europeans who administered these vast territories and populations: perhaps 20,000 British soldiers and civil servants on the ground to govern a South Asian domain of 300 million. Twenty-one thousand French and 14 million natives in almost 5 million square kilometers of French West Africa. The system of imperial rule could not afford to "waken" the intermediaries into claimants for national self-government.

How long such a balancing act could be maintained without either revolt or violent repression remained a lurking if often unexamined question. The debates that followed episodes of upheaval and suppression brought the issues to the surface. Early in the interwar years, the idea of liberal empire still seemed possible. In the aftermath of the so-called Amritsar massacre of April 1919, where British commanders and their Gurkha soldiers unflinchingly emptied their rifles at a crowd of 1,300 protesters in the Punjab, killing about 400, to take perhaps the most notorious example, the fervent defender of empire, Winston Churchill, argued in Parliament that Britain could maintain its rule in India only by forswearing "frightfulness." The secretary of state for India, Edwin Montagu, asked whether Britain would keep its hold on India "by terrorism, racial humiliations and subordination, and frightfulness, or are you going to rest it upon the good will, and the growing goodwill, of the people of your Indian Empire." The Labour Party MP Ben Spoor wanted to see the people of India "really free" and "in the Empire on equal terms, so far as their ordinary rights are concerned, with every British citizen."[9] Revealingly, no MP in the debate suggested that Britain should divest itself of its colonies. Rather, the interwar period was filled with projects for imperial reform and piecemeal concessions that might sustain an imperial equilibrium. Such a search meant that colonial powers rarely had the political "space" to become project-states at home, although in the French case, the Popular Front did attempt to produce a major colonial reform. The requisites of the colonies weighed on domestic alternatives. Efforts involved in maintaining an empire helped dampen energies for radical renewal in the democratic metropoles, even as a decade later they served to cement domestic solidarity in the fascist or authoritarian states.

Although both the metropole states and sometimes their colonies were shaken by labor unrest and harsh political conflict in the years after the war, by the mid-decade stability seemed to have returned to postrevolutionary and long-existing regimes. So, too, after waves of agitation and rebellion, the colonial powers managed to subdue challenges to their rule even though anti-imperialist activists and Communist Party parliamentarians in the metropoles sought to sustain opposition. The "Wilsonian moment" remained but a moment.[10] The mandate system of the League of Nations helped inscribe a new, largely racially or ethnically based status quo that envisaged different grades of indefinite tutelage. The reorganized colonial regimes were not always accepted quietly. Military resistance flared in Spanish Morocco, and the Rif leaders inflicted a major defeat on Spanish forces in 1921. Druze and then Arab rebels raised a serious revolt against the new French colonial occupiers of Syria; Bedouin forces resisted the British in Iraq. The new imperial rulers resorted to aerial bombardment—including the French bombing of Damascus in 1926 which killed 1,500—to suppress these uprisings and establish control. Force or the threat of force remained the ultima ratio of empire. But it did not preclude the emergence of organized opposition—nationalist, communist, and in many cases across the broad swathe of lands from northern Africa through the Middle East to South Asia and Indonesia, Islamic.

Conflict between the colonial powers over their respective imperial possessions and ambitions was also put on ice for about a decade. After some squabbling, the British and French shared out the Ottoman provinces at San Remo in April 1920 and distributed Germany's African colonial territories to themselves and to South Africa. German Samoa went to Japan and the United States; the Kiaochow lease on the Shandong peninsula went to Japan; South Africa received German Southwest Africa, today's Namibia, as a protectorate. In the areas where conflict threatened over colonial domination—the Middle East and North China—precarious agreement was also reached for a decade. Needless to say, this was agreement among the overlords; not all the peoples disposed of were willing to remain acquiescent.

From a global perspective, the stabilization of colonial rule outside Europe by the mid-1920s after the suppression of local revolts formed a counterpart to the postwar treaty settlement within Europe and its adjacent territories. The Treaty of Riga in 1921 ostensibly settled the Russo-Polish border (even as it effectively confirmed Bolshevik control of Russia). The Treaty of Lausanne (1923)—which replaced the 1919 Treaty of Sèvres with the Ottoman Empire—established the territory of the modern Turkish Republic but likewise reconfirmed the Ottoman Empire's territorial losses. The Washington Conference treaties concluded in 1922 froze battleship tonnage in the Pacific arena and ostensibly kept Japan from further encroachment on the internally contested Chinese Republic. The temporary suspension of reparation annuities in 1924 (the Dawes Plan and Treaty of London) and the Locarno treaties a year later seemed to promise pacification in Europe. The promise of postwar recovery thus linked territorial and military settlements with a restoration of an international economic and financial order. The colonial realms appeared to be an important stake in that effort to re-equilibrate global politics and economics. Perhaps the wealth of the "third world" might help compensate for the heavy costs left by the first world's war of the early twentieth century.

Colonies were thus not to be relinquished but rather integrated into supposedly more encompassing institutional structures—empires, supposedly of almost but not-quite equals. On the political side, this meant administrative and legislative reforms suggesting unification within some common uniting sovereignty. The British Commonwealth of Nations (suggested by Jan Smuts in 1917) emerged in states with the Anglo-Irish Treaty of 1921, the Balfour Declaration at the 1926 Imperial Conference, and was formally constituted by the 1931 Statute of Westminster. The Dutch revised their constitution in 1922 to stipulate that "the Kingdom of the Netherlands comprises the territory of the Netherlands, Netherlands India [today's Indonesia], Surinam, and Curaçao." They followed with a long-discussed East India Government Act, enacted in 1925, which sought to rebalance power between the king and his governor general (comparable to the viceroy of India), the States-General (the Dutch parliament) and minister of colonies, and the Volksrad or elected parliament in Batavia. The States General retained control of the budget although with the obligation of consulting the Volksrad. Much was left unresolved—a domestic balance of power is often just a constitutional conflict in hibernation. Underlying the Dutch settlement, though, was the fact that "in

none of the colonial nations has the possession of a dependency so saturated the whole life of the country."[11] The French Popular Front proposed
reforms in 1937, and Charles de Gaulle announced his version of a supposed
encompassing unit, the French Union, at Brazzaville in 1944. All these projects were efforts to avert simple independence of the roughly billion colonial
subjects involved, and all were in a race with the rising nationalism within
the colonies. In terms of implementation, however, they remained hostage
to the deep resistance of conservatives at home, who remained convinced
that concessions would only encourage demands for home rule and that
shorn of their dependencies, their countries would become second-rate
powers.[12]

Integration of the colonial economies (and of the dominion economies
in the British case) was the counterpart to achieving new political superstruc-
tures. This should have meant trying to invest in the colonies, to advance their
economies, and thus also to assure the resource flow from periphery to metropole.
Insofar as international economic exchange was to be established after a war
that had destroyed much of it and a depression that was threatening a second
rupture, it would be reconstructed on the basis of protected imperial zones.[13]
At the same time, concepts of imperial economies also provided a new possibility for reconstruction. The colonies had long beckoned as a supposed source
of wealth even when the calculations proved illusory, and the returns that
did flow to the metropole were skewed to narrow classes of beneficiaries. Burdened with postwar debts, the colonial powers—or the pressure groups that
agitated on behalf of empire—set even greater store on the economic benefits
that overseas domains would yield. Drawing economic advantage rather than
merely pursuing territorial expansion was up to date. But that required a greater
effort to invest in enterprises in the colonies. Albert Sarraut, centrist politician
and editor of *Dépêche de Toulouse*, coined the phrase *mise en valeur de l'empire*
for the French colonies, which meant in practice state investment and subsidies—to be sure in mines or rubber plantations but also in the railroads and
roads and harbor infrastructure needed to exploit colonial resources.[14]

Mise en Valeur

Mise en valeur was a catchy slogan, but it is not easy to measure the degree
to which the empires "paid" the colonizers. Neither is it easy to determine to
what degree the colonies themselves might have benefited in terms of
development—such as was claimed, for example, in the case of Indian railroad

construction during the Raj—or were merely exploited, despoiled, and directed toward prolonged misallocation of resources. That issue, however, cannot be explored here. As for the European rulers, scholarship has come up with different answers, to a degree dependent on the colonies involved but also the question addressed. Some economists and historians have focused on the costs and benefits to the colonizing *societies*. They have asked whether the businesses and citizens of the metropoles were relatively enriched by colonies or potentially made worse off, whether because of the defense and development costs they had to accept or (a more speculative counterfactual question) the possible foreclosure of more profitable investments at home to pursue the alleged benefits raised in the colony. Other researchers have focused on the costs and benefits to the colonizing *state*, whether costs to be covered by taxes at home or costs to be covered by revenues from the colony. This was the fiscal issue and it depended on whether the colony itself could be administered as a paying proposition; what it cost the imperial power in terms of military and police forces and economic infrastructure, and how much might be raised in revenue, labor contributions, or military levies from the imperial domain—in short, which colonies might pay for the privilege of being ruled by Europeans and which could not.[15] The colonizers originally liked to claim that the costs of running India or any of the other possessions should be met by the colony itself; thereafter, they liked to demonstrate how much they were investing. It is not easy to determine which of these contradictory propositions was true.

At the same time, the fiscal issue cannot be cleanly separated from the more general questions of economic gains and losses. The aim of colonial state expenses was to enhance the economic welfare to be gained, hopefully within the colony and for the *colons* or settlers but certainly by the metropole's economy. In this way, late nineteenth- and twentieth-century colonies differed from, say, those of the sixteenth and seventeenth century, when extraction of colonial products (gold, silver, tobacco, indigo, etc.) was monopolized by the European states or the trading companies they chartered. Leopold II's personal colony—the Congo Free State, existing from its recognition by the Conference of Berlin in 1885 to 1908, when the Belgian state took it over in the wake of its horrifying abuses—came the closest to that model of extraction. Probably the greatest relative gains accrued to Belgium and the Netherlands, which each had one large colony—the Congo and the Indies (Indonesia)—that they exploited in different ways differing in objectives and methods.[16]

There has always been a third set of questions, which has also attracted passionate attention but are not addressed here—namely, the redistributive issue of which "classes" at home and in the colonies bore the tax burdens directly or indirectly (perhaps through wage or commercial competition with colonial labor), and / or received the benefits. This inquiry attempts to combine the fiscal and the societal bookkeeping, the direct costs to the state and the taxes that covered them, with the impact on national income and wealth. One authoritative account suggests that the British Empire was a device for mildly distributing British national income upward.[17] Assuming this calculation is correct, it cannot resolve the issue of whether the differential rewards to the elites of the metropole might be disproportional or unjust. We come finally to the issue of benefits and costs: was development of a colonial industry—say, rubber, mineral mining, or farming and forestry—a gain for the colony, and if so, what share of the rewards should have accrued to the colony and what share to the metropole's enterprises? This question has become entangled with another about the impact through time—whether the economic potential of primary producers must normally lead to their remaining in a relationship of dependency and relative backwardness and vulnerability.

The material or economic issues deserve the best answers possible, but they may also be beside the point. Until the years after World War II, the colonial powers were committed to their empires, whether they brought material rewards or imposed new costs. The psychological returns of having an empire were important in their own right, whether for Brits who lustily sang "Land of Hope and Glory . . . God made thee great and mighty, may he make thee mightier yet"; or for the French who cheered their aviators, as did Antoine Saint-Éxupéry in *Vol de Nuit*, who flew heroically from one outpost to another across the vast reaches of the Sahara and West Africa; or for the Italians who claimed a Mediterranean and East African destiny. The empire brought memories of heroism and sometimes martyrs, spiffy naval uniforms, parades and Sunday brass band concerts, grand global expositions—the Colonial Exposition of 1931 in Vincennes drew 34 million visitors[18]—and even serious anthropological studies, tropical products in northern groceries, touching testimonies of cultural deference, the satisfaction of building hospitals or railways, or bringing Christian faith. Empire was fulfilling. Only when the metropoles became enmired in long colonial wars or had to contemplate harsh budget sacrifices at home from the 1940s into the 1960s did material bookkeeping play a major role.

Historians during the Cold War who were intent on critiquing Lenin's analysis of imperialism as a stage of capitalist development liked to demonstrate that both in terms of trade and investment, Britain and France had far more economic intercourse with nonimperial areas abroad than with their own dependent possessions. It is true that the highest degree of international trade took place between countries with highly developed industrial sectors, such as Germany and Britain. But the trade within an imperial unit was of a particular sort: an exchange between the commodities of the colonies and manufactures or value-added products of the mother country. In the earlier stages of the Industrial Revolution, Britain bought raw cotton and crude cloth from the American South, India, and later Egypt to become the textile center of the world. Rosa Luxemburg captured the nature of this exchange when she defined imperialism as a relationship between an industrial metropole and commodity-producing colonies.[19] In 1913, the empire provided well over 50 percent of Britain's imports of foodstuffs and key raw materials (although only 3 percent of raw cotton and 8.4 percent of iron ore).

Colonies allowed the metropole's agents to monopolize sales of manufactures, financial services, and infrastructural equipment to the colony. In 1913, over half of the British exports to the empire (37.2 percent of its total exports) were comprised by manufactured goods. "In the special case of capital goods, it was axiomatic, though unpopular in India, that governments would order from Britain."[20] As Paul Bernard, chair of the Société Financière Française et Coloniale, a holding company for Indochina investments understood, thanks to tariffs, France provided the lion's share of Indochina's imports.[21] The "mother country" could also structure the legal institutions (including formalization of property rights along Western lines and at the cost of collective and customary rights) and the labor markets (such as contract labor migration) for a favorable trade outcome. From the turn of the twentieth century on, the colonies, or subservient quasi-client states such as Persia, beckoned as commodity and labor preserves for Europeans and Americans, all the more so as rubber was needed for the burgeoning auto industry, petroleum for the conversion of ships from coal to oil.

Pause for a moment on the case of rubber. Unlike oil, it required a labor force, one rounded up and then often retained under brutal conditions before World War I. Production in the Congo depended on extracting labor from the vines; in Brazil (not a colony but a state unable to control exploitation), the latex-yielding tree (*Hevea brasiliensis*) allowed tapping and produced 60 percent of the world's supply between 1867 and 1910. Brazilian seeds and the plants made their way originally via Kew Gardens to sites scattered across the Dutch East Indies, Malaya, and Vietnam, as the production of autos and trucks took hold. The Europeans (and the American Firestone Company in Liberia) envisaged the plantation as the rational and profitable form of exploiting land and labor. Plantations, of course, were not merely large tracts for monoculture; labor needed to be centralized, roads built, and hygiene assured. Most fundamentally, indigenous, often collective, property rights had to be transformed into individual concessions to colonial developers—just one component of the ongoing advance of private property regimes under way in Europe, Mexico, and the Americas since the sixteenth century. By and large, throughout the vast global borderlands where Europeans and their offspring met peoples of color, the process was inexorable. In the case of rubber cultivation in the Indies and Malaya, however, small estates (defined as under forty hectares or one hundred acres) remained competitive. The French brought rubber trees to Vietnam in the early twentieth century; by the 1920s, the privatization of the land was well under way, although the colonial authorities occasionally decided in favor of customary rights. By the 1920s, the Michelin plantations became a site of large-scale rationalized production—planting, tapping, processing—drawing on a harshly disciplined labor force. It was logically enough a focal point for encouraging labor resistance by the later Communist revolutionaries, the Viet Minh, who managed to organize a major strike in 1930, part of a more general series of strikes and, as discussed below, a decisive step toward ultimate decolonization.[22]

From 1900 to 1930, writes Jacques Marseille, the economic historian of the empire, the colonial domain offered significant opportunities for French capitalism. Total French investment in colonial enterprises by 1914 reached almost 7 billion francs or $1.3 billion. From the late 1880 to World War I and through the 1920s, the colonies in general provided a source of profits. The good times resumed after the Depression and World War II for another decade and a half. Essentially, Marseille sees a mechanism where the French state budgets and thus the taxpayers financed colonial government and sometimes firms, but through the 1920s thereby provided lucrative returns for the country's investors.[23]

Modern capitalism in general makes it difficult to separate costs and revenues attributed to private enterprises from the state's provision of infrastructure, spillover from military innovation and contracts, tax subsidies, and social services. The colonial context made it particularly hard to disentangle public and private returns. European colonialism required the support of public budgets—that is, taxpayer revenues—to sustain the conditions for firms to prosper. The Dutch scholar Ewout Frankema has focused on taxes across the British Empire, largely to contest recent claims that high colonial taxation in the extractive colonies—as supposedly opposed to lower taxation in the "settler" colonies with a large British presence—left a legacy of weak public institutions and underdevelopment. Rather, he argues, low rates of colonial settlement made it harder to raise taxes and create an enterprise-friendly state. Frankema finds, not surprisingly, that tax capacity varied widely across the empire (in which he includes the wealthy self-governing dominions as well as the massively populous Raj) and that the African colonies "remained fiscal and financial backwaters after the First World War."[24] Surprisingly perhaps, wages of unskilled workers were significantly higher in West Africa (including the Gold Coast and Nigeria) than in East and Southern Africa with their settler colonies and in India. Most useful, perhaps, he provides the working-day equivalent for the annual per capita fiscal burden, and he comes up with a range of one to three days in West Africa and seven to thirteen days in East Africa.

Frankema's indices focus on cash transfers, which characterized British dependencies, but the colonial world in general also raised significant off-budget resources through labor conscription. Long after the formal abolition of slavery, colonial landlords, mining enterprises, and public authorities demanded the recruitment of indigenous labor paid at minimal rates. In French Africa, local levies were assigned to rail construction at tremendous human cost and then deployed to extend the road systems in West Africa. The League of Nations felt compelled to take up the question of forced labor in 1926. Responding to a League survey, representatives of France, Belgium, and Portugal expressed their "formal willingness to suppress this mode of labor except for maintaining it for reasons of public interest during a transitional period" and then quickly added a further list of exceptions including military service, fiscal obligations, and private firms working for public works, to prevent famine or "sometimes to create a source of wealth for the population." The Dutch, British, Spanish, and Italians agreed to sign on, but it took several more years of controversy before the International Labour Organization convened a conference to pass a convention on forced labor in June 1930. As their delegate to the conference, the French government produced a native Senegal citizen, Blaise Daigne, to argue that his countrymen were not ready for such legislation, and after it was passed, the French refused to adhere. They argued in particular that their so-called secondary contingent—the draftees not sent to the military units of the Tirailleurs sénégalais but assigned to labor battalions (those for whom "the implement replaced the rifle")—fell under their prerogatives of national defense. In 1932, the governor of France's Ivory Coast denounced the hypocrisy: "We need to call things by their real name. We can't pretend to be following a free labor regime with respect to the natives when it is a question of recruiting the manpower that private individuals require. If we want to give in to the demands of the *colons* it will amount to forced recruitment with all its abuses. We have to choose."[25]

Forced or semicoerced labor remained widespread. The British colonies could avoid the most coercive forms by contracting for labor contingents with chiefs with a suggested maximum of thirty to fifty days. It is not easy to quantify the tax or wage equivalent that it provided. Marlous van Waijenburg has provided the most recent effort to estimate its contribution to the administration of the colonial state by calculating the length of the annual corvée, the percentage of the populations that were subject, and the prevailing wage rates. The value of conscripted labor in 1913–1915 and 1920 amounted to nearly half the size of the budgeted money taxes and then fell to about one-quarter by 1930. In the early years of the century, its contribution was probably greater. The more recently organized the colony, the higher was the fiscal value provided by corvée, as the colonizers could build fiscal capacity only gradually. Formally, the French requirements seemed to average about ten days per year, but in practice it might go up to thirty or more. Building on Ottoman precedents, the French imposed thirty days of labor services over a five-year term in Syria and Lebanon. Sixteen days per year were required in French Indochina in the late 1920s. The corvée obligations in the Belgian Congo and the Portuguese colonies probably extended to sixty days per year.[26] All in all, labor taxes contributed a significant nonmonetary component of the costs of maintaining infrastructure.

Pre-1914 conditions had seen more abusive situations. Under the nineteenth-century "cultivation system," the Dutch East Indies (today's Indonesia) provided half of the Netherland's state revenue as early as the 1850s, while the riches of the Congo, extracted under brutal conditions, were rewarding the Belgian firms and investors granted concessions by Leopold II. By the end of the century, the wealth from the Congo's "red" rubber, then from ivory, diamonds, and gold, was enriching a wide circle of Belgian investors. Copper would add to the stream of mineral riches between the wars, as would uranium and cobalt after World War II—all of it dug out by African workers who received a fraction of what their mining counterparts in Europe eked out. They were sometimes conscripted to overcome their supposed *paresse*, or sloth, if no longer lashed or amputated. Long after the violence abated, wages in the colonies were small fractions of what workers in the metropole could earn.

Forced labor put at the service of the *colons* was only the most egregious contribution of the colonies to private investors and businesses. Wealth also flowed from the businesses that settlers from the metropole ran in the colonies—factories, banks, transportation facilities. Dividends rose accordingly. Shares in Belgian colonial companies rose an average of 7.2 percent yearly for the thirty-five years from 1920 to 1955.[27] The Dutch Empire—its colonies officially designated as a component of the Kingdom of the Netherlands—offered material awards second only to India. The infamous cultivation system had given way in 1901 to the so-called ethical policy, which envisaged less coercive arrangements but no less remunerative. Annual Dutch capital investment in the Indies rose from 600 million guilders ($150 million) per year between 1910 and 1914, to over 1,400 million guilders yearly from 1920 to 1924, then to 1,800 million guilders yearly by 1925–1929, then plummeted back to about 600 million guilders from 1930 to 1934. Accumulated foreign direct investment in the Indies rose from 750 million guilders ($187 million) as of 1900 to 1.7 billion guilders (ca. $425 million) as of 1914 and to 4 billion guilders by 1930 (perhaps $2 billion in 1914 terms). Investment by Dutch firms headquartered in the Netherlands—the NHM (Nederlandse Handels Maatschappij) and KPM (Koninklijke Paketvaart-Maatschappij)—replaced the earlier trading companies based in the Indies as economic powerhouses. Unsurprisingly, their considerable investment went to plantations and oil resources and shipping, and not to industrialization. The secondary sector remained at 12–15 percent, even until the late 1950s, although the number of factories and workshops doubled.[28]

The vigorous colonial commerce of the late 1920s was all the more important given the reduction in international trade during the recovery from World War I. By the second half the 1920s, the major national economies had caught up to and were advancing beyond the levels of gross domestic product (GDP) they had achieved on the eve of World War I. However, the proportion of international trade in that output lagged far behind the domestic gains. British exporters were handicapped by restoration of a sterling exchange rate that overpriced its manufactures with respect to those of other countries including the United States. France in contrast had stabilized its currency after 1926 (formally since 1928) by locking into a "low" exchange rate that provided an incentive for exports. By the 1930s, however, as the British and then the Americans abandoned their earlier linkages to the gold exchange standard of the 1920s, the French, too, would face serious international financial difficulties, and the stocks of gold they had accumulated by the late 1920s to the consternation of the United Kingdom and United States were swiftly depleted. There were longer-term structural difficulties as well.[29] The terms of trade had become adverse for rural producers as commodity prices declined relative to industrial ones, and the still-substantial agrarian sectors faced stagnation, indebtedness, or sometimes foreclosure and outright impoverishment. These difficulties afflicted farmers in the grain belts of North and South America but even more acutely for the myriad small holders of Central Europe and Japan, and the peasant tenants of the colonies, such as Vietnam. Family farms could not lay off workers until better times returned, and migration faced new borders and other obstacles such as the severe US restrictions imposed in 1924. Confronting all these impediments to international commerce and migration, it was logical enough that the idea of imperial economic regions, protected from foreign competitors and locked into preferential trade arrangements with their mother countries, beckoned strongly as an alternative.

As globalization—already interrupted in 1914, partially renewed in the late 1920s, but interrupted anew by the Depression—faltered, the arrangements that German geopoliticians called common economic regions seemed to offer salvation. No longer were the colonies to be conceived just as sources for extraction of labor power, commodities, and minerals or even markets (although that vision persisted) but now as components of common protected economic and political zones along with the metropoles. The world was throwing up walls again but walls that would enclose imperial regions and not just single countries. The French, British, and Dutch in particular envisaged their dependencies increasingly as part of a territorial conglomerate needed to maintain their geopolitical standing and as an economic preserve to maintain economic stability.

Politically, too, the growing sense of economic and geopolitical insecurity made European publics and political leaders more enthusiastic than ever about their overseas dominions. That included the majority of the French Socialist Party (SFIO) who called for an "altruistic" colonialism to secure the loyalty of the *indigènes*. Even Communist Party member Maurice Thorez declared in 1937 that the right to a divorce did not mean the obligation to get divorced. The Communists did not want colonial issues to undermine the politics of the Popular Front. As they piously declared, for the colonial peoples to fight for independence would mean undermining the broad struggle against fascism. Unsurprisingly in alignment, the Dutch Communists declared they were dropping the slogan "The Indies free from Holland" in view of the menace of Japanese fascism.[30]

The Balance Sheets Change

In retrospect, two opposed developments can be discerned at the same time— on the one hand, intimations of the end for colonial empire and on the other hand, a heightened effort to make the system more viable. Decolonization as a quasi-inevitable historical development is usually dated from the upheavals of World War II. By mid-1942, the Japanese subjugated the white colonial rulers of Southeast Asia, and by war's end the Soviets had magnified their influence in world politics by virtue of their role in defeating Nazi Germany while the British confronted international financial exhaustion. The decisive point of inflection, however, probably came earlier with the world economic crisis of the early 1930s. Prices for the agricultural staples—rice, wheat, cotton, and coffee produced by the colonies and by the rural regions of Europe and the Americas as well—plunged and rural living standards with them.[31] Economic difficulties rekindled the radical protests and strikes of industrial labor, for instance in Indochina. The Depression also brought into the public arena a new generation of colonial youth who, after a decade of intellectual preparation, often in Europe, were no longer willing to abide by the clientelistic bargains that their elders had struck with the colonial overlords. Naturally, their aspirations collided with the enhanced importance that the empires held for the colonizers.

The international accounts of the colonies reveal the change in their role from the 1920s to the 1930s. France's annual exports outside the colonies fell from 7.78 billion francs in 1927 to 2.66 billion (reckoned in constant-value 1914 francs) or a decline of 66 percent, whereas sales to the colonies declined only from 1.35 billion to 1.33 billion or about 2 percent.[32] But the colonies had to pay for these French exports. Their own exports covered part of the bill; credits from the metropole covered the rest, increasingly extended from the public purse. Paris was thus subsidizing its own exporting industries by expanding their colonial markets, but it was not alone. Paul Schmelzing, a historian of finance, has traced these statistics for twenty of the British, French, and Dutch colonies. The balances changed proportion with the Depression. The favorable colonial balance of trade in the 1920s indicated the vigor of commerce; by the 1930s, it was the flow of capital from the metropole that increasingly kept the colonial economies viable. The balance of investments testified to diverse impulses—early on, the expectations that commercial firms and their investors expected to reap from the colonies but increasingly government investment in infrastructure, or the need to bail out national firms with subsidies.

The surpluses on international trade for the colonies grew robustly through the 1920s; by the 1930s they disappeared and capital investment replaced it, presumably from private investors and governmental authorities in the metropole. From 1922 to 1925, the balances of trade rose from $200 million a year to close to $1,000 million, thence to decline progressively and slip into negative territory from late 1929 until 1935 (and again in 1938). In contrast, capital imports for the twenty colonies tracked by the League of Nations (including India and South Africa) increased from 1927 to 1937, from slightly under $90 million current US dollars to almost $620 million by the mid-1930s, thereafter falling to below $400 million in 1938 and 1939—a decline probably attributable to the significant increases in defense budgets for Britain, France, Belgium, and the Netherlands. The aggregate capital and trade balances for the British colonies rose from $211 million in 1923 to about $250 million in 1929, then after a slump in 1930, to over $500 million from 1933 to 1936, before slipping in the late 1930s. British India and the Dutch East Indies remained the steadiest in terms of their balance of payments. The investment figures roughly accord with the trend noted by Marseille—the decreasing role of trade and the increasing role played by investment. Policymakers and economic decision makers were viewing the colonies not as a resort to be milked but as a costly investment good needed to maintain an imperial economic bloc. Colonial governments allowed the colonies to book significant gains—whether in the tariff rates conceded at Ottawa or greater investment authorized from the metropole—for the sake of imperial cohesion.

Under conditions of depression, the effort to build tariff walls around metropole and colony became attractive. This was a neomercantile strategy that echoed the efforts of eighteenth-century empires, including the British, to construct a quasi-autarkic imperial conglomerate with tariffs and preferential treatment. Joseph Chamberlain had staunchly advocated this policy before 1914, and as we have seen, Albert Sarraut became its French champion

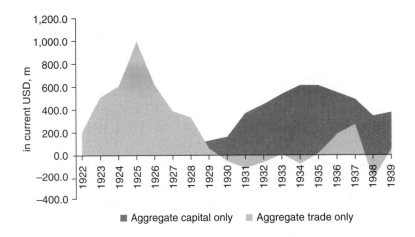

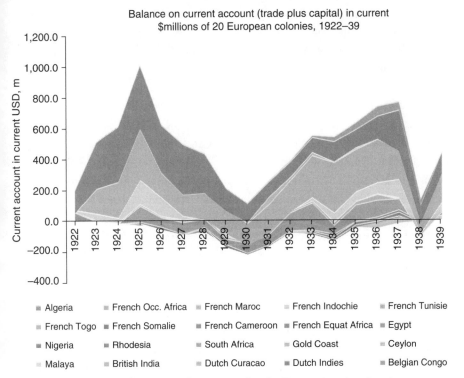

Balance on current account (trade plus capital) in current
$millions of 20 European colonies, 1922–39

Figures 2.1–2 Graphs and tables of supporting data for Figures 2.1 and 2.2 have been pre-
pared by Professor Paul Schmelzing of Boston College and if cited are to be credited to him.
The detailed data for these charts—Aggregate Trade + Capital Balance in Current USD
(Millions) by Colony; Aggregate Trade + Capital Balances in Current USD (Millions) by
Colonial Power; Aggregate Trade + Capital Balance in Current USD (Millions) by Colony;
Aggregate Trade + Capital Balances in Current USD (Millions) by Colonial Power—are
available by request from the author.

during the interwar era. After World War I, the terms of trade turned increasingly against agricultural commodities (i.e., agrarian prices declined with respect to the prices of manufactures), a trend that worsened dramatically with the Great Depression and ultimately fed back on the demand for industry. The balance of trade became increasingly adverse for the colonies (as well as for farmers within the metropole). This development drew together the dominions as well as Britain into a protected system of common tariffs and mutual exemptions, the so-called Ottawa system constructed in 1931 just as the United Kingdom levied a general tariff against those countries not in the system. (Germany, shorn of colonies, would turn to its "near abroad" in Eastern Europe to construct a similar zone.) Opening the December 1934 Conference on the French Economy at Home and Overseas (Conférence économique de la France métropolitaine et d'outre mer), Sarraut called on the country to organize its overseas domain—that is, follow the British example and impose an imperial tariff bloc, "a sort of autarky as a defensive system," uniting the colonies and the metropole into "a privileged regime permitting the French to send the colonies its manufactured products and to absorb colonial production."[33] French cotton manufacturers, for example, who with their capacity augmented by the acquisition of the formerly German factories in Alsace faced strong competition not only from synthetic fibers but from the Japanese and other new competitors, were particularly avid supporters. They managed to sell 40 percent of their output abroad in the 1920s, but the colonial share itself increased from 40 percent of these exports in 1925 to 90 percent in 1938 as they lost out in other markets.[34] Conversely, the French market cushioned colonial exporters of agricultural products, who doubled their sales (in constant 1914-valued francs) from 1928 to 1938. "In the interwar period, the empire became the leading commercial partner for France; it furnished almost all her imports of agricultural primary products [including vegetable oils] and absorbed the essential of her exports of cotton cloth, soaps, sugars, and cement, and permitted the auto industry, and metallurgy in general, to maintain their export capacity."[35]

In theory there was an alternative strategy: that of developing the colonies' own industry, which found some favor among expat businessmen in the colonies before independence. What was intended, of course, was the development of the settlers' enterprises, not of any autonomous indigenous production. Examining the Vietnamese economy, Paul Bernard denounced the "absurd paradox" of colonies buying from the metropole without selling to them: "Many of our compatriots have not yet understood that our great

Asian possession has crossed the threshold from being a simple trading post able to provide spices, exotic fruits, and trade-fair articles for the metropole or an ordinary market where French industry can find a large clientele that is not very picky." Instead, Indochina should become a veritable second metropole or distinct economic unit. The British, he argued, had followed this policy in India. Indochina had the resources and labor. If France provided capital, the colony might well achieve the same sort of development as had Japan. As for competition with French industries, although certain branches might suffer, the general demand for French goods would increase. This would require, Bernard understood, a new investment policy as well as dismantling restrictions. Depend on private capital from the metropole to enhance production, he urged, and not false theories of underconsumption. Bernard criticized the focus on state development projects over the previous half century, just as he objected to the left's focus on theories of underconsumption in general. Develop productive resources and redeploy labor from the overpopulated north of Vietnam (Cochin China) to the relatively underpopulated south; allow private investment and consumption would rise. France had tried too long to develop public works especially railroads that were never fully utilized and left the colony with a crushing debt burden.[36]

As world commodity prices plummeted, however, Bernard's policies found little support among the Franco-Indochinese rice exporters who dominated the colony's exports. In good times, trade and profits for colonial exports grew, but their proportional importance grew even more in bad times as overall business shrank. Although as recently as the 1920s, Indochinese grain, corn, and rice producers had sent over 80 percent of their product (amounting to 63 percent of the colony's total exports) to neighboring Asian consumers, by the late 1930s almost three-quarters went to France with prices supported by protective tariffs. By 1938, the colonial export needed the guarantee of a protected French market and were prepared to accept in return the tariffs on imports that Paris wanted to impose across the empire. From 1930 to the end of the 1950s, the strategy of protected high tariffs remained the principal reason for the *colons'* support of an autarkic policy. Wars aside, French exports to the colonies continued to grow long term at a faster rate than exports elsewhere.[37]

The same protected security of the empire attracted capital. Both France and Britain focused their overseas investments far more intensely in their empires between the war. Marseille has followed some 469 firms in the colonies, who raised capital for investments and estimates that on the eve of World

War I, 25 percent of French overseas investment went to Russia (12.4 billion francs), 8.4 percent to Latin America, and in third place, between 4.1 percent and 7.5 percent to the colonies. After the war, with Russian investments wiped out and others liquidated to finance the huge conflict, the colonies rose to first place with estimates of a total of 15–26 milliard gold francs by 1929 in a shrunken overseas portfolio. The share of *nouvelles émissions*—roughly IPOs—for firms organized outside of France fell from 30 percent in 1913 to 10 percent in 1930. But colonial issues climbed to 70 percent of that total from 25 percent in 1913, and by 1939 they represented 50 percent. In the 1920s, 208 new firms were founded for colonial business, roughly doubling all the previous numbers, and a total destined to shrink to 48 between 1930 and 1957.[38] But of that new foreign investment, colonial shares increased from 25 percent to 70 percent. To take just the salad days of the 1920s, new issues of shares in colonial corporations amounted to 6.75 billion current-value francs, while they peaked at 3.25 billion for corporations operating elsewhere abroad. Accumulated investments in colonial enterprises by 1929 amounted to 6.3 billion francs (1914 value), and probably 10 billion if one included government-financed infrastructure (equipment)—perhaps one-third of total foreign investment, according to Marseille. "The empire had thus become the privileged area for French capital exports."[39]

Critics have argued both for Britain and France that the investments poured into colonial administration and infrastructure and enemies might in the long run have been more profitably directed toward the home economy. That may be true; after decolonization by the 1960s, the national economies of France, Britain, and other colonial powers soared, and their cross-border trade and investment would recover the shares they had enjoyed before World War I. But decision making was based on the interests of particular constituencies, not a homogenous national society. The returns on colonies paid key political interests very well, as the returns on capital indicated. In 1927–1929, the rate of profits for mines was 18.4 percent, for industries 17.4 percent, for finance 11.9 percent, while plantations had dropped to 9.5 percent and transport 7 percent—still healthy returns. Marseille argues that investment in firms with colonial business was lucrative and remained so in the 1920s but less so for trading companies than firms that produced for the colonies. The largest profits, measured in current francs, in 1929 accrued to the Bank of Indochina.[40]

The break in continuity came with the composition of investment and chronologically with the 1930s. Essentially, state investments including

Table 2.1 French Capital Invested in the Empire (in Billions of 1914 Francs)

	Private Capital (public shares only)	State Loans	State Budgeted Infrastructure	Totals
Cumulative pre-1914	2.0	2.1	2.4	6.5 (ca. $1.3 billion)
1915–1929	1.6	0.7	0.23	2.5
1930–1939	0.8	3.4	0.54	4.7
1940–1958	2.0	—	10.0	12.0

Rounded off from Marseille, p. 105

The private investments in the colonies before 1914 were comparable in magnitude to those in Russia and Spain. At 1914 exchange rates (1Fr = $0.20 and £0.04) the 1914 total of 6.5 billion francs equaled about $1.3 billion or £260 billion, approximately 20–25 percent of British investment abroad. Marseille estimates that total private capital figures, and not just the series based on quoted securities, would raise the private share significantly. Nonetheless, on the basis of these latter figures, the share of private French capital invested in the empire would have risen from about 30 percent pre-1914 to about 64 percent from 1915–1929—presumably largely during 1919–1929—and then dropped to about 17 percent for the years after 1930. The state stepped in, first to make the colonies viable during the depression, then to keep them French after 1945.

subsidies had to substitute for private investment. That share included an increasing participation by public authorities whether for infrastructure or budget support and subventions to private firms for railroad and telegraph extension. Public investments played a substantial role throughout, but from 1930 until the end of empire, they clearly took over the preponderant role and outpaced new private issues by five to one. By then, the disproportion between state aid and revenues earned was causing anxiety and leading to the disenchantment with the empire that Marseille characterizes as a divorce.[41]

French public authorities invested more in that sunset era than in the previous seventy years, although the budgeted expenses for the colonies (3.5–4 percent) were lower than the 6.5–7 percent from 1900 to 1914. It is not clear how much of the post-1945 sum was required for military expenses, which US aid largely compensated for. Of course, the state budget claimed two or three times the share of French GDP after World War II than it had before World War I so that as a percentage of French GDP the colonial expenses dropped. This does not mean that French "capitalism" was losing out to state enterprise; capitalists, as Adam Smith recognized, have always required a framework of state legislation to extract material rewards from their own inventiveness, luck, or hard work. Capitalism in the modern era has also rested on an interweaving of public and private funds. In the postwar United

States, a massive military budget and development initiatives helped sustain the prosperity for which capitalist champions claimed credit. In the interwar and indeed from the nineteenth century, guaranteeing empire played an equivalent role.[42]

British investments in empire were far larger than the French. D. K. Fieldhouse, following other authorities, has summarized the trends.[43] Like France, Britain focused its overseas investments far more intensely in its empires between the wars. In 1914, accumulated British investment overseas amounted to about £3.6 billion (approximately $17.5 billion) of which the empire absorbed almost one-third (£1.148 billion / $5.6 billion), whereas the public and private capital invested in the French Empire amounted to about $1.3 billion or less than one-quarter the British. The French sunk massive investments into Russia and East Central Europe, most of which would be lost. Of the British placements in its empire, over 90 percent went to the dominions, which were politically autonomous although tied by commerce and sentiment to the Crown. Of the £443 million invested in the dependent empire, £287 million or almost two-thirds was placed in India.

Just as the value of new capital issues for French firms active in the colonies strongly outpaced the investments for French firms in international business in general, so too did British investments become more targeted. Between 1910 and 1914, an average 39 percent of new overseas investments went to the empire and 61 percent outside, such as to the United States and Argentina. But the empire's market for new overseas investments climbed to 66 percent annually for the four postwar years 1919–1923 and amounted to 59 percent annually for 1924–1928. As overseas investment shrunk in the Depression, the empire's total claimed an average annual 70 percent during 1929–1933 and 86 percent between 1934 and 1938. Ottawa Conference duties allowed the empire to increase its proportion of imports to Britain by 14 percent between 1914 and 1938, while British exports to the empire grew as a proportion of the whole by 6 percent. When Britain introduced its 10 percent general tariff in 1932—a fundamental reversal of the free trade policies that had largely prevailed since 1847—the dominions and colonies were exempted. The British Commonwealth was evolving into a very effective semiautarkic bloc. In an era of shrinking international trade (the United States had passed its high Smoot-Hawley tariff in 1931) as overall exports dropped 28 percent with respect to 1913, the empire played an ever more significant role. It was even more important as an arena for investments: 61 percent of the total value of quoted overseas securities in 1936 were empire issues (of which about two-thirds emanated from the dominions) versus 39 percent of the overseas investments of 1914—a reversal that reflected the net spending down of US investments in World War I.[44] Fieldhouse explains the attractions of empire: the dominions and colonies did not default on interest payments, and between 1918 and 1931, companies found an increasing proportion (almost half) of their issues subscribed to in the colonies. The empire, including dominions, thus consolidated a protected market for their exports and in return allowed a safe haven for British capital at a time when other arenas were prone to private or public default.

During and after World War II, this relationship became even more vital. Britain financed its war against the Japanese in Burma and India by payments in pounds from these British-administered dependencies, who accumulated the blocked credits in London as "sterling balances," an arrangement made compulsory for continuing members—the colonies—in 1939. By 1945, the British deficit on current account amounted to £10 billion, half of which was defrayed by lend-lease and another quarter by sterling area credits. They would remain on the British international accounts but were never to be called for repayment in gold or dollars. British dependencies used currencies that were pegged to the pound and since 1920 held their reserves in gold in London or British government securities, and then were members of the "sterling area," a trade zone whose members, which excluded Canada but encompassed Argentina, Eire, along with several smaller European countries among them Portugal and Sweden. Egypt, Thailand, and Iraq settled accounts in sterling, pegged their currencies to the pound and held some reserves in London. This insulated currency area became the target for American treasury officials who continually urged dismantling it and lowering the tariff as a price for lend-lease and postwar aid.[45] By the late 1950s and early 1960s, the empire was ebbing fast as a source of economic advantage: like the poet on Dover Beach, London could only hear its "melancholy, long, withdrawing roar."

Postscript: Postcolonial "Development"

The years after World War II radically changed the geopolitical possibilities for preserving empire. The swift Japanese occupation of British, French, and Dutch colonies in Southeast Asia in the name of Asian leadership of the region was blatantly hypocritical but undermined European claims to stewardship. The Italians lost their African "empire" to the British by 1942. The French and British soon became mired in long and brutal wars both in Asia and then in some of their African colonies to reassert their dominion, and the Dutch had to relinquish the Indies after a four-year effort to retain control. The United States played a wavering role, reluctant so long as Franklin Roosevelt remained president to side with the French and British but reluctant to disavow them as Cold War conflicts firmed up. Only vis-à-vis the weaker Dutch between 1947 and 1949 did Washington actively threaten economic sanctions and then again in 1956 by demanding the withdrawal of the British-French-Israeli effort to reconquer control of the Suez Canal. As for the formal American colony of the Philippines, it was advantageous to turn it over to pro-US elites in 1946. The American effort to regain influence over Cuba after Fidel Castro's revolution, ostensibly to keep his new regime out of the Soviet orbit, proved a miserable fiasco in 1961. The French accepted a divided Vietnam in 1954; the United States accepted a Communist South Vietnam between 1973 and 1975. Hoping to retain at least Algeria, where there was a substantial French settlement (just under one million of the 9.4 million total inhabitants in 1954), the French felt compelled to come to the conference table in 1961–1962. President de Gaulle, the greatest master of defending his nation's interests and of recognizing reality, finally understood that the costs of maintaining empire would tear apart his country. In 1940 France had lost a battle but not a war. By the early 1960s it might have won some battles, but it could not win the war. So too, Prime Minister Harold Macmillan recognized "the winds of change" in tropical Africa. As Todd Shepherd has recognized, decolonization might itself become a mission for the colonizers, just as once accumulating empire had been. The Belgians announced in 1960 they were quitting the Congo, but the Union Minière sought to encourage the secession of its wealthy mineral and copper region under Moïse Tschombe, who charmed European and American supporters by his dapper dress and knowledge of polo. The charismatic leader of resistance to the Belgians, Patrice Lumumba, had been conveniently flown to a provincial site under Central Intelligence Agency auspices where was he assassinated by Congo adversaries.

Economically, the European project helped to replace the colonial tribute. In fact, many of the economic flows were reconstructed, as they might have been earlier, without political possession. Formal empire might have ended; neocolonialism, underdevelopment, resource exploitation, the vast differentials of income did not. The former colonies who had achieved independence by the time of the 1955 Bandung Conference emerged for a while as the "third world," with connotations of neutralism, poverty, and underdevelopment. But they were still the site of a preponderance of essential mineral resources. By the mid-1950s, they were coming to be envisioned no longer as the "backward" economies but an attractive investment arena if properly organized. The World Bank stepped in to coordinate private investment under the aegis of its International Finance Corporation. The Rockefeller report, *Partners in Progress*, provided a blueprint. By the end of the century, former colonies were "emerging markets."[46] The realm of governance—foundations, NGOs, the intellectual architects of development studies—endorsed the objectives of capital.

But despite the high stakes of oil, commodities, and minerals, the premise of the European empires since 1918 had not been mere economic reward. It was also the conviction that retaining domination of less developed colonies conquered a century earlier was necessary to sustain a claim for their countries' status in international politics. In the turbulent interwar world, the resource empires—usually preoccupied by efforts at conservative stabilization at home and thus disinclined to mount great efforts at reconstructing society—sought to assert a political mission by prolonging and exalting what they claimed were benevolent associations of commerce, interest, and loyalty. They did so by conjuring up supranational projects in which their homelands would be guaranteed the keystone role in lieu of simple empire—the French Union, the British Commonwealth (later just the British Commonwealth of Nations or, informally, the Commonwealth), the enlarged Kingdom of the Netherlands. These associations were to replace continued use of force: dominion without domination, usufruct without exploitation. Some historians have claimed that these reformed structures might have awakened real loyalty among the peoples whose allegiance they hoped to consolidate and head off what happened—the rise of simple postcolonial national fragmentation.[47] A circle of sympathetic intellectuals was moved by the project, in the French case preeminently Aimé Césaire and Léopold Senghor, who could adapt it to their own celebration of *Négritude*. Other envisaged futures advanced by the postcolonial intellectuals in Africa and the West Indies reached for ideas for international economic integration and equality and not just formal sovereignty.[48] As discussed in Chapter 7, their programs would remain largely aspirational given the ideological polarities of the global cold war and the accumulated disparities of economic power.

What remained of the empires as territorial units after the 1970s were the British Commonwealth, the French Union, and a few remaining overseas territories ruled from Amsterdam, London, and Lisbon. The Soviet Union and the United States created different sorts of hegemonic structures, which achieved coordination by different means. The resource empires bequeathed cultural legacies, sometimes condemned as postcolonial, and important economic ties. Like each of the forms of global organization that have characterized our epoch, the resource empire was not hermetically sealed from the other institutions that tended to sociopolitical organization. It served states and it served capital even as it drew on their resources. Descended from empires of conquest, even in its fading stages it persisted as an institutional form that evoked great loyalties and provoked bitter resistance. It drew on nonterritorial resources along with the assets of hard power to insist on a territorial existence. It convinced anti-colonial elites that to become sovereign required controlling the resources that Western firms had brought on stream.[49] Even after formal rule ended, the inequalities that empire had built on and sought to perpetuate remained. Formally independent states would accept or call on the industrial and financial institutions of their former masters and sometimes their armed forces as well even as they conceived projects for autonomy. The postcolonial world was not postimperial. It is the nonterritorial sources of organization we must next consider.

3

The Realm of Governance
and the Web of Capital

WHERE DOES HISTORY, at least the history of political life, happen? Historians have traditionally looked within individual territorial states, at the institutions and people that ran them, or the wars they fought. Increasingly, however, other sites of power and influence have also claimed importance, some established by treaties among states, others by nonstate actors, professional or philanthropic, often working with governments, but often on their own initiative. "We send this New Year Greeting on January 1, 1914," wrote the philanthropist and steel magnate Andrew Carnegie, who three years earlier had established an endowment to advance international arbitration and the settlement of disputes, "strong in the faith that International Peace is soon to prevail, thru several of the great powers agreeing to settle their disputes by arbitration under International Law, the pen thus proving mightier than the sword." Carnegie ventured this optimistic prediction six months before some of the same great powers lurched into a four-year global war that cost between 10 and 20 million lives. His confidence was all the more remarkable given that key personnel of his ambitious foundation were deeply involved in investigating the savage wars that had just ended in the Balkans. Its chairman and moving spirit, Nicholas Murray Butler, concurrently president of Columbia University from 1902 until 1945, had already organized about twenty economic experts in Bern in August 1911 to ponder the connections between war, history, and economics. The Endowment's international commission, organized in 1913, was to issue its unsparing report on the Balkan violence a few weeks before Sarajevo. One of his field investigators, Samuel Dutton, wrote Butler a month or so after his New Year's message: "It is certain that another war is taking shape in the near future; it will be as cruel and bloody as the last."[1]

It is easy sport to make fun of Carnegie's hope for international law on the eve of war, especially a war in which earlier agreements to refrain from inhumane practices were increasingly discarded. But it is more important to understand the hope that he and his foundation staff invested in strengthening the agreements, and institutions intended to constrain state violence. Nor was it only the force of law that might restrain the recourse to war. Those less trusting in international treaties and arbitration perhaps found the British journalist Norman Angell more convincing when he argued in his 1910 book *The Great Illusion* that the densely woven trade and commercial connections of the international economy made war irrational and thus unlikely to take place. The realm of law and the webs of material interest would supposedly overcome the destructive tendencies of the modern nation-state. Alas, the ties they provided were gossamer, not gold or iron, and the history of the early twentieth century revealed their fragility. Nonetheless, they came to constitute a dense field of aspirations and discourse, if not of accomplishment, and have become increasingly fascinating for today's historians. Attention is warranted even if the historiography easily becomes overshadowed by hypotheticals, a history in the subjunctive.

War, of course, was not the only horseman of the apocalypse. Famine and pestilence still galloped across borders, and nineteenth-century reformers had added slavery, addiction, and prostitution to their list of scourges to overcome. Environmental degradation was beginning to be targeted inside national boundaries although climate catastrophe was not yet sensed as a menace. What was new—conceptually since the Enlightenment, organizationally since the mid-nineteenth century—was the transnational resistance to these social plagues. It was to be coordinated not only by governments through treaty arrangements, but increasingly by nonstate actors invested in combating each scourge—and not only by going on the defensive. New initiatives sought to reduce disorder and unpredictably as a whole, controlling political and social risk through international arbitration and the reach of international law, or by ensuring global hygiene and health, and even taming economic cycles. Late nineteenth- and early twentieth-century thinkers increasingly envisioned society as a plasmic whole, sometimes in terms of elites and masses, knowable and controllable through statistical science, biological and legal interventions. The audacity repelled many at the time and certainly social historians in the century since, but the ambitions constituted a major historical force and deserve empathetic understanding.

Premises of Governance

The state, the project-state in particular (see Chapter 1), was one powerful instrumentality for influencing social outcomes, but the state had territorial limits and could be captured by allegedly irrational or even demagogic leaders. Although the proponents of international law and treaties of arbitration (its most tangible form in the early twentieth century) clearly felt they were citizens of particular nations, they invested efforts and hopes in creating a sphere of norms that might bind state action. They sought to construct alternatives to unbridled violence and disorder by calling on the resources of states to build nonstate reservoirs of influence. As such, they subscribed to and indeed inhabited what historians often term not merely an international but a transnational domain. Even as the United Nations (UN) has confirmed a global legal order based on the sovereignty of 194 states, increasingly our species works, inhabits, and fantasizes not only within and between states but in a global space that evades and at times defies the nation-state structure.[2] This domain possessed no legislative or executive capacity unless assigned by voluntary treaties, but it has conferred influence, legitimation, and recognition, if not always power. It included sites for debating the normative and ethical frameworks of international activity, such as international courts of arbitration, or religious organizations that operated internationally as well as charities. Its actors created a society of values that occupied and shaped the international or transnational realm, somewhat like the increasingly dense radio transmissions were said to fill and even shape the so-called airwaves or ether. International associations—first the League of Nations, later the UN, at the same time powerful corporations, ambitious foundations such as Ford and Rockefeller based in the United States (later the German party foundations, humanitarian nongovernmental organizations [NGOs], scientific networks, and not to be overlooked, quasi-confederal associations such as the European Union)—fill the international domain with a continuing discursive buzz of peaceable intentionality. Historians have increasingly traced their activity.[3] I consider them here as a *realm of governance*.

I use the idea of governance and not that of internationalism to tie together the initiatives under consideration. Both concepts suggest alternatives to the exercise of power by territorial states. Both locate the capacity to shape or at least interpret ongoing development in a domain that cuts across the states that occupy the globe. Both, however, still posit implicit spatial dimensions of thought and action. Historians of internationalism have emphasized the negotiated sites—such as the League of Nations and the UN—and the agents of activity, including NGOs or self-declared collective identities—as they grew and continue to grow more numerous and denser in the modern era. They focus on actors cutting across national lines, seeking to tame national power, even when recognized and organized by nation-states. "At the turn of the twenty-first century," claim the editors of a first-class collection of essays designed to exemplify the new scholarship, "historical interest in internationalism ... is gradually becoming the norm in a relatively short space of time."[4] But their dialogue is with Leopold von Ranke, whereas mine is with Max Weber. By using the concept of governance, the account here aims to emphasize less where efforts to organize social outcomes are constructed than how they are constructed when they cannot draw on potentially coercive enforcement. What seems critical to me is less the authority that international agents possess than the power they must do without. The idea of governance represents a challenge to the politics that takes place within states as well as between them.

"Governance" has become a very fashionable and even reassuring concept. At its most rudimentary level, it refers merely to the procedures prescribing the behavior of organizations that have no legal coercive power. At the same time, governance is supposed to suggest rules that conduce to decent collective action and to policy that is free from corruption, "transparent," independent of special interests, and decided on by rational debate. We could perhaps but do not usually refer to the governance of the Mafia or the Zetas. Governance relies on expertise and scientific reasoning, without which disaster can loom, but it also conduces to deference, less essential but very pleasurable.[5] Foundations love to support it; policy advisers aspire to find it. International organizations such as the International Monetary Fund measure it and suggest how to achieve it. It claims to represent benevolent policy that is designed to convince without deploying state power or, as Claus Offe has suggested in a probing discussion, without political persuasion.[6] Like "civility," governance keeps disagreement within bounds. As critics understood, invoking governance could have the effect of stigmatizing forceful efforts to challenge the status quo, protect privileges of class and race, and prolong the inequalities of international life.[7] Later historians have emphasized the social conservatism of the major foundations.[8] Critics view governance as a fig leaf for conspiratorial rule by elites. I would not go so far, but it is, in effect, an effort to govern without relying on a state and without incurring traditional bureaucratic or electoral competition. In fact, the ideal of a pure scientific expertise remained unrealizable. The realm of governance was suffused with political contention, nor could it be otherwise. But that is no reason to doubt the intense activity advocated and fought for in the name of rationality and science. The realm of governance existed, in part as mirage, in part as regulatory horizon.

The policies that governance prescribes do not depend on elections for legitimacy. They presuppose that individuals and the groups they lead can rise above personal or even collective preferences to lay down guidelines that benefit society as a whole. It recommends procedures and criteria for achieving such norms including expertise in the activity to be governed and calm discussion among the experts assembled in committees. It privileges rationality and tends to dismiss "will"—the raw preferences of the masses—as irrelevant when not misguided. Democracy is allegedly preserved by allowing an interested public to comment on the policies proposed but not necessarily to veto or change them. The organizations of governance replenish their personnel through co-optation, a process that unsurprisingly excludes uncomfortable dissenters.[9]

The behavior sought represents a venerable aspiration, praised from Plato onward. Georg Wilhelm Friedrich Hegel believed that the Prussian monarchy's bureaucracy exemplified governance and functioned as a universal class, transcending the particular interests of a complex civil society. When the bureaucracy had the king's ear, so to speak, the result was supposedly a benevolent and ethical state—a government and law whose rationality transcended the mere reconciliation of interests that could be achieved by civil society. When, in the early twentieth century, American educated classes feared the populist results of urban political machines, they appealed to the institution of city managers so as to give political power to governance. The dream of expertise (technical and political) has been a recurrent aspiration from Saint-Simon and Auguste Compte's nineteenth-century call for rule by experts to Thorstein Veblen's hope for a Soviet of engineers at the end of World War I. Governance depended on and encouraged the growth of what political theorists have called epistemic communities—whether in law, administration, medicine and public health, or finance.[10] But the politics of governance also gave rise to organizational rivalries as did the politics within governments.

Advocates of governance vaunted its nonpartisanship, but it rested on underlying political assumptions in early twentieth-century political society: fear of the far left and of those today we consider populists. Revolutionaries and pronounced socialists supposedly excluded themselves on the left; nationalist authoritarians were out of bounds on the right. The realm of governance provided a transnational buffer for assuring the continuity of re-source empires (see Chapter 2) and dampening the shocks that project-states might deliver to the international domain. It represented a compromise between the reformist ideas of pre–World War I international liberalism— exemplified in Britain by the political philosopher L. T. Hobhouse and the *Manchester Guardian* and in the United States by the Progressive movement— and the aspirations of conservatives to uphold the status quo of a peacefully accepted inequality of peoples and races. As throughout the twentieth century, it functioned in the West on the basis of cooperation between non-revolutionary spokesmen for organized working-class interests and reform-minded traditionalists and entrepreneurs. By the 1920s, they included trade union representatives, such as Albert Thomas, who populated the new International Labour Organization (ILO) and were repelled by "Bolshevism," religiously motivated do-gooders, reformist businessmen with technocratic visions of capitalism, such as Herbert Hoover's ideas of "associationism," the foundations concerned with public health and governmental reform and the social scientists affiliated with them, although like so many of the modernist advances in culture and social activism, they had clearly emerged in the years before World War I.

Governance organizations proliferated, of course, within national socie-ties. Many were the voluntary associations, as Alexis de Tocqueville had ob-served with respect to America's public life from the 1830s on, but they thrived elsewhere as well. Antislavery movements intensified even as the institution thrived under the conditions of plantation agriculture and as the demand in-creased for the commodities it provided—sugar, coffee, and cotton. After abolition, British and French public life became increasingly populated with organizations aspiring to goals they conceived as publicly benevolent. Some of the most powerful were committed to temperance, a cause that mobilized women who otherwise were excluded from public service. Many focused on the disturbing visible poverty generated in new industrial cities, such as the Quaker-inspired Hathaway and Cadbury Trusts or the American settlement house movement. Many were religious in motivation, such as London's Toynbee Hall, or the German Inner Mission. Other religiously inspired efforts combined missionary effort with educational and medical institutions. When they focused attention abroad, they were notably active in the ageing empires where governments had not yet implanted Western-style social projects—such as China or the Ottoman Middle East, even though a rich fabric of educational and social foundations existed under Muslim auspices.

International Law and Rights

Two major approaches to governance—one legalist, the other functionalist—marked the activities of the 1920s. The former, preeminently focused on tempering international violence, aspired to strengthen legal institutions that had international scope. Their founders aspired to work alongside and through governments to bind the power of states when they threatened violent conflict. Certainly, the concept of international law—the law of nations—claimed recognition explicitly since the seventeenth century. As a notion of civilized practice for war and sieges, the immunities given to ambassadors, the sense of common cause against pirates, or the recognition of treaties, the germs of international law hearkened back to Roman concepts of a jus gentium and later to scholastic theology developed by Aquinas, who attributed these supposedly universal norms to the share of rationality that humanity shared with God, so-called natural law. Inscribed into treaties that protected noncombatants and limited violence, these norms supposedly could be accepted by states and, once accepted, had to be adhered to: *pacta sunt servanda*, treaties must be (or at least should be) observed as the sixteenth-century Dominican philosopher Francisco de Vitoria stated. The European conquest of the Americas in the sixteenth and seventeenth centuries and their competing expeditions to Asian seas encouraged profound and wide discussion of international law and usages. Vitoria and the Dutch legal theorist Hugo Grotius fifty years later contributed major doctrinal statements to this emerging discussion as it successively encompassed the claims of conquest, conversion, and commerce. Indeed, according to the reactionary Carl Schmitt, international law arose as a code to avoid conflict among the Europeans in their imperial land grabs. The need to settle religious civil wars in the European heartland and the eighteenth-century struggles for dominance or even security in a crowded continent encouraged further efforts to make the world safe for princes. Emer Vattel attempted to codify usages in the mid-eighteenth century. The era of the French Revolution and its aftermath added nationalist passions and aspirations for popular government to the rivalries even as railroads and telegraph allowed a new intensity of claims to statehood.

The decades from the late 1840s through the 1870s saw a series of wars in Europe and the Americas, less cohesive and protracted than the long struggle against Napoleon but producing a world of competitive states and unified nations that seemed more brutal than ever. Darwinist-derived concepts, such as the struggle for species' survival, allied with racialist ideas provided the ideological justifications for the competitive global "order" of the latter nineteenth century. But the new order was also one that recognized government by discussion: the ordaining or modifying of constitutions so that liberal bourgeois elites might have a voice in government. Was it not possible, then, that resources of discussion and legal expertise might claim a role in reining in the recourse to violence and conflict internationally? By the 1870s, a society for international law had been founded. Special institutions were also emerging. "Mixed commissions" that might arbitrate disagreements over treaty provisions became a more frequent recourse, inscribed into the treaties themselves. After the American Civil War and the many wars of national emergence that marked the 1850s through 1870, national delegations convened at Geneva and The Hague to find agreement on laws of war that would set limits to violence.[11]

Internationally negotiated agencies worked when they had territorial states behind them that at least temporarily had overlapping interests. Special purpose associations, such as the International Postal Union, or commissions to combat sexual trafficking or opium smuggling also emerged out of international conferences. An effective international regime for limiting opium traffic depended on the mobilization by reform-minded NGOs but also the fact that Japan's emerging imperialist ambitions were benefited by joining in an effort at control.[12] Similarly they began to subscribe to a series of international courts and judges that might, it was hoped, resolve disputes.

The recourse to international association and arbitration was mixed with the pursuit of special or national interest. Between Leopold II of Belgium, who claimed to protect missionary activity in Equatorial Africa, the British who wanted commercial access in the region, and Otto von Bismarck who thought to ensure that newly united Germany would not be excluded, the colonial partition of Central Africa was consummated under the guise of multilateral agreement at the enforcement of international debts. A language of human rights emerged, sometimes sponsored by monarchs whose own regimes hardly demonstrated a concern for them. Still, a rhetoric of supposedly binding law emerged to replace the appeal to a common Christianity that agreements in the early modern era had often cited. The concept of "civilization" suggested a common Western domain of rights and usages even as it justified continuing subjugation of nonstate polities in Africa, Asia, or the vast continental interior of Central Asia and the Americas. As the chair of the Carnegie Endowment insisted in its 1927 yearbook, "There is no greater fallacy than to suppose that all peoples wherever situated and of whatever background are equally competent for orderly self-government."[13]

These ambiguous effects have thus enabled historians to narrate this history in very different ways. Earlier chroniclers could take the advance of associations, courts, and treaties at face value as a story of real progress and advance. A subsequent generation might unveil the very particular motives behind each claim and see only a cynical pretext, much as the German emperor William II greeted Czar Nicholas's summons for a conference to limit war as the consequence of Russian military inferiority, or Marxist historians could condemn bourgeois hypocrisy. What substance, after all, did the norms and the treaties really possess? Japan would walk out of the League of Nations in February 1933 when it was rebuked for aggressive behavior in invading Manchuria; Germany would exit at the end of 1933, denouncing the allegedly one-sided efforts of arms limitations; the partial sanctions imposed on Italy after Benito Mussolini's invasion of Ethiopia did not preserve the country's independence. Was law without enforcement really law?

Most recently, a cycle of younger historians' interest in international law or institutions has suggested that even initiatives that might fall short of proclaimed intentions did help sensitize opinion and prepare for later advances. In a world of imperfect institutions, all these advances had a merit in themselves—often the way an imperfect UN has been thought to represent an advance over a world without such an association. As the author of the history of the mandates system writes, "Inadvertently, by seeking to 'internationalize' empire, the League ultimately brought a world of universal and normative statehood nearer."[14] On the other hand, does it make sense to accept the recent assertion that the 1928 Kellogg-Briand Pact whose sixty-three pre–World War II signatories renounced any recourse to war was a milestone on the path to peace?[15] More generally, does the new interest in the development of international law, human rights, or claims for international economic redistribution (see Chapter 7) slight the distinction between norms and practices and provide a consolation for the meager results attained?

Nonetheless, by the interwar period—with the formation of the League of Nations, the reorganization of overseas empires, the recourse to continued arbitrations and expert commissions—an active realm of governance occupied public energies alongside the realm of states and government. Just as the globe increasingly pulsated with the energy of radio communication,[16] so too it was energized by efforts at global governance, initiatives often sponsored by the states whose *sacro egoismo* the new institutions and organizations were designed to mitigate. Niccolò Machiavelli and Carl von Clausewitz had supposedly written the rules for global politics from 1500 to 1870. Might it not be the moment for Andrew Carnegie and the international lawyers to provide an alternative?

The League of Nations offered the institutional umbrella for these efforts. The Permanent Court of International Justice convened in early 1922 at the Peace Palace in The Hague—the structure Carnegie had funded for his arbitration efforts.[17] Its judges were chosen by the Assembly and the Council of the League and the League funded it. By 1939, it was recognized in 600 treaties as having arbitrating authority for disagreements. The Mandates Commission provided the institutional forum designed to supervise and carry out the new rules that the imperial powers accepted to put a decent drapery on empire. No equivalent minorities commission emerged to enforce the treaties made by the League Council with the new states of Eastern Europe. Rather the Council received the grievances and appointed three-member committees to hear the issues and either accept the promised remedies or bring them publicly to the council.[18]

Notable among the Europeans who contributed to the efforts to develop international law in the interwar period were Jewish lawyers educated in the Austro-Hungarian Empire, who found refuge in Britain and the United States in the 1930s, among them Hans Kelsen and Hirsch Lauterpacht. The cumbersome imperial structure of Austria-Hungary had exposed both the power of ethnic nationalism and the continuing, if ultimately unsuccessful, effort to find a framework—prenational and postnational at once—that allowed for ethnic diversity within a federative polity. Although they were enthusiastic supporters of the republics that succeeded the Habsburg Empire, the international lawyers remained vulnerable given the anti-Semitism that infected many of the national communities of Central and Eastern Europe. They faced an immediately urgent problem as the collapse of the prewar landed empires in Europe along with the devastation of war and the aftermath of the Bolshevik Revolution created masses of refugees formally stateless. The fledgling League usefully invented a solution for provisional documentation under its own authority, the so-called Nansen passport named for the Norwegian explorer and activist Fridtjof Nansen.[19]

The effort to guarantee ethnic and religious minorities in the new European states through "minorities treaties," which granted their spokespersons the right to petition the League to preserve linguistic and other rights within their new nations, was an ambiguous gift. Originally pressed by Jewish agencies fearful of how their coreligionists would fare in the new nations of Eastern Europe, the minorities treaties came to serve Magyars awarded to Romania and Germans seeking to protect school rights and threatened landed property inside restored Poland.[20] As Natasha Wheatley has argued, the richer texture of internationalism or international governance produced not merely the associations that arose under League auspices, whether through the mandate system, the ILO, or organizations contesting plebiscites. It involved the spread of claims to collective recognition, whether on the part of self-proclaimed nationalities or other groupings that sought recognition through the league or in terms of legal personality. International lawyers had generally insisted that only states had standing in international law; now in the 1920s, they vigorously questioned this narrow criterion.[21] National territories were no longer the only ground for legal subjecthood. But this hardly guaranteed that such groups could really defend themselves in the realm of governance.

There were other approaches, however. Nicholas Murray Butler thought the approach of international law was too feeble. He envisaged that his section of the Carnegie Endowment, the Division of Exchange and Education, could play a stronger role by encouraging an "international mind" in America and abroad. He pushed the Endowment to fund splashy rebuilding projects such as the library of the University of Louvain (Leuven) and organized conferences and studies. As Germany and France eased tensions in the mid-1920s, Butler financed conferences and publications to urge reconciliation, notably by sponsoring the publications of F. W. Foerster, a notable German critic of his country's clandestine rearmament who infuriated nationalist opinion at home. Under pressure to sever ties with Foerster and the pacifist Helmut von Gerlach, the trustees hesitated but did decide to gradually withdraw their financial support. Foerster in turn criticized the Endowment's unwillingness to take a stand against German violations of the peace treaties, which led to Carnegie's statement that it was not its policy "to adopt any attitude toward questions of internal politics of any country."[22] When the National Socialist government clamped down on the Hochschule für Politik, the Endowment found itself without any basis for action. Its ambitions for southeastern Europe—a Balkan union to be prepared by a series of Balkan conferences bringing together Albania, Bulgaria, Greece, Turkey, and Yugoslavia—proved similarly a bridge too far, as the diplomat and social observer David Mitrany warned in 1930. A Balkan entente pact was signed in 1934 but not because of the conferences. Formal structures had to rest on shared interests emerging from civil society.

The Functionalist Vision

More than the lawyers, Mitrany sought to develop a theoretical framework for the activities of governance and the public-private domain in which they operated. His "functionalism" was not high theory, but it did articulate an effort to get beyond the formalist concepts of law and sovereignty. It represented in effect an international version of the legal theories developed by Léon Duguit in the decade before World War I, which envisioned law as the instrument for governing society's pluralist group interests.[23] Others have seen a decisive precedent in the inter-allied economic arrangements and councils during World War I that Arthur Salter described in his history of wartime control of shipping work for the Carnegie series on the social and economic history of the war.[24] Whatever the origins, Mitrany's term *functionalism* well describes the second major manifestation of governance initiatives. The idea suggested that efforts to create political unions on the basis of nation-states should yield to the organization of associations for specialized common purposes that would bring together peoples organically. Charitable foundations and NGOs operating within states had followed functional lines, focusing on education, health, urban reform, and the like. The interwar era extended these efforts internationally. The International Labor Organization, attached to the League, moved vigorously from the outset, although its ambition to secure international adoption of the eight-hour day remained out of reach. By 1926, however, the ILO did persuade national governments, as cited in the previous chapter, to sign agreements designed to prevent forced labor and disguised slavery. The League's health organization, headed by the energetic physician Ludwik Rajchman—later first chairman of UNICEF—pursued an active public health agenda, often overlapping, as shown below, with the largest private initiative, the Rockefeller Foundation's International Health Service. Mitrany's career illustrated how the juridical and functional approaches could be pursued in tandem, for even while espousing his ideas of functionalism he remained close to the Carnegie Endowment's juridical endeavors. As he wrote in the early 1930s, "The founders of modern international law, Vitoria and Suarez, were among the first to point out that the natural social tendencies of man involve as natural a sociability among states." Sociability justified the fashionable ideas of planning, which so characterized the project-states under conditions of world depression. "Planning rests on a profoundly different state of mind from that which prevailed at the beginning of the nineteenth century; a change in communal psychology which swings the pendulum of political gravitation from the individual to the social, and in regard to government from negative order to purposeful action, cannot fail to re-open also the wider question of the communal organization of world affairs."[25]

Like the international lawyers and Rajchman, Mitrany was born into a Jewish family, not in the Habsburg monarchy but in neighboring Romania—formally recognized as independent by the 1878 Congress of Berlin. However, he definitively left behind both his religious identity and the new state whose political leadership had virtually defined its emerging national personality as anti-Semitic. Jews could not become officers although they had to serve in the military; they could not own farms or hold public office. "Yet in spite of all that I could not bring myself to embrace Zionism," Mitrany confessed, although he recognized that it was "both proper and necessary that the Jews should have homeland of their own."[26] Mitrany worked and studied as a young man in Hamburg and then shortly before the outbreak of war moved to England, where he found a position as become an unofficial apprentice to C. P. Scott, the editor of the liberal *Manchester Guardian* before finding a post at the London School of Economics. He envisaged his program as a sort of transnational Fabianism.

He retained his interest in Romania and southeast Europe and wrote two major monographs in the Carnegie series on the impact of the war on the country and the larger region but more generally on their social structure, above all the poverty and subjection of its peasantry. Although he had found it productive to work with the Fabian left, he found the doctrinal reluctance of liberals and democratic socialists—and certainly the new communist parties—to work with agrarian parties devastating for democratic development. The need in postwar Europe was for "the two sections of the working masses to join with the liberal bourgeoisie and consolidate their new democratic prospect. Instead, the Socialist parties at once and in the worst Marxist tradition turned against the Peasant parties and groups, only to find themselves later helpless against the two extremes of Communist and reactionary pressure. The dogmatism of progressive intellectuals was a clear counterpoint to that central premise of 'the relation of things' which has been the base of the functional idea."[27]

Once in Britain and affiliated with Labour Party, worker educational institutions and the New Europe, a group agitating for the breakup of the Habsburg Empire and the extension of nationality to its diverse peoples. In 1916, he became a member of the first League of Nations Society, but as his memoir stated, he was less concerned with the production of sovereign states or with formal regional unions than with bodies that would deal with regional problems and local needs "and so help to turn the often endemic regional hostility, as in Latin America and the Balkans and elsewhere, into ways of local cooperation."[28] Throughout his long career he remained skeptical of new federations—somehow countries and whatever supranational associations might be negotiated should remain concerned with purpose-driven tasks.[29] The accent differed from later elaborations of functionalism, identified with Jean Monnet or the émigré political scientist Ernest Haas, which argued that such initiatives could generate ever more extensive associations of supranational government by virtue of their "spillover" effects.

From 1922 to 1929, Mitrany worked as assistant European editor under James Shotwell on the Carnegie Endowment's *Economic and Social History of the World War*. As he edited the different manuscripts, "one particular background picture began to assert itself: it showed how under the impact of the new kind of warfare, which had made economic resources and industrial potential a decisive factor, the belligerents had all adopted much the same ways and means for dealing with problems of supply and production and distribution under conditions of war. Here was a rare thing in social experience—a plain demonstration of a general concept, in this case revealing the close working relation under given conditions between the function of government and the structure of government." The answer to problems "were improvised by countries which differed greatly in their material and technical resources, and by countries with very different systems of government and administration."[30]

In 1932, while visiting Harvard, he lectured on "The Political Consequences of Economic Planning" and ventured to Yale to expound his ideas for a "Communal Organisation of World Affairs" within the framework of the William Dodge Lectures of 1932, "The Progress of International Government." Mitrany's lectures reviewed the theorists of sovereignty and international law in the sixteenth and seventeenth centuries. He noted the paradox between the stress on state sovereignty and possibilities for international regulation. "State equality thus became before long the central idea of the political world. Yet from that moment the international branch of political philosophy seemingly took a vow of abstinence." Democratic movements limited the autocratic state but nonetheless thereby extended state power, a tendency to which both the Reformation and theories of sovereignty contributed. The late nineteenth century had brought "some thirty bodies, like the International Postal Union, working smoothly and efficiently for the world at large." The increase in the number of independent states and the growth in democratic sentiment led to a further step in international progress, "which brought us to the threshold of a genuine international society." "The two Hague Conferences of 1899 and 1907 transferred the discussion of general international problems from the directorate of the Great Powers to a common council of all independent states of the world." Despite the paucity of political results, "the Hague Conferences nevertheless represented a central advance in the organization of the civilized world."[31] But the right direction was not to unify territories but functional associations. "To widen the territory is merely to 'rationalise' nationalism. . . . A new philosophy for a world society must indeed begin by asking that we renounce the pagan worship of political frontiers as the source of our public law and morals."[32]

For the same reason, he rejected Count Koudenhove-Kalergi's plea for "pan-Europe," whose deeply conservative tincture of protecting Europe from both Bolshevism and American "materialism" could not serve to advance genuine global peace. "The core of the Pan-European scheme thus consists of certain economic aspirations, to be surrounded with a protective covering against the competitive and the envious."[33] The same denunciation applied for national planning. "The epidemic of schemes for economic planning which started in Russia and is now raging in almost every Western country has at present a national bias" and offers "a very doubtful means toward a more stable international peace." It was mercantilist and likely to become just an instrument of political power. "Yet the most hopeful prospect arises precisely out of this transformation of the state into an instrument of service. . . . Instead of slicing up government into hierarchically subordinate geographical area we need for our new ends rather to dissect its tasks and relevant authority on functional lines." States would remain in being but apparently become stake holders in a diversity of economic and social councils. States were not equal but all deserved representation; there would be a "scheme of devolution: secondary bodies could be set up in various parts of the world as international organs of regional groups of states; they would not include any of the actual Great Powers but would be connected with and subordinate to the central organs of the League." The regional councils could grapple with the problems left as nations were carved out of old empires. Thus the League would include the great powers directly represented, secondary states with group representation, and smaller states with panel representation. Feasibility was evident "by the significant way in which frontier disputes, which in the past have given rise to any a conflict, have almost passed out of the political field."[34]

Mitrany did not lose his faith with the outbreak of war in 1939. In 1941, he submitted a memo to the British Foreign Office that repeated his ideas. He remained skeptical about plans for federation, which the Foreign Office envisaged as a counterweight to German power. They would be either continental—in which case, dominated by a hegemon—or ideological, as exemplified by Clarence Streit's well-circulated proposal for a union of democracies. But then, "what will be done if one or more members were to go fascist, and so lose their qualification for membership [a conundrum facing the European Union today]. All these difficulties rise from a fundamental confusion as to the real issue involved. The criterion of selection is based on existing or professed democratic form, whereas the only test that could satisfy is that of democratic performance."[35] The solution was "to organize governments following specific ends and needs, and according to the conditions of their time and place, in lieu of the traditional organisation on the basis of a set constitutional division of jurisdiction and rights and powers." Common interests would be bound together. Railroads could be continent-wide; security would be met by an American "safety zone." Social security, health, the drug and white slave traffic, (control of) subversive movement, aviation, and broadcasting were all spheres ripe for transnational governance. "The functional *dimensions*, as we have seen, determine themselves. In a like manner, the function determines if appropriate *organs*." Nothing in such functional beginnings would prevent their evolving into a federal system.[36] Frontiers would no longer have to be changed; "the functional method denies by implication that there is any progress in changes of frontier." States would not need to claim a formal equality since through functional development "the system would make for that equalization of social conditions and outlook which, better than any constitutional device, might in time provide a solid foundation for political union." He advanced the same ideas publicly in his 1943 tract, "A Working Peace System." Probably sensing the coming domination of the four or even two great powers, he sharply rejected any formal world assembly based on democratic principles. "One aim is to create a forum for the expression of progressive world opinion; the other aim is to build up an effective instrument of common policy. . . . It is not an unprincipled or an unwise compromise to err if need be on the side of working democracy rather than of voting democracy."

Lurking beneath these convictions was a skepticism about guaranteeing human rights that today's readers might find tendentially dangerous. Could an international institution guarantee individual rights? Mitrany had already decided that the idea of guaranteeing collective minority rights was imprac-tical.[37] But by the second postwar period, he also came to argue that no inter-national authority could guarantee individual "negative" rights—the protec-tions against state interference—and the newer "positive" rights, such as claims to social security: International action could be effective in guaran-teeing these positive rights by sanctions on those states that withheld them. But individuals were bound to lose their rights as a result just of economic change. "The functions and powers of the state are growing apace even in normal times through the widening practice of national planning. This is bound to curtail many individual and local rights, and therefore cuts across attempts at establishing or reviving internationally the rights of individuals and groups."[38] At the 1954 International Political Science Conference, he con-ceded that "the social trend which is revolutionising the whole concept of and complex of human rights is *irreversible.*" A declaration of human rights should be welcomed, but "there is an impossible contradiction between the would-be protection of individual rights through international authority, and the all-inclusive control of the whole complex of economic and social life by the national state."[39]

Social Health

The realm of governance encompassed more than efforts to civilize legal in-ternational behavior and to reconceive national politics. Perhaps the most conspicuous sphere for the exercise of functional governance was that of public health. Nineteenth-century cholera epidemics had prompted confer-ences on international quarantine procedures but without significant agree-ment until an International Sanitary Convention was founded in 1892, followed by establishment of the Paris-based Office international d'hygiène pub-lique. Colonial medicine as well as the health of increasingly urbanized socie-ties at home became a major preoccupation for imperial powers. With the world depression of the 1930s—in this respect too, a decisive twentieth-century turning point—came a major internationalization of the public health agenda across India and Southeast Asia but not only in colonial Asia.[40]

The Rockefeller Foundation's International Health Commission (IHC), established in 1913, was already active in Latin America and Eastern Europe (although working under a succession of different names until 1951). Its funding and influence set it up as a power alongside the League of Nations Health Organization (LNHO), also committed to a public health agenda though less focused on the technologies of eradication. The Rockefeller's health establishment had grown out of the oil magnate's aide's interest in medical philanthropy and research, leading to an Institute for Medical Research in 1901 and then in 1909 to the Rockefeller Sanitary Commission for the Eradication of Hookworm Disease, a debilitating anemia caused by parasites absorbed into the intestines. The original target was the American South, but the ambitions of the directors soon led to envisaging an international campaign and the founding of the IHC. Many of its doctors and directors had practiced in the Philippines after the United States had taken over the islands from Spain and found themselves engaged in suppressing Emilio Aguinaldo's anti-colonial resistance. Although the first director, a former college president, Wickliffe Rose, envisaged the hookworm campaign as part of a broader effort to recruit local authorities in a grassroots campaign for public hygiene, his physician successors saw their mission as wiping out one illness after another.[41] The energetic manager of IHC efforts, Fred Soper, sought to follow the "intensive method" of eradication that Colonel George Washington Goethals applied to suppress yellow fever in the Panama Canal Zone. It involved systematically mapping the country, lecturing villagers (in this case on the importance of building and using latrines), repeated medical exams, and treatments when needed. Eradication was and remains a controversial strategy. Although the Rockefeller Institute's anti-hookworm campaign "introduced modern hygiene and laboratory-based medical examination and treatment, to a significant portion of the non-urban people of Nicaragua at a time when neither the medical profession nor the state was capable of doing so, or inclined to try," it met resistance.[42] Local villagers distrusted a campaign supported by the conservative government, while intellectuals blamed the United States for helping to overthrow the prior liberal regime. The IHC's campaign against tuberculosis in France was supported by French authorities but also proved disappointing. TB did not respond to the medication then available; it was a milieu disease spread at home often by infected soldiers on leave.[43] In Italy and in India, the Rockefeller Foundation's anti-malaria campaign ran into resistance from the league's Malaria Commission, which stressed alleviating the poverty of the regions where malaria was prevalent.

Yellow fever and malaria promised more satisfactory targets than TB; the mosquito was an identifiable vector. The International Health Board had begun anti-malarial work in the South in 1915 and within a few years expanded its interventions in Brazil, Nicaragua, Puerto Rico, El Salvador, the

Philippines, Palestine, and from 1928 to 1951, in Italy. Eradication of the mosquito by spraying breeding pools, in the 1920s through the copper-arsenic salt known as Paris green, and with DDT by the 1940s, promised mass attack. For the Rockefeller commission, eradication of the mosquitos continued to promise a far more direct response to the disease. Nonetheless, results were still mixed. Malaria did decline, but was it because of spraying? Rockefeller authorities saw their task much as a military mission; Malcolm Gladwell has compared Soper, one of the most dedicated advocates of species eradication, to General George Patton; but General William Westmoreland—who always called for more soldiers to ensure success in Vietnam—might have been a more appropriate comparand. Lewis Hackett, director of the Rockefeller Malaria Mission in Italy, was impatient with the more holistic approach urged by most of the Italian experts: quinine for sufferers, land reclamation for the region, a continuation in effect of the fascist project for draining the Pontine marshes. Likewise, Hackett rejected the idea that squalor caused the disease instead of the inverse: the League of Nations commission's solution, he wrote the Foundation's director in New York, was "to treat the malaria of Italy with roast beef."[44] Eradication of the malarial mosquito species by spraying seemed initially to promise success in northeast Brazil and in wartime Egypt, where a major infestation of the disease had cost perhaps 100,000 lives in 1943. But eradication was rarely permanent, and the Sardinian campaign after the European war ended suggested that the disease could be controlled without a zero-malaria campaign.

Directors of the foundation remained adamant in their goal of species eradication. Although despite the recourse to DDT, they could not claim they had eliminated mosquitoes, they did take pride in the elimination of malaria: "failure as success," according to one internal report.[45] Just as significantly, by the time the Foundation yielded its field initiatives to the World Health Organization (WHO), founded in 1948, it had waged dozens of campaigns, supported twenty-five schools and institutes of public health, and financed graduate public health study and schools directly.[46] It flanked the LNHO, and after the League's organization was phased out during the second war, Rockefeller's public health experts played important roles in establishing the United Nations Relief and Rehabilitation Administration—the umbrella UN postwar relief organization that operated until 1947.

As Anne Emanuelle Birn outlines, the relationship between the emerging WHO and the Rockefeller alumni was delicate. Rockefeller's Soper had become head of the oldest public health organization, the Pan American Sanitary

Bureau (PASB), and worked to magnify its financial base and independent functioning, forcing "WHO into a decentralized structure, based on geographically-organized regional offices (with PASB remaining the largest and most independent of these)." WHO drew on Rockefeller International Health Board personnel, approaches, and strategy; as the program director Lewis Hackett noted, "To a greater or lesser degree, all the international organizations have adopted the policies and activities in which the IHD [International Health Division] has pioneered." "The things they did are now the basis of WHO work."[47] Although the scientific directors felt this provided the basis for fruitful cooperation, the Foundation's trustees decided to move on. Perhaps they understood that their public health activity had enjoyed a privileged moment in which medical technology seemed to favor its program of eradication and during which the United States' powerful sphere of influence allowed an arena for intervention. The time had come to dismantle the IHD, focus on medical education and scientific work within a Division of Medicine and Public Health, and move toward supporting the Green Revolution in agriculture and population issues.

Debt, Depression, and Capital

A global or an international economy is a vulnerable economy, and a global economy overtaken by war is doubly in jeopardy. It is vulnerable to the direct costs of war: physical destruction and depreciation of industrial plant and housing and exhaustion of agriculture; diversion of production to goods suitable only for military purposes; the physical winnowing of the most energetic elements of the labor force; special burdens created by refugees and the injured and often by famine and disease. But it is further vulnerable beyond the end of outright hostilities to costly legacies—the disruption of peacetime exchanges and supply chains that cannot be easily restored, an end to the flow of labor migration, diminished consumer demand, continuing debt burdens (on which more below), and the political rancor generated by the effort to distribute the debt burdens among different economic classes.

The world economy had reached an impressive degree of globalization on the threshold of the war. The concept of global and international interdependence had been explicitly emphasized before the war and optimistically cited as a deterrent to war.[48] Distant corporations operated and bought colonial plantations for commodity producers. Forest products, minerals, oil and coal, iron ore, precious and useful metals, and commodities such as wheat, rice, sugar, coffee and tea, cotton, and tobacco were ferried across the oceans. Industrial firms sold their automobiles, electrical equipment, optical goods, and chemicals to foreign buyers; others contracted to build transportation facilities or to operate subsidiaries. States accepted labor from beyond their borders—perhaps 45 million Europeans migrated to the Americas, perhaps 20 million Chinese to Southeast Asia, close to 29 million Indians crossing the Indian Ocean or the Bay of Bengal under terms of indenture.[49] Alongside the physical products and the workers that streamed across and within borders were the financial instruments, the sacramental pieces of paper that gave rights to present and future income. These pledges served as the fluid in which all the physical exchanges floated, and facilitating their continuous renewal was itself a source of tremendous and dignified income. In Western societies, the men who thus occupied themselves wore more elaborate and formal clothes, while marriages and often families were constructed around possession of these paper claims if not control of land directly.

The national incomes of the countries who fought World War I, at least in the West, would largely recover their prewar level by 1924. However, the prewar share of international trade in gross national product would not be attained again until the 1960s. Still, observers could find that celebrated firms were active throughout most of Europe, Latin America, the United States, Japan, and the British dependencies. Multinational firms operated across borders with sales agencies and production facilities in countries and colonies far outside their headquarters, among them General Motors, Ford, Bayer, International Harvester, Singer sewing machines, Unilever, Goodrich, De Beers, DuPont, and Siemens. Innovations were coming thick and fast: commercial radio and aviation, expanded automobile ownership and telephone use, the cinema as a mass entertainment—there was indeed a diffused awareness of a global economy and a truly mass society.

The major shadow side of the global economy was agriculture. World War I had summoned an immense productive effort that left an excess capacity for many branches for peacetime. Despite the fact that wheat exports from Russia and the Danubian countries would shrink from over 40 percent of the global total to just over 6 percent, farmers in Canada, Argentina, the United States, and the relatively high-cost producers of Western Europe faced steep price declines.[50] The American South watched cotton prices sink. The Depression was to hit these commodities disproportionally, and basic industrial commodities, iron and steel, also languished. Tariffs beckoned as a solution, as did cartel agreements within countries and across borders. The

Treaty of Versailles restricted German tariff sovereignty until 1925, but by the mid-1920s, heavy industry firms were seeking to extend such production agreements across borders. Autarky beckoned for authoritarian states, and for the mandatory powers, as we have seen, empire promised vast protected zones even if most colonies could not offer mass markets.

Weighing on all these other legacies of what was now known as the Great War was a mountain of debt—debt that each belligerent had piled up to finance its own war production and recruitment of military forces, and debt that the Allies had incurred to purchase materiel from the Americans, and debt finally that the Allies had laid on the defeated Germans. The debt was poorly understood: many viewed it as the cost of the war transferred to future generations. But the real ongoing costs of the war had to be paid in large measure from current blood and labor exertion and civilian consumption foregone. Countries cannot make a future generation pay for the goods they need to fight a current war any more than they can conscript their unborn babies for the trenches. But they certainly can deplete the savings they might have passed on. They can labor longer hours to manufacture weapons that have no purpose except for inflicting harm on an enemy instead of what they would make in the absence of that need. They can cut back on their leisure time and conscript female labor or transfer it from households to factories, which may or may not be counted as desirable. They can defer the maintenance on industrial equipment and housing and the application of fertilizer to their fields. And they can ask their allies or foreign suppliers to give them materiel in return for IOUs. After the war, societies will have to pay to renew exhausted lands and depreciated industrial capital; they will have to pay continuing disability costs and pensions. And they may have to transfer real resources to the foreigners who insist on collecting debts—whether these were owed by the Allies to the Americans or the postwar reparation debt owed by the Germans to the victorious Allies. Until the world depression largely liquidated any pretense to collection, countries continuously bargained and quarreled over who would pay what. Despite countless hours of acrimony and political posturing, the Americans settled for collecting about 50 percent of their loans in real terms, and the Germans ended up paying only a small fraction of their theoretical burden, although by pointing to the nominal sums that the Allies brandished, they convinced themselves they had been outrageously put upon.[51]

The debt accumulated at home and abroad was the counterpart of household and corporate savings that had been silently liquidated (often without recognizing the fact) to pay for the war. After decades of general monetary stability through 1914, price levels rose two to three times—not even taking into account the catastrophic episodes of hyperinflation in Central and Eastern Europe. This meant not only a continuing hemorrhage of real income but also a drastic amputation for the middle and upper classes of future inheritances, fixed interest payments, and life insurance policies. As between countries, so too at home: classes and interest groups bargained and quarreled over who would bear these losses. The burden of repaying internal debt—for example, war bonds subscribed at home—had to be distributed among different social groups, whether through taxation or through inflation, which itself operated as a form of implicit and indirect taxation. Taxation might reduce inflation but would provoke resistance from elites and perhaps provoke a recession as investment dried up. Inflation meant that patriotic purchasers of war bonds would be implicitly expropriated. The hyperinflations that followed the war started with wartime borrowing but were exponentially aggravated as governments and their compliant central banks kept printing money to meet their bills in the face of a continuing price spiral. In that sense, the recourse to new paper was the only public finance resource available. At a certain point, it became self-defeating and the actual volume of depreciated money no longer met the continuing need for a means of exchange.

How were the international claims to be adjudicated—whether in terms of debt payments or currency revaluation—after the prewar gold standard had been abandoned? This issue brought to prominence a whole new cadre of economic experts, sometimes serving on national committees, sometimes organizing new institutes for studying economic issues, sometimes traveling abroad at the behest of governments as "money doctors" to help stabilize currencies. In addition, the international activity of private economic associations grew denser, and in the second half of the 1920s, major cartel activities increased—always seeking favorable state policies but functioning as a network with its own judgments and interests and claiming to act in the public good. They operated sometimes in tandem with states and sometimes as part of the realm of governance. Their influence grew from 1920 to 1930, was partially eclipsed by the impact of the Depression and recrudescent nationalism, then reemerged after World War II to surge finally unabated from the 1970s until the first decades of our current century. In the terms used in this book, some of this economic leadership operated within the realm of governance—seeking public interest settlements that would revive and advance national economies and their notion of general welfare. But they were often recruited from the web of capital, seeking over their lifetime to sustain and increase the value of their firms' portfolios. In the pages that follow, we follow both governance and capitalist dimensions.

There was a constant element in all the money doctors' prescriptions. In each case, the political deadlock had to be resolved by concessions on the part of the trade unions and parties of the left, who had come out of the war in strong positions but were under tremendous political pressure to surrender to the austerity demands of the center and right, giving up recent limits on working hours, generally the eight-hour day, losing control of finance ministries and other cabinet positions, and forswearing deficit spending. In some countries, they would have to give up price controls on food, abandon the indexation of wages to consumer prices, and accept the reduction of employment in the public services such as the railroads. In return, capital from abroad was to be granted to guarantee the value of a new currency or later to make new borrowing from abroad feasible. And in the long run, price stability and new investment would supposedly stabilize employment. These compacts, repeated throughout the 1920s and not only in Europe, became foundational compromises for Western stability. Even as American officials along with the representatives of the Morgan bank, notably Thomas Lamont, were busy renegotiating and floating loans in Europe, they were busy seeking compromises over oil concessions and loan repayments with the Mexican government. They usually entailed intervention by international coalitions and the major delegates of private international finance. In Europe, the pattern was replicated in the late 1940s, the 1980s, and most recently during the euro crisis. In Latin America and ex-colonial areas, they were tied into negotiations on the exploitation of oil resources.

As of the 1920s, there were new forums that facilitated these parallel efforts. Alongside its supervision of mandates, public health, the League developed a significant governance capacity in economic and labor questions. It arose both from national interests and the need to confront humanitarian crises. The representatives of the Allies' Supreme Economic Council, organized in 1916, agreed to continue their activities after the armistice. The French, in particular, under economics minister Étienne Clémentel envisaged a continuation of economic burden sharing, in large part as an effort to secure American financial help beyond the war. With the rising tide of anti-European sentiment from 1919 on, Washington resisted, much as until recently the Germans and Dutch have resisted the calls for internationalization of euro debts urged by the Mediterranean states and for similar reasons.

At the same time, the Western governments and aid organizations were facing the misery in Central Europe. Civil war and the Bolsheviks' introduction of "war communism" had produced a humanitarian crisis in Russia, and the relief effort was led by Herbert Hoover and an American relief mission. Patricia Clavin has emphasized the role of the Austrian economic crisis in catalyzing international action.[52] With the continuation of the Allied blockade after the armistice and the breakup of the Habsburg Empire's political and economic unity, conditions became dire in the imperial capital, which was home to 2 million of Austria's 7 million population. Malnutrition worsened as did de facto starvation in the cold, gray, and grandiose city along with infant mortality, typhus, TB, and abbreviated life spans for the elderly. British humanitarian groups foregrounded the threat to children. Government-affiliated economists and businessmen, including Arthur Salter who had organized British shipping in the war, Jean Monnet, the cognac salesman who had headed the French purchasing committee in Washington, and John Maynard Keynes, civil servant turned dissenter at the Paris Peace Conference, helped organize concerted action for Vienna and pressed for continuing coordination through the newly constituted League of Nations. Their urging led to the first international financial conference held in Brussels and to an Economic and Financial Organization established under League auspices. Salter became its first secretary, and it developed into one of the major League committees. For the rest of the decade, its officials and economists, flanked by leading bankers from the private sector, were supervising stabilization programs for Poland, Greece, and Hungary.[53]

Negotiation of an Austrian rescue package in October 1922, sealed by the Geneva Protocol, set several important precedents. The League's Austrian committee with British, French, Italian, and Austria's own participation agreed not to provide intergovernmental loans, but to guarantee a significant infusion of private capital. It sent a commissioner-general to Vienna to supervise the austerity program that was required but that was to be guided by a committee that included J. P. Morgan, Paul Warburg of the Kuhn-Loeb banking firm, and Benjamin Strong, president of the New York Federal Reserve Bank. The Austrian loan came at a price of an Economic Commission that fired 50,000 workers of the Austrian civil service, admittedly from a bloated bureaucracy designed to administer a great empire but now reduced to a poor state of 7 million inhabitance. The national budget was removed from parliamentary control for two years. Conditions for the loan also meant that the Austrian Socialists, who resisted the terms but essentially abstained, had to yield their political power to the Christian Socials in the national government, although they retained a dominant role in Vienna city politics. But the krone was stabilized.[54] When the young Austrian woman who was to marry the later celebrated economic historian Alex Gerschenkron traveled on a vacation to Germany, which for another year would remain in the throes of hyperinflation—so she recalled to this author about fifty years later—she found that her now-stable currency increased daily in terms of the meals and accommodations she could enjoy throughout the trip.

An even more momentous mediation came with the so-called Dawes Plan of 1924. Following the deadlock on reparations from during 1921–1922, the French had sought to occupy the Ruhr region in January 1923 as a tactic to compel the German government to resume payments. Both sides hardened their stance until late in the year: Berlin called on the coal miners not to work while it supported them with the unlimited printing of paper marks. Already at a million to the dollar in January, the currency continued to plunge. Finally, a new great-coalition cabinet led by Gustav Stresemann, confronting the possibility of communist rebellions and the secession of the Rhenish region under French control, decided to back down in November and resume negotiations with Paris. A new transitional currency issued with a fictional backing at a value of one trillion to one old mark managed to preserve its value. By this time, the American financial community and administration were willing to intervene. Secretary of State Charles Evens Hughes announced Washington's intention to get back to help negotiate a way out of the reparations clash. Europeans accepted mediation by a new committee nominally chaired by Judge Charles G. Dawes but dominated by the new experts on international capital. Key to the deal was a dramatic reduction of payments for five years and the promise of a loan, secured in theory by a lien on the German state railroads, that would be floated by the firm of J. P. Morgan to help launch a new stable currency, the reichsmark.[55]

The political price was the acceptance by the German Social Democratic Party of the end of its prized social gain from the revolution of 1918: the eight-hour day. The French, who had grown disillusioned with the meager results of their policy had to accept withdrawal from the Ruhr and at Locarno in 1925 had to renounce the possibility of unilateral intervention across territorial lines. For all the bitter pills swallowed by both sides, the Dawes loan opened a period of American enthusiasm for investments in Central Europe that more than covered German transitional payments and reinvigorated capital markets and investment until the Depression. Governance and capital seemed in perfect alignment: the political position of the German Social Democrats and organized labor was clearly reduced, but the start of real growth seemed compensatory. Later in 1926, the Polish currency would be bailed out by the bankers and the League. Increasingly, too, the major central bankers Benjamin Strong and Montagu Norman sought to coordinate the conditions for maintenance of a stable international currency regime.

As historians have emphasized, they did so under a set of rules that assumed almost fetishistic importance: the gold standard, or technically after the 1922 Geneva Conference, the international gold exchange standard.[56] Adherence to the gold standard, as it developed before 1914, meant that a nation pledged to maintain its currency's value in terms of a fixed quantity of gold, which meant in practice that a country would keep its foreign debt limited, its domestic budgets in balance, and implicitly, the division of its national income between wage earners and recipients of dividends and interest largely stable. Wages might rise but no faster than productivity gains warranted. The system was depicted as operating automatically. If a country's foreign or domestic debt grew rapidly, gold supposedly flowed out to reduce domestic money supply, raise prevailing interest rates, and constrain consumption and wages in the improvident country until its trade and budget deficits fell back in line with what might be justified. Implicitly, the system was maintained by the capital surpluses of Great Britain, to a degree by France, and Germany, which could fund investment in less developed countries. London functioned as a lender of last resort, its currency accepted as good as gold, and its own balance of payments sustained by the returns of a century of capital invested abroad (less the fifth or so liquidated during the war to buy supplies). Supposedly, as the bank's famous Cunliffe interim report of 1919 outlined, when it urged a rapid return to the gold standard, the rules applied to Britain as well. But they hardly constituted a real burden since if the Bank of England moved to raise its interest rate to counteract any outflow of gold, other countries increased their deposits in London. Before 1914, India in particular helped to provide the surpluses needed to support Britain and many countries chose to deposit their own surpluses in London. The rules were suspended during the war, but responsible financial opinion thought they should be renewed as soon as possible, and at the Geneva economic conference in 1922, central bankers agreed, though allowing US dollars as an additional reserve alongside gold. Since the United States was now an international creditor and global liabilities had ballooned beyond the fractional coverage the precious metal might provide, American dollars promised to serve as a stable basis alongside the precious metal.

Most of the belligerent countries, who had suspended their adherence to the gold standard, were not ready to yoke their currencies to its discipline right away, so the value of their moneys really depended on the ratios with which they traded against each other, which in turn meant that the money markets of London, New York, and a few other capitals such as Amsterdam served to signal how economic trends might be read. The currencies of the defeated countries and revolutionary Russia would depreciate disastrously until stabilized at various points up through 1924, often as in the case of Russia and Germany, by writing off savings, insurance policies, and other financial assets.[57] Meanwhile, the vulnerable classes faced cold and penury. As is well known, this hit the classes who had invested in their states' war debt particularly hard. Austria was stabilized by a League of Nations loan; the Soviets halted their "war communism"—essentially, a massive requisitions program and a suspension of money wages in favor of direct ration stamps to its working-class supporters. Under the New Economic Policy from 1921 on, local markets were revived and private business tolerated, peasant production was purchased, not confiscated, the currency stabilized, and foreign investors welcomed.[58]

By mid-decade, this great bonfire of worthless claims had gone far enough for countries to consider returning to the gold standard, but it was difficult to find the appropriate levels. Britain led the way in 1925 but at a value (vis-à-vis the now-powerful dollar) that required maintenance of a national interest rate which inhibited industrial growth and investment in housing stock. It was less the fact of returning to gold that burdened the mid-1920s economy than the fact that the financial community wanted to approximate the prewar rate at a time when international competition for manufactures was severe and the price level of British goods at the revived exchange rate made its goods about 10 percent higher than competitive American ones. The industrial interests of the Midlands protested but were overruled by the representatives of finance and the Bank of England who argued that to maintain its position as a reserve banking center, the new sterling rate must not amputate the real value of foreign banks and governments who banked in London. "I would rather see Finance less proud and Industry more content," Chancellor of the Exchequer Winston Churchill argued, but he gave way, nonetheless. Even that gadfly spokesman who feared deflation, John Maynard Keynes, was relatively quiet before the decision, though persuasively denouncing it soon afterward. Germany did not pledge itself to gold but to maintenance of its new currency, the reichsmark, at a rate that would allow it to meet the new transitional burden of reparation payments. (In fact, American capital was now flowing into Europe and made the burden of these transfers negligible until the Depression struck.) France, which had undergone its own fierce inflation from 1924 to 1926, though never as devastating as the German one, finally stabilized de facto in 1926 and de jure in 1928 at a "low" gold content that left the franc and French goods underpriced with respect to other countries' currencies, especially sterling. For the next few years, it became the country that accumulated gold reserves at a rapid rate, thus vexing the British and leading to a mini-crisis of payments.[59]

At the same time, the "real" economy of commodities and manufactures also had to master postwar turmoil and the conditions of the 1920s. Here, too, basic sectors such as coal and steel faced glutted markets by the mid-1920s, and corporate leaders reached across borders to attempt to stabilize quotas and market shares. Both official trade treaties and corporate agreements were negotiated in parallel across national lines, as was the case between France and Germany and Belgium in 1925–1926. Each also entailed the international investments that were reknitted across country lines: French interests in newly Polish Silesia, Austrian and German capital in the new countries of East Central Europe—international firms investing across borders.[60] What was emerging was a network or a web of capital, allied with home governments and often supported by them but constituting a nexus of interests and loyalties in its own right.[61] It was hardly monolithic, but its very divisions helped weave its members together in continual conferences and negotiations. American economic competition meant that Europeans had to act concertedly. So too the Japanese were a new actor in Asia. Whether the Europeans' cross-border agreements could subsist if national conflict resumed remained an open question.

The background of policy disputes, conferences, conflicts over reparations, and decimated currencies that had to be stabilized or replaced meant that a new coterie of economists and bankers emerged both to advise national governments and to constitute an ongoing set of supposedly wise men who spoke for the stabilization of European and even global capitalism. Their clients were national governments, but they also saw themselves as stewards for a world economy. The League of Nations was serving as an economic clearing house, just as it was in the field of public health. Its ILO emerged as a major coordinator, not of revolutionaries but of union and socialist party leaders who relished collaborative efforts to regulate the labor markets of wages and working conditions. ILO economists led by James Bellerby also criticized any deflationary effort to restore prewar price parities; rather, he urged, use monetary management (in the 1920s, they were not yet endorsing fiscal policy) to accept the levels of inflation that wartime had brought and to preserve high employment.[62] Although the ILO delegates could not redress the uneven political balance between labor and capital in mid-1920s, they did succeed in speaking out against forced labor.

The edifice of capitalist governance—so we might describe the interlocking networks—was crowned just as it was about to crumble by the Bank of International Settlements (BIS), founded in 1930 as part of the new reparations arrangement that was evidently required as the Dawes Plan came to its five-year term. There was no realistic prospect that the reduced payment schedule of 1924–1929 could revert to the original schedule of payments, and a new conference stretched out the payments once again. The new BIS, based in Basle, was to serve as the transfer agency for remaining reparations and as a coordination center for the national central banks (those of Britain, France, Germany, Italy, Japan, and the United States) that were its shareholders, nominated its directors, and contributed its capital. Governments could not receive credits, although central banks were eligible. France played a major role since the objective was to monetize the reparation obligations, owed mostly to France, and sell them on the private market. The head of the Bank of France's economic research bureau, Pierre Quesnay, became the first general manager of the BIS. The key international department of the Banque de France, the Mouvement général des fonds, insisted that it be given a voice about decisions to be taken in BIS, and French finance officials kept tabs on BIS through French economists working at the Geneva institution. The Americans kept an arm's-length distance; Federal Reserve directors were prohibited from serving as directors, and the Morgan bank became the Americans' transfer agent. As it turned out, the growing implosion of the capitalist economies meant that the German obligations were effectively wound up at the Lausanne Conference of 1932, and remaining interest payments were suspended as of July 1, 1934.[63]

The BIS could do little more than be a spectator as the world economy slid into depression. Its more important role was as a recognized center for thinking through the changing conditions and requisites for global capitalism. Alongside the ILO, it emerged increasingly as a forum where a new generation of economists might puzzle out how economies might malfunction and what remedies might be appropriate. Seconded by the new Basle institution, the ILO pressed for a new world economic conference to "consider how the conditions for a successful restoration of a free gold standard could be fulfilled."[64] It convened in the spring of 1933, shortly after Adolf Hitler had become chancellor and had been voted full executive powers and Franklin Roosevelt was confronting a disastrous collapse of the American banking system. It was the Americans who decided that they would not participate in this conference, having just left the gold standard and fearing the constraints on monetary reflation. (By 1936, the Roosevelt administration, having devalued and reestablished a new gold value for the dollar, would be willing to enter a tripartite agreement to stabilize currencies with the French and the British.)

The BIS was not a Keynesian institution. Its chief intellectual guide, Per Jacobsson, head of its Monetary and Economic Department, was deeply influenced by Knut Wicksell, the outstanding Swedish economic theorist of the prior generation who had emphasized that financial equilibrium based on monetary values was achieved in a domain separate from the real economy, including levels of employment. Keynes pursued these insights as he developed his own argument in the years leading up to publication in 1936 of *The General Theory*: the orthodox notion that labor's unwillingness to accept wage cuts was the cause of persistent unemployment, he argued, was deeply flawed. Workers defended a money level of wages; they would accept a lower real wage as prices rose and the system reflated. Normally, central banks might use monetary expansion to lower prevailing interest rates sufficiently to encourage reflation of prices, industrial expansion, and full employment. Keynes, though, was further to conclude by *The General Theory* that monetary policy alone might well not achieve this result; rather, governments had to use fiscal policy—that is, accept deficit funding and public spending.

Basle, however, in the early 1930s was tasked with trying to preserve or recover the international economy that was then in free fall. Jacobsson's Monetary and Economic Department considered the BIS an institution for governance, protecting the ideal of the gold exchange standard in a time when credit and liquidity were collapsing. If not "Keynesian," this certainly represented a broader mission than the BIS's banking department, which looked for returns on the Bank's investments. Rather, the monetary and economic unit asserted in its May 1931 report to its board that the Bank was a public interest organism that "strives to eliminate imperfections in the current currency system instead of trying to profit from them." As early as 1930, the BIS governing board decided to study transforming short-term credits into midterm credits, an expedient that entailed central banks' lending to each other in foreign currency reserves. The bank also experimented with accepting the gold deposits on its own accounts held in member banks ("earmarking") as a basis of credits—in effect, a form of credit swaps. Over the next years, BIS came to be seen as a nexus for facilitating lending among central banks and thereby the national bank networks they followed.[65]

Such a development, often described as a chapter in central bank coordination, gave the banking community a stronger claim to play an important role in the realm of governance. Restoring international finance in the economic turbulence of the interwar years could be understood and presented as a global public good and not just a contribution to national strength or to the mere accumulation of wealth. New centers for research and policy studies such as the Brookings Institution or the Kiel Institute for the World Economy added to the presence of economic "science." Their members straddled the networks of government and banking. They were part of the web of capital at the same time. Capital and governance shared, so to speak, the same church—the former concerned about the collection plate, the latter about the prayers.

The networks of capital, especially of finance, unsurprisingly came under attack from the left but also from an anti-capitalist right, which still found strong voices in fascist movements. Even as Mussolini and Hitler sought to assure industrial leaders that they appreciated their leadership of the economy and worked to disarm socialist parties and trade unions, a strong current of hostility to finance, above all supposed Jewish international finance, percolated through their movements. Gottfried Feder's tract denouncing "interest rate slavery" was one conspicuous artifact. Italian fascist labor unions and Nazi factory councils asserted their autonomy, although after their respective movements came to power, their resistance to industrial leaders had to be muzzled. That story is now well known.[66]

More relevant for the history here is the fact that as the Depression dragged on, national governments were compelled to assert their ambitions to restructure economies. Even under conservative auspices, they retreated from commitments to the gold standard and the price stability it was intended to guarantee.[67] Working-class electorates joined farmer voters in bringing more reformist policies to fruition, as in Sweden and the United States, or else accepted populist remedies.[68] Schacht and Keynes represented two varieties of national response. Schacht signed on to make autarky work through bilateral deals with the hard-pressed agrarian economies of East Central Europe. Germany accepted its agricultural commodities on a quota basis, froze its proceeds in reichsbank accounts, and applied the credits to purchases of German industrial goods. Only when by 1937, when Germany was straining its national balance sheets to import the raw materials needed for rearmament under its new Four-Year Plan chaired by Hermann Goering, did the "wizard" Schacht dissent from policies that could claim his paternity. Keynes preached the virtue of domestic production, limits on the free flow of capital, and the exercise of national demand management, congratulating Roosevelt in 1933 for having torpedoed the World Economic Conference. Keynes, like Roosevelt, remained a liberal to his marrow and understood that the American president was saving democratic capitalism while Schacht was a political cynic willing to advance National Socialist plans to achieve predominance in Europe. But in the relationship between states and capital, both Schacht and Keynes advocated an expanded role of state policy to set the conditions for renewed capitalism. US policymakers looking across the Atlantic in the late 1930s saw both Britain and Germany as exploiting their respective spheres of influence to exclude American commercial interests.

By the 1930s, it was time to talk as well about national planning and rearmament. Planning, as seen in Chapter 1, was an effort to restore the control of the economy from the autonomous forces of capital to the supervision of the state. It had democratic enthusiasts in the British Labour Party, New Deal agencies, and the French Popular Front. It also had nastier practitioners. The Soviets, who had allowed a partial reopening to the international economy—at least openness to foreign investment—reverted in 1928 to a Five-Year Plan, then to the decision to collectivize agriculture, and increasingly to Joseph Stalin's horrors of famine, gulag, and mass political trials. In Japan, Inoue Junnosuke, the finance minister who had helped his government accept the gold standard (and sign on to international commitments for naval disarmament and a significant role in the League and BIS), was increasingly marginalized in the 1930s as the military tightened its grip on politics and pressed expansion into Manchuria and defiance of the League. He was assassinated in February 1932 by a young recruit of the Blood Pledge Corps, a right-wing terrorist circle.[69] As war approached, in Manchuria and then China proper, in Ethiopia, in Spain, in Poland, the spokesmen for both governance and capital worked in the shadow of state projects—some benevolent, others agendas for territorial aggrandizement. The balance between project-states, the realm of governance, and the web of capital would shift once again at the end of the 1930s. States reclaimed their dominance. Still, no particular distribution of public authority was likely to remain static: the dancers remained entangled even as one or another took the lead. How long were states and their territorial resources to remain preponderant?

The quarter century from the beginning of World War I to the beginning of World War II (in Europe) was an immensely fecund period for institution-building across the world. States, nonstate claimants of governance, and increasingly networked agents for capital and finance all took qualitative leaps forward to master the exponentially growing complexity of turbulent social transformation. The world wars and the Great Depression forced innovative responses—some claiming expansion of democratic control, others urging salvation through party discipline and the subordination of individual claims to those of national collectivities. The claim of this book is that by following these three strands, we are better equipped to understand the public world we have inherited.

But this does not mean that these collective agencies acted alone. They each drew on the resources of the others—capital required the state, the intellectual resources of the realm of governance lived off the web of capital and not surprisingly tended to define conditions under which capital prospered. Both governance and capital had finally to admit—despite their ideological pretensions—that without the residual power of states and regimes, they would remain in a flux of good intentions or condemned to economic equilibria that would not achieve full employment. This fabric of mutual need or codependence revealed itself in particular in the territorial peripheries—the lands of empire or de facto dependence—where representatives of competitive states, initiatives of governance, and the web of capital were all seeking to expand their activity. Once again, global war would change both the territorial units of world politics, undermining empire, changing ideological balances, and concentrating state power.

PART TWO

Mid-Century Ambitions

4

Projects for the Postwar

Nations, Empires, and Governance, 1940s–1960s

Although victory had not brought the relief and freedom that were expected at the end of the war, nevertheless the portents of freedom filled the air throughout the postwar period, and they alone defined its historical significance. . . . Thinking of [Moscow], this holy city and of the entire earth, of the still-living protagonists of this story, and their children, [Zhivago's friends] were filled with tenderness and peace, and they were enveloped by the unheard music of happiness that flowed all about them and into the distance.

HOW DOES THE HISTORIAN reconcile this lyrical ending of Boris Pasternak's great novel, completed during the Soviet "thaw" of the mid-1950s with the turbulence of the postwar years? (How does one read Pasternak's coda in 2022 against the background of Russia's "special military operation" that is devastating Ukraine?) The historian must listen for the music not just of happiness but of conflict and change. By the mid-1960s the Italian sociologist Alessandro Pizzorno ventured an explanation of why that music became so audible in Europe: "After 1945 the reaction of European peoples was quite different from that which followed 1918. Historical self-deception was more difficult, because despair was more profound. Europeans in those years felt something that it would be hard to define, but something nonetheless important for all that: what we might call the ideological orientation of social goals. By this we mean that for a certain period individuals preferred to think of their own lot in terms of the lot which they imagined or desired for the collectivity. Like all great ideological moments in modern societies, this too was filled with egalitarian claims.... In critical moments, when the very bases of collective life are threatened, the value of equality is posed once again."[1]

The observation was valid for areas beyond Europe, although expectation of change was more powerful than despair. Between 1937 and 1949—that is, between the start of World War II in Asia and the Cold War—global politics shattered and formed anew. If we look at which states dominated world politics, the great contests that had produced such intense rivalries since 1905 or even since the 1890s seemed provisionally resolved. Two great powers, Germany and Japan, that had wagered on military and political domination of their respective continental regions were reduced to occupied territories. Two others that had initially claimed disinterest in this traditional form of rivalry, the United States and the Soviet Union, emerged as wary global leaders. They would hold on to that preeminence, locked into their own new rivalry for forty-five years.

If we focus on the collective actors introduced in the previous chapter, significant change had also taken place. The French, British, and Dutch held on to their extensive colonial possessions or intended to reacquire control, but their claims were far more tenuous than after World War I. During the two decades after the formal end of World War II and despite their efforts—painful alike for their own self-image and the peace of the people they ruled—their expectations for productive and profitable rule dissipated. The new hegemons, Russia and America would organize frameworks that were also imperial but without the former trappings of legal sovereignty, coordinated instead by military missions and alliances, preferential economic exchanges, and ideological recruitment of sympathetic adherents.

States Revived

Despite predictions that the era of national states was fated to give way to international confederations, states remained the fundamental institution of global politics. The major powers reclaimed economic initiatives from independent sources of capital once mobilization for World War II took off in earnest in the late 1930s. Business and banking were compelled to yield key aspects of economic decision-making capacity to their home governments. National authorities moved to prevent a relapse into depression or the burden of post-World War I debts that had dragged down their interwar economies. Governments also devoted resources to rebuild institutions for global governance; they understood that their countries were regrouping in a difficult environment—reconstructing statehood among ruins, poverty, mass migrations, and anguishing personal losses. States and civil society—often conceived in liberal thought as layered entities, or as structure and superstructure—embraced more closely, almost merged or fused.

Wartime and cold war thus changed the balance among the historical agents introduced in the previous chapters. For about two decades after World War II, states and imperial structures rebounded as energetic historical protagonists. Newly independent countries emerging from formal empire sought to define economic systems that steered a course of noncapitalist development and also independence from the rival alliance systems. The United States and the Soviet Union expanded their spheres of control beyond their own borders and defined objectives that spilled far beyond their own frontiers such that they became imperial actors, if not empires, in the traditional sense. The two superpowers constructed different systems for coordinating their respective spheres of influence: the Soviets relied effectively on cloned Communist Parties that with some notable episodes of deviation aside, largely deferred to Moscow's wishes. For Washington, the objective was less to ensure a monopoly of power by one or another of the plural parties than to exclude the Communists from any real control. Restructuring the international economic system, above all its financial linkages, became integral to Washington's programs for coordinating its larger zone of influence. This effort would mean a long secondary tug of war with Great Britain, which aspired to restore the international stature it inherited from the preceding hundred years. Both countries shared aspirations for a vibrant international economy, but the British were also concerned with sheltering their economic sphere, the "sterling block," with its restrictions on sales of sterling, from being steamrollered by the dollar.

So, too, the major organizations relied on for governance were increasingly captured by the member states and above all by the superpowers. It was to be states that took charge of reconstructing the major institution of global governance, the United Nations (UN), and states, too, that negotiated a new international backstop for the web of capital—namely, the International Monetary Fund and the World Bank, destined to throw the surviving economic agencies of the League of Nations, now reconstituted within the UN, into a secondary role. Project-states were thus to recapture policy initiatives and construct unprecedented institutional solutions, only to have this vigor abate by the late 1960s. The war, not surprisingly, strengthened national sentiment—not the competitive nationalism dominant from 1870 through the 1930s, but the affirmation of the value of a threatened community held by many ordinary folk, certainly by intellectuals, participants in the resistance movements, anti-colonial activists, and war leaders seeking to inspire their populations. Hence the paradox bequeathed by the epic struggles that spread across the world of 1945: a recommitment to individual fatherlands (or sometimes, as for Russia and India, motherlands) and simultaneously a conviction that humankind must transcend the destructive divisions of nationalism and embrace wider associations.

At the same time, the second war—as had World War I but with more durable results—encouraged efforts to overcome class divisions if only to assure unstinting production efforts from labor even to the point of direct intervention in the labor market—capping wages, prohibiting strikes, and limiting the right to switch jobs, in Britain as well as Germany. The war effort logically led to plans for a postwar welfare community, as it did for a postwar international order.[2] Sometimes analyzed as an opportunity to halt the reforms of the 1930s, the wartime experience served in many ways to secure them within a new class equilibrium. Working-class leaders sought to lock in a new durable hold on politics within their societies, financial and commercial leaders to recover a favorable environment for trade, and intellectuals to anchor a legal order for rights, individual and collective. The AFL remained the much larger labor federation with strength in construction, garment workers, and other often-artisanal trades, and its leadership (much like that of the British Trades Union Congress) distrusted state-supervised corporatist arrangements, preferring to act as a collective agent in the labor market. CIO leaders, especially Walter Reuther of the Steel Workers, envisaged cooperation with liberal business leaders and creation of a virtual industrial commonwealth. But the New Deal faced a conservative pushback in the 1938 congressional elections; the racial issue divided organizational efforts in the South, and by late in the war, the threat of Communist Party influence in some of the unions pushed Reuther toward more traditional objectives and more segmented industry-specific campaigns.[3] The war's most decisive legislative legacy in the United States followed from a national, not class, project: the GI Bill of Rights. Still, throughout the industrialized world, World War II and the defeat of fascism suggested that the modern state had to be "democratic" in one way or another, whether through elections and multiparty competition or anti-fascist programming. It had to recognize "rights" even as it ignored obvious exceptions, whether those of a political opposition as in

Eastern Europe or African Americans in the United States. In Europe, these aspirations had to play out in the shadow of wartime destruction, the mass uprooting of refugees, and soon enough, the ominous possibility of a new world war.

Can we date these transitions with greater precision? The institutional innovations of the earlier project-states lost momentum by the late 1930s even where they were not forcibly annulled. Still, these earlier changes provided a springboard for renewal once World War II came to its conventionally perceived ending. The second half of 1941 brought the entry into the great war under way of the superpowers hitherto on the sidelines, the United States and the Soviet Union. Both of these countries faced initial disastrous military surprises, but their vast resources quickly set limits to Axis conquests even if they did not ensure the eradication of the Nazi and Japanese empires. But the world they would seek to make politically predictable and advantageous—an effort epitomized by the Yalta Conference of February 1945—would have to pick up the threads of the period before the war.

Within the chronology of military events, late 1942 and early 1943 brought a decisive reversal of fortune. Impressive Axis advances could not be sustained and were thrown back as the allied coalition won decisive victories. The Russians defeated the Germans and their Romanian and Italian allies at Stalingrad and Kursk; the British joined by the Americans compelled the Germans and Italians to retreat west from Egypt and surrender in North Africa. The German U-boat threat to Atlantic merchant shipping, which had reached ever more menacing proportions up to late 1942, declined precipitately in the same months. Japanese domination of the Western Pacific became a vulnerable holding operation after the naval defeat at Midway and the American landing on Guadalcanal. Tokyo still retained its prewar acquisitions of Taiwan, Chosen (Korea), and Manchukuo, along with the coastal provinces of China, Thailand, and the extensive colonial territories it had overrun in Southeast Asia and was searching for forms and justifications of rule that would enlist local collaborators. In Europe, national resistance movements became increasingly active as the ultimate defeat of the occupying forces seemed more likely. Still, for the years or months that the Axis armies remained in control of their conquests, the experience was ever more excruciating in terms of repression, deportation and genocide, and the ruthlessness of local collaborators. Killing continued until the end. The final phase of the struggle—what can be termed the war for the

Axis succession—was the cruelest of all for subject populations who had survived the first onslaught of Germans and Japanese. Ultimately, it became the cruelest, too, for the enemy soldiers who had to fight their hopeless war and for the urban inhabitants of the once-arrogant conquerors, now subject to relentless aerial bombing.

Every contending country defined its participation in terms of postwar projects, even as its troops on the ground focused just on survival or overcoming the enemy. By 1943, it was clear to most except those whose political fate had tied them irretrievably to complicity with the occupying armies that the war would end sooner or later with the defeat of fascist and Japanese militarist regimes. As the Axis's geopolitical projects collapsed, the forces that sought to occupy the post-fascist political space included not only old rulers in exile but also resistance movements and parties seeking to create new polities or renew old ones. In theory most agreed to subordinate their claims to the overriding goal of victory, but serious fissures existed, above all between Communist-affiliated and non-Communist movements in Poland, Yugoslavia, and Greece, and at times in Italy. Those whose conflicts had been temporarily put on ice, as in China, resumed their mutual enmity after the war. The Soviets and their Communist Party adherents called for the installation of people's democracies in liberated Europe—new regimes at least temporarily based on all anti-fascist parties and supposedly to be ratified by free elections. Was this merely a charade designed to lull liberal democratic suspicions until the time when total party control might be realized? The issue has been continually argued over seven decades. In any case, Franklin Roosevelt and for a year or two the Truman administration as well as Western European leaders sought to prolong the coalitions of convenience whether in Europe or China and to avoid global partition. By 1947–1948, both sides decided it was impossible.[4]

Even as so many public figures insisted that the coming world order must transcend nationalism, the nation-state ideal, beckoned with a renewed luster. International initiatives did not weaken or delegitimize nation-states emerging from the war. Advocates for international cooperation and institutions presupposed that reviving the nation must be foundational. Resistance movements and leaders, sometimes in exile, had taken up their crusades in the name of the nations that had been invaded, and in the case of collaborationist regimes, betrayed. Partisan fighters on the ground took mortal risks to oust occupying soldiers and their opportunistic collaborators from their home countries. National polities had already taken on new responsibilities during the Depression; wartime compelled further intervention and programs, most visibly perhaps the evacuation and relocation of families from targeted cities. Thus, World War II was to endow the nation with a renewed lease on life— as a second-generation project state—though not always animating the same countries it had earlier in the century.

At the same time wartime and postwar programs stipulated vigorous international participation. The Axis occupiers and collaborationist regimes had sought to justify their conquests in transnational terms—the National Socialist New Order and the Japanese East Asia Co-prosperity Sphere—even though these collapsed by 1945.[5] The victors likewise stressed the encompassing coalition their redeemed nations would take part in. A recent collection of essays on transnational and indeed transcontinental trends rightly emphasizes "a global moment in the middle decades of the twentieth century . . . the important continuities of thought, organization, and personnel that continued from the age of empires to the age of the superpowers."[6]

And not only states had ambitious plans. Project activism marked the empires that had survived the war or were reconstructed. On the one side, those who claimed independence had a vision of community that was simultaneously encompassing and selective and often competitive. Across a great belt from the Caribbean to East Asia, postwar activists offered *Négritude*, African socialism, pan-Arabism, Zionism, Islamic statehood, Hinduism, Soviet-oriented Communism, Maoism, each tinctured with nationalism.[7] On the colonists' side, the interwar notion of "valorization" of colonial assets gave way to the imperative of just reestablishing control—although this often meant offering a new concept of remote rule, such as the French Union or the Commonwealth or Greater Netherlands. If these formulas failed to win "hearts and minds" (a phrase invented by Gerald Templeton, the British commander in Malaya), then military rule or even a war of reconquest remained a recourse.

The expanded role of the postwar state meant that agendas for governance and projects for capital remained overshadowed under state or interstate umbrellas. The new UN—the institutional instantiation of the wartime alliance—reflected global ideals but was bound to become a site of national rivalry and, as Mark Mazower has emphasized, an opportunity structure for prolonging empire.[8] Its early agencies, created to deal with the human misery left by the war, the United Nations Relief and Rehabilitation Administration (UNRRA) and the United Nations Educational, Scientific, and Cultural Organization (UNESCO), would become arenas not only for international governance but also of state rivalry and activity. So, too, officially created international bodies, whether under UN auspices or separately negotiated, would succeed the League's economic commission and seek to take over the tasks that private bankers had exercised in the 1920s.

Ambitions for the Postwar State

If we go by the rhetoric of liberation, then in Europe eradication of Nazism and fascism and punishment of those who collaborated with the occupiers—loosely called *épuration* or a purge (not to be simply identified with the purges that marked Communist rule in Russia or its "satellites")—would rank high on the list of projects. These were different from the Allies' trials of enemy soldiers and policymakers they viewed as violating the laws of war or even crimes against humanity. The initial International Military Tribunals in Nuremberg and Tokyo tried about fifty major offenders and executed ten German and seven Japanese military and political leaders. The Americans followed up with twelve trials of concentration camp guards, SS officials, diplomats, doctors, and other identified groups. Many others Germans faced trial by the individual allies and countries that had been occupied; Norbert Frey tallies 95,000 trials, a majority in eastern Europe. The British, French, Dutch, and Americans also tried about 5,400 Japanese soldiers in their Southeast Asian colonies and executed a total of about 950.[9]

Going beyond the trials of enemy soldiers, the Allies could agree (with some British and French hesitation) that planning and waging aggressive war was a punishable transgression of international behavior. Agreement on the terms of the international war crimes trials required a major negotiating effort, reinforced at a moment when agreement seemed elusive by the translation into English of Aron Trainin's book *Hitlerite Responsibility under Criminal Law*.[10] The discussions finally yielded the 1944 Charter for the International Military Tribunal at Nuremberg and its counterpart for the Tokyo military tribunal. The supporters of these postwar trials saw them as a decisive impulse to international governance. In theory, the major war crimes trials conducted by the Allies were to adjudicate the behavior of the Germans and Japanese in the territories they occupied outside their own country during wartime. And not just for combat but also violations of the accumulated laws of war in combat, including crimes against humanity, and the new category, so important for the Americans, of conspiring to wage aggressive war.

Within the liberated countries, political purification, the term that probably best conveys the supposed intent of the purges, was an announced project that was to be the premise of reconstruction. Several motivations reinforced the postwar reckoning. Punishment of collaborators, after all, seemed fundamental for reestablishing legitimate justice in the recently occupied countries, and it could be severe in the Netherlands and Norway. It was also a policy that could cover the ambiguous ambitions inherent in Soviet "popular democracy." Prosecutions soon merged with the goal of rendering powerless and intimidated those leaders in Soviet "liberated" countries who looked to the West, and not to Moscow, for political support.

Judicial procedures against the collaborationist wartime regimes and their hangers-on was left to the countries emerging from occupation. Once a wave of lynch justice or "popular" revenge was over, it was subordinated to national tribunals. As such, it faced all the problems of assigning guilt that might have been expected. Communists often wanted these to do the work of tarring other party leaders with guilt, as happened in the areas of Europe they controlled. Noncommunist procedures soon ran into imponderable questions: was a factory owner who produced vehicles for the Germans a collaborator if he hoped thereby to keep a workforce fed and knew that his plant would be run directly by the occupiers should he refuse? Louis Renault was removed as head of his auto company, which was nationalized; in Italy, Vittorio Valetta, FIAT's manager was removed but reinstated after a year.[11] Gradually, the trials wound down. But punishments were severe in Norway, Sweden, Belgium, and the Netherlands. In Bulgaria where Communist control was complete, Nikola Petkov, a major pro-Western political leader was convicted implausibly and executed for collaboration as late as 1947. In Italy, the trials were largely wound up by 1947. Even though Communist Party leader, Palmiro Togliatti, was serving as minister of justice, prosecutions were not particularly harsh. The party's strategy was to advance its role through coalition politics. Italians, moreover, had to face, or more usually evade facing, the unpleasant fact that their ruling groups had long supported the country's own fascist regime which had fought until 1943 as Germany's principal ally in Europe. It was more satisfying to try the German officers who had conducted atrocities once the Nazis had marched into most of the country in September 1943, after Benito Mussolini's ruling circle had attempted to remove the dictator and switch sides. Even in the most notorious case of the Ardeatine cave massacre of hostages, the conviction of SS general Erich Kriebke would be reversed.[12] Whether judged as too harsh or too lenient, as an exercise in vengeance or a demonstration of human rights—a verdict often dependent on political orientation—the purges in Western Europe, at least, were a statement that nation-states were resuming sovereign status.

Advancing the protections of citizenship in the economic realm—enhancing the "welfare state"—is usually identified as the major achievement of project-states in the postwar. Certainly, there were powerful continuities of postwar reforms with prewar policies, including those carried out by fascist as well as democratic regimes. Some of the major flagship reforms were identified with the US New Deal in the 1930s—preeminently the Wagner Act's recognition of labor union organizing rights (soon to be diminished under a GOP Congress in 1947), and the construction finally of a national old-age pension scheme established by the Social Security Act of 1935. But to make it politically acceptable, Social Security was presented as an individual worker's payback after decades of his or her own savings (although employers had to contribute equally), and not as a social entitlement. It was also keyed to what workers had earned during their career. The leftist energies of the New Deal coalition in any case had refocused by the late 1930s on the problem of monopoly, and fiscal policy soon dissipated; Roosevelt had moved his energies to mobilization for eventual intervention at the end of the 1930s and announced the subordination of Dr. New Deal to Dr. Win the War. Whereas industrial leaders were tainted by collaboration in Europe, they emerged as self-sacrificing dollar-a-year men in the United States. Nationalization marked French and British working-class demands but not those of either branch of the American union movement—and of course there was no longer a significant socialist party in the United States. The American left's postwar effort to confirm legally the maintenance of full employment into law was moderated in Congress to a far more innocuous Employment Act of 1946. The distinctive American welfare achievement remained the GI Bill of rights, offering college tuition to veterans, but it identified eligibility with national service, not income needs. Harry Truman's effort to secure national universal health insurance in 1948 failed and reemerged only in 1965 as the Medicare and Medicaid programs for those over sixty-five or destitute.[13]

In general the welfare state came to be identified with social insurance—that is, schemes paid for variously by payroll taxes and employer contributions and state budget allocations and providing compensation for industrial accidents without concern for negligence or fault, old-age pensions, and as programs grew more comprehensive, unemployment support, and sometimes medical insurance. It is perhaps identified most conspicuously with the 1942 Beveridge Plan in Britain and its call for so-called cradle-to-grave welfare protection, later with the Labour government that campaigned on its proposals in 1945 and then enacted key nationalizations and social insurance schemes during its five years in office.[14]

Certainly there were powerful continuities with prewar policies. Bismarck had introduced retirement pensions since the 1880s, in good part to reduce the apppeal of the growing Social Democratic Party. Lloyd George's great reformist government had made a start with insurance against illness in 1910 / 11. Unemployment insurance schemes had been introduced by middle-of-the road non-socialist coalitions in Germany, France, and Britain in the mid-1920s. On the continent Christian Democracy had long sought and partially achieved family-oriented welfare schemes, including aid for *familles nombreuses*. These were to be administered in France by employer-employee *caisses*, not the state. Even where social democrats in northern Europe pressed to enlarge the welfare systems, such policies had long been in the works, and the Swedes had pressed their own coalitions since 1932.[15]

But plans for the postwar period came with a new ideological impetus. The chief British advocates, whether Beveridge himself, affiliated with the Liberal Party, LSE professor Richard Titmuss, or the sociologist T. H. Marshall sought to identify the ideas with a new phase of democratic civic inclusion. As Marshall set out in a classic lecture, the meaning of citizenship had advanced beyond the civil rights won in the eighteenth century and the political rights such as the suffrage wrested in the nineteenth century to the attainment of social rights, with their claims on education, health, and welfare in the twentieth. The trade union movement was the major agent in this campaign, but the vision of expanded citizenship was based not on class conflict but an expanded sense of community. It was implicitly socialist but socialism understood as an effort to overcome class divisions—class being a capitalist artifact such that "in the twentieth century citizenship and the capitalist class system have been at war."[16] Titmuss derived his inclusive vision from Britain's wartime experience, including the evacuation of children during the Blitz.

That response under the bombs revealed the social fractures of British society as London's inner-city waifs arrived in middle-class homes and the possibilities for community responsibility.[17] Politically, the conditions were ripe for expansion of social insurance, including protection against the risks of ill health.

The war had revealed the working classes in the allied countries as key contributors to victory. Their representatives in exile or underground had collaborated with other party delegates in the coalitions of the resistance. In Belgium, France, and elsewhere, they negotiated social compacts with non-socialists (the charters of the resistance) that augured well for the establishment of a mixed economy, including collaboration with trade unions and factory councils and nationalization of basic industries. The conservative and industry interests that might earlier have resisted their demands were compromised by collaboration: they could not present a vigorous opposition, and in fact, many accepted the program as a new and promising start. The result was to be significant expansion of the social constitution of the postwar state that could last largely into the 1970s without significant backlash. Just as significant as the extension of pensions and insurance schemes was the fact that the postwar struggles transformed many of them from occupational or religiously based plans into national projects that supposedly wove together the entire society.

Postwar Germany had to build on an ambiguous legacy. National Socialism had inherited earlier welfare provisions even as it smashed independent trade unions and abolished non-Nazi parties. The regime had established a unified Labor Front to control the workforce within a pseudo-representational structure, and it had developed ideas of the "factory community" in which managers and workers labored in harmony under the oversight of the "trustee of labor," who ensured productivity. The war made it all the more urgent to increase labor output, especially since after the continent was subdued by June 1940, Britain still remained undefeated and the war threatened to continue. Nazi authorities envisaged a further major overhaul of social policy on the basis of populist (*völkisch*) ideology once they entered the war. Eventually, 6 million non-German workers would be enticed or coerced to work in the factories of the Reich under brutal conditions. However, in the fall of 1940, looking forward to victory, Adolf Hitler empowered the head of the Labor Front, Robert Ley, to work out an extensive postwar program encompassing old-age care, health and leisure provisions, vocational education, social housing, and a national wage framework. In the programmatic statements of the Arbeitwissenschaftliches Institut (AWI or Institute for Labor Science), the new program was intended as well to motivate the population through the second winter of the war; it was a "social" objective of the war to be distinguished from Britain's allegedly plutocratic goals.

Since war production and the draft for the armed forces led to labor scarcity, wage competition and labor mobility was potentially threatening to production. But private wage bargaining was excluded; the state had to determine the "just wage" for every activity that would lead workers to decide freely on their appropriate workplace. Wage differentiation could take place within factories but not between them. Under the new program, the worker was to be motivated to stay at his job by wage premiums, and nonpecuniary motivation. The discrepancy between industrial wages and office-work salaries was slated eventually to be overcome. Social policy became part of an encompassing ideological harnessing of labor power.[18] Of course with the reversals on the battlefield and the heavy bombardment of German cities, the urgency of just holding together a workforce became ever more demanding. Rationing, evacuations, and bombardment imposed their own brutal thrust. The labor ministry's plans were vetoed by the finance ministry. As defeat loomed, the ideological concepts collapsed, but under Allied occupation and within the limits of an impoverished and badly housed country, work continued under the longer-term structures of social insurance.

With the defeat and occupation came new challenges and the chance for major reform. First of all, 10 million refugees had to be absorbed into West German society and income provided for 4 million invalids, widows, and orphans. The Allied Control Council planned a new welfare reform that would unify the fragmented social insurance funds for different occupational groups. Although the Soviet could impose an integrated social insurance law in East Germany, the Western powers failed to overcome the contending interests in their zones. With the currency reform of 1948, the provisional UK-US bizonal—and then after, France joined, trizonal—legislative assembly, the Wirtschaftsrat (Economic Council) took over the efforts to reconstruct the inherited patchwork, but this protoparliament found its effort resisted by the West German state governments and delayed further by the Allied military governors who claimed it would overburden the budget. Updating the system would have to wait for the Bundestag of the Federal Republic of Germany, free of military rule, after 1949. Political party and bureaucratic wrangles then intervened, and only in the early 1950s, did the Adenauer government start reconstructing the welfare system. The postwar Deutscher Gewerkschaftsbund (DGB), a unified federation of pre-Nazi Social Democratic and Catholic labor movements, hoped to secure the equal treatment of wage workers and salaried employees, but this venerable distinction, supported by employer associations, was preserved in the new proposals. Although it involved a long and arduous debate over details, the Social Democratic Party and the Christian Democratic Party (see below for their evolution) agreed on the need for comprehensive and encompassing reform on social insurance, a task that would extend past the elections of 1954 and be completed only by 1957 with a major increase in pensions at its center—a "dynamic" pension, increased by 65 percent and keyed to the growth of national income. "The result was an epoch-making structural reform" that adapted the traditionally rigid pension structure and a new intergenerational norm.[19]

The history of these postwar debates in Germany, so caught up in interest group divisions, reveals that social insurance was not a project that excited or carried a particularly socialist valence. Rather, it was the wearily elaborated product of a state built as much as on professional and interest group divisions, including after 1945 refugees from the east and the mass of veterans and dependents left by the war.

The reform that incorporated the most programmatic and public excitement, the one we might best describe as a sociopolitical project was that of *Mitbestimmung* or codetermination—that is, representation of unions on corporate boards, which was passed in 1951. Such a reform had been written into the Weimar Constitution along with the idea of *Arbeitsgemeinschaft* and factory community—unfortunately, an elastic concept that right-wing employers, with the support of judges, managed to turn into a notion of authoritarian factory relationships, solidified by the National Socialist concept of *Führerprinzip* and the labor law of 1934.[20] But the postwar DGB was prepared to take up the reform once again. When employers and the Christian Democratic Party parliamentary delegates resisted the extension of codetermination to the fundamental coal mining and steel industries (*Montanindustrie*), long united in overlapping stock ownership and corporate connections, the unions staged a remarkable general strike in 1952 to secure passage of the reform.[21] Codetermination might seem a momentous rebalancing of social forces, but it was also a channeling of the more disruptive threat of plans for factory councils, which had played a brief disruptive role in European industry at the end of World War I when they challenged not only industrial proprietors but older and more bureaucratic trade unions. Codetermination kept working-class representation safely in established union hands. Militant factory councils appeared in northern Italy during the final weeks of World War II, but in general they could not sustain pressure for their challenge to managerial capitalism against the distrust of the Allied military commanders and thereafter the Communist Party and its affiliated trade unions, also determined to control factory-floor volatility.[22]

Nationalizations and Planning

The other major demand—for nationalization of industries—remained blocked in Germany in contrast to Britain. During the early postwar years, the left-wing Socialist Victor Agartz pressed for nationalization and workers' control in a program of "economic democracy," as did the Christian Democratic Party organizations in industrial North Rhine–Westphalia. Agartz, however, lost traction in the Social Democratic Party, and as head of the Bizone, Konrad Adenauer had waited out the brief influence of the collectivists of the Christian Democratic Party. Advocates of nationalization in any case had to contend with the opposition of the US military governor, Lucius Clay, who declared that nationalization of the industry in the state of Hessen was premature and should await an all-German decision. He likewise stalled the Hessian legislation on codetermination, but his successor, John J. McCloy, acceded in April 1950. The British zonal authorities were also unhappy with the equivalent German plans in North Rhine–Westphalia, which contained the mines and furnaces of the Ruhr, but they remained nominally responsible to a Labour government in London that favored public ownership. However, once the financial pressures of supporting their zone led them to accept a bizonal fusion in late 1946, they deferred to General Clay. In any case, trade union energies across the political spectrum mobilized more easily around the goal of halting the dismantling of factories that the Allies carried out until 1949–1950.

Similar aspirations marked other socialist movements until the Cold War inhibited them. In Belgium, the Netherlands, and France, working-class representatives had played a strong role in the resistance organizations and helped negotiate social "compacts" with the other factions that were supposed to govern new post-fascist governments. Although there would follow much contestation over details, the thrust of postwar policy was expansion of social rights. Nationalization demands could sometimes be channeled into the sanctions against industrialists seen as collaborators, as in the case of the Renault works. As a general policy for socialist control, Britain and France were most consistent in nationalization of what British socialists like to call the "commanding heights" of the economy—the national bank, the railroads, coal mines and the steel industry, road transport. In Britain, the Labour Party carried out the nationalizations between 1945 and 1950, only to have the Conservatives denationalize them until Harold Wilson's 1964 government could take them over once again.

But what did nationalization mean besides a shift in paper shares (compensated) to public title? British socialists such as Evan Durbin (who died in a 1948 accident at age forty-two) and Herbert Morrison had thought through the forms of nationalization in the 1930s and were committed to public companies managed by experts and run on the basis of planning to assure maintenance and development.[23] Labor delegates might have a voice, but workers were not to be exclusively entrusted with enterprise management. This separated the structures envisaged after World War II from the council movement or the "guild socialism" that appealed to labor activists after World War I. Conflicting priorities would remain as they did for the American Tennessee Valley Authority (TVA). Were the new nationalized industries supposed to run in the black without subsidies from the state budget or to deliver power and services at low prices for the public? Should they assure high salaries for their labor force or emphasize technological improvement and increases in productivity? Were the overall results of the nationalized sectors different in kind from the still nominally Italian private firms whose shares had been purchased in the 1930s by the Italian state holding company—the Institute for Industrial Reconstruction (IRI)? Or the postwar state energy conglomerate, the Ente nazionale idrocarburi (ENI), with its nationwide network of gas stations (and their six-legged fire-breathing dogs), all reorganized out of the Mussolini era's AGIP by the entrepreneurial Enrico Matteo, affiliated with the Christian Democrats? Or the postwar state development agency for the south, the Cassa per il Mezzogiorno, fond of showy industry installations, so-called cathedrals in the desert, and crucial for the Christian Democrats as a source of patronage?[24]

Economic planning was also an objective inherited from the 1930s, when it was advocated by Socialists, labor union leaders, and even the problematic "neo-Socialists," such as the Belgian Hendrik DeMan, who would support the wartime collaborationist regimes. In the United States, regional planning helped motivate TVA and left-wing circles in the Department of Agriculture; it seemed more legitimate for the natural resource sector than for industry.[25] Generally popular on the left, planning enjoyed a revival of interest after 1945 but gained little real traction in the Western capitalist world outside of France, where Charles de Gaulle had established the Commissariat du plan and installed Jean Monnet as its head. Herrick Chapman's long research emphasizes that in France, nationalization, planning, and a degree of workers' control could be instituted together. The provisional government nationalized Renault, the aircraft engine manufacturer, Gnôme et Rhône, and the coal firms of northeast France by decree upon the liberation; a year and a half later, following upon a strong Communist and Socialist showing in the elections for the National Assembly, the four major banks were made government property, followed by the Électricité de France and the Gaz de France, half of the insurance companies, and the remaining coal mines, now reorganized with the earlier takeovers as the Charbonnages de France. Comités d'entreprise were instituted as part of the reorganizations and allowed Communist and Socialist trade unions a voice in production, and leading trade union leaders were named to sit on the boards. Nowhere else could the left institute all three dimensions of economic transformation— state ownership, planning, and workers' codetermination with a voice on the factory floor. As we shall see, the achievement did not last.[26]

Of course, in the Soviet Union and later its satellites, central planning along with public ownership of enterprises had been declared the defining characteristic of the economy since the end of the 1920s. State agencies were to set production quotas and prices and allocate raw materials and industrial labor. Non-socialist governments elsewhere might claim these prerogatives in wartime but only as emergency grants of power to be dismantled once peace returned. (Briefly during the financial crisis after 2008, non-socialist states would nationalize parts of their countries' financial sectors to avert their catastrophic collapse.) But assuming governments did not transform industries into state enterprises or take an active managerial role in firms whose shares they had acquired in the depression, they still had to have investment funds to plan goals for a national or regional economy. Monnet could muster these for favored projects and so could Pasquale Saraceno at the Cassa per il

Mezzogiorno and David Lilienthal to a degree at the TVA.[27] In West Germany, the agency that distributed Marshall Plan funds could exercise some steering capacity for projects the government favored, but by 1950, such funds were a small fraction of the capital investment raised by domestic sources. However, targeting projects was a dominant approach. Modernizing steel production through the construction of "broad band" rolling mills was a favored objective for the Italian IRI and Monnet's Commissariat du plan. In Germany, the Thyssen work sought approval and funds to reequip its steel plant, but the Allies still had to give their permission for such a project until 1953. The "technocratic" managers in Italy, installed originally under Mussolini's regime, in particular Oscar Sinigaglia, continued to serve as key modernizers after 1945.[28]

In contrast, "planning" surprisingly disappeared as a Labour Party objective during its tenure in office from 1945 to 1951 despite enthusiasm for the slogan between the wars.[29] Recalling the unemployment of the interwar years, the party's economists placed their trust in Keynesian fiscal policy to sustain full employment rather than sectoral intervention. So-called demand management could replace industrial planning as outlined in the sequel to Beveridge's first report in 1945, *Full Employment in a Free Society*. Keynesian budgets—characterized by their willingness to accept deficit spending—appealed in the United States as well and could unite the progressive Republican industry leaders in the Council of Economic Advisers with liberal Democrats. An all-star cast of economists published a wartime manifesto for an activist economic policy to follow victory. Alvin Hansen, the major exponent of Keynesianism in the United States warned that in the modern world no system could survive which permits the continued recurrence of serious depressions. And as the volume's editor argued, "Why if, under the impetus of spending for war, we can attain a position of full employment and (despite the large output for war purposes) the highest standard of living in the history of the world—as we have in 1941–1942—can we not achieve them in peacetime?"[30]

Economic planning, however, requires more than compiling a wish list: it has to be an exercise in overcoming painful constraints—insufficient investment capital or foreign currency, scarce raw materials, and labor concentrated in older, less productive sectors. Besieged wartime Britain from 1940 to 1942 had learned that painful lesson; it developed linear programming and operations research as tools to cope with scarcities. Aneurin Bevan on the left of the party had learned from the war that "the language of priorities is the religion of socialism." For Britain in World War II as in World War I, man-power shortages had loomed as the main constraint when the armed services and the needs of production were stretched to the limit. Durbin, most con-sistently of the Labour leadership, tried to think through what democratic planning entailed when industrial production remained a major bottleneck after 1945 and the government was no longer willing or able to resort to con-scription or direct controls. The only recourse aside from moralistic ap-peals—"We must all mitigate our claims in order that others may mitigate their claims against us and that by compromise we may all win," Durbin wrote—was a policy of wage incentives. Short of compulsion, differential wage policies provided the only answer to the "undermanning" of industry and socialist planning in general. As Anthony Crosland on the party's right agreed, only a wages policy could prove there was a halfway house between laissez-faire and totalitarian planning.[31] But state intervention in collective bargaining was anathema to the Trades Union Congress, which accepted a voluntary wage freeze in 1948 but rejected any effort to tamper with labor market bargaining.

Outside Europe and the United States, planning still beckoned as the key to economic advance. Among the newly independent nations, it appealed as a rapid path to development without the creation of a dominant capitalist class. Leaders of the newly independent nations—Sukarno in Indonesia (1949), Jawaharlal Nehru in India (1947), Habib Bourguiba in Tunisia (1954), Kwame Nkrumah in Ghana (1957)—exemplified the approach, perhaps Nehru above all. The Congress had instituted a National Planning Com-mittee in 1938; in 1944, the (British) government of India set up a depart-ment for planning and development, and after independence the Congress worked out an Industrial Policy Resolution in 1948. Three Five-Year Plans followed (1951–1956, 1956–1961, 1961–1966), although only in 1955 did the Congress Party openly commit itself to socialism.[32] The first plan prioritized agriculture but named transport, irrigation, and power as investment targets. A fifth of the funds committed were allocated for education, health, and housing, and only 5 percent allocated for industry (of which two-fifths were to go to village and small-scale industry—a bow to Gandhi's values). Basic and small-scale industries were the major targets of the second plan, which included three giant government-owned steel mills and helped unleash an industrial boom; industry and agriculture, including irrigation, were objec-tives in the third plan. The plans brought the multiplication of government offices, licensing requirements, and hardly advanced socialism and Nehru himself noted that disparities of wealth and poverty were increasing. From the early 1960s, criticism increased from Indian businessmen and the World Bank; Nehru's successor, Lal Bahadur Shastri, was responsive to pressures for liberalization and the preparatory documents for the fourth plan suggested that market forces must play a greater role.

The other great Asian land power, China, fell into open civil war by 1947. Chiang Kai-shek's Nationalist government eschewed outright collectivization but had instituted a Three-Year Plan for industrial development in 1936. Following the Japanese takeover of Manchuria, as William Kirby describes, its mission focused on readying a war economy and then by 1942–1943, outlining a state-controlled postwar economy under a National Resources Commission (NRC), initially as a secret agency and after 1938 as a key public bureaucracy.[33] Planning efforts were endorsed by a forum of bankers, academics, and industrialists, the Chinese Economic Reconstruction Society, but viewed warily as too technocratic by the ruling Kuomintang (KMT) party. Nonetheless, the objective of state control and technocratic management prevailed at two interministerial conferences in April 1943 and October 1944, which established postwar production targets but contingent on infusions of $20 billion of foreign capital, predominantly American, over five years. Grandiose plans projected against a backdrop of wartime misery characterized the Nationalists' approach. US War Production Board director Donald Nelson, who organized an American Productive Mission in China in 1944, waxed enthusiastic about a Yangtze dam project that would emulate the TVA. But the Nationalists' emphasis on state development and control of industry alienated much of the potential American support. Agreement with China on limiting American and British extraterritorial privileges in 1943 was not calculated to remove American business mistrust. The Americans on whom success must depend were divided both about Chiang's military effectiveness and his economic plans. The needs of the regime, whether for UNRRA aid or US assistance were enormous, but the prickly generalissimo made collaboration difficult. For Chiang Kai-shek and the KMT, the daunting national task included overcoming the long record of diminished sovereignty, defeating the Communists, and establishing territorial control in areas where the KMT had never really ruled effectively, as well as resisting the Japanese. But natural catastrophes, wartime destruction, and the misery of refugees overstrained the regime's overblown ambitions.[34]

For Jian Tingfu, the Columbia University–trained economist who liaised with the UNRRA mission, the urgent overwhelming challenge was to alleviate human misery and poverty. The State Department and other advisers pressed for more "liberal" or private development plans including a freer hand for American firms to operate in China. All the projections on paper were belied by the devastation that remained after the Japanese surrender, including the significant industrial development and coal mines that Chiang hoped to recover for China by moving quickly into the north and Manchuria, a move that overstretched his real control. Of the dream of billions from Washington, a nominal $500 million credit authorized by the Export-Import Bank dribbled in for individual projects. US firms not associated with the joint ventures of the NRC opposed subsidizing Chinese "socialism," and Socony and Caltex blocked credits to the Chinese Petroleum Corporation. Joint plans for the Yangtze dam project were canceled in 1947. The NRC was granted ministerial status and its director, Weng Wen-hao, a leading exponent of industrial planning since the 1930s, was named by Chiang as premier under the new 1948 constitution, only to preside over a disastrous monetary reform that rendered the currency more worthless than before, with all the social misery this entailed. Once open civil war flared, Chiang's military hold crumpled disastrously such that by 1949, his forces had to flee the mainland. The NRC personnel ended up either in Taiwan or with the Communists where the enterprises they controlled were peacefully transferred to the Communists.[35]

Latin American states presented a complex picture. Brazil remained wedded to a national corporatism inspired by interwar models, including Mussolini's corporativist institutions. Mexico was forging ahead with a populist model most successfully instituted by Lázaro Cárdenas. So long as Franklin Roosevelt remained president, these institutional experiments could persist without bringing down the opposition of the economic colossus to the north—the "Good Neighbor Policy" had some substantive content. Indeed, Washington remained most preoccupied by the fascist models (as they tempted Argentina and Brazil during the war), not yet the socialist ones. The interaction of US reformers and Latin American economists played an important role in the 1940s. Latin American economists contributed to the ideas for the Bretton Woods institutions, and American economists went south to advise on projects. The chief risk was the alienation of the military at home. By the 1950s Latin American populist coalitions seemed far too Marxist within the context of the Cold War. Nonetheless, models for development generated in the 1950s and 1960s impacted not only ideas for a redistributive new economic order but also devolution of planning to private agencies.[36]

Christian and Liberal Alternatives

It is easy to forget that emerging from the years of war and privation, the securing of a welfare state, in particular one framed as part of a socialist or social democratic political future, was not the only project that prevailed across the industrial world. Whereas Socialists could reemerge as a party that had suffered persecution in prisons and concentration camps, Christian Democrats essentially had to refurbish an ideological tradition that had been badly compromised and provide a respectable tent for the vast majority of citizens who had stayed silent during the dark years. Christian Democracy presented itself as a newly energized political coalition designed to gather the middle classes and non-Marxist workers under the banner of Christian humanist values (including the sanctity of private property), which they argued that fascists had betrayed. Precedents existed from before the war in different forms although often tainted as organizations by compromises, both tactical and ideological, with the encroaching fascist movements of the 1930s. On the other hand, the parties could count notable and heroic anti-fascists among their ranks, and they could also differentiate themselves in Germany and France from narrow prewar Catholic denominationalism.

Earlier intellectual traditions, whether nineteenth-century social Catholicism or French "personalism," with its effort to foreground individual rights, provided a resource for renewal.[37] The Catholic Church hierarchies in France and Italy—tainted by their support for the Vichy occupation regime or the collaboration of the Vatican with Mussolini—had delicate and sometimes thorny relations with the respective Christian Democratic Parties, while the German version self-consciously reached out to Protestants.[38] A Christian Democratic Party gained traction in Chile—whose parties echoed those in the European spectrum—with greater independence from a burdened past. The Christian Democratic political project was ideological—opposition to Marxism and Communist rivals in particular—but there was also a social project, less oriented toward the economy than the private sphere. Left Christian Democrats supported the revival of "Christian" unions, and in 1949 the German Catholic Congress (Katholikentag) had welcomed codetermination although Pius XII and conservatives warned that it was incompatible with natural law. During the overhaul of the national pension legislation in 1956–1957, Adenauer was persuaded by his son Paul and socially minded Catholic civil servants to change the concept for national pensions from one that envisaged individual workers saving for their own retirement to that of an intergenerational compact in which retirees would draw their share of a growing national product, a so-called dynamic pension. As James Chappell emphasizes, by the late 1950s, the tensions within the Catholic social project could be reconciled with a view of economic development and the expectation of continued growth that allowed Catholic activists suspicious of capitalism and those hostile to collectivist tendencies to find a common ground.[39]

Sanctity of property was not the only social project. Before the Italian and German Christian Democratic Parties and their French equivalent, the Mouvement Républicain Populaire (MRP), hovered the project of reconstituting traditional male-led families, respect for marriage, bringing up children in the Catholic Church, resistance in Italy to divorce (abortion was suppressed as a theme), and control of their share of school systems or at least revenues: "A Catholic modernity, it was presumed in the long 1950s, would be made up of prosperous and hygienic families following traditional gender norms and obeying Church precepts in their sexual lives. . . . The state and the economy were now tasked, above all, with enshrining the rights and needs of the consuming family . . . that emerged as the presumed agent of social and political life . . . instead of, for instance, the individual citizen, the working class, the race or the nation." The theme, of course, extended beyond the Christian Democratic Parties, but it became their project par excellence; as an MRP spokesperson declared in 1947, "'We recognize the family as the most intangible and the most sacred' of all human groups."[40]

Secular "liberals"—to use the term in its European sense—also had to generate a postwar project—largely to forestall trade union and social democratic political domination in a postwar world where socialism seemed such a cresting wave. Liberals had organized notable conferences in Paris in 1938 and were influential in the Geneva-based Graduate School of International Studies and in neighboring agencies of the League of Nations. Friedrich Hayek had found shelter at the London School of Economics alongside Lionel Robbins. The most cohesive intellectual project would emerge in German-speaking Europe, gathering Austrians, Swiss, and German theorists, and become known as ordoliberalism. Ordoliberals claimed to be rejecting the state interference in the economies that the fascist regimes had imposed, even though some had been involved in Germany with planning a postwar future. A national economy must be based on free competition—private and public cartels were both rejected. But economic competition had to be structured within a sociopolitical order, an *Ordo*, that provided individuals with basic social protections, what became known as the social-market economy.

The social order needed to anchor the market economy, to make it broadly acceptable—but also to preclude any experiments in collectivism, or union claims for economic democracy. Given the National Socialist regime's mixed economy and extensive wartime regulation, Ordoliberals could present their call for depoliticizing the economy as anti-fascist and thus immune from criticism; but shorn of its rhetoric, their doctrine was largely a way of re-packaging a managerial capitalism under the mantle of social reform and preventing any inroads of Keynesian budgeting until the recession of 1966. Their glory moment came when Ludwig Erhard became head of the Verwal-tung für Wirtschaft, or nascent finance and economics ministry in the West German Bizone (1947–1949), and refused to impose price controls with the currency reform of 1948, successfully wagering that an acceptable currency would encourage production and provision of agricultural goods to forestall inflation.[41]

Across the Atlantic the leading state of the "developed world" by the latter 1950s and 1960s would focus on two overriding projects: national security and the consumer society. Walt Whitman Rostow's *Stages of Economic Growth* (1960) linked the two with a stylized history of economic development that argued "mature" industrial economies reached a level where they must choose either collective and militarist goals, as had Nazi Germany and the Soviet Union, or a peaceful and democratic plateau providing citizens high mass consumption. In fact, the more germane policy choice was the one between private and public goods that John Kenneth Galbraith had outlined two years before Rostow in *The Affluent Society* (1958). The United States had used the Eisenhower years, Galbraith implied, to retreat from public goods, except for its interstate highway program, until the Soviets' launching of Sputnik in 1957 proved a wake-up call. Americans could easily afford and should purchase more public goods—civilian and military—argued Galbraith, as did his ad-visee, presidential candidate John F. Kennedy, in 1960. The preoccupation with national security—in fact, American leadership—united both parties.

Both Galbraith and Rostow, however, were proposing agendas for highly prosperous countries, projects for the wealthy. They did not probe terribly deeply the inequality that was taken for granted in the United States. The Italian sociologist Alessandro Pizzorno, cited above, pointed out a few years later that even in Western Europe, the levels of family income were hardly so satisfactory as the Americans took for granted.[42] And the massive popu-lations of Asia and Africa were nowhere near the European level. In some ways, their collective project was the most demanding of all, for it united the geopolitical aspiration to stay clear of the communist and anti-communist international blocs with their respective ideologies for development. The global division gave them an opportunity as well as a mission, for they could seek foreign assistance in return for their continued neutrality. When the leaders of newly independent states met at Bandung, Indonesia in 1955, they confidently defined themselves as a neutral bloc, the "third world," just as many of them sought to assert socialist planning as a socioeconomic path between capitalism and communism. Their moralism often grated on the Western powers especially since the legacy of colonialism was the historical past that most shaped their political ideologies. Their ambitious third world project—not yet the New International Economic Order of the next decades but an assertion of a global historical role—illuminated the changing nature of empire.

New Imperial Frameworks

In the wake of World War II, formal empire would end. Government from a European metropole over faraway peoples organized into dependent territories became impossible to maintain. The interwar idea of "valorizing" empires— that is, assuring a net flow of resources to the benefit of the colonial power— gave way to the rhetoric of development and the reality of military commitments. But possession of an empire still seemed precious. The ultimate objective for many in the French and British political classes, military establishments, and civil service was less to reconstruct their home society than to hold on to great power status and overseas economic assets. To do so, however, required strenuous interventions in colonial administration, social and religious arrangements, and even the ecological status quo. For each of the major imperial powers in Asia, it meant an effort to reconquer colonial states that had preexisted their arrival, had then been lost to the Japanese, but were now rudely claimed by indigenous parties. In Africa, it meant resistance from those who claimed they were entitled to independent statehood. In these efforts, all the powers attempted efforts at territorial rejiggering—federation, protectorates—that might prove more serviceable. In line with the overarching ideologies of modernization and development, they offered major new projects. Demands for sovereignty, that abstract concept painfully disengaged from overlapping authority in sixteenth- and seventeenth-century Europe, could no longer be finessed by the colonial powers with formulas that sought to conceal unequal claims to decision making. Strong independence movements built on their interwar predecessors and, when necessary, fought persistently, often ruthlessly to raise the costs of colonialism.

For the imperial soldiers, these were thankless wars, usually fought not in pitched battles but police operations, requiring violence against populations and often finding disapproval and opposition at home. Communist adherents, whether domestic or represented by Soviet delegates at the UN, predictably denounced the efforts. But the Americans, too, remained skeptical, indeed hostile, until anti-Soviet considerations trumped the arguments for independence. The concept of UN trusteeship, which replaced the mandates, did not provide the carrying power that the mandates had and seemed to be relevant only in the case of scattered island or minor possessions. Besides the demoralizing military operations—which outside of Indochina did not end with battlefield defeat but foreign pressure or civil strife at home—the end of the European empires shattered often foundational myths about their own political systems. Suez demonstrated that Britain no longer had a special world-power status; the end of the Algerian War put paid to the notion that the colony was part of a France whose universal values erased particu-larities of place, race, and faith; the Dutch had to abandon the memory of the Indies as a site of productive racial fusion. Those unwilling to shed these beliefs, cultivated so long as national faith, sometimes gravitated toward far-right ideologies. Those accepting the new reality often marveled at how long their societies had maintained them.[43]

The creakiest and most neglected possessions, those of the Portuguese and Spanish, would remain the longest; but the British, French, Dutch, and Belgian colonial territories became independent between 1947 and the mid-1960s. Independence was conceded without the metropole's armed resistance in some cases—the British partitioned the Raj in 1947 and India and Pakistan emerged; Ghana was granted independence in 1960—the accession of these countries to voluntary association in the Commonwealth (at least for a while) allowed a certain consolation. The Palestine mandate with its apparently insoluble ethnic division between Arabs and Zionist settlers was dumped into the hands of the UN in 1946–1947. The French withdrew from the Levant (Greater Syria) in 1946, Tunisia in 1954, and Senegal in 1960. However, they fought tough and unsuccessful wars to retain control of Vietnam from 1945 until 1954, then of Algeria from 1954 to 1962. The British fought as well, to retain Malaya, where they did suppress a rebellion and then Kenya, with brutal judicial as well as military tactics. They stayed in Zambia and Zimbabwe longer (Northern and Southern Rhodesia) but largely to preclude the white supremacist successors from setting up racialized rule as was happening at the same time in South Africa.[44] With British troops initially serving as the new occupying force, the Dutch sought to reestablish their rule in the Indies. As it became clear to the Japanese their brief domination over Indonesia would soon end, they sought to turn over the islands to the nationalist leader Sukarno and his colleague Hatta, who were readying a declaration of independence under the occupier's approval, but under pressure from younger and more radical activists, moved up the date to announce independence a few days before Tokyo's surrender. The vast archipelago meant that control was contested in local milieus stretched across 1,000 miles. The British left and the Dutch remnants returned, often to British scorn.[45] They sought to expand their area of control in a so-called police action; the Americans brokered an armistice in 1947 but fighting resumed until Washington threatened a cutoff of Marshall Plan aid. The Dutch finally recognized Indonesian rule in 1949, although they remained in Papua New Guinea until 1954.[46]

But if prewar colonial empires had to be renounced as a cartographic vision—territorial sovereignty with homogenous colors on a map faded—or as an imagined pipeline with resources flowing from periphery to metropole, that is, as a resource empire, other forms of international domination would be adopted by the two powers that emerged strongest from the war, Russia and America. Finding the right vocabulary to describe their respective forms of preponderance has been difficult—was it imperial? hegemonic?—especially since they differed in intention and impact. When de Gaulle challenged the United States, Washington pouted; when Hungary and Czechoslovakia challenged Moscow, the Soviets invaded. Both the Soviet Union and the United States denied any imperialistic intent. Each found justification in the action of the other. This is not to equate the instruments of control within the two spheres; they were very different. The Communist sphere relied on waves of arrests, trials, and exemplary executions, thus rested on a political police, uniformity of the press, and an archipelago of forced labor camps. It did not tolerate dissent whether within the Soviet Union or the states governed by Communist parties. Through the late 1940s, Moscow reserved its most acute denunciations for the heretical Marxist dictatorship that would not acknowledge Stalinist supremacy, Marshal Josip Tito's Yugoslavia. Titoism replaced prewar Trotskyism as the offense that called for humiliating self-abasement in a "show trial," often to culminate with a bullet to the brain. US policymakers remained committed to significant pluralism within recognized limits, although in periods of heightened political or international rivalry they relied on financial aid to friendly editors and intellectuals, goodwill trips, the mobilization of the foundations discussed in Chapter 3, occasional threats of public disgrace before Congress, loss of jobs, and criminal penalties for perjury and contempt. Both systems believed that voluntary adhesion to publicly proclaimed values was critical, and both used indexes of economic achievement to demonstrate their superiority. But the logic of their counterposed power moved them to create international structures of adherence and domination and to explain their behavior in terms of systemic values—that is, ideologies. The Soviet expansion followed from 1944 to 1948 as their armies conquered and remained in Eastern Europe. It rested primarily on the loyalty of Communist Parties to Moscow's decision making. Indeed, from the morrow of the Bolshevik revolution, ruling Russia itself was envisioned as only one component, even if the most essential, in a transnational structure of loyalties.

A somewhat analogous situation had characterized prerevolutionary Russian history: the country was both empire and nation, periodically emphasizing the one strand of loyalties or the other. Joseph Stalin, both because of personal formation and tactical considerations in the succession struggle after Lenin's stroke and death, had emphasized Russia as the beleaguered site of socialist revolution, and the Soviet culture industry revived traditional Russian national themes when the Germans attacked. But with impending success in the war, the transnational linkages of a centrally controlled party rose in importance once again.

The United States moved into a dominant role in Western Europe with only rare and uncomfortable moments of acknowledgment that its position was hegemonic. Under the Roosevelt administration, while Washington still depended on Soviet participation in the European war and hoped for it as well in the war against Japan, cooperation with the Soviet Union seemed essential. American policymakers hoped that the political systems restored or established in Europe would be based on broad-based post-fascist coalitions that the Soviets could accept. The Soviets claimed to want anti-fascist popular democracies but aspired to much more decisive roles for the Communist Parties. Each side clung to ambiguous notions of democracy to allow for working together. The real difference between them emerged once Soviet troops moved into Poland in the fall of 1944 and insisted that the Communist Poles who had found refuge in Moscow should be recognized as the new government, not the broad non-Communist coalition of exiles based in London. The compromise reached at the Yalta Conference in February—Roosevelt's last international intervention—reflected the facts on the ground: Britain and the United States could control Greece and Italy, as Stalin recognized; the Soviets dominated eastern Europe. The London Poles were granted only one quarter of the new government's offices, but supposedly "free" elections would follow to ratify or amend the negotiations among them. Over the next two years, American efforts to patch together communist and non-communist coalitions under guarantees for pluralism came to naught. So, too, the mirage of compromise between Communists and KMT failed in China as civil war flamed. The 1945–1946 American mission under General George Marshall could not bridge the determination of each side to overcome the other.[47] Ethnic and/or religious differences, tamped down under European imperial rule in Africa and Asia, also proved unreconcilable. Territorial partition—the Iron Curtain—replaced the wartime alliance; national partition as in the Raj or mandatory Palestine replaced colonial divisions, and communist–non-communist divisions within Western European states in 1947 replaced the coalitions emerging at the liberation a couple of years earlier.

The European Recovery Program, the formal name for the Marshall Plan, initiated and pushed through Congress from June 1947 through April 1948, as American partisan division increasingly yielded to fear of further Communist expansion, demonstrated that Washington's role had become decisive, but less for Western European economic viability than political coherence. The Soviets decided that their own central planning system and control of Eastern Europe was incompatible with the American vision of an international open economy. They hunkered down and revived the prewar Third (Communist) International's notion that the German working class would reorient even the western zones of occupation toward Moscow. This proved an illusion. The introduction of a common West German currency, the deutsche mark to replace the vastly depreciated reichsmark, confirmed Soviet views that Washington was seeking to control an anti-Soviet formation. Moscow responded with the blockade of the land routes to West Berlin inside their zone of occupation, and the United States countered with the famed airlift. The two sides carefully avoided hostilities, but the territorial division of Europe was reinforced. By the fall of 1948, Britain and Benelux leaders recognized that security threats were as likely to emanate from Russia as from any revival of German military power, and they asked Washington to reorient their early project for a Western European alliance concerned about future German aggression with an Atlantic pact preoccupied by Russian intentions.

Truman's policymakers were happy to second the initial steps for a military alliance. State Department officer Phillip Bonsal counseled Averell Harriman, the European coordinator of the Marshall Plan, that the United States was not taking on a new role—which of course it was—but just pursuing "the logical sequel of the basic executive decision taken in September 1940 with the bases for destroyer deal and the legislative decision of March, 1941, when Lend Lease was approved." Americans should rapidly approve the proposal for a North Atlantic alliance that the Europeans would be proposing (although it would be wrong to treat Germany "at this stage politically and economically as a friend and political ally"—a caution that would be dropped within a year). Bonsal also pondered the fact that "in Greece our people were admitting . . . that they are in fact running the Greek Government. It seems to me that this creates a dangerous and eventually untenable situation."[48] The implicit issue was whether America might support a permanent alliance (itself a departure from earlier traditions of reluctant geostrategic noninvolvement) without taking on an imperial position. As the German proverb had it, wash me but do not get me wet.

The Soviet response to this division, to which they had contributed so powerfully by 1947, was to eliminate pro-British or pro-American elements, including democratic socialists as well as old-fashioned liberals, from the governments in Eastern Europe. The Kremlin had secured communist control in Romania and Bulgaria; it could not relinquish Hungary after the Communist Party had fared badly (25 percent) in the 1946 elections, nor Czechoslovakia, which under Prime Minister Edvard Beneš and President Tomáš Masaryk, was tempted by Marshall Plan aid. Finland was not worth fighting to subdue since Helsinki's neutrality commitments and occupation of the Petsamo naval base sufficed for geopolitical security in the Baltic. Conditions in China could be left to the forces under Mao Tse-tung, for whose peasant-based Communism Stalin had little sympathy. At Yalta, Stalin had agreed to recognize the KMT government and probably banked on a durable partition of the country once the Japanese were ousted, and the Soviets accepted another partition in Korea as the Japanese surrendered. Originally agreed on as a line to separate the Soviet troops entering Tokyo's former colony from the north and the Americans from the south, the 38th parallel would become the most durable legal frontier of the Cold War, although overlaid by the armistice line of the Korean War in 1953.

Each superpower could construct a plausible narrative that it was responding to the deepening territorial and ideological divisions even as its policies helped to foreclose them. Confronting an apparently irreversible trend, the preemptive strategy for the American government envisaged encouraging the friendly states of Western Europe into some sort of integrated structure. The goal of "integration" rose to prominence in 1949 among the Marshall Plan bureaucracy in part as a slogan to secure the congressional appropriations for the second year of a four-year commitment. Public relations required a new achievement once the emergency of 1947–1948 was overcome and the supposed threat of communist takeover in Italy and France was averted. Integration recommended itself as a noble aspiration with an economic logic.[49]

For London, however, Washington's aspirations also collided with its own claim to equal status and global influence. "Integration" threatened to mean the end of a privileged relationship with Washington and relegation to second-class status. The planning for what emerged in the summer of 1944 as the Bretton Woods agreements for reconstructing a postwar international monetary system and the subsequent negotiations for a new American loan had already revealed the divergences. Both sides wanted to restore a system of stable exchange rates to revive international trade and investment. John Maynard Keynes was acutely aware of the pressure that the international commitments could place on Britain's domestic economy: to keep export prices competitive would require high interest rates and deflationary pressure at home and a continual drag on employment. "To suppose that there exists some smoothly functioning automatic mechanism of adjustment which preserves equilibrium if only we trust to methods of laissez-faire is a doctrinaire delusion which disregards the lessons of historical experience without having behind it the support of sound theory," he prefaced his initial sketch of a clearing union.[50] He proposed a common fund in which countries with export surpluses—that is, the United States—would accumulate their credits and from which deficit countries—that is, the United Kingdom—would automatically draw. American negotiator, Assistant Secretary of the Treasury Harry Dexter White, held fast for a fund that would negotiate the terms of any stabilization loans and impose the conditions for the domestic economy. Washington prevailed. In the arduous negotiations for a postwar American loan, which would supplant expiring lend-lease aid, the American Congress insisted that Britain and the Commonwealth eventually remove the discriminatory tariff preferences of the 1931 Ottawa Agreements and remove the restrictions on selling sterling—that is, move toward "convertibility" for the shielded currency. London Treasury officials were not convinced that the terms they had to accept were worth the loan, but the short-term needs were desperate.

Anglo-American financial differences played out within the context of an overriding community of geopolitical interest., but they were real nonetheless. By 1947–1948, the British felt renewed financial pressure. In a brief for the upcoming Marshall Plan negotiations and a sixty-page internal memo R. B. E. "Otto" Clarke attributed the world's dollar shortage to the US price inflation in 1946–1947, which despite Britain's own vigorous export performance in the same period, created an unsustainable crisis. Clarke outlined drastic and probably fanciful alternatives to the world dollar shortage. The easiest solution would be for the United States to double the dollar price of gold (from \$35 to \$70 an ounce) and then earmark half of the \$20 billion in Fort Knox for other countries.[51] Another plan would be for the United States to buy the Egyptian and Indian credits (sterling balances) piled up in the Bank of England for dollar or gold reserves.[52] London found little solace in the short term. Finally buckling to pressure from Washington, the Treasury announced that the pound would be convertible into gold or dollars in July 1947 but was quickly compelled to reverse the action to staunch a sharp run on reserves. Americans understood that they had probably pressed London too hard but continued to urge "integration" in an Atlantic economy. UK Treasury officials and the embassy staff in Washington, however, tried to find comfort in what they believed was the difference between the supposed pro-integration zealots in the Marshall Plan administration on one side and the State Department on the other side, which supposedly was not asking for "surrenders of national sovereignty."[53]

Robert Hall, a senior civil servant at the Treasury (arguably the most important definer of policy options in postwar Britain, regardless of which party was in power), set out the differences in a lucid memo at the beginning of 1950. "There is some ground [to believe] that many of the people concerned in the U.S.A. have in the back of their mind some form of political union, and when they press for closer economic relations they are really wanting these as a means to a wider end." As an economic goal seeking freer trade and opposition to cartels, their goal was unexceptional. "This is what integration in the sense in which Adam Smith would have used the word if it had been fashionable in his time." The United Kingdom, Hall wrote, albeit with emollient exaggeration, "has constantly affirmed ever since the original lend / lease agreements that it was in favour of a world of this kind," although we would move more slowly. "There is of course a long-standing illogicality in American views on this matter. For historical reasons they have a certain innate hostility to the Empire; they very much disliked the Ottawa Agreements for Imperial preference: ... On the other hand there is some evidence they want a united Europe, partly to relieve them of some of the calls now made upon them, and that they think this can only be a success with the participation of the U.K."[54] British embassy personnel tried to dissect Washington opinion even more finely: Paul Hoffman allegedly was relatively benign, but others within the Marshall Plan's directorate, the Economic Cooperation Administration (ECA) "have in mind is an economic integration which clearly involves some central authorities requiring political integration." Happily, the State Department was applying less pressure.[55]

The British reporter was partially right; American opinion varied—poised in a transient stance of creeping hegemony. Arthur Schlesinger, the historian periodically turned policy adviser, writing from Paris, believed Washington should bet on Britain; only Britain in Europe could serve to in this role.[56] However, Undersecretary of State Dean Acheson, seconded "integration" and insisted that "the key to progress toward integration is in French hands; even with the closest possible relationship of the US and the UK to the continent, France and France alone can take the decisive leadership in integrating Western Germany into Western Europe." While Acheson remained critical of the ECA pressing so hard for integration, he did want the French and Organisation for European Economic Cooperation (OEEC) to decide "on a timetable for the creation of supra-national institutions. ... In my opinion, they would fall short of the needs of time if they did not involve some merger of sovereignty."[57]

This was in fact the objective of the Schuman Plan for a supranational coal and steel authority (conceived by Monnet) in May 1950. Although, the trajectory of events over the next few years was still unclear, "integration" essentially meant harnessing West German economic and then military potential for a US-blessed architecture of Europe. As different authorities have pointed out, the economic implications were that the Americans would let Germany recover its industrial power, cancel its debts, and take on a full role in balancing European deficits to the United States. For the next several years, the Germans would exploit French desire for its coal and American desire for its military manpower and industrial potential to make a case for restoration of sovereignty.[58]

Faced with the Franco-German initiative of May 1950, the UK Foreign Office declared it was an admirable idea except for the supranational authority, which of course lay at its core. In fact, Britain was fighting to keep the residue of its imperial influence, and US power was the major threat, even when political values and personal connections among the two countries' governing classes kept them aligned. The US political system was tricky to deal with: State Department personnel with their Ivy Leaguers were eminently clubbable for London's civil service, but congressional representatives, some with Irish background still resentful of London, others from Midwest provinces, provided a less predictable interface. Conservatives feared that American aid went to subsidize British "socialized medicine" while those on the left worried that assistance was helping to meet the costs of the empire. While Americans would not put pressure again to declare the pound a convertible currency as they had in 1947 with disastrous results, the US Treasury strongly argued that sterling was overvalued (it had been reset in 1940 at an equivalent of $4.03) and should be devalued. This recommendation made sense from Britain's balance of payments situation—the country's exports would be more competitive, its imports more expensive (but rationing could finally be lifted)—and Britain decreed a 30 percent devaluation for a new parity of £2.80 in September 1949.[59] Devaluation was welcomed by Washington and it did relieve an unsustainable balance of payments situation.

But the danger persisted that the foreign holders of sterling balances at the Bank of England (preeminently the Indians, newly independent since 1947, but members of the sterling bloc more generally, including Argentina and some non-Commonwealth nations) would unload their pounds for dollars or other currencies. The monetary consequences of Washington's vision of "integration" seemed a further threat for the British imperial residue. What British officials called a "two world" system (the dollar and sterling zones) threatened to implode into an American-led international economy. As Edward Playfair at the Treasury wrote in early 1950, "Whatever we may decide is only a beginning. We are sliding towards some kind of different world. It will be clearer what world it is when crucial issues are no longer avoided by a bribe of Marshall aid.[60]

Negotiations for the general renewal of Western currency convertibility became the next chapter in the construction of new monetary and security architecture. From the outset of the ERP, Washington had pushed for "viability" of Europe's overall balance of payments with respect to the United States—that is a rough current account balance that could be sustained without American aid. It soon became clear that this was too optimistic a goal. The ECA did facilitate currency clearance agreements in 1948 and 1949 by allowing a portion of Marshall Plan aid to flow toward direct defraying of intra-European imbalances but pressed for a more durable payments union, tantamount to convertibility. This required a central fund that might let each country borrow to meet transitory deficits and into which it would be required to bank surpluses—a significant achievement that the ECA pressed for and paid for in part by further foreign assistance in 1950–1951. The 1951 European Payments Union, which lasted for seven years until full convertibility could be resumed among its members without a backup fund, was a major step toward "integration" of Western Europe that along with the North Atlantic Treaty Organization (NATO) in effect rendered America a guarantor of the European currency area.[61]

The year 1950 brought a change in the mix of military and security concerns. The Soviets had exploded a nuclear device in 1949; two alliance systems had emerged in divided Europe; in June 1950, the North Koreans had invaded South Korea, and Washington responded with a commitment of combat troops. Even earlier, the Truman administration had decided to call for a major increase in its military budget under the terms of the policy paper NSC 68. It decided on a crash program to develop a fusion weapon, the H-bomb. Concern mounted about a war with the Soviet Union; demagogic members of Congress and the Senate fanned the flames of domestic anti-communism. By conspicuously joining the Americans with military forces in Korea, the British in effect diverted Washington's attention from its dissatisfaction with its laggard response to European "integration."[62]

Washington also turned its attention to upgrading the North Atlantic Alliance. Signed in 1949, it had remained largely a commitment on paper without a real military structure. Despite concern that a rapid defense buildup would set back general economic reconstruction, in light of the crises during 1949 and 1950, members agreed that they must devote serious effort to rearmament, and the way to measure their contribution had to be in terms of national income. For many of the states, national income accounting was still rudimentary, so the new effort compelled a standardization of economic analysis. A Temporary Counsel Committee was established in the fall of 1951 to review each country's national budgets to move them toward comparable contributions, arrangements ratified at the Lisbon meetings of February 1952. National income statistics—now standardized under Anglo-American and NATO oversight—allowed a more integrated coordination of Organisation for Economic Co-operation and Development (OECD) economies.[63]

By the fall of 1950, the Americans were ready to propose West German rearmament—a development unforeseen as late as 1948. The Christian

Democratic government of the Federal Republic of Germany pressed this development behind the scenes. Not included in the original Atlantic Pact (which had emerged after all out of concerns about German revival), Adenauer's government felt threatened or claimed to feel threatened by the military arrangements being taken by the new German Democratic Republic and wanted permission to raise its own units. Adenauer also understood that with every new responsibility asked of the Germans—whether for coal and steel integration or for military units—his government could reclaim steps toward fuller sovereignty.[64] Now it was the turn of the French to pose obstacles. Interim proposals that would integrate German with French battalions in a European Defense Community claimed countless meetings during 1951–1953 at the same time as the Germans sought to use the demands for their troops to preserve their domestic coal and steel cartels, which the French participants in Coal and Steel Community insisted on dissolving, and which the Americans finally insisted must be removed. But the French still could not swallow the European Defense Community and defeated it in the French Assembly in the summer of 1954. British foreign minister Anthony Eden patched together a more modest solution—German military units would simply join NATO as a national contingent. The French finally gave in; Germany hardly seemed threatening and it recovered full sovereignty in 1955.

The Korean War brought a decisive increment of American intervention in East Asia. The war with North Korean and Chinese Communist forces that followed from June 1950 to summer 1953 prompted the West's peace treaty and security pact with Tokyo and proved a major contribution to Japanese economic recovery. The former powerful military adversary now began a thirty-year period of remarkable economic growth, shielded from military expenses. The threat of a leftist assault on its economy had already been averted by the so-called reverse course of the occupation. For the historian John Dower in 1975, "The occupation did not merely attempt to lay bare the workings of the old economic system and tinker with them a bit, but particularly after 1947 actually concentrated on the creation of a new or neo-capitalist structure. This was necessarily supra-national, linking what are now the two giants of international capitalism." Dower saw US "imperialism" as a central issue, although by the 1980s many Americans worried that Japan was exploiting the relationship to wrest industrial dominance."[65]

We confront the issue of how best to define the frameworks of influence, ideology, protection, and advantage that Washington wove in the decades after World War II. Geir Lundestad chose "empire by invitation" for Europe.[66]

Americans developed a quasi–civil service of economic and political advisers who staffed foreign embassies and realigned economies and currencies (most notably the West German and the Japanese but indirectly the British and other European parities). Whereas in the 1920s, the "money doctors" had come from the banking networks or the League of Nations, in the 1940s and 1950s they operated through major official agencies—the traditional ones such as the Treasury and State Department and the newer ECA, which morphed into the Mutual Security Agency by 1951–1952, and then later into the Agency for International Development. These networks reflected the policy differences within American politics more generally: the Treasury and its powerful voice in the International Monetary Fund, Andrew Overby, spoke for economic orthodoxy with its potentially deflationary consequences; the ECA for the more expansive Keynesian approaches.[67]

The new balance of imperial influence became starkly evident in October 1956. After refraining from active intervention in the Polish "bread and freedom" demonstrations, which brought the formerly disgraced national Communist Władisław Gomułka to power, the Soviets forcibly crushed the Hungarian revolution at the end of the month. The nationalist Polish Communist leadership did not threaten to break their military ties with the Warsaw Pact, but the new Hungarian government, carried away by the élan and violence of their own revolutionary movement, mooted an affiliation with NATO. When ideological loyalties failed, the ultima ratio of the Soviet control was military, and it remained military until the end of the 1980s, when Mikhail Gorbachev accepted the end of Soviet control of Eastern Europe. (More than thirty years later it has become military once again.)

In the same weeks, the British and French, alongside Israel, sought to reassert their voice in the Middle East by seizing the Suez Canal back from the Egyptians. London and Washington had cooperated three years later in helping to undermine the nationalist Iranian prime minister Mohammad Mossadegh from power and maintaining the rule of the shah. In 1954, Washington had used its secret services to help remove Colonel Jacobo Arbenz in Guatemala and safeguard US interests in Central America. It had wisely refrained (for the moment) from helping the French to avert their military catastrophe in Vietnam and their withdrawal from the now precarious division of that country. In October 1956, however, the Eisenhower administration threatened the British with undermining the pound and compelled Eden's humiliating withdrawal from Suez. His successor, Harold Macmillan, recognized the "winds of change" blowing through Africa in his celebrated speech to the South African parliament in 1960. Thus, by 1960, two old empires were decisively compelled to retreat while one new one was created and reaffirmed by military intervention and another reached hegemony largely through financial power.

American ascendancy, of course, did not rest on financial resources alone; these were the assets deployed but behind them rested the country's armed forces and nuclear arsenal. For both the United States and the Soviet Union, both project-states aspiring to reshape their societies in the 1930s, the overriding state project by the 1950s became security—and increasingly an aspiration to total security. In so evolving, their rivalry worked to produce overarching imperial structures for regulating an international environment, including economic systems and ideological frameworks. In contrast to the end of World War I, there was no general peace conference in which great power status could be ratified. By the late 1980s, when the smaller national states who had been dominated by Moscow were escaping from that subjection, their intellectuals interpreted the Yalta agreements as the charter of a Soviet-American condominium over the European world and China. But there was also the UN, formally established at the San Francisco Conference in the summer of 1945: it started as the institutional expression of the antifascist alliance embodying all the contradictory aspects of that coalition, above all by conferring veto power on the two new military superpowers, the two major colonial states, and the most populous nation in the globe whose affiliation was to be tested by civil war. The new UN thus represented a world suspended between capitalist and state-socialist development, colonialism and decolonization, but infused, too, with the promise of global governance.

Plans for Governance

Historians have suggested that the UN was designed to provide a soft landing for decolonization.[68] But new states could also find their forum: India, then Indonesia, later Ghana, could assert their presence either alone or as a group. So, too, advocates for global governance could see it as a vehicle to advance human rights and economic development. The UN and international organizations helped merge the aspirations of the project-state with the realm of governance.[69] UNRRA from 1944 to 1947, the International Labour Organization, Food and Agricultural Organization, World Health Organization, and UNESCO conceived of as permanent organizations were important resources. In 1956, Secretary General Dag Hammarskjöld launched a UN Program for

Operational and Executive Personnel, ultimately absorbed into the UN Development Programme by 1965. The idea was to provide an international advisory agency for developing the civil service of newly independent states. In the long ensuing discussions, the Communist countries raised the specter of neocolonialism, the British beheld an interference with their own hopes to shape the civil service of their ex-colonies, and Egypt and India felt that in effect the proposal was patronizing and were concerned about being displaced. Gradually, the proposal was cut back from envisaging a permanent UN civil service at the disposition of new states to the temporary seconding of technical experts (OPEX). The Congo crisis in 1960 not only highlighted the need for administrative expertise but also encouraged the former colonial powers to offer the equivalent.[70] It showed the urgency of the need and ironically led to the death of Hammarskjöld in a plane crash.

Outside the UN, supposedly independent governance institutions, the nongovernmental organizations involved with political and economic affairs, also found their interests and goals shaped by the ideological strength of state projects. The year 1949–1950 was an inflection point in the construction of an American domain across economic, military, political, and cultural fields. Even as newly inaugurated President Truman called for a new program of technical assistance for developing nations, so-called Point Four,[71] Paul Hoffman, for instance, went from the ECA and Marshall Plan to head the Ford Foundation from 1951 to 1953 but seemed to envisage that powerful and wealthy institution as a sort of paragovernmental agency. Rowan Gaither, director of the Rand Corporation, who would succeed Hoffman as president of the Foundation and had written the foundation's overall mission statement in 1949, now prepared a memo for him on goals and objects, suggesting that "the most important problem confronting the world today is the maintenance of world peace," from which it followed that "the political, economic, military and ideological strength of the non-Soviet world must be increased to provide a basis for resolving unsettled issues, to supply a deterrent to aggression, and to prepare for any future eventualities." For the Foundation to be effective, activities had to be evaluated "either in: a. Lessening tensions between the United States and the U.S.S.R., or in b. Enhancing the relative strength of the West vs. the East." Official initiatives of the United States faced limits; private studies of the Soviet system, of communications, "support for comprehensive studies of the particular non-Soviet areas of greatest importance in the cold war (e.g. India, Pakistan, Indonesia, Iran, the Philippines) in order to ascertain what factors (political, economic, military, ideological) are most

important in each with respect to Western policy, and what Western economic, political or other measures will be best calculate to achieve the goals
of Western policy. In particular, this project should determine the adequacy
of our present or proposed economic and political policies with respect to
the ideological war.... Existing knowledge of human behavior [should] be
utilized as effectively as possible by policy-makers and administrators in government, industry and elsewhere, particularly in making the decisions required by the national emergency."[72] The Rockefeller Foundation hardly
lagged behind Ford in encouraging international relations theory as a key
tool for global management.[73]

Such commitment did not exclude independent scholarship but reflected
an agenda emerging within what might be viewed as the gravitational field
exerted by bipolarity. As one scholar summarizes, "in the constellation from
the 1940s to the late 1960s the convergence of political and scientific concepts
made possible a philanthropic activity that was both in the service of American foreign policy but was not determined by it."[74] The Ford Foundation
went on to fund the Social Science Research Council's area studies programs
(from which this author benefited in the 1960s and 1970s), devoted to
"strengthening democracy," and nurturing university programs in "behavioral
science" resting on large-scale data about political behavior.[75]

The political theory of the 1950s congenial in such a milieu helped confirm a
model of pluralism and polyarchy or competitive interests and resources
(with many variants) as the defining characteristic of Western democracy.
Theorists of pluralism deployed it, among other purposes, to criticize
C. Wright Mills's theory of a unified power elite, which liberal scholars perceived, correctly, as a fundamental critique of American democracy.[76] Inter-
estingly, the same methodological starting points led to revisionist analysis
of the National Socialist and Soviet regimes that departed from the model of
a coherent totalitarian form of government. Scholarly analysis had unin-
tended paths and consequences, often transcending the premises from which
it originated.[77]

Rockefeller and Carnegie remained hospitable to critical intellectuals, and
the former's long activity abroad moved from medical interests to promoting
"development" and "modernization." As noted in Chapter 3, Rockefeller
wound down its regional health offices—focusing its work on disease in the
New York Rockefeller University—and moving toward projects trying to
shape population outcomes on a large scale, namely the Green Revolution
and population control. Still interested in the provision of community health

care in the immediate postwar, Rockefeller Foundation officers shied away from funding public health ventures in Eastern Europe by 1948. The Communist takeover of mainland China ended the Foundation's long work in that country; and a major review of its International Health Division (IHD) in 1950–1951 led to shutting down the IHD and focusing on "human ecology," with its emphasis on population control.[78]

Was there a counterpart to the notion of social science in the Communist world where Marxism-Leninist "diamat" or dialectical imperialism in the postwar period was enshrined as the official paradigm for historical and sociological knowledge? By the 1960s, it can be ventured, "cybernetics" appeared as an allegedly useful tool for applying social science to politics and economics stimulated in part by the advent of computers and the growing fashion of "convergence" theories on both sides of the Iron Curtain.[79] Communist and democratic systems would supposedly grow more similar as variants of a common model of "industrial society," with similar structures of production and provisions for welfare. The realm of governance saw its boundaries dissolve into an encompassing domain in which the principles of science might join that of a tepid social democracy.

Thus, the postwar world offered a unique moment for activist states to reassert command of global order. Colonial wars only increased the claims for "stateness"—whether on the part of the newly independent countries such as Indonesia, Ghana, Algeria, or Vietnam or as a consequence of the expanded welfare-state agendas of long-established nations. Conversely, powerful states needed agents to help with governance; the United States in particular required interlocutors within the Atlantic alliance who were more than vassals. The construction of governance was a realm that the states of the 1950s might delegate to the UN and its agencies, to the OEEC (and then the OECD) as an economic think tank emerging from the European recipients of Marshall Plan aid, and to a world of foundations only too happy to second their affirmation of global needs and processes.[80]

For a brief period, too, the web of capital was subordinated to the project-state and security empire. Capital was controlled to a degree by American domination of a reserve currency and the country's willingness to provide the capital and foreign exchange that it had left to the private banking community between the wars. On what basis was global or regional and national economic performance to be reorganized? States had learned that economic welfare could not just be left to business and finance. What had to be defined was not merely a post-fascist political order but a post-Depression economic order.[81] The Depression had disillusioned many with the global capitalism that had preceded it. The economic catastrophe of the 1930s, and the challenge of World War II left states not always with enhanced capacities but certainly renewed missions. Finance seemed far more under control of the project-states than it had been before the Great Depression. Capital was bruised by the catastrophic performance during the Depression, then subordinated to wartime economies. Nation-state and UN interventions marked the reemergence of peacetime preoccupations in 1943–1944. Bretton Woods was an effort to put it back together with nation-states playing the key role in international economic reconstruction.

Social systems followed political power, Stalin allegedly told the Yugoslav Communist intellectual Milovan Djilas. For decades, historians debated whether Stalin and the Soviet leaders took their ideologies seriously as a basis for action. Of course they did, but the stakes of ideological prediction were not primarily about the future, which after all was rather open ended and could arrive tomorrow or decades hence. Ideology was a weapon for the present.[82] The stakes were about enforcing loyalty and commitment at home. As the edgy joke that circulated in Eastern Europe had it, the future was absolutely predictable, but the past was subject to unexpected change. Ideology played a role in demonstrating that changes in political strategy and tactics all had a long-term logic, appearances to the contrary notwithstanding. In any case, a caste of Communist clerics would demonstrate that Western capitalism would fall into crisis, a prediction useful for cleansing the Party of "wets" (to use Margaret Thatcher's later term for those without the courage of their convictions) but not for debating with Roosevelt, Truman, or Winston Churchill. At the end of the war, the Hungarian Eugene Varga was the theorist most in vogue and most sophisticated about demonstrating capitalist crisis. American social theorists duly responded over the next twenty years with alternative analyses that we cite below.

The British and Americans all realized with a shock by 1947 that postwar capitalist arrangements were not going to prosper without sustained political effort. The British had to accept that they could not preserve a protected area of international finance. Americans realized that their allies' or clients' economies were more fragile than they had hoped for if they wanted to revive a vigorous system of international commerce and payments. And the Soviets understood by 1947 that the vigor and expansiveness of an American-led capitalism might become far more dangerous to their own enclosed sphere of state socialism than they had reckoned. It was not that the Americans were demanding Russia abandon its own centrally planned state socialism as a condition for a voice in an international economy. It was just that the conditions Washington seemed to require for Marshall Plan aid—open markets in Eastern Europe—would preclude Soviet political control.

Global trade and payments could be organized along open or closed lines; and the Americans and the Soviets would choose different alternatives. The ownership and control of *national* productive assets could be organized with more or less state control. As much as public or private ownership of industry, economic policies divided over openness or closure, an effort to break down boundaries for trade and enforcement, or to reinforce territorial control. The fascist version of autarky or the German concept of *gemeinwirtschaftliche Räume*—closed economic zones such as Hjalmar Schacht had negotiated for the National Socialist government when Berlin agreed to purchase agricultural goods from the countries of Eastern Europe with credits that were kept in Berlin and used for industrial purchases—emerged tainted by the experience of 1933–1945. The British version had been established at the Ottawa Conference of 1932 and comprised preferential tariffs for the Commonwealth. Both offended US policymakers, although the German zone embodied far greater relations of dependency. As the "arsenal of democracy" and with an extraordinary productive record from 1940 through 1945, the Roosevelt administration called for the virtues of a free-trade world, much as the British had done in the mid-nineteenth century. The British and French versions of trade and investment within their respective imperial frameworks became harder to maintain, although the initial postwar continuity of their empires gave them some hope. As the war ended, the coming battle to maintain some, if not full, control of their dependencies seemed critical for maintaining zonal protected economies. In the Atlantic world, however, they were not in a position to resist the American thrust for lowering tariff barriers and eliminating currency zones.

There was a milder and nonimperial version of economic regionalism, often endorsed on the left. Gunnar Myrdal, director of the UN Economic Commission for Europe—and obviously responsible to a global organization that included the Soviet Union and its allies—sought to maintain an economic region that remained free of American pressure to absorb US exports, would allow a relatively protective zone for economic planning, and would include the Soviets. The United States offered the politics of productivity and the Marshall Plan and was supported by the OEEC/OECD, which it helped to create and nurture. Myrdal, sought to prevent a hardening of economic lines. British officials, even under a Labour government, despised Myrdal's soft socialism. By the 1970s, these issues would feed into the campaign for a New International Economic Order.[83]

The first global order of the second postwar era lasted perhaps twenty years. It fell apart between 1968 and 1973—with the insurgencies of the student movements, renewed labor radicalism, inflation and the oil crisis. The project-states lost their balance: the Western-oriented liberal ones were buffeted by new claimants with apparently radical programs—for example, the student movements and demands for racial equality.[84] The socialist sphere faced insurgency because it was unable to provide economic welfare enough to compensate for its authoritarianism. At the same time, the older imperial frameworks—prolonged into the 1960s by very favorable oil contracts, ideologies of modernization and secularism—would also fall apart. Could the allure of the nonterritorial forces of capital and governance provide enough binding energy to provide coherence? These questions provide the issues for the next two chapters.

5

Countervailing Power?

Capital's Projects and Their Limits, 1948–1960s

CAPITAL, TOO, HAD ITS PROJECTS in the 1950s. Of course, the term *capital* is an abstraction, a shorthand for business leaders who represented finance and industry in the public eye and asset owners and managers who directed privately owned firms. The intellectuals who examined their relationships, privileges, and influence brought the term to life, often critically in the wake of Karl Marx. Sociologists had made its characteristic activities—industrial production methods and wage labor, markets including financial markets, and decentralized reinvestment of profits—into the defining characteristics of a social system: capitalism. The world depression had multiplied its critics, but by the end of World War II, others celebrated its achievements and worked to disarm its detractors. By the mid-twentieth century, they popularized a new armory of concepts to highlight its global promise: productivity, growth, modernization, and development, among others. The historian needs to listen in. We have to listen also to the workers employed by economic enterprises, were essential for their functioning, and remained conflicted about their collective role within the system—proud of their skill, contesting their dependency.

In 1952, the economist John Kenneth Galbraith sought to explain in effect why American capitalism, at least as curated by the New Deal, was safe for liberals.[1] Galbraith was not a researcher at the frontier of economic theory as it was emerging in ever more mathematical notation with the advent of general equilibrium models. Nor was he an avid and meticulous student of business cycles—a branch that had been energized by the Great Depression, studied in notable German institutes, and marked by distinguished contributions from Gardiner Means, Joseph Schumpeter, and others. As a

Canadian from Ontario, he had begun as an agricultural economist and became involved with American price control administration during the war, and then in assessing the effectiveness of the US air war in the Strategic Bombing Survey, which suggested (perhaps incompletely) that despite the thousand-plane raids and urban destruction, massive air attacks had not really devastated Germany's industry or shattered its people's willingness to prolong their combat.

Like John Maynard Keynes, Galbraith had a rare gift for communicating with the public and a capacity and desire to skewer what he called "the conventional wisdom." He followed in Thurman Arnold's path of exposing "the folklore of capitalism," though without the grating, almost-cynical tone that had characterized that New Dealer's critique of fifteen years earlier. American liberals had long identified monopolistic tendencies as poisonous for democracy as well as economic fairness. In 1937–1938, the New Dealers, alarmed by the onset of a second wave of depression, fastened on the alleged role of oligopoly and monopoly in cutting off recovery. They could find support in the formal theory of "imperfect competition" developed by economists Joan Robinson in Britain and Edward Chamberlin in the United States. In contrast to the agricultural sector with myriad farmers and small businesses who were "price takers," oligopolists—including the great names of American industry—were price makers: that is, they could sufficiently limit the competition they faced such that they did not have to produce all they could have to achieve maximum net returns. They would earn their highest profits at a lower threshold by exploiting their market power, a term Galbraith used to suggest the political dimension to economic outcomes. Might the oligopolists who restricted production have contributed to the renewed depression during Franklin Roosevelt's second term? The Democrats had established a Temporary National Economic Committee to investigate monopolies in 1938, and Roosevelt's legislative message even identified fascism as an outgrowth of the "private power" exerted by monopolies. The administration's antimonopoly stance (so different from its corporatist initiatives earlier in the New Deal) proved short-lived once American rearmament made the industrial prowess of big business seem essential.[2]

Now at the beginning of the 1950s, Galbraith suggested that the earlier alarms about monopoly had been misguided: capitalist competition was assured not because multiple firms competed to keep prices down but because producers prompted wholesalers or consumer cooperatives or labor unions to curtail the abuses of monopoly. Americans, he rightly recognized, had always been obsessed with the specter of monopoly—originally attributed to bankers' schemes from the administration of Andrew Jackson on and later to the industrial "trusts." But the critics of the banks or America's huge corporations, according to Galbraith, had looked to the wrong remedies: In theory the threat of price competition limited the power of the big firm. "It was to the same side of the market and thus to competition that economists came to look for the self-regulatory mechanism of the market." This was misguided. The restraints on private economic power "were nurtured by the same process of concentration which impaired or destroyed competition. But they appeared, Galbraith argued, "not on the same side of the market but on the opposite side, not with competitors but with customers or suppliers. It will be convenient to have a name for this counterpart of competition and I shall call it *countervailing power*." In the typical modern oligopolistic market of a few sellers, the active restraint was provided not by competing suppliers but from the other side of the market by strong buyers. Although competition among sellers was regarded as a self-generating force since rival producers entered the market wherever there were still profits to be made. "Countervailing power is also a self-generating force and this is a matter of great importance."[3] This distinguished countervailing power from George Kennan's notion of containment, articulated five years earlier. Both expressed the binary imagination that peaked in the 1950s, but Kennan's containment, as he emphasized, required constant conscious policy even if venerable theories of the balance of power suggested it would have been provoked spontaneously.[4]

Galbraith's analysis, we can recognize in retrospect, made sense for a particular phase in the history of capitalism—the "Fordist" decades of mass production, scarred by memories of the Great Depression but reaffirmed in global war. Significant by its absence in the book was any reference to the intellectual scrutiny of the capitalist system and indeed of economic society developed during the previous decade by Karl Polanyi and Peter Drucker, who both started from Viennese backgrounds and a framework based in an anthropological holism to reach diverse conclusions—Polanyi believing that market society and mechanisms disastrously abstracted economic activity from society and had led to fascism, Drucker coming to rely on the modern corporation in effect to revive society and protect it against an overweening state.[5] Galbraith accepted the mass production economy developed by the American corporation. It provided three or four decades (ca. 1940–1980) during which tangible investment in massive mechanization to turn out standardized output available to a broad consuming middle class characterized industrial "modernity." The system rested spatially on core regions with a cohesively organized working class educated with manufacturing skills and willing to trade radical aspirations to collective ownership or political domination for a consensus on maintaining the active role of the project-state to centralize welfare and fight a recurrence of mass unemployment, support advanced technology and contract for its manufactured output. This chapter provides a glimpse into its operations during its "glorious" years. As later chapters show, it would advance, or perhaps recompose, to a new phase whose geographical, managerial, and public policy parameters would transform the organization of its firms, working classes, and of capital itself.

Social Partners, Social Adversaries

The system of countervailing power, Galbraith continued, was "seen with the greatest clarity in the labor market where it is also most fully developed." Citing the 1937 Wagner Act, which established the legal rights of unions to organize, Galbraith declared that "in fact, the support of countervailing power has become in the last two decades perhaps the major peacetime function of the federal government."[6] Precisely in its sanctioned "countervailing" role, postwar organized labor in the United States was an integral player in Galbraith's vision of capitalism. Although it often acted in light of its own interests and claims, when well organized and disciplined labor, it was the basic asset of capital—not for nothing had Marx described the compensation paid to labor as "variable capital."[7] This discussion thus includes labor in its ambiguous or dialectical role—as an asset of capital, as a countervailing adversary in the economy, and sometimes as political administrators of states that preserved capitalist enterprises.[8]

Caught up in the force field of the Cold War—although in part a cause of it and certainly a major stake—corporations had recovered a vast degree of self-confidence since World War II. Schumpeter famously asked, "Can capitalism survive?" in 1942 and had answered, "No, I do not think it can."[9] By the 1950s, it was surviving very well, at least in Western Europe and the Americas. Nonetheless, as a consequence of World War II and then Cold War competition, the agendas of new emerging nation-states, and the reinvigoration of interstate associations such as the United Nations (UN), the web of capital was overshadowed as a global agent at least for a decade or two. In some instances, states simply nationalized independent enterprises. In others, they imposed legislation that restricted or expanded businessmen's independence of action; in still others, they prescribed processes of shared or corporative decision making (often with representatives of organized labor and government representatives). The working classes were not an adversarial force in that structure but in fact a raw material for capitalist production. Assessing these tendencies from the mid-1960s on, analyses of twentieth-century politics and economics would emphasize the triangular relationship of state, capital, and labor—each sometimes an adversary of the others but often an implicit partner, certainly a component of national and global capitalism.[10] Workers were strategically organized in most industrialized societies but, precisely because of that cohesion, could normally be counted on as a restrained collective actor, motivated by economic rationality—if not, as in colonial societies or precapitalist regions, by deference or coercion. From the perspective of working-class incorporation, the outcome was progressive and facilitating the so-called mixed economy in which private and state-owned enterprises might coexist, along with what would also be called the Keynesian welfare state.

In some cases, firms willingly traded their liberty of action for the sake of more assured income. After all, except for stubborn old leaders or families, they were in business for profits, not to insist on unrestrained domination. Nonetheless, even as the web of capital seemed to give up some societal power, at least for a while, the socioeconomic system that historians and sociologists call capitalism continued to evolve. What is more, because global politics seemed increasingly to pit the capitalist world against the socialist world in an epic confrontation, the leaders of the large capitalist firms gained enhanced prestige and in some cases deference. Cold War rearmament responded primarily to geopolitical tensions, but its scale in the United States during the 1950s and 1960s helped cement an alliance of advanced sector industries, commodity producers, and an ambitious defense establishment and foreign service. Ideas among Democratic Party lawmakers and policy advocates to have the government nationalize steel production or directly intervene to sustain a demand that had seemed to flag in 1949 could be superseded as massive defense orders took hold. As Tim Barker has demonstrated, the Korean War proved a decisive step in welding a community of policy between state and capital. The Office of Defense Mobilization, he suggests, became America's Commissariat du plan.[11] Rearmament served as a crucial component for sustaining prosperity and full employment in the early 1950s. Mutual Security Assistance seamlessly replaced Marshall Plan aid with the United States paying for the European rearmament it encouraged through so-called offshore procurement. North Atlantic Treaty Organization (NATO) scrutiny of national budgets in the early 1950s functioned as a form of indicative planning on the transnational level.[12]

In the 1950s, Western capitalism operated more in a neo-mercantile than neoliberal context—that is, nation-states insisted on the political mobilization of their economic activity on behalf of international competition. Doctrinaire demands to dismantle political supervision of economic activity enjoyed less traction than they would twenty years later. As discussed in Chapter 4, project-states made greater claims on their national economic agents; they called on them to help prepare for and fight an arduous world war, to expand systems of welfare and national planning (including the improvement of statistical capacities), and sometimes to replace formal sovereignty over colonies. Multinational firms were still closely tied to national states and dependent on their support. The multinational was anchored in a home country and had subsidiaries abroad, such as General Motor's Opel in Germany; it was not just a headquarters with interlocking operations and complex supply chains. Industrial innovation often depended on military requisites, as in the aerospace industry. Indeed, President Dwight Eisenhower, increasingly deprecated as dim old Ike, identified the problem of economic power in 1960 more acutely than Galbraith in 1952: the civic danger derived from the guaranteed patronage of the national state for the industries involved with national defense—preeminently aerospace, aviation, and missiles but increasingly electronics, and the engineering faculties and think tanks.[13]

In terms of spatial or geographic dimensions, the emblematic industries were still crucially organized around coal, steel, and oil—ecologically demanding assets, fixed in particular locations, and in the case of oil often extracted from politically controlled territories. (We follow them more closely in the next chapter.) National states thought they might steer these productive forces through civilian and military planning authorities, but the policy dependency often went the other way—as Eisenhower's warning of a military-industrial complex implied. These were signature industries, just as William Blake's "dark Satanic mills" with children passing the shuttle between warp and woof had been in the early 1800s; then replaced a century later by George Orwell's coal mines—"You and I and . . . all of us *really* owe the comparative decency of our lives to poor drudges underground, blackened to their eyes, with their throats full of coal dust"; and then yielding anew Ford's assembly lines. It is not that the iconic industrial processes quantitatively dominate national output: the intricate networks of wholesale and retail trades, the crafts, construction, logistics, and transport remain crucial: New sectors, however, make a qualitative contribution to national productivity growth owing to key technological or organizational improvement.[14] But of course, the iconic industries keep changing, and the twenty years after World War II was a period of decisive transformation that deeply impacted all levels of social and political organization from international relations "down" to family and gender roles.

Wartime conditions encouraged ideas among labor leaders for full incorporation into a system of corporatist capitalism. Industrial labor played a dual role within the terms used by this book: it was a major source of ideas and pressure for project-states, and even when unions remained adversarial, or in Galbraith's term, a countervailing power, organized labor often functioned as an asset of capital. High employment in the war, the apogee of mass-production industry, and the claims of patriotism assimilated labor into the organization of corporate capitalism. The Second World War, like the first, had led states, both democratic and authoritarian, to give unions a role in the factories and enterprises needed for production. Italy's "internal commissions," conceded to labor during World War I, had been suppressed by the fascists in 1925; but in his last year in power, while ruling the north under German occupation, Benito Mussolini instituted "management councils" (*consigli di gestione*) that were claimed as sites of workers' control upon liberation. They did not last beyond the recovery of the right during 1947–1948, when a new and tamer version of "internal commissions" were sanctioned instead. Vichy France had decreed a "charter of labor" with vertically integrated "organization committees"; National Socialists had appointed "trustees of labor." With the liberation on the horizon, leaders of industry hardly believed they could recover their prewar economic domination. French industrialists, for example, convening in November 1943, agreed they would have to find "an equilibrium solution" between "the capitalism of yesteryear and the collectivization of the means of production." The future would belong to the "organized profession, not the owners of capital."[15] At the same time, the director of the firm must retain his historic supremacy. In Britain and the United States, the recruitment of union representatives into wartime production committees and their acceptance of no-strike pledges (with the exception of John L. Lewis's United Mine Workers) bound them more closely to the productivist framework. Even the United States seemed to advance toward a corporatist structure with the War Labor Board and the Office of Price Administration. Congress of Industrial Organizations (CIO) president Philip Murray proposed an Industry Council Plan that would have had labor set production plans and investment decisions alongside business leaders in major industries. Walter Reuther, head of the United Auto Workers, wanted a tripartite Aircraft Production Board that would have extensive powers, a scheme blocked by the automobile industry and earning George Romney's description as "the most dangerous man in Detroit."[16] Just as industry executives often balked, so often did old-school labor leaders. The American Federation of Labor (AFL) heads and British Trades Union Congress (TUC) leaders feared that collaboration would limit their capacity to exercise countervailing market power. Nonetheless, during the wartime conditions that still prevailed as occupied Western Europe was being liberated, industry and labor representatives formed solidarity pacts under resistance authorities that would assure production, index wages, and—so important an objective for labor—workers would not be laid off even if demand dropped. These pacts bought a respite for capitalism as the war ended, but they weighed heavily on the future as wartime orders ceased. Unions saw the defense of employment levels as a priority while industry feared an unsustainable burden.

Corporatist initiatives played out against the general inflationary trends that marked the years from 1938 on, when rearmament started driving up demand. Inflation, Galbraith recognized in his analysis, undermined the dynamic of countervailing power. In a milieu of inflationary demand, countervailing power might give way to a de facto collusion in which employers granted high wages to labor and passed their cost on to consumers: "Under inflationary pressure of demand, the whole structure of countervailing power in the economy dissolves" even if "the full coalition between management and labor" was disguised by "the conventional [rhetoric] of animosity and by the uncertainty of management how long the inflation would last."[17] Inflation was lasting a long time.

The Limits of Countervailing Power

World War II, like World War I, unleashed a process of hyperinflation when government authority collapsed as countries were invaded or fell into civil war. China's currency collapsed in 1947. Germany's and Japan's currencies became almost worthless (although retained as accounting units until drastic reforms in 1948), but hyperinflation overtook other countries as well: Greece and Hungary, savaged by the war as the Germans retreated, descended into hyperinflation—Hungary achieving a depreciation even greater than Germany's in 1923. The process was a vicious circle: governments printed money to cover expenses as tax collection failed; the agricultural sector withheld produce from urban purchasers as cash depreciated and price controls were attempted, usually unsuccessfully. As legal or black market prices rose, unionized wage earners pressed for salary increases which prompted further price increases from employers; whatever tax receipts a government might extract as it lost territory and taxes failed ever more lamentably to cover expenses including civil service wages . . . and the cycle continued. In Western Europe, France and Italy also descended into rapid inflationary spirals—governments printed money to cover their expenses; employers and employees were caught in a spiral of catch-up adjustments. As after World War I, the increase in prices served as the arena in which society fought its distributive battles.[18]

Reformists understood that suppressed inflation inherited from the war would ravage currencies after hostilities, and they proposed various schemes for monetary reform, such as freezing of bank accounts or long-term forced loans. The Belgians adopted such a scheme in 1944, and Pierre Mendès France sought to institute one for liberated France, but Charles de Gaulle feared that the social and political unrest it would provoke among labor was too risky, and the plan was vetoed. Italy postponed its monetary reckoning until 1947, but then with the exit of the Communists from the governing coalition, President Luigi Einaudi and the head of the Bank of Italy choked off the easy credit that allowed companies to invest and meet wage demands but stabilized the lira for almost twenty years. In Japan and Western Germany, the occupying Americans imposed monetary reform in 1948.

Monetary reform in West Germany entailed abandoning the old reichsmark as legal tender and replacing it with a new deutsche mark, freezing bank accounts and then converting them, and providing Germans enough pocket money in the new currency to get through the transition. Monetary stabilization was never politically neutral. As in the 1920s, it required—and perhaps was intended to provoke—the exit of the left from the postwar coalitions. Currency stabilization thus accompanied the decisive break with Communist Parties under the Marshall Plan. But not before inflation surged in the United States as price controls were relaxed during 1946–1947. Indeed, the rise in American prices played a major role in the Europeans' dollar crisis that Washington had to answer with the Marshall Plan. The outbreak of the Korean War added a further impetus to inflation in 1950–1951, and by the 1960s, a systemic inflationary dynamic seemed at work. Lyndon Johnson chose to finance his increased military commitment in Vietnam from 1965 on with deficit funding—that is, government debt, which fed back into wage-price spirals. The efforts of the American state were going less into maintaining countervailing power than to supporting the rewards of both parties—industry and labor. In the United States and Western Europe, which did not face the collapse of the state and open civil war, the most conspicuous agent of inflation seemed to be the wage-price spiral as organized labor fought during the postwar years to catch up with price increases and simultaneously business leaders sought to defend their earnings against wage increases.

Inflation prevailed from the end of wartime price controls to 1949, then spiked again with the Korean War. The inflationary conjuncture, which Galbraith viewed as an exceptional condition that turned what should have been countervailing power into collusion among producer coalitions, would resume again from the mid-1960s through the 1970s. Like the global misery produced by the Depression of the 1930s but with opposite effect, the pervasive inflation would disorient routine politics (as Chapter 6 demonstrates). Where the 1930s helped strengthen the project-state, the inflation would eventually help to deconstruct it by the 1960s and 1970s. But in the 1950s, the inflation left by wartime had apparently abated. Currency stabilization would help to prevent the collusive behavior that Galbraith had discerned as the impediment to countervailing power. It assured that once the wave of postwar radicalism and labor's dreams of structural sharing of power ended, wage and hour issues would return to a central place in industrial relations.

Maintaining real income as price controls were lifted became a second priority for labor alongside preserving wartime employment levels. These were harsh concessions for industrialists but initially the apparent price for their continued ownership of their enterprises. It was a delicate negotiation of reciprocity to be tested in 1946 as postwar inflation surged and military orders ended. Employers on the continent chafed at having to retain what they saw as bloated workforces. But the model of collaborative relations initially held becausen Communist-affiliated unions urged their workers to accept wage restraint and continue the "battle for production" while the war went on and even into 1946. In France, it was the Socialists, and their new union federation Force Ouvrière that pushed strike militance whether in industry or the civil service; the Communists, party chair Jacques Duclos insisted, had to prove "that democracy is a regime of order, a regime of tranquility and of work."[19] By spring 1947, the French Communists felt compelled to stand behind a strike at the nationalized Renault works, which gave Paul Ramadier, Socialist prime minister in France, the opportunity to remove their ministers from his cabinet, a step soon followed in Belgium and then Italy. Ramadier sought to strike a balance: "We have to work to the utmost to get prices down to break the infernal cycle we have been trapped in; The first social reform, the [first] measure for *salut public* is lowering prices. On the other hand we can't tolerate miserable wages that don't even secure the daily bread." In Italy, Communists and the left also called for discipline: "We all seek socialism," exhorted the secretary of the Milan Camera del lavoro; "But do you believe we can socialize poverty?"[20] The harsh winter of 1946–1947 tested this discipline, and Communist union members responded to grassroots pressure to strike for salary increases or, as in Belgium, to continue the price freeze on heating fuel. The geopolitical wind was shifting in the spring of 1947 as Americans announced their aid to Greece and Turkey and prepared the intervention that became the Marshall Plan. For American policymakers, the moment had come to wager on social democracy to exclude the Communists: "The trend in Europe is clearly toward the Left," a State Department official minuted. "I feel that we should try to keep it a non-communist Left and should support Social Democratic governments."[21] The leaders of the American labor movement's two federations were coming to agree but still with significant difference in tone. For Irving Brown and Jay Lovestone of the AFL, removing the influence of the Communists remained the urgent objective. The CIO agreed but tended to remain more concerned with the actual struggle of the industrial workers for tolerable factory and living conditions.

By 1948, American labor representatives were integrated into the new trade union offices within the Marshall Plan's Economic Cooperation Administration (ECA) and its country missions.[22] The CIO and AFL maintained major international offices and developed a whole new realm of activity in effect, often as spokesmen for US foreign policy, working with Marshall Plan offices, which themselves were integrated into the embassies' economic divisions. These opportunities often intensified competition between the two labor federations. Their rivalry abated only when the CIO's rising hostility to the Communist currents within its own affiliated unions—primarily the United Electrical Workers (whose Irish leader James Carey was himself trying to purge his red elements) and the Longshoremen headed by the

West-Coast militant Harry Bridges—impelled emerging CIO chief, Walter Reuther, toward greater cooperation with George Meany's conservative federation. Nonetheless, the CIO remained more critical of American policy toward European labor than the AFL.

The CIO understood the costs of encouraging the labor union schisms even if they deplored the Communist influence over the major federations in France and Italy. In both countries, workers continued to support the major trade unions. In Italy, the General Confederation of Labor (CGIL), close to the massive Communist Party (PCI), faced a secession by Catholic workers, who formed a "Christian" federation (CISL). A social democratic current also split from Pietro Nenni's Socialist Party, which it viewed as in thrall to the Communists. With this split came a new social democratic trade union movement, the UIL, patronized by US policy makers and the AFL. Similar splits also characterized the French scene where the CGT faced the Socialists' Force ouvrière (FO) and the Catholic-oriented CFTC (later CFDT). In both countries, the Communist-affiliated federations remained far stronger, as American labor representatives recognized. In a lucid report to the CIO Committee on International Affairs a few years later, Victor Reuther (Walter's brother) argued that American propaganda had been ham-handed. Activity in Paris was too concerned with summitry and "too little preoccupied with the basic bread-and-butter issue which unite all French workers"; it had relied "to a dangerous extent on a too-simple and too-negative anti-Communism." Whereas in France, Washington was supporting the weaker FO against the more viable Catholics, in Italy, Americans had an opportunist Catholic secession, the CISL, which even more than FO (in France) "has won the unenviable reputation of being a political strike-breaking agency with a sterile anti-Communism for its program." American policy was paying a heavy price for the Italian Christian Democratic electoral victory over Communism in April 1948. In Germany, the American High Commission was closer to "reactionary employer groups" than to the German Trade Union Confederation (DGB).[23]

In contrast, to the French and Italian scene, the British TUC, the Swedish LO, and the West German DGB managed to remain united national labor federations. In Germany, the memory of common persecution by the Nazi regime, the presence of Allied occupying forces, and the example of the progressive subordination of labor to the Communist authorities in the east all worked to preserve a German union federation (DGB) that overcame the Catholic-Socialist divisions from the Weimar Republic.

But even these encompassing union federations faced what they saw as pro-Communist or "fellow traveler" domination of the postwar World Federation of Trade Unions (WFTU), originally organized within the League of Nations framework and including Soviet as well as American delegations. By 1948, the split was becoming glaringly inevitable. The AFL denounced the proposed appointment of Walter Schevenels as secretary of the Trade Union Advisory Committee because he allegedly worked "hand in glove with the Communists."[24] British and American trade union representatives found Louis Saillant, general secretary of the WFTU, little more than a dupe of the Communists. The divisions within the WFTU came to a head when its Executive Bureau convened in Paris in January 1949 and bitter denunciations were traded by the British and the Russians and the TUC delegates moved to suspend the organization. Giuseppe Di Vittorio, then president of the WFTU as well as general secretary of the CGIL, pleaded that there should be no hatred among workers and tried to smooth over the division. He could not resist adding, however, that when the Marshall Plan was originally under discussion, it was a fine idea, "but it was soon transformed into a military plan destined to lead to world domination by certain capitalistic interests," to which Arthur Deakin of the TUC and previous president of the WFTU replied that some of Di Vittorio's s points were "repulsive": "We have not expressed hatred. But we have been long suffering." James Carey of the CIO called for formation of a new federation. "At this point," admitted the CIO's careful notetaker, "the meeting became an uproar ... everyone was talking at once: Kuznetsov shouting 'no, no, no; Di Vittorio quite angry, shouting about dictators, democratic farces, etc.; Saillant stood up, waving the Constitution in Deakin's face ... and Deakin picked up his papers and his coat, waved, said 'Goodbye" and walked out of the room" along with the other British and the entire CIO delegation.[25]

These conflicts, which divided the ILO at the same time, were not only proxy conflicts of an overarching international Cold War.[26] Even as they found a place within that encompassing geopolitical conflict, they were genuinely local struggles. All levels of party and workers' organization were engaged simultaneously. Italian and French enterprises had "internal commissions" set up in the Resistance; the Germans enterprises had workers' *Betriebsräte*, which were more directly responsive to shop-floor grievances. The first battle in Italy was over layoffs. Industrialists believed that under pressure from the left, they had been compelled to hire labor during and after the liberation beyond what economic demand justified; by 1947–1948, they were seeking to trim what they saw as bloated workforces. With Communists removed from the coalitions, Alcide De Gasperi's Christian Democratic government supported industry leaders and indeed sent police to break up protest strikes. CGIL-affiliated workers saw a fundamental assault on their federations and attacked the unwillingness of the dissenting Christian unions (the CISL) to join their protests. As one insisted, "Our country is going through a tragic and difficult moment on both the political and labor-union level. Confronting the destiny that the capitalists and landlords are preparing for us we just can't accept the permanent immobilization of the working masses." Wage scales were a crucial stake, above all because of the impact of continuing inflationary pressures.[27]

With funding from American government agencies, including the Central Intelligence Agency, the American and British federations organized a new International Congress of Free Trade Unions (ICFTU) as a rival pro-Western force. Nonetheless, given the fundamental and irrevocable split, was organized labor really in a position to be a countervailing power to capital on a global scale? In the United States, it was clear that the GOP congressional majority that controlled the 80th Congress after the midterm elections of 1946 was a hostile force, while the Truman administration represented their best hope for progress. The Taft-Hartley bill that passed in 1947 over President Harry Truman's veto rolled back some of the gains of the Wagner Act. It still confirmed the right to organize a union if there was a majority vote of a plant's workforce, but it also prohibited the union's right to restrict employment to union members (a power known as the closed shop) and it allowed the federal government to delay a strike for eighty days in an industry it defined as critical for national security.

The fact was that labor in the West was too divided and unprepared to offer an alternative vision to the managerial capitalism that triumphed in the 1950s. The most ambitious plans, on the one hand, for industrial collaboration in the United States, on the other hand, for nationalization in Italy and France were shelved; neither were Communists making this a cause for industrial action.[28] Motivated by Moscow's calculations, they struck to oppose the Marshall Plan, not to restructure the economy. This did not mean that trade unions—whether CIO or AFL or TUC or FO or the West German unions—did not tenaciously defend labor interests in the workplace and discussions of social policy. Neither did it mean that the Communist-affiliated unions in Italy could not genuinely pursue labor aspirations. Nor did it mean that within the Communist countries, the trade unions ever really became an autonomous force; they remained a party emanation until the 1980s in Poland.

Nonetheless, postwar unions carved out a sphere of workers' collective dignity in the workplace. Industrial workers enjoyed representation in "internal commissions" within the factories and by 1951–1952 in West Germany, on corporate boards, after the DGB successfully mobilized a general strike to press the Adenauer government to finally push through codetermination for the coal and steel industries. Union objectives came to focus by the end of the 1940s less on overthrowing the capitalist order or on institutional transformation than on conditions of work and compensation, and circumstances conjoined to make these major contests through the mid-1960s. Wage scales were a crucial stake, above all because of the impact of continuing inflationary pressures. But this issue, too, opened up major divisions within the union movement and exposed the question of how labor was to be valued—within capitalism and state socialism. Who would pay for advances in productivity?

Wages and Productivity

Roughly speaking, wage systems divided between those that rewarded output (e.g., piecework) and those that paid according to labor time, with allowances made for differing levels of skill and seniority. As inflation grew more rapid, it leveled wage differentials since authorities conceded catch-up increases not as percentages of base pay but in absolute terms without regard to the underlying differentials. A catch-up pay hike equal for all had the effect of compressing the wage structure, in particular the differentials between workers hired en masse for industrial shop-floor jobs and those employed at supervisory or clerical tasks. As the director of the Renault firm, appointed by de Gaulle and soon to be confirmed as head of the nationalized enterprise, wrote to the minister of the economy in newly liberated France, "Every measure taken by successive governments since 1936 [the Popular Front] has favored firm members at the lower levels and the raises have always been less and less significant the higher one is in the hierarchy."[29]

Communist union and party leaders generally endorsed this effect; social democratic unions sought to restore hallowed differentials. The impact the system had can be seen more clearly by flashing forward to the quasi-revolutionary labor agitation of 1968–1969, when the issue arose again and the more egalitarian choice was sustained both in terms of wage hikes and then wage indexation (in absolute terms) for over a decade. In 1969, as Italy entered the "hot autumn," the FIOM (Federazione impiegati operai metalmeccanici—a category that included workers in basic steel production and the applied engineering industries such as auto or machine-tool production) demanded equal salary hikes for all their labor ranks. The sociologist Aris Accornero, committed to the labor movement, would highlight this choice as the major cause both for the union successes achieved and the ultimate demoralization and decline of Italian labor unity. The policy was not a long tradition for Italian labor, he argued: it was an ideological choice that responded to the demands of the radical student movement and the need to integrate the new influx of unskilled labor from the south, and over the course of the 1970s, it nurtured grievances among workers who had labored to elevate their skills.[30]

Analogous, if not the same, forces were present in the late 1940s and early 1950s. No rebellious student movement had yet emerged and the great migrations to Turin from the Mezzogiorno were just beginning. But the struggle against fascism and occupation had energized organized labor and intellectuals, and the Communist Party sought to press an activist policy. The great sorting of the organized working class into those who felt supported by Moscow and those who feared and rejected Communist loyalties took place not only in the arena of high politics but also in workplace struggles over pay and the conditions of work. In 1948, the Communist Parties and their large sympathetic union federations—the CGT in France, the CGIL in Italy—had engaged in major strike movements over their countries' participation in the Marshall Plan. In 1950, industry issues became paramount, but as the Paris embassy's economic observer noted, French employers in the private sector and the hard-line managers in the nationalized sector felt strengthened by "the weakened condition of the divided labor movement."[31] Signature contract negotiations arose for all the auto and metal-working industries in France and Italy in late 1950. At stake were complex mixes of base minimum wages and differentials for seniority (of primary concern in France) and productivity (contentious above all in Italy). The French employers sought a low but encompassing minimum wage for manual workers that allowed for differentials up to 70 percent by skill ratings. The French negotiations for the Paris region concluded at the end of October with a complex compromise that the non-Communist unions—FO and CFTC—accepted but which the CGT bitterly denounced as a betrayal of the originally agreed-on demands by all the unions and workers' advocates. All these controversies were keenly watched by the American labor representatives attached to the ECA mission, who in fact believed that the employers had won "the more substantial victory."[32]

The negotiations in Italy revealed the impact of the Marshall Plan's campaigns for productivity as the key to rising prosperity for business and labor alike. The priority took concrete form with the European Productivity Agency (EPA) organized within the structure of the Organisation for European Economic Cooperation (OEEC) in 1953 and wound up when the OEEC morphed into the Organisation for Economic Co-operation and Development (OECD).[33] Productivity did not refer merely to the level of output, which would become measured by gross national product (GNP, or alternatively by national income) and was also a key index of competition between the American and the Soviet spheres. Productivity, like efficiency, was a numerator with a denominator: the measure of output per worker or hours worked and, in conjunction with ideas of growth, the growth of output per worker. Rising productivity for Western or "bourgeois" economics was the answer to the harsh distributive conflicts envisaged by Marxists and pressed by militant labor unions in the 1930s. "If it weren't for possibilities of increased productivity," according to the research director of the Committee on Economic Development, "the struggle between capital and labor would be more severe and dangerous than it is."[34] Growing productivity supposedly meant that labor would benefit in growth proportionally to capital; the pie would grow and did not have to be sliced differently. American production in World War II had been a triumphant demonstration. The social democratic interlocutors of American trade unions had responded positively in general, and productivity missions that followed in the wake of the Marshall Plan had brought European workers and employers to the auto showcase of Detroit and elsewhere. But there was also suspicion that the celebration of joint effort and benefit concealed unequal sacrifice. Joint committees, such as the Anglo-American Council on Productivity, were fine, but industrialists, so labor spokesmen argued, supposedly saw productivity only in terms of minimizing labor costs and securing the consent of union representatives. If so, they did not really succeed; real wages seem to have risen in line with productivity at about 3 percent per year until the mid-1960s, at which point wages began to outpace productivity gains—a significant change of trend discussed in Chapter 6.[35]

Still, as Stefan Link points out, the point of the missions with their travel, dinners, and drinks together was to get "buy-in" from European labor and management on a collaborative or "human relations" approach to industrial production. Henry Ford had structured a factory around flow technology, and he paid workers well to subordinate their efforts to the imperatives of the assembly line, even as workers and foremen enjoyed a limited sovereignty on the shop floor. His grandson in the postwar period, Henry Ford II, subordinated the industrial process to the art of managing a multidivisional company, smoothing conflict, sublimating, as management guru Peter Drucker put it, "the concept of mass production" into "the concept of the corporation"—in less abstract terms, helping the Ford Company transition into a multidivisional firm along the lines of Alfred E. Sloan's General Motors. Drucker separated the governance of the "plant" where workers, contrary to Taylorist ideas, should determine the conditions of labor from control of the enterprise where management had clearly to retain oversight. The Americans organizing this effort did not think in Galbraith's terms of countervailing power but of supervised collaboration.[36] Their unacknowledged goal was to obscure conflict.

The concept of productivity had (and continues to have) an implicit corollary—namely, that national economies must remain inherently competitive on an international scale. From Marx to Molotov during the initial Marshall Plan discussions in summer 1947, critics emphasized the restless, expansionary nature of capitalism. Industries had to be more productive because ultimately, they were involved in a world market. Firms had to be able to export or remain competitive at home. The Marshall Plan had to be justified in terms of making national recipients "viable"—that is, capable of prospering without continual aid—in other words, by achieving a favorable international balance of payments (what would be made more precise decades later as their balance on current account). How all countries should achieve this in a zero-sum world remained unclear. But for the prophets of productivity, competition in the international arena, even the West European arena, hovered as a whiplash for prosperity, above all in Italy, Germany, and Japan.

Spokespersons for labor, on the other hand, such as the CGIL's Di Vittorio clung to national development strategies and stressed the need for raising wages to develop the internal market, preferably within the framework of a national plan such as the CGIL's Piano di lavoro.[37] Planning as such could be neutral and technocratic; it claimed to function in the realm of governance. Nonetheless, even in the case of the French planning agencies, headed by Jean Monnet, the optimal economic zone implicitly ex-

panded beyond the national territory to include German coal resources—
hence the expansionary logic that surged outward from the national plan of
1944–1945 to the Schuman Plan of 1950 for a Coal and Steel Community.
Latin American economists would make import substitution the centerpiece of their development strategies, paradoxically with the support of
American economists.

Productivity was a ruthlessly simplified metric. In the very years it was
being vaunted at FIAT, the sociologist Alain Touraine was conducting a long
study of the nationalized Renault works in Paris. Like some of the American analysts in the 1930s, he focused on the enterprise as a social unit but
without appealing to the mystique of the director, explaining that as the
postwar French auto enterprise produced for a mass market and shed its diverse prewar auto models, the logic of the factory changed. Paradoxically,
the "new system of labor, because it is technical, is entirely social"; it gave an
"illusion of technocracy." Yes, the worker was "increasingly directed, integrated
[*encadré*], subjected to precise instructions, subordinated to an administra-
tively complex technical hierarchy." Whereas workers in the ancillary tool
shops might retain skills, on the assembly line there was a "massive degradation
of labor." The skill needed by the assembly workers was only the capacity to
integrate himself into a social group."[38] Given the complexities of what Touraine called the structure of labor, how could one pin down the sources of
productivity growth? Touraine, working in Renault from 1948 to the mid-
1950s, avoided the term even as it became a magic formula throughout the
Marshall Plan orbit. But its ideological attractiveness for highlighting how
classes might collaborate (or demonstrating where they would not) won the
day and simplified the narratives for both capital and labor.

In that way, it complemented the other powerful algorithmic approaches
to political economy such as GNP (later gross domestic product [GDP]) and
economic growth. Entrepreneurs claimed that productivity derived from capital investment and refinement of productive processes. Labor feared that it
derived from extracting more labor per unit of compensation from the worker:
numbing tempos on an assembly line, what the French referred to as *chro-
nométrage*, longer hours, and heightened discipline. The unions referred to
Taylorism, but the role of Taylorite production developed before World War I
specifically speaking was vastly overestimated; Fordism was a concept
standing in for assembly-line and mass production.[39] Nor was the approach
absent under state socialism, where managers and party officials sought to
regulate and increase output according to "norms" of production—essentially,

quotas by units of time—a system that led to a major rebellion in East Berlin in June 1953, two years after the simmering controversies in the West.[40]

In Italy, wage workers felt that these schemes of supposedly Taylorized or Fordist labor practices amounted to a way of imposing what American workers knew from assembly-line labor as a "speed-up." The Italian unions were to call them *supersfruttamento* or "hyperexploitation" based on the manipulation of piecework rates (*cottimo*) so as progressively to make them labor longer or faster to maintain their compensation. Two revealing discussions took place within days of each other in Turin, Italy's auto city, in April 1951, almost as if a staged debate across class lines. At the annual meeting of stockholders on April 10, 1951, the general manager of FIAT, Vittorio Valletta, stressed the importance of productivity gains. Looking back to the results of 1950, the auto firm had booked sales of 150 milliard lire (then about $250 million), 35 milliard more than in 1949. "The significance of this figure lies in the fact that most of the increase is owed essentially to an *increment of productivity*. With the previous year, 1950, FIAT can be said to have completed the hard road started in 1946 to recover from the war." Valletta insisted that "maximum productivity does not mean, cannot mean, exploitation of workers. On the contrary it tends to value them morally and technically as an essential factor of production, as a citizen of the factory." The rapid rhythm of work "permitted by the modern machine tool is a determining element in lowering costs and thus multiplying the potential of labor. "Moreover, the more rapid rhythm of work is transformed by means of premiums and incentives for production into a higher wage. That can be verified despite the fact that in almost all sectors of the Italian engineering [*metalmeccaniche*] firms we are still far from the 'machine tempos' and the productive rhythms of American industry. . . . Trying prejudicially to represent the increase in production as a form of 'supersfruttamento' offends the consciousness and good sense of the worker himself. Yes, exploitation exists but exploitation of the prodigious machines . . . [far more so] than manual labor would allow."[41]

The FIAT stockholders also heard an updated concept of enterprise management at their annual meeting. It did not contradict affirming the value of private initiative, Valletta said, to argue that the single firm could no longer stand alone; it had to be supported by society in general and as a state responsibility. Export assistance was particularly important: credits, insurance, favorable trade agreements, and tax relief were all needed. Italian industry had had more than a third of its plant destroyed in the war; it faced high wages and charges for social insurance. America had provided Marshall aid;

now it could help with technical assistance. "The fabric of contemporary social life is sufficiently complex that in every economic sector and every country state intervention in production has become inevitable."[42]

Three days later, from April 13–15, the CGIL held the first national convention against *supersfruttamento* at labor headquarters (the Camera del lavoro). The labor spokesman denounced the "progressive colonization of our country on the part of foreign capital in general and American capital in particular." US policies of "subjection and extortion" had allegedly prevented Italian economic recovery; American aid was a front for "continual commercial penetration by colossal dumping"; it had created a situation of uncertainty and semi-stagnation. Workers' wages were keyed to the quantity of output, not the hours worked, exploitation climbed as a function of piecework (*cottimo*). The CGIL, he insisted, was not against productivity, but productivity should increase as a result of further mechanization. The unions did not want to go back to the wartime and early postwar conditions of 1945, but the government's statistical data revealed that from 1948 through 1950, production had risen by 19 percent in manufacturing and by 42 percent in extractive industries, owing largely to increasing hours of work. "It would require a long time to explain all the forms of exploitation in today's Italy. . . . The industrial *signori* have demonstrated an unsuspected fertile inventiveness in the field of hyper-exploitation." The methods included accelerating the pace of production and reducing the pay per unit of output, downgrading the workers' skill grade, using apprentices, outsourcing of tasks (*appalto*), and violations of contract as a condition for employment. "Hunger and poverty are driving workers to sell their labor power for a price lower than the necessities they require. . . . This can't be tolerated: the unions and the factory committees have to be able to intervene whenever the employers try to adopt these sorts of symptoms."[43]

Nor was it only the Italian left unions that saw dangers in productivity drives. American labor observers raised similar issues. By 1953, CIO observers of were charging "that the American Mutual Security Agency [the successor to the Marshall Plan] was overlooking that German management was trying to pervert the program for its own purposes." It was misguided for the agency to argue that workers' wage increases were unjustified since advances in productivity would be reflected in lower prices." And as far as "assurance against speed-up is concerned . . . such assurance is obtainable in the last analysis only on the basis of the workers retaining the right and having the ability to strike in self-protection if necessary. . . . From the very beginning of the talk about the productivity program in Germany, the DGB was given good reason to be suspicious of the program."[44]

My account focuses on Western Europe and North America—what would become known as the OECD countries, emerging from the OEEC that had been formed among the European grantees of the Marshall Plan. The 1950s proved a decade of robust growth and recovery of national income, often at the cost of reconstituting housing, unrenewed if not bombed out during the war, its squalid conditions often shocking American labor delegates.[45] Rebuilding of industrial plant was prioritized. *Les trente glorieuses*, the remarkable growth from the late 1940s into the 1970s, were hardly glorious at first for the working classes, whose growing welfare waited until at least until the mid- or late 1950s.

We can follow the interaction of capital and labor trends in developed and developing countries outside the North Atlantic area, in particular Japan in Asia and Brazil in Latin America. As in Europe, initial postwar Japanese conflicts arose over the efforts to shed labor that seemed redundant when wartime production needs collapsed. In contrast to France and Italy, no wartime resistance coalition existed to supervise solidarity pacts between unions and employers. Nonetheless, labor organizations waged a major rail strike and work stoppage at Toshiba to defend against mass sackings. Unions turned to "production control" tactics akin to the Italian "occupation of the factories" in 1920–1921 and the French sit-down strikes during the Popular Front of 1936. Each of these produced a far more bitter reaction than did mere strikes. (Now-retired American professors reading this chapter might recall their own shock and unease at student takeovers of their classrooms or university administration buildings in 1968–1970.) But control of a classroom in 1968–1969 would not prove equivalent to control of a complex university, and similarly in the late 1940s, control of the factory floor—even with workers dutifully accounting for all their materials and output—had a limited leverage on Japanese capitalism supported by the occupation authorities. "In the first two years after the war, organized workers gained far more than even their maximum prewar demands, as they built on the earlier desires for job security, wage security, and higher status within the firm and society. In this heady period of 'production control,' successful strikes, and rapid organizational gains, Japanese workers very nearly established a labor version of the Japanese employment system: guaranteed job security, an explicitly need-based seniority wage, and a significant labor voice in the management of factory affairs." As in Germany—but with no need in Japan to consult with British occupying authorities answerable to a Labour government in London—the American occupation regime (Supreme Command of the Allied Powers or SCAP) quickly turned from relatively benevolent support of Japanese labor to alarm at its leftward course. "The New Deal reformers who held sway during the period of initial post-surrender policy helped stimulate a labor offensive which far exceeded American expectations and brought major changes to both Japanese politics and labor relations within the enterprise.[46] SCAP grew alarmed at Communist inroads and in February 1947, prohibited a planned general strike and in 1950 fired 12,000 workers considered Communist Party members. The mid-course shift in American policy likewise helped management regain the upper hand. Management in the late 1940s and early 1950s defeated radical labor and rejected the labor version of Japanese employment practices.

The occupation regime also halted the breakup of Japanese industrial combines with the so-called reverse course and encouraged a new trade union federation, the Sohyo, to replace the radicalized labor organizations of 1945–1948. SCAP allowed the rebuilding of a powerful Federation of Employer Associations (Nikkeiren), which led the fight to reconstruct labor relations around new decentralized unions on the plant level. Pay issues became acute as a ravaging inflation raised rice prices sixtyfold by 1948. During 1946, labor had gained a larger role in winning uniformly rising wages. Unions "sought to reduce or eliminate the significance of output pay, and make those portions remaining as secure as possible"—hence ineffective as incentives. They also narrowed the gap between blue-collar and white-collar workers. As in Italy, the more militant unions called for fixed wage increases across all ranks; employers resisted and proposed to minimize those across-the-board components of the wage package "paid without reference to the quality of an individual's labor" and pay as much as possible according to factory performance.[47] The galloping inflation, which was conducive to wage levelling, was staunched at the end of 1948 with the so-called Dodge Line, a currency reform akin to that introduced by the Allies in West Germany the preceding spring, although provoking a far harsher stabilization crisis until the Korean War (and the Communists' victory in China) gave Japan a privileged role as America's strategic base in East Asia.[48] Over time, employers succeeded in reducing what the unions labeled livelihood wage; in their "Three Wage Principles" of 1954, the employers sought to tether wages to the profitability of the firm and gains in productivity rather than inflation and standards of living.[49] But as inflation abated, Nikkeiren also retreated from insisting on incentive-based pay so that it might bargain on the base wage. "The logic of capital, a wage reflecting the ability to pay," Andrew Gordon summarizes, "prevailed over the logic of the labor movement, a wage according to need."

The process was more brutal or at least harsher on unions than in the West. Between 1949 and 1952, Japanese exports and profits increased and a new credit squeeze in 1955 facilitated further rationalization and modernization of equipment, which rose from 4 percent to 10 percent from 1955 to 1961. The share of fixed investment rose from 19 percent of GDP in 1955 to 33 percent in 1961. Gross income from profits rose concomitantly from 31 percent to 39 percent and pretax business profits from 17 percent to 24 percent; employment in construction and electrical machinery grew sharply. But wage levels suffered for younger workers entering the labor market. Overall, however, wages rose as the Japanese economy, zealously shepherded by Ministry of Finance credits and Ministry of International Trade and Industry bureaucrats, forged ahead in the world. Essentially, labor gained welfare and security at the cost of collective power. The period 1949–1953 was one of harsh labor conflict, but by the mid-1950s a new employment relationship was solidifying: management dominated, but workers got assurances of employment and security. Dramatic strikes at Nissan in 1953, the Oji Paper firm in 1958, and Mitsui's Miike Coal Mines in 1960 with 100,000 policemen squaring off against union supporters ended in the acceptance of company unions.[50]

Had Galbraith written his book on Japanese capitalism, he would have had to emphasize a very different dynamic: not successful countervailing power but co-opted collaboration. Nationally, growth came in Japan, as in West Germany, with wages reduced as a share of national income but growing welfare as GNP rose rapidly—the premise of the politics of productivity. Performance encroached on the livelihood wage—seniority became a criterion on which both sides could settle. "By the mid-1950s wage bargaining in Japan followed the same basic pattern it has ever since." Thanks to investment, hourly labor productivity increased far more rapidly than wages did between 1950 and 1955.[51] The Japanese settlement had its own special emphasis, an assurance of "belonging" to the factory community—that double-edged concept that could not only enhance workers' sense of inclusion but also suppress their capacity to bargain. But if we compare the long-term results with Britain, where unions fiercely resisted the factory-community ideal, the result was indeed what the Americans had promised for productivity—a vast increase in economic growth.

The Brazilian case suggests that without US oversight, the politics of productivity was not easy to stabilize. Workers' legislation developed in the 1920s and 1930s and codified under the Estado Novo by the corporatist labor laws (CLT) in 1943 supposedly granted worker rights. In fact, it allowed employers to crack down on unions, especially after Brazil joined the UN Relief and Rehabilitation Administration in 1944, as part of the global anti-Axis crusade. Nevertheless, wartime inflation and industrial conflict exploded in 1945–1946 and workers gained substantial wage hikes. But by mid-1947, the conservative government—Vargas had been voted out in 1945—cracked down on the unions. It established a new organization, the Social Service of Industry (SESI), advocated by the São Paulo industrialists as a defense supposedly against Communist control of the unions. To finance its activities, the government imposed a 2 percent national payroll tax and assigned the resources to the employers' national organization. Proceeds were used to support a chain of subsidized food stores for union members, designed to put the workers' co-ops out of business. By 1960, SESI shops had expanded enrollment from about 700,000 to 4.6 million workers.[52] Dissolution of the Communist Party followed in May 1947—at the same moments the national Communist Parties were being extruded from Western European governments.

Vargas, however, returned as a pro-labor candidate in 1950, and his government restored the freedom of union elections in 1952. In the state of São Paulo, producer of about half of Brazil's industrial output, a new encompassing labor federation was formed in 1951 and brought the city to a halt during March and April 1953. In 1953, the government appointed João Goulart as minister of labor from the Brazilian Labor Party (BTB); he would be removed in 1954 but remained influential. Vargas faced a mutiny from military units and committed suicide in the same year, leaving no leader with equivalent power in a system that traditionally relied on personalist and regional authority. Successive governments oscillated between efforts at repression and accommodation; to cite a student of the country's industrial relations, the basis for a corporatist accommodation between labor and management, which could turn the upsurge in productivity in an equivalent increase in real wages and welfare, seemed precarious during the 1950s and early 1960s. The effort by the US-sponsored ICFTU regional bureau to stabilize social democratic labor organizations was unsuccessful; Brazilian moderates gained little traction and could not split the larger unions. Even when less accommodating governments were in power during the 1950s, the left retained its local positions of power. But the left could not close the gap between real wages and productivity gains even as it retained control of the labor movement. The United States gained support for hard-line anti-communism but not for a more stable coalition with social democratic leadership.[53] Labor representation would soon be on the defensive. "Troublesome" workers would be fired; major strikes were frustrated. The unions would reassert their demands for industrial democracy and control in the second half of the effervescent 1960s, only to have the military take power and impose a brutal dictatorship until the 1980s.[54]

More generally, labor's postwar élan was fading. The heroic worker of Popular Front murals gave way to the visionary entrepreneur and businessman. The 1950s saw the industrial leader—whether an owner of his firm or a professional manager—reclaim prominence as a figure of heroic proportions, celebrated not only by himself and his colleagues but business schools and journalists alike. The trend had started, of course, much earlier, as noted particularly by American social critics, but emphases changed. The iconic business figure from before World War I until the world depression (1910–1930) had been the organizer of mass material production, often an engineer who combined innovative technological acumen with a sense of the mass market personified by Henry Ford. By the 1930s, he was reenvisioned as a skilled psychologist and motivator of a complex organization, a master of "industrial civilization." His task was to motivate the collective masses. The German Goetz Briefs, now forgotten but influential between the wars, saw the proletariat as a psychological mass that had to be reconciled to modernity. The management guru Elton Mayo and his follower F. J. Roethlisberger of the Harvard Business School argued that "the function of management, in its most general terms, can be described as that of maintaining a social system of the industrial plant in a state of equilibrium such that the purposes of the enterprise are realized." The rise of fascism indicated in the interwar years that the reigning view of human nature was darkening, the vulnerability of the masses to irrational impulses required leaders who could shape motivation and organization psychology.[55]

Postwar recovery and the dominance of the US economy changed the valence of management once again. Industrial society needed to steer between murky fascist appeals and Marxian socialism: the manager—now the executive—strode to the top as the expert on preserving a political equilibrium as well as an expert in productivity. He was not a reactionary: the industrialists grouped in the American Committee on Economic Development, including Paul Hoffman of the ECA (and briefly the Ford Foundation) welcomed interventionist budgeting to avert depression. "We must participate in the formation of public policy, even though the specific issues may not have an immediate influence on our individual businesses," and overcome group interests, argued one writer in 1951.[56] The claims made for him by business school analysts, journalists, and sometimes sycophants grew more and more exaggerated. "In many respects the role of the policy-forming executive in a business enterprise is unenviable," the *Harvard Business Review* told its apparently under-rewarded readers. "It is a perpetually demanding role; its rewards, both economically and socially, are rarely commensurate with the sacrifices it entails. . . . Only the exceptional and dedicated individual is truly fitted."[57] The robustness of recovery in Germany, Japan, and Italy and the competition with the Communist model meant that the executive was the natural leader. *Leadership*—revived in our own times today with all its ambiguities of irrationalism—was a requisite for capitalism, for democracy, for dictatorship, and for warfare.[58] The Weberian aura of charisma, which had played so troubling a role in interwar politics, was channeled in the 1950s into the rhetoric of capitalist economic leadership—with an occasional titrate of bureaucratic "iron cage" pessimism.

Productivity, Growth, and Development

The European and Japanese growth rates of the 1950s and 1960s seemed to confirm the Marshall Plan's emphasis on productivity. "The improvement of productivity, in its widest sense, remains the fundamental problem of Western Europe," intoned the OEEC. "Great emphasis is placed in the United States . . . upon public relations efforts by management in acquainting worker with their plant, its problems, and its place in the economy."[59] The question for business and industry was what combination of technological and organizational improvements and lowering of unit input costs (including wages) would best secure productivity advances. The question for labor was whether they would have to bear the greater burden. Experts talked about technology and moving labor into the areas of high growth; and in fact, the migrations from country to city, and in Italy from south to north, were a chief motor.[60] The migrations reflected the fact that agricultural productivity surged as robustly as industrial productivity, such that—as had occurred a century earlier in Britain and Belgium—a far smaller percentage of farmers produced the needs for West European families. Commentators recognized German, Italian, and Japanese "economic miracles" by the late 1950s. Some observers attributed them to American interventions, whether the Marshall Plan or the decision to incur a major military operation in Korea. Others perceived the need for these populations to work together to overcome the destruction they had suffered in the war. Few speculated as to whether the fascist and military regimes might have somehow inculcated a heightened discipline on the part of labor, if only because their subjection in the 1930s and 1940s bequeathed a continuing sense of vulnerability.[61] Remarkable, too, was the fact that although there were minor recessions in 1957, no major economic slump ended the decade of growth from the end of the 1940s to the end of the 1950s—the trend would continue through the 1960s. Further political interventions helped forestall what until then had seemed the normal ten-year life span of an economic cycle; these included the restoration of full convertibility of Western European currencies in 1958, the creation of the European Common Market between 1957 (the Treaties of Rome) and 1963 (the Common Agricultural Policy).

The central, indeed magical, indicator of this surging prosperity was no longer the employment rate or even the steel tonnage but the rate of economic growth. Economic growth theory had been explored by British and American economists right before the war, at a moment that growth hardly seemed to function. Being able to conceptualize it, whether in the form of national income statistics or as an input-output table, was an epistemological achievement that could be said to originate with Sir William Petty's protostatistical efforts at "Political Arithmetick" in the late seventeenth century. Interwar economists had begun to quantify national outputs and also to conceive "the economy" as a global system in its own right, an insight that Schumpeter's posthumous *History of Economic Analysis* traced back to the physiocrats' notion of an annual cycle of harvests, consumption, and surplus for reseeding. Commercial censuses carried out by national and American state governments assigned quantities of outputs and inputs. Keynesian theory placed an emphasis on grouping such components of economic activity as savings and consumption, investment, and government spending. Estimating their quantity as components and as a whole required statistical refinement especially when the goal was to compare them from one year to another. How much larger or wealthier was a society in the present than at a chosen point in the past? Totally new products made their appearance and societies place much more effort or less in producing them. Relative prices changed—one might compare intertemporally if one held prices constant (but with respect to which year?) or quantities but one could not do both—the economists' version of Werner Heisenberg's uncertainty principle. There were differences between capitalist societies and the Soviet economy, which did not really like to assign quantities to services. And then, once consensus might be reached on measurement, how should a society assure economic growth and not merely full employment or prosperity?[62] Economists in the late 1930s explained why it was so hard to guarantee: if a society saved too much at the expense of consumption, falling demand would choke off expansion; if it did not save enough, inflation would eat up any surplus in nominal dollars. Economies climbed along a precarious "knife-edge" trail and could easily fall into the abyss on either side.

The apparently prodigious performance of the economy during the war and further reflection on the New Deal loosened the constraints. After the war, Robert Solow demonstrated that technological innovation made the path to growth less precarious, more of a smooth gradient the economy could count on ascending. Truman's head of the Council of Economic Advisers, Leon Kayserling, was perhaps the first policymaker to evoke the promise, not just of recovery from the Depression or wartime destruction but of continuing year-on-year growth.[63] Economic growth allowed a policy of allocative neutrality; workers as well as managers would benefit from the size of the pie and would not insist on cutting wider angular slices, which would have to come at the cost of others' shares. America's unions accepted wage-price guidelines, agreeing to limit wage increases to productivity gains. The notion of increasing productivity became the leitmotiv of American ideology. It was incorporated into the ECA's Productivity Missions and soon became the dominant theme for the European recipients organized as the CEEC and later as the OECD. Productivity growth was the prerequisite of economic growth.

But was growth equivalent to development? The idea of development suggests a qualitative change in a society's output to higher value-added production—crudely put, to an economy of less muscle and more brains. Matthias Schmelzer's study of the OECD shows how that statistical agency, originating as the Europeans' office for coordinating their response to the Marshall Plan, became a major nexus of economic knowledge about growth and development. The forerunner organization of 1947–1948, the OEEC came to depict the Marshall Plan as a development program for Europe, whose lessons its successor of 1959–1960 would transmit to former colonies in the third world. "Development" as such, though, I would suggest, had become implicit in what I would term the "second" Marshall Plan of 1950–1952, when European integration and concern with backward regions became leading preoccupations. The first phase of the European Recovery Program, what I would term the "first Marshall Plan," had responded to the frightening setbacks in early 1947 to postwar recovery as coal shortages, rail and canal shipping breakdowns, labor unrest, and the congealing division of Germany all seemed to threaten an economic implosion. After that emergency was averted by 1949–1950, the ECA had to convince Congress that European economies could return to "viability," that is, a balance of payments equilibrium that would not require a continuing supply of dollar credits.[64] Washington ECA officials and the European recipients both sensed that ideas of productivity and development should be added to the goals of foreign aid. The OEEC economies would move to higher levels of efficiency and more modern technologies. They would "develop" along American lines.[65]

The concept of development and development assistance unsurprisingly had earlier origins. Alexander Hamilton clearly had a notion of development in mind when he advocated transforming the agrarian American republic into a commercial and industrial power that could emulate Great Britain. Albert Sarraut's concept of *la mise en valeur* of the French Empire implied the need to develop colonial economies but for the benefit of the metropole. So too Western takeover of customs collection was designed primarily to secure debt repayment in China or Turkey. As Jamie Martin's study emphasizes, the new idea that League of Nations agencies might help secure and supervise development assistance was controversial. The league reluctantly accepted the innovation, originally to help Greece resettle the refugees arriving from Turkey as stipulated by the 1923 Lausanne Treaty. Arthur Salter, who had served in Vienna to oversee the league's stabilization loan would travel to China a few years later to supervise the League's mission there. As Sara Lorenzini points out, Sidney Caine of the Colonial Office introduced the idea of development planning with his noted memorandum of August 1943. Citing the Soviet Union and Tennessee Valley Authority, Caine called on the state to become a planning agency for the empire and bring about a decisive rise in productivity. The British Colonial Office drew up plans for a new Colonial Development Corporation based on the revenues from the marketing boards that imperial civil servants were helping to initiate.[66]

Ultimately, the idea of development thrived alongside that of growth and productivity. "Modernization" would join this cluster of concepts. In his inaugural address of January 20, 1949, President Truman floated what became the celebrated Point Four program, an extension of Marshall Plan foreign assistance to help develop the third world.[67] The reorganized OECD of 1960 (of which the United States became a member), the UN Development Programme, and the International Bank for Reconstruction and Development (which would be rebaptized as the World Bank) became centers for development economics as would the US Agency for International Development. Point Four itself aroused a lot of enthusiasm, but it became less transformative than the Marshall Plan. The US agencies in charge looked for discreet small-scale economic interventions and always stressed its Cold War role as an alternative to Communist appeals. Funding was sparser and the projects were often explicitly linked to private investment schemes. The Kennedy administration would focus these efforts as the "Alliance for Progress" targeted at Latin America. But this program, too, had clear limits of funding. And with only slightly less innocent ignorance about Latin America than it had for Africa, Washington presupposed a "third world," easily oversimplified as a realm of underdevelopment, war, military dictatorship, and irrational economic schemes. With some notable exceptions, Americans and retreating colonial authorities found it hard to listen to the aspirations of societies they were no longer ready to control by military compellence.

But return at the end of the 1950s to the "Atlantic" area, largely governed since the start of the decade by the GOP, the Tories, Christian Democrats, and centrists of various stripes, according to local contexts. Cast a glance, too, at Japan, safely under Liberal Democratic Party management. During most of the 1950s, they all enjoyed a golden age of a system that looked much like what conservative German economists had dubbed ordoliberalism. Among the larger countries, it worked best in the United States and Germany. Significant sectors of socialist parties and intellectuals were renouncing Marxist collectivism: Anthony Crosland's *Future of Socialism* (1956) rejected the Labour Party's commitment since 1918 to nationalization of the leading sectors of the economy, relying instead on the power of sustained economic growth, and the party itself lost its third general election of the decade in 1959, prompting much soul-searching about its remaining orthodox commitments.[68] The Social Democratic Party's Godesberg Program of 1959 signaled peace with capitalism and private ownership. The massive strikes of the early 1950s in Europe and Japan lay, it seemed, decisively in the past. Labor's representatives wanted more in the way of workplace control than employers were happy to give and they bargained for higher wages but not necessarily a higher share of national income than productivity advances supposedly justified. (And in the state-socialist world, labor was even more under control of a state party, having traded most independence of action for a regime nominally acting in its name, and when challenging the Communist status quo in East Germany in 1953 and Hungary in 1956, crushed by force. Only in Poland after the Bread and Freedom demonstrations did Moscow allow a more autonomous but still loyal leadership to emerge.)

If one surveyed the United States and Western Europe, Galbraith's idea of countervailing power might be judged to be a broadly applicable principle of equilibrium, effective within but also far beyond the shores of the United States. Inside America's boundaries, the long Democratic Party regime—reformist on issues of labor, frozen (except for desegregation of the armed forces) on issues of racial injustice that seemed increasingly unsustainable—had been succeeded by the center-right GOP. And beyond American shores, the approximately ten years after 1958 brought a rare equilibrium of forces balancing states that still maintained social welfare projects; ambitious centers of governance—whether lodged in the UN, established by national governments or by private foundations; and the networks of capital—still regaining confidence after the war and its rupture of trade and commerce. At the end of the decade, Daniel Bell—a creative bellwether among social scientists, his antennae always quivering to detect the political currents of the day—published his essay, "The End of Ideology: On the Exhaustion of Political Ideas in the 1950s," essentially an obituary for American radicalism.[69]

The "third world" was a different story: it seethed with overt or potential struggles for the future of Cuba, South Vietnam, the Congo, and Algeria as the calendar ticked toward and into the 1960s. Was the new regime of Fidel Castro to remain within the economic and political possibilities blessed by Washington and ensuring a safe dependency (albeit one less reliant on casinos and American tourists), or would Havana gravitate toward Moscow's orbit with the implications for domestic suppression that that choice would entail? And would Washington, France's heir as protector of non-Communist Indochina, compel the South Vietnamese finally to hold the plebiscite on unification with the North promised by the Geneva Accords of 1954, or recognizing the de facto subversion of the south, agree to postponement and a forever war? Would the emerging Congo follow the charismatic *Marxissisant* leadership of Patrice Lumumba, or could the Union Minière manage to rescue its copper and mineral interests in a secessionist Katanga under the West's courtier Moïse Tshombe? (Belgium had long been an anomalous construction: it had, and it needed, projects to precariously hold together its Flemish and Wallonian halves; its monarch in World War I had enhanced its status by courageous resistance; its monarch in

World War II had undermined its cohesion by rapid surrender. After World War II, administration of the Congo on the one hand and conspicuous leadership of the European Community on the other hand provided the projects. Both entailed an outsize influence for the institutionalized forces of Belgian capital—the Société Générale and Union Minière and indirectly the respected Banque Nationale. The European project also allowed scope for enthusiasts for governance. Brussels would walk away from its colony brusquely in 1960, without taking responsibility for the debris left behind, preserving varnished memories in the racialized exhibits at the Tervuren colonial museum, and paying the price only in the intensified internal conflict that the end of its colonial role bequeathed its Flemish and French communities.) As for Algeria, would General de Gaulle's fledgling Fifth Republic manage a face-saving autonomous status for what it maintained was a component of France itself or have to accept that the terrorist tactics of the National Liberation Front could not be overcome in a world of transnational sanctuaries? (The decolonization of Black Africa and the Antilles were easier: the French cultural capital accepted by the colonial authors of *Négritude* did allow peaceful separation and clientelism.)

In retrospect, we can ask whether the particular equilibrium among states, capital, and the realm of governance could have been long preserved. Project-states were likely to strengthen the role of capital at home, whether intentionally through the ideologies and interests that motivated the conservative party custodians who governed in the 1950s, including rearmament contracts, and ultimately by provoking resistance to the programs of the left who came to power in the 1960s. Resource empires—a form of state—had become retreating empires, seeking to preserve their privileges through negotiated or quasi-coerced economic ties such as oil and mineral concessions, thus often by fusing their interests with those of capital. Then, too, the equilibrium of the 1950s might come to feel oppressive in its own right—the last hurrah of a surviving generation from the interwar and wartime years, continuing to call for political and social discipline and bound to provoke a demand for youthful cultural liberation at home. There were signs of this in the serious rioting that met the visiting vice president of the American hegemon in Latin America in 1958 and the even more disturbing Anpo protests against the security arrangements with the United States that rocked Japan a year later.

By the late 1950s, the global "order"—if in fact it was an "order" and not just a moment when countervailing powers had reached a brief stalemate—incorporated two moments of force. The one lay along a metaphoric east-west axis: the Cold War that opposed an American-led community of states with mixed economies against the state-socialist bloc. The other was constituted by the metaphoric north-south tensions that were the legacy of empire and colonialism. Some differences were fought out, or at least to a standstill along the east-west, and others on the north-south, but most of the important issues raised elements along both axes. In the UN, the communist countries lost no opportunity to align themselves with the voices of the global south, while the countries of the global north would claim they were defending the West in seeking to perpetuate their quasi-imperial preponderance. The conflicts could not remain orthogonal to each other. Neither, moreover, could they remain contests only between national state units. The contending forces were hardly black boxes. Rather, the international countervailing powers pulled the social forces within states into their own confrontational alignments, as if they were iron filings caught within a magnetic field. The balance of forces might prove very ephemeral. As of the late 1950s and early 1960s, these nested contests appeared to have reached a tense equilibrium, the isometric standoff that Galbraith believed defined American capitalism or that Kennan urged on Americans to pursue the Cold War. Again the question arises, could this parallelogram of forces, east and west, north and south, domestic and external, have long endured?

Changing moral assessments of colonial hierarchies would continue to erode whatever presumptions of legitimacy even a reformed colonial order retained. In the spring of 1958, for example, reacting to the French pursuit of Algerian forces in neighboring Tunisia—and the "collateral damage" it produced after the bombing of the hospital at Sakiet Sidi Youssef—the young senator from Massachusetts John Kennedy threw his weight behind bringing that colonial war to the UN, despite the NATO alliance. The realm of governance remained something of a wild card. At the same time, the evolution of technology and distribution of material resources could exert incentives for change. The web of capital (and in the socialist world, of state capital) continued its own inexorable pressure.

6

Contesting the Postwar Order

Coal, Steel, Oil, and Dollars, 1950s–1970s

Prelude: Looking Back from 1968

Sometime around the mid-1960s, the social equilibria, West and East—attained under conditions of austerity in the 1950s and cemented by the ideological discipline of the Cold War—began to shake apart ever more discernably. Cultural shifts provided the most dramatic indications of an approaching earthquake, its rumblings audible before the ground heaved. If you were young and living in what the left termed the capitalist world in the 1960s, you were into music and movies. If the most popular new music came from America and Britain, the vanguard "cinema" was identified as a product of continental Europe, supposedly as a "new wave" that bestowed on enthusiastic cineasts two decades of revelatory films from the mid-1950s on, including, among others, Ingmar Bergman's brooding Swedish ruminations on death and aging, Federico Fellini's depictions of postwar Italian wealth and anomie, and as ideology grew urgent, Jean-Luc Godard's *The Chinese Girl* (*La chinoise*) in 1967. Except that she wasn't Chinese but a young French university student from a middle-class background who lived with her boyfriend and another young man from the provinces who would find it increasingly hard to accept their carelessly adopted violent radical politics, and with a young woman, in from the farm, trying to latch on to the urban scene and finding her place as a sort of unavowed servant girl to the others. All of them were continually discussing how to exist in their allegedly hopelessly unjust society even as they lived off the inequalities they found so intolerable in theory. The Communist alternative that Russia represented had become bureaucratic and repressive, and only Chairman Mao Tse-tung, whose simplistic aphorisms were inscribed in the "little red book"—dozens of copies of which were the main prop on the set—had a genuine commitment to ongoing revolution. Mentored by a tolerant liberal left professor who proves unable to say that killing in the name of revolution is wrong, Godard's *chinoise* and her complaisant boyfriend become convinced that only Maoist rituals of violence can bring down an unjust bourgeois order—as they were supposedly doing in China.

Godard listened in at a moment during which postwar radicals were looking toward a rural-based revolutionary activism that they associated with the North Vietnamese struggle against the Americans in Southeast Asia, with Che Guevara's effort to replicate Fidel Castro's revolutionary seizure of power in mainland Latin America, and finally with the unparalleled Chinese turmoil of the Great Cultural Revolution. Make two, three, many Vietnams, Che had urged. Régis Debray proclaimed Latin America as the theater for ending American imperialism. In Mao's effort to rekindle what he remembered as the fervor of his early movement, tens of millions of city dwellers would be denounced and bullied and sent for reeducation at harsh village labor sites, and perhaps millions would be lynched after kangaroo court hearings. In the West, the fans of such terror were a small though disquieting minority. As a member of a student faculty committee summoned in 1967 to repair the growing polarization at my own American university, this author listened carefully too. Not to the local Maoists who were no more than a fringe, but to the far wider discontents that were cresting across the universities of the globe. Radical student movements had made headlines by their provocative demonstrations on behalf of flaunting bad language in Berkeley in 1964, but they soon moved to protests against the war in Vietnam, animating what became the nationwide Students for a Democratic Society and their slogan of "participatory democracy," supposedly an exertion of direct action in public spaces because the routines of electoral democracy seemed to change so little.

The sources of radicalism were multiple. The postwar university—with its vast expansion of students in Europe and in some of the American states like California—was a privileged site of origins but simultaneously a center for widespread generational insecurities. European students focused on American "imperialism" but also envisaged a problematic personal future. The new universities were part of a decisive expansion of postsecondary school education in the 1960s. They consisted often of upgraded normal schools, new campuses of older venerable institutions in urban settings, and the additional layer of schools variously called polytechnics in Britain, community colleges in the United States, and their equivalent.[1] Preparing the qualified middle classes of the future, they also incubated the discontented of the present. Clark Kerr, president of the University of California system, developed the concept of the multiversity: higher education would train the new administrative elites for the technocratic society at hand.[2] Many students found this vision uncongenial: were they being prepared only as cogs in a well-functioning machine?

More fundamentally perhaps than the immediate aftermath of World War II, the global sixties resembled the years 1917 to 1921. Between 1944 and 1948, the victors in World War II had set a limit to revolutionary passions. They had channeled demands for vengeance into trials, and would-be revolutionaries had agreed that the needs of reconstruction were imperative—from motives of Stalinist *Realpolitik*, the Soviets had managed to keep hold of the left. The French and British offered reform projects but seemed determined to retain ultimate control of their colonies; US policymakers had overcome any lingering doubts about maintaining an active role in occupied Japan and Germany. From the mid-1950s to the mid-1960s, the forces of radicalism appeared to settle in the so-called third world. The Bandung Conference of 1955, the socialist and nationalist programs of Gamal Abdel Nasser in Egypt, Kwame Nkrumah in Ghana, Castro in Cuba, Ahmed Ben Bella in Algeria— all patronized by Soviet and Chinese policy—suggested that the global south was at the vanguard of world-historical transformation.[3] By the mid-1960s, radical enthusiasm had blown back to ignite students and minorities across the first world as well. State managers and elites seemed caught off balance when a new cohort of radicals surged into the streets in the late 1960s. In effect, popular intervention and demands flooded like a rampaging river over the banks of the institutions that had been built in the aftermath of World War II. Among those threatened were the competing political parties that had channeled popular and elite aspirations from the early nineteenth to the mid-twentieth century. What the Germans called the extraparliamentary opposition claimed to be the force of the future. Parties were weakened not only in democratic regimes. Soviet suppression of rebellious Czechoslovakia had sacrificed the ideological resources that world Communist Parties provided Moscow. The Italian Communist Party refused to endorse Leonid Brezhnev's insistence on socialist solidarity (the Brezhnev Doctrine), and the emergence of "Eurocommunism" received a decisive impetus.

White America and its students in particular were aroused most by America's commitment to the Vietnam "quagmire." The Geneva Conference of 1954 had divided the former French colony at the 17th parallel and provided for elections to take place in the south to resolve its future. Supported by the United States, the military rulers of the south postponed the elections as they faced infiltration from the north and its support for an armed National Liberation Front, soon to be known as the Viet Cong. President John Kennedy, captivated by the new doctrines of guerrilla struggles for the "hearts and minds" of the peasant population, had sent military advisers to little avail; in February 1965, his successor, Lyndon Johnson, committed a major increase of ground troops. Only by 1968 after the Viet Cong's Tet Offensive and mass demonstrations against the war in the cities and on university campuses did Johnson decide there must be negotiations and that he must refrain from running for another term given the turmoil in the country.

The passionate divisions over the purpose and conduct of the war brought American university students into activist politics. But it was hardly the entire reason for a movement that caught up Europe and Latin America as well. Mass action in America had already mobilized around the civil rights movement. The "nonviolent" civil rights marches of Martin Luther King Jr. threatened to be eclipsed by the less patient rallies of Black Muslims around the talented leader Malcolm X, soon to be assassinated, perhaps at the behest of the patriarch of the movement, Elijah Muhammed. King's own leadership was challenged by "ghetto" revolts in Detroit, New York, and central Los Angeles (Watts) in the mid-1960s, and King himself would be assassinated by a white racist in May 1968. In the spring of 1968, triggered by the school's closing of a gym that bordered the glacis separating it from Harlem, student protests paralyzed Columbia University for several weeks,

Restiveness had already made its way to the large student populations of Berlin, where protests against the shah's visit in 1967 led to serious clashes with police and the death of one student. French student unrest erupted in the bleak new university of Nanterre (today's Paris X), and the seizure of Nanterre spread to the most spectacular student revolt of all in Paris, which the government hesitated to suppress until it threatened to bring down the Gaullist regime. The Mexican authorities faced a summer of demonstrations until in early October they finally left hundreds dead in the Tlatelolco quarter of Mexico City. Universities became the site of upheavals in Latin America, Italy, Britain, Africa, and Indonesia. Many students resented the self-righteous radicalism of their activist colleagues, but it only took an organized core to paralyze classes, intimidate professors, abolish grades, and press for a voice in university governance (as well as classroom organization), above all where university administrators decided to summon the police. Even after the takeovers ended, the organizations persisted and demonstrations resumed with the American incursion into Cambodia in 1970. The most disaffected would migrate over during the course of the 1970s into the hard core of America's Weather Underground or the diverse Red Brigades of Italy and Germany who embarked on a half decade of shooting industrialists and political leaders. The practitioners of class terror would thus join the cohorts of those killing in the name of national liberation such as the Irish Republican Army or the Basque ETA.

The protests of the 1960s were hardly conspiratorial. Nor were they confined to students. We could begin a survey of 1968, not with Columbia University in April or Nanterre in May but with the garbage piling up for ten days on the streets of New York from February 2 to 12, as angry sanitation workers denounced their union leaders' settlement and refused to collect trash. Or with the Memphis, Tennessee sanitation strike that began on that day and drew Martin Luther King to rally the African American trash collectors in their demands for union recognition in February and March and to his assassination on April 4. Race and class converged in these strikes by workers at the bottom of the social pyramid. So, too, many of the European proletariat came from the Italian south, or the Turkish provinces, or the relinquished colonies. They were new to the industrial cities, found the factory discipline oppressive; and the older established trade unions were challenged by newer "autonomous" organizations, ready to support the agitation of 1968. During the "hot autumn" of 1969, strikes and protests brought Italy's industry close to paralysis.

Nor were the European Communist states unaffected. Dissidence had been growing since Nikita Khrushchev's "secret speech" of 1956 denouncing Stalinist excesses and subsequent thoughts of reform. In the countries where the regimes depended on the presence of Soviet troops, restiveness grew, not yet to challenge the Warsaw Pact outside of Czechoslovakia but certainly there in a major way in 1968. By the spring of 1968, multiple foyers of protest ignited and flared. Nonetheless, the revolution had misfired at best. Brezhnev who early on had seemed hospitable to reform decided that he could not tolerate the Czechs following their separate path. Their demand to leave the Warsaw Pact clinched his determination to suppress the reform movement. In Paris, Charles de Gaulle seemed to hesitate, but his prime minister, Georges Pompidou, argued that order must be restored, and the army supported this program. Workers in France and Italy won major wage increases—with the Grenelle Accords, the French CGT agreed to return to work, leaving students on their own. The students at Columbia University won some committee discussions but were forcibly removed from the campus buildings, as were those at Harvard and elsewhere in 1969.

The upheavals continued elsewhere, at least for a while. Salvador Allende led a Socialist-Communist coalition to electoral victory in Chile in 1970, displacing Eduardo Frei's Christian Democrats whose slow pace of reforms had increased impatience in the electorate. Three years later, the Chilean military, supported by a broad swathe of the country's middle classes, had liquidated Allende's Latin American experiments. The military governments in Argentina and Brazil decided that the whole leftist student culture of their countries must be arrested and, indeed, many of its members physically liquidated. And while counterrevolutions clamped down in the Southern Cone, militant revolutionaries were taking over in the Middle East from rulers they believed far too compliant with European and American paymasters. How had this degree of turmoil come to pass? What brought so many societies to the earthquakes of the late 1960s? And to signal the concerns of the next chapter, what would be different after 1968?

Systemic Change

If Montesquieu had been around in the 1960s and 1970s, he would have diagnosed a seismic slippage in what he meant by the spirit of the laws—a reseating of social relationships on a global scale, legal and material, comparable to other profound shifts that had marked world politics at intervals of roughly a century—epochal caesuras in the late 1700s, then the 1860s and 1870s. Prime Minister Harold Macmillan evoked the "winds of change" gusting through Africa in 1960. But the winds were blowing as strongly through the global north and south alike for an entire generation. The cyclical rhythms of political events, the pendulum swings from right to left and back again took place against the continuing progress of irrevocable transformation. In the 1960s and 1970s, the early postwar equilibrium of project-states, residues of empire, resources of capital, and the realm of governance came under fundamental strain and had to be fundamentally renegotiated. How and why that happened is the subject of this chapter and the next. Was it that the long subordination of individual fulfillment to the collective discipline generated by World War II and then the Cold War finally gave way as a new generation came to maturity? Was it the very success of postwar growth that suggested that aspirations for fulfillment here and now might finally claim their due against decades-long deferrals on behalf of society's future? Historians find it difficult to answer at that level of generalization. This chapter will examine more measurable phenomena, including the collective claims on the economic growth of the 1960s and resistance to the perceived outworn patterns of domination.

Much of the 1960s came as a surprise. Looking back, however, the historian can sense the ground beginning to tremble at the end of the 1950s. The staunchly anti-communist Pope Pius XII was succeeded by the reformist John XXIII in 1958, who initiated a series of *aggiornamenti* or updatings that would impact hundreds of millions of Roman Catholics internationally as well as the frozen Italian political spectrum. The last two years of the Eisenhower presidency and the death of Secretary of State John Foster Dulles brought a modulation of American foreign policy from the "rollback" bluster that seemed bankrupt with the suppression of the Hungarian revolution of 1956. China's "Great Leap Forward" was ending in the disaster of mass famine. But in the West, the economic expansion from 1948 on (with an interruption in 1956 and 1958) was to remain vigorous for another unprecedented decade: private American investment continued abroad, while the Europeans launched the European Economic Community in 1957 and returned to convertible currencies in 1958. Labor costs in Europe continued relatively low as agricultural productivity enjoyed a major boost from mechanization and chemical fertilizers, and workers left for urban employment.[4] Energy costs, as we see below, remained favorable, once Anglo-Americans intervened to unseat Iran's prime minister Mohammad Mossadegh in 1953, and the new oil producers' cartel, Organization of Petroleum Exporting Countries (OPEC), did not flex its muscles until the early 1970s, though then with tremendously unsettling impact.

Growth continued in the 1960s, prolonging the reconstruction boom of the 1950s; "more was produced in that quarter century than in the previous three quarters, and many times more than in any comparable period in human history."[5] But after a decade and a half of reconstruction and social "discipline," the 1960s brought a change in relative collective preferences from capital accumulation to social and individual consumption. Renewal of housing, the advent of television and mass auto ownership, and vacation travel became possible for many in Europe. New political coalitions oriented more toward social spending on welfare and university expansion came to power, whether under the Democratic administrations of Kennedy and Johnson in the United States, Harold Wilson and the Labour Party in Britain, the "Opening to the

Left" that would include Pietro Nenni's Socialist Party in Italy, the Grand Coalitions and then the Social-Liberal government dominated by Willy Brandt's Social Democratic Party in West Germany, the left Christian Democrats of Eduardo Frei, followed by Allende in Chile, and Janos Quadros's populist regime in Brazil. Some of these experiments would come to grief, but by the mid-1960s it appeared as if the project-state was to be infused with a new breath of life by ambitious political leaders, impatient with the defensive anxieties of the 1950s and eager to transform society. Some advanced redistributive programs and new plans for sociopolitical inclusion whether in terms of race or class, such as Johnson's Great Society, or projects for public investment and development at home—Wilson's appeal to the "white heat of technology."

For a decade or more, from the mid-1950s until the late 1960s, reputable social theorists were talking as if class conflict and worker militancy were features of the past erased by the Cold War and postwar prosperity. But by the 1960s, the ideological commitments that social scientists had pronounced moribund were reviving. Far beyond the Communist Parties, intellectuals were renewing Marxist analyses, less the political economy of *Capital* than the earlier philosophical treatises, such as the 1844 *Manuscripts* that suggested socialism would overcome "alienation" and restore human solidarity and autonomy. Herbert Marcuse, by origins a German Marxist, updated these ideas in an accessible tract—in many ways, Rousseau-like in inspiration—that became a student bible, *One-Dimensional Man*. Marcuse, also a critic of Soviet Communism, proposed that Western liberalism might be superficially open to dissent but in fact rendered it impotent by its consumerist rewards and "repressive tolerance." Capitalism suffocated its opponents by allowing them to vent their grievances and consenting to superficial reforms.[6]

Symptomatic of the flux, the ambitions, and the desire to reinvigorate the project-state as a reformist project was the popularity of the idea of "convergence," popularized by intellectuals such as Raymond Aron and Daniel Bell—the notion that the socialist systems and Western capitalism were converging toward a shared "industrial society"—a model of modernity in which capitalist and socialist economies might both ultimately operate on the basis of technical and bureaucratic rationality.[7] "Planning," that perennial slogan of the left, popular in the 1930s and revived in the postwar years, resurfaced. But planning itself remained a rather multivalent term, frequently invoked but with many implications. In the state socialist systems, where economic activity was not supposed to be independent of central planning agencies, the 1960s saw revivals of Oscar Lange's claim that a state socialist system could use shadow prices to introduce a market logic to determine output, rather than the cumbersome input-output tables that had found their way as well to the West in wartime "operations research." The Czech economist Ota Šik, who served in Alexander Dubček's brief government during the Prague Spring, sought a "third way" combining market and plan.[8] Disappointingly, these and other efforts to reform central planning—Liebermannism in Russia and the New Economic System in the German Democratic Republic—could led to blockages and rivalries for scarce materials that undermined their rosy predictions by the late 1960s. And after the Prague Spring of 1968 in which Czechoslovaks challenged the legitimacy of one-party rule, enterprise autonomy was condemned for undermining the regime.[9] Šik fled to Switzerland as the Soviets moved in to crush the Czech experiment and ended as a professor at the St. Gallen business school.

In the West, the agile John Kenneth Galbraith claimed to discern the direction of current political economies in his new book of 1967, *The New Industrial State*. Planning, he announced, was central to the "the world of the technically dynamic, massively capitalized and highly organized corporations that dominate the modern industrial economy. . . . The planning system, in turn, is the dominant feature of the New Industrial State."[10]

In capitalist societies, the planning system was no longer embodied by a heroic manager or entrepreneur but the group of engineers and managers and skilled workers who formed what Galbraith called the technostructure. Indeed, the proletariat was fading as a preeminent object of interest for social observers of a reformist bent; instead, "the white-collar worker" hove into view. Modern sociology has populated the social landscape with classes constructed conceptually to explain evolving political trends from early modern revolutions through fascism and populism. French sociologists focused on *les cadres*, or the ranks of white-collar workers in government and large enterprises. The term has no precise English equivalent, including as it does middle-level management, engineers, and office workers, recognized as a separate labor category since the late 1930s and the Vichy regime.[11] The cadres replaced the "lower middle class" (*Kleinbürgertum*, petits bourgeois, sometimes *classes moyennes* or *ceti medie*) who had been spotlighted as complicit with fascism from the 1930s through the 1950s. Their discontents and those of the students who felt they were being educated only to fill their faceless ranks allegedly contributed to the explosions of 1968. Bureaucracy itself was rediscovered as a decisive social actor, no longer just a Weberian executor of political decisions but a shaper of them as well, whether in Western histories of the Nazi regime, analyses of Soviet Communism, or administration at home.[12]

Even as reform economists of state socialism in Eastern Europe pleaded for a devolution of planning from the central state to within the socialist firm—a model supposedly operational in Yugoslavia—Galbraith and others argued that the capitalist economy had actually become a planning society where decision making was already localized within the enterprise. Galbraith's concept of planning, however, remained oriented toward maximizing a firm's profits; he did not advocate a system of national democratic planning much less central planning that determined material inputs, career possibilities, and prices. Galbraith's technostructure had capitalist clients and objectives, whereas French civil servants in the Commission du plan, or in Britain's weaker agencies, or the Italian SVIMEZ (designed to develop the Mezzogiorno) envisaged a state project.[13] Nonetheless, by the late 1960s, foreign observers thought that French "indicative" planning exerted little impact on the country's economic performance, while in Britain, as noted, the term was applied often merely to describe policies such as Keynesian demand management or investment in education. In Germany, the vague precepts of the Freiburg school (preeminently Walter Eucken who died in 1950 and A. Müller-Armack who worked with Finance Minister and then Chancellor Ludwig Erhard) emphasized "the competitive order." Planning was tainted in theory by the Nazi economy as well as the Communist model. It imposed supposed restrictions on cartels but made room for exceptions, subsidies, and a high degree of trade association coordination. Common to all the national discourses on economic management and planning was the acceptance of the fact that the realm of capital and the contemporary state were deeply intertwined. Critics of this interpenetration would remain in the minority through the decade.

The developments of the 1960s and 1970s can be depicted as an "opening" and then partial reclosing of participation in political decision making and of policies contesting the global distribution of wealth. Conceive of the trajectory as one of inclusion and then hardening, a tentative opening of the civic borders to new claimants for a voice followed by an alarmed reshutting of the gates. But this did not happen before the redistributionist thrust of the 1960s project would lead to a powerful wave of inflation that would discredit reform coalitions.

Claims for redistribution did not just take place within national societies. They also involved a surge of demands from the less industrialized economies for global redistribution, thus creating a perfect storm for public order, as conservatives understood it, by the end of the decade. Hence, following on the brief period of *apertura* or opening, to use the Italian word for the 1963 inclusion of the Socialists in a Christian Democratic–led ministry, ensued a long drawn-out countermovement—a reorganization of political constituencies, a reassertion of religious authority, a revision of economic ideas and theories, and in some places, military takeovers. Together, the political and economic movements comprised a profound multidecade cycle of reform and stabilization—of anticipation for a global left and then disappointment. The trajectory of the 1960s would thus in some ways parallel that of the 1930s—initial rekindlings of project-states with ambitious social programs that soon generated second thoughts and opposition. Different, however, from the denouement of the 1930s, there was no fascist reaction in the advanced capitalist societies. Counterrevolutionaries would, however, conspire to wrest power in the global periphery: in Greece, then Argentina and Brazil and by 1973 Chile (and India if one counts the Emergency). There were rumors of plots in Italy and a madcap attempt at a coup in Spain, but overall momentum on the left died at its own hand, as we shall see later in the chapter.

In the realm of international high politics, the custodians of the East-West Cold War attempted to crawl back from potential geopolitical danger and unpredictability, to discipline the arms race, and to control a world where their clients in the third world might otherwise drag them into dangerous, even nuclear, confrontations. But cutting across this effort at superpower stewardship (of which Henry Kissinger would emerge as the supreme practitioner by the 1970s) was the complementary effort by the industrial countries of the global north to control socioeconomic and even moral dangers. For the stewards, such as those in the Trilateral Commission, such perils could arise from a social-democratically inclined left—exemplified by Gunnar Myrdal at the Economic Committee for Europe in the 1950s and 1960s and then by Willy Brandt's championing the ideas of a New International Economic Order, which envisioned a transnational redistribution of wealth. The momentum of the 1960s reforms, followed by the limited results that they yielded and the reactions they spawned, aroused in their turn the pathologies of a terrorist far left, whose adherents drew inspiration from Mao's revolutionary career and peasant movements of the third world. More significantly for subsequent political developments, the disappointments of the 1970s undermined the programs and parties of global social democracy.

Out of power, they would undergo a process of self-criticism and "reeducation" facilitated by new paradigms of economic theory—preeminently the monetarism that fascinated the conservatives who took their place but just as influentially by softer doctrines that stressed the role of "expectations," and the unavoidable verdicts of "the markets." Even as they retained their nominal affiliations of the 1960s and 1970s, the social democratic successor generation absorbed new lessons and became the stalwarts of economic and social discipline ready to preach the lessons of what would be called neoliberalism. Helmut Schmidt and eventually Gerhard Schroeder replaced Brandt; Tony Blair made the Labour Party a vehicle for an earnest piecemeal reform agenda; Bill Clinton's personal warmth conquered the Democratic Party—all leaders apparently confident that their respective parties had largely achieved the basics of social justice such that they could fraternize with representatives of global capital. In the Communist world, Brezhnev's administration became a byword for stagnation, while Deng Xiaoping, the most consequential of the decade's leaders, opened China to market reforms.

The social democratic drift of the 1960s and the reactions that would accumulate in successive decades took place against fundamental long-term transformations of global society. They did not necessarily generate movements to the left or to the right, but they emerged as challenges to which both left or right were likely to respond with different diagnoses and remedies. The most salient in retrospect included a massive rise in world populations—African, Latin American, and Asian in particular across half a century until birth control options became widespread—and their migrations. Paul Bairoch noted not just a moderate acceleration of population growth in the third world from 1910–1920 until mid-century but thereafter a "genuine demographic inflation,"[14] even as oral contraception became available after 1960. The surge in population was accompanied by the growth in migration from the third world to the more industrialized countries of the global north. In the nineteenth and early twentieth centuries, the human flows had streamed from Europe to North and South America, from India across the Bay of Bengal and the Indian Ocean, and from China to Southeast Asia or Manchuria.[15] Outright formal empire became increasingly unsustainable after World War II. But its retreat left claims to citizenship or to residence in the metropole that many of the formerly colonized could make upon their one-time rulers. War and ethnic violence led to streams of refugees from Southeast Asia to Europe and North America: Pakistanis to Britain, Indonesians to the Netherlands, French and Arab Algerians and Vietnamese to France—

and the last to the United States as well—and Palestinians to refugee enclaves outside Israel. But the flow had economic as well as political causes. As early as the 1950s, contract labor schemes, drawing Turks and Yugoslavs to West Germany (*Gastarbeiter*) and Latin Americas to the United States (*braceros*) became numerically significant; and European efforts to encourage the immigrants to return "home" after the recruitment of foreign workers ceased in 1973–1974 did not have much success. In 1965, the United States decisively liberalized its immigration regime with the Hart-Celler Act that allowed for family reunion, and in the mid-1970s the numbers from America's war in Vietnam increased significantly.[16]

Urban concentrations of the newcomers also increased: African American laborers in the deep South—increasingly displaced by mechanical cotton pickers, introduced in the 1930s but deployed en masse only after the Depression and World War II—resumed their migration to northern cities. In Latin America, Africa, and South Asia traditional subsistence agriculture yielded to commercial monocultures designed for exports, displacing countryside dwellers into the peripheral shanty towns of rapidly expanding cities. Altogether, the number of internal migrants the world over vastly outnumbered international settlers. Still, internal migration or the early intra-European migration from Italy and Yugoslavia did not attract the same attention or pose the same dilemmas of cultural integration as did the arrival of Turkish, Asian, and African migrants. In quantitative terms, the growth of the foreign born in the West (Western Europe, the United States, Canada, Australia, and New Zealand) or global north who had migrated from the global south and Eastern Europe rose from 4.9 percent of the region's population in 1965 to 7.6 percent in the 1990s. The trends would increase into the new century.[17] The United States took in 322,000 immigrants as a yearly average in the 1960s, 423,000 in the 1970s, 586,000 in the 1980s, and 770,000 in the first half of the 1990s, and the number hit 814,000 at mid-decade.[18] Of those totals, the number arriving from developing countries rose from 42 percent to about 80 percent. The percentages were comparable for Britain and the Netherlands;[19] Germany drew more from Eastern Europe. Of the world's "migrant stock," 75 million in 1965 and 120 million by 1990, Western Europe became the home for 16 percent in the mid-1960s and about 19 percent by 1990. The United States and Canadian share went from about 17 percent to 20 percent. Southern, Western, and Southeast Asia—that is, Asia exclusive of China and Japan (which admitted hardly any migrants)—dropped from 41 percent to 36 percent of the aggregate stock of migrants even as its absolute number grew from 31 million to 43 million.[20] These demographic changes caused alarmed reactions. Global population was increasing quickly and swelling fastest in the poorer societies of the global south. Even more disquieting for some observers, these populations were heading north to the wealthy societies of the first world. The reactions included a concern, voiced by the Club of Rome, that global natural resources would be exhausted and a concerted campaign for population control.[21]

Other shifts were becoming noticeable as well. Based on the decline in religious observance among many of the European and North American elites, commentators analyzed an encroaching secularization as the most notable change in mentalities. But just as notable was the revival of religious loyalties among other religious traditions, social classes, and geographic regions—a trend itself often simplified as a rise in "fundamentalism." By the late 1960s, a rising concern about environmental degradation made itself felt as well. The first Earth Day was inaugurated in 1970; concern with nuclear power and atmospheric pollution intensified, and the formation of new Green Parties suggested the political impact these issues might exert.

All these developments contributed to a breakup of Cold War ideological glaciation. Geopolitical struggle was becoming more complex; East-West rivalries were being overlaid by North-South tensions. The message of the 1955 Bandung Conference, dominated by Jawaharlal Nehru's India, was independence from the Cold War alliances that helped prolong the geopolitical ascendancy of the old colonial powers. The formation of OPEC in 1960 and the final wave of decolonization in the early 1960s encouraged a sustained critique of alleged neocolonial exploitation by industrialized Europe and North America, increasingly designated as the first world. But "dependency" did not require a recent colonial background. Its leading theorists based in Latin America explained that the international division of labor worked to keep agricultural or extractive economies at a permanent disadvantage with respect to more industrialized economies. Their terms of trade remained more vulnerable; their wage levels would lag; investment to develop industry would seem less remunerative than similar projects in the first world; and their elites would find it easier to draw rents and payments by serving as intermediaries (*compradors*) for foreign investors than as entrepreneurs at home. The remedy proposed as of the 1950s, as suggested by Raúl Prebisch at the United Nation's (UN's) Economic Commission for Latin America and others, had been "import substitution." This entailed using tariffs and subsidies to develop domestic industrial capacity even though it contradicted the logic of comparative advantage in the short run. Faced with disappointing results, the developing countries represented in the United Nations Conference on Trade and Development would press for political interventions in international trade on their behalf, including tariff preferences for their products by countries in the global north—a so-called New International Economic Order (discussed in Chapter 7).[22] For the 1960s and 1970s, however, the regional distribution of wealth continued to flow the other way.

Resources in Transition: Coal, Oil, and Steel

States have always been called on to intervene in the supply of basic and strategic commodities—sometimes to assure an adequate supply when domestic output fails or imports are restricted, occasionally to regulate inhumane labor conditions at the sites of production, frequently to soften the impact of oversupply on prices and employment. In the nineteenth century and through the world depression of the 1930s, issues arising from cotton and wheat cultivation threw political life into profound conflict. In twentieth-century wartime and during the last third of the twentieth century, coal, steel, and oil set new challenges for project-states and their creation, the European Economic Community.

Despite decolonization, international disparities of power persisted in the search for resources, especially petroleum. Until the formation of OPEC in 1960, the noncommunist oil economy seemed safely organized by what we might call the agents of petro-empires, state-sponsored companies who had acquired the rights to explore, drill, and refine the oil of former colonies. Western oil companies (whether government owned or private) served their home states and the realm of capital, much like the great trading companies of the mercantile era. Increasingly, they might be compelled to share their surpluses with the new sovereign custodians of petroleum wealth, who, however, were often satisfied to reserve it for a narrow group of national clients. In general, as Bairoch noted, the extractive sector (including mining as well as oil) underwent an annual rate of expansion between 1948 and 1970 of more than 9 percent but for the benefit of the industrial world, not the development of the lands from which the natural resources were drawn.[23] For the beneficiaries, the petro-empires raised no moral problems. As George Kennan disdainfully observed about Venezuela, "The local population had not moved a finger to create this wealth, would have been incapable of developing it, and did not require for its own needs the thousandth part of what was apparently there."[24] Formal empire—even in the form of the mandates or the resource empires of the interwar era—was ending; but the effort to cling to its bounty, whether for state power or wealth, would continue, all the more so since among the great trends under way was an evolution of material and technological possibilities usually described as an energy transition: in this case, the ongoing shift in global fuel sources from coal to oil.

Historians measure an energy transition as the growth of a new energy source from 5 percent to 80 percent of energy consumption in sectors such as heating, power, and transport, and they find that they usually take half a century or longer.[25] The hydrocarbon transition began early in the twentieth century, but the decades from the late 1950s through the 1980s claimed particularly dramatic political conflicts and outcomes. The underlying fact was the increase in global energy consumption and production during the postwar decades.

Sources provide quantities of energy use or supply use in different forms: million tonnes of oil equivalent or trillions of watt-hours (terawatt hours, TWh).[26] A terawatt hour equals the energy that would be drawn by 1,000 hundred-watt bulbs burning for about 1,141 years. If Charlemagne had switched on 1,000 hundred-watt bulbs to celebrate his coronation as Roman emperor on Christmas Day in 800, a terawatt-hour of energy would have kept them lit until almost three months after the German half of his progeny invaded Russia in World War II. World energy consumption in millions of tonnes of oil equivalent (Mtoe) rose from 948 in 1920 to 1,772 in 1950, 3,011 in 1960, 4,001 in 1970, and to 5,127 in 1980, an approximately fivefold linear rate of increase from 1920 to 1980—and a threefold increase from 1950 to 1980, thereafter starting to decline slightly. These figures represent final use—that is, they do not include the 30 percent or so of total primary energy supply (TPES) that goes into refining or transporting fuels for final use. Since 1980, world energy production and final consumption have each nearly doubled to reach 14 Mtoe and 9,700 Mtoe, respectively. Increasingly, the hydrocarbons in final use went to generating electricity. As Europe and Japan recovered from wartime destruction and industrial development came to the rest of Asia and haltingly to Latin America and parts of Africa, the postwar US share of energy consumption naturally declined even as it burned two-thirds more oil, gas, and coal over the interval.

In contrast to today's energy transition from hydrocarbons to renewables, the leading energy story from the world wars to 1980 was the trajectory from coal to oil. Not only did oil displace coal over time; its consumption grew decisively with the expansion of automobile and air transportation and then

Table 6.1   World Energy Consumption

Primary Energy Consumption by Selected Regions in Terawatt Hours
(1 TWh–1 Billion KWh)

	1950	1980	2021
USA	10,600	14,750	23,050
Europe (West + East)	6,500	12,810	22,880
USSR / CIS	3,000	8,660	11,200
China + CPA	1,532	6,847	43,790 (China only)
Japan	380	2,680	4,930
India + SA	1,713	3,813	9,840 (India only)
World	28,300	62,450	165,320

Note: China + CPA includes China, Taiwan, and North Korea; India + SA includes India, Pakistan, and Bangladesh. I have converted the source's data in exajoules (10^{18}J) into terawatt hours (TWh = 10^{12} kilowatt-hours).

Data sources: For 1950 and 1980 statistics, C. G. M. Klein Goldewijk and J. J. Battjes, *A Hundred Year (1890–1990) Database for Integrated Environmental Assessment*, Report 422514002 (HYDE, version 1.1), table 21, p. 36. National Institute of Public Health and the Environment, Bildthoven, downloaded from PBL Netherlands, Environmental Assessment Agency. For 2021 data, BP, *Statistical Review of World Energy 2022*, https://www.bp.com/en/global/corporate/energy-economics/statistical-review-of-world-energy/html.

the vigorous economic growth of postwar Europe. Even before World War I, Winston Churchill, then First Lord of the Admiralty, ordered British ships to convert from coal to oil; the expansion of car and truck transport in the interwar years drove the process forward, and World War II required vast amounts of oil and gasoline. Coking coal remained important for transforming ore to iron in blast furnaces and then iron to steel in Bessemer converters, but steel production in Europe increasingly smelted its steel from scrap iron in open-hearth furnaces. In terms of greenhouse gas emissions, the transition from one form of hydrocarbon to another (as opposed to their overall growth) made relatively little impact (although it certainly reduced noxious smog in London and other population centers). But in terms of politics and society, the switch had major ramifications.

Coal had fueled the era of nation-state competition as well as industrial development in the 1800s and reached its zenith in Western Europe at the outset of World War I. It provided the energy for the project-state. In its "glory days," hundreds of thousands of laborers toiled in the mines, often in dangerous conditions. The United Kingdom counted about 1.2 million employed in the coal industry (above ground and below) in 1920, 700,000 through the 1940s and most of the 1950s, about 600,000 in 1960, and then a

Table 6.2   Coal Production in Terawatt-Hours (TWh)

	1950	1980–1981	2016–2019
UK	1,505	971	16
Germany	1,389	1,731	351
Europe	4,675	4,894	1,811
USSR/Russia	2,161 (1965)	4,028 (1981)	2,556
US	3,827	5,455	3,972
China	241	4,051	22,171
Japan	299	113	5
India	209	742	3,536
World	ca. 15,000	20,968	46,500

For column 3, the production figure is for average annual output within that range. 1 TWh = 122,835 TCE (tons of coal equivalent); 1,000,000 TCE–8.141 TWh.

Data sources: Ritchie, Roser, and Rosado, "Energy," online at *OurWorldinData.org/fossil-fuels*, https://ourworldindata.org/Energy (for data since 1965); and from *BP Statistical Review of World Energy*, https://www.bp.com/en/global/corporate/energy-economics/statistical-review-of-world -energy/primary-energy.html. Data from 1950 derived from *Our World in Data* from the Shift Data Project Portal, https://www.theshiftdataportal.org/energy. The Shift Data Project draws in turn on Bouda Etemad and Jean Luciani, *World Energy Production 1900–1985* [library copies listed as *1800–1985*] (Geneva: Droz, 1991).

Note: I have used production rather than consumption figures in this table. Both reflect the energy transition under way, but the decline of coal production in Europe and North America had a more conspicuous impact on politics. The decline of coal mining disoriented the traditional left in Europe and the United States (see Chapter 9), while the growth of Soviet and Middle East oil transformed geopolitics.

steep decline: 200,000 in 1980, 50,000 in 1990, and perhaps 700 today.[27] Thousands of railroad cars shipped coal and iron ore every day, usually within national boundaries and between abutting regions of iron ore. Along with steel—for the production of which it still remained a major input as of 1950 along with iron ore—coal provided the backbone of industrial societies, while given the arduous and often dangerous demands on their labor, coal miners (and later steelworkers) still proved major protagonists for contests over union rights and the provision of social welfare. Not every country possessed coal reserves, but a great belt ran from northwest to southeast— from Wales and northern Britain, to Belgium, northern France, the Rhine- Ruhr area. In Eastern Europe, German, later Polish Silesia, and the Don Basin had important reserves; North America had major coal fields along the Appalachian chain, while across the Pacific the Japanese were mining significant fields in Manchuria, mines that would revert to China after 1945. By the 1960s, this iconic industry was in steep decline in Britain and by the new century would be shutting its pits throughout Europe.

Table 6.3   Oil and Gas Production in Terawatt-Hour Equivalents

	1950 Oil	1950 Gas	1980 Oil	1980 Gas	2019 Oil	2019 Gas	1980/1950 (Growth of Oil Output)	2019/1980 (Growth of Oil Output)
USSR / CIS	2,820	1,875	7,015*	4,122	8,366	8,582	2.5	1.2
US	3,102	1,928	5,585	5,251	8,670	9,300	1.8	1.6
Europe	114	64	1,667	2,286	1,840	2,352	14.6	1.1
China	2	0	1,230	144	2,218	3,084	615	1.8
Nigeria	0	0	1,182	16	1,176	493	—	1.0
Saudi Arabia	1,289†	1.5	5,919	92	6,462	1,112	4.6	1.1
Iran	1,113	35	861	45	1,835	2,414	0.8	2.2
Venezuela	2,138	86‡	1,363	156	541	256	0.64	0.4
OPEC (formed 1960)	NA	NA	15,249	730	23,400	7,936	1.5	—
World	18,201	2,154	35,900	14,285	52,070	39,762	2.0	1.5

1 TWh = 0.0860 Mtoe = 86,000 tonnes of oil equivalent = ca. 632,353 bbl.

* 1981 (closest year available)

† 1970 (closest year available)

‡ 1970 (closest year available)

Data sources: Ritchie, Roser, and Rosado, "Energy," online at *OurWorldinData.org/fossil-fuels*, https://ourworldindata.org/Energy (for data since 1965); and from *BP Statistical Review of World Energy*, https://www.bp.com/en/global-corporate/energy-economics/statistical-review-of-world-energy/primary-energy.html. Data from 1950 derived from *Our World in Data* from the Shift Data Project Portal, https://www.theshiftdataportal.org/energy. The Shift Data Project draws in turn on Bouda Etemad and Jean Luciani, *World Energy Production 1900–1985* [library copies listed as *1800–1985*] (Geneva: Droz, 1991).

Note: I have used production rather than consumption figures in this table. Both reflect the energy transition under way, but the decline of coal production in Europe and North America had a more conspicuous impact on politics. The decline of coal mining disoriented the traditional left in Europe and the United States (see Chapter 9), while the growth of Soviet and Middle East oil transformed geopolitics.

Shutting down coal mines was expensive. Workers had to be supported; sometimes a ravaged landscaping had to be ignored.[28] Oil, in contrast, entailed different geopolitical and social developments. Early in the twentieth century, local oil fields brought wealth to national firms or those companies, supported by their home countries, who won concessions from foreign states. By World War I, Russia developed major reserves in its Caucasus region; Austria enjoyed a boom in its Galician territory north of the Carpathians. These regions remained small in comparison with John D. Rockefeller's Standard Oil Company, which was compelled to dissolve into thirty-four component oil firms under the Sherman Antitrust Act in 1911. The successor firms, of which a few, familiar today across many name changes, extracted, refined, and marketed the petroleum wealth of Pennsylvania, Texas, Oklahoma, and California and quickly moved to develop reserves abroad in the years through World War II.

Socony (Standard Oil of New York, later Mobil) and Esso (Standard Oil of New Jersey, later Exxon) remained refining and marketing giants. By the end of World War I, American authorities became alarmed about depletion of reserves at home and faced "impregnable" British control of foreign oil fields.[29]

The alarm was misplaced both with respect to reserves and exclusion from sources abroad. Standard Oil of California (later Socal, today's Chevron) had acquired a foothold in Bahrain and then developed the petroleum fields of the Saudi Arabian mainland to form the core of the Arabian American oil company or Aramco. It acquired the Texaco company built on the discoveries of the Spindletop wells in Texas and would ultimately merge with Gulf Oil—a firm financed by the Mellon interests on Pittsburgh (who also controlled Alcoa) which united fields in Texas with refineries and facilities on the Gulf of Mexico as well as a foothold in Kuwait.[30] Gulf, Texaco, and Socal would dominate the rich Venezuelan oil fields, and the South American country remained the largest exporter of oil until after World War II. It became the model for the "petrostate," possessed of reserves it could not consume, governed by a narrow elite, often authoritarian, relying on oil royalties to replace domestic taxation, and sometimes indulging in massive arms acquisitions that its oil clients were happy to sell. Mexico was a prewar exception. Despite the major grip of British firms on its oil, that country's government, aware of its revolutionary heritage, nationalized the industry in 1937. It would remain a defiant holdout against the pattern of foreign control in most of world—the United States, Brazil, and Russia aside.

British and Dutch capital kept apace. The 1907 merger of the Royal Dutch Petroleum Company, which was developing the oil fields of the future in Indonesia, with the Shell transport and trading company of London produced the new Royal Dutch Shell company. In 1913, Shell bought significant oil assets in Russia and Romania to which it added major Mexican holdings in 1919 (nationalized in the 1930s). Based on discoveries in 1908 in Iran, then Persia, the Anglo-Persian (after 1935, the Anglo-Iranian) oil company benefited from Winston Churchill's order to convert the Royal Navy from coal to oil and constructed a huge refinery complex at Abadan Island in the Persian Gulf. During World War I, it took control of the sequestered German-owned British Petroleum Company (BP), which provided the name that the firm took after its Iranian assets were nationalized in 1953. BP controlled the British Iraqi holdings, the development of Nigerian oil fields, and by the 1960s and 1970s its major holdings in the North Sea and Alaska.

The French predecessor of TOTAL, the Compagnie française des pétroles—incorporated with a French state share of 35 percent—had secured a quota of Mesopotamian oil after 1918 in return for transferring Mosul with its oil resources from France's new colony of Syria to British-controlled Iraq. It would be Algerian oil possibilities that beckoned later. The discovery of oil in the Algerian Sahara became a stake in the Algerian struggle for independence, and although Paris authorities lost that battle in 1962, they did protect the rights of their state-sponsored firms to develop the promising reserves beneath the sands. Elf-Erap, a subsidiary of Elf-Aquitaine, retained a highly advantageous revenue-sharing agreements until the late 1960s.[31] The public Italian energy firm ENI, formed out of the fascist state's oil portfolio holdings, the AGIP, and still today running the ubiquitous service stations in Italy with the fire-breathing six-legged dogs, also engaged in a somewhat mysterious search for oil sources in the Middle East but by posing as an alternative to the majors. ENI director Enrico Mattei denounced economic colonialism and praised the oil states for their struggle "against fatalism and resignation" and offered a 75–25 split in profits as part of his effort to challenge the "Seven Sisters." At the same time, he and FIAT director Gianni Agnelli were negotiating contracts for oil and gas from the Soviet Union, opening a FIAT plant to produce the Togliatti model FIAT in Russia, seeking to reassure President Kennedy that Italy was not deserting the Western alliance and hoping to midwife what would become the "opening to the left" political coalition.[32] No surprise that his death in the crash of Mattei's private plane in 1962 fueled all sorts of conspiracy theories.

Petroleum extraction thus brought with it implications for issues of law, politics, and contests over sovereignty very different from the coal-based economy that had preceded it in the West. The oil industry came to post–World War II maturity as a product of state-supported European and American firms that built much of their oil wealth in the interwar resource empires and then negotiated networks of control over compliant elites outside Europe who wanted to exploit the hydrocarbon wealth within their borders but required foreign expertise and resources to extract it. Mexico and later Brazil successfully resisted foreign control over their petroleum reserves. Venezuela, governed by a leftist Acción Democrática (AD) party since a 1945 coup, amended an earlier hydrocarbons law in 1948 to assure that the Venezuelan state receive a 50 percent share of the net oil companies' revenue. Fifty-fifty promised labor peace and seemed inherently equitable to the American firms as well; it supposedly guaranteed them against threats of nationalization.

US firms could also acquiesce since the American tax code allowed them to credit their Venezuelan tax payments against corporate taxes at home.[33]

By 1948, the United States was a net importer of oil, in fact would grow to become the largest importer in the world. American entrepreneurs presented the Middle East as an indispensable strategic asset in the Cold War.[34] They had successfully resisted an American government effort during the war to extend the purview of a wartime Petroleum Reserve Corporation to Saudi Arabian oil supplies.[35] What might have been a more rational government policy was significantly frustrated by the competition among American oil firms.[36] But without state-owned oil companies, Britain and the United States had to work in partnership with the independent majors, who in turn were locked into profitable relationships with the petrostates. Aramco, Anglo-Iranian, Chevron, Sunoco, Esso, Exxon, and Gulf enjoyed a role in global capitalism akin to such private-public fusions as the British or Dutch East India Companies. As would be pointed out during the 1973–1974 oil crisis, in effect they made much of their revenue essentially collecting taxes from American consumers to pay for their privileged position in the Middle East.

The Saudi monarchy was willing to accept its 50–50 share of industry revenues with the Americans, but the Anglo-Persian had a stormier relationship with Shah Reza Pahlavi who had seized power in 1926. When the company cut its annual payment in 1932, he revoked the concession; the company immediately appealed to the International Court of Justice which upheld the sanctity of treaties. A new agreement secured the firm's concession until 1993 and the Tehran government traded its share of profits for a guaranteed payment per barrel. Calls for "Iranization" aside, the Iranian government remained in a state of total "subalternity."[37] When Mohammad Mossadegh, the histrionic premier, threatened nationalization, the British wanted joint action to have him removed, but the Truman administration resisted. However, in 1953 when the Republicans came to power in Washington and Mossadegh threatened the institution of the monarchy, calculations changed. With the assistance of the Central Intelligence Agency (CIA), the new young shah Mohommad Reza Pahlavi went briefly into self-exile, Mossadegh was ousted, and a new agreement was reached. The taste for intervention—partially disavowed by the New Deal with the Good Neighbor Policy of 1934—returned in the 1950s. A year after their derring-do in Iran had secured a compliant regime in Tehran, CIA activists helped United Fruit arrange the ouster of allegedly "leftist" Colonel Jacobo Árbenz in Guatemala.

The states endowed with oil who became increasingly assertive about re-capturing control, whether in 1930s Mexico or Iran unsuccessfully in the early 1950s, finally produced their own counter cartel. Countervailing power, yes. But the majors also began to lose control to the "independents," the smaller oil firms who started to strike their own deals with the petrostates.[38] The politics of oil—made salient by the energy transition of the postwar—allowed for redistribution but only to a small number of states with vast degrees of inequality.

Cartelization would challenge the imperial structure of oil production and pricing for both the West and the East. In effect, the price of petroleum was determined as much by international politics as by the forces of supply and demand. Through the 1950s, national producers were relatively compliant toward the Western interests that pumped, refined, and marketed their underground wealth. An oil elite grew wealthy by forming consortia with the Western firms that marketed and refined their oil, as was the case with Aramco and Anglo-Iranian. The massive presence of the majors and the weak power of the oil producers had kept petroleum relatively inexpensive in terms of what oil importers might be compelled to pay. Relatively cheap energy provided a basis of vigorous postwar economic growth in the West.

That was to change between the late 1950s and the early 1970s as the oil-producing countries began to realize that they might potentially get much more for the essential resource they controlled and the political temperament in Latin America moved to the left. Elections in Venezuela in 1958 returned a coalition headed by the populist party, Acción Democrática, and the Caracas government unilaterally raised the earlier 50–50 settlement on oil revenues to 64–36. The new president, Rómulo Betancourt, who was installed several months later, faced pressure to nationalize the industry from a left-wing schism in the AD. Choosing to crack down on the Communists (who were emboldened by the recent victory of Castro in Cuba), Betancourt was able to win Washington's toleration and make the new division of revenues stick. The architect of his oil policies, Juan Pablo Pérez Alfonzo, articulated a policy of no further concessions, higher taxes on the foreign companies and formation of a state oil company, and cooperation within the new OPEC cartel. In 1971, he published *Petrólio y dependencia*, a scathing attack, as Giuliano Garavini says, on the UN's development model and that of the Alliance for Progress of the 1960s. According to Pérez Alfonzo, the oil companies extracted superprofits in implicit collusion with a national bureaucracy that could spend without taxation. "Creole capitalism" had to end, and

Venezuela needed to take the lead among the Asian and African nations seeking to end neocolonialism.[39] The days of worry-free exploitation were coming to an end.

So too in the Middle East. The flash point of Middle Eastern politics, though, was the Arab-Israeli conflict. In 1967, the Israelis had fought a brief preemptive Six-Day War against Nasser's threats to blockade their Red Sea ports and perhaps launch his own invasion. Brilliantly successful in military terms, Israeli troops surged beyond the frontiers prevailing since the initial Arab-Israeli war of 1948–1949 and occupied the Jordanian half of Jerusalem along with Jordan's territory west of the Jordan River (the West Bank), the Gaza Strip previously held by Egypt, and the Golan Heights taken from Syria—borders that are still in place and still contested as of this writing four decades later. It would be the West that ultimately paid the consequences of Israeli triumph and Arab humiliation. As part of what Garavini aptly calls "the petrostate's 1968," the Ba'ath Party seized power in Iraq in July 1968, and a year and a half later, a young officer's coup overthrew the monarchy in Libya. Algeria signed on to OPEC in 1969. Britain's Labour government decided to pull out of the Persian Gulf sheikdoms it had hitherto protected and controlled, leaving Oman and these mini states—who knitted together a fragile United Emirates—unprotected before Communist agitation and Iranian ambitions, now represented by a shah with dreams of a revived Persian Empire.

At the same time, the oil exports from the Middle East surged: Saudi exports rose from 13 percent of the world's total to 21 percent. Libya and Iran followed the Venezuelan example with price rises in 1970–1971. The United States and its oil companies came out relatively unscathed given American domestic consumption and the inelasticity of demand for the refiners' gasoline. And when the United States devalued on August 15, 1971, it passed some of the burden back to the oil-exporting states that had just imposed price increases in dollars.[40] During these tug-of-wars, major oil states decided they must nationalize the oil companies' holdings: Algeria in February 1971, Iraq in June 1972, Libya during 1972–1973. The Saudis pressed for partial ownership—"participation"—but were rebuked by OPEC colleagues for demanding too little. Iran replaced the consortium with a National Iranian Oil Company that would take ownership of the facilities, including the Abadan refinery, and sell the oil to the consortium that would run the installations. Control of their petroleum destiny, however, also brought them concerns about maintaining prices.

In October 1973, Anwar Sadat tried to reverse the humiliating results of the 1967 war with a surprise attack that caught Israel relatively unprepared on the Jewish Day of Atonement. Still, after initial shock, the Israelis rallied in the Yom Kippur War and within a few days were poised to cross the Suez Canal and destroy the Egyptian army. In the framework of the Cold War, the Soviets threatened vaguely to intervene on behalf of Egypt, which provoked Secretary of State Henry Kissinger, preeminently concerned with the global balance of power, to place American forces on alert to deter the Soviets. Ultimately, a cease-fire was reached that left Israeli boundaries intact but still allowed the Egyptians to feel they had somehow salvaged their military honor after 1967. On that basis, the US administration of Jimmy Carter could later broker the Camp David agreements of 1978, which brought an Israeli-Egyptian peace treaty that still prevails.

At the time of the Yom Kippur War, however, the other Arab governments announced an embargo on oil sales to countries allegedly supporting Israel. The instrument was difficult to coordinate and struck unevenly but created alarm in Europe and the United States. Premonitions of petroleum scarcity had already manifested themselves; given the voracious appetite for oil, the underground oil reserves were likely to be limited: the world, influential experts argued, was in the years of "peak oil."[41] What had seemed the infinite and inexpensive flow of oil from the Middle East dried up; Americans had to line up for fuel at their gas stations and talked darkly of energy dependence. With the end of the brief war, the oil producers restored shipments, but in January 1974, their newly powerful cartel, OPEC—including not just Iran, Saudi Arabia, and Iraq but Venezuela and Nigeria as well—announced a more-than-threefold increase in the price of the oil they sold. The official price of Arab light crude oil was raised from $3.29 to $11.58 per barrel, based on the $7.00 / barrel return that the producers claimed as their own. Discussants at the OPEC conferences in late December 1973 raised the idea, not only of exploiting current market opportunities but recognizing oil's "intrinsic value"—that is, as a depletable, finite resource. At the end of the 1970s, oil prices surged once again, although no longer under the full control of the cartel. By 1981, OPEC agreed on a reference price of $34 for Saudi crude, up from $14 in early 1979. In the ten years from 1970 to 1980, the world price of crude was to rise from $1.80 to $39 per barrel. As a cartel, OPEC was increasingly fractured over pricing policies and according to its historian, "next to irrelevant" in this second leap of world prices.[42] By the mid-1980s, petroleum prices were falling quickly, but during oil's frothy decade, they were a source of tremendous strain, not least on the new imperial hierarchies they had helped to sustain and their oil-endowed hegemons.

The imperial structure of the oil industry—oligopolic control over vast resources at home and among semi-sovereign polities abroad—had been important for constructing the respective alliance structures of the global hegemons. With the OPEC price hikes, it became a major strain on their coherence. It took as great a toll in the socialist world as in the capitalist. When obstreperous suppliers threatened to cut off oil supplies as at the end of 1973, the Soviet Union, despite vast reserves, found it more and more of a burden to deliver oil to its Council for Mutual Economic Assistance, i.e. Comecon partners, at subsidized prices. Before 1973, the Russians had set their prices on a rolling five-year average of world market prices and had also sold to Western clients. As prices rose in 1974 and again in 1978–1979, they made the adjustments more quickly. They also resented the political need not to be able to sell outside the bloc, even as they faced material constraints on their capacity to pipe petroleum to their East European dependents. By the end of the 1970s, Moscow was reproaching its allegedly ungrateful clients for their supplications, while East Germans and Bulgarians resented their Soviet patrons' stinginess and were having to resort to Western loans to buy the oil they needed—increasingly from OPEC providers as Soviet supplies remained limited and rose in price.[43]

The political economy of oil contrasted with that of steel as well as with coal. As with both coal and steel in the pre-1914 era, the expansion of steel output after World War II was to become a trumpeted achievement of the project-state. Before World War II and into the 1950s, coal and steel seemed inseparable companions. Coal fed the blast furnaces that smelted ore into crude or pig iron ingots as oxygen blasted out impurities. Then the pig was remelted with coke and desired additives, then pressed into plate or bars and rails or drawn into wire, thereafter to be shipped to the auto and machine factories and shipbuilding wharves at a greater distance. But increasingly coal's tasks seemed humbler in the chain of adding industrial value; it went into electrical generation, and its direct use in manufacturing steel diminished as the electric furnace and use of scrap increased. Coal was burdened with the image of the dangerous and dirty underground mine and later with the ravages to the landscape of the open-pit mine.

In Europe and North America, coal and iron ore were distributed in proximity or conveniently with access to water transport. Along the borders of what once had been the middle kingdom of the Carolingian Empire—that is, Belgian Wallonia, French Lorraine, the Ruhr basin and the Saarland—the coal and iron regions were close enough to facilitate dense rail networks to bring them together and to networks of the engineering firms that shaped the semifinished products. Lorraine steel firms processing minette ore required Ruhr coal as well as Saar deposits. Saar coal, whether controlled by France (1918–1935 and 1945–1955) or by Germany was important for south German engineering firms. Further afield, the engineering firms that processed steel plate into autos and ships and beams flourished in the Genoa-Turin-Milan triangle in Italy. In the United States, Appalachian coal and iron ore were exchanged along the Ohio River, with Pittsburgh and Bethlehem, Pennsylvania as important nexes, and through the Great Lakes where Minnesota Mesabi range taconite could reach the blast furnaces of Gary, Indiana and Cleveland, Ohio. In Russia, the Don Basin on the Black Sea became a major center early in the twentieth century.

Even in authoritarian regimes, governments had to accept some mass organization of labor. They might subvert it or subject it to party control, but they could not simply dissolve it. Unionization and collective bargaining were outgrowths originally of perils inherent in mining, where safety depended on the collective cooperation and alertness of the labor force. European miners had long organized into *compagnonnages*, *Knappschaften*, and other benevolent associations. They were militant—in effect, combining the artisanal formation of old craft workers with the newer mass consciousness of industrial labor. Steelworkers had organized later under the conditions of industrial unionism. In the United States, John L. Lewis's coal miners and steelworkers, adhered to the new Congress of Industrial Organizations, the militant federation of industry-wide unions organized in the 1930s to challenge the American Federation of Labor. The engineering and auto industries that transformed these products also became a heavily unionized labor force with skilled and unskilled components. As indicated in Chapter 5, American labor federations saw their rival organizations, not their employers, as their chief adversary. Militant trade unionists were strong among the Pacific Coast Longshoreman and for a while the electrical workers, but these would confront hostile legislators and unsympathetic national executives in the 1950s. In Europe, the events of World War I and the Bolshevik revolution had produced a fundamental rift between Communist and Social Democratic unions in France. The Popular Front brought them back together in 1936 in a fragile coalition as did the rightist reaction under the Daladier government of 1938–1940 and then the persecution under Vichy. But as fascism was overthrown, relations frayed. In theory, unity of action was promised; it did not last. By 1946, as discussed in chapter 5, the Socialist union federation Force ouvrière, the communist CGT, and the reformist Catholic-oriented CFDT asserted their claims to speak for the working class. So too in Italy, while the CGIL remained largely committed to its Communist Party allies, Socialists and independent federations would reemerge by 1947–1948.

For the first five years after the war, the Allies attempted to limit German steel output with level-of-industry agreements of which the allowed ceiling on German steel was the most important. At Potsdam, the quotas initially put forward by the Allies ran from the British proposal of 11 million tons to the Soviets' suggestion of 3 million tons, which in fact was all that West Germany managed to produce in 1947.[44] (The excess plant capacity was to be dismantled and shipped as reparations.) Germany in 1938 had produced 23.3 million tons of crude steel, 70 percent of it in the Rhineland and Westphalia (of which the Ruhr was a district). But to feed the blast furnaces, it mined 5.8 million tons of iron ore on its own territory and imported 15.7 million tons or almost three-quarters, over half of that from Sweden. The Marshall Plan, then the Schuman Plan, and concerns about Soviet military strength changed the calculus. Germans, implicitly supported by the American High Commissioner, continually pushed for raising the allowed ceiling (although they were nowhere able to meet it), while the French had to be persuaded that their former enemy should be allowed to contribute its resources to the North Atlantic Treaty Organization (NATO).[45]

The Schuman Plan of 1950 promised to solve that issue by establishing a common coal and steel authority, which the Benelux countries and Italy would soon join. It reassured France and allowed Konrad Adenauer's government and the German coal and steel firms to shake off the French voice over Ruhr coal by superseding the International Ruhr Authority.[46] Steel output became an early symbol of Cold War prowess.[47] But even as Allied limits were taken off steel production and the International Ruhr Authority with its French veto was dissolved, the technology was changing such that coal seemed less important. Electric furnaces using scrap were replacing the coal and iron linkage. Postwar steel production worldwide took off as of 1950—from a total of almost 200 million tons to about 716 million tons in 1980, a growth rate of 5 percent per year, consonant with the recovery in Europe and Japan and the robustness of American and Soviet output.

But the vigor of Asia meant anguish for Europe. The renewal and modernization of plant under the aegis of the French "plan," the European Recovery Program, and the Schuman Plan's Coal and Steel Community represented a final two-decade surge for this signature sector of the Atlantic economy. From the mid-1970s, the established industries in Europe and North America were buffeted by the oil crisis of 1973, the inflation and recession that followed, and their renewed whiplash at the end of the 1970s. In February 1980, Roy Jenkins, the president of the European Commission, sounded the alarm for Europe's industrial future. The firms that had grown so vigorously during the 1950s and 1960s entered into a steel crisis that lasted into the 1980s, marked by dizzying corporate sell-offs and reorganizations, mass layoffs, and the abandonment of the mines, smelters, and furnaces in the British Midlands, the Ruhr and Central Germany, and the rust belt along the Great Lakes and the industrial Midwest.[48]

Japan from the 1970s and South Korea from the 1980s, in contrast, were becoming major competitors; they enjoyed convenient access to ocean ports and lower wages although higher US labor productivity compensated for higher wages. As of 1982, if the US worker's productivity was indexed at 100, the Japanese worker's productivity was 141, the German worker's 108, French worker's 100, and British and Korean workers' about 70. The United States and the European Union (EU) under the direction of the Belgian Étienne Davignon, the community's commissioner for industry, responded in the late 1970s and early 1980s with varieties of protectionist measures—voluntary restraint agreements, quotas on production within the EU, mandatory minimum prices, and subsidies. Western steelmaking remained viable in smaller specialized plants such as found in the Brescia region in Italy or in US mini-mills, but raw steel output moved offshore in the West. Employment in the American industry dropped from a peak of 650,000 in 1953 to 236,000 in 1984 and from close to 800,000 in the European Community in 1974 to under 450,000 a decade later.[49] From the turn of the twenty-first century, growth in raw steel was dominated by China primarily for its own phenomenal industrial and urban development—steel production had left Europe: the major producer countries after China were India, Japan, the United States, South Korea, Russia, and Germany.[50] China, Japan, India, and South Korea, which counted for 13 percent of global steel production in 1967, would produce 36 percent by 2000 and over two-thirds of the global steel output by 2019. The Indian firm Mittal would also own the largest steel producer based in France, Belgium and Luxembourg, Arcelor-Mittal, while

Table 6.4   Steel Production in Leading Countries (Millions of Metric Tons)

	1967	1980	1990	2000	2019
US	115.0	101.4	89.7	101.8	87.9
USSR / Russia	96.9	147.9	154.4	59.1	71.6
Germany	41.3	51.1	44.0	46.1	39.7
Brazil	3.6	15.3	20.6	27.9	32.2
China	14.0.	37.1	66.4	128.5	996.3
India	6.3	9.5	15.4	26.9	111.2
Japan	62.0	111.4	15.0	106.4	99.3
S. Korea	0.3	8.5	23.1	43.1	71.4
World	497.2	716.4	770.4	850.1	1,869.9

1 metric ton (or tonne) = 1,000 kg or approximately 2,200 lbs.

Data sources: https://en.Wikipedia.org/wiki/List_of_countries_by_steel_production, based on various years of the *World Steel Association: Steel Statistical Yearbook* online. For Europe, see also European Commission, Eurostat, 50 Years of the ECSC Treaty; Coal and Steel Statistics: Data 1951–2000. Where there are discrepancies, I have used the Wikipedia entry with its extensive list of sources.

Tata would be the proprietor of the largest UK steel company. Just as Germany had thrown down the steel challenge to Great Britain before World War I and surpassed its output by 1910, so the Asian countries would advance in the late twentieth and early twenty-first centuries.

Growth and Inflation, 1966–1974

It is against the backdrop of the long-term reallocations of hydrocarbon and steel resources that we can better appreciate the agitated currents of political economy in the era. We described in Chapter 4 how the tensions between the global North and South and the so-called first world and the third overlay the East-West conflicts of the Cold War. Overlapping that set of divisions were two great distributional struggles taking place at the same time during the 1960s and 1970s. The one, followed in this chapter, pitted the states used to controlling the oil reserves of the Middle East and Latin America against the countries that sat on those oil reserves. The United States and the Soviet Union shared attributes of both. The Soviets were to use the increased world market price of oil to keep its satellites dependent on the discounts they enjoyed from their Russian supplier. The United States would use its resources to rally European allies to an International Energy Agency and reinforce a primacy that its abandonment of fixed exchange rates for the dollar had put into question two years earlier. (Whether these results were clearly envisaged even by so impressive a strategist as Henry Kissinger cannot be determined, but that the crisis of 1973–1974 could be thus mastered is tribute enough.)[51]

The other struggle, ongoing throughout the century, took place within first world countries as capital and labor contended for shares of income, each side convinced that the other was benefiting unduly under the conditions of inflation (to which ironically their rivalry contributed). From a systemic perspective, the recurrent wage bargaining sometimes amounted to a collusive shifting of national income to both sides jointly at the expense of less organized economic sectors. It related to the other long-term development discussed above, the diffusion of coal and steel production. Steel was not a scarce contested resource as oil often was. But it was the product that stood for industrial development, and its continued increase revealed the spread of industrial prowess, as did the development of an Asian auto industry. Growth in Asia, where wage levels were still lower than in Europe and North America, was increasing at the cost of Western coal and steel industries that had been central to the labor movement since the interwar era. Economic growth remained the condition for preserving social cohesion by materially rewarding the different classes of society. It was easier to debate how to distribute the increment of the social product—whether for social services, public higher education, military security, or infrastructure—than to contest an unchanging output and certainly less calamitous than to fight over a declining national income as had occurred in the early 1930s.

Growth in real terms, however, required an agreement over the division of national income between labor's wage share and the rewards to capital, which could be maintained only if the social partners felt they were not losing out. It was precisely that confidence that eroded in the late 1960s.[52] In the turbulence of 1968 and 1969, strikes and the occupation of factories increased alongside student unrest. Governments tended to approve large wage rises for unions so they did not join student rebellions in the street. In France in 1968, the workers won a major wage increase. In Italy the next year, one would see a major series of strikes on the part of the industrial workers called the hot autumn. But rising wages meant rising prices and created what was known as a wage-price spiral. Employers believed they could pass on higher labor costs to consumers. No one was better off at the end.[53]

Inflation complicated the problem since monetary gains in wages or dividends were not real gains. When growth faltered, inflation had often assuaged the distributive conflict by disguising the outcomes in terms of real income. But above a certain rate, inflation lost that mystifying function. Inflation spiked in 1947–1948, again during the Korean War, then eased during the later 1950s, but it did not, could not disappear. It was not necessarily harmful; indeed, during a period of growth, prolonged through the 1950s and then into the 1960s, it probably contributed to overall stability in Europe. By the 1970s, it had become the most agonizing of problems for making economic policy.

What were its sources? The impact of the oil price increases in 1974 and 1979 would raise prices in the short term of perhaps 4–6 percent.[54] But the pressure on wages and prices was there long before. On the one hand, it apparently arose from ambitious government spending—President Johnson's decision not to seek new taxes as he committed more troops to South Vietnam in 1965 and the German Social-Liberal government's decision to ward off a threatened recession in 1966 by deficit spending. Critics attacked the ambitious social programs of the social-liberal coalitions. Conservatives attributed the rise in prices to a growing share of government expenditure that was funded by monetized debt purchased by the central bank. Governments of the left in Scandinavia, the Federal Republic of Germany after 1966, the United States, a British Labour Party back in power, the Socialist-Christian Democratic *apertura* cabinets in Italy after 1962, and Johnson's Great Society seemed culpable at first glance, although the correlations were ambiguous and social-democratic coalitions could also appeal for restraint from their labor union allies. Ambitious government programs sponsored by governments of the left also contributed, as their costs often outran tax revenues or households' willingness to hold government debt. Public expenditure in the OECD countries as of 1950 amounted to a median 34 percent of national income, but by 1965 it had risen to 41 percent (without wartime expenses) and by 1973 would reach 49 percent.[55]

The newly fashionable monetarist economics claimed tautologically that inflation was no more than a monetary problem and would end when acquiescent central bankers refused to buy government debt. But there were social and electoral pressures on public spending during a decade of social-democratic ascendancy. Along with the growth rate of the economy, the major metric for economic analysis became the Phillips curve—an empirical correlation presented by economist A. William Phillips, which revealed in the case of Great Britain, but was supposedly applicable to capitalist economies in general, that the lower the rate of wage increases over time, the higher the rate of unemployment. By the mid-1960s, the policy conclusions ran the other

Table 6.5 Average Annual Rates of Inflation in Five Countries (Consumer Prices) during Selected Years, 1950–1981

	1950–1959	1960–1969	1970–1979	1973–1975	1979–1981
FRG	1.9%	2.5%	4.9%	6.2%	5.7%
Italy	3.0%	3.8%	12.2%	16.5%	17.8%
Japan	4.0%	5.4%	8.7%	16.5%	6.2%
UK	3.6%	3.6%	12.4%	18.2%	13.9%
US	2.1%	2.4%	7.0%	9.6%	11.3%

Data source: Charles S. Maier, "Inflation and Stagnation as Politics and History," in *The Politics of Inflation and Economic Stagnation: Theoretical Approaches and International Case Studies*, ed. Leon N. Lindberg and Charles S. Maier (Washington, DC: Brookings Institution, 1988), 11, table 1-2, based in turn on International Monetary Fund, *International Financial Statistics*, vol. 37 (October 1984), line 64.

way; governments could lower persistent unemployment, so economists on the center-left argued, by allowing a higher rate of inflation through deficit spending.[56] The prescription was neo-Keynesian, although Keynes had argued that economies needed only a discrete shot of deficit spending to lower unemployment, while the Phillips curve suggested the stimulus must be inscribed permanently.

The difficulty was that whereas into the 1960s an inflation rate of 3 percent might stabilize unemployment at no greater than 4 percent (its floor in the early 1960s), by the administration of President Johnson, administration economists were suggesting that it would require 5 percent inflation to keep unemployment down to 5 percent. The trade-off would be seen as ever more adverse, although economists friendly to Democratic policy responses suggested that these results represented only a short-term Phillips curve. What supposedly were the causes for this inconvenient worsening of the Phillips curve by the late 1960s? That was unclear; what was evident was that the problem seemed self-reinforcing. Labor would bargain for wages or welfare benefits whose purchasing power partially evaporated in the next cycle, so they would have to ask for even higher wages. They suffered from a "monetary illusion"—namely, that a higher paycheck yielded greater purchasing power. And although unions in the product sector might eventually prove less powerful than they once were, the new service sectors wanted more: police and firefighters, sanitation workers, hospital employees, teachers, and so forth. And if one group won wage increases, then others sought them as well.

Herein lay the problem, conservative critics would respond by the 1960s. Ever greater rates of inflation would be required to reduce unemployment

beyond some level postulated as the NAIRU, or the nonaccelerating inflationary rate of unemployment. What that rate supposedly depended on was
structural supply-side factors—the frictions of the economy, inhibiting taxation, changing technologies, the simple inertia involved in transitioning
workers from one sector to another. Milton Friedman and others at the University of Chicago enjoyed a new influence. Friedman argued that governments
could never produce long-term increased employment rates by the device of
government deficits that central banks would be required to "accommodate"
by buying treasury debt and thereby increasing the money supply. Once an
economy reached that point, Friedman was to argue, the Phillips curve
became a vertical line: trying to overcome these limits by stimulating demand
through government spending would just push prices up and up without ever
lowering the unemployment rate.[57]

The growing response of center-left governments was the adoption of what
some sociologists termed a political wage—that is, the recognition of trade
unions as partners in the public determination of wage increases in return
for pledging their restraint, a policy approach that became celebrated as neocorporatism.[58] The Swedish trade union organization, the LO, and employers' federation agreed to a series of wage-price agreements, Haga I, II,
and III, named after the castle where they were negotiated. When the Nixon
administration suspended gold convertibility in 1971, it imposed a ninety-day
price and wage freeze, then a series of negotiated controls, the so-called Phases
I, II, and III. Another response was tried in Italy and Israel and to a degree
in other countries: indexation of wages in terms of prices—that is, an effort
to guarantee real wages. This would supposedly calm workers' fear of losing
purchasing power, but it tended rather to lead to a continuing ratcheting
upward of wages and then prices. It was precisely the scenario that Galbraith had said would destroy the mechanism of countervailing power.
Rather, unions and compliant employers—private and public—would accommodate each other's demands at the cost of the massive numbers outside
the unionized industries—whether self-employed or pensioners and all those
on fixed income.

But the monetary turbulence was not easily quelled and reverberated in
the international arena. The pressure from the unions culminated in France
and Italy in 1968 and 1969. The French unions' protest was attached to the
student explosions that rocked France, but once the unions won a nation-
wide wage hike of about 15 percent, they returned to work. The French government, in any case, followed up the wage concession with a devaluation

that largely nullified their nominal effect. The Italians did not. Major governments had to face the consequences of inflationary pressure throughout the postwar era. The Bretton Woods agreements required maintenance of exchange rates in terms of dollars and gold, although one-off devaluations were allowed. The Italians had sharply restricted funding of their government debt and private firm borrowings in 1947 and managed to hold the value of the lira at around 600 to the dollar. The British had devalued from $4.03 to $2.80 in 1949 and were constrained to devalue again in 1967. President de Gaulle had accepted a devaluation of the franc from about 350 to the dollar to 500 when he came to power in 1958 and then cut off two zeroes from the rate to end up at a rate that looked superficially the same as the 1914 ratio of 5:1.

Only Americans had been spared an adjustment primarily because through the 1950s, Europeans had faced a chronic dollar shortage. The delegates of Allied governments meeting at Bretton Woods, New Hampshire in 1944 had agreed that the dollar would serve as an international reserve currency alongside gold. National treasuries would have to accept dollars as an international means of payment, but the United States accepted the potential obligation of redeeming foreign accumulations of dollars with gold. So many countries needed American goods (and therefore, American dollars to buy them) that it was presumed that the dollar would always hold its value, almost like a credit card that never had to be paid. In 1959, however, the Belgian-born Yale economist Robert Triffin identified the underlying "dilemma" that was overtaking American policy: for the United States to fund dollar needs of its partners in the Bretton Woods system, it must simultaneously run a continuing current-account deficit and thus undermine the value of the reserve currency it was providing. America was running a deficit in any case by the end of the 1950s. More Americans were purchasing European automobiles and vacations. The United States maintained troop commitments in Europe and South Korea. In 1965–1966, President Johnson sought to finance escalation in Vietnam without resorting to new taxes;- later in 1971, President Richard Nixon wanted to stimulate the American economy as he headed toward a campaign for reelection.

The American capacity to export its own inflationary tendencies onto other countries committed to holding American dollars was becoming irksome. Critics charged that the dollar was overvalued at $35 per ounce of gold—a parity established in 1935—with respect to European prices and currencies. So called Eurodollars—that is, dollars originally sent abroad to buy European goods or pay the costs of US troops kept in NATO countries—

accumulated in the European banks or were used to purchase European assets; Jean-Jacques Servan-Schreiber, publisher of the *Time*-style *L'Express*, claimed in *Le défi américain* (1967) that the overvalued dollar, with its reserve-currency privilege, was facilitating a systematic American takeover of European firms. The Eurodollar accumulation became the basis for a robust Eurobond and Euroloan market, and the conditions set on borrowing became progressively easier. Dollars abroad provided loans for American firms as well; commercial banks, not central banks, opened the sluice gates of these reserves, thus feeding the inflationary expansion of credit. President de Gaulle's adviser Jacques Rueff argued that gold alone could serve as a common reserve, and in 1965 / 1966 de Gaulle announced that he would not allow an increase in French dollar reserves. The German government felt more dependent on American security and had to accept the currency, thus expanding the Bundesbank's monetary reserves and potentially feeding domestic inflation, a development that the Germans feared from their experiences with hyperinflation after the two world wars. By September 1969, the Bundesbank revalued the deutsche mark upward, from 4 DM to 3.66 DM per dollar. This did not relieve the inverse pressure on the dollar. By 1971, the trends had become impossible to control. The pressure on the Federal Reserve Bank's reserves built up until Washington announced it could no longer exchange dollars for gold on August 15, 1971.[59]

Over the next year and a half despite agreements, no fixed ratios seemed stable. Strikingly, the dollar held most of its values as new exchange rates were renegotiated, notably in the Smithsonian Agreements of spring 1973. This effort could not outlive the OPEC oil price increases of early 1974. By the mid-1970s, all efforts to key diverse currencies (including the dollar) to a fixed gold / dollar ratio were abandoned and the world economies entered the period of freely tradable currencies, such as still exists today (though European currencies were partially unified with successive efforts to establish limits on their divergent values and then finally a generation later to merge them into today's euro). Freely trading currencies, it was argued, should prove no more inflationary than the abandoned gold standard. Nonetheless, the new system removed a transnational scaffolding on price movements in each country. And it encouraged workers and international capitalists to continue seeking their own welfare through price and wage rises.

In any case, the inflationary fillip given by these settlements was soon overshadowed by the OPEC increase of posted petroleum prices in January 1974. The petro-empire that the West had enjoyed was suddenly upended.

The action presented a policy puzzle for each oil-importing economy. Did the new price for oil represent an inflationary burden for the Europeans and Americans that required compensating by reduction of public expenditure? Or was it really a tax being imposed by OPEC that would induce a recession unless it was offset by government spending? Different governments decided the issue differently or oscillated from one reaction to the other.

There was no sharp economic crash as in 1929 and no onset of economic misery as in the 1930s, but the global economy entered a period in which the remarkable progress of the preceding two decades seemed to vanish, perhaps irretrievably. New concepts and terms testified to harsh dilemmas. Following Richard Cooper's use of the term in 1968, "interdependence" was identified as a critical element of economic relations.[60] Interdependence-implied that national policies to stimulate employment or to curtail inflation failed because they tended automatically to provoke countervailing financial pressures from abroad. The economists Robert Mundell and Marcus Fleming had each already demonstrated that efforts to rebalance economic aggregates in any one country could be nullified by the ramifications on the nations with which it traded and had financial relations. Any country, they pointed out, was able to secure at most two, but not all three, of the parameters that it might wish to secure (high employment levels through monetary policy, control of capital flows, and a desired exchange rate)—what the economist Maurice Obstfeld later labeled as a trilemma. The Bretton Woods agreements left states the power to limit capital movements but committed them to maintain fixed exchange rate parities, which effectively restrained their monetary policies. With the 1960s, the G-7 governments and the European Community loosened the restraints on exporting capital. Freedom to invest abroad or buy foreign currencies became the priority, but the pressure to raise interest rates or adjust exchange rates could grow correspondingly. In the terms this book has suggested, this might have been seen by representatives of capital as an important gain, but it was also a weighty transition for the project-state, which increasingly focused on economic and financial growth indicators as its measure of success—at the very moment that the days of relatively unproblematic postwar growth were ending.[61]

For the rest of the 1970s, the economies seemed intractable. Inflation proved disturbingly stubborn. As the Princeton economist Phillip Cagan argued, what was new was not that a supply shock drove up prices but that the "core rate" persisted through the recessions of 1975 and 1978–1990.[62] Since the OPEC countries priced their oil in dollars and the dollar slowly inflated, the United States suffered less from the price increase than the Europeans; and in effect, the Americans lived more easily. Their major oil producers could always sell the oil they bought at a profit and had little incentive to oppose the cartel. Nonetheless, by the end of the 1970s, the OPEC countries realized that a large percentage of their higher dollar receipts since 1974 had eroded in real terms, and they imposed another sharp increase in 1979, soon dubbed OPEC II.[63]

By the end of the decade, the conclusion spread that inflation could simply not be allowed to continue. In the United States, "inflation has the kind of dominance that no other issue has had since World War II," the pollster Daniel Yankelovich determined. "It would be necessary to go back to the 1930s and the Great Depression to find a peacetime issue that had the country so concerned and so distraught."[64] A newer doctrine amplified the supposed correlation between the quantity of money and inflation: "rational expectations." Ending inflation did not just require that central banks be freed from the requirement of buying government debt so states could cover their spendthrift programs. It was the public's belief that in the end, the central bank would "accommodate"—that is, monetize or cover government deficits—that had to be changed. The banks must make it clear they would not restart the printing press.[65] Painful but hopefully brief recessions could provide the springboard for renewed growth. By the 1980s, central bankers would become the policy heroes in the United States, Italy, Germany, and Japan. But the politicians who acted on these theories also understood that credibility required exemplary confrontations with established civil service constituencies and industrial unions.

Although few might have sensed this at the time, the turmoil of 1968 and 1969 represented in fact the transition to a new era that closed the postwar period. Inflation in the advanced economies tended to mount—never so extremely as during the great hyperinflations after World War I and World War II, when the German currency, among others, became worthless—but up to 10, 15, even 20 percent per year. Unemployment rates remained stubbornly higher than during the 1960s, and the concept of "stagflation"—a tendency toward simultaneous price inflation, which undermined any nominal economic growth and persistent joblessness—became commonplace. The extraordinary growth of the postwar had been the material premise of political stability. Now it was ending in an era of claims and counterclaims within first world societies and between countries of the first and the third worlds. Who would pay for the ambitious social programs funded by growth, including the higher education of the very student classes many of whom now seemed to reject the whole achievement as coercive? Even more gloomy was the danger of absolutely diminishing resources envisaged by the Club of Rome in 1972. Night was falling in the gardens of the global north. If the project-state appeared fundamentally overextended, the profitable legacies of empire under attack, and the resources of capital—whether inexpensive energy or Western industrial dominance—now tenuous and shaky, might the agencies that spoke for governance now come into their own?

PART THREE

Contending Projects
since the 1970s

7

Deploying Governance

CONSIDER TWO VERY DIFFERENT PHENOMENA of the 1960s and 1970s. First, what many observers, and not just those on the right, beheld as a disintegration of public order: strikes, student occupations, terrorist activity, and growing demands for redistributing wealth and authority—an explosion of contentiousness acted out throughout much of the world, developed and less developed.[1] Second, just beginning, a change in political language in the global west, more striking in retrospect than as it was occurring: the rapidly growing adoption of the hitherto rarified term *governance*.[2] In English-language books it revealed a point of inflection in the mid-1970s and by the mid-1980s and 1990s would grow exponentially. (See figures 7.1–2.) This was no coincidence. Government stability seemed threatened in the streets, and wealthy countries faced emphatic claims for a fairer international distribution of wealth from poorer ones. "Governance" suggested an approach to administration that promised to rise above the divisions and defuse the assault—rational rules and procedures that guided private organizations and that, in the public domain, should command assent without state enforcement.

"Governance" Takes Off

The realm of governance, as I use the term, was a domain of norms, ostensibly based on science, considerations of justice, or calculations of utility. Policy intellectuals and policymakers claimed to act on behalf of expert knowledge. They deployed the language of public affairs supposedly in terms of the common good and not just on behalf of a particular party or interest. The policies advocated were supposed to transcend that of a mere transaction or compromise. They claimed if not "scientific" objectivity, conclusions dependent on empirical findings and disinterested debate. In terms of organization, the realm of governance comprised many different institutional forms: new political associations, public interest lobbies, and international organizations whether official or nongovernmental organizations (NGOs). The issues they tackled were to be negotiated or defended in new forums, no longer states but associations and international agencies. Of course, many of these forums tended to gather like-minded analysts, often dismissive of those who might press "unsound" policies of too ideological a bent. For all its measured discourse, the realm of governance remained permeated with ideology.

Can we trace a genealogy for this strand of public intervention? Alexis de Tocqueville famously recognized American democracy was long hospitable to multilevel government and independent organizations. Chapter 3 has cited precedents between the wars, The League of Nations and the United Nations (UN) responded to humanitarian emergencies and then to more general needs arising from labor, gender, and health issues. European analogues had developed from other traditions. Nineteenth- and early twentieth-century German jurists and historians stressed the legacy of local and corporate "self-administration" (*Selbstverwaltung*) or guild regulations.[3] In France "associations" including formal religious institutions were treated as governed by the state and codified in the laws of 1884 and 1901. The legislation derived from centrist political efforts to defuse revolutionary politics by encouraging the organizational capacity of society itself. Youthful leaders who began on the radical left and in opposition become moderates or reactionary as regimes changed, and they sought to escape confrontations they condemned as outdated by political and economic progress. French thinkers and political figures from François Guizot to Hippolyte Taine on the right, through the legal theorist Léon Duguit and the centrist politician Pierre Waldeck-Rousseau, who sponsored the Laws of Association, emphasized society itself as a source of cohesion and possible reform. The idea hearkened back to Montesquieu's "intermediate bodies" and sought to overcome the French revolutionaries' rejection of such associations as subversive.[4] Sometimes dubbing themselves progressive rather than socialist or radical or "liberal" with connotations of economic orthodoxy or dislike of anticlerical measures, they could urge a more rightist or leftist course according to circumstance. The French reckoning with May 1968 brought out the differences between this tradition of autonomous reform, a self-styled second left, from both Marxists on the left and self-proclaimed liberals on the right. As in the United States, the latter were emphatically anti-communist, repenting of their own youthful Marxism, and often contemptuous of the third world; their journal *Commentaire* took inspiration from the American *Commentary*, which followed a similar trajectory.[5] Appeals to associational efforts such as the new "clubs" let the reformist "second left" avoid the ideological confrontations that comprised the legacy of 1968. The post-'68 Unified Socialist Party (PSU) under Michel Rocard, which split from the established SFIO, seemed hospitable to this new direction, in effect promoting a turn toward governance *avant la lettre*. The hour of the "clubs," however, soon faded; the Socialists produced a Common Program with the French Communist Party in the mid-1970s, recalling the Popular Front of 1936 and advocating a traditional program of nationalization and increased taxation. The left's coalition, however, still lost the March 1978 legislative elections to the two conservative parties in President Giscard d'Estaing's presidential majority. Nonetheless, by the presidential campaign of 1981 François Mitterrand could capture the presidency—only to have to scuttle his reformist program in 1983 as the business community took alarm, the balance of payments worsened, and inflation increased. Mitterrand turned instead to close monetary collaboration with Helmut Kohl's Germany, disillusioning many who had supported him. The reformist Socialist leaders of the late 1970s and early 1980s, Michel Rocard and Jacques Delors, would take their energies elsewhere.

By 1980, the sites of governance were multiple and increasingly aligned around a neoliberal agenda. They included the international organizations set up at Bretton Woods, the World Bank and the International Monetary Fund (IMF). The UN Economic and Social Council (ECOSOC) and the Economic Commission for Europe claimed the same moral authority, but they had quickly become caught up in the ideological rivalries that divided the organization.[6] Originally brought into being as a response to the Marshall Plan, the Organisation for Economic Co-operation and Development (OECD) had established itself as an advocate for governance, as had the earlier League of Nations institutions between the wars. Other sites included the dense thicket of domestic foundations and nongovernmental institutions recruiting members by co-optation, such as the Council on Foreign Relations, the Brookings Institution, the Hoover Institution, Chatham House, the Atlantic Council, the Kiel Institute for the World Economy, such periodicals as *The Economist*, the *Financial Times*, the *Neueste Züricher Zeitung*, the *Frankfurter Allgemeine Zeitung*, *Nihon keizai shimbun*, *Il sole 24 ore*, *La Folha de São Paulo*—all those publications the French described a century earlier as *bien-pensant*. The point is not that they were partisan, but that in light of the distress of the 1970s, they and many others and the columnists they re-cruited represented or claimed to represent a wisdom or knowledge that tran-scended any identification with party. Behind them stood intellectuals who had long urged the policies now coming into fashion—notably the rarified Mont Pèlerin Society and think tanks that claimed objective proceedings even as they admitted affiliation with partisan institutions or points of view, such as the German party foundations, the British Institute of Economic Affairs, or the American Enterprise Institute.[7]

Government bodies might establish special commissions, sometimes to re-solve ad hoc issues on which opinion differed, sometimes to gather decen-tralized experts in one place as a continuing resource. Wealthy donors could establish foundations, as had John D. Rockefeller and Andrew Carnegie early in the century, supposedly at sufficient arm's-length from the funder, that were dedicated to specialized branches of knowledge. Private voluntary organ-izations (PVOs or NGOs) sent substantial aid abroad from the 1960s on; by the 1980s, there were 4,600 agencies distributing assistance—totaling $4.7 billion in 1980—to 20,000 organizations in developing countries. These sums were far outmatched by public agencies ($37.8 billion) and corporations ($13.3 billion), but they could work with alacrity and interface with local groups. Even when they were funded in part by first world governments, they could pursue an agenda that stressed left-leaning social and political participation.[8] Increasingly from the 1960s on, the new foundations or think tanks became known for competing claims to expertise. The Rockefeller Foundation funded an Overseas Development Council, close to the Democratic Party, staffed by former officials of the Agency for International Development (AID) and chaired by Notre Dame's president, Fr. Theodore Hesburgh. Germany and the United States had set up bodies of economic advisers that supposedly fur-nished nonpartisan expertise: the President's Council of Economic Advisers and the Congressional Budget Office in the United States, the Sachverstän-digen Rat or Council of Wise Men (Experts) in Germany. Private foundations and think tanks also claimed a role in the governance space. Some were of long standing and devoted to nonpartisan analyses (itself a restricted spectrum), such as the Brookings Institution or the Council of Foreign Relations in the United States and the Royal Institute of International Affairs (Chatham House) in Britain. Others represented particular interests whether on the side of business (the American Enterprise Institution) or labor unions. From the 1970s on, as this chapter will suggest, political and economic elites could mobilize the realm of governance; they could deploy the foundations and organizations that claimed scientific independence and authority to reorient the discourse of entitlements and equality that had set the agendas of the 1960s.

Under the slogan of governance, experts were mobilized to temper the turbulence of the 1960s and early 1970s—and not just for an evanescent moment of stability but ultimately for almost a half century. They proposed ideas; they needed networks with political or economic power to adopt them. And the reverse question remained open—whether their ideas would sustain their nonpartisan force or be instrumentalized by their patrons. This had been the concern of social-democratic intellectuals on the left two decades earlier. Then, in the terms that Jürgen Habermas had introduced, capitalist interests tended effectively to smother the possibilities for governance and social rationality and, in his picturesque metaphor, to colonize the lifeworld.[9]

Historians have emphasized the international dimension of these policy networks and intellectuals. Many cut across state borders in an epoch of growing globalization. Some were established as special commissions by national governments, others by international agreement. Still others claimed a role as nongovernmental institutions or NGOs. Their number roughly tripled between 1968 and 1981.[10] To be clear, they did not mobilize just on behalf of capital. As the Italian constitutional lawyer Sabino Cassese has emphasized, governance associations claim a sectoral role, whether regulation of public health, economic transactions, arms control, or environment.[11] Their proposals supposedly addressed a social ill in the interests of all parties collectively; they were intended to command respect as inherently compelling, whether according to criteria of social justice or economic rationality. They divest the state of the burden of massive regulation, indeed over time might replace state presence, or even become important instrumentalities for states that were jealous of their sovereignty but hoped to off-load some of its burdens.[12] During the long 1970s, there was a vigorous expansion of governance institutions overall—some established by international negotiations, others by a proliferation of NGOs. They all had to establish a claim to legitimacy, not only by virtue of the authorities that established them but by their appeal to a nonpartisan domain of high-minded values. The invocation of "governance" revealed the new terms of debate.

"Governance" was related to another neologism: "governability." By the mid-1970s, governability—the capacity to peacefully administer a society and to overcome open unruliness—seemed in peril. Although the term appeared far less frequently than governance, its usage oscillated more rapidly. According to Google n-grams, the use of "governability" surged sixfold with respect to

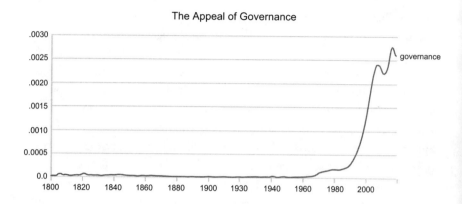

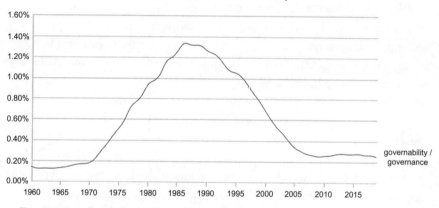

Figures 7.1–2   Google Books Ngram Viewer

"governance" by the late 1980s. The figures suggest that the idea of governance diffused fairly steadily ever since the 1970s, while in all likelihood a sudden panic about governability took hold among the "commentariat" from the 1970s into the last decade of the twentieth century.[13]

For the participants in the Trilateral Commission, funded by David Rocke-feller and directed by Zbigniew Brzezinski in 1973, who published *The Crisis of Democracy* in 1975, governability signified the ability of the political re-gime to resist being overwhelmed by the demands of its citizens—those whom social commentators in earlier decades might have called the masses. Governability was endangered by the weakening capacity of the state to hold in check the "demands" of social groups. Michel Crozier, whose major work in the early 1960s highlighted the destructive tendency of French bureaucratic actors to hoard information, emphasized a decade later that the European political systems were "overloaded with participants and demands," and the bureaucratic cohesion they required to meet these demands fostered "irresponsibility and consensus." Samuel Huntington had identified a similar danger of special-interest domination he termed *praetorianism* in his major book *Political Order in Changing Societies*.[14] The 1960s had made it far more acute, in large part because of a generational break. "In all three Trilateral regions, a shift in values is taking place away from the materialistic work-oriented, public-spirited values toward those which stress private satisfaction, leisure and the need for 'being and intellectual and esthetic self-fulfillment." Huntington emphasized "the tremendous expansion of the nondefense activities of government," and he cited John Adams: "'Democracy never lasts long. . . . It soon wastes, exhausts, and murders itself. There never was a democracy yet that did not commit suicide.'. . . The pursuit of the democratic virtues of equality and individualism has led to the delegitimation of authority generally and the loss of trust in leadership."[15] Similar laments surfaced throughout Western societies. Samuel Beer, a liberal in politics, affiliated with the Americans for Democratic Action, analyzed the 1960s and 1970s in Britain at the beginning of the 1980s: "It was in [the 1960s] that the pressures generated within the collectivist polity substantially and visibly escaped from public control. By the later sixties what had appeared as the common ground of a new social and economic order began to look like a swamp of pluralistic stagnation." "The traditional bonds of social class," he quoted another observer, "party, and common nationality are waning and with them the old restraints of hierarchy and deference."[16] Looking back at these analyses, one sees both familiar tropes and significantly different analyses from today's concerns. The critics of the 1970s emphasized a cascading of special-interest demands; they were less the product of coherent class claims than of undisciplined groups each bidding for a greater share of the national product. They failed, as Mancur Olson put it, to be encompassing enough to discipline social partners.[17] Inflation and public service strikes provided the visible evidence. Beer used the term *populism* to suggest the breakdown of organizational discipline in favor of mass demands and participation, not the cultivation of exclusionary ethnic consciousness, such as implied today.

The Trilateral Commission soon became viewed among those inclined to conspiracy theories as an elitist cabal, but its influence derived rather from the participation of venerable liberals, such as Arthur Schlesinger Jr., alongside the conservatives who discerned a crisis of governability. The generational vector remained important if unspoken: trilateralism expressed a demand not only to recover control from the supposed political and social excesses of the 1960s but to assert a concept of political maturity. In the United States, it implied a reaction to the spectacle of the Democratic Party Convention of 1972, where the agenda seemed dominated by militant demands for gender equality and lifestyle issues. Trilateralists in effect rallied against Woodstock as well as leftist unrest; it was time for grown-ups to recapture the political initiative. But trilateralism was not simply a new holy alliance to quash domestic unrest. Its very sober and socially conscious reports represented a responsible mobilization of experts for global economic governance. They gained force from the fact that the trilateral powers amounted to approximately two-thirds of global economic output. At the same time, they were also a response to the dispersion of global power and resources from the one-time imperial powers to third world challengers, their growing influence made manifest on the one hand by calls for a New International Economic Order, on the other hand by the Organization of the Petroleum Exporting Countries' (OPEC's) new militancy. Following the Huntington-Crozier *cri de coeur*, which did not discuss developing countries, the majority of its early reports focused on north-south relations and called for more aid to developing countries; as of 1974–1976, this aligned with Henry Kissinger's effort to keep OPEC and the third world from consolidating ranks.[18] It was supported by Helmut Schmidt, Willy Brandt's successor as chancellor, more hard-nosed both in his view of the Soviets and third world romanticism. But it was still too soft for the emerging neoconservative critics, such as Irving Kristol, who condemned these policies as "liberal chic." The issue, Kristol asserted, was not a potential class war or the champions of poor nations against the wealthy West seeking a fairer distribution of resources, but an assault of communist, socialist, and even neofascist agitators (in Africa) against liberal capitalism.[19]

International Redistribution?

Certainly, claims for recognition, respect, and resources saturated the public arena, which extended from schools and neighborhoods up to the UN General Assembly. Some of the claims were couched in the language of rights that had been transgressed or rights that needed to be recognized. Political philosophers took them up in the language of obligations.[20] Interest group and class claims had after all continuously motivated politics within states and continued to do so. Now as former colonies and developing countries asserted an international role, they waged similar struggles with the industrial countries of Europe and America. For the new nations of Africa and Asia as well as those long established, the inequality of wealth and their perceived vulnerability vis-à-vis the "first world" remained major concerns. Especially when long-standing analyses of exploitation suggested that the wealth of the first world derived from the third world.

The UN, as historians have now documented, provided the ready forum to articulate their claims.[21] By virtue of their sovereign presence in the General Assembly, which provided theoretically equal representation, the countries of the global south had a voice they lacked individually or in the agencies derived from the Bretton Woods agreement, the OECD, and the European Community. Accepting their role as developing countries, the ex-colonial countries, whether defining themselves as a geopolitical bloc (as in Bandung) or an economic force, wanted to strengthen recognition of their rights as collective actors. The UN's ECOSOC, like the Economic Committee for Europe in the late 1940s and 1950s, provided an institutional forum for the socialist world and the nonaligned developing countries to articulate a program critical of the Western powers including the United States. Yugoslavia provided early leadership in the 1950s; once OPEC became a player, Algeria's president also staked a claim.

In Cairo in 1962, delegates from third world countries organized what emerged as the UN Conference on Trade and Development (UNCTAD). Its first conference took place in Geneva in 1964, with 4,000 delegates from 120 countries. As Johanna Bockman points out, the ideas put forward by UNCTAD sounded more liberal than socialist. Ernesto Che Guevara called for access to markets and an end to tariff barriers. What the third world producers needed immediately was access to the markets of the first world.[22] This was precisely what was difficult to achieve. Agricultural surpluses remained one of the major American domestic policy concerns during the Truman administration and after.[23] Given a Congress that overrepresented rural interests, the United States was still unable to overcome its own agricultural sector's commitment to quotas and protection. It had already rejected the proposed International Trade Organization (ITO) in 1948 in favor of a less ambitious General Agreement on Tariffs and Trade that remained more of a wealthy countries' club for industrial trade. And only with great difficulty did the EU finally manage to negotiate its own "internal" Common Agricultural Policy in 1964. The EU did accept the Yaoundée conventions of 1963 and 1969 that gave tariff concessions to African ex-colonies. The accession process of the United Kingdom, Ireland, and Denmark to the European Economic

Community (EEC) in 1973 would raise the issue for a wider group of countries, including British colonies that would lose privileged access to a Commonwealth trading system. The former colonizing powers had their particular clients for low-tariff privileges but would hardly welcome Che Guevara's manifesto for free trade.[24]

Free trade alone, however, was not designed to solve the problems of the global south. UNCTAD's Geneva meeting called continually for a vague "structural adjustment." The origins of the concept and the policy controversies it aroused went back to the late 1940s and 1950s when the particular difficulties of the global south claimed attention. The UN Economic Commission for Latin America's economists Hans Singer and Raúl Prebisch, who would serve as secretary general of UNCTAD from 1964 to 1969, would each claim credit for what became known as the 1950 Prebisch-Singer thesis that over time, deteriorating terms of trade for agriculture—the falling ratio of prices of primary products to manufactures—would favor industrialized nations at the expense of agrarian exporters. Interwar trends had already suggested the concept, and by the 1940s it had found supporters among US economists including Charles Kindleberger and briefly even Paul Samuelson. The idea was potentially explosive and certainly contested but was seized on by economists of the so-called periphery, or the global south, and it would become central to so-called dependency theory. For sympathetic economists, it demonstrated that the global north continued to exploit the south and that imperialism lived on in the form of neocolonialism. Singer's notion that the developing countries should be eligible for soft loans with easier conditions was staunchly opposed by Eugene Black, president of the World Bank, and Singer had to content himself with the establishment of a Special UN Fund for Economic Development (SUNFED), bitterly opposed by conservatives in the United States. For economists in general, it suggested that import substitution and industrialization were key to the economic progress of the third world.[25] The need was for development as well as trade, as the MIT economist and Kennedy adviser Walt Whitman Rostow also recommended, and the new president duly called for a UN Decade of Development. Rostow himself regretted the invocation of the UN, which he saw controlled by radical economists, even as Prebisch himself retreated from his earlier gloomy analysis and became an enthusiast for John F. Kennedy's "Alliance for Progress." That effort was conceived in part as an alternative to Fidel Castro's dramatic appeal in the early 1960s. Despite evocations of the Marshall Plan, it remained underfunded and fell victim to the division between advocates of land reform on the left and industrial development.[26] By the late 1960s, the decade of development was largely forgotten. The Johnson administration was mired in Vietnam and the United States bitterly divided. Rostow had shifted his optimistic energies from describing the process of "takeoff" to defeating guerrilla warfare. Intellectually contested meanwhile by other economists and historians, the easy path to a rapid "takeoff" was hard to document in terms of gross domestic product.[27] In an era of highly charged ideological conflict, spokespeople for the global south would call for redistribution.

The third world was becoming an ever more difficult arena from the viewpoint of US policymakers. The number of UN member states increased from sixty to one hundred members in the 1950s, most resisting an East or West alignment. Under General Secretary Nikita Khrushchev, the Soviets put more resources into economic competition. By 1966, Latin American delegates managed to enshrine a declaration of economic and social rights on a par with classical political rights. At the 1972 Santiago meeting of UNCTAD— convened in Prebisch's hometown during Salvador Allende's Marxist presidency of Chile and dedicated to a new international economic order—accusations of neocolonialism based on dependency theory became the centerpiece of third world laments.[28] During the next two years, the fact that the third world was divided between oil producers and consumers (at the same moment that OPEC was drastically intervening in the price of oil) probably strengthened the bidding up of radical rhetoric. OPEC members, in particular Venezuela and Algeria, did not want to be viewed as belonging to the club of industrialized exploiters. Rather, as the Venezuelan delegate to the OPEC conference of March 1973 congratulated his fellow petroleum pumpers, "while the general clamor of the Third World for fair prices for their exports of raw materials went unheeded, they, in OPEC, through their unity and determination showed the way by securing a fair return for their oil. They had served effectively as the spearhead for their developing brothers."[29] Their brotherhood was less evident when they quadrupled the price of oil ten months later, but third world countries felt the pain far less than the industrialized nations, and OPEC funneled significant payments to aid institutions. Algeria, a relatively minor oil producer, played a key role in making this implausible (Kissinger would say "unholy") alliance function.

Three groups of countries emerged as contending actors during the 1973– 1974 crisis: the OPEC members who decided to exploit their privileged resource position; the Western powers angered by OPEC but divided between

US concern about continuing leadership and France's Gaullist reflexes; and the large Group of 77 (G-77) in the UN who could exploit the energy vulnerability of the Atlantic powers to press common claims against the wealthy West. The oil majors attracted the wrath of the American Congress as willing OPEC accomplices but were passive players. The oil price hike served as some grand prisoners' dilemma game, inviting each to seek its own advantage. As Marino Auffant's dissertation research stresses, it threatened a further wrench to the US-anchored international monetary system, already threatened by the shakiness of the dollar.[30] US Secretary of the Treasury George P. Schultz had denounced the price increase at the IMF's G-20 meeting in January 1974. The IMF had been developing its plans for Special Drawing Rights (SDRs) as a supplementary reserve, but the United States was reluctant to share its own reserve currency privileges. Now the chair of the IMF further envisaged that the Fund would serve as the agency for distributing the glut of petrodollars that the OPEC producers would have to recycle to consumers. This was also unwelcome. Kissinger, always preoccupied by independent initiatives by NATO allies—whether Willy Brandt's Ostpolitik in the late 1960s or Paris's continuing unwillingness to remain subordinate to Washington's proposals—proposed a conference among the major importers at a Washington conference for February 11. The Federal Republic could be counted on to second Washington because of its need for American troops, but Britain and France were in a stronger position to bargain with oil-producing countries. Kissinger stressed the need for multilateral coordination, by which he intended American leadership of the Atlantic nations. Michel Jobert, President Georges Pompidou's foreign secretary, saw the conference as another overweaning US initiative to impose a world energy order. The French did decide to attend, but Jobert so bitterly denounced the American policies that he found no support from other delegates. A resolution was patched together that allowed for some French exceptions.

The G-20 powers represented only one bloc. The question remained whether the third world countries could retain some unity as raw material exporters given the divergence of interests between OPEC and the far more numerous oil consumers. Well aware of the potential tension, the Algerian leader Houari Boumédienne, serving also as president of the fourth conference of the nonaligned states, called for a special UN session, not only on oil but also on the conditions for trade and raw materials in general. Opening the session in April 1974, he accused the industrialized countries of having accepted self-determination for their colonies only after having won control of the world economy. The UN G-77 announced their program for a New International Economic Order (NIEO), soon approved by the General Assembly, based "on the principles of equity, sovereign equality, interdependence, common interest, cooperation and solidarity among all States." Only slightly less lofty were the specifics: full sovereignty of each state over its natural resources, bilateral and multilateral aid to promote industrialization, reform of the international monetary system to advance development, and terms of trade more favorable to commodity producers.[31] In specific, it called for the developed countries to share technology, to accept linking raw material prices to those of manufactured goods, forgive debts and provide assistance for finance and development.[32]

Lawyers and philosophers might debate whether these were claims or rights. Did they mean, "we demand" or "we deserve"? In the postwar world, the distinction soon faded. The UN had inscribed the right to have rights in its 1948 Declaration of Human Rights. But these were the liberal rights, supposedly inhering in human nature according to Stoic and Christian concepts of humankind and reaffirmed in Anglo-American and French claims since the seventeenth and eighteenth centuries: freedom of expression and belief, protection from torture and infringements of liberty, and from being murdered, whether as an individual victim or—what the Genocide Convention had spotlighted—as part of an ethnic mass. European conservatives had been eager to enshrine human rights in part as a response to Soviet concepts and in part to avoid any recognition of the more troublesome economic rights.[33] Beyond Kissinger's awareness that America had to give lip service to them, they never really weighed in his calculus of the global balance of power. Unfortunately, their blatant transgression at the outset of the 1970s made them hard to ignore. Human rights emerged dramatically on the global stage with the unsuccessful Biafran effort at secession from Nigeria (1967–1971) and then with Islamabad's campaign to retain East Pakistan (1971), which resulted in the formation of Bangladesh. Richard Nixon had personal sympathy for the Biafran secessionists, but he and Kissinger essentially looked on as Britain (and Shell Oil with extensive Nigerian oil installations) supported the federal government while it starved the Biafrans into submission. In Asia, Washington unsuccessfully "tilted" toward its Pakistani ally and against neutralist India and East Pakistani rebels despite the quasi-genocidal conduct of Karachi's unsuccessful campaign to recover its territory on the other side of India. Indian intervention on behalf of emerging Bangladesh effectively brought the war to an end.[34]

These struggles with their immense human suffering stimulated an outpouring of Western sentiment for human rights, enlistment of celebrities, and mobilization of NGOs. Although they raised support for alleviating suffering, their impact on state conduct was limited. This was in the nature of the problem: it took atrocities well under way to arouse public opinion. "Never again," alas, usually meant "Never in time." By the mid-1970s, at the same time as the NIEO was being negotiated, the Soviets felt that nominally endorsing "rights" was harmless enough so that they might sign on to them in the Helsinki process in return for consolidating the borders of a divided Europe. Jimmy Carter's presidential campaign of 1976 and his subsequent administration inscribed human rights as a centerpiece of its foreign relations but could press for them only marginally even in the Americas. The cynic can say that hypocrisy is the compliment that virtue pays to vice. But democracy could not subsist without the claims of rights. Governments alone could not guarantee them even when inscribed in constitutional documents: the realm of governance provided the networks and legal forums where these ideals might be defended. Surprisingly, the "basket" of human rights that Leonid Brezhnev believed he might safely accept in 1975 would serve Eastern European dissidents as they organized for what became their surprising success at the end of the 1980s.

The status of economic rights was far less clear, certainly outside the domain of labor law where many had been recognized, not least by the League of Nation's International Labour Organization between the wars. If the extension of such rights to a nation-state as such seemed questionable, a further argument was at hand: the West or the global north had despoiled the third world. Economic rights were a form of reparation or rendering justice. American and Western European spectators of the rhetorical dramas at the UN might well believe that since the poor nations outnumbered the wealthy, they were using their majority to impose a guilt trip on the successful developers. The communist countries were happy to assist in ritual shaming. By the 1970s, however, influential British and American economists were to push back, not at the UN itself but rather in numerous essays published in hospitable journals such as the *Journal of Political Economy* or in staff discussions at the State Department. In 1970, the OECD published an influential critique of import substitution industrialization based on the comparative performance of less developed economies, soon to be followed by other indictments.[35] In any case, the NIEO was to run into the harsh and skeptical headwinds of what was soon being called neoliberalism.[36]

Facing this conjunction of OPEC's oil price increases and the third world's moral offensive, the EEC, recently enlarged by British, Danish, and Irish membership, signed the Lomé Convention at the end of February 1975, opening access to European markets for the forty-six members of the African, Caribbean, and Pacific (ACP) countries. Did the pact change the relations of dependency? The program included aid provisions but gave the European Council access to ACP mineral and energy resources and reinforced European access to natural resources and markets.[37] Lomé was one of several dozen regional trade agreements for preferential trade negotiated from 1960 through the 1980s: Central Africa, West Africa, the African Great Lakes Countries, Latin America, the Southern Cone, the Arab States of the Gulf, the Maghreb. Association of Southeast Asian Nations (ASEAN), and Central America were among the networks envisaged. UNCTAD facilitated some multilateral clearing arrangements just as the United States had helped finance the European Payments Union at the end of the 1950s.

What about outright aid? How responsive was the global north? Bilateral aid from the capitalist countries constituting the Development Assistance Committee (DAC) amounted to 88 percent of total official financing between 1956 and 1960, of which the US share constituted two-thirds at first and three-fifths in 1960. (Foreign aid from communist countries remained a very minor source of financing.) The 1960s brought an expansion of multilateral aid through governance agencies: the International Bank of Reconstruction and Development, the International Finance Corporation, and the UN. But instead of a special UN fund for economic development, the underdeveloped countries got a soft-loan window at the World Bank and a series of regional development banks founded from 1959 to 1970.[38] Overall, the results that the NIEO countries hoped for were disappointing.

Part of the difficulty was that the Marshall Plan, highly regarded as a success story, above all in the United States, was a misleading model. The $13.5 billion of 1948–1951 had flowed to developed countries, not to the less developed world; it served to remove temporary postwar blockages to trade and industry and lack of foreign currency reserves. The human resources required for development, skilled labor, and engineers, were already present in the European recipients. Aid recipients in Africa and Asia required a qualitative transformation. American efforts to extend aid to developing countries whether in Harry Truman's Point IV program of 1949 or Kennedy's Alliance for Progress in the early 1960s aroused enthusiasm but involved a far lower commitment in real current dollars than the European Recovery

Program (ERP). They were also bilateral loans and grants and did not envisage the same important role for trade among the recipients as had the ERP and later the American-primed European Payments Union.

The inequalities within the so-called third world or global south further complicated the idea of redistribution from the haves to the have-nots. The haves included the wealthy Petrostates, even if within those fortunately endowed countries the vast differences between a privileged elite and masses of impoverished citizens persisted. Primarily Saudi Arabia and Libya recognized the need to recycle dollars into the Western economies to avoid a serious world economic contraction, although they also expressed their obligation to assist their oil-bereft Arab neighbors. The first challenge was largely met; oil dollars were deposited into Western banks, which by virtue of fractional reserve requirements that allowed them to lend far more than the cash they held, were able to extend significant credits to third world government programs. American and European drivers, after impatiently waiting in line to fill their gas tanks, had the privilege of contributing to build a luxury hotel in Caracas, buy a new Mercedes for prerevolutionary Tehran *jeunesse dorée*, or helping to staff a hospital in Lagos. The higher world market price for crude meant, too, that the oil-rich Soviet Union had to increase its oil exports to its Communist dependents at below the new market prices. Meanwhile, the OPEC price hike led Kissinger to remain focused on keeping the Western Europeans from breaking ranks with the United States and striking independent energy deals. In 1973, having had little substantive results, he corralled them as fellow petroleum importers under the aegis of the OECD into an International Energy Agency.[39]

A Decade of Inflation

Inflation or "stagflation" within the first world seemed more preoccupying than the claims of the NIEO. The inflation of the 1970s did not reach the same orders of magnitude but lasted longer and was far more internationally transmittable than the ravaging hyperinflations after World Wars I and II. Inflation in the OECD countries averaged almost 10 percent per year from 1974 through 1979, as against 4 percent for the previous decade.[40] Moreover, inflation did not bring a reduction in unemployment, which continued at an average 5 percent, compared with 3.2 percent from 1960 to 1973. Price levels and the mass of credits and money aggregates had increased in several leaps from the late 1960s. They rose throughout as central banks were called on to fund budget deficits, then at the end of the 1960s to satisfy the demands of a militant labor movement (in turn seeking to catch up with corporate earnings and the previous round of price increases) and shortly thereafter as a consequence of OPEC price increases. Where indexation or cost-of-living raises had been built into pensions and wages as in Italy and Israel—sometimes in hopes that unions would not press for more than the rate of inflation if they could count on staying abreast of price changes—this had simply lubricated a wage-price spiral.

The stagflation itself opened up some fundamentally divergent analyses of democratic capitalism. Its persistence and strength challenged economists and policymakers alike. Social scientists on the left—often those outside the economics discipline narrowly conceived—became convinced that the neo-corporatist experiments under way would replace market capitalism with a far more state-managed economy. Conservative commentators, on the other hand, suggested that democracies tended inexorably toward inflation and slower growth since they had to appease so many pressure groups. Inflation allegedly resulted when governments and their central banks gave way to the same sort of claim-mongering that the third world countries were pressing through the UN. Public choice theorists, applying economic analyses to political outcomes, argued that inflationary tendencies were likely to become chronic in democracies: Loosening monetary restraints and allowing budget deficits to deliver welfare benefits or tax relief did not seem to visibly cause pain and met much less opposition from parliamentary bodies than did tightening interest rates or raising taxes. Ambitious government programs fixed for the future—so called entitlements sponsored by governments of the left—also supposedly contributed, as their costs often outran tax revenues or households' willingness to hold government debt.[41] Public expenditure in the OECD countries as of 1950 amounted to a median 34 percent of national income, but by 1965 it had risen to 41 percent (without wartime expenses) and by 1973 would reach 49 percent. Close examination revealed, however, that no simple correlation existed between government spending and the rate of inflation.[42]

As inflation became endemic, social scientists initially took different positions. For James Tobin of Yale, identified as a liberal Democrat, it was not very concerning. The only aggregate welfare loss it imposed, he joked, assuming earnings kept pace with prices, was on the shoe soles eroded by more frequent walks to the bank. Pensioners were increasingly protected by cost-of-living adjustments or, in American usage, COLAs. But Tobin underplayed the sense of dislocation that noticeably rising prices inflicted on particularly older citizens.[43] (This writer remembers how taken aback his mother, then in her sixties and certainly well-off, seemed when he told her that a restaurant meal had cost almost twenty dollars.) For conservatives, the rising prices testified to an underlying social or moral rot. James Buchanan and Richard Wagner perceived a zeitgeist of permissiveness: "increasingly liberalized attitudes toward sexual activities, a declining vitality of the Puritan work ethic, deterioration in product quality, explosion of the welfare rolls, widespread corruption in both the private and governmental sector, and, finally, observed increases in the alienation of voters from the political process." Inflation played a role in this deterioration. "Inflation destroys expectations and creates uncertainty; it increases the sense of felt injustice and causes alienation." It shortened time horizons. " 'Enjoy, enjoy'—the imperative of our time—becomes a rational response in a setting where tomorrow remains insecure and where the plans made yesterday seem to have been made in folly."[44]

For the first time since the 1930s, Western commentators expressed doubt about the value of democratic government. Some contended that wage earners, at least as their voices could be aggregated by labor unions or left parties, no longer understood the need to accumulate capital for investment but demanded permanently excessive wages and welfare entitlements. Modern capitalism had lost the impulse to save that had created wealth to begin with. It was concerned predominantly with consumption. The "moral basis" required for a functioning capitalism had supposedly eroded. But what was its moral basis? If judged by the character it required, then presumably, the work ethic and the willingness to defer gratification for the sake of future returns— the qualities Max Weber had believed constituted "the spirit of capitalism," or perhaps Joseph Schumpeter's "animal spirits." If judged by its fruits, then supposedly a certain fairness of reward and of life chances. Not equality of outcome but equality of opportunity, insisted liberals in Europe and America.

It would take a subsequent generation to stress how utopian this standard could prove in the face of the structural inequalities of race and poverty. John Rawls's influential *Theory of Justice* (1971) proposed two criteria for social policy that he believed took account of political reality but would satisfy most progressives. First, any redistribution in terms of wealth or income must make the most disadvantaged citizens—and not just the average citizen—better off. Second, when they designed policy, all advocates should act as if they operated behind "a veil of ignorance" and did not know which social class they actually belonged to or whether they might personally benefit. In effect, no expert wanted to deny equity as a standard to which capitalism must adhere, but determination of how much redistribution or public spending might be needed usually ended up following Goldilocks's guideline of "just right": distributions of income and wealth should not be "too" skewed but not really much more equal than they already were in the OECD countries. The grounds for egalitarian principles of justice—within and between societies, on the basis of humanitarian individualist obligations or historical reparation—were sharply debated in light of Rawls.[45] But up to what point redistributive corrections should be made remained unclear. To assure survival? To return to some allegedly precolonial status quo? Certainly not for absolute leveling, but then why not?

As we have seen, for social commentators of the 1950s in the developed world, growth promised to attenuate feelings of inequality without altering national shares of income or wealth. So long as wage increases did not outpace productivity growth, capitalism would remain viable. Sadly, probably inevitably, so critics argued, the willingness of the masses to restrain their consumption or social welfare benefits to assure growth had apparently dissipated. So had the readiness of their representatives to vote the taxes to cover social programs.[46] But even were legislators prepared to fund traditional and new income-maintenance programs, the expansion of higher education, or the rising cost of national health plans without deficits, these provisions, editors and experts warned, threatened to "crowd out" productive investment. Redistributive policies without balancing the budget threatened inflation, but imposing additional taxes to fund these programs or selling government bonds could also forestall innovation and investments. The voices of governance continually reminded citizens that the future must not be sacrificed for present consumption. But the consumption so often targeted was hardly the discretionary spending of the wealthier classes, who instead would soon benefit from the tax reductions of the 1980s.

Suggested remedies for the persistent inflation depended on diagnosis of its causes. For Hayeckian liberals, Keynesianism was responsible for the inflationary proclivities of the modern economy, and there should be no license to worsen inflation with further regulation such as price and wage controls. The prevailing middle-of-the road explanation was codified in a report by the so-called McCracken Report, commissioned by the OECD—*Toward Full Employment and Price Stability*, which concluded that "conventional economic analysis" could largely account for the experience: "the most important feature was an unusual bunching of unfortunate disturbances unlikely to be repeated on the same scale, the impact of which was compounded by some avoidable errors in economic policy."[47] The analysis was careful, well-reasoned, mature, judicious, and virtually tautological—bad things happen in the economy from time to time. No extraordinary regulatory measures need be taken: the state could be acquitted and sent home.

As significant as the findings, perhaps because it trended to be taken for granted, was the OECD's claim that the judgment was delivered by "a group of independent experts." The world of allegedly "independent experts" was into its own once again with the great inflation, recovering the influence it had in the 1920s and 1930s when it rallied to get capitalism back on track. The realm of governance was to play a major role in the great reorientation of economic policy that began in the 1970s. The OECD itself was a paradigmatic center of expertise, norms, and ideas, an enlarged perpetuation of the Marshall Plan recipients that formed the Organisation of European Economic Cooperation.[48] It claimed specialized knowledge and access to a truth supposedly guaranteed by objective or scientific knowledge. Experts made truth claims in many spheres of life, but as we have seen in earlier chapters, international affairs, public hygiene, and economic performance were domains in which their authority seemed most important. The rapid development of military technology had prompted the establishment of new bodies, often of scientists and strategists. In the United States, the Atomic Energy Commission played a key role once nuclear weapons were under development, and as president, Dwight Eisenhower had appointed a special scientific adviser to the president in 1957. James Kilian, the president of MIT, and then George Kistiakowsky, an eminent Harvard chemist, served as first appointees. Legal expertise had a different status based on appeal to previous findings of law, statute, or supposedly accepted norms of equity. Communist states in theory insisted on its class basis but recognized the principles of "bourgeois" and international law. In any case, most societies had long institutionalized legal governance within a system of public or religious courts.

Claims to expertise and governance would become increasingly politicized, but in the 1970s and 1980s they were politicized in the same prevailing direction. As Matthias Schmelzer's study of the OECD makes clear, this was a complex process, and the OECD from the late 1970s on became committed to market ideologies. "Faced with declining growth rates, the OECD started to analyze social expenditures as an obstacle to growth, criticized the 'welfare state in crisis' and increasingly promoted the privatization of social services." By 1980, Keynesian views had been largely expunged from the OECD

Secretariat and its reports. The new formula called for strengthening competition, freeing international trade, cutting budgets, strengthening "the personal responsibility of individuals and families and reducing generous social security benefits."[49] By the 1980s, to look ahead, the import substitution model earlier promoted for less developed economies was in full retreat. Critics admired instead the emerging "Asian tigers," who were quickly developing on the basis of exporting advanced electronic products (and mass clothing items). In 1983, the National Bureau of Economic Research issued an influential study of international trade that focused on the successes of the Pacific countries.[50] By then, as we shall see in the next chapter, a serious foreign debt crisis would be afflicting some of the countries that had been hit by oil costs and the need to borrow. "Structural adjustment," including privatization and budget cutting, would become the mantra for governance.

The mid-1970s were the political turning point (as Chapter 8 sets out in more detail). The analysis of inflation quickly entailed an attack on redistribution in general—national and international. The major achievement of the postwar project-state—encompassing social welfare systems—soon came under attack. The criticism articulated in the 1970s and 1980s under conservative auspices would be taken up by American "New Democrats" and British "New Labour" in the 1990s and culminate with "reforms" at the turn of the millennium. In particular, unemployment benefits came under systematic criticism as too generous, supposedly disincentivizing the unemployed from seeking new employment. By 2003, German Social Democrats would accept a major effort (so-called Hartz IV) to limit unemployment payments (see Chapter 9). Unsurprisingly the reaction against redistributive policies undermined the chances for a New International Economic Order. No matter the appeal of the NIEO to recent historians, at the time they grated on many in the Western camp. Whereas the moral force of arguments in favor of greater equality held sway through the 1960s and into the 1970s, it was turned around at the end of the decade.

Despite eloquent appeals, aid did not prove—or perhaps was never sufficient to provide—the panacea for national underdevelopment in the 1950s, nor for any of the following decades, although it could prove important for discrete interventions for education, public health, and particular projects.[51] From the 1950s on, however, economists associated with the Mont Pèlerin Society contested the development paradigm, most ardently perhaps Peter Bauer, who would remain active long enough to become a favorite of Margaret Thatcher and to oppose the Brandt report of 1980.[52] Bauer, born in

Hungary in 1915, migrated to Britain in 1934 to attend Cambridge and profiled himself as early as the 1950s as a critic of development economics. Bauer's papers at the Mont Pèlerin Society conferences in the late 1950s, packaged for the business public in *Fortune* magazine in May 1958 ("Economic Growth and the New Orthodoxy"), attacked state-led assistance. He rejected the concept of a specifically underdeveloped world, criticized comparative national income statistics as too undifferentiated, insisted that agriculture and commodities as well as industry could lead to national wealth, and lashed out at Gunnar Myrdal, the perennial punching bag of those critical of UN woolly-mindedness. Most of these points were defensible, but their combined thrust—along with similar arguments by many others—was intended to justify what might best be described as the self-satisfaction of the deserving rich. From the mid-1970s, Bauer took to the pages of *Commentary*—the once left-leaning monthly of the American Jewish Committee that was then evolving into a forum to attack the effort by neutralist and NIEO states to condemn Israel and thereby to attack the idea of the NIEO itself.[53]

The critiques entailed more than a criticism of mistaken Keynesian policies at home or development policies abroad. Once redistribution was at stake, critics implied that deep-seated societal flaws were involved, including racial pathologies. The American controversies surrounding Daniel Patrick Moynihan's 1965 analysis of the Black family, allegedly dysfunctional because deprived of male heads, revealed the pitfalls, political as well as intellectual, of ethnocultural specification.[54] As with subsequent interracial statistical correlations, the numbers seemed revealing, but the causal context far too oversimplified. On an international level, it was taken up with implicit critiques of the societies of the global south. Far less doctrinaire an intellect than Bauer, Moynihan was still determined to be an outspoken ambassador at the UN when appointed by Gerald Ford, and he often clashed with Kissinger, who now headed the State Department. In March 1975, Moynihan published his attack in *Commentary* on third world ideologies and the Western guilt feelings that had allegedly encouraged them.[55] The State Department headed by Kissinger, he averred, was set on appeasement, when the United States should be asserting a principled opposition against the creeping socialism and anti-Zionism of the now-majoritarian forces of the third world. Kissinger shared much of the analysis even if he held his tongue in public. "We are now living in a never-never land, I am certain," he had told his staff at the time of the OPEC price rise, "in which tiny, poor and weak nations can hold up for ransom some of the industrialized world."[56] The attacks on

Zionism would send many among the Jewish intellectual circles far from their inherited Democratic Party affiliations toward what soon become known as neoconservatism. The critique of Zionism from the global south not only isolated the United States as a supporter of Israel but also made itself felt at a moment that the Democratic senator Henry "Scoop" Jackson was critiquing Kissinger's détente policy as mollycoddling a Soviet Union intent on cracking down again on human rights and impeding the emigration of Soviet Jews.

Race was not always involved although quasi-racial attributes had long been posited to account for group behavior that resisted market rationality:[57] Quinn Slobodian cites the ordoliberal Wilhelm Röpke's defense of Apartheid and his criticism of the New Frontier as a wedge for international planning. Anti-imperialist in the 1930s, he defended colonialism by the 1960s. Foreign aid was the mechanism by which "the ideas and methods of collectivist policy are carried into the world economy."[58] Even the most sympathetic anthropological analyses of third world communities celebrated virtues that confirmed their subjects' tribalism and resistance to market logic. Earlier critiques of African communities among British colonial officials and others had focused on the persistence of common lands; but increasingly, the association with race became a subtext. The attitude was echoed by US conservatives, hunkering down to resist desegregation.

The critiques were formidable. Did not aid reinforce dependency rather than overcome it? Did it not just reinforce clientelism and corruption? But the issue ran deeper than aid. The political scientist Stephen Krasner, who twenty years later served as head of the State Department's Policy Planning Staff under President George W. Bush, comprehensively outlined the confrontation as a younger "realist" professor in the mid-1980s: The West, he argued, wanted to cling to a model of market allocation and capitalist rationality. The third world sought to use the power of states—reinforced by the UN regime of so-called Westphalian sovereignty—even when their behavior seemed to violate their economic interests: "From a realist perspective, the defining characteristic of Third World polities is vulnerability. This vulnerability has not been reduced by economic growth. . . . The most strident period of Third World demands, which occurred in the early 1970s, followed the most rapid period of Third World economic growth. . . . The principle of the sovereign equality of all states has legitimated Third World challenges to the dominant market-oriented regimes favored by the North; international organizations created and funded by the North have become forums where such challenges can be voiced; the weakness and vulnerability of developing countries compels such challenges to be made." Krasner was pessimistic. The third world could attack and undermine existing international regimes, but it could not destroy or replace them. "The North-South conflict will be an enduring characteristic of the international system. There are some problems for which there are no solutions."[59]

A Governance Unicorn: The European Economic Community in the Years of Stagflation

Defining what sort of institution the EU was (and is) has always been a frustrating exercise. Political scientists would argue whether it was really just an intergovernmental organization or a quasi-government. It was not a state, but it exercised state-like functions. It was created by sovereign states and possessed delegated powers but was hardly sovereign, although it would sign the Helsinki accords (formally the Conference on Security and Cooperation in Europe) in 1975 and the final act on German unification in 1990 as an international entity. When it was negotiated as the European Economic Community (EEC) in early 1957, it provided for a parliament with very limited powers, a commission, which the Dutch envisaged as a nonpartisan body of experts who would pursue "objective politics," and a council of ministers, representing national preferences and convening a few times per year.[60] These organs roughly paralleled those established a few years earlier for the Coal and Steel Community, the supranational entity created by the Schuman Plan, which remained in being though increasingly subordinate to the EEC. EEC national members retained theoretical sovereignty although they ceded large areas of authority over their own legislation. It provided for a common external tariff and the progressive reduction of internal tariff barriers. By the early 1960s, it created a Common Agricultural Policy by which subsidies and price equalization members protected high-cost producers, especially the large French farming sector, from harsh internal and external competition. EEC Court decisions in the early1960s established that Community law could override national rules and that individual citizens and firms and not just member states were subjects of EEC legislation.[61] The growing role played by its heads of government meeting as the European Council from 1974 on, enhanced efficacy but made it harder to define.

The year 1973 also brought the first wave of enlargement for the EEC with the adhesion of the United Kingdom, Ireland, and Denmark. This meant that a wider range of policies needed to be accommodated both in terms of governance institutions and monetary reconciliation. Whether under Tory prime minister Edward Heath (1970–1974) or James Callaghan when Labour came to power in early 1974, the British remained leery of too federal a European structure. British policy in general remained tempted by that half-century will-o'-the-wisp, the "special relationship" with the United States. But the United States did not make such a policy easy for Europe, especially when the OPEC oil embargo and then the almost 400 percent price rise hit in the same period and Kissinger sought to align Europe behind Washington's confrontation with the Arab states. Valérie Giscard d'Estaing, Callaghan, and Schmidt all were new in office in the spring of 1974. The French believed correctly that Kissinger wanted any European project to remain subordinate to American leadership; NATO, not the EEC, must always remain the preeminent association. Still, French president Giscard believed that American cooperation was needed in light of French economic difficulties, and so the Europeans dropped their plans for their own closer political union, while Washington reaffirmed its commitment to NATO.

As of the 1970s and 1980s, the EEC might best be described as a one-of-a-kind governance organization. By December 1974, Schmidt and Giscard had agreed on the role of a new European Council (not to be confused with the Council of Europe, organized in 1949 to safeguard human rights), which would bring together the heads of government with the president of the Commission every few months empowered to take decisions by majority votes. Its first meeting in Dublin in January 1975 produced no miraculous transformation, but it would gain in traction. Giscard felt compelled to backtrack on strengthening EEC institutions in light of the pressure from the Gaullist stalwarts in his majority, who were always wary of ceding French sovereignty to a supranational construction. No real advance toward realizing the earlier ambitious plans for a common foreign and defense policy and European Political Cooperation emerged during 1975–1976. Nonetheless, the Community's parliament gained important leverage vis-à-vis the Council of Ministers and the Commission in 1975 and began the struggle for influence over the budget and policies. The European Council also agreed on introducing direct elections for the European Parliament by 1978.

The mid-1970s were not an easy period in which to stake a clear identity. Yet precisely in these years of monetary and institutional challenges, the EEC might provide a unique organism for transnational governance. Currency and budget affairs were clearly traditional domains for sovereign action. But in the shadow of United States and the ambitions for a common economic zone, coordination of monetary policies had to bear in mind the requirements of the Community as a unit. The Common Agricultural Policy, negotiated in 1962, with its complicated monetary units of account designed to cushion Europe's agricultural sector—and increasingly to shift the costs of keeping high-cost French farming viable in the face of imports from outside Europe—had already revealed the difficulties of achieving monetary harmonization. By the 1970s, the system of monetary exchange had to be rebuilt as a whole. It was to be constructed in two major phases. The first was the creation of a European Monetary System (EMS) of coordinated exchange rates, negotiated by 1978. It produced a common notional unit of account, the European Currency Unit (ECU, also the name of the major coin of the French ancien régime), as the central strand for aligning each country's exchange. The second would be the creation by leading EEC members—though not the UK—of a common European currency, the euro, whose phased introduction was inscribed in the Maastricht Treaty of European Union in 1992. This section focuses on the first, admittedly short-lived, accomplishment; the following chapter will cover the second phase.

Two sources of European monetary tension above all had to be accommodated in the 1970s—one between the EEC as a whole and the United States; the other between the strong-currency states, preeminently Germany and the Netherlands, and the more inflation-prone states, at this time, France in particular. Resolving these tensions of course involved national goals and conventional sovereignty issues. Maintaining a currency was, after all, along with defense, a primary prerogative of statehood. But resolving the tensions simultaneously to keep the Community together and recover equilibrium on the money markets had to be a governance issue as well. It required compromises on behalf of a multinational system.

An early 1970 scheme to reduce currency fluctuations and work toward a currency evaluation fund and even a common currency by 1980, the Werner plan, fell victim to the inflow of American dollars in 1971 and the revaluation of the deutsche mark as a defensive response. By the late 1960s German policymakers continually felt pressure to raise the exchange rate of their own currency in order to limit the flood of American dollars exchanged for deutsche marks and deposited in German bank accounts as a hedge against US inflation.

The United States had benefited from the fact that at Bretton Woods, the dollar was confirmed as a reserve currency to be accepted by Western national banks at its legally fixed value in gold. From the end of the 1950s and through the next decade the dollar gave signs of being overvalued with respect to other currencies, especially the deutsche mark and the yen. The costs of Vietnam and its NATO military commitments, the American taste for European (and later Japanese) autos or vacations, its businesses' search to acquire foreign subsidiaries meant that European firms and ultimately the central banks accumulated dollars, which added to their own domestic inflationary pressure. Germans reluctantly revalued their currency upward in small doses but worried that a more expensive deutsche mark would make their vigorous export industries less competitive. (Remarkably the taste for German goods did not diminish through all the DM devaluations.) Europeans mostly sought to exchange their dollar surpluses back at the Federal Reserve for gold as doubts grew about the sustainable value of the American currency. With elections looming in 1972, the Nixon administration did not want to devalue the dollar formally, but rather pressured the Germans and Japanese in particular to revalue their currencies. As this pressure on US reserves intensified, the Nixon administration suspended "convertibility" of dollars into gold on August 15, 1971, effectively nullifying its Bretton Woods commitments. Simultaneously it imposed a temporary tariff on imports and a ninety-day wage-price freeze, a move designed to brake inflation at home. Who would prevail in this mano-a-mano? Europe, Canada, and Japan (the G-10 at that point) and the Americans agreed in the December 1971 Smithsonian Agreement to try to stabilize fixed rates by sharing the costs of adjustment. The United States formally devalued by 7.9 percent with respect to gold, while the Germany and Japan raised their currencies by about 14 percent and 17 percent, respectively, vis-à-vis the dollar and all agreed to keep their currencies within a band or "tunnel" of 4.5 percent above or below against the dollar.

The committee of European Central Bank governors also felt the need to better coordinate their own currencies, a goal sought as well by the Bank of International Settlements and the EEC Commission. At Basel in April 1972, EEC members (including the three new members about to join) further agreed on "the EEC snake in the Smithsonian tunnel," a picturesquely named effort to keep their own currencies tethered to each other with 2.25 percent allowable wiggle room, and they established a credit facility that the weaker currencies might draw upon.[62] But currency turmoil continued. US wage and price controls ended in January 1973; Washington felt compelled to devalue again by 10 percent in February 1973 and then simply to let the dollar float in terms of gold, a decision that ended the tunnel. The Bundesbank decided that Germany could no longer defend the dollar by keeping the deutsche mark low but would let it float upward. Pressure on the pound and the franc compelled London and Paris to uncouple from the snake. So long as the United States as the major reserve currency provider found it difficult to discipline its own economic policies, no international system that depended on its restraint was likely to work. The oil price rise of early 1974 redressed the weakness of the dollar since OPEC demanded payment in dollars for oil. Nonetheless two years of European currency turbulence followed until French president Giscard d'Estaing (Pompidou's successor after May 1974) decided to rejoin the snake in May 1975, and even then, France was ill-prepared to defend any fixed exchange rate.

"The overall political drive of policymakers in the EEC countries," Harold James remarks, "was to think of an alternative, on a global level, to the dollar as a reserve currency."[63] But what should serve as the substitute, and even if the Europeans pooled reserves, what should be the common unit of account? French finance minister, Jean-Pierre Fourcade, proposed a European unit based on a basket of EEC currencies weighted according to the size of the respective national economies. Expert committees and bankers proposed using a weighted average of exchange rates. The Commission thereupon proposed a concerted floating, or a renewed snake, and perhaps a common bond issue. A committee of notable experts called for a parallel currency, the Europa, to circulate alongside national currencies.[64] Still, no concrete progress toward monetary union followed. The heads of government at the European Council insisted "that in this field their will has not weakened and their objective has not changed."[65] But as of March 1975, the respected former head of the Commission Robert Marjolin warned that Europe had made no real progress and that hope for monetary union was actually regressing.

Halting steps toward common action alternated with setbacks. In April 1975, convergence was defined in terms of a European Unit of Account—again a weighted average of European currencies in potential competition with the IMF's special drawing rights (SDR), an emergency reserve credit for countries facing currency crises that included a major dollar component and was thus hardly independent of American involvement. The Bundesbank still favored the snake as the basis for coordination. By June 1975, the Commission's *Report on the European Union* urged that eventually, "monetary policy would become an exclusively Community policy domain, in the same way as trade policy and common external tariff" with a European central bank and a parallel currency alongside the national ones.[66] Meanwhile it responded to national political priorities. As premier, Chirac had chosen the twenty-fifth anniversary of the announcement of the Schuman Plan, May 9, 1975, to announce over objections from key advisers that France would rejoin the snake; however, within a few months with an eye on the elections scheduled for 1976, he and president Giscard d'Estaing decided on a stimulus program of tax cuts despite the warning of French treasury and central bank officials. By April 1976, a chastened Giscard had to announce that France was quitting the snake a second time, drawing a harsh rebuke from Schmidt: "'Monetary acrobatics' can't override the need to tell the truth to one's parliament, trade unions, or industry."[67] Exchange rates seemed to follow laws as inexorable as gravity.

European negotiations bore more fruit by 1977. French policy embarked on a decided course of stabilization when Chirac retired and was replaced with Raymond Barre, who embarked on a policy of "disinflation" by reducing wage increases and targeting the money supply. Chancellor Schmidt, confirmed in office with new elections, insisted that "the root of all current evils was inflation" but became more determined to work with France as he became angrier with new president Jimmy Carter, who was urging Germany to loosen its monetary policy and become the "locomotive" for economic recovery. The new commission president, Roy Jenkins, reopened discussion of economic and monetary union in late October 1977 with a notable speech at the European University Institute in Florence. Progress in choosing among the various schemes under consideration, so the central bank governors reported at the end of their review of alternatives in June 1978, now depended on political decisions at a Community level.

The EEC finance ministers agreed and proposed a system that would include all Community currencies—even before the differences in rates of inflation and balance of payments were entirely resolved. The European Council of heads of government agreed a few weeks later to create a European Monetary Fund (EMF) that could support currencies under pressure—which meant essentially a commitment from the Germans to support the franc. But the heads of government had to convince their national banks since the EMF was to rest on central bank cooperation. The chancellor appeared before the Bundesbank council on November 30, 1978 to plead for its urgency. He told the Bundesbank that it would not be exposed to unlimited interventions to prop up other currencies, although he did not want that concession made public. He stressed that the proposed institution was useful primarily to give France a cosmetic pretext ("swimming trunks" or "makeup") to return to a snakelike arrangement. However, it was also crucial for Germany in light of the country's division and the burdens of its history: "We are doubly vulnerable and will remain so far into the next century. Vulnerable on account of [divided] Berlin and the nation, and secondly ... vulnerable on account of Auschwitz. All the more so we remain reliant on ... the Common Market. A European Community without an efficiently functioning common economic market will decay."[68]

The European Council reached agreement between December 1978 and March 1979 on a new EMS. The fund did not materialize, but each participating country pledged that it would intervene to prop up its currency by interest rate increases if it diverged more than 2.25 percent from the ECU, the notional currency, with its name a concession to French pride, and based like the European Unit of Account on a weighted average or "market basket" of the currencies in the scheme. The current floaters, which included the Italians, were allowed a 6 percent deviation before being obliged to deflate. The British and the Dutch declined to enter the new EMS, although their currencies still counted in determining the value of the ECU. The system provided essentially that the Bundesbank back up the weak-currency countries in return for the latter accepting constraints on their own spending. As the Gaullists and the left in France argued, the system confirmed German domination of the EEC currencies. The burden of adjustment would fall on the countries in deficit, but this had been the implication of Bretton Woods as well; despite Keynes, it remained in effect the unwritten monetary rule for postwar American-led capitalism. But it was a rule destined to be broken, as if in a cycle of sinning, confession, absolution, and penance.

Hard bargaining was required not only between countries but also within them. German industry objected to the tolerance for French devaluation that the agreement envisaged. Giscard opposed his own Finance Ministry to support harsher constraints. The French finally agreed that when 75 percent of the permissible deviation from the ecu was reached, the treasury would intervene to correct the depreciation. Britain finally refused to join the system, although sterling could be included in the basket of currencies. Ireland broke its peg with sterling to join; Italy tried to extract greater commitments but also finally agreed to sign on. The French Gaullists resisted and Chirac denounced Giscard's concessions. A deal to lower and then end the side payments (the monetary compensatory account) that French farmers had to pay German farmers, which compensated for the lower farm support payments that appreciation of the deutsche mark had entailed, had also to be thrown into the bargain.[69]

The agreement would soon have to confront the impact of the second major OPEC oil price hike, the Iranian revolution, and a major new surge of inflation. By 1983, the central rate adjustment had been triggered seven times: the deutsche mark revalued upward on four occasions and the French franc's parity reduced on three occasions. The moment of truth for the EMS came when Mitterrand won the French presidential election in 1981 on a left-wing program of higher taxes on the wealthy and increased public spending. He soon faced the choice of leaving the EMS or reversing his electoral program and submitting to austerity. As we shall see, he chose alignment with Bonn. The constraints of capital, largely supported by those speaking for governance, prevailed over the left's version of a project-state.

From one perspective, the monetary travails of the 1970s revealed the fragility of the EEC, but from another perspective, they demonstrated that after a quarter century, linked currencies had become a scaffolding for European governance. As the Committee of Central Bank Governors understood, their institutional preferences—representing both governance and capital—required the intervention of national political leaders, especially Chancellor Schmidt. But this intervention rested in turn on the continuing debate among central bankers and the arduous refinement, sometimes in wearying detail of technical policies, and the pressure from major business leaders and economists. The process strengthened a dense network of institutions and a career civil service and a sense of loyalties, like the other governance institutions of the latter twentieth century: the IMF, World Bank, UN and its agencies, and the international courts of justice.[70] By the mid-1980s, the EEC was poised for another rapid surge of institutional integration under the impetus of commission president Jacques Delors and a cohort of industrial leaders who saw that Europe faced Japanese as well as American competition. Governance, as Chapter 8 will demonstrate, was deployed by the mid-1980s no longer primarily as a brake on the left; that threat had faded. It was an institutional counteroffensive on behalf of capitalist modernization.

The history of the EMS thus not only raised the question of whether governance activities that involved a search for enhanced economic welfare (at least as measured by national income) could be effective without the simultaneous intervention of states and capital. But it also raised the issue of how the realm of governance might represent the broad strata of society it allegedly served. The European Community and its monetary travails revealed the potential for and the limits of governance. It brought together experts around a project that combined knowledge and persuasion. It produced or strengthened a community supposedly aligning a common agenda with the enlightened self-interests of states. It outlined a path from the "chaos" of competing sovereignties to an overarching unity. It suggested a new form of "order" that respected the power of states and the rights of capital. It renewed the hope of an enlightened elite, an epistemic community, a club of the wise. But the Community also remained burdened by the problem that became known as the democratic deficit, which was raised by Shirley Williams, a great supporter, and by many others. What gave its institutions legitimacy? Perhaps this was a misplaced demand if the EEC did not aspire to statehood. On the other hand, could the mission of governance ever be devoid of politics? These questions still persist.

When Governance Did Not Suffice

With political parties—democratic and authoritarian alike—less capable of providing order or satisfying mass demands, centrist and conservative voices needed to regain control of the policy landscape, at home or internationally, as they had in the 1920s. They could do so by capturing the state, legally through elections or extralegally through military takeover. In some societies, conservative forces, fearful of social revolution and economic radicalism, which they simplified as Moscow-inspired communism, felt they could not tolerate party competition and imposed military dictatorship. In Latin America, the familiar recourse to military intervention became particularly tempting. Following an electoral victory by the left in 1964, the Brazilian military had stepped in to oust President João Goulart in 1965 and imposed a harsh dictatorship that would last until the early 1980s. Chile had the most "European" political system, with analogues of the European left and right contesting elections. But in Latin American tradition, it maintained a military that played a far larger political role. Following moderate Christian Democratic electoral victories in the mid-1960s, an avowedly Marxist admirer of Fidel Castro, Salvador Allende, was voted into power in 1968. His policies rapidly polarized the country, which had a strong middle class that resisted his turn toward socialism. The private entrepreneurs, spearheaded by the truck drivers who plied the long roads that knit together Chile's long north-south geography, and supported by the American administration and presumably intelligence, connived in the seizure of power in 1973 by General Augusto Pinochet and the military. Allende died fighting off the attack on the presidential palace: another hero for a left-wing pantheon, another death in the minds of students and the left to chalk up to the machinations of the Central Intelligence Agency. In Argentina three years later, the military returned to claim power from the widow of Juan Perón, who had returned to power for the third time in 1973. The Argentine generals and admirals, like the Chileans, instituted a brutal repression against any suspected "left" elements in the media or among the students. Thousands of suspected radicals were imprisoned, tortured, and often made to "disappear," sometimes as bodies dropped into the sea. Uruguay did not fail to be inspired by its neighbors especially after confronting an urban guerrilla movement. Landlocked Paraguay had long had a military dictator and did not need the prompting of its neighbors. By the late 1970s, the Southern Cone seemed safely in the hands of ultraright armies, whose military activity was directed only inward. But like the Communist regimes in Eastern Europe, they would all become vulnerable less to a revolutionary opposition than an inner loss of purpose and conviction.

In the wake of the civil rights movements, followed by waves of feminist mobilization, a growing insistence on acceptance of open homosexual relationships, and recognition of the needs of the disabled, a culture of rights would liberalize Western legal systems from the 1960s on. Divorce and abortion became lawful alternatives even in Catholic redoubts such as Italy and Spain. The successful though often partial conquest of rights accompanied the widespread acceptance of nonviolent mass political action, championed most conspicuously by Mohandas Gandhi in interwar India, then inspiring Martin Luther King Jr. and sit-in leaders in the United States, and influential voices in the African National Congress in the Republic of South Africa.

But nonviolence had not won the independence of Algeria or the overthrow of the Battista regime in Cuba or the transformation of China. Out of the turbulence of the 1960s, there also emerged small clusters of urban intellectuals and students and radicalized workers, who became convinced that mass action without outright violence was futile. These too became a phenomenon of the 1970s even if claiming only small circles of adherents. Among the legatees of Italy's Hot Autumn and Germany's radical students were those who felt that bourgeois society was so hopelessly bureaucratic and privileged that it could be reformed only through violence. Capitalism was such a pervasive system that the assassination of its leaders, and their alleged government servants, came to seem a legitimate tactic. Terrorist assassination had become a tactic of anti-colonial struggles since the 1940s, and now in the 1970s, of movements fighting for territorial statehood: the Irish Republican Army, the Basque ETA, the Palestinians who slew Israeli athletes at the 1972 Munich Olympics. But the German and Italian terrorist groups attacked to overthrow a supposedly repressive capitalism, not to claim a territorial state. In Italy and the Federal Republic of Germany, a host of "red brigades," cells of conspiratorial radicals that formed, fissioned, and re-formed embarked in the mid-1970s on a campaign of assassination which deeply tested the strength of their postwar liberal institutions. Many dozens in Germany including the head of the industrialists' association and various ministers were murdered. Perhaps a thousand kneecappings and shootings took place in Italy; Christian Democratic prime minister Aldo Moro, who had led his party's "Opening to the Left" with the Socialists in 1963, was kidnapped in March 1978, soon after securing implicit Communist support for a latent *compromesso storico* coalition and assassinated two months later. Such a wave of terrorism was hard to wipe out. Some on the left reacted ambivalently, expressing sympathy for the activists' sincerity or recognizing the social injustice that supposedly motivated the deeds. Gradually, police work came to prevail. Arrests were made. The Italians used laws of "repentance" that forgave those who would testify against accomplices and held several massive trials that ultimately put perpetrators in jail for many years or life. The Germans moved against the most spectacular group—the so-called Baader-Meinhof gang, several of whose members committed suicide in prison.

Faced with such vigorous protest movements in the areas of race, gender, and working-class representation, the older structures of political representation in the 1970s appeared rather moribund and dead. Even in the United States, the Democratic Party seemed particularly vulnerable to mobilization on the left. At the Chicago convention of 1968, Mayor Richard J. Dailey had mobilized Chicago police against the admittedly violent assaults of the street. The party nominated Hubert Humphrey, the hapless heir to a hapless Lyndon Johnson, but gave a spectacle of being under siege. Four years later, in 1972, the balance had changed; the party adopted such open rules for the accreditation of state delegations that its Miami convention seemed a fairground for every group claiming political recognition, whether militants for racial equality, feminist legislation, and gay rights. The party conclave outran American opinion in its apparent hospitality for disorderly politics and, under George McGovern, suffered its most decisive defeat since 1920.

Where one-party rule was enshrined legally as in Communist countries, the problem of dissent in the aftermath of the 1960s returned with a vengeance in the 1970s. Brezhnev's government initially seemed to continue the tolerance for dissent and ideas of modifying central planning. But in the wake of the Czech effort to allow for pluralism and to defect from the Warsaw Pact renewed crackdown began and such dissenters as Andrei Sakharov faced punishment as did their counterparts in Prague (Charter 77) or the German Democratic Republic. To claim a monopoly for a single party really allowed the ruling elites little room for recognizing the legitimacy of alternative voices.

In one instance—but by far the hugest country of all—the China of Chairman Mao, the supreme leader who incarnated the People's Republic, had himself grown discontented with the tendency of party to become routine and institute a self-perpetuating bureaucratic rule. This led to the astonishing convulsion of 1966 and the next decade—the Great Cultural Revolution—in which an aging Mao, his wife, and his closest advisers decided to mobilize the activists and press the party to demolish the country's persistent hierarchies from the outside. For almost a decade, university academics, officials, and enterprise officials were systematically denounced, terrorized, and removed from their positions and exiled to rural labor if not killed, as young activists were incited to follow the precepts of Mao and his loyalists for a sort of revolutionary renewal—the phenomenon that excited those in the West whom Jean-Luc Godard had filmed. Millions of qualified professionals were degraded and dispersed. Ultimately, the constant effort to renew revolutionary energy and level the hierarchies that survived 1949 wreaked great economic damage; it could not be sustained. The patient associates of Mao had to bide their time, but as he aged and the excesses became visible, they prepared to take power and impose discipline on the turbulence. Within five years, more moderate voices gradually reconsolidated the claims of expertise and hierarchy, above all when the chance to play a new role in world politics beckoned. International politics and nation-state rivalry had helped to unleash the impatient social forces of protest; but might they not also help to channel them?

Also disturbing was the fact that the most populous political democracy in the world, India, which seemed to have successfully inherited British parliamentary institutions, apparently cast them aside. Reconciling new liberal institutions with the single-party domination that has often followed revolution or nation-state formation has traditionally proven challenging, whether in the United States, Mexico, India, or elsewhere. Opposition can appear implicitly seditious. Prime Minister Jawaharlal Nehru, the architect of the Indian republic and its leader since independence, died in May 1964. Undoubtedly one of the twentieth century's great democratic statesman, he piloted a huge country riven by caste, religious and language differences, equipped with strong regional centers of power and still beset by vast reservoirs of poverty, to regional military prowess and international prestige. His successor, Lal Bahadur Shastri, likewise died in office after a trying year in which he successfully rebuffed a Pakistani attack on Kashmir followed in turn by arduous Soviet-sponsored negotiations. Nehru's daughter, Indira Gandhi, was selected as prime minister and, after a shaky start in disciplining her sprawling party, called and won elections in 1971. Victory was precarious, however. The oil crisis hit India hard, in part by raising the cost of the fertilizers on which the Green Revolution depended. A railroad strike in 1974 and, most disabling, a court decision that called in question the electoral results put her administration in critical straits. Faced with the alternative of stepping down or ruling by decree, she had the president invoke emergency powers, suspended civil liberties with constitutional amendments, and resorted to preventive detention of opposition leaders in 1975.

In his study of the Emergency, heavily influenced by critiques of the interventionist state, Gyan Prakash links Mrs. Gandhi's and her son Sanjay's projects to a renewed push to impose "high modernist" projects, including a heavy-handed sterilization drive to control population growth, and urbanistic projects such as clearing the slum districts of old Delhi: "Powerful international institutions and rich organizations, like the Ford and Rockefeller foundations had guided India in this endeavor. But these had not achieved the state's objectives. . . . It is against this background of failure that the Emergency appears as a last-ditch attempt to salvage with exceptional means the global and elite-driven projects of modernization. Sterilization and slum demolition were its instruments, applied with the knife and the bulldozer."[71] Although she postponed the parliamentary elections a year, Congress lost in early 1977 to a union of diverse opposition forces who temporarily overcame fragmentation to form a unified People's Party (Janata). Mrs. Gandhi managed to extract another parliamentary victory in 1980 but after an explosion of Sikh violence and its forcible repression, died at the hand of a Sikh assassin at the end of October 1984.

The crisis of parliamentary politics in India differed from those in Iberia, Greece, Latin America, and the Middle East. Not the army (which imposed dictatorship in Pakistan, the twin nation separated at birth), but a police force that responded to the government was the instrument of repression. Behind Prakash's critique lurk familiar analyses reminiscent of James Scott and Antonio Gramsci's notion of "passive revolution." "Underlying the state's attempt to command and control the people directly was a deeper failure—the failure of postcolonial politics to cultivate a democratic polity and society."[72] That is, a failure to overcome quasi-feudal hierarchies and deep cleavages of ethnicity, privilege and wealth, and in the Indian case, of caste. The criticism echoes the Italian left's history of national unification according to which liberals produced a unitary state but left the south in the grip of clientelism and oppressive landlords. For Gramsci, the fault derived from the absence of a historical agent equivalent to the French Jacobins. Society remained too refractory; the state and the party foo weak. Western foundations, notably the Ford Foundation office in New Delhi, wagered on access to the elites who ran the state.[73] Interventions for population control—and not only contraception but sterilization—became one of the iconic projects from the 1970s on, where it found a ready reception among Indians feeling threatened by the reproduction of the lower castes. The realm of governance and the project-state reinforced each other's programs.

Still, the historian needs to interrogate the underlying critique. Was the project of grassroots democratic development historically feasible, whether in the Mezzogiorno of 1860 or in independent India after 1947? Was the alternative to state development, with all its dangers of narrow elite control and clientelistic politics, likely to be a broadly supported social democracy, or would it have been stagnant landlord control as persisted in the post-bellum American South, the interwar Balkans, and arguably, interwar rural China? The variants of state-imposed development have indeed left visible wreckage—whether the wreckage of Joseph Stalin's terror, or later Middle Eastern dictatorship, or India's brief experiment with the Emergency. Perhaps it is impossible to resolve the counterfactual issue when we envisage a society divided between elites whom we can identify, and a residual "mass" population whose politics we find hard to make sense of. Are we not always going to find flaws with the historical outcome once we frame the issue in terms of elites and masses? And this is just to ask about secular scenarios; religious loyalties were always in the mix and potentially volatile.

Authoritarian seizures of power seemed hardly feasible in the democracies of Western Europe and the United States although the idea of a military takeover provided the plot line for a popular movie of the time, *Seven Days in May*, and rumors persisted of neo-fascist plots in Italy (including those supposedly emanating from the Masonic lodge P-2 or authoritarian "sleepers" in an obscure movement called Gladio), and indeed there would be madcap coup attempt in the Spanish Cortes. Nonetheless, party government seemed to falter in different ways. If one looked around the globe, single-party systems seemed a durable form of rule—in Communist societies, of course, but also in Mexico, India, and many of the African states. In Italy and Japan, the electoral hold on power of a single party after World War II also seemed almost unshakable.

With time, however, and the appeal of neoliberal alternatives to corporatist institutional inheritances, the dinosaur parties loosened their hold. The Mexican Institutional Revolutionary Party would face challengers to the right and left; the small "lay" parties of the Italian center would lead the governments of the 1980s, the factions within the Japanese Liberal Democratic Party would make the overarching party canopy count for little, and a Hindu populist party, the Bharatiya Janata Party (BJP), would challenge the Congress. The authoritarian regimes would also crumble. The Greek colonels whose practices of torture and repression captured by Costa Gravas's film *Z* were obtuse enough to try and invade and annex the island of Cyprus in 1973, which had been divided in the wake of long conflict into Greek and Turkish sectors and administered under UN auspices. Their invasion failed, and their dictatorship collapsed in disgrace, taking down the acquiescent Greek monarchy with it. A conservative politician unsullied by collaboration, George Karamanlis inaugurated a republic, and within a few years Greece returned to modern democratic norms, marked by the alternation of conservative (New Democracy) and socialist (Pasok) parties.

So, too, despite fears that the hatreds of the civil war might resume, a peaceful transition took place in Spain. Although Francisco Franco did not relinquish an authoritarian regime, under the official carapace of one-party rule, change was taking place, especially after he slipped into a long terminal illness. Franco had already stipulated that he should be succeeded by a restoration of the monarchy that had collapsed in 1931. The young heir to the throne, educated abroad, had absorbed the liberal norms of Western Europe. Spain had prospered and developed as an industrial country in the 1960s and 1970s, its transformation paid for in part by the military assistance that accompanied American air bases, economic association with the European Community, and the vacation boom on its Mediterranean coast.[74] The official trade unions might still provide the workers' only legal representation, but they had been burrowed into, in effect, by a new generation of social democrats and communists. The Communists, too, had changed. Officially the party was in exile in Paris; but in the 1970s, its membership took the lead, alongside Italians, of articulating a new "Eurocommunism," which declared independence from Moscow dictates and accepted peaceful transformation. A new generation of conservatives, who did not want to endanger international investment and of academics who yearned to be full members of the international intellectual community, worked toward reconciliation in the twilight years of the dictatorship. The prime minister, Admiral Carrero Blanco, resisted these silent changes but was assassinated, probably by Basque terrorists, in a spectacular car bombing in 1975, and the shock prodded the political classes not into reversing liberalization but hastening transition. In 1976–1977, parliamentary government was restored and political parties (including the Communists) were legalized, Juan Carlos returned as monarch, and as in Greece a moderate conservative prime minister worked for reconciliation. At the same time, legalized trade unions and employers concluded a set of framework negotiations—the Moncloa Pact—that assured the transition in the economy could take place without destabilizing conflict: it was perhaps the most successful of the neocorporatist agreements that were being concluded throughout Western societies in these years.

The adoption of democracy was stormier in neighboring Portugal, the poorest of the non-communist countries but also the last European colonial power—mired, however, in fighting rebellions in Mozambique and Angola on the two coasts of southern Africa. Army officers and conscripts saw no end to these wars and little purpose either; on April 24, 1974, the army deposed a dictatorship that had also grown discredited at home and long since in Western Europe. This "revolution of the carnations" took place peacefully, indeed joyously, but it was unclear which currents in Portugal and its armed forces would prevail. Conservative military leaders such as General Antonio Spinola, who had fronted for the revolutionaries, and moderates, such as future president António Ramalho Eanes, faced a younger group of officers, Castroite in orientation, inspired by Allende's regime that had been crushed a year earlier. For the better part of 1974, it appeared that the radicals, with strong support among the agricultural workers of the southern Portuguese large estates, might prevail. Kissinger was convinced that a Cuban fate awaited

Portugal, but in fact, the moderates with strength among northern small farmers prevailed, and within two years Portugal, too, had a government in which a more conservative "Social Democratic" party that alternated with a more social-democratic but officially named Socialist party. The army moderates retained a tutelary role for a couple of years and then relinquished it.[75]

In all these cases, the realm of governance stepped in on the side of democratization. The German political party foundations, the human rights organizations, provided funds and moral support and shelter, in a sense, for the democratizers. This was a change from earlier in the decade when they had been preoccupied by supposed radicals. But governance organizations were also often convinced that the way forward required the new economic wisdom supposedly taught by the experience with inflation—that is, diminishing the role of the state over economic policy. The Western state project of the 1980s would become the neoliberal turn: turning toward the market, slimming welfare and bureaucracy, and clearing the way for the financiers and industrial leaders who spoke for capital. The institutions of governance would manage to convert key leaders of the social democratic, reformist left to accept the importance of redressing economic policy and public finance.

By the late 1970s, all Western governments were unpopular, as were their efforts at union-management "concertation" or neocorporatism. As inflation eroded the real value of its dollar revenues, OPEC announced a second threefold oil price increase at its Dubai meeting in December 1978. OPEC II proved as destabilizing as the first oil shock. President Carter acknowledged American unhappiness with public affairs in his famous "malaise" speech (though that was not his term) of July 1979. The American public and Congress saw the oil majors effortlessly raking in huge profits. Carter envisaged letting the domestic price of petroleum rise to world market levels while taxing away the higher profits that would result. The oil companies lamented their being made a scapegoat and regretted the days when Democratic congressional notables from the oil states—Lyndon Johnson, Tom Connally, and Sam Raeburn of Texas, and Robert Kerr of Oklahoma led a compliant industry-friendly party.[76] Meanwhile, inflation at the end of the 1970s rose to double digits in Europe; Labour prime minister Callaghan presided over the public service strikes that marked the second winter of discontent in 1978–1979. (See Table 6.5.)

In theory, the West's pain was the petrostates' gain. They could embark on rapid development of infrastructure, health facilities, urban development, expensive arms purchases, and investments in Europe and North America.

Life expectancy gained. At the same time, the new wealth was very unevenly distributed; agrarian backwardness remained while urban glitz proliferated. Migrant labor in the Gulf formed a new subproletariat trapped in domestic service and menial jobs. Emerging authoritarian leaders, Mu'ammar Gaddhafi in Libya and Saddam Hussein in the Ba'ath republic of Iraq, emerged with dictatorial power. Iran modernized, but the arrogant luxury displays of the privileged provoked growing strikes and unrest, threatening oil production, and led to the flight of the shah in January 1979.

In national elections, voters tended to rebuff every ruling coalition or party. Swedish socialists were ousted from power in 1976 for the first time since 1932. The luckless, if not feckless, Callaghan would lose to Thatcher in 1979.[77] A year later, Ronald Reagan asked Americans whether they felt better or worse off than four years earlier and swept into office. The wind did not always blow from the right, but where the left prevailed, they did so less as a consequence of economic issues than as an impulse to replace the conservative disciplinarians, Adolfo Suárez in Spain, Eanes in Portugal, Charles de Gaulle and his successors, Georges Pompidou and Giscard in France, Karamanlis in Greece, each a modern Lycurgus, who had governed since reestablishing constitutional regimes. In 1981, the French Socialists defeated the Gaullists who had ruled since the inception of the Fifth Republic in 1958; Spanish and Greek Socialists displaced the conservative governments that had sat since the restoration of democracy in their respective countries, and Portugal wagered on a Socialist prime minister after its military's "revolution of the carnations." in 1974. These results revealed the desire to get beyond their nations' respective founding moments. Elsewhere, impatience with the left's incapacity to master inflation took its toll. By 1982, the German Christian Democrats had replaced the ruling Social Democratic Party after over a decade of a left-center coalition. In Italy, the Christian Democrats' coalitions with the Socialists were restructured, and prime ministers from the "lay" parties—Republicans with a reputation for relative fiscal probity—served as prime ministers (technically, presidents of the Council of Ministers) for the first time since 1945. But equally important (and prefiguring the way "civil society" movements would displace Communist authorities in the 1980s), associations proposing policy in the name of governance offered a path to stabilization.

8

Reinventions, 1978–1990s

THE PROJECT-STATE HAD MOBILIZED public energy to wage war, overcome the interwar depression, attempt to retain empire, and construct social insurance schemes for old age, unemployment, and varying degrees of medical coverage. But governmental activism seemed to run into pervasive difficulties by the 1970s. Persistent stagflation in the West, ratcheted up again by a second threefold Organization of the Petroleum Exporting Countries (OPEC) price hike in 1979, frustrated macroeconomic management. Labor unrest dominated British public life and made air and rail travel a chancy venture in Italy and France. The state-socialist planned economies were becoming more and more indebted, and the Soviet Union became ensnared in a difficult guerrilla campaign in Central Asia. Hardline political conventicles were pursuing terrorist campaigns in Germany, Italy, Spain, and the United Kingdom and finding broader sectors of opinion "understanding" their motives. Military rulers remained determined to eradicate any possible opponents in Latin America. Many Americans perceived their cities as subject to pervasive crime, encroaching decay, and uncontrolled graffiti. The nuclear balance of terror was threatening to break down. Civil war would soon cost several hundred thousand lives in Angola and Central America a half decade after raging in Nigeria and Bangladesh.

In fact, policy responses were starting to change course. The Carter administration also pushed through a policy of airline decontrol under Alfred Kahn that presaged the initiatives to follow under the Reagan administration. And Carter's choice as chair of the US Federal Reserve, Paul Volker, imposed a brutal hike in interest rates in late 1979 to throttle the apparently unrelenting inflation. These changes could not reverse the impression (all the more vivid when the mission to rescue American hostages in Tehran proved an embarrassing fiasco) that the Democratic administration was flailing both at home and abroad. Neither President Jimmy Carter nor Prime Minister James Callaghan, each elected in a final effort for the battered coalitions of social liberalism, seemed capable of mastering the economic disintegration taking place on his watch. The former admitted public frustrations in his famous "malaise" speech; the latter merely rejected imputations of crisis: "Crisis? What crisis?" he snapped back at journalists. But observers might certainly be pardoned for sensing governments losing control.[1]

"Tendenzwende": Global Reorientation

Political and economic institutions can recover but rarely without some fundamental resetting of the equilibrium among the state, the sources of capital, and the monitors of norms that we have called the realm of governance. Two fundamentalist leaders who came to power in early 1979 had radically different concepts of how to govern society but were both prepared to seize states at hand precisely to overcome politics as usual and clear the way for other forces of human fulfillment. Each was dedicated to beliefs that scorned the less rigorous philosophies of a prior generation. Each was determined to infuse the state whose levers they might control with a transformative project designed precisely to reverse the moral sloth they believed was corrupting it. At the same time, both claimed that their ideas had a universal validity transcending individual countries. Their respective causes and dedication— religious zeal and energetic capitalism—assured them ardent followers and overshadowed their adversaries at home. These general commitments, moreover, were claiming political energies the world over for the rest of the twentieth century.

Culminating months of turmoil in Iran, the Ayatollah Ruhollah Khomeini returned from Paris to assume the leadership of an Islamist upheaval against the authoritarian program of secular modernization on the part of Mohammed Reza Shah Pahlavi and his British and American sponsors. The Iranian kingdom was anomalous, preserved as a buffer by rival great powers but with a noisy parliament after 1906, and by World War II a young and pretentious monarch, the second of an upstart dynasty. First Russia and Britain, with its oil interests, later Russia and the United States alongside Britain, jockeyed for decisive influence. After the war, the nationalist left-wing Tudeh Party, based in the Azerbaijan province where Russian influence remained strong, became more assertive. It supported Prime Minister Mohammad Mossadegh as he threatened nationalization of the Anglo-Iranian oil interests only to be checked in 1953 by the UK and US covert intervention. Despite support by a feared secret police as well as American arms, intelligence, and financial aid, the shah's power evaporated; by 1978, he could not trust his military to intervene against growing mass hostile demonstrations and he flew into exile. The mullahs, as they would be labeled abroad—their religious culture formed in the Shia center of Qum, not in worldly Tehran—inherited a powerful state with dictatorial capacities. Their new republic established a Council of Guardians granting the religious dignitaries supreme power to intervene in elections and other political matters. And as an instrument to control the grassroots, including the business community, they established a paramilitary Revolutionary Guard.

Far away, climaxing a campaign to win control of the British Conservative Party, Margaret Thatcher not only defeated a hapless Labour Party in the general election after four years of inflation, labor conflict, and financial buffeting; she led the Tories from their mellow toleration of the welfare state to a strident reassertion of market-based outcomes. There is no alternative, she would proclaim. She transformed the British Conservatives into an enterprise-oriented party with the help of bright self-confident ministers—perhaps most assertive, Keith Joseph, an energetic Oxford-educated spokesman for a vigorous capitalism. The decisive event at home for the Thatcher government was the bitter strike of the coal miners contesting the shutdown of coalpits. Given the personal clash between United Mine Worker head Arthur Scargill and the prime minister, Thatcher was able to frame the conflict—echoing the rhetoric of the 1926 general strike—as an uprising against the general interests of the nation. Two years later, she sent a major naval strike force to retake the bleak Falkland Islands from a clumsy Argentine effort at seizure by an unattractive military junta. The wakening of a populist nationalism served her well—almost three decades after the ignominy of the Suez debacle, Britain could claim an imperial victory. Privatization policies followed thick and fast. Being British, Thatcher accepted the rules of party government, ultimately having to yield to Tory notables for whom electoral viability was always the supreme principle. But in the three intervening electoral cycles, that she could dominate, she imposed a direction almost as marked as the Labour government of 1945–1951.

The ayatollah and the "Iron Lady" were not the only transformative leaders of the late 1970s and 1980s. The state was back—so long as it was in the service of entrepreneurial capitalism, faith, or party. These events of the late 1970s opened a decade of worldwide epochal reversals of policies. Reviving the ideological fervor that Barry Goldwater had aroused among conservatives in the mid-1960s, Ronald Reagan won a resounding presidential victory in 1980, espousing the same principles as Thatcher. Reformers in the 1980s also promised to break open the political stalemates in Italy, to replace the conservative Gaullist succession in France, to liberalize the cautious founding generation of post-authoritarian leaders in Iberia and Greece, to reenergize the process of European integration, and to democratize Latin America. The years of stagflation, violence, morose politics, and efforts to reinforce capitalist economies on one side and socialist on the other yielded to new departures and ideological reversals.

As often the case, the history of what Germans called a *Tendenzwende* or a break in trend—in their case, the 1982 replacement of a Social Democratic Party (SPD)–led government by the Christian Democratic Union (CDU)— meaningful changes had begun earlier. Even before the 1970s ended, prodded by West German chancellor Helmut Schmidt and the inclinations of its own national security adviser, Zbigniew Brzezinski, the Carter administration embarked on a decisive response to Soviet upgrading of intermediate-range missiles in Europe with plans to station American medium-range weaponry within range of Soviet targets. In the calculus of deterrence, such theater deployment would supposedly allow a credible American response to Soviet attacks in Europe, whereas threatening to unleash US-based intercontinental weapons that would provoke a Russian counterforce response on the American homeland would not. North Atlantic Treaty Organization foreign and defense ministers agreed in December 1979 to the so-called double-track decision. Negotiations would be undertaken with the Soviets until the end of 1983; if Moscow did not yield, over 100 Pershing II and 464 Cruise missiles would be deployed. Indicative of the political realignments under way was the fact that the parties of the non-communist left in Western Europe split: traditional Social Democrats and Christian Democrats followed Schmidt and Carter in accepting the need to place new weaponry in Europe, while the left (e.g., the Young Socialists in West Germany) and concerned Protestant reformers throughout northern Europe staged mass demonstrations to protest.[2] The demonstrations did not derail the new missile emplacements, but they may have contributed to the atmosphere that led to major arms reduction agreements by the late 1980s.

The most significant transformation was under way in China where Mao Tse-tung's successor, Deng Xiaoping, began to open his country to experiments in enterprise autonomy, confined at first to privileged geographic zones but soon to expand rapidly. The Soviets, in contrast, would cling to their economic and geopolitical formula—authoritarian state management—through the end of the long Brezhnev regime and the brief last effort at orthodoxy by his successor, Yuri Andropov. Both remained mired down in their drawn-out effort to defend a Marxist government in Afghanistan against Muslim rebels, while their efforts to redress a creaking economy finally impelled Mikhail Gorbachev after 1985 to unleash a process of "restructuring" and "transparency" (perestroika and glasnost) or liberalization. Part visionary, part sorcerer's apprentice, he could not control the acceleration of reforms, which culminated with the fall of Communist Party rule throughout Eastern Europe and the dissolution of the Soviet Union in 1991.[3]

Commentators and historians would seize upon the remarkable unraveling of the European Communist regimes at the end of the 1980s as the decisive event of the epoch. Many would attribute the apparent exhaustion of the left in the West to the disorientation provoked by the end of the Soviet Union and Communist Party rule. But the Soviet Communist model had already sacrificed whatever residual attraction it had retained after Stalin's death and the invasion of Hungary in 1956 by its intervention in Czechoslovakia in 1968. The party no longer aroused the fervor or even the willingness to accept Kremlin discipline among Western intellectuals or workers that it had from the 1920s through the 1950s. Among Communist Parties in the West, only the French seemed to soldier loyally on under mediocre leadership.

But disorientation on the left went far beyond disillusion with Moscow. Soviet senescence was itself a product of a more general ideological enervation. It was not the collapse of Communism in the East that undermined the West European Left but rather the reverse. The fact that the new post-communist regimes in Poland, Hungary, and the Czech Republic would take up neo-liberal policies revealed the systemic strains that assailed the socialist vision. By the end of the 1970s and early 1980s, the vocation of democratic socialism had collided with the apparent imperatives of a global economy, and the leadership of the Communist Parties in the East caught the disease of disillusion. Many socialists had already lost faith in state ownership by the late 1950s—witness the SPD's Bad Godesberg Program or a manifesto such as Anthony Crosland's 1956 tract, *The Future of Socialism*. Their preferred term, *social democracy*, implied a commitment to advancing the welfare state and egalitarianism, perhaps to public ownership of essential public services or natural monopolies, but no longer to general nationalization as a program. But this program—not yet infused as it would be later by racial, gender, or ecological issues—seemed largely accomplished by the late 1960s. Even more of a handicap, the policies it had instituted throughout the West seemed to have contributed insidiously to the sad decade of stagflation. At the same time, the social and electoral base of the old Western left would change. The industrial labor force in Europe would decline; public service unions, such as French schoolteachers, would remain, but the subculture of the parties would diminish. Was it enough to sing the traditional songs— "Jerusalem," "Bella Ciao," or even "We Shall Overcome"—at party conferences or the local Festa dell'Unità?[4]

The surge of inflation from 1969 to 1974, then again in the late 1970s when OPEC II hiked oil prices from $13 to $35, plus the new labor contracts, would threaten the fiscal bases of the welfare state. By the early 1980s, the beleaguered reformist left would turn toward liberal technocratic approaches to public policy and then to invigorating the European Economic Community (EEC).[5] Jacques Delors, the president of the Commission, defined Europe as a social project. Certainly, the EEC helped to establish welfare democracies as the standard for European administration. But at the same time, it strengthened its industrial and financial voices. Increasingly, the EEC was taking shape as a somewhat dirigiste but capital-friendly instrument. Free market liberals, especially in Britain, complained about the directives taken by Brussels. Their lament overlooked the fact that the concepts and mechanisms of governance it enacted were shaped by market needs. Good governance did not suggest ongoing state intervention as much as it did the restoration of market incentives. With the last decades of the century, the web of capital came to dominate the ideals of public government—and not only in its traditional heartland but in Eastern Europe and China as well.

Associations of religious faith, embracing literal scripture readings and fervent practices, also emerged as powerful political forces. In the Islamic world, as noted, the Iranian revolution posed a powerful new center of religious activism, rivaling the earlier promises of secular nationalist leadership, whether Gamal Abdel Nasser's Egypt in the 1950s, the Ba'ath revolution in Iraq, or Algeria's rallying of the third world in the 1960s and 1970s. And the long struggle of Afghan mujahideen—religiously inspired guerrillas supported by the United States and combatting the pro-Soviet government foisted by Russia—opened a campaign of paramilitary Sunni offensives certainly willing to support attacks on civilian populations. But religious enthusiasms burgeoned also among Evangelical Christians in the United States, Latin

America, and Africa, where they would become important forces in shaping political opinion. A new Polish pope, John Paul II, visited his homeland in 1978, where his charismatic presence helped arouse active impatience with the party and the regime. Looking ahead to the surge of these trends at the end of the century, an observer might wonder whether the twentieth-century state would retreat before the forces of capital or fervent religiosity.

"Reinvention" seems the appropriate term for these efforts to shape a society that Western middle-class opinion saw as threatening to slip out of control in the 1970s. Ultimately, reinvention entailed the coordination of efforts by national governments, the spokesmen for capital, and the traditional international and national advocates of economic governance. All these agencies—organized in theory with separate institutional missions—were to become increasingly bound together during the 1970s in an effort to sustain the political economy of global capitalism (and the final decade of state socialism). The events of the late 1970s and 1980s were to press home once again—and by the next generation even more so—that the smooth functioning of the world economy depended not only on labor and commodities provided in the present but equally on anticipations of the future embodied in the extension of credit and the accumulation of debt. An international economy that had been transfixed by inflation was to be restructured on the basis of debt. Accumulating it and extending it was to be the silent prerequisite for the policies known as neoliberalism. We follow these developments in this and the next chapters.

Debt's Dominion, 1

As noted in the previous chapter, domestic policies could not really be taken in isolation. Despite American renunciation of convertibility in 1971, its currency still remained the medium for international transactions, including OPEC's staggeringly higher oil bill. The fear that this windfall might be "sterilized" (i.e., deposited without being loaned for new investment) in Middle Eastern treasuries did not come to pass; nearly half a trillion dollars would be recycled over the course of the 1970s into European and American bank accounts.[6] From bank balance sheets, they could serve as the fractional base for far larger loans to third world countries, preeminently to Mexico, Brazil, and to Eastern Europe in the 1970s, in particular Poland, whose new government led by Edward Gierek needed to defuse working-class anger at recently decreed price increases. Willy Brandt's Social-Democratic government, committed to normalizing existence with Communist Eastern Europe, increased loans to Poland and to the German Democratic Republic (GDR), both of which went heavily into debt to finance the consumer goods needed to appease their dissatisfied citizens. But the new liquidity spread far more widely as well.

While the OPEC powers were upending the power relations inherent in the international economy, the proponents of the New International Economic Order, inscribed as a United Nations (UN) objective in 1974, would at least temporarily win a fistful of dollars that the flush commercial banks in the West were eager to lend for ambitious development plans. Yes, there were hazards involved: the new Basel Committee on Banking Supervision, convened under the aegis of the Bank of International Settlements that same year of 1974 by sober central bankers, began to focus not only on the exposure of core country banks to loans to the periphery but also the overall "country risk" that might arise. Walter Wriston, the head of Citibank, might say that countries could not go bankrupt; he did not say that they could default (although in the 1930s, remarkably few had). The country risk under discussion threatened not from the imprudence of individual banks but from the possibility that borrower countries might freeze bank accounts or suddenly devalue.[7] As so often in financial crises, the worthy bankers recognized the risks but were reluctant to interfere with market mechanisms that they counted on to crimp credit when individual banks seemed improvident.

Two years later in 1976, Mexico came perilously close to default. The country had pursued an ambitious course of industrial development in the 1960s and 1970s under PRI leaders increasingly educated and socialized in US business circles. To sustain the pace of investment without cutting social spending, they turned increasingly to American banks. Between January and August 1976, Mexico's foreign currency reserves had fallen 85 percent. President Luis Echeverría excluded devaluation but felt compelled to accept conditional loans in negotiations with the International Monetary Fund (IMF) and the US Treasury in the first of the later notorious "adjustment" programs.[8] The rescue required a fusion of state and private bank efforts as well as an IMF loan needed to persuade the private banks to chip in. Successfully resolved, it did not halt the momentum of third world indebtedness.

The late 1970s brought a capitalist world awash with monetary claims issued to cover OPEC oil prices, militant union demands, continuing profits, and extended welfare and education expenses. Since the recycling of petrodollars back to Western and Japanese banks after OPEC I had proceeded without the anticipated difficulties, it led banking supervisors to keep a light hand on the private bank sector, which accelerated its lending to the less developed world. Although many in the financial community viewed this as a market-driven adjustment, state intervention was also crucial. The United States and other countries relaxed credit controls so that OPEC revenues deposited in American banks could be recycled more quickly; the official special-purpose export-import banks in the United States, Germany, Britain, and Japan guaranteed the debts that developing countries piled up to finance their imports. The IMF created a special facility in 1978 for developing economies hit by OPEC's second oil price hike. By helping the world's economies to continue paying for expensive oil, and thus lubricating, as it were, the recycling process, these measures would provoke greater difficulties for the international financial community than the increases of 1974.[9]

Beyond prompting official easing of credits, the OPEC crises impelled private banks to assume a far larger role in lending to the less developed countries. By 1972, central banks and governments, according to Carlo Edoardo Altamura, were facing possible legal crackdowns on the flow of Eurodollars after the monetary upheavals of 1971 and the breakdown of Bretton Woods. "A growing number of politicians and central bankers appear determined to tame the 'Euromonster' which they hold responsible for the monetary upheavals of the past year," warned the *Financial Times* in March 1972.[10] The OPEC price hikes deferred that threat. IMF and other officials and bankers were aware how severely the price increases would impact the less developed countries and wanted the oil exporters' surpluses recycled as efficiently as possible to the consumers. Indeed, a major expansion of lending took place and soon became an apparently lucrative business. As large international private banks competed to place loans in the developing world, a practice called loan pushing that increased the volume of lending from a yearly average of $14 billion between 1974 and 1977 to $22 billion in 1978, $35 billion in 1979, and close to $40 billion in both 1980 and 1981. Until they might have to be written off as unperforming, such loans inflated the asset sheets of the lending banks. Large banks would syndicate loans, spreading not only risk but also exposure. Between the eve of the first oil price rise at the end of 1973 and the end of 1982, loans from first world banks to the non-OPEC, less developed countries rose from $32 billion to $247 billion and loans to Eastern Europe rose from $9.5 billion to $53.3 billion. Of this almost $300 billion outstanding, US banks held 40 percent, Japanese banks 25 percent, UK, French, and German banks 15 percent, 8 percent, and 7 percent, respectively. The Crédit Commercial de France was heavily invested, as were Midlands and Lloyds

Table 8.1   Foreign Direct Investment Outflows (Selected Years, 1970–2000)
in Millions of USD

Year	World Outflow	Developed World	US Outflow*		
	(per UNCTAD)	(per UNCTAD)	(per OECD)	(per FRED)	(per OECD)
1970	$ 14,158	$ 9.812		$ 9,607	
1975	$ 28,607	$ 28,090		$ 30,407	
1980	$ 53,674	$ 51,089		$ 57,349	
1985	$ 62,163	$ 57,964		$ 31,207	
1990	$ 233,315	$ 241,470	$ 216,589	$ 83,306	$ 37,180
1995	$ 356,404	$ 337,973	$ 306,649	$221,813	$ 98,748
2000	$1,379,493	$1,328,690	$1,271,544	$361,263	$159,214

*The OECD sources, available from 1990, provide foreign direct investment (FDI), including portfolio investment in foreign shares and development of branches of American companies abroad; the FRED data also include acquisition of foreign financial liabilities (government and private debt).

Data sources:

For world and developed world outflows, 1980–2000: *UNCTAD Handbook of Statistics*, cited in "Global Policy Forum, Foreign Direct Investment." (Alternate source from 1990 to 2000 from OECD.Stat: FDI Series of BOP and IIP Aggregates, Outflows: World.)

For the US outflows: Board of Governors of the Federal Reserve System (US), Table: "Rest of the World: Total Financial Liabilities and Foreign Direct Investment: Equity Transactions" (BOGZ1FA264194035A), retrieved from FRED, Federal Reserve Bank of St. Louis, https//fred.stlouisfed.org/series BOG Z1FA264194035A/, July 8, 2022. (Alternate source from 1990: OECD.Stat: FDI Series of BOP and IIP Aggregates, Outflows: US.)

with 205 percent and 165 percent, respectively, of their capital exposed by 1983. US bank loans to Latin America rose to 97 percent of their capital by 1981.[11]

In effect, states and banks arrived at a mutual accommodation during the 1980s. As governments came under the control of center-right coalitions, they moved to curtail budget deficits, not by raising taxes but seeking to curtail spiraling welfare payments largely at the behest of the world of finance, which decried profligate spending. At the same time, the Federal Reserve allowed banks to expand their lending at home and abroad. With consumer credit made widely available (and not just keyed to mortgages or installment payments on purchases), household debt could climb. Foreign direct investment across borders also ballooned. Each loan extended made a bank balance sheet seem more impressive.

The immediate peril, however, arose for the countries that indulged in the borrowing spree since the loans were denominated in dollars and required servicing at prevailing (London Interbank Offered Rate [LIBOR]) interest rates, which were to rise steeply once President Carter's new chair of the

Federal Reserve, Paul Volcker, decided that a drastic increase in the Fed's discount rate was needed to counteract the new surge of inflation at home. Market interest rates rose in response from 7 percent to 7.5 percent to 11.5 percent in 1980 and above 14 percent in 1981. Prime interest rates rose to 20 percent before the Fed relaxed its policies in 1982. But the "Volker shock" did its work. Inflation fell from 14 percent to 3.5 percent, and this despite the income tax cuts of the incoming Reagan administration and the growth of federal budget deficits from 1.2 percent under Carter to 3 percent and 3.5 percent by the mid-1980s. Deficits would continue for a decade until the Clinton administration. An orthodox financier such as Peter Peterson, Richard Nixon's secretary of commerce in 1973, later chair of Lehman Brothers and the New York Federal Reserve Bank from 2000 to 2004, would make it his mission to decry the deficit, but it seemed to matter little to American economic performance, largely because the rest of the world—and increasingly China— would finance it by buying Treasury bonds.

Similar trends were produced elsewhere. The coming of North Sea oil and Thatcher's policies pushed sterling up, but British gross domestic product (GDP) fell by 5.5 percent and unemployment doubled. Carter had hoped in 1978–1979 that the West German economy might serve as a "locomotive" to stimulate world production, but Germany was tightening its monetary policy as was Japan.[12] Both countries measured their success in terms of exports and sought to lower their internal budget deficits. Their combined current account positions went from a deficit of about $24 billion in 1980 to a surplus of $137 billion by 1987, while the American international current account dropped from a surplus of $2 billion to a deficit of $168 billion, four-fifths of it accounted for by the German and Japanese surpluses. These two countries persisted in their mercantilist economic convictions, whereas the United States seemed unlikely to curb its foreign purchases. What it sold increasingly were its own Treasury IOUs—promises to pay with a bit of interest in the future.

Demand for American "treasuries"—that is, government bonds—was sufficient for the dollar to move higher in foreign exchange markets—7.5 percent in 1982, 10.3 percent in 1984—thus less developed countries that had borrowed in dollar-denominated loans from banks engorged with the dollars recycled from the OPEC countries found themselves in great distress. Even before the Volcker shock, the difficulty of foreign debtors was far more noticeable, further squeezed by appreciation of the dollar until concerted action by the United States and the G5 powers started a decline. By 1987, following the so-called Plaza agreement with the G5, the dollar started to descend.

For the first time since World War I, America became a net debtor between 1986 and 1988. The development led to the US Treasury raising interest rates and then to a massive stock market sell-off in October 1987, a fall as sharp as in October 1929 but without the same devastating link to the underlying economy. Foreign purchases of bonds and deposits covered the tax reductions that the Reagan administration delivered. Inflation seemed yesterday's problem; so was labor unrest.

Unemployment did rise in both Britain and the United States as domestic interest rates were raised. But in the long run, it was the less developed countries, especially in Latin America, that bore the costs of halting inflation. After OPEC I, from 1974 to 1978, the cumulative current account deficit of oil-importing countries still amounted to no more than $180 billion. Although the new OPEC II oil levy of 1979 was largely recycled, the dollars flowed back to the commercial banks of the developed world, which lent in turn to the less developed countries. The inflationary pressure produced by OPEC II led to the tightening of interest rates in the advanced countries and a rise in interest costs from 9.2 percent to 16.7 percent in 1981. Mexico, already in difficulty in 1976, entered dangerous waters once again in 1981–1982.[13] The new president, José López Portillo, indulged in massive spending; the budget deficit doubled and the current account deficit rose from under $2 billion to over $16 billion. Creditors offered some accommodation in the summer of 1982, but the finance minister announced a three-month moratorium on loan repayments (not just interest) in late August. Banks in response cut back their loans to major debtor countries—from $54 billion in 1981 down to $19 billion in 1985. Combined GDP fell about 15 percent between 1981 and 1984. The impact on American banks, whose loans to the debtors amounted to almost twice their capital, threatened runs on US banks. López Portillo announced a nationalization of the banks in September, converted dollar accounts into pesos, imposed exchange controls, all the while threatening to organize an international debtor cartel and criticizing the IMF—bravado that intensified capital flight. But the constitutional limitation on presidential terms meant that López Portillo was already slated to yield office to his chosen successor, Miguel de la Madrid, who championed an orthodox program. The PRI dominated organized labor and could assure the conversion to a neoliberal program. Jacques de Larosière, director of the IMF, helped defuse the crisis, approving an IMF loan conditional on contributions from private banks in a move toward "concerted effort." Loans were patched together and Mexico signed an IMF agreement in November; private banks ponied up even more and agreed to a further moratorium. Still, net transfers (new loans less payments on the old ones) amounted to $37 billion for seventeen large debtors, which meant their economies plunged into depression to meet payments. Mexico's GDP in 1985 was 26 percent below 1980. The World Bank estimated that for the years 1980–1988, capital outflows—repayment and capital "flight"—amounted to $64 billion from Mexico, $35.6 from Brazil, and $39.5 from Argentina.

The growing debt crisis was not just an affliction of Western capitalism. It hit Eastern Europe as well. As OPEC prices rose, Soviet prices—oil keyed to a lagged world market price index—also rose. For East Germany, who helped secure Valuta or Western currencies by refining Soviet oil and selling it to the West, this represented a great danger. Industrial pig rearing provided another major export item, but the more pork exported, the higher the meat prices at home. Poland was also afflicted primarily because to prevent mass unrest as it repressed Solidarity, greater consumption had to be allowed, including Western imports. Borrowing from the West was the only recourse.[14]

"Follow the money," "Deep Throat" told *Washington Post* reporters Bob Woodward and Carl Bernstein in 1973. He was talking about Watergate perpetrators, but the advice would have proved opportune for the crises of the 1970s and 1980s. In effect, the developed world's resources transferred to the OPEC countries would derive from the less developed countries via the intermediation of Western banks. But the banks were hardly just a disinterested pipeline of liquidity. Western banks had taken an active role in so-called loan pushing and were themselves at risk as precarious creditors, which is why national governments found themselves so involved. On the borrower side, crises, according to the statistical study carried out by Jeffrey Frankel and Andrew Rose, were to be more prevalent as commercial bank loans replaced the credits extended by multilateral agencies and as lenders sought out portfolio investments rather than new enterprises. Less developed countries that relied on foreign commercial loans were more vulnerable than those in debt to multilateral agencies such as the IMF or World Bank. Budget deficits seemed less important than usually believed.[15] By the mid-1980s, it was difficult to separate the financial institutions, US government officials, and the agencies of governance, who all collaborated on the script for financial retrenchment. At the Seoul meeting of the IMF and World Bank in October 1985, Treasury Secretary James Baker proposed further loans in return for "structural reforms." These included liberalizing import controls, welcoming direct investment and privatizing state enterprises. These measures were in line with the almost century-old recipes of American foreign economic policy, whether with respect to the Open Door in China, British imperial preference, and postwar foreign aid. Of course, they presupposed a world where private enterprise should prosper.[16] Two years later in 1987, the Americans added debt-equity conversions to the mix of proposals. US banks would sell their loans at a discount in local currency to the countries that had contracted them and then would use the proceeds to buy stock in local enterprises or other assets. The American lender could claim it was relieving the burden of debt on Latin America; the cynical historian might say that the Reagan administration and its business supporters was using the financial pressure on the debtor nations to acquire local assets. American capital, presidential power, and international governance converged to create a new financial order. The New International Economic Order envisaged at the UN in 1974 could have belonged to ancient history. Latin American countries adopted the "Washington consensus"—the policies recommended by the Treasury, IMF, World Bank, and the think tanks. Augusto Pinochet's Chile had pioneered in application of the reforms; its University of Chicago–trained economists, the "Chicago boys," zealously applied their monetarist lessons at home without having to worry about working-class opposition.

Why did not simple default seem a better option for the indebted countries? In the interwar period many countries had defaulted. After the 1970s, not even leftist governments in Cuba and Nicaragua did so. Jerome Roos explains, however, that the creditor-debtor balance had shifted. President Franklin Roosevelt himself had attributed the defaults of the interwar years in part to the banks' cupidity.[17] In the 1920s and 1930s, moreover, foreign debts had been marketed widely and ownership was dispersed, whereas in the second postwar period, they were held by a few large banks that were supported by their national governments and could work with IMF resources to negotiate relief short of default. The result was that although payments of principal might be temporarily suspended under IMF-brokered agreements, interest payments continued and no state risked renouncing the obligation to repay. Would partial or total default have risked their being shut out of the international capital market? Financial historians disagree on the likelihood of this sanction. More of a deterrent perhaps was the likelihood that default would be accompanied by a massive devaluation that would not only have proportionally spurred commodity exports but simply imposed harsh costs on the general populations. This was the upshot of the Thai and Russian devaluations in the late 1990s.[18]

Debt was to remain a problem, with Mexico again in 1994, with Thailand and Russia in 1997–1998, Argentina in the early 2000s, and most recently with Greece within the Eurozone. But until the last, it proved to be a transformative problem, cementing into place the so-called Washington consensus. International debt from the mid-1920s to the 1930s had been contracted during a period in which leading currencies had been stabilized and, in the case of the British pound, overvalued. (See Chapter 3.) Among developed countries, it had rarely been repaid in full. Russia had repudiated its debt after the revolution. Europeans had renegotiated their debt with the United States during the 1930s, and Washington extended direct aid in the UN Relief and Rehabilitation Administration and Marshall Plan periods. Often denominated in pounds sterling or in dollars, its burden was ultimately alleviated in an era of inflation.

The crises revealed that there was no single set of values available for judging the debt relationship. Economists spoke as if there was no alternative to painful stabilization programs, while critics presupposed that they imposed intolerable sacrifices. Moral considerations could be claimed by both creditors and debtors, which is why the institutions of governance—among others, the IMF on one side and the proponents of the New International Economic Order on the other side—had no transcendent authority and faced contested legitimacy. International lending did facilitate technological development in the third world. Most participants in the debt relationship, including debtors, nominally accepted an obligation to repay when they accepted a loan. Creditors argued that repayment in full, rejecting what since the Greek euro crisis of 2010 have been called "haircuts" or debt write-downs, was necessary to avoid "moral hazard," the possibility that the precedents of debt forgiveness would be claimed by others and ultimately the commitments that kept lending viable would collapse. *Pacta sunt servanda*, pacts must be observed, the maxim of international lawyers in the sixteenth century, should apply to contracts as well as peace treaties.

Both capitalism and socialism rested on "great expectations," not of bequests but of economic growth and technological change. Both were still relatively free of the environmental pessimism (or realism) that has since become so important a consideration. Loans were a wager on mobilizing otherwise unused productive capacity. Although they might draw on prior savings, the system multiplied accumulations. Banks created credit lines, assuming that the productive capacity when mobilized would reveal that the loan had justified the wager. The defenders of capitalism claimed that lending at interest assured that current capacities would be mobilized without state compulsion to realize these expectations. On the other hand, argued advocates for the debtors, hadn't the banks imprudently pushed the loans on the borrowers, often offering sweetheart deals or kickbacks to rulers who accepted them? There was room for rancor on both sides.

Sovereign debt—loans to national governments—muddied the normative waters even more. Many of these loans (similar to the case of American loans to Central Europe in the 1920s) did not go to productivity-enhancing enterprises in the capitalist sense. They went to state projects that had civic culture or even public employment as one of their goals. They often entailed corruption and payoffs. Even when devoted to infrastructure, they perpetuated privileges, economic rents, and waste. Insistence on repayment could thus mean a healthy pressure for modernization and reallocation of resources.

Thus, too, it meant confirming the rules of neoliberalism for better or worse: discharging masses of workers from public services (some admittedly inefficient and bloated), cutting welfare benefits, privatizing nationalized industries. But it also meant imposing huge degrees of misery on subaltern sectors of the population. Coupled with the rising import prices produced by devaluation, it brought impoverishment to the countryside, to those thrown into unemployment, to the elderly. It brought the attrition of public services, the denial of education, and increasingly in the late 1970s and 1980s mass migration of the dispossessed to the barrios of sprawling cities where they looked for casual employment and sometimes had to settle for mendicancy and violence augmented by the profits and violence of the drug trade. In the longer run, it may also have helped produce an expansion of life expectancy and a rise in general global incomes—not even counting the transformations under way in East and South Asia. Weighing short-term costs against long-term gains must again be a subjective exercise.

The balance of social forces and ideological commitments had changed from the 1960s. Ending inflation in the 1970s and 1980s required reversing the political and social factors that seemed to follow from governments tilted toward the left, as it had during the 1920s. It seemed to require limiting the power of trade unions; it militated against extensive welfare provisions. Delinking the automatic adjustment of wages to prices—usually instituted in indexation schemes, particularly entrenched in Italy and Israel—usually had to override union preferences. Communist Party economists in the West

Table 8.2 Government Spending as Share of National Income (All Levels of Government and Including Interest Payments on Government Debt)

Country	1960	1970	1980	1990	2000	2010	2020
France	22.2%	20.5%	46.0%	49.6%	51.7%	56.6%	62.4%
Germany	22.9%	39.5%	48.2%	44.7%	45.1%	47.9%	51.0%
Italy	16.5%	32.3%	40.8%	52.9%	45.9%	50.3%	57.3%
Sweden	24.4%	29.5%	41.0%	40.0%	55.1%	52.3%	53.0%
UK	33.1%	42.0%	47.6%	41.1%	36.8%	50.6%	50.3%
US	28.3%	32.3%	34.3%	37.2%	33.9%	42.5%	46.2%
Japan	18.4%	20.3%	33.5%	30.1%	37.3%	39.8%	46.7%

Data source: For 1960–2010: IMF Data Mapper, "Government Expenditure as Percent of GDP" and Paolo Mauro, Rafael Romeu, Ariel Binder, and Asad Zaman, *A Modern History of Fiscal Prudence and Profligacy*, IMF Working Paper No. 2013/005 (Washington, DC: International Monetary Fund, 2013), https://www.imf.org/externa/datamapper/datasets/FPP. For 2020, Wikipedia (source not listed). The 2020 data include significant jumps in some cases as a consequence of the COVID-19 pandemic.

understood that it was necessary, but one supporter, Ezio Tarantelli, paid for his advocacy when he was gunned down by a leftist assassin in 1985. Governance representatives tended to split: the Brandt report of 1980 showed that governance might speak out on behalf of the less developed world, but the policies remained in the realm of good intentions where they would again rouse the disagreement of Peter Bauer and those who thought like him.

Reduction of public budgets and deficits was a priority for the governments of the 1980s and 1990s. On an overall measurement, reduction of the government spending share of GDP became an aspiration and was partially successful. But in this process, social welfare expenditures loomed as a particular target, especially for the Thatcher and Reagan administrations but for the moderate German Social Democrats as well. Provision for old-age insurance, Social Security in the United States, and periods of unemployment, health insurance—that is, all the vicissitudes of income through life aggregated as risk—became a target for "reform"—that is, for restricting the socialization of risk in favor of the privatization of burdens. Paul Pierson has documented, however, that pension systems were hard to dismantle after the previous generations of expansion.[19] In the United States, the Social Security Act of 1935 seemed almost a constitutional right, and cost-of-living adjustments in an inflationary era had significantly expanded its cost. But it was identified as a quasi-universal entitlement, not particularly identified with a working class. To make it acceptable in the mid-1930s, it was paid for by special taxes on employees as well as employers; its benefits had been keyed to lifetime earnings, and they were sequestered in a separate trust fund. Congress refused President Carter's proposal to beef it up with general taxation, and there was a great deal of panicky rhetoric that the Social Security Trust Fund would soon be bankrupt (a rather irrelevant fear since general taxation might always be drawn on).

For all their achievements in national healthcare provision, the British system of pensions had been unified into a basic state pension plan (State Earnings Related Pension Scheme [SERPS]) only in the 1970s. The Thatcher government limited indexation in 1980 but still worried about the expansion of the plan and proposed to abolish it over time and replace it with mandatory employer-provided plans or individual personal pensions. The Trades Union Congress (TUC) and Labour Party protested, as would be expected, but so did employers and occupational pension funds. Women who might have a much shorter period of lifetime employment faced a particularly stringent future. The government retreated but did pass a reform by 1986, retaining SERPS but encouraging private schemes. Together with sale of hitherto public housing (council houses—30 percent of households lived in public housing in 1979) and privatization of key industries, these policies helped to consolidate a wide social bloc with middle-class interests, electorally significant enough so that the Labour Party could not simply override their appeal. In the United States, David Stockman, Reagan's Director of the Office of Management and Budget, proposed a sharp and sudden reduction in benefits for early retirees in an effort to reduce social expenses. The Senate voted unanimously to oppose any "unfair" cuts. A bipartisan commission did agree on a 1983 compromise that delayed cost of living adjustments and extended the compulsory program to other payers. Long-range benefits were slowly to taper down—by the new century it was understood that this cornerstone of old-age insurance would need to be supplemented by private pension plans. Overall, "the Reagan administration's effort to restructure state pensions was largely thwarted."[20] But this was not the whole story over time. The longer-term evolution of American social security was not a cheering one. As Jacob Hacker explained, conservatives prevented reform—most spectacularly dooming the admittedly complex Clinton national health insurance plan in the 1990s—such that existing public programs provided less and less coverage of life-cycle needs.[21] As Chapter 9 discusses, by the 1990s the parties of the left in the major democracies signed on for the same program.

Unemployment insurance and income maintenance was the most obvious target for Thatcher and Reagan reform. These benefits always came burdened with suspicion of encouraging malingering; this despite the 12.5 percent rate of joblessness in Britain by 1983 and the possibility of other alternatives. Little by little, the Thatcher government diminished universal benefits and threw recipients on means-tested supplementary benefit. "Wasteful" child allowances were also a target, although how children's benefits could "undermine the will to self-help," as the government spokesman suggested, was hard to see.[22] It was the universality of the program that aroused Tory hostility—as poor relief had traditionally done since Poor Law reform in 1834. The premise of universal eligibility came under attack. Reformers suggested a negative income tax, but the scheme would have required higher general tax rates—a red flag for the Tory constituencies. Overall, reform proved hard to achieve but there was "a gradual erosion of the universal systems of unemployment insurance and child allowances." But the changes were slight; more visible were the cuts in income tax on the wealthy—a universal tendency of the decade. In the United States, food stamps and Aid to Families with Dependent Children (AFDC)were the signal targets of the Reagan administration although a thorough-going reform would have to wait for the Clinton presidency in the 1990s. The administration, with a Republican Senate majority and enough conservative Democrats in the House, seemed to enjoy a mandate and had success in 1981 but not subsequent years, as recession took hold. The states, which shared in Aid to Families with Dependent Children, cut more, letting the burden fall on the exclusively federally funded food stamps program. In 1986, all benefits were made fully taxable. Mostly, however, the Reagan administration sought to throw the burdens of unemployment insurance and income maintenance on to the states under the slogan of New Federalism. "Workfare" requirements had a superficial appeal across the aisle: for conservatives, as a way of compelling the work-shy back into employment; for liberals, as a possibility for empowerment. But the latter would have required more resources for childcare. The Earned Income Tax Credit for the working poor was "the great political success of the retrenchment era." The administration was hostile at first, but the program grew. "Popular hostility to programs for the poor, which had helped to elect Reagan and Thatcher, dissipated rapidly. . . . Over time both administrations found themselves considerably expanding the most palatable targeted program— supplements for working families with low incomes."[23] Nonetheless, the rhetoric of unworthiness for the poor and unemployed persisted, the fear that women and children living hand to mouth might be gaming the system, the hostility to unions all persisted. And most remarkable, the rhetorical and legislative climate persisted among the left-center leaders who succeeded in the 1990s, whether Tony Blair and New Labour or Bill Clinton and New Democrats, or the Gerhard Schroeder SPD government that was elected in 1998 after sixteen years of Helmut Kohl's chancellorship.

The "Grand March" in Disarray: Labor's Transformation and Ideological Disorientation

In 1978, the historian Eric Hobsbawm, never willing to renounce his hope for socialist progress but coming to terms with disappointments, delivered a major lecture in London titled "The Forward March of Labour Halted?" He pleaded for the Labour Party to reach out to the expanded middle classes in an encompassing left. The Czech author in exile, Milan Kundera ended his 1984 novel, *The Unbearable Lightness of Being*, with a harsher view of the left's march: "The fantasy of the grand march . . . is the political kitsch joining leftists of all times and tendencies. The Grand March is the splendid march on the road to brotherhood, equality, justice, happiness; it goes on and on, obstacles notwithstanding, for obstacles there must be if the march is to be the Grand March."[24] The different mood—disappointments with setbacks versus cynicism about the idea—reflected not only the authors' very different political stance; it captured a historic rupture.

Historians, including this one, have found it plausible to sympathize with the grand march. But aside from Kundera's irony, shaped by his experience in Communist Czechoslovakia, there were other reasons to modify the narrative. Capitalist labor relations were bound to be adversarial. Almost by definition, social classes are dialectical concepts, defined by their contrasting interests. Business leaders might take pride in providing work for men who came to their factories or offices five or six days a week. From management's perspective, these subordinates had limited comprehension of the system that fed them. Workers, especially younger and less experienced ones, rarely understood why they could not receive higher pay than employers would settle for. In the West, they had entered the 1970s still militant and all the more edgy because inflation threatened the wage packets they negotiated. Governments, as seen, had resorted to concertation or corporatist arrangements—inviting union leaders to cooperate with public officials and industrial representatives in calculating just and tolerable wage increases, in return for price controls or keying taxes to real wages. But these agreements had not been popular on either side. Labor delegates who had been persuaded to sign on for restraint watched firms achieve profit surges that went to dividends or executive pay. Employers saw resentful workers compelling their union or even shop-floor delegates to engage in destructive work stoppages to extract higher pay, require redundant manpower, or relax on the job. In their view, labor delegates seemed not to comprehend that if they pressed too hard, competitors would drive their firms out of business. Some failed to sympathize with the higher rewards that the market allegedly dictated managers and owners should receive—indeed, a gap that would only grow over the half century after 1970. Many found their repetitive tasks demoralizing, while those who took pride in their skill wanted greater recognition. Some of their spokespersons even entertained visions of removing private owners and placing industries under some form of collective ownership, although state firms would face many of the same constraints.

Over the course of the late 1970s and 1980s, the preconditions for these sometimes stubborn positions changed considerably. They did so both in the workplace and the halls of party politics. The forward march, as Hobsbawm recognized, was not going well. FIAT manager Cesare Romiti fired sixty-one outspoken activists after the assassination of a high-ranking firm official on September 21, 1979. Other setbacks followed. Within a year, it was the workers themselves who attacked strike organizers. In 1980, an attempted strike at FIAT provoked a clamorous counterdemonstration by workers who did not want to shut down the plant.[25] In 1984, Thatcher went to the mat against the coal miners striking against mine closures and prevailed. Reagan defied the air controllers and won.

Some brilliant essayists and sociologists explored the discontents of the working class and came to diverse results. In an analysis that distressed many in the Socialist milieu of the Mitterrand years, André Gorz declared that the workplace was no longer and could no longer be a site of fulfillment: "Workers are there and fall in with the work that *is done*. They do not do it themselves. . . . All that matters is the wage-packet at the end of the week or month— especially since [employers] don't ask anything else of [them], no decisions or initiative. They're expected to be passive? Well then, let's be passive. Or more exactly, let us use passivity as a weapon against those who imposed it. . . . The language of proletarian resentment is also the language of impotence." The answer for Gorz, who always nurtured an emancipatory streak, was to reduce the role of work and have society shuttle between the sphere of necessity and that of autonomy. The state was needed to delineate and patrol the dualism.[26] Aris Accornero, close to the Italian General Confederation of Labour (CGIL), was more nostalgic about the community that labor had created and indeed the great confrontation: "During the whole twentieth century the relation between the great actors, capital and labor, and their great objectives, profit and wages, appeared nested and intertwined as perhaps we shall never see again in the West. The firm was revealed as a place where both a 'system of domination' and a 'structure of cooperation' coexisted and where any prospect of overcoming the contrasts so that the conflict might be reintegrated seemed unrealistic. "What is changing under our eyes is not just the incontestable industrial imprint that the world of the factory [*impresa*] and of production had given to work and to the workers ... at least in the West. In fact an era is fading, which for labor and for the workers will bring consequences as profound as those encountered in the transition from agriculture to industry and then from industry to services [*terziato*]."[27]

Diagnoses throughout the West echoed these mournful conclusions. In Germany, Theo Pirker, on the left of the movement, reissued his critical study of the German labor unions with a bitter critique of their co-optation and bureaucratization. The earlier struggles for codetermination in the early 1950s had only reinforced their domestication.[28] But as during earlier critical eras, labor and the left were fundamentally split between reformist and radical strategies. The vision of the Popular Front continually beckoned but was hard to maintain, even when "defeats" seemed imminent. All the more so, when the Communist Party component remained compromised by the experiences of Soviet-dominated Europe and most recently the suppression of the Prague Spring.

But perhaps the grand march, at least as judged by social democrats, had actually been successful. Welfare states had been significantly expanded in scope. Access to education and vacations had multiplied. Indeed, in the advanced countries, the achievements were part of the problem. How did one find a new agenda that provided the same moral cohesion? Labor was on the defensive as automation claimed jobs and manufacturing moved to Asia. Why did the horizons for labor in the West seem to crumple so dramatically at the end of the 1970s and early 1980s? Yes, heavy industry and mining no longer provided as many workplaces, and the processes of manufacturing changed. Automation eliminated many jobs on the assembly line. Standardized mass output was yielding to a greater array of differentiated products. The very imprecise term for the transition was the advent of post-Fordism. The great unified factory that operated on "flow" principles was increasingly decomposed with far more separation of production units and increased outsourcing. In itself, that should not have been fatal. Fordism or assembly-line production, strictly speaking, had never numerically dominated industrial production, and militant workers were found in mines, construction, printing establishments, and agricultural work.[29] The German printers' union, I. G. Druck, went on strike in 1978. Public services including teachers were strongly organized in France. The challenge for labor unions was to organize the substantial numbers of migrants and of women who entered the workforce:[30] Turks in Germany, North Africans in France, South Asians in Britain, Congolese in Belgium, Indonesians in the Netherlands, Sicilians in Turin, a renewed wave of African Americans in Detroit as the mechanization of cotton picking impelled their move north, Mexicans throughout the United States as emigration was liberalized, and Vietnamese as the Americans finally yielded the south to Hanoi. But organizing this imported population was not a natural task since the "new" members of the working classes often challenged places and attitudes that had long been held by the historic "proletariat." Racialization was one response.[31] The line in France between skilled and semiskilled became one between white and less white. Gender issues also moved into the forefront— women's promotion, wage equality, security of job tenure were disturbing causes for male-dominated unions. Shop-floor organizations claimed autonomy from industry-wide organizations. Intensifying all these dilemmas, labor union membership continued to decline in Western societies.

These adverse trends had a major impact on the unions' historical affiliates, the parties of the left. Whether the Communists in France, Italy, and the Low Countries, or the Social Democrats / Labour in Britain, Germany, and Scandinavia, or the Democratic Party in the United States—they no longer maintained the same sense of ideological cohesion; indeed, they were ferociously divided for a generation or more. Working-class organizations, moreover, no longer existed in their symbiotic relationship with their historic party homes, whether social-democratic or communist. Matthew Myers, who has followed European left parties and the unions in this era, argues that in the years from the late 1970s to the early 1980s, political leaders somehow dismantled the working-class left. Marc Lazar cites the "personalization" of leadership by Bettino Craxi, François Mitterrand, Enrico Berlinguer, or Georges Marchais as one factor for the party changes.[32] British Labour Party electoral autopsies attributed the losses of the party to class "dealignment." As the future premier Tony Blair argued, "There are growing numbers of young often socially upward-moving people who are simply not prepared to accept our basic ideology just because their forefathers did."[33] Similar diagnoses were made throughout Western countries. In Italy, the phenomenon of terrorism made the critiques more anguishing. Giorgio Amendola on the right of the Italian Communist Party criticized the CGIL and his own party's tendency to excuse the *autonomisti* and factory violence: "Who can deny that there is a direct relationship between factory violence and terrorism? There are forms of struggle which we see in Turin but which are widely used outside factories: road occupations, intimidating marches, vandalism, destruction of cars and businesses, . . . which distort the very character of the class struggle." The unions had to limit the recourse to strikes against the general interest.[34] Between Pirker's diagnosis of bureaucratic self-suffocation and Amendola's denunciation of adventurism, perhaps no reconciliation was feasible.

But Amendola's perspective would prevail. The new leadership emerging among the left parties was convinced as well that not only the excesses in the factories but also in public finances had to be brought to order. Central banks won greater independence from their national governments and could resist funding government deficits. On the morrow of his election victory in 1997, Blair freed the Bank of England to set interest rates as its Monetary Policy Committee advised, not as his Treasury would recommend. New Democrats in the United States and New Labour in Britain along with the tough-minded Social Democrats first under Helmut Schmidt, then Gerhard Schroeder, were determined to run a tight fiscal ship. Walter Wrister brought the pension system for civil servants in order in Germany. Mitterrand reversed course in 1983 to chain himself to the Bundesbank mast, rejecting the sirens of socialism from his ranks. President Clinton declared in 1992 he would "end welfare as we know it," which meant ending the Aid to Families with Dependent Children program. Even the Scandinavians tacked in light of their export dependency. The growing competition from the "Asian tigers"—Japan, South Korea, Taiwan, Thailand, and Indonesia—meant that labor and welfare costs had to be kept under control. Globalization became a justification for a new lean regime. The best way to measure results—though very imperfect—was to measure the shares of national income that went to wages and salaries versus investment. After the expansion of the wage share in the 1960s and 1970s, the trend reversed: returns to capital outpaced returns to labor.[35]

Emerging out of the pressures of the 1980s and 1990s was what might be termed a non-left left. Its Anglo-American ideology will be considered in more detail in Chapter 9. But we can summarize its general characteristics as it was to emerge. They included a silent abandonment of any further redistribution of income beyond the alleviation of outright hardship. A technocratic mindset on the part of leaders who in many cases became personally wealthy through politics and the honoraria it brought after power and saw no conflict of conscience in enrichment. Pierre Rosanvallon saw analogies with "le moment Guizot," putting the best face on the nineteenth-century minister of the "bourgeois monarchy," who had advised becoming wealthy but also supported a government of engineers and experts. An acceptance of the premises of what was being called neoliberalism—reliance on the market to manage society—even if they shied away from labeling their policies as such. Insofar as enthusiasms were concerned, ecological issues mobilized youth and reformist middle-class recruits.

By the 1980s, two major but related ideological transformations were under way on the left. On the one hand, lifestyle or identity issues seized attention, brought into focus by the AIDS epidemic erupting in the 1980s and the focus on gay rights. And relatedly, the emphasis on traditional "human rights," whether those of speech and dissent emphasized in international relations by the Helsinki agreements of the mid-1970s, the search for racial equality in the United States, and the emergence of feminist issues. This was an extraordinary transformation in the ideological history of the West. It brought a significant risk: by moving beyond the causes familiar to the electoral communities reared in a political culture represented by traditional parties of the left—socialist, communist, American Democrats, working-class Labour—and leaving these communities ready for the messages that would be called populism

The international constellation of ideas also worked to transform the left. The new salience of human rights that the Helsinki process of the mid-1970s helped to mobilize an intellectual left was mobilized against Marxist regimes. The "new philosophers" in France, with an immense talent for media self-celebration, rediscovered the oppressive history of Communism, as if everyone else had forgotten it. Charter 77 in Czechoslovakia—defending liberal rights and reviving the spirit of the Prague Spring—was followed by the formation of Solidarity, the Polish union uniting the protesting workers of the Danzig shipyards with a core of intellectual dissidents that became the first organized mass opposition under a Communist regime. Solidarity in Poland offered a vision not of "more" (whether more socialism or more pay) but of citizen participation, and it succeeded in creating an enthusiastic Western audience—not yet linked by social media but by T-shirts and interviews and theoretical elaboration of its ideas. The movement would be driven underground by the regime's crackdown in 1981 but generated the "vibes" so that under the carapace of an authoritarian regime, the autonomous associations of "civil society," such as the unions, the church, the public intellectuals, created the potential for emancipation. Youth culture, the underground seminars of the "flying university," and above all, the Dionysiac appeal of rock music created a new milieu.[36] Exhilarating as it was, this new emancipatory community left open the question of what sort of order it would construct if it succeeded to power.

"Ever Closer Union": States, Capital, and Governance Create a European Regime

The mid-1980s brought decisive steps in integrating Europe after half a decade of wearying disputes over the distribution of costs and benefits. Any vision for Europe by the early 1980s was giving way to protracted haggling over the differential payments from the 1 percent of national value-added taxes (VATs) that supported the EEC budget and its redistribution through the common funds. Of these, the largest portion went into the Common Agricultural Policy's (CAP's) price supports that preeminently benefited France and to the Structural Adjustment Funds that assisted the member states with lower per-capita national incomes. Too wealthy to be eligible for the latter but having to pay EU tariffs on food imports that it continued to receive from the Commonwealth, the UK was the largest net contributor to the EU budget. Taking over as prime minister, Thatcher stridently insisted, "I want my money back." Over the advice of the Foreign Office and British Commission president Roy Jenkins, she resisted Chancellor Schmidt and President Valéry Giscard d'Estaing's counteroffers over the next two years. When he succeeded Giscard, President Mitterrand was willing to raise the VAT but not to cut the benefits to French farmers; Schmidt was willing to pay more but not to the CAP. A French and British compromise on price supports was pushed through over Thatcher's objection in 1982, but her stubbornness paid off with a June 1983 compromise and she could announce, "I have my check."[37]

According to the fashionable bicycle metaphor, the EEC could remain upright only if continually pedaled forward. But it was a bicycle built for two, and although the French and Germans generally pedaled vigorously together, the British sought to slow the teetering vehicle. Nonetheless, pedaling became vigorous from the mid-1980s on.[38] Hans-Dietrich Genscher, who had continued as the Free Democratic Party's foreign secretary when the Free Democrats joined the CDU to replace the Social Democrats, seconded by Italy's Christian Democratic minister Emilio Colombo, decided to press for a treaty on the EU that would seek a common European foreign policy and further development of a monetary union. Chancellor Kohl decided to make this initiative his own.

The decisive inflection point came in March 1983 as President Mitterrand had to decide whether to press on with a relatively leftist fiscal program, which would compel France either to abandon the "snake" or to jettison Socialist Party plans to increase taxes that were provoking an attack on the franc and a flight to the deutsche mark. Bonn proved willing to limit revaluation of the deutsche mark on its part, and by the end of a dramatic week of conferences, Mitterrand announced France would do what it took to keep the besieged franc in the Exchange Rate Mechanism (ERM). This entailed a modest devaluation, a limitation of the EEC agricultural subsidies that France received, and a cancellation of planned taxes on the wealthy—in sum, a renunciation of the left's electoral program in 1981. Kohl agreed to raising the VAT contributions to the EEC budget—not a doubling as the commission had wanted, but from 1 percent to 1.4 percent—and he announced in May 1984 that he was supporting the Genscher-Colombo initiative for a new Community treaty. Mitterrand was now emerging as a committed supporter of Europe's *relance*.

"During 1983 his Presidency's great project was redefined as Europe ... the project around which the Presidential majority was to be refounded, based on a rallying of the center-left and centered around the Socialist Party."[39] This meant a program much more in line with some neoliberal remedies—corporate profitability, decentralization of wage bargaining, strengthening the banks' role in financing—along with the older tradition of state-encouraged modernization, linking with Germany but by emulating Japan. By July 1985, the French Finance Ministry moved to liberalize the money markets, utilize open-market operations, and end exchange controls.

The second half of the 1980s brought remarkable reforms to Europe, East and West. Gorbachev succeeded to Soviet leadership and unleashed the stunning reforms that would lead to the disintegration of the Soviet Union by 1991. EEC members would develop the institutional structure of the Community and advance toward monetary union—both efforts culminating in the Maastricht Treaty of 1992 and a common currency by 1997, even as the Federal Republic of Germany swallowed a collapsing East Germany. These strands were distinct but intertwined. EU institutions changed slowly, but the Commission was energized with Jacques Delors's appointment as its president in spring 1984. The EC's Committee on Further Development of European Institutions and Cooperation convened at Fontainebleau to consider the Parliament's draft "Treaty on European Union" in discussion since 1981.[40]

Over the next year, Mitterrand and Kohl and the Commission pushed forward a program for market liberalization coupled with majority voting. The right of a member state to veto a proposal that affected its vital interest had been enshrined as the Luxembourg compromise after the crisis in the 1960s over the CAP. But the right to veto meant that progress on integration would always remain hostage to Britain's opposition, a single dissenting state. At the end of June 1985, the Council met again, now in Milan, where the majority led by France and Germany voted for an intergovernmental conference to amend the treaties. The vote was defined as a procedural one and thus not subject to a member state's veto. Thatcher was furious but was persuaded to acquiesce: the United Kingdom would benefit from the commercial and trade reforms, which might be held up if veto powers were retained by the member states. There was no dissent on the final list of trade reforms, and the final list would be ratified as the Single European Act. The Milan Council also enacted a proposal for "the Europe of the Citizens" that encompassed free movement of peoples and goods, a European passport, and expansion of educational exchanges under the Erasmus program; and it approved Commissioner Étienne Davignon and Karl-Heinz Narjes's "White Paper for Completion of the Internal Market," calling for the elimination of all the nontariff barriers to free trade, such as national subsidies to home industries, special tax benefits, and "qualitative" border controls, based on alleged special standards by EC nations.

Complementing it was a "Delors package" agreed to by the European Parliament over the course of 1987. Two-hundred sixty-four commission proposals became directives of the council and were sent to the member states, where 70–80 percent were enacted as national legislation.[41] That no longer meant the reduction of internal tariffs, which had been largely completed, but rather the removal of nontariff barriers to trade. The liberalization got an important boost by a decision of the European Court in Luxemburg over the status of Cassis de Dijon, the fermented French blackcurrant spirit that West German distillers had sought to exclude from their domestic market on the pretense that its alcoholic content was less than the minimal 25 percent German regulations mandated for brandy. The court's decision established that aside from health regulations, any member state's product allowed for sale at home had to be eligible for sale in the other states. The commission got the right to approve or reject mergers. Capital movements were to be freed from general restrictions in 1999, and banks of one country got the right to operate in the others.

Establishing Europe on market principles required it to strengthen its state-like attributes such as a larger bureaucracy and more directives. It took time to overcome many impediments. Agreement on VAT convergence at 15%, reduction of freight paperwork, elimination of border checks on individuals (resolved at Schengen in 1985 although implemented only a decade later)—all produced an increase in legislation by the Council of Ministers and an expansion of the commission's civil service from 5,000 in 1970 to almost 13,000 by 1990.[42] In a favorably received speech at the TUC's annual convention, commission president Delors promised an internal market "beneficial to all," with social conditions secured by European-wide legislation. Thatcher, however, was increasingly disquieted by the trend and especially by the Franco-German push to expand majority voting (rather than reserved veto rights). She was no longer to be mollified and denounced the trend toward a European "superstate" in a notable speech at the College of Europe in Bruges in September 1988. With her hardly veiled hostility to impending German reunification the following year and her disastrous proposal for a poll tax (a flat tax on households), she lost support within her party and was ousted from the leadership in November 1990. Beginning as an advocate for entrepreneurialism and breaking the power of labor, she ended deserted by the advocates of modern capital.

Thatcher failed to recognize that the capitalist energy she had begun by promoting was no longer so supportive of national institutions. New industrial organizations supported the Delors program: Europe, like the United States, was feeling the pressure of Japanese imports and it seemed important to complete the internal market. Although Japan and the United States might have large enough economies to forge ahead, no European state could do so acting alone. Also important was the decision by key industrialists—including the vigorous Commissioner Davignon—that the European industrial heartland must be transformed around the incentives of internal demand. The temptations of neocolonial enterprise were traded for modernizing industry at home.[43] Working to take advantage of the institutional collapse of the German Democratic Republic in the fall of 1989–1990, Chancellor Kohl supported these initiatives in part because he wanted to complete national unification without incurring European opposition but also knowing that the reunified Germany with 80 million citizens would be the dominant national power. The interests of capital aligned with the demands of governance—a nonparty program of rational reform that could perfect the common efforts of labor and capital. As the 1990s opened, it appeared that the EC, now to become the EU, was itself a sublimated quasi-project-state.

Crucial to both operations—German unification and European integration—was monetary union. The prospect of merger into an all-German economy with the deutsche mark as a national currency was a major factor in 1989–1990 in moving the majority of the East German population beyond any concept of a confederal structure for East and West Germany toward enthusiasm for full adhesion to a unified state. Most immediately, the prospect of German currency unification seemed essential to forestall a mass migration from east to west and to secure CDU viability in the scheduled spring 1990 elections for the German Democratic Republic's national legislature. By the autumn of 1989, Chancellor Kohl and Foreign Minister Genscher were pursuing two objectives simultaneously: moving toward German unification without losing French and British acquiescence despite the former's unease and the latter's hostility, and encouraging the European monetary union desired by Mitterrand without arousing the opposition of German and Dutch critics.[44] The internal treaty of unification in the summer of 1990 provided for conversion of East German marks on par with the deutsche mark in current transactions. So far as Kohl was concerned, such an expanded German currency had to flow into a unified European one. Hardly an abstract theorist, he understood that the country he was re-creating as the most populous west of Russia had to be anchored in a wider institutional framework to remain a tranquil component of an enlarged Europe.

Once Mitterrand opted for monetary alignment with Germany in 1983, the greater the role that the Bundesbank played in securing French currency levels, the better; conversely, the Bundesbank president Karl Otto Pöhl remained hesitant about weaker financial ministries being able to draw on German strength. Since the 1970s, the French had maintained that a common monetary policy framework created by aligning with Germany would discipline and stimulate their economy. The Germans, on the other hand, wanted convergence on economic conditions—labor costs, inflation rates, budget stability—only following which might a unified currency "crown" the structure.[45] West Germany and Belgium did agree to a slight revaluation of their strong currencies in early 1987 rather than push the French to devalue. Foreign Minister Genscher wanted more active support than did the Bundesbank; political union in the EU seemed at stake. For Genscher, the Gorbachev reforms currently under way in the Soviet Union made it important for Europe to become more cohesive. Buoyed by the German role in passage of the Delors package, he called for establishment of a European monetary area with a European Central Bank. This was not a cabinet decision, but Kohl supported it, as did representatives of German industry and commerce, and he won approval in the Council for a committee of central bank representatives, chaired by Delors, to advance monetary union. Kohl predicted success in establishing a central bank by the year 2000.[46] He proved to be on target. Crudely put, the EU and monetary union would advance as the project traditionally had, as the product of German money and French ideas.

The Delors committee met in connection with the Committee of Central Bank Presidents and agreed despite the unhappiness of Pöhl on a three-stage process to begin with the free movement of capital in 1990. Delors was a skilled and energetic operator, helping to bridge a committee of conservative bankers with ambitious political leaders.[47] A European central bank, much less a unified currency, was hardly envisaged at the outset. Mitterrand, though, wanted to ride on to German financial power and tame any unilateral political temptations. For a while, he despaired of prompt action when in late 1989 Kohl put off the government conference intended to move toward the next stage of union. The French president also worried that Reagan's United States might be making its own deals with Gorbachev as it strove for "Star Wars," a missile shield for the American continent but not for Europe. At Reykjavík in December 1986, Reagan and Gorbachev agreed to eliminate all nuclear weapons within ten years, raising the Europeans' anxiety about their exposure to Soviet conventional forces, but the German, French, and British agreed on the elimination of the medium-range missiles that had been installed with such controversy a few years earlier.

Thatcher saw the German problem through the lens of World War II, Mitterrand through the dangers of World War I. As he told Genscher, if German unification preceded European unity, fear of the new and powerful nation would provoke a new Triple Entente, the anti-German alliance of 1914.[48] Monetary union was the substantive step needed to prevent this careening into a rerun of 1914's alliance politics. Fears were alleviated when at the end of the year, the Strasbourg Council adopted a charter on social rights for workers and a conference to move ahead on monetary union. The chancellor still deferred making a post-unification commitment to accept the post-1945 Oder-Neisse border with Poland (already enshrined into treaties by each existing German state) even though he realized that it would be necessary, and Mitterrand hoped that Gorbachev would slow the process down. When the Russian leader declined to do so, Mitterrand accepted that German reunification was a fait accompli.[49]

In the wake of the euro crisis of 2012–2015, it became commonplace to suggest that since the EU could not impose a common fiscal or spending policy, it had been foolish to take on the task of managing a single currency. But this neglects the powerful handicaps that afflicted partial monetary union—pegging exchange rates when capital could flow without hindrance. The decline of the dollar also acted as an elephant in the room. In the second half the 1980s, the American currency continued to decline with respect to the deutsche mark, and Treasury Secretary James Baker continued to press the Germans for greater domestic spending to slow their currency's ascent with respect to the dollar. German policymakers also were anxious about the impact of a more expensive deutsche mark on their exports. Locking their currency into a structure with weaker currencies would take some of that pressure off. In early 1987, the Germans, Dutch, and Belgians each revalued their currencies slightly to ease pressure on the franc, but the French still had to borrow from the European Monetary System's (EMS's) emergency facility: to keep the franc from falling out of the ERM's "target zones." Partial linkage meant tremendous pressures on currencies: the EMS was a house of straw. And as some pointed out, when capital movements were freed completely in 1992, the gales would blow even stronger.

By September 1987, the deutsche mark was hitting the top of its allowed band within the ERM, and Baker threatened that the United States might allow the dollar to fall further to deter Germany—where, he alleged in mid-October, policy was controlled by a "little clique of monetarists" in the Bundesbank—from raising its interest rates. Pressure on the dollar hit the stock market the following Monday, which suffered it largest one-day fall ever, shedding 23 percent of its value. The German government grew concerned and successfully pressured the Bundesbank to roll back interest rates by

0.5 percent, leading to a truce in the German-American currency wars.[50] But the tension with France was still palpable. French Finance Minister Édouard Balladur kept pushing the Germans; Italian Foreign Minister Giuliano Amato argued that the fundamental problem was that the EMS had no "engine of growth" because German domestic demand was lower than the average. This irritated Pöhl but inspired Genscher to call for a European bank and currency area. The Bundesbank responded with a less grumpy but still stubborn insistence that to develop the EMS quicker than a convergence of economic conditions justified would be futile. In a subsequent memorandum, Pöhl insisted that "the EMS rested on an agreement between central banks and not between governments." The Bundesbank would not participate in the EMS's Monetary Committee. Moreover, in a monetary union with irreversibly fixed exchange rates, "the weak would become ever weaker and the strong ever stronger." Kohl agreed that the central bankers must be included in the committee, but he decided Delors should chair it—a decision that Pöhl deplored and British chancellor Nigel Lawson later deemed a disaster. Thatcher, however, believed that Pöhl would prevent any risky changes. Pöhl remained unhappy; Kohl told him essentially to chill.[51]

The Delors committee met seven times between September 1988 and April 1989. Harold James has provided the narrative of debates, which ranged over how to organize the stages for further cooperation, how to preserve the role of the banks and whether market forces alone could lead to convergence of exchange rates or formal rules, such as limits on budget deficits and overall government debt, would be necessary. The latter view prevailed, and the confidence that rules would guarantee convergence when markets did not remained an article of faith. Odysseus might be bound to resist the sirens, but gale-force winds were now threatening to snap the mast to which he was tied. Pöhl suggested what would become the 3 percent limit on deficits almost en passant. The report laid out the implications of what a central bank and zone must imply. It laid out a path to monetary union—that is, "a currency area in which policies are managed jointly with a view to attaining common macroeconomic objectives." To which the committee added that the adoption of a single currency, "while not strictly necessary for the creation of a monetary union, might be seen for economic as well as psychological and political reasons as a natural and desirable further development of the monetary union."[52] It would make management easier and would testify to the irreversibility of the union. The revised draft of the report in April mollified Pöhl: it stipulated that price stability was the major objective of the new banking system—a formulation that would become a continuing point of controversy and criticism during the history to date of the European central bank.

The central bank governors were to manage the transition to a unified monetary policy, lock in respective exchange rates to the new currency, and manage the rates in common vis-à-vis outside currencies. At a Madrid summit, the heads of government accepted the report as the basis of future work. Pöhl was satisfied that the political leaders would not be brought into the process too early. Whether the United Kingdom would accept the later stages of institutionalization remained unclear. Both Delors and Pöhl agreed that the Committee of Governors needed to preserve their independence vis-à-vis their governments. The European Council's Ministers of Economy and Finance (ECOFIN) decided on November 13 to entrust the Committee of Governors to go ahead with designing the institutions they were recommending. Four days earlier, the Berlin Wall had been breached and it became clear over the next months that Germany would have to accept a far greater financial commitment than it had hitherto foreseen.

After the inflationary experience of the 1970s, central bank independence had become viewed as the crucial dike against the political pressures of legislatures to spend money and incur deficits. The concept and how to measure it generated a huge literature.[53] The Federal Reserve, the Bundesbank, and the Swiss and Dutch banks seemed to be models. The American occupation authorities had inscribed it into the statutes of the 1948 Bank Deutscher Länder. Statutes did not always guarantee policy. The Italian central bank had won independence in 1981—that is, it had shed the obligation to fund government deficits by buying treasury notes, a "divorce" that the US Fed had won thirty years earlier. The Bank of France would win statutory independence in 1992 so it aligned itself better with the new European Central Bank and met the criteria for Bundesbank assistance.[54]

For the Delors committee and the follow-up drafters of legislation, the issue was how to preserve the new bank from political pressure to indirectly accommodate national deficits. When it met jointly with the Monetary Committee which grouped finance ministers and was charged with preparing the amendments to the Treaties of Rome that would establish the bank, there was more wide-ranging debate. French Treasury Director (the chief permanent position within the Ministry of Finance) Jean-Claude Trichet did not want the new bank to report to the European Parliament but also feared the new institution would be biased against growth. Hans Tietmeyer, Trichet's counterpart at the German Ministry of Finance (and later president of the Bundesbank) was more single-minded. Unfortunately, so he claimed, the whole history of European integration was one of resisting discipline, or in bankers' language, of weakening conditionality. "It must be clear that the member countries do not stand behind each other's debts." As Pöhl stated again a year later when the design of the bank was presented to ECOFIN, the bank would take account of the multiple objectives of financial policy, but if there were a conflict between price stability and other economic objectives, "the governing bodies of the system will have no choice but to give priority to its primary objective. There can be no compromise in this respect."[55] This differed from the US Federal Reserve which in 1977 had inscribed price stability as one objective in 1977 but also established high employment the other. It was expected that the criteria for EU countries to join the Eurozone—limits on budget deficits and public debt—would make member banks single-minded. Governments in the EU had the prerogative of setting exchange rate policy, but the new statute (incorporated in the Maastricht Treaty the following year), required the EU to get the consent of the European Central Bank. The bank was not intended to serve as a lender of last resort.

The Committee of Governors saw itself as a voice of governance. As Tommaso Padoa Schioppa argued, the emphasis on central bank independence was part of the new acceptance of minimal government and the primacy of markets.[56] As an institution designed to assure stability, it also represented the interests of capital. Its mission to defend monetary stability presupposed that the interests of wage earners could not intrude on the returns to capital. The inflation of the 1970s, not the Depression of the 1930s, was the proximate trauma that stuck in its founders' minds. Its safeguards were of a piece with the so-called Washington Consensus, the neoliberal menu recommended by Americans for stabilizing Latin American and other weak currencies although the enforcers were located not across the Atlantic but in the other central bank nearby in Frankfurt, the Bundesbank. Happily when a 1931-type crisis was to loom again in 2008–2010, the guardians of the euro used the escape provisions that had also been inscribed to disregard their rules and step in as a lender of last resort.

By September 1990, the plan for the European Central Bank was ready and presented to ECOFIN. Discussions in Europe inched along in 1991, during which period the new British prime minister, John Major, made it clear that the United Kingdom would not support an upgraded EU that did not provide for an opt-out on a common currency. The German and French governments managed to narrow the British insistence from a general escape clause to a special concession to the British. The Committee of Central Bank Governors agreed on the convergence criteria for joining the common currency: a national debt under 60 percent of GDP, a budget deficit no greater than 3 percent, and interest rates within 2 percent of the lowest three in the EU. How would the future members get from here to there? In negotiations at Maastricht, December 9–10, 1991, it was agreed that a European Monetary Institute, a sort-of proto–central bank, would govern the transition to the European Central Bank during the period in which the upgraded monetary union was to become irreversible. If by 1997 no date had been settled on, then the new European Monetary Union (EMU) would begin on January 1, 1999. All these provisions along with the still-valid monetary agreements were written into the Treaty of Maastricht in February 1992.

For the historians of Maastricht, Mitterrand's achievement was to lever French influence with Germany inside the Union and with the United States by means of the Union. Inside France, his accomplishment was to align the Socialist Party with an EMU that "might be not so much a shield and protector against the forces of the global market as a means of institutionalizing its imperatives."[57] In other words, to align French socialism with German capitalism. For Kohl, as for Schmidt before him, the political challenge was to co-opt the obstreperous independence of the Bundesbank, which was legally anchored in the ordoliberal institutions that the Americans had encouraged for postwar Germany and which the chancellor recognized were respected by German public opinion across the board. EMU for Kohl was above all a commitment to a Europe that would accommodate a united Germany, and as of 1991–1992, the commitment meant irreversibility and a timetable.

But this did not mean smooth sailing for the upcoming third stage of the transition to the new central bank to be. The members of the still-existing EMS would experience a thorough drubbing in the run-up to the euro. At the center of the new system, German unification had saddled the Federal Republic with immense fiscal burdens as well as the guarantee of East German bank accounts. To meet these obligations without deficits required high interest rates. The Bundesbank believed the German government's mark-for-mark guarantee unwise; Kohl publicly insisted on it for the sake of reunification and to staunch the flow of East Germans to the West ("If the mark does not come to the East, the East will come to the mark"). But Kohl's commitment to the East appeared to disparage the Bundesbank and compelled it to raise interest rates from the eve of unification in late 1990 through July 1992, in turn antagonizing Britain and the US authorities. Even more of a vulnerability, speculators bought the debt of EU countries with weaker currencies and high interest rates in the expectation that the new central bank would have to support them. Britain joined the EMS and its exchange rate mechanism on October 8, 1990, even though it planned not to accept the euro as a currency. London, however, insisted on setting a relatively high level for sterling in terms of the deutsche mark, thus becoming alongside Italy and Spain a destination for funds attracted by the prospect that membership would provide immunity of these inflation-prone countries to adverse currency speculation. Not surprisingly, their currencies soon became targets of those who believed their exchange rates could not be maintained.

As for the Germans, the new director of the Bundesbank, Helmut Schlesinger, faced open dissent on the Maastricht commitments from four of the regional bank presidents. Meanwhile, the Danish electorate narrowly rejected the Maastricht Treaty (though they would be persuaded to approve it on a second plebiscite), and Italian industrialists denounced the anti-inflationary straitjacket entailed by the high interest rates imposed by the Bundesbank as it met the costs of incorporating East Germany into the Federal Republic. In short, the deutsche mark exchange was maintained by rising interest rates while the Italians, Spanish, and British clung to maintain the exchange rates that adhesion to the ERM required, which meant the obligation to buy sterling if offered. The commitment became more and more unsustainable, and on Black Monday, September 16, 1992, London withdrew from the EMS. Italy followed suit. For some in the United Kingdom, it seemed a humiliation almost as great as the Suez retreat in 1956, and they were quick to blame it on George Soros, who had massively shorted the pound. Recriminations were hurled back and forth between the major and lesser powers.

The crisis resumed in July 1993, now with the franc as a target. For a while, it seemed as if the EMS might break in half, with a German, Dutch, Belgian, and Danish cluster defending their exchange rates, and a team of weaker currencies sanctioning inflation. The French were angered over the maintenance of high German interest rates; the Germans dug in their heels to defend their monetary "sovereignty." At the end, the crisis was weathered by allowing currencies to have a greater margin of fluctuation before defensive interventions had to be taken.[58] For skeptics, the difficulties indicated that a common currency would mean a permanent deflationary pressure; for those committed to the reform, it seemed to demonstrate that a single currency was needed so that devaluation was impossible.

In 1999, currency values were locked in and the euro became the virtual currency for Eurozone members alongside their national moneys. On January 1, 2002, new notes and coins replaced the old with six months given to trade in francs, lire, and the sacred deutsche mark. Bank machines were out of commission for a weekend; this author remembers paying for his family's entry into the small museum of Cefalù in Sicily with the new coins—10-euro sample envelopes had been available from banks—to the wonder of the museum attendants. As the historian of the euro writes, "Some of the most intractable problems of European cooperation—exchange rate and monetary policy issues—were solved as it were by the waving of a wand. . . . The European Monetary Institute successfully formulated the basis for a common monetary approach." But as always when a monetary hegemon sets the terms for international exchange, it thrust the burdens of adjustment on the weaker economies and those countries with greater domestic inflationary tendencies to face massive calls for austerity—as would become evident with the Greek crisis of 2010–2012 (see Chapter 9).

State interests, the interests of capital, and the processes of governance all converged in the creation of the Eurozone. Given the requirements for countries that joined the Eurozone, it represented a commitment to growth and accumulation without sanctioning a growth in wages at the expense of profits. It endowed the EU with a new and important attribute of statehood: the creation of a currency but one evolving from extensive debate and reconciliation of interests. Insisting on debt and deficit limits was meant to assure that the share of profits and capital would not be shaved in a distributional struggle. Even the debts of the third world might be mastered, so it was believed when the United States made a commitment to avert financial catastrophe in Mexico in 1994. And, as the next chapter details, when it came the turn of the left center to come to power again—Clinton's New Democrats at the beginning of 1993 and Blair's New Labour in May 1997—they offered no intellectual challenge to the neoliberal "gospel of wealth"—to borrow a nineteenth-century affirmation. President Clinton ran balanced budgets and restructured a welfare system he felt perpetuated dependency. When it came time for the SPD to return to power in 1998, its new chancellor, Gerhard Schroeder, rolled back the unemployment benefits with the program known as Hartz IV.

By the end of the century, indeed of the millennium, Americans might enjoy an extraordinary confidence that global politics and the world economy was headed into a period of happy equilibrium. "The global taming of inflation was a huge success.... [It] has dropped to levels that, only two decades ago, seemed frustratingly unattainable."[59] US policy intellectuals were brimming with awareness of the country's unipolar moment. "Instead of becoming the 'ordinary' country that some anticipated, facing a world 'after hegemony,' the United States found itself in a position of preponderance unseen since the Roman Empire."[60] Its armed forces were absolutely dominant, its former adversary now struggling to institute democracy, was starting to climb out of an unparalleled depression. No serious Western intellectuals or policymakers believed in central planning; the market was the best aggregator of society's preferences. The realm of capital and the realm of governance were tightly aligned. The EU was privileged in particular; its interior frontiers virtually done away with for the first time since 1914, its institutions gradually maturing, and its reach becoming more extensive. Parties of the extreme left hardly existed; parties of the center left governed and carried out the policies of the center right.

Had history stopped at the end of the twentieth century, the new spirit of the laws—to recall Montesquieu's term for underlying sociopolitical consensus—would have been a fusion of brash capitalists and supposed social democrats enchanted with their discovery of the market, as well as a phalanx of governance institutions—foundations, nongovernmental organizations, official agencies. The vital forces of government no longer seemed the state but "civil society": the labor unions, churches, religious and ecology groups, brave journalists and writers that had allegedly liquidated authoritarian regimes. Russia had felt compelled to quit Afghanistan. China was embarking on economic transformation and embracing modernity. American politics seemed so satisfactory that the country could occupy itself with the pressing issue of whether the suspected erotic pleasuring of its president by a White House intern constituted "sex" or not, and whether his denial of it constituted grounds for removal from office. Of course, the Clinton impeachment was about more. It testified to the fact that the most powerful country on earth was loosening the ground rules that tamed its periodic proclivity for ferocious domestic conflict over social, moral, and religious issues. It suggested that its ideology of universal opportunity was becoming threadbare in the glaring face of new wealth, educational, and rediscovered racial disparities. The challenge opened by Newt Gingrich's "contract for America" and his ruthless opposition was opening a political rift that within a quarter century would fundamentally divide US politics.

9

Convergences and Catastrophe

States, Governance, and Capital

Triumphalism was a pejorative term on the left in the 1990s; it seemed too crude to celebrate victory. If we focus on the Cold War, however, the West did seem to have triumphed by the mid-1990s. The Communist regimes had collapsed in Eastern Europe and across Russia. The Soviet Union itself had ceased to exist after seventy years. A new reunited Germany just moved its capital back to Berlin. Other changes were also sources of satisfaction. An apparently 1930s-style act of aggression—Saddam Hussein's seizure of Kuwait—had been defeated and traditional territorial order reaffirmed. The apartheid regime in South Africa was dismantled and Nelson Mandela installed as president in 1994. Alliance politics are not the theme of this study, but in the flush of Cold War success, the United States overlooked the careful stance it had negotiated about moving its forces into Eastern Europe at the time of German unification, when it had won the right to integrate the German Democratic Republic (GDR) territory into the North Atlantic Treaty Organization (NATO).[1] Under the notion of partnerships for peace, it extended NATO membership to the Polish and Baltic states—who could object, after all, to a defensive alliance moving to the borders of its former, now shrunken, adversary?

Economic developments also generated confidence. Champions of international trade, including President Bill Clinton, could celebrate the North American Free Trade Agreement of 1993 and a successful intervention a year later to shield Mexico from a debt crisis that might have set off a cascade of bankruptcies. Successive financial crises in South Korea, Russia, Thailand, and Argentina would admittedly inflict major losses on the citizens of those countries; but they were far away and could be contained without global contagion. Economic leaders, parties of the moderate left and right, and re-spectable opinion leaders all affirmed that globalization—a process whereby the flows of goods, labor, and capital subjected even the most powerful states to benevolent transnational forces—had become the destiny of the world economy. Confident but careful economists such as Ben Bernanke, director of the Federal Reserve Board, and Olivier Blanchard, then of MIT and later director of research at the International Monetary Fund (IMF), would soon point to the "great moderation" in the swings of business cycles that marked the current era. Heading toward a new century, it appeared that kumbaya capitalism was set to succeed the casino capitalism that British political the-orist Susan Strange had fretted about a decade earlier.[2]

A certain magical thinking seemed to explain all this success—punctuated by some dissenting voices. "Civil society"—the nonstate organizations of labor and capital and religion—would be building this new world with a minimum of state control.[3] Markets, after all, supposedly provided a coercion-free mech-anism to coordinate human aspirations (which assumed that the discrepan-cies in wealth and power between the buyers and sellers of labor did not count as coercive). They had the marvelous capacity, now celebrated by social demo-crats as well as market fundamentalists, to produce the optimal collective choices from millions of individual preferences or so-called utility functions. Self-interest motivated a harmonious cybernetic or self-steering path toward economic welfare and transcendence of politics. Social welfare systems—even the left came to believe—should be overhauled to end the long-term depen-dencies that state assistance allegedly produced. Where states remained necessary, new streamlined procedures would make them far more efficient. Governments should divest themselves of state-owned enterprises that would be run as private firms with less waste and leaner payrolls and be less sus-ceptible to political patronage. Separating the state from capital, however, was not really possible. Neither could the realm of governance really claim a to-tally disinterested perch. Lines of convergence brought them ever closer together.

Uncivil Society and the Limits of Governance

Poke a little closer, too, at global developments. "The contemporary world transformation . . . with all its intense pressures and unforeseen conse-quences," pronounced the leading NGO concerned with peacekeeping, "tends to pull people toward strongly supportive groups. These groups, in turn, particularly with charismatic, inflammatory leadership, may easily become harsh, separatist, and depreciatory toward others. A deadly combination of severe social stress and distinctively hateful, fanatical leadership can produce mass killing, even genocide."[4] During the very same years of the mid-1990s in which theorists were celebrating the forces of civil society and business and financial leaders were asking to be free from state regulations, civil society seemed to disintegrate entirely in parts of Africa and the Balkans. The imminent breakup of Yugoslavia as the 1990s began had led to a brutal civil war. Western diplomats faced the crucial choice in 1990–1991. Should they attempt to patch up this Balkan federation that only Josip Broz Tito's prestige and constitutional rigging had seemed to rehabilitate after World War II, or was the task so hopeless that the powers should preside over as peaceful a partition as possible? Slovenia, the northeastern Yugoslav republic wedged between Austria and Italy whose people seemed to feel themselves in the European Union's cultural zone, had seceded in late 1990 and handily defeated the Serb-dominated federation army sent to force its secession. Franjo Tudjman's Croatia decided to escape the federation as well, and Germany hastened to recognize it in December 1991. Slobodan Milošević's Serbia believed it should restore its domination from the interwar period. Both leaders would be happy to accept a breakup of Yugoslavia if they could split the hapless Bosnian republic with its Muslim population. Religious differences supposedly motivated each side but had long since been transmuted into justifications for nationalism and authoritarian longings. The EU looked on fecklessly at this first war on European soil since 1945 raged on until American mediation produced a truce in late 1995—the Dayton Accords—and then a 1999 Serbian evacuation from its own province of Kosovo (populated, however, largely by ethnic Albanians whom Milošević appeared determined to humiliate). The German Social Democratic government finally overcame its hesitation about intervening in conflicts outside its boundaries: Foreign Secretary Joschka Fischer transformed the Social-Democratic slogan, *Nie wieder Krieg* into *Nie Wieder Auschwitz*.[5] But slogans of "Never again" always implied the reality of "Once again, too late."

Meanwhile in East Central Africa, the accumulated ethnic controversies between peoples whom Belgian colonial authority had designated as Hutu and Tutsi ethnicities boiled over. The Tutsi, somehow depicted by the Belgians as the favored race—taller, martial, worthy of subordinate office—had occupied a precariously privileged position. Hutu demagogues labeled them as exploitative and parasitical, and they urged on a campaign of paranoid genocide. The Organization of American States and Western powers hesitated to intervene and perhaps 700,000 Tutsi were massacred before the furies ebbed. Western theorists and governance organizations drew lessons about from Bosnia and Rwanda justifying humanitarian intervention and how it should trump the respect for sovereignty. But similar dramas would be repeated for the next twenty years. Violence continued, between ethnicities, communities, within states, and even in the United States where mass shootings surged periodically. The magma of murder could seethe as always underneath the mantle of "civilization."[6]

Two striking interpretations suggested the ambiguities of the decade, Francis Fukuyama had referred to the disappearance of the powerful Soviet Communist challenge as the end of history. It was easy to deride his message as Pollyannaish; but just as important for his scenario was the uneasiness that with the supposed end of rivalries between systems, a miasmic fog might settle over the landscape of history and lead to the disappearance of a Nietzschean vitality. Samuel Huntington, Fukuyama's teacher and Harvard professor who had celebrated a third historic wave of democratization between 1974 and 1990, discerned a different peril a decade later: the replacement of ideological conflict with megacultural conflicts—the clash of civilizations. In the late nineteenth and early twentieth century, "civilization" had been the term used to summarize the ineffable superiority that justified imperial control; now it served to explain the eruptions of intercommunity violence and "terrorism." The categories were muddied but essentially were an effort to essentialize the religious clashes that seemed to have been left when communism disappeared. Marxist regimes had collapsed; Islamic fundamentalism had moved into the vacancy to provide the continuing antagonisms that Huntington's worldview—despite his own apparent personal serenity—seemed to require.[7] The gentle authors of the Carnegie Commission's report might dissent from its message, but the clash of civilization had a certain crude simplicity.[8] As of the late 1990s, it was becoming evident that the new political divisions separated those groups benefited by globalization and the advance of digital knowledge, and those who clung to familiar territorially constructed communities. The difficulty was that the party systems of the West were largely constructed around old issues of class and economy and, as a result, could not provide coherence for these newer fault lines.[9] The politics of class and stratification—including the efforts to work across those lines such as characterized by American presidential politics or British New Labour—seemed to be giving way to the politics of identity.

Race and religion remained particularly hard aspects of identity to assimilate. This is not to argue that they intrinsically lay at the basis of communitarian politics, but they provided visible signs of accumulated separation, economic disadvantage, and a politics of exclusion. With race in the United States, no matter the advances in legal desegregation, centuries of slavery and prejudice had produced persistent disadvantages in housing, income, education, and the tax base for local education and facilities. Even if the language of racial inferiority or superiority were avoided, economy and society had worked to perpetuate these into institutional form, and they lurked behind politics. Sociologists such as William Julius Wilson recognized the connection, but when finally endorsed by Democratic Party politicians or school boards in the second decade of the twenty-first century, the analysis would arouse anger among opponents as "critical race theory," which allegedly accused everyone as complicit in racial prejudice. In Europe, postwar immigration, often from former colonies, produced similar communal disadvantages inscribed in education or patterns of residence. Believers in market solutions rarely addressed its long-term impact on urban geography.

Religion remained perhaps the second greatest tag for discrimination in the global north after skin color and perhaps the most divisive factor in Asia and Africa. Prohibitions on the exercise of faith were rare, but religious practice involved public acts that intruded on space or practice and tested commitments to cultural pluralism. In Europe, the height of minarets or the wearing of veils in schools aroused resistance. In the United States, religious loyalties motivated major opposition to abortion and interventions for preferred presidential candidates. In a country such as the Netherlands where confessional distinctions had firmed up over centuries but racial markers had hardly existed, so-called pillarization (*Verzuiling*), theorized rather complacently as "consociational democracy," might produce a stable pluralism. Catholics and Protestants supposedly lived contentedly in their respective silos—but what happened when darker-skinned Muslims arrived? Elsewhere, peaceful toleration was more precarious. Religious compartmentalization (Sunni and Roman Catholic) had been built into the distribution of offices for independent Lebanon but had broken down in the 1970s and led to a long and terrible civil war. But religion was also a proxy marker—a readily identifiable label—for conflicts, as in India at partition or Northern Ireland in the 1980s, which were rooted in political distrust and conflict itself, communities of memory and grievance, networks of political organization, and ambitions to dominate or escape domination.

"Culture" became an overused term in the mobilization and explanation of the supposed conflicts over identity. Identity issues were harder to compromise by adjusting taxes and / or subsidies—the old politics of who got what, when, and how, which had structured parties since at least the Great Depression. They required restraint and different sorts of accommodation. Territorial identity, the search for what Germans called *Heimat*, might be conciliated with regionalist assemblies or even autonomy, even if not in every case. Language primacy in the school systems and / or public announcements was an inherited source for grievances. Canada ceded Québec its rights to a predominantly French identity but not without much tension. In Belgium, the end of colonial control over the Congo in 1960 had ended a common imperial project that had helped to bring together Dutch-speaking Flemings and French-speaking Walloons, and it took a decade to devolve almost all internal administration into Wallonia, Flanders, and the capital Brussels, mostly Francophone but enjoying the prestige of being capital for the country and the EU. The Spanish state might grant Catalonia extensive regional powers but not the independence that the most fervent Catalans demanded, and Madrid was unwilling to yield to the armed Basque militants insisting on Euzkadi. The Scots got a regional parliament, but Scottish nationalists hoped for independence. The Italian Northern League despaired of what they viewed as southern sloth and criminality and built a party on their prejudices, even while Italy's regions won greater control over tax resources. Either regional wealth or regional poverty could encourage middle-age intolerance and young extremists' violence. Some conflicts burned themselves out. Northern Irish Unionists and the militants in favor of Ulster's merger with the Republic of Ireland settled for an accommodation that at least ended the recourse to terrorism and retail civil war—the Good Friday Agreement of 1998.

Throughout these lethal clashes, governance organizations sought to step in to mediate the violence and, above all, the quasi-genocidal internal wars that were wracking the Balkans and the global south. The mid-1990s saw a major effort by new NGOs, such as Médecins sans Frontières, and UN agencies, including armed peacekeepers, to alleviate the human cost. The International Crisis Group founded in 1995, ultimately had representatives in fifty-five conflict zones documenting the violence by 2015 and trying to liaise with Chatham House, the Council on Foreign Relations, and other groups. Documenting what happened and trying to apply what was called restorative justice when international or domestic criminal prosecution threatened to derail a negotiated transfer of power might be chosen as path toward settlement.

Notably in the case of South Africa, the establishing of "truth commissions" and amnesties for confessions of human rights abuses under apartheid persuaded the white minority to yield power to the African National Congress. But truth commissions were efforts at somehow reconciling victims and perpetrators *after* explosions of murder and atrocity. Prevention proved more elusive.[10]

The Carnegie Corporation made an effort to use economic as well as humanitarian initiatives together, creating the Carnegie Commission on Preventing Deadly Conflict in 1994, convening scholars and policymakers and issuing their final report in 1997, a survey of nuclear dangers, military clashes, and internal or civil war. Impressive though it was, the Carnegie study and subsidiary reports revealed the contradictory pressures on its governance efforts. The commission declared it had developed a comprehensive approach to forestalling internal wars and genocides when minorities, immigrants, or governmental officials become targets of irrational, hateful, or extremist responses. The long-term solution was "to promote democracy, market economies, and the creation of civil solutions that protect human rights."[11] The report rejected Huntington's idea of a fateful clash of civilizations, urging a strategy of prevention—"creating capable states with representative governance based on the rule of law, with widely available economic opportunity, social safety nets, protection of fundamental human rights, and robust civil societies."[12] The only difficulty was that the medicine presupposed the absence of the illness.

The commission envisaged that the World Bank could play a major role in a post–Cold War world "that is increasingly pluralistic and vulnerable to volatile social, technological, and other forces . . . that tend to be nonlinear in their nature and consequences, hard to anticipate and difficult to comprehend." Major donor nations had signaled "a new determination to link development assistance to preventing deadly conflict." But this would not be easy. Donor countries were cutting back on funding through the Bank. Increasingly, the Bank had to take account of the private sector as a source of funds and of preferences. Private foreign direct investment had climbed from $44 billion in 1990 to $175 billion in 1995 and $230 billion in 1996, whereas World Bank commitments in 1995–1996 were limited to $21.5 billion and overall public lending amounted to only 40 percent of what the twenty-four wealthiest OECD countries invested.[13] The Bank's 1997 World Development Report, "The State in a Changing World," implied that the Bank and its donors would take into account that assistance, "subject to well-considered conditions," could offer troubled governments "the incentives to develop still-fragile national political structures in ways that allow politics to triumph over force in resolving domestic issues. . . . During the Cold War, the politics of containment sometimes caused the bank to bend its economic terms in order to influence a borrower' international alignment. Since 1990, curbing corruption and promoting good governance and respect for basic human rights— actions that can also be construed as political interference—have become more prominent concerns of Western donor nations. . . . Bad governance by weak states appears increasingly to be the cause, rather than the result of ethnic and other deadly intrastate conflict that threatens economic development."[14] But this did not allow the Bank itself to impose criteria for loans. Within the Bank, "considerable dissent" existed on tying lending to political demands. Conflict prevention was in effect subordinated to retrospective assessment folded into postconflict reconstruction.[15] For the Bank to focus directly on human rights as a criterion for lending would be considered by the majority of shareholders as violating the prohibition in its founding agreement on political interference. Focusing on corruption became a substitute. "Corruption has become for the World Bank what human rights violations have become for the United Nations, a key indicator of a troubled state."[16] The realm of governance and the domain of capital were increasingly hard to disentangle in the post-1989 world.

Living with Neoliberalism / Modernizing Social Democracy

Issues of political economy remained fundamental in the global north, even as a new consensus on policies seemed to prevail. From the 1980s until the financial crisis of 2008, the salient political trend in the developed or "advanced" capitalist economies was the effort to roll back the state's role in tempering the harshness, or if one prefers a more neutral language, the diversity of economic outcomes—that is, the gap between the rich and the poor within countries. In most economies, that meant reversing efforts both to regulate capital, above all the financial sector that was generating new wealth, and to redistribute the wealth so accumulated. As long as overall growth continued, efforts at redistribution were to be focused on the very young and especially the old outside the labor market or those temporarily compelled to unemployment. Accompanying this widespread consensus was the belief that the state should offload the economic enterprises it had accumulated over decades of wartime and peacetime interventions. To do so, it often had to take over their debts or quarantine them in new structures that could be liquidated or combined with concessions enough to find private takers.

The term for this bundle of policies, of course, was neoliberalism. The label is fraught, however, often signaling in academic circles instinctive disapproval. It also tends to ignore the multiple meanings of the term liberalism. In the United States it described the forces at any given moment seeking to dismantle political restrictions while simultaneously advancing programs for economic or racial equality, whereas in Europe liberal parties have resisted the latter. As of the 1940s, Friedrich Hayek and John Maynard Keynes could both claim the designation of liberal with legitimate reasons—Hayek because he was convinced markets provided a collective allocation of resources that no planning authority could ever manage, Keynes because he shunned conventional socialism. The German ordoliberals also laid title because they wanted to corset markets in a firm legal defense of property. Neoliberalism actually has retained a more coherent meaning than liberalism. Everywhere, it has implied a political project to remove state intervention whose effect, if not intention, might be to limit the accumulation of private property.[17] For some advocates, the motive was simply the belief that redistributive policies were confiscatory; others believed that they were ineffective or counterproductive. They burdened the economy with excessive bureaucracy. In the eyes of others, redistributive policies targeted those who did not possess the education, "culture," or character traits to participate effectively in a modern economy.

The major parties of the conservative center argued that allowing the greatest feasible scope for private saving and investment must produce the economic growth that would benefit all. Neoliberalism brought with it a reconceived image of society and its divisions: the class structure envisaged by Marxist-inflected sociology, which served the "Fordist" or mass production era, yielded to a vision of a society in which all were middle class except those "excluded"—the very poor, the homeless, migrants, the ill, and so forth. Networks started to replace classes as the imagined elements of social structure, and it was no longer the proletariat but the marginalized, the "disaffiliated," or precariously attached who appeared as the deserving subjects of social assistance.[18]

Which brings us to the paradoxical result of the neoliberal decades—the development of a state project precisely to extricate the state from policies that might limit the aspirations of capital or, as neoliberals argued, would interfere with the collective rationality of markets. The project implied three major initiatives in the 1980s and the 1990s: cutting taxes, reducing welfare burdens, and privatizing state enterprises. They fulfilled a convergent agenda: the wishes of capital, the advice of policy foundations, and the enthusiasm of political leaders. But there were many contradictory elements to such a program. As one political scientist summarized, although privatization—the term replaced "denationalization" in Thatcher's Britain—sought to shape economic outcomes through regulation rather than ownership, it did not shrink the state but transformed it. In so doing, however, it made regulation a more difficult task. Private governance used self-regulation to preempt government rules. International and varying national rules were exploited to secure exemptions.[19]

This program in fact ran parallel with the redefining of capital's goals so as to focus on maximizing its net returns. Milton Friedman described them pithily in 1971: the goal of the corporation must be to maximize returns for its shareholders. Of course, not all business leaders were so consistent; some hoped to make their companies benevolent social institutions. Their goals had been shaped by their involvement with public policy for community or national objectives. Entrepreneurs had not become cultural icons in the United States or in Europe by defining their objectives as making money pure and simple, any more than sports heroes had by fighting for outsize salaries and advertising revenues. Nonetheless, earnings and market performance claimed a far more prominent place in judging the success of the enterprise. What is more, the institutions of governance concerned with economic welfare implicitly accepted much of this agenda as bystanders. It did not hurt that many of those who reaped outsized gains also made large philanthropic gifts to nonprofit institutions such as universities, museums, orchestras, or hospitals. Benevolence justified plutocracy.

Remarkably enough, during the 1990s and first decade of the new twenty-first century, parties of social-democratic persuasion (including the American Democratic Party in this admittedly vague category) embraced, indeed celebrated, these aspirations. In a survey of Tony Blair's Britain, two sympathetic authors summed up: "The pragmatic post-war social democratic arguments for a mixed economy have given way, rightly or wrongly, to the celebration of competitive markets and private enterprise. The privatization of public assets and services has continued under Labour. The Blair government has become the champion of public-sector reform. Labour is business-friendly as never before."[20] In fact, the new dispensation had been germinating during the previous decades. German Social Democrats in 1959 had dropped their Marxist-derived commitment to nationalization. The party entered a great coalition in 1966 and led a social-liberal government with the then-reformist Free Democrats from 1969 to 1982. Preoccupied by rapprochement with East Germany (*Ostpolitik*) and then environmental issues, it developed a new basic program by 1989, which recognized that collectivism and solidarity no longer attracted the middle-class electorate to which it had to appeal. The Norwegian Labor Party had a "freedom debate" in the late 1980s, as it cooled its heels in opposition. The British Labour Party jettisoned its commitment to public ownership (Clause IV) that dated from 1918. Both the American Democrats and British Labour needed ideological reorientation after twelve years of GOP presidents and eighteen years of Tory prime ministers in Britain. Both parties decided that new public preoccupations had contributed to their long exile from power: failures to guarantee law and order, foreign policy setbacks, and the allegedly rising cost of welfare payments to the unemployed. Traditional American liberalism and British class politics seemed to have run their course.

Explaining the "conversion" of social-democratic parties, whether in Britain and Europe, or the Democratic Party in the United States has prompted a massive social science literature. The sociologist Stephanie Mudge attributes the shift primarily to the changing role that economists played—from the grand theorists of capitalism and socialism whose ideas informed the collectivist programs in the early twentieth century, to the academic advisers such as Keynes, who argued for the demand management adopted through the 1960s, to those finally she terms the "transnational financial economists," who interpreted market behavior and were integrated into the social-democratic parties as they consummated the neoliberal turn. "There is a genetic link between the social situation of party experts and the way left parties speak."[21]

But surely, there is a demand side to economic knowledge as well as a supply side. The redefinition of goals seemed a necessary adjustment to changing socioeconomic conditions no longer under national control. The Phillips curve premise of economic management—trading a tad higher inflation for a boost to employment—had slipped out of control. The stagflation of the 1970s, described in Chapters 7 and 8, demoralized and chastened social democrats. With the rise of imports from Asia in particular, many union and left party leaders felt they had to bargain not only to increase wages but also to retain jobs for their workers within a wider and more constraining framework of globalization.[22] To be fair, more than a forced adjustment seemed at stake. Labour did not continue budget cutting; government spending would go up to over 40 percent of gross domestic product (GDP) by 2002–2003, halfway through Blair's tenure in office.[23] His successor, Gordon Brown, promised to invest further in education and public transport. The Clinton administration pressed on with racial, educational, and environmental programs.

Still, the social democratic or center-left seemed to develop a fascination with the process of capitalist growth itself, the vigor of new technologies and profits, the outgrowing of the dreary smokestack industries whose workers had formed a basis of the party. The decision to let the Bank of England determine interest rates without consulting the Treasury, which followed within days of Blair's 1997 electoral victory, signaled reassurance to capital. It was an application of supply-side economics, garnished with the rhetoric of the "information age." Not all liberalization counted as "neo." More parental options for their children's education, prison reform, and regional devolution constituted part of the package. Underlying them all was the axiom of expanding choice and it had ambiguous effects. Charter schools in the United States gave ambitious parents in inner-city ghettos the chance to get their kids a more rigorous education but at the price of further stratifying the public school systems that had once played so important a role in the construction of a multiethnic democracy. Liberals who vowed to get tough on crime at a time that drug use seemed an unstoppable trend expanded what some termed the "carceral state" and its racially skewed targets.[24] The bleak detritus of abandoned factories was the inevitable price for progress.

The cost of welfare payments to the unemployed seemed to strike a special nerve. Reduction of this burden appeared to be the economic policy that would prove social-democratic competence—one is tempted to say manhood. In practice this meant, above all, getting the residual unemployed back into the labor market. "Labour is promoting work not welfare. There is," as Gordon Brown, then chancellor under Blair, announced, "no 'fifth option' of staying home for those capable of work. To this government any job is better than a life of dependency on the dole."[25] As governor of Arkansas, Bill Clinton had also spotlighted the alleged deformation of the 1935 Aid for Dependent Children—stigmatized by the 1970s as creating "welfare queens," ostensibly African American single mothers—and announced his goal of "ending welfare as we know it." His 1996 program of Temporary Assistance for Needy Families (TANF) offered block grants to states that would contribute their own funds to the mix. At the same time, individuals were limited to two years of consecutive welfare payments or five years over a lifetime. Federal welfare

TANF grants, moreover, did not entice southern and conservative states to allocate the full measure of matching benefits. The favorable economic conditions until 2008 cushioned the law's potentially catastrophic impact; however, the new emphasis on getting women to work, while downplaying the burdens of single motherhood, indicated how far the center-left had moved since Lyndon Johnson's War on Poverty of the early 1960s.[26]

The other major debate on unemployment insurance and social welfare payments took place in Germany. Social Democratic Party (SPD) chancellor Gerhard Schröder, running for his second term in 2002, had promised to enact the recommendations of the commission headed by Peter Hartz, the personnel director of Volkswagen, which came into effect from 2003 to 2005. The fourth recommendation, "Hartz-IV," was particularly controversial. It envisaged merging social welfare assistance with unemployment insurance with a reduction in overall benefits, means testing for eligibility, and provision for sanctions for not accepting employment. The fact was that from 2001 to 2005, Germany (like France) could not stick to the Maastricht criteria of keeping the budget deficit below 3 percent. The benefits were designed specifically to remain below the net wages so as to incentivize employment. From 2005 until 2018, the unemployment rate sank from 11.7 percent to 5.2 percent and in East Germany from 18.7 percent to 6.9 percent. But the cuts in benefits seemed particularly harsh. If recipients of unemployment insurance found part-time work, their earnings were deducted from their benefits; family members' payments also could count against unemployment benefits. Over time, the majority of eligible recipients were migrants. A larger number were elderly.[27]

The political impact helped undermine the long postwar German political party equilibrium consisting of the moderate left (SPD), moderate conservatives (Christian Democratic Party [CDU]) and the small, sometimes idealistic, sometimes opportunistic Free Democratic Party that could determine whether SPD or CDU might form the next government. Now, over the next decade, a regrouping took place; a new "Left" united disgruntled SPD members in the West along with ex-GDR socialists still mourning the regime that had been swallowed up; the Greens became a viable alternative; the three postwar parties continued their decline, and by the 2010s an ugly populist Alternative for Germany, including some apologists for the National Socialists, entrenched itself in the East. By 2019, the electoral results would start to resemble the distribution of the late Weimar Republic.[28]

Whom, then, did New Labour, the adherents of the third way, or the New Democrats believe they represented? The rhetoric around these plans was revealing. "Classical" liberalism in the nineteenth-century Europe sense presupposed a society of rational and literate adults—that is, property-holding males until the twentieth century. The "new liberalism" in Britain ca. 1900 or the Progressive era in the United States had added economic rights to political ones but still with an individual subject. Social democracy traditionally conceived of a collective subject—the working class or the trade unions. The New Deal had legally recognized labor as a collective actor, and along with European social democracy, its programs aimed to endow unions with equal strength in the face of a capitalist entrepreneurs. From the 1990s on, however, many in these very parties despaired of these collective constituencies, saw them as rent-seeking organizations seeking to hold back the rewards of innovation-spurred growth to protect antiquated payments.[29] But whereas old Democrats, old Labour, and the SPD had built parties based on preexisting social constituencies, the New Democrats, New Labour, and their similar parties and intellectuals had to create the constituencies and communities for their parties. The question for twenty-first-century politics was whether they could successfully do so. Similar uncertainty beset the successors to François Mitterrand who had reshaped the French Socialist Party as it did the divided left, fragmented after Bettino Craxi's administration, the scandals unearthed by the investigations of Mani Pulite (Clean Hands) in the 1990s and Silvio Berlusconi's populist ascent.[30]

For a pair of critical French observers writing a decade into the Blair years, although the Labour government insisted on the new conditions imposed by the logic of globalization and the knowledge society and declared it would rely on partnerships, cooperation, and networks rather than hierarchies, the self-description was not accurate. Instead, it was a hybrid policy mix that presupposed "the need for permanent training and flexibility in the job market, the adoption of managerial modes from the private sector, and privileging competition and incentives." It was a "societal project for the middle classes, organized around work, winners, and consumption." Modernization had become its mantra, but that included "a mobilization of the state" to deal directly with the citizen and consumer and community "at the expense of intermediate organizations and bodies." "Political modernization" in fact resulted in the exclusion of institutions and groups in favor of communications, professionals and politics focused on image and spin—an example, Colin Crouch said, of "post-democracy."[31] For Anthony Giddens, who emerged as the major theorist of the program, the third way was a response to globalization and heightened individualism, "associated with the retreat of tradition and custom from our lives," in an age of "moral transition."[32] Social Democrats, he urged, should be promoting a new democratic state, with devolution to local government and direct democracy, renewal and transparency of the public sphere, and administrative efficiency. In a similar vein, the influential German sociologist Ulrich Beck wrote, "We are sliding into a *new* society, not into a changed society, neither into a 'post-industrial' nor a 'late capitalist' society . . . but into new type of social framework (*Gefüge*), for which we have no concept and therefore no vision."[33] Beck's remedy was less political—although the Greens might have been the most appropriate rescue vessel—than a call to take the discussion out of technocratic hands and democratize discussion and knowledge. Further planning as such had only authoritarian possibilities.

Giddens indulged in the same incantatory summary of new values but clearly signed up for New Labour. He had already redefined equality in his tract *Beyond Left and Right,* and the argument was indicative. He advocated a concept of positive welfare for an age that was overcoming scarcity. Welfare had to be more comprehensive than just supporting the poor. "Security, self-respect, self-actualization—these are scarce goods for the affluent as well as the poor. . . . A generative model of equality, or equalization, could provide the basis of a new pact between the affluent and the poor. Such a pact would be an 'effort bargain' founded on lifestyle changes . . . on the part of both the privileged and the less privileged, and a *wide notion* of welfare, taking the concept away from economic provision for the deprived towards the fostering of the autotelic self."[34]

Mark Bevir summed up, "Although the state can no longer promote social justice and prosperity by means of the Keynesian welfare state, it can do so through a Third Way that combines supply-side interventionism with welfare-to-work programs to create a greater equality of skill-based assets and to render more equal the outcomes of the market economy." Although "for a large part of the 1980s the story was of Labour lagging behind its sister European social democratic parties in the march toward modernization . . . remaining attracted to nationalization, Keynesianism, unilateral nuclear disarmament, close links with the unions and a less than fulsome embrace of European integration . . . by the 1990s Labour is seen as having leapfrogged European social democracy in the race to 'modernize.'"[35]

On the continent, similar agendas motivated the German Social Democrats, Felipe Gonzalez who steered the Spanish Socialists (PSOE) away from Marxism and served as prime minister from 1982 to 1996, the Italian Socialist Giuliano Amato, premier in 2000–2001, and Dutch Labour Party prime minister (1994–2002) Willem Kok. Kok remained perhaps the most traditional social democrat given his origins in the trade union movement and he embraced Keynesian measures to reduce unemployment even as he supervised privatizations urged by his Liberal coalition partners. Most were intellectually attractive and telegenic, appealing to a new educated postindustrial middle class. In effect, they completed the trajectory begun a century earlier, when Social Democratic "reformists" diverged from orthodox Marxists.

Public and Private, State and Society

"Modernization" of social democracy meant the embrace of capitalism based on market societies. These latter two terms were often used as equivalents but were not the same. Market societies implied the dismantling of state-controlled planning and centrally imposed prices.[36] Capitalism required not only prices determined by supply and demand but also the capacity to acquire rights and ownership from either private owners or state concessionaires, hence the creation of a new class of wealth holders who often had access to sweetheart deals or foreign backers or, in the Soviet Union, political favoritism. The choice seemed to lie between a quick change of property rights and free prices—so-called shock therapy—favored by homegrown staunch neoliberals such as Lesczek Balcerowicz in Poland and Václav Klaus in Czechoslovakia, Václav Havel's successor as president, and many Anglo-American economists. It would impose admittedly the pain of sharp rises in prices and probably massive transitional unemployment but offered the promise of a quicker reprise of activity. The Polish reformers of Solidarity signed on for Balcerowicz but underestimated the pain. Shock therapy would mean painful unemployment—in effect, the furloughing of workers in late middle age. Balcerowicz foresaw a shrinking of GDP of 5 percent, but it turned out to be 18 percent in 1990–1991.[37] Still, by 1992, recovery was under way. The alternative to shock therapy—trying to keep old industries afloat with state subsidies—promised a gentler transition but the danger of never achieving a competitive economy in an age of globalization. As theorists such as János Kornai demonstrated, it could keep workers on at obsolescent plants and ultimately drag down economic recovery. United Germany was a wealthy enough society to replace the income for East German workers made redundant, although by the end of the 1990s, that price seemed excessive and provoked the welfare reforms under Social Democratic auspices. But the costs in human dignity led to resentments at the new "elbowing" society and sentimental recollections of the former communist regimes—hence the support for the party of The Left, heir to disgruntled SPD voters in the west and ex–Socialist Unity Party members in the East and, ultimately after another decade, the basis for a party of national resentment.

The major effort along with restructuring welfare was privatizing state-owned enterprises. The arguments for doing so were not solely ideological, although ideology and party ideology had probably played the major role in Great Britain repeatedly since 1945. When the Conservatives succeeded the Labour Party, they reversed the nationalizations that Labour had imposed— road transport, coal, steel, the Bank of England. But these nationalizations had left the management of these industries in private hands; the government had effectively purchased the shares. Labour had renationalized some in 1964, and the Thatcher government had sold the shares once again after 1979.

In Italy Benito Mussolini's government had effectively taken over ownership of bankrupt firms after 1929 as a bailout and by 1933 created the Institute for Industrial Reconstruction (IRI) as a major holding company. IRI would come to hold shares worth approximately half the value of Italian industry and banking and be responsible for 470,000 employees. IRI had become a great source for patronage for the Christian Democrats in particular, and its president and later Italian prime minister, Romano Prodi, felt caught between the pressure to divest and the politicians' resistance as Maastricht approached. He resigned in 1989, and Guido Carli took over the negotiations as treasury minister. German delegates wanted privatization to be included in the Maastricht Treaty, but French and other delegations joined Italy in successfully excluding it. IRI had created a special holding for oil and gas, the ENI (Ente nazionale idrocarbone), which, as mentioned in Chapter 4, grew aggressively under Enrico Mattei and survived his death. Both IRI and ENI lost money and required government aid, which Brussels resisted as a violation of competition policy. A showdown came right after Maastricht over the loans to the third IRI holding, EFIM (Ente participazioni e finanziamento industria manifatturiere), the office for financial support of manufacturing industry, which competition commissioner Karel van Miert described as part of a "closed and incestuous" political and financial system.[38] Van Miert, a Belgian socialist, made it his mission to reduce state support and ownership of national enterprises when it came to EU policy; leveling the playing field became a major argument for privatizations. The Amato government had transformed IRI, ENI, and EFIM into joint stock corporations with shares held by the treasury and pleaded that without the state guarantee, IRI with its 400,000 employees would go into default. The commission retreated, and an agreement in the summer allowed Italy to continue its guarantee, while the government agreed to taper off its aid. The European dimension precludes seeing any great ideological victory for capital. "The perception was that Europe needed a new economic 'organization' and a 'public hand' on a regional [European] scale in order to foster growth and structural change at the national scale."[39]

Norway and Britain had created national firms to develop their large-scale oil reserves. France had nationalized its railroads under the Popular Front after a long history of providing bailouts, and it had nationalized the Banque de France at the same time. It was a substantial shareholder in many sectors, such as aerospace, the Électricité de France, and the Elf-Total oil enterprise. West German federal states had organized banks with public support. Austria had a national oil industry. Capitalist states had large public sectors. The United States had finally organized a public national banking network, the Federal Reserve System, in 1913 and strengthened it in 1933. It had developed a major hydroelectrical network, the Tennessee Valley Authority (TVA) in the 1930s. And, of course, it retained a major military sector for the development of nuclear power and the National Aeronautics and Space Administration for space exploration. By and large, what was known as the entrepreneurial state was alive and well in the capitalist world. This is not to mention housing where local governments in Britain, Austria, and elsewhere were major owners (until the Thatcher government sold houses to renters) and in the United States where the federal government backstopped the mortgage market.

But criticism became more effective in the 1970s. Such public enterprises were plums for political patronage—in Italy, it seemed, above all. Their objectives were muddy: Were they intended to keep prices down (whether for electricity as in the TVA, or oil and gas as in ENI) for consumers and firms? Were they intended to boost local development and employment, extract profits to defray government deficits? Were they expected to employ large labor forces to work against unemployment or to shed workers and run lean and mean? There were legitimate questions as to their utility, and there were powerful private interests as well who wanted to get their hands on profitable monopolies. Not least, selling off public property provided one-shot injections of revenue for national budgets at a time of persistent deficits. The EU as an entity had emerged as a business- and finance-friendly institution in the 1980s, and although it was not a property holder, it certainly proposed no obstacles to privatization. Rather, the rules it developed for making the single market and then the currency union encouraged divestment.[40]

The case for retaining public enterprise was clearest when the enterprise rested on "natural monopolies" or the resources involved seemed inherently public, such as the offshore oil fields in the North Sea that Britain and Norway could both exploit. In some cases, such as Britain, the state retained radio and television broadcasting monopolies and only slowly allowed private competitors. In the United States, the government auctioned off spectrum space (the proprietary right to use specified wave lengths). As heirs of a civil-law tradition, Mexico and France, among other states, sold private companies the rights to develop postwar highway systems as toll roads. But accumulated state enterprises were often burdened with sunk costs or environmental liabilities and were not just cash cows, so finding private investors was not likely to be a simple matter. Tax concessions often seemed necessary. Their new owners were not so desirous of private ownership that they did not want the state to absorb all the potential for losses.

The state socialist countries faced a more dramatic divestment and more choices. There was no capitalist sector; ministries of planning and economy ran enterprises directly. Who was to inherit the state enterprises? How should a private sector be created? Poland underwent what was called shock therapy, supported by Western economists such as Jeffrey Sachs and caried through by the rigorous liberal Balcerowicz. In Russia, the liberals favored by Boris Yeltsin, such as Yegor Gaidar, who served as acting prime minister for roughly the second half of 1992, presided over a vast divestment of state assets, often to the applause of Western economic advisers. The buccaneering and rudimentary legal framework led to a steep if transitory decline in output, a devastating depression and hyperinflation for much of the 1990s. Russia's wealth in oil and minerals ended up in the hands of a cadre of leaders, some of whom who would help cement the rise to power of Vladimir Putin, others of whom would be imprisoned for their new privileges. The transformed economy would recover from 2000 to 2009, thanks in part to the boom in energy and material prices. Throughout, World Bank governance indicators for accountability, rule of law, and control of corruption gave Russia significantly lower rankings than the middle-income countries in which category it fell and even the low-income countries.[41]

In the final months of the GDR, 8,000 large and small socialist enterprises were placed into a trust agency, the Treuhand-Anstalt, which briefly became the largest managerial enterprise (in terms of assets) in the world. The original decree of March 1, 1990 was a wager to preserve unitary oversight and raise capital from the West, but as of summer, it was reconstructed and broken up with the mission of finding purchasers. "Privatization is the best restructuring," its administrator believed. Just to find purchasers at bargain-basement prices was difficult, however. Obsolete units had to be liquidated; others came with legacies of environmental pollution and had to be given to West German firms against pledges of keeping them in business. The real estate holdings of the former firms became the most valuable asset. But the mission of the Treuhand was to liquidate itself, which it did by selling or giving units and plants to West German firms. The prices set were low, sometimes at zero, because the equipment and expertise that had made the GDR an apparent industrial powerhouse within the Soviet bloc now lost their former Eastern European state markets and found it hard to sell to the West. East German productivity was much lower and its technical level far behind, say Siemens or IBM, while its Trabi autos soon became a national joke. Indebtedness to the GDR Staatsbank became debt to the Bundesbank, and although the nominal face value of accounts beyond a family minimum in deutsche mark had been halved by the currency union, the real burden was now far higher. The 1:1 conversion of western and eastern marks for current transactions rendered labor expensive, such that West German auto assembly lines were established in Hungary and Czechoslovakia but not in the new East German federal states. The former East German *Kombinate*, which at least had internalized supply chains and work teams, were now dissolved. Layoffs and furloughs even as new positions in public administration and universities were taken over by "Wessies." By mid-1992, industrial employment was less than 1 million as against 3.2 million in 1989. The logic of privatization seemed inexorable but claimed a heavy, if temporary, sacrifice in morale.[42]

For the course of world history in the current century, the most momentous choice was that of China, which had embarked on an experiment of enterprise zones under Deng Xiaoping at the end of the 1970s. As Isabella Weber's account of the long debate documents, the Chinese came close to shock therapy—privatization, liberation of prices—in the second half of the 1980s. But as inflation rose sharply, threatening a recurrence of the disastrous hyperinflation of the civil war in the late 1940s, the regime reversed course and continued its gradualist policy of allowing the development of a private sector, while preserving state enterprises, and reaffirming political control, whether brutally at Tiananmen Square in 1989 or by methodical recentralization under current chairman Xi Jinping.[43]

If we tally all the privatization of state-held land and firms into personal or corporate assets, the 1980s and 1990s probably saw the greatest conversion of collective property since the massive secularizations of Catholic Church lands throughout Western Europe and Latin America that had extended from the late eighteenth century into the 1860s. It was neoliberalism's greatest wager. For those with a commitment to the older habits of a shabby or sentimental collectivism, the downside was the growing inequality of wealth, even as overall welfare could increase, particularly so since a technological revolution was in full swing with the advent of individual computers, cell phones, and digital technology in general. The new capitalism was no country for old men.

Could another choice have been made at this historical juncture? That question has been raised also with respect to the early Industrial Revolution. Perhaps. Would it have been less painful for so many people? Again, another subjunctive history. Welfare and utility have to be measured in many dimensions, of which income equality is only one. The decades of neoliberalism brought significant liberal advances in terms of race and gender rights, educational access, and just acceptance for the variations of human experience. As for issues of political economy, there was no effective counter-capital party in the West organized along traditional lines by the end of the twentieth century. As the chair of the US Federal Reserve put it, by 2007, "it hardly makes any difference who will be the next president. The world will be governed by market forces."[44] But for Asia, Africa, and Latin America, there clearly were counter-capital social movements. Resistance to triumphant market society was no longer embodied in the Soviet Union or even Communist China but in the tribal uprisings or urban guerrillas or the diverse movements and parties that contested the policy consensus that had achieved dominance. At the end of November 1999, perhaps 40,000 protesters, including AFL-CIO union members, environmentalists, and militants on the left mobilized against the World Trade Organization meetings in Seattle. The street clashes signaled that globalization could arouse a major resistance—not yet in political party form but potentially able to disrupt what seemed a triumphant consensus, as had the popular parties in Bolivia and Latin America.

Echoes of Empire

The most advantageous political framework for capitalism's potential to create wealth (or transfer it from others) transcended the nation-state. Political confederations, common free trade or protectionist economic areas, or empires had all reflected that logic. Capital was inherently expansionist, and although business groups welcomed the support of their respective nation-states in terms of tariffs, subsidies, and purchases, they also remained impatient with the strictures that territorial sovereignty imposed. In conventional terms, colonial empires no longer existed by the late twentieth century. Chinese incorporation of Tibet remained perhaps the major forcible imperial domination of a large territory with a resisting population, at least until Putin's moves against Ukraine in 2014 and 2022. The emancipation of Eastern Europe from Soviet control had appeared to many as the final stage of decolonization. But from the perspective of critics across the world, the ambitions and reach of American military bases, industrial products, and investment funds could appear as a new form of empire, especially when America's military reach seemed so tightly woven with the influence of capital.[45] The United States had had an ambiguous relationship to the European resource empires. It had pressed for the dissolution of their formal structures from World War II on, going to war against the Japanese Empire and the Third Reich in the cause of liberating the countries the Axis had conquered. President Franklin Roosevelt had prodded the British to move toward Indian independence and might have resisted resumption of French control of Vietnam. The Truman administration lost patience as the Dutch attempted to regain their domain in Indonesia. Nonetheless, Washington found that its preferred successors in Asia, as in Eastern Europe, could not stabilize the territories they moved into after European and Japanese moved out. Region by region—Eastern Europe between 1945 and 1947, East Asia in the late 1940s and 1950s, Africa in the 1960s and after, the objective was to prevent European decolonization or just challenged regimes from opening vast areas of the world, with all their economic potential, to potentially Marxist movements.[46]

Each major area of the world presented a different challenge to Washington's view of its interests and values. Historically, American administrations felt it their right to protect American firms' investments in Latin America and resumed active intervention by removing the Arbenz administration in Guatemala in 1954 and then trying to abort the Cuban Revolution.[47] In Western Europe and East Asia, the threat of military invasion by Russia and China—ideological and strategic rivals—led to the buildup of military power deployed locally and supported by the implicit threat of retaliation by air. In the Middle East, a religious dimension augmented the threat. American support of Israeli territorial independence in 1948, which had been established at the cost of uprooting a Palestinian population of 700,000, made normalization of relations with the Arab powers difficult—a situation compounded by the failure to secure an acceptable peace after the war of 1967. At the same time, the massive petroleum holdings of American firms created a huge material interest in precluding any Arab nationalist challenges. The Islamic Republic of Iran founded in the revolution of 1979 beheld the United States as a core threat to its religious values as well as the security of its regime. Africa seemed a more open situation, and the United States had made it clear that it rejected British and French plans to retain domination of the Suez Canal and Algeria. But when a radical and charismatic nationalist, Patrice Lumumba, threatened to become the leading actor in the Congo as Belgium announced it was giving up its colony—though hardly its mining interests—the United States helped place him in harm's way, where his rivals could assassinate him. Twenty years later, Washington moved to support friendly claimants to power in the colonies evacuated by Portugal, while Cuban forces supported by Moscow sought to support Marxist nationalists. Ultimately, Washington realized it was less costly to accept neutralist national movements as in Angola than to support military strongmen who promised compliant regimes at the cost of continual involvement. The difficulty of the American situation was that the United States read the global situation correctly: it was engaged in a global rivalry with adversarial forces that often defined themselves as nationalist *and* Marxist and, in the Middle East, as representing Islamic-inspired polities. America's global preeminence had made this confrontation "structurally" inevitable. Losing a local struggle, as it did in Vietnam, however, did not have to doom Washington's overall strategic viability, although it obviously frustrated its goal of keeping its local allies a viable force.

For many of its enemies, the United States embodied an in-your-face secular materialism, and their opposition took the form of anti-capitalism or religious fundamentalism. Increasingly, they resorted to violence against non-military targets—that is, to terrorism, a strategy developed through the twentieth century in Ireland, Palestine, Indochina, and Algeria, not to mention the earlier struggles in the German-occupied territories during World War II. Terrorism was defined as the use of lethal force against civilians or off-duty military delivered by opposing civilians or militias. It was designed explicitly to make civilian forces pawns in asymmetric warfare and thus contravened the codified rules of war. The use of aerial bombing against civilians had aroused pangs of conscience or recrimination before World War II but had been assimilated as an acceptable recourse since the victors as well as the defeated had steadily expanded its scope. Terrorism became the excruciating dilemma for America's global preponderance and indeed its security at home. Domestic terror exercised by unhinged or resentful, perhaps psychopathic, individuals against racial minorities or schoolchildren within the country crystallized no real national response: gun control ran into the country's deeply fractured ideological stalemates. But terror successfully mobilized by aggrieved Islamic opponents produced rare unanimity. The cruel and stunning destruction of the World Trade Center towers on September 11, 2001 provoked a major response: the PATRIOT Act, along with sharpened surveillance in public assembly points, above all airports, as well as authority to convoke military tribunals for suspected terrorists. Few Americans, in shock from 9 / 11, questioned the need for these measures. But the atmosphere also seemed to legitimize the most fervent supporters of executive supremacy in the new George W. Bush administration.

September 11 catalyzed the most recent project of the American project-state. As after December 7, 1941, citizens responded to a direct assault. Reestablishing security at home and security projected to those turbulent areas of the world that bred terrorism became the American project. National security, it can be argued, had become the uniting theme of US foreign policy since 1940, when the country seriously geared up for global conflict.[48] After a short interlude of postwar satisfaction, national security appeared endangered again by 1947–1948. The fact that postwar America was the preeminent global power did not ease this preoccupation; it made conflict and rivalry throughout the globe seem all the more threatening. Soviet power and ambitions loomed as the central challenge, and until Moscow's interventions in Hungary and especially Czechoslovakia, Communist Parties still could kindle a glow of socialist loyalties throughout the globe. Social revolutionary aspirations everywhere testified to the dangers that Washington and the circles who felt a stake in foreign affairs perceived and to which they responded with foreign aid, efforts at subversion, ideological persuasion, and commitment of military forces for the rest of the century. This is not to argue that the country was imagining these threats; they existed, but the nation's policies confirmed them. And in so doing, they wove them into the fabric of domestic politics and intellectual life as well.[49]

All this might have suggested that as a global hegemon, the United States was following the trajectory of conventional empire—built on force and maintaining supremacy by battles at the edge of empire, some of which it won, others lost. The *limes* or frontier of the American supremacy ran along the Iron Curtain, most dramatically at the Berlin Wall and demarcating what those in its sphere considered their shared values—toleration of peaceful political disagreement and protection of the individual against arbitrary arrest or expropriation. Once Vietnam was abandoned and oil seemed so threatened, the focus of American attention shifted to Africa—and after 9 / 11 to Central Asia and the Arab Middle East. It was the George W. Bush administration that created this project, less perhaps the somewhat befogged president himself than his close advisers, Vice President Dick Cheney and Secretary of Defense Donald Rumsfeld, while his activist White House lawyers, John Woo and David Addington, sought to exploit the emergency, quickly titled the War on Terror, to endow the presidency with far-reaching emergency power, putting forward the most coherent project for executive supremacy since the Federalist founders.

US global preponderance during the second half of the twentieth century rested on an unconventional profile. American power had depended on its economic prowess and protected continental position in wartime. It had its own huge resource endowment and population that provided an industrious and patriotic mass labor force. By the 1980s, however, US ascendancy no longer rested on the Fordist economic organization it had harnessed to national and military purposes from 1940 to the 1960s. By the end of the twentieth century, it exploited a symbiotic relationship with a rising China (fittingly dubbed Chimerica by Niall Ferguson), which worked to develop overseas consumer markets for its developing state capitalist industrial development and to encourage American investment by funding America's balance on current account and its growing domestic deficit.[50] The energies of the Chinese population as guided by the powerful ruling party allowed the United States to transition to become in effect an empire of consumption— the Keynesian motor of global aggregate demand, which China, following Japan and Germany, needed for its respective export-oriented policies. Peter Petersen, chair of the Council on Foreign Relations, fretted for at least two decades about the public debt, saying its growth portended catastrophe. It had been the Reagan administration that had lightheartedly let the deficit increase in order to reduce taxes in the questionable conviction that lowering the top marginal rates would mobilize production—a wager unsuccessfully sought by the brief incoming British government of Liz Truss in the fall of 1922. The Clinton administration brought the deficit down. But in the wake of 9 / 11, the George W. Bush administration let it increase again. Republicans who had opposed the "tax and spend" economy of the Democrats had little aversion to the "borrow and spend" economy. The country's budget or fiscal deficit, as the financial journals continually stressed, transmitted itself into its debt to foreigners, who bought the Treasury's promises to pay and ultimately provided the funds that filled the budget gap at home. In theory, it was possible that the Chinese might dump their American Treasury bond holdings on the market, but that would certainly have diminished their value for Beijing. Given the proportion of products China was selling in the West and Western investments in the spur to industrialization, they had little motive. Creditor and debtor's mutual embrace had the potential for disaster but a larger stake in their co-prosperity. The smaller debtor countries faced a different danger, as the defaults and devaluations of the late 1990s sadly proved. Capital, and the international ascendancy of the American state, continued to converge; and after 9/11, no argument that they might be separable was likely to gain traction.

Debt's Dominion, 2

The transition to an "empire of consumption"[51]—a shorthand formula, of course, because the United States remained a center of digital innovation and services if no longer of unchallenged Fordist mass production—went along with another transition in American capitalism—namely, the growing share of financial activity in the economy (and a corresponding decline in manufacturing) since World War II. Financial services had represented about 10 percent of American economic activity in 1945, 15 percent in 1960, and had grown to 20 percent by 2006. Both American parties smiled on this development. But those numbers represented the income claimed by banks, investment houses, and insurance companies, not the paper assets they created. As explained in Chapter 8, the great monetary tightening that ended the protracted inflation of the 1970s had been achieved at the price of an implicit trade-off. The money distributed by central banks to government finance ministries had been tourniqueted. But the potential for money creation that inhered in a banking and securities system as it made loans remained uncurtailed. Even as the Clinton administration managed to balance the national budget, it unleashed restraints on the banking system. The Depression era's Glass-Steagall Act, which separated ordinary banks that kept deposits and extended loans for businesses and the public from investment banks that took equity positions, was repealed in the Financial Services Modernization Act of 1999.[52]

To a degree, the new credits extended by financial institutions represented the counterpart of productive potential in the economy, but they exceeded any physical expansion of output or growth in productivity. It is unclear whether they proportionally increased the growth of intellectual capital and innovative processes although the case has been made that they have flowed into intangibles that are harder to assign values to.[53] A far larger share of the Anglo-American economic effort went to processing the purchase of paper claims on future income and wealth—that is, shares of corporations (often by other corporations) and on mortgages and, most intriguingly, just on wagers in the form of "derivatives" that those underlying claims would appreciate. Investors could buy shares in index funds—investment vehicles based on the value of the stock market indexes for different sectors of industry. Derivatives were bets on bets, much as the proliferation of casinos might represent, although without even having to hire the construction crews. This activity did not yield higher real wages for workers in the economy for goods or nonfinancial services. It was transformed into private and institutional savings by an inflation of asset values—including the stock market and real estate—as well as the sharply rising prices of university education.[54] Although this wealth was distributed very unequally, a great deal was held in widely diffused assets—professionally managed pension funds for teachers, municipal workers, trade unions, and the homes of 70 million Americans, some owned free and clear but others hypothecated for large portions of their purchase values.

Financialization, in effect, was both a consequence of and a contributor to removing the state as an inhibiting force on markets and profits.[55] The financial services industries—with their epicenters in New York and London and lesser nodes in Tokyo and Frankfurt—grew as a percentage of domestic "product." Financial sector profits amounted to about 20 percent of nonfinancial corporate profits through the 1970s but then rose to almost 45 percent in 2007.[56] By 2008, the pyramid of credit had reached what the economist Hyman Minsky, who studied the history of credit cycles, defined as a Ponzi phase and what others called a Minsky moment—that is, one when new investors would continually have to be brought in to redeem the debts of the previous ones.[57]

The consequence was that the impact of Americans' private sector debt was potentially far more perilous than the country's public debt to China, which had no real motive to dump US Treasury bonds. Domestic debt included above all household mortgages to banks and specialized savings and loan institutions, although an increasing amount of "leverage" was accumulating on consumer credit cards. Examining peak years of the business

Table 9.1   US Gross Credit Market: Debt Outstanding

	GDP ($ Bils)	Total Credit Market Debt ($ Bils)	Total Credit/ GDP (%)	Financial Sector Debt ($ Bils)	Financial Sector Debt/ Total Debt (%)	Nonfinancial/ Total Debt (%)
1973	1,382.3	2,172.7	157.2	209.8	9.7	90.3
1979	2,562.2	4,276.4	166.9	504.9	11.8	88.2
1989	5,482.1	12,839.2	234.2	2,399.3	18.7	81.3
2000	9,951.5	27,137.6	272.7	8,157.8	30.1	69.9
2007	14,028.7	50,875.7	362.6	16,218.4	31.9	68.1
2010	14,526.5	53,353.1	367.3	14,141.8	26.5	73.5

Data source: Thomas J. Pelley, *Financialization: The Economics of Finance Capital Domination* (Basingstoke, UK: Palgrave Macmillan, 2012), 22, table 23; Economic Report of the President, February 2012, table B-1; Flow of Funds, table L.1, Board of Governors of the Federal Reserve, March 8, 2012; and author's calculations.

cycles, total US debt (including the federal debt) more than doubled from 157 percent of GDP in 1973 to 363 percent in 2007, of which financial sector debt rose from about 10–32 percent of the total.[58] The decade after 1979 brought an almost threefold increase. Mortgage debt roughly doubled from 1989 to 2000, then doubled again to 2007, climbing from 65.4 percent of GDP to 67.9 percent, then to 103.5 percent of which 95 percent was household mortgages.[59] Meanwhile, European banks got into the American home mortgage securitization game, funding 58 percent of asset-based commercial paper sold in dollars, of which German banks alone held almost 20 percent of the total, or over one-third of what US lenders held. What this meant was that when the crisis hit in 2008, the Federal Reserve would have to extend credits to the vulnerable European banks so that they did not liquidate their US holdings.[60]

In 2007, household debt reached 98 percent of GDP. But given the rising price of real estate, the public's feelings of wealth increased and they felt freer to leverage their house values at a higher rate. In the wake of the crisis, commentators suggested American home purchasers were acting improvidently. Home ownership, however, was always one of the major themes of the American dream. (I recall my solidly Republican father-in-law, a firefighter, investor, and national credit union officer in Saint Paul, telling me that homeowners had a stake in the city that renters did not have.) Just as banks had "pushed" loans on emerging-market countries in the 1980s and 1990s, so home-loan corporations pressed mortgages in the 1990s and 2000s to swell their assets.

Would-be homeowners took on "subprime" mortgages, often enticed by a low introductory interest rate that would "balloon" to a much higher rate after a few years. Corporate behavior seemed to follow households: the value of new stock issues diminished $600 billion from 2000 to 2005, while new borrowing rose $400 billion.[61] Riskier debt brought higher interest payments; they were designated as "junk bonds"—but how risky, purchasers calculated, could they really be? The riskier higher-rate loans could be bundled into nominally independent corporate shells (special-purpose vehicles) that in theory did not encumber the books of the parent institutions.

Lending to families seeking to buy into the American dream was hardly adventuresome enough for the large lending institutions that were extending loans. The originators of home mortgages, including local savings banks, generally sold them individually to more specialized institutions such as WaMu (Washington Mutual Bank, a savings and loan association) or used them as collateral with the US government-sponsored enterprises designed years before to stabilize a larger mortgage market and nicknamed Freddie Mac and Fannie Mae. Fannie and Freddie held or guaranteed mortgage-backed securities nominally valued at $5.5 trillion but with equity backing of $54 billion.[62] Their bonds were then sold to investment banks that sold them to individual investors or other dealers. Following the dot-com crash of 2001, the Fed dropped interest rates to 1 percent, encouraging a vast wave of mortgage refinancing at the lower cost.[63] Adding to the froth were new instruments that banks devised to package and sell mortgages, mortgage-backed securities. Mortgage acceptance houses sliced up the mortgages by risk and interest rates—from high-risk and high-interest tranches to much less risky paper— and moved them into the aforementioned special purpose vehicles separated from their regular balance sheets and for which the parent firms had to hold collateral at only 10 percent of what otherwise would have been required. They could then peddle the slices as "securitized" debt (asset-based commercial paper or collateralized debt obligations) to the public and to each other. Not to miss another opportunity, the larger investment houses also devised individually tailored insurance policies—credit default swaps (CDS)— that lenders could buy to hedge against default by their borrowers or to resell at a premium if another lender felt that it was in a risky situation.[64] But not only lenders. Any purchaser could wager on another company going bankrupt even were the CDS buyer not its creditor. Yet until late in the game, the danger of outright default seemed so slight that selling CDS seemed almost a risk-free business.

The industry itself had long pleaded to weaken the guardrails. By international agreement finally achieved in 1988, the so-called Basel I framework, the United Kingdom, United States, and Basel Committee (which we met in the previous chapter) agreed that OECD-based banks must retain enough capital to cover 8 percent of their conventional loans. Mortgage loans, however, needed to be counted at only half the amount of other loans. In 2004, the new Basel II regulations, proposed largely by the industry's trade association, lowered the provision for counting the mortgage loans that had to be covered from 50 percent of their nominal value to 35 percent. Although the crisis would unroll in the American heartland, increasingly the world of international banking became a club of lenders finding assurance in the loans that they traded with each other. The web of lenders and brokers, outside the traditional banking system—known collectively as the shadow banking system—including investment banks, mortgage lenders, money-market funds, hedge funds, insurance companies, went largely unregulated (and still remains so to a large degree) and magnified the role of credit and private money creation. Regulated banks ventured deeply into the new activities as well. The large European banks (Deutsche Bank, UBS, Barclays) piled up loan-to-deposit ratios of up to 50:1, while their American counterparts were at 20:1.[65]

The multiplication of claims on paper that could serve as money can be arcane for the layperson. The essential was that by passing paper back and forth between investors, banks, and investment bankers, the credit system could self-inflate . . . until it could not. Alongside other loans, banks, financial houses, and mortgage lenders were linked together by "repo" or repurchase agreements. These substituted short-term, even overnight, back-and-forth sales of financial assets, including securitized mortgages for short-term borrowing. A bank desiring short-term cash, sometimes foreign currencies, could sell its government securities to another lender, agreeing to repurchase them within twenty-four or forty-eight hours at a slightly higher price, discounted in advance and known as the haircut. The margin would provide the equivalent of an implicit overnight interest payment. Between September 2007 and late 2008, the average haircut calculated as an annual rate rose from below 2 percent to 45 percent. It is hard to know the exact amounts, but the repo markets may have reached $10 trillion in the United States and $11 trillion in Europe and the United Kingdom. Commercial banks did not rely on this facility, but the brokerage and investment houses such as Goldman Sachs and Lehman Brothers were heavily into this new and volatile source of liquidity. Although the drying up of repo, as measured by the haircuts demanded, drew a lot of attention, the sale of short-term corporate debt (commercial paper) probably played an even greater role in the contraction. Once the process of failure, or rumors of failure, started, valuations fell quickly. How should a "nonproductive" loan or mortgage be valued? Banks did not really want to be in the business of foreclosing on real estate they could not sell. And with securitized mortgages, there was often no way to attach a given property to a single loan. Although some banks made provisions on their balance sheets for nonperforming loans, most refused to "mark to market"—that is, declare values that were fractions of the nominal loan, indeed for which a market had disappeared. Without a value on the loan, it could not be collateralized. A chain reaction of default threatened to work itself through American and then European banks.[66]

Americans looked into the abyss in September 2008, when the Treasury refused to give JPMorgan the guarantees the firm demanded to refinance Lehman Brothers, the venerable overextended financial firm, which for many months had dawdled over offers for a takeover as insufficient. The Treasury's decision not to facilitate the bail-out of Lehman—justified in terms of "moral hazard" or the negative example set by rewarding bad behavior—sent a further crisis of confidence shuddering through the system.[67] Ben Bernanke later wrote that September and October 2008 was the "worst financial crisis in global history, including the Great Depression."[68] Testifying before Congress on October 23, 2008, previous Fed chairman Alan Greenspan professed to be in a state of "shocked disbelief" that banks had been so imprudent.[69] Fans of the film *Casablanca* might have remembered the cynical police chief played by Claude Rains expressing his "shock" that gambling was occurring at Rick's bar. But Greenspan had himself implicitly changed the regulatory principle of American central banking after the dot.com crisis—from keying interest rates to the balance between full employment and currency stability to the continued rise of the stock markets. When Wall Street faltered, rates had been loosened.

Only massive intervention by the Treasury in 2008, authorized by Congress, prevented a systemic collapse. In the United States, the transition from Bush to Obama made little difference—policymakers continued the bailouts—there was no long period of hostility between an overwhelmed GOP administration and an incoming Democratic administration as had happened in 1932–1933, although Republican legislators were clearly not on board with the Bush administration's emergency response. The outgoing

Treasury secretary, Hank Paulson, and Obama's incoming secretary, Tim Geithner, followed the same prescriptions as did Bernanke, the chair of the Fed who was retained by both administrations. They did well in containing the crisis. Paulson won authorization to prop up the de facto bankrupt federal mortgage authorities, Freddie Mac and Fannie Mae over the vote of three-quarters of the GOP congressional delegation. The Democratic Party had felt compelled to rescue Wall Street even as the GOP continued its populist swing to the right. Officials midwifed the purchase of Merrill by the Bank of America and of Bear Stearns by JPMorgan. Lehman's collapse turned the tide in favor of averting the next threatening catastrophe, the looming bankruptcy of reinsurance giant AIG, which teetered on the brink of bankruptcy in September. On September 20, the administration requested authority to purchase up to $700 billion from any US-based financial institution free of judicial or congressional oversight. Congress balked, but in mid-October after the European banking system threatened to implode, the Treasury won approval for an alternate program, less dismissive of Congress: the Troubled Asset Relief Program (TARP). TARP authorized the Treasury to purchase or insure distressed assets, pre-2008 mortgages, and other obligations if "necessary to promote financial market stability." Banks that were selling assets to TARP and receiving cash had issued warrants to purchase nonvoting shares and to surrender preferred stock—in effect, to accept a short-term nationalization.[70]

By March 2009, the Federal Reserve had committed almost $8 trillion to the financial system, over half the GDP of that year. The price of rescuing the banking system and the well-compensated group that made it function seemed to many a moral scandal even though a ceiling was set on bank executives' compensation. To justify the bailout, advocates argued that the government was averting a crisis of liquidity, not of solvency. It made no sense, according to the banks, to value their assets merely at what an emergency sale might yield. They were just strapped temporarily and required the Treasury's backing until their portfolios rose toward a more stable evaluation. Wile E. Coyote just needed to avoid looking down until he reached the other side of the canyon.

The subprime crisis quickly impacted Europe. The greatest volume of private credits flowed between the United States and Europe. Europe's bank claims on the United States had grown from $1.05 to $2.63 trillion between 2002 and 2008. European banks had invested massively in the American mortgage market. They issued asset-based commercial paper dollar-denominated loans via "conduits" with lower capital requirements than their banks. Collectively, what were known as shadow-banking assets (held off the main bank balance sheets) grew from near zero in 1980 to $15–$20 trillion in 2008.[71] The Dutch proposed a joint emergency fund for rescues, but the Germans vetoed the proposal despite the fact that Germany's major mortgage lender, Hypo Real Estate, was in grave trouble. Most in danger were the Irish banks, which had inflated a real estate boom by taking on loans worth seven times the country's GDP. The Dublin government decided to extend a blanket guarantee, thus taking the country's treasury and taxpayers hostage. One of the afflicted Irish institutions, moreover, was essentially a branch of Germany's troubled Hypo Real Estate and threatened to bring it down alongside the Irish wreckage. Chancellor Angela Merkel and Finance Minister Peer Steinbrück, the SPD's leading coalition member, together felt it necessary to reassure German savers as to the health of the country's banks by extending a €68 billion line of credit in early October. Outside Germany, it was taken as a message that everyone who was not a German should worry about their deposits and their equities, which lost $2 trillion in value the following day. In Britain, the Royal Bank of Scotland seemed on the verge of collapse. The Labour cabinet, which had a solid majority, pushed through a scheme that amounted to quasi-nationalization if the big banks chose to accept its guarantees: up to £50 billion in cash for bank stock and £450 billion for debt guarantees and purchase of distressed asset-based securities by the treasury.

The European banks were also deeply threatened by the US crisis even as their travails threatened American institutions. European central banks faced dollar demands they could not cover without dumping dollar-denominated assets in the United States. What helped to save the transatlantic financial network between 2008 and 2010 was the Federal Reserve's massive deployment of "swap" agreements. The Fed accepted the European central banks' domestic loans, and above all the European Central Bank's (ECB's) loans made to national banks, at their face value in euros and provided dollar loans in return. To the degree that Europe required dollars, the Fed became its bankers until the European positions could be redeemed. If American banking recklessness (certainly matched by irresponsibility in Ireland and elsewhere) had helped to create the crisis of prodigal banking, American officials at least invented the expedients to extinguish the blaze.[72] They were very aware of the catastrophic implosion at home in 1929 and the international financial system's collapse in 1931 and ended up providing 3½ to 7½ times the liquidity that had been considered available in the Great Depression.[73] Looking ahead in the chronology of rescue, there was a kerfuffle of signals in 2013 that the Federal Reserve might try to pull back on its stimulus, but conditions seemed too precarious. In the fall of 2013, the temporary swaps among the six major banks—the Fed, the ECB, and the national banks of England, Japan, Canada, and Switzerland—were extended indefinitely. Emerging markets were guaranteed indirectly as the Bank of Japan offered expanded swap facilities to India, Indonesia, and the Philippines and potentially Singapore, Thailand, and Malaysia.[74] Papa Fed and Mamma ECB helped their prodigal children to survive but not without a large dose of suffering.

The cost of the crisis was immense. Over 9 million US homes were lost as mortgages were foreclosed. Chrysler and General Motors went bankrupt— the enterprises would be refloated, but the value of existing equity was wiped out. The Bank of America teetered on the edge. African-American unemployment rates doubled. Mexican exports, employment, and remittances from the United States dried up. Japanese autos, Toyota in the lead, and electronics fell. The advanced economies plunged from about a 3 percent growth rate to a 3 percent contraction; emerging market and developing countries dropped from about 8 percent to 4 percent. German exports fell by a third. American household wealth, according to different estimates, fell from 22 trillion to 19 trillion, as if Americans had lost one and a half times all that they had produced during the year before the great recession began. Gross world capital flows fell from 30 percent of global GDP in 2007 to under 3 percent in 2008 and 2009.[75]

As in 1929–1931, there had been no way to contain the crisis. The Eurozone would spend the next several years agonizing about its internal imbalances. Banks began to suspect each other's solvency from August 2007, and the interest rate discrepancies widened between their interbank loans and solid "sovereign" or national debt (German ten-year bonds, known as Bunds, were the gold standard). The aggregate deposits of Eurozone commercial banks to each other fell from €2,800 billion to €643 billion between the summer of 2007 and summer of 2012. Banks hunkered down and moved their assets to the national central banks and the ECB.[76] But state credit was also far from immune.

Between fall 2008 and early 2009, the Irish state decided it must bail out its vastly overextended banking sector including nationalization of the Anglo Irish Bank, thus taking on almost €500 billion in liabilities. The Irish had benefited hugely from EU development funds since entering the European

Economic Community and enjoyed a boom in housing and hotel building. Banking sector assets rose from four times GDP in 2004 to eight times GDP five years later. Only Iceland, with a tenth of the population, borrowed and lent more lavishly.[77] By 2010, the Irish government went tail between its legs (and divided) to the ECB. The ECB was willing to help Dublin and the central bank of Ireland bail out its banks—but only if the government would compel taxpayers to "lean in"—that is, to pledge public funds to meet the debt to the degree necessary. Otherwise, they reasoned, Ireland would become the Eurozone's Lehman, as the head of the Irish central bank argued it had the potential to become. This was, according to the sharp judgment of the *Financial Times'* chronicler, "a preposterous comparison. Lehman . . . was a global bank with a balance sheet in the trillions . . . at the heart of the world's financial plumbing. Anglo, by contrast, was a small racket on Europe's financial periphery, busily and exuberantly losing its investors' money in the time-honoured way of lending more for houses than they were worth."[78]

From the tempests of the Irish Sea to the seductive waters of the Aegean: the Greeks had piled up state debts from the 1980s on as the country basked in EU membership. Tax avoidance was easy sport for the wealthy. Much of Greece's debt had been contracted in drachma which might have been devalued or inflated away before 2001. Once the euro replaced the drachma in 2001, Greece acquired the capacity to import far beyond the value of its exports or tourist services it offered, but its foreign debt was in a currency it could no longer manipulate. The Greek Socialists, PASOK, replaced the conservative New Democracy in October 2009, after the latter party had revealed that the country's budget deficit was almost 14 percent, way beyond Maastricht criterion. By late 2009, the government's debt was 130 percent of GDP; its budget deficit was close to 16 percent and its current account deficit about the same. Rolling over earlier loans from foreign lenders would have brought punishing interest payments.[79]

The fragility, moreover, extended beyond Greece. National banks in the Eurozone (which continued to function in effect as regional banks even after the establishment of the ECB) had to step up lending to their own country's commercial banks and borrowed from the ECB to do so, while national banks that had built up surplus lent to the ECB. By 2012, the Bundesbank surplus rose to 739 billion, while Spanish and Italian deficits rose to 404 billion and 265 billion, respectively—not as high in percentage of GDP as Greece's but disquieting nonetheless. American swap lines, which had buffered the Eurozone banks' exposure to the subprime crisis of 2007–2010 were reopened but played much less of a role in the Eurozone's own crisis of 2011–2012. As they extended loans to their national commercial banks, the consolidated accounts of Eurozone national central banks, rediscounted in effect at the ECB, grew by almost 60 percent between June 2011 and July 2012, reaching the equivalent of one-third of the euro area's GDP.[80] And the small Greek financial system was the crater where the Eurozone threatened to blow.

What followed was a long melodrama that almost ruptured the Eurozone.[81] Given the fact that Greek national income was only 4 percent of the Eurozone's, its impact cannot be understood without understanding that Europe's banks were all each other's creditors and Spain and Italy's banks were also potentially shaky. All required creditors to roll over loans to their debtors. Loans to Spain, Portugal, Spain, and Greece amounted to $2.5 trillion or about $2 trillion, and Spain like Ireland had a vastly overextended real estate sector in debt. By May 2010, Greece was unable to borrow on the capital markets and negotiated a three-year economic adjustment program financed by the EU, the IMF, and the ECB, the so-called troika, a policy that Adam Tooze calls "pretend and extend." Bringing in the IMF was a confession of weakness the Europeans did not like; nonetheless, IMF director Jean-Claude Trichet's ominous warnings were accompanied by a new facility to Greece of €110 billion and €750 billion for a reserve for other European governments. Germany accepted the package as a final recourse, an ultima ratio, but insisted on saddling Greece with supervision by the troika representatives to monitor its behavior. Of course, the more that austerity was applied with its increase of interest rates, privatization of state enterprises, and paring of public employees, the less able Athens would be to meet its terms of payback. Even had it miraculously turned the corner, the stock of overhanging debt made commercial loans impossible. The debt burden grew as the GDP fell, Athens would have to pay 7 percent of its GDP each year to its creditors, a transfer burden higher than any imposed by reparations after World War I. Austerity policies fixated on labor costs, but they would be lightened by sacking workers. Public sector employees remained protected because they could not be effectively leaned on.

By July 2011, it was understood that the original program could not be met. The IMF recognized that the debt must be restructured with "private sector involvement"—that is, a reduction of the sum owed or a "haircut." Bondholders—many of them German banks—would have to agree to some "voluntary" reduction of the money they had lent, whether by extending the payoff date, or reduction of interest payments, or in the worst case which soon proved necessary, by outright reduction of the principal. By July 2011, the IMF urged voluntary rollovers or deadline extensions. The EU summit in September agreed to a 21 percent reduction of the debt's present value by means of lowering the interest payments and extension of maturities, assuming bondholders signed on. As recession deepened, all these projections seemed clearly unfeasible. Meanwhile, a major American firm, MF Global Holdings, with its large holdings of Greek debt, filed for bankruptcy, following the Franco-Belgian Dexia SA bank a year earlier, victim of its overextension into real estate.

The Greeks wanted an outright reduction of the face value of the debt. But this was hardly the German or Dutch point of view. Northern Europeans paid their debts; why should their industrious citizens have to cover the improvident borrowing on the part of the dolce far niente folk of the south or even the hearty drinkers of the incestuous financial community in Dublin? (The idea of charging the virtuous burghers of the north an EU sunshine tax to enjoy Costa Brava or Aegean beaches, tacked on, say, to Mediterranean hotel bills, lay beyond the imagination of sober bankers.) The ECB claimed to fear unilateral debt reduction on the grounds that the bank could not accept sovereign bonds of a defaulting country as collateral. This problem was solved, however, by activating an exceptional liquidity assistance facility, a new EU mechanism for backing up commercial debt with a layer of public debt.

Athens still retained the leverage of threatening desperate measure. The Greeks might find a majority of debtholders to agree to a haircut and then compel the unwilling minority of creditors to go along by introducing so-called compulsory action clauses. Unilaterally imposing a write-down on the holdouts, however, would constitute a "credit event" that would allow the purchasers of credit default swaps to collect on the policies. So, too, would a unilateral Greek crashing out of the Eurozone, although German finance minister Wolfgang Schäuble suggested that if the Greeks did revert to the drachma, devalued the national currency, and then rejoined the Eurozone at a lower drachma-euro rate than the first time, it would have been a preferable solution.

At this point, non-Greek agencies wanted an agreed-on solution and were negotiating a new rescue package. Prime Minister George Papandreou's announcement in late October 2011 that the package being negotiated would be put to the voters in a referendum infuriated the creditors who pressed him into modifying and ultimately withdrawing the national poll in favor of a parliamentary vote. It was up to the G-20 meeting in Cannes in November 2011 and the EU summit a month later to find a solution to recapitalizing the Greek debt and finding a "safety net" to keep Italy and Spain from sliding into insolvency.

A new debt restructuring agreement aimed at reducing the country's debt-to-GDP ratio from 165 percent to 120 percent by 2020 was hammered out in March 2012. It would require Greek government bondholders to exchange their paper for new bonds with a face value of 31.5 percent of the old debt to mature between ten and thirty years along with a sweetener of short-term notes amounting to another 15 percent. In total, €198 billion of old bonds were exchanged for €92 billion of new European facility notes (15 percent and Greek bonds 31.5 percent), while €106 billion or 53.5 percent was to be annulled. The CEO of the German Commerzbank commented that the new agreement was as freely consented to by creditors as "a voluntary confession at the Spanish inquisition."[82] The market value of the new bonds, moreover, fell to about 20 percent of face value, so the write-off was far higher than the nominal 53 percent. Even so, this amputation hardly provided a long-term rescue for Greek finances, and the grinding pressure on the Greek economy continued. The exchange wiped out €106 billion of old debt—of which Greek banks held 36 percent—but added €30 billion of new debt. The burden of interest payments diminished. The holdout creditors were in fact paid off fully to avoid the complexities of outright default. In the eyes of one of its chroniclers, the Greek debt buy-back and haircut supposedly demonstrated that "an orderly default can take place within the euro area."[83] This white-knuckle financial ride, however, certainly stretched the meaning of "orderly," but it could have been accomplished with less Sturm und Drang and misery far earlier.

The political and social fallout in Greece over the next few years was hardly orderly. Two national elections formed a vivid political backdrop. Contenders included a new apparently radical party, Syriza, and a neo-Nazi party, Golden Dawn. The first vote in May 2012 yielded no parliamentary majority; the second on June 17 produced a three-party coalition that kept the new left-wing Syriza from office. Debt sustainability seemed further away than ever and compelled the Eurogroup by November to postpone interest payments and to allow the Greek debt agency to buy back half the debt it had issued at the vastly lower prices now prevailing. The Germans, however, insisted on further austerity programs even as Greek unemployment mounted and public services such as health care deteriorated. Syriza won the elections in 2015 but emerged as less frightening than it had earlier appeared; its leader, Alexis Tsipras, was committed to staying in the Eurozone.

Even the Germans had to realize that austerity would only raise unemployment and make it ever less possible for Greeks to balance their budget. But their difficulty to apply this insight resembled their inability to grasp that not every country in the world could have a net positive balance on current account. Berlin kept insisting that the Eurozone could not be a transfer union. But if German financial officials refused to sanction the principle of debt forgiveness, they did agree to extend further euro loans. This not only saved the Eurozone from a potential collapse of the joint currency but also precluded a more fundamental reform. A survey of Atlantic monetary history since the Bretton Woods system came apart at the beginning of the 1970s suggests that the strong fiscal powers never relinquished their power to inflict hardship but would draw back from absolutely bankrupting the currency periphery since so many of their own credit institutions were involved. Just as China and the United States were locked into, a pact of mutual dependency that would hurt both if disavowed, so euro debtors and creditors were locked into their own unhappy marriage that limited the agony they could accept and impose.

Respectable conventional opinion would soon argue that instituting the common currency had been a great error since at the European level, no common fiscal responsibilities could be imposed while at the national level, no single-currency devaluation was possible. In fact, the pain inflicted on outside countries with a laxer fiscal system was not so different. The joblessness, hunger, and misery in Thailand, Russia, and Argentina proved as bad as the lingering austerity within the Eurozone. The voices of fiscal rectitude blamed irresponsible borrowing for half a century, whether by Latin America in the 1970s and 1980s, or by American home buyers in the 1990s and 2000s, Greeks and Italians in the years through 2012. But for half a century, the ability to print money equivalents had been effectively delegated to private lenders who made their profits by placing loans at interest, getting commissions on the syndication, selling the credit instruments as if they were far solider investments than they were and, finally, surrounding their claims with the aura of sacred writ. "At the root," one of its most clear-sighted and optimistic historian writes, "the eurozone's crisis is a result of ideological resistance to writing down debts—whether those of the banks or those of sovereigns."[84]

Looking back over these crises, it could be argued that the great project of the neoliberals who dominated the capitalist world of the 1980s for at least a generation was not really one of reducing the role of the state in the economy or enlarging the scope of markets. It was rather one of redistributing income to those who had been able to gather financial claims on the future from those who had to accept lower earnings in the present. The reluctance to envisage or acknowledge this result testified to a shift in values among the center-left parties who should have been committed to preventing such an outcome. It followed the discovery that by financializing the future, so to speak, and selling its imputed value in the present, society could transfer wealth to those who understood how to profit. One did not have to save in the present to spend in the future. "Pie in the sky by and by" could become "Cake to take here and now," a process of financial alchemy and upward redistribution. The representatives of governance, capital, and the state seemed tacitly to endorse this process or at least did not know how to prevent it. And since the aggregate material welfare of global society managed to increase over the long term thanks to its industry and technological inventiveness, they deemed the distributive consequences of less importance.

What followed in the years after America's "subprime crisis" and the euro's Greek drama was a half decade or more of stagnating real incomes labeled "austerity" in which the advanced economies fared the poorest, until all were hit by the relatively exogenous economic shutdown forced by COVID-19 in late 2019. The consequences of the aftermath will be taken up in the following chapter, but we should briefly ask how we can best think about the decade or so of capitalist crisis after 2008. Within the United States, the Democratic Party had done more to rescue capitalism than the GOP— in 2008 as in 1933. The international economy had been saved from the effects of a financial Chernobyl because the American government refloated the banking system, and the ECB under "Super Mario" Draghi kept the euro afloat. Saving the financial armature of the Atlantic economy had seemed the most urgent task. Had it not been done, the suffering on Main Street would doubtless have been far greater.

The realm of capital had in fact dominated the political economy since the 1980s; the American state—Congress and the president, the Treasury and the Federal Reserve—had defined their role as clearing away the obstacles for the economy throughout. The government became a booster, cheerleader, and finally, a rescuer for finance. The costs were high, above all in minority communities. Whether myth or memory, the American social ballast of industrial craftsmen morphed into an army of big-box store clerks, call-center respondents, private security guards, and indispensable health-care workers. As a counterpart to "hoop dreams" for minority kids, McKinsey consultancies and Goldman Sachs internships motivated privileged youth. Similar trends prevailed in Europe, where the United Kingdom's financial community, and German exporters set the rules for rescuing the Greeks and others from outright misery.

Insofar as "austerity" dictated the terms of rescue for "the periphery" or the global south (which, as of the new century, began in Greece), it carried on the stratification imposed by earlier resource empires. The currency union was in some senses halfhearted. Greece, Portugal, even Italy were deemed the periphery; no one talked of the periphery for the dollar or the pound. Even the Germans had worked to make sure that the former GDR would not be a financial periphery inside their reunited country. (They did less well in recuing East Germany's real economy.) But they could not overcome their own sense of a frontier within the EU. Greece was a place to vacation. Meanwhile, the mandarins of governance divided, many ratifying the new power of capital, others fretting that its victory seemed so costly for the poor.

Had there been a resilient social democratic coalition less haunted by the momentous transformations of the 1970s or a conservative-centrist coalition less concerned about possible moral hazard, these social losers might have pushed through the policies advocated by the left half a century earlier and in fact partially instituted during the Ur-crisis of 1929–1936 and the postwar recovery years from 1945 to 1950. By 2015, a left populist party in Greece, Syriza, achieved power by running against the policies imposed by the EU; but once in power, they too had to yield to imperatives of EU supervision. Their finance minister, Yaris Varoufakis, who delighted in scaring the Germans by his rock star appearances on television, was quietly disavowed by Prime Minister Tsipras, much as Germany's Social Democratic chancellor Gerhard Schroeder had pushed aside his theatrical left-wing party comrade Oskar Lafontaine after their victory in 1998. On a European-wide scale, the Communist left had imploded and the non-Communist left might win elections but could not impose a more egalitarian economy after the wreckage of state socialism at the end of the 1980s. Nor did they really want to. Having instituted welfare state reforms, the social-democratic center-left believed it had completed its economic program and now had to tend to noneconomic issues—gender, race, sexual expressiveness, and the fight against terrorism.

Other forces, however, would capitalize on the sense of grievance that the great crisis and recession had bequeathed. The drama of populism and the authoritarians who exploited it would reveal the legacy of the convergences cemented in the early twenty-first century.

10

The Populist Assertion and the Return of Authoritarianism

Viktor Orbán, Hungarian prime minister from 1998 to 2002, again since 2010, and reconfirmed in power by a two-thirds majority in April 2022, recognized the connection between the financial tsunami of 2008 and his era's political transformations. Fresh from his decisive electoral success in 2014, he told his Fidesz party adherents that the crisis of 2008 was a regime changer comparable to the upheavals of the previous century: "For our generation the regime change is the generational experience to which we compare everything, against which we measure everything, whence we start to define everything that happens around us." In the twentieth century, "there were three major world-regime changes. At the end of World War I, at the end of World War II, and in 1990. . . . When the changes took place it was clear for all of us that we were going to live in a different world overnight. . . . The basic point of my talk here is that the changes in the world nowadays have similar value and weight. We can identify its manifestation—that point when it became clear—as the financial crisis of 2008, or rather the Western financial crisis."

What lesson had to be drawn? The most important issue was not a race for economic competitiveness. Rather, it was the race "to invent a state that is most capable of making a nation successful. . . . This is why a trending topic is understanding systems that are not Western, not liberal, not liberal democracies, maybe not even democracies. . . . Today the stars are Singapore, China, India, Turkey, Russia. . . . We are searching for . . . ways of parting with Western European dogmas [and finding] the form of organizing a community that is capable of making us competitive in this great world race. . . . We needed to state that a democracy is not necessarily liberal." Liberal democracy could not protect the nation or its weaker members. The "Hungarian nation is not a simple sum of individuals, but a community that needs to be organized, strengthened and developed, and in this sense the new state that we are building is an illiberal state, a non-liberal state."[1]

Orbán's speech—as coherent and ideologically grounded as any provided by the leaders we think of as populist—sets the agenda for the final chapter of our history. He compels us to interrogate what today's populism represents and its relation to nation and state. The Fidesz leader's speech presupposed the existence of a Hungarian or Mágyar nation, but it was not nationalist per se. Nationalism has been and remains a powerful force, but the community that nationalism conjures up identifies itself in opposition to other external nations, and it seeks a state to provide a protective political structure for a people or *Volk*. Orbán was not demanding, at least not in this statement, political rights for the Hungarian-speaking irridenta in neighboring Romania, as Hungarian nationalists have periodically called for since the 1919 Treaty of Trianon that reduced their historic kingdom. Populists can be nationalist in this sense, but the community they usually invoke is already understood to exist as a nation, albeit one beleaguered and in peril. Globalization threatens, but the right sort of community could prosper in a multicultural world—witness Singapore, China, India, and Turkey. Ethnic cohesion was important, but Orbán was not singling out minorities such as the Roma as a preeminent danger; antisemitic tropes might linger in the background but they were not central. The peril that had to be overcome derived from liberal ideas, the attractions of cosmopolitanism, and the right to adversarial politics.

And what of the state Orbán envisaged? Was it a project-state in the sense used in this book? Orbán may have believed so, but the project was reduced to protection of the ethnic community. Some persuasive critics would describe Orbán's achievement as "the post-communist mafia state."[2] This chapter will return to the typology of states at the end. Populism, its relationship to a revived authoritarianism, and the options for the state are all intertwined. They constitute the knot that this chapter must struggle to unravel.

Creating the People

Populism had a long history on many continents and revealed many variants; by the twenty-first century, journalists and social scientists struggled to pin down its elusive common elements. The term had a venerable past, suggesting the collective political power of the people, usually counterposed against a smaller privileged group in the same political unit: ancient Rome's state was summarized as the Senate and People of Rome, SPQR, a designation still stamped by the municipality on the manhole covers of the Eternal City. In the mid-1870s, enthusiastic Russian students had decided they should go to the people, the *Narod*—that is, undertake peasant community organizing. The Narodniki formed part of a continuing debate as to Russia's destiny: whether to become liberal and "Western," or to nurture its Slavic, Orthodox, and communal virtues. In the United States, populism referred to the political "People's Parties" that developed out of the movements of agrarian protest in the South and West during the 1880s and 1890s. They had organized as the terms of trade turned strongly against agriculture in the late nineteenth century and as a twenty-year deflationary trend in currency values made it harder to pay off their mortgages and the seasonal loans they so depended on. In a vast region where transportation of their grains to market was so dependent on railroads, they protested, too, against the pricing policy of the railroads, which effectively charged sparsely populated states and counties higher rates than those that bore a denser traffic. In Wilhelmian Germany, Volksparteien with pronounced anti-Semitic rhetoric emerged in rural Bavaria and Hessen as agricultural prices declined in the late 1870s. They were connected with the movement to develop alternative sources of credit, such as the Raffeisen banks, to the urban banks they saw as exploitative.[3] Piles of debt often provide the backdrop for the populist drama.

American populists saw salvation in inflation of currency through the un-limited coinage of silver, which until 1896 remained less restrictive a reserve medium than gold. They generated communal institutions and a critique of capitalism.[4] As third parties, they won local elections but could not over-come the electoral system to win a national presidential poll. Nonetheless, they managed to influence the Democratic Party sufficiently to nominate Williams Jennings Bryan in 1896 and make the election a fundamental refer-endum on the economic direction of the country: an orientation toward debtors and agrarian production or a reaffirmation of an industrial future. As Richard Hofstadter famously pointed out, a vast current of conspirato-rial thinking swirled up with this confrontation.[5] Populist rhetoric criticized remote eastern bankers sometimes identified as Jewish and counterposed their manipulative urban ways against the wholesome and beset agrarian producers of the heartland. Henry Adams supported the Silverites against the gold forces, which he along with less genteel protesters sometimes iden-tified with Jewish capital. Hard-pressed agrarian producers yielded to the worldview across Europe, among them Prussian Junker landlords, who managed to have the grain futures market suppressed for a decade after 1896. Thirty-five years later, Ezra Pound would recycle the rhetoric into a frenetic advocacy for Benito Mussolini's Italy: "Jefferson and / or Mussolini," which praised the supposed similarity of the two leaders: "When a single mind is sufficiently ahead of the mass a one-party system is bound to *occur as actuality* whatever the details of form in administration. . . . When a corrupt oligarchy of any nature controls a country, they will very probably set up in theory a two-party system, controlling both of these parties."[6]

Not all invocations of the people in the first half of the twentieth century were populist in the contemporary sense. In the brief and ideologically fractured democratic years after World War I in Italy, the emerging Catholic party, simply designated as *clericali* before the war, organized itself as the Popolari, spanning a spectrum from conservative landlords to firebrand priests. In the Americas, the first real populist manifestation arrived arguably with the Peruvian elections of 1931 when both presidential candidates mobilized the socially marginalized against a supposedly "self-interested antinational, oligarchical elite."[7] The appeal to the virtuous people was too useful not to be claimed by the Third International as its leaders blessed Popular Fronts in the mid-1930s, or at the end of World War II sponsored "People's Democracies in Eastern Europe" to cover their Communist Party sympathizers' seizure of decisive political control.

But the most fraught legacy of populism has remained that between today's movements and classical fascism. Mussolini had built a real regime by the late 1920s; the German National Socialists would make their electoral breakthrough in September 1930. In Latin America, a latent fascist movement emerged with Argentine general José Félix Uriburu who seized power in 1930.[8] Outright fascism (including the Nazi variant) and contemporary populism have been fluid movements and have shared many elements, but fascism stressed military virtues and the vitality produced by conflict. Fascist party success was made plausible by the Great War and Communist revolutions, whereas earlier populist movements could arise as a more general response to relative economic deprivation. The movements of the 1930s and 1940s led historians and social scientists to discriminate between movements such as Huey Long's or the Peróns' populism and European fascism. More recently, some separate a "left" populism including the Kirchners of Argentina or the Peruvian Apristas from a "right" populism that embraced neoliberal policies from the 1980s and 1990s, even as they vociferously attacked economic elites.[9]

What distinguishes contemporary populist ideas is not just the belief that some core of good, familiar folk form a nation but that there exist at least two sorts of people in any polity: a virtuous, usually ethnically uniform core and a collection of ultimately parasitic hangers-on, whether intellectuals or immigrants or politicians—a mass infestation of updated "caterpillars of the commonwealth."[10] In fact, no parasites, no people. The "people" are summoned into life when the nonpeople, the exploitative outsiders, somehow fundamentally alien, are conjured into existence. Populism is a dialectical term that evokes enemies, whether intentional or not. Those who use the term are precisely those who feel themselves impugned, often as intellectuals and cosmopolitans, hence condemned as an elite by virtue of education if not great wealth.[11] Populism thus envisages society as a "dipole," the term used to describe a magnet with its two poles, north and south, each of which can exist normally only as one of the pair.

But populism involves a dipole in a further sense. It requires a people's tribune or political entrepreneur, a would-be strong man, a leader waiting to summon the people or at least define it as a political group. Antiquity provided the model for Caesarism; Karl Marx and Friedrich Engels elaborated a case study in *The Eighteenth Brumaire* and conveyed the striking image of the French peasantry as potatoes in a sack: a class *in itself*—that is, possessing common socioeconomic traits—but not yet *for itself*—that is, without the capacity and collective insight to act as a class. It was the genius of Louis Napoleon to mobilize this political potential, to have himself elected president of the Second French Republic, then to undermine and eliminate its parliament, and to use the plebiscite, or polarized yes-no vote, the ancestor of our referenda, to make himself emperor. But even plebiscitary elections have become unreliable. The opposition is forced into silence or threatened with reprisal. Results are contested, and if they go against the incumbent, they are denounced as fraudulent or stolen. Nicolás Maduro of Venezuela and Alexander Lukashenko of Belarus insist they secured robust majorities in 2018 and 2020, respectively; Donald Trump remains confident that he could not have lost in 2020.

It is the apparent bond between the leader and his supporters that initially seizes attention among the current movements and regimes. A crowd assembled for a rally apparently confirms the resonance between the leader and a national people supposedly victimized by elites and globalization; it demonstrates legitimacy enough. The historian needs to recall the emotional power of crowd action: that brief fusion of individual wills that occurs in moments of crisis, such as the beginning of a war, confrontations in the street, perhaps civil rights marches, or enthusiasm for a leader—recall even the enthusiasm at old-fashioned American political conventions. Populist movements require continuous efforts at organization, but participation in them often rests on genuine collective and liminal experiences as outlined by classical sociologists such as Émile Durkheim or Victor Turner. Participants have the sense of making history, of tearing down the Bastille or the Berlin Wall or of listening to Martin Luther King Jr. on the Washington Mall. Such experiences make political participation seem urgent, transformative, and transcendent. Without that possibility, they would not change history or make it so dangerous.[12]

Movements and Political Entrepreneurs in the Twenty-First Century

The success of populist leaders does not rest solely on the personal magnetism of the leader. The ideological menu has been critical. The appeal to nonmaterialist values, whether nationalist or religious, has been key to the success of movements, which have had little choice since the late nineteenth century but to compete under conditions of mass suffrage. Those recruited have recognized that playing the values or identity card conventionally thought of as right-wing—whether religious loyalty, or nationalism and xenophobia— can overcome collectivist or redistributionist economic programs. Witness authoritarian nationalism in the French Third Republic, or Tory Democracy in late Victorian England, or the adhesion of landlords and industrialists to interwar fascism and Nazism, and the loyalty of American Evangelicals to the Republican Party.

Alongside shared ideas and values, populist coalitions represent complex networks of interest with different stakes in economic outcomes. As the history of populist movements in Turkey and India reveal, it also requires attention to the ground-level networks and political deals underlying what appear as monolithic ideological movements and thus, too, the premises of state authority.[13] The populist regime depends on electoral success, and this is achieved molecularly by putting together different coalitions, appealing to the mosaic of interests within different federal states or local constituencies, as documented clearly in the case of the Bharatiya Janata Party's (BJP's) success in the world's largest electoral democracy, India.[14] Energized by their hopes in the leader who promises political redemption, parties serve as the workhorses for populist success. But once the regime is established, they are often left to become cogs for patronage and management: Italy's fascists,

France's Gaullists, Mexico's Institutional Revolutionary Party (PRI), India's BJP, and Trump's Republicans reveal comparable trajectories.

The populist movements of the late nineteenth century arose in a particular economic conjuncture of tightening money and depressed agricultural prices. In its most recent phase, populism benefited from the aftermath of the financial crisis. But gifted, often demagogic political entrepreneurship was critical. For a leading American analyst of Peruvian populism, the key element in its emergence was not the structural conditions of a stratified society and exploitative economy but the inventiveness of the contending candidates.[15] Juan and Eva Perón in Argentina and Getúlio Vargas in Brazil were attracted by fascism and ideologies of the corporative state and convinced of their electric rapport with the people—as was Huey Long, in that picturesque United States variant of Latin America, Louisiana. Peronismo invented its mass collective interlocutor, the *decamisados* (*sans chemises* in French, an updating of *sans culottes*, might be more suggestive than "shirtless"), but the Peronist movement and party also penetrated the highly developed associational life of this most European of Latin American societies.[16] In Argentina, ethnic identity and skin tint played less of a role than elsewhere in the Americas where ethnic awareness played a massive role, whether as a motif for reclaiming an indigenous heritage or uniting against ethnic enemies. In Mexico, affirmation of indigenous identity played a huge role during waves of reform, and it helped let Lázaro Cárdenas perfect a mass democratic movement without recourse to militarist repression. As of the 1950s, the APRA (American Popular Revolutionary Alliance) of Peru led by Alan García from 1985 to 1990, remained probably the most coherent populist challenge, and outside of Latin America there was little reference to the phenomenon. With the economic difficulties of the 1970s, it returned and after the relatively liberal interlude of the 1980s returned again in the 1990s in the form of "electoral authoritarianism," sometimes contending with a Marxist guerrilla left: Alberto Fujimori in the wake of the Sendero Luminoso (Shining Path); Hugo Chávez, president of Venezuela, followed by Maduro; Evo Morales in Bolivia; Rafael Correa in Ecuador.[17] As single-party regimes unravel, whether in Poland or Mexico, the opposition that emerges is entrusted with a degree of authority that often succumbs to a populist temptation over time, as occurred with the strand of Solidarność that held on to power and became the Law and Justice Party (PIS), or Mexico's populist challenge to the PRI, originally the Party of the Democratic Revolution (PRD) in the 1980s led by Cuauhtémoc Cárdenas and represented today by Andrés Manuel López Obrador (AMLO).

Eastern Europe proved a receptive region for populist authoritarianism. Poland's post-1989 trajectory was predictable enough. The opposition of the 1980s to the Communist state rested on uneasily allied currents: on the one side, the fusion of workers and intellectuals represented by the Workers' Defense Committee (KOR), the Gdańsk shipyard workers led by Lech Wałęsa, and the newspaper *Gazeta Wyborcza* edited by Adam Michnik along with Western-oriented dissidents; on the other side, the forces of rural and Catholic traditionalism. Wałęsa uneasily straddled the two currents but could not prevent the formal division of Solidarity. The more liberal wing kept the presidency of the country for a decade but then lost to the populist PIS dominated by the Kaczyński brothers. In Czechoslovakia, it was logical enough to put Václav Havel in Prague Castle as president in 1990, but the Civic Union that had led the demonstrations soon divided: Catholic traditionalism was weaker, but neoliberalism grew stronger—all the more so after the autocratic leaders of its two constituent republics agreed on the dissolution of the overarching nation created in 1918. Havel's successor, Václav Klaus, aligned the Czech Republic with the Thatcherite program he had learned from the 1980s. Slovakia, permeated by the survivors from the Communist days, supported an earlier reform Communist Party official would-be strong man, Vladimír Mečiar (1990–1991 / 1992–1998) and built an industrial economy with close ties to German manufacturing in the formerly more agrarian half of the country. Neoliberal development policies remained compatible with populism, in Slovakia, Hungary, and Latin America. They allowed the new political leadership to develop private industrial clienteles at the expense of the older party-oriented elites.[18]

Most remarkable in Europe was perhaps the transformation of the Fidesz party that had pressed the transition in Hungary in 1989–1990. Given its two-thirds majority from 2010, the Hungarian government was able to gut social welfare and remove social and tax legislation from the scrutiny of the constitutional court. All this was accompanied by a continuing background of denunciations of interference by the European Union (EU) and George Soros and the alleged hostile political influence of the Soros-funded Central European University.[19] Orbán, however, has brought or at least claimed to represent not merely a regime but an idea of the state and a vision of history, whereas other would-be authoritarians who have occupied this political space such as Jair Bolsonaro have made little effort to construct a transformative state. Put differently, their "project" goes little further than perpetuating their own power.

Mostly, they have sought to detour around their existing state institutions and evade judicial oversight, to deal directly with an electoral audience and win their adulation. Some see the need for a party to reach a point where they can cathect directly to the people, but the party is ultimately an instrument for a regime that is highly personalized. The leaders construct the people they need to call on them to rule.

Perhaps the formula has worked best, at least for now, where voters claim affiliation with a leading religion—Recep Erdoğan's patronage of Muslims after secularist Kemalism supported by the military lost its grip on the Turkish electorate and Narendra Modi's mobilization of a cross-class Hindu coalition that successfully demonized the large Muslim population of northern India.[20] "The tyranny of the elites is over," Erdoğan announced after his 2011 electoral victory. His victory did result from the Justice and Development Party's (AKP) rural traditionalists apparently disrespected by Kemalist policies. But according to one of the most penetrating analyses, Erdoğan did not simply construct a free-floating movement as mayor of Istanbul and a rising Islamist politician. He tailored his appeals alternately between two contending Islamic networks, both of which were proscribed by the secular Kemalist and military establishment. One was an emerging sector of entrepreneurs based in Anatolia, committed to a vision of social Islam and supporting Muslim banks and charitable foundations. The other was a religiously motivated movement inspired by the cleric Fethullah Gülen that focused on educating a rising generation of civil servants, teachers, and businessmen linked to the Turkish diasporas in the United States and Germany and the Turkic republics of post-Soviet Central Asia. Gülen himself emigrated to the United States in 1999, but his adherents joined with Erdoğan in forming the AKP in 2001 and winning the parliamentary elections the following year. Both groups prospered during the flush years of economic advance and Arab investment. Erdoğan cultivated both circles to sustain an ambitious regional foreign policy. Gülenists built an impressive international trade network and the country's foreign trade increased after the crisis. But Gülen, ensconced in Pennsylvania, distrusted Erdoğan's increasingly militant Islamist displays and foreign policy, including the unsuccessful gesture of supporting the Palestinians in Gaza. The symbiotic relationship soured quickly, and Gülenist officers attempted a military coup in July 2016. The follow-up was a series of trials and purges of officers and bureaucrats—the rumored alleged "deep state" believed loyal to the spiritual leader over the ocean—and Erdoğan's tighter embrace of autocratic rule and gesture. By the end of 2021, it was not at all certain that his idiosyncratic ultralow interest economic policies designed to unleash a new wave of growth would do more than intensify an impending hyperinflation.

In India, Modi, according to the revealing account by Prashant Jha, created Hindu allegiance by evoking a Muslim enemy and encouraging violence; and he won loyalties among the poor for inconveniencing the rich even as his demonetization of cash caused great hardship among modest shopkeepers. In the massive northwestern state Uttar Pradesh, he could seamlessly build on the paramilitary anti-Muslim networks of the Rashtriya Swayamsevak Sangh (RSS), somewhat as in the late nineteenth century, the recovering Democratic Party machines in the American South could count on the Ku Klux Klan. Modi threw himself into winning elections and managed to keep the loyalty of upper-caste voters even as he won the allegiance of the "untouchable" Dalits. The formula for success in Gujarat, where Modi had built his power base and could brandish his persona as successful industrial leader, differed from the emphasis needed in poor Bihar. "We are still not the natural party of the backwards and Dalits," his lieutenant reported. "We are no longer untouchable for them. But it's fragile. . . . Unless they see us take their side in battles against upper castes, they will not fully trust us."[21] In the meantime, Modi worked to neutralize any potential sources of opposition, intimidating journalists, disempowering local ombudsmen, rebuffing and cowing the state's investigative agencies, and hammering the supreme court into submission. The emerging regime relied on what was early on described as a "deep state" inside the government and a "parallel state" of Hindu nationalist vigilante groups outside, "who have no official government position, but nevertheless advise BJP ministers or chief ministers." Since the elections of 2014, vigilantism and anti-Muslim violence have continued, while the alleged "deep state" came out into the open.[22]

In India, as in Hungary and the United States, the construction of a cross-class alliance has been both essential and, at first glance, implausible. Political entrepreneurs skillfully mobilize the countries' economically marginalized or threatened groups—whether Dalits in India or industrial workers in Europe and the United States displaced by globalization—to create an electoral bloc but then pass tax and welfare "reforms" that benefit the well-off. Populism thus appeared to India's elite as an antidote to caste politics that had empowered plebian groups. The decay of the Congress Party facilitated BJP success. Tied to a declining Gandhian dynasty, it often disdained the voters from the states that Congress activists saw as the "cow belt." By the 1990s, its secular vision no longer functioned even among the economically successful, who signed on to a Hinduist movement whose rhetoric seemed designed to demonize them.

As this book went to press, it was unclear whether the success of populist movements had crested or will still run strong. The strong man's dynamic assault on left-right politics might either run against the reefs of financial reality as in Turkey or have to settle into a more workaday authoritarianism as in Hungary, or even try to behave as normal political contenders. Electoral calculations still matter. In late 2021, even Prime Minister Modi had to withdraw his proposals to encourage agrobusiness before the robust opposition of farmers and the prospect of important state elections. On the other hand, Hindu crowds still call for violence against Muslims.[23] Bolsonaro narrowly lost a run-off presidential election to the left's candidate, Lula. He had built no institutionally based regime.[24] Populism reveals the power of societal networks and interest groups, the need to aggregate constituencies and not just carry away mass sentiment. Thus, it also demonstrates the autonomy of politics and the decisive role of political work. It recalls the brutal importance of what Carl Schmitt, perhaps the most penetrating right-wing theorist of the last century, described as the struggle between friend and foe, us and them. Schmitt, however, assumed that that distinction had to be inherent in a world of states. The populist leader took no chances and understood it had to be groomed and nurtured.

No one can predict whether current reversals or wavering indicates the general exhaustion of populist politics or just a temporary phase that the leader will resolve by another bout of dramatic authoritarian measures backed by mass rallies. At the end of 1924, Mussolini's still-ambiguous dictatorship was shaken by the political class's reaction to his lieutenants' murder of the Socialist opposition leader Giacomo Matteotti. Faced with a mounting wave of disaffection, the fascist leader decisively and publicly opted to wipe out the vestiges of liberalism. Many observers were convinced in 1936–1937 that Adolf Hitler's regime was reverting to ordinary authoritarian politics only to have to deal with Kristallnacht and the Sudeten crisis in 1938 that culminated in Munich. Nonetheless, Mussolini could wager successfully on the support of the monarch in his months of difficulty, and Hitler had already decisively altered the German constitution and its institutions. The very extemporary nature of the populist initiatives of the early twenty-first century had not, as of this date, resulted in institutions. The gutting of the judiciary in Poland, Hungary, Turkey, and India is not yet complete. Compared, say, to the rule of the Egyptian or the Myanmar military or the Chinese Communist

Party at the end of second decade of the twenty-first century, the illiberal populist state was not yet cast in concrete.

The reader will note that this account avoids the term totalitarianism even in discussion of very brutal regimes. Are we not entitled to call the North Korean, the Chinese, and according to some, the government of Vladimir Putin totalitarian? The problem for the political analyst is that the word's meaning has so evolved since appearing toward the mid-twentieth century. Originally, the term was applied by Italian Communists and Socialists as early as the mid-1920s to Mussolini's fascist government; thereafter, the concept was applied to the profoundly violent National Socialist and Soviet regimes as well. When Hannah Arendt and then Carl Friedrich and Zbigniew Brzezinski wrote their works, they envisaged governments that "atomized" the associations of civil society and made arbitrary terror as well as party-led "mobilization" major instruments of rule. The concentration camp and the gulag became the key sites of power, the single party and the political police its controlling device. A suffocating ideology dominated public communication. George Orwell's *1984* served as a literary allegory. By the last third of the century, this continued mobilization of terror and ideology seemed to fade, at least in Europe, while outright military rule without the pretensions of mass enthusiasm, as in Brazil, Chile, Argentina, Egypt, and Syria, loomed as even more cruel. The concept lost purchase as some theorists on the left found totalitarian potential in all states while meticulous historians pointed out the internal divisions and rivalry within the Third Reich and Stalinist Russia. The instruments of communist rule were also reinterpreted. Pervasive control of the media and the attempted monopoly on information became the key to repression. Thus, when the dissenting voices and movements that gained traction in Eastern Europe in the late 1980s revived the term totalitarian, they emphasized less terror than the pervasive warping of the public sphere. The instruments of control had changed: pervasive spying, censorship, prison sentences at times, control of privileges, and access to education as in East Germany but less reliance on the sudden inexplicable singling out of enemies. A decade of liberalization followed after 1989, often with huge opportunities for corruption as public property was privatized and thereafter in some of the successor states, a crude populism and even a renewed authoritarianism. Across the world, as this book goes to press, different modes of consolidating dictatorial power have made themselves felt—prison, "reeducation," censorship, corruption, assassination—all the more cruelly applied in the case of beleaguered rulers or party armies seeking to prevail in a civil war.[25]

Dimensions of Inequality and Revolt

Populism benefits from a two-fold sense of alienation, socioeconomic and cultural. On the one hand, it is a manifestation against the widening gulf between groups hit hard by economic change and those raking in ever greater fortunes, a revolt against the web of capital such as motivated the US "Occupy Wall Street" movement or the Seattle protests against the WTO. This widening gap can be documented statistically. But just as profoundly it is also a revolt against the realm of governance. It springs from a disaffection with what is perceived to be the arrogance of knowledge and expertise. It is manifested, say, in the resistance to prescribed medical procedures such as vaccination or the vote for anti-system parties and even the abstention rate in elections. Consider for example most recently the jump in abstentions as well as the vote for Georgia Meloni's Fratelli d'Italia in the Italian parliamentary vote in September 1922. Consider the revolt against capital and the revolt against governance sequentially.

Not the inequality itself but its manifestation condenses the discontent into usable politics.[26] The populist leader understands how to exploit the moment of disillusion: "We"—hardworking farmers or factory workers or small businessmen—cannot make ends meet while the lords of finance are rolling in wealth and immigrants get handouts. All the while, spokespersons for capital are lightheartedly praising "disruption" or Joseph Schumpeter's "creative destruction." Much of the distress was attributed to the globalization that gathered momentum again in the 1980s and 1990s. Classical economics had long marshaled its partial derivatives to demonstrate that the international division of labor as determined by natural resources and labor skills would yield the greatest degree of global wealth. Development economics after World War II relaxed the dogma; countries and regions could change their skill set and move toward higher value-added production. Free trade agreements multiplied: the EU's Single Market, Mercosur, North American Free Trade Agreement, potentially the Trans-Pacific Partnership. But their progress seemed to leave obsolescence and unemployment in its wake, whether in the rust belts of the Great Lakes or Wallonia and Lorraine as steel production and shipbuilding and auto production moved to Asia; and finally even the abandoned local bookstore or corner pharmacy succumbed as former clients ordered from Amazon and filled prescriptions at CVS.

Firms were taken over, wound up, and stripped of their assets. Globalization might benefit emerging economies but not the industries at home. Global finance benefited those plugged into transnational financial networks, not the masses of working people, and indeed, this view gained persuasive adherents far before the crisis.[27] The doctrines of "neoliberalism" that had prevailed from the 1970s on, the apparent role played by automation and robotics, and the growing financialization of economic wealth brought home the misery to the "advanced" economies. Whether for wages, lowering the government deficit, and privatizing state assets so that the afflicted economy could reduce its debt burden, make foreign payments and reenter the global bond market. Austerity was a punishment that supposedly made a moral point—living beyond one's means through excessive imports should not be rewarded—but punished very selectively. It inflicted hardship on those fired from government or private jobs and often on the old whose savings had been depleted and in many cases, Greece most recently, led to a continuing downward spiral of employment, lower government revenue, and diminished social assistance. There was no shared viewpoint from which to judge its efficacy. If one followed the hardship inflicted on the unemployed and their families in order to satisfy the world's savings classes, the policies seemed heartless and probably ineffective. If like *The Economist* magazine, one looked at the economies humming once again after a decade of misery and purged of so many redundant workers—where had they gone?—or unproductive bureaucrats, it was a harsh but benevolent medicine.

Latin American populist regimes began with expansionary programs and generous wage policies. But when inflation surged out of control, populists could apply neoliberal remedies, such as attempted by Peronist Carlos Menem (1989), Fernando Collor de Mello in Brazil (1990–1992), and Alberto Fujimori in Peru.[28] Orbán's Fidesz presided over a 13–14 percent decrease in social spending from 2008 to 2012, while at the same time it centralized education and health care and reaffirmed "traditional family values," thus combining neoliberal and traditional conservative measures. Private pension funds were also nationalized (as in Argentina). Unemployment support was tied to work requirements including public works if necessary; as of 2012, local authorities in Hungary could deny social assistance to the unemployed if they did not keep their houses and gardens tidy, and local authorities could deny public works employment, an exclusion that hit the Roma communities hard.[29] Erdoğan went the other way: from neoliberal beginnings in the 2000s to corporatist state economy; the logic was holding on to power. If socialism was ruled out, populist rulers either had to bow to the logic of the international market or try to construct a national capitalism on the basis of a quasi-autarky. In neither case, was it possible to resist the logic of capital and the market?[30] Ultimately, for the authoritarian leader, the priority was not the economic program but holding on to power. Identifying himself with the people's interest, as Maduro managed to do in Venezuela, his continuation in power was indispensable.

Not only populists pointed out the discrepancy between the fate of the displaced and the success of the newly enriched. Inequality of wealth and income significantly increased within the major economies from 2000 to 2020. Thomas Piketty deservedly shot to celebrity status in 2014 with his vast treatise documenting the exponential increase of inequality since 1980 and a longer-run tendency through most of the twentieth century (the world wars excepted). He attributed it to the fact that although the rate of return on capital was relatively stable over the long term, it generally exceeded the rate of economic growth (his lapidary formula was $r > g$). Hence, capital must claim a greater share of national income over time, all the more so when the greater rate of saving (and thus returns on savings) among higher earners were calculated. Since the wealthy derived more of their income from capital than from work, inequality must increase. If this were not disquieting enough, Piketty pointed to the phenomenon of "super managers"—that conspicuous, often lionized group of executives who managed to jack up their salaries and fringes (many of them titles to capital) in a self-referential game of competitive compensation, which justified each other's pay hikes by the increases offered to their peers.[31]

Piketty's analysis won enthusiastic agreement from many, unsurprisingly on the "left"—although even supporters admitted that really long-term trends could not be extrapolated from the half century (1970–2010) he documented. His famous inequality, $r > g$, was not axiomatic. It was an empirical correlation that Piketty found holding in earlier centuries and then the neoliberal years, such that the countertrend toward greater equality was a brief artifact of the world wars and the construction of welfare states. Piketty advocated remedial measures (increased taxation of the wealthy and higher inheritance taxes). Critics mounted a robust but scattered opposition.[32] Nonetheless, for the recent decades, his findings were largely corroborated by a study no one would suspect of leftist sympathies. According to the McKinsey Global Institute's probing examination of the national balance sheets for ten leading economies—the United States, China, Japan, the United Kingdom, France, Germany, Sweden, Australia, Canada, and Mexico, together accounting for 60 percent of the world's income—the two decades that witnessed the financial crisis, interest rates at record lows, massive central bank intervention, and the hit from COVID-19 also brought a significant change of wealth. Striking was the fact that wealth had diverged far more than income. Statistics on global wealth are rare, so the McKinsey report bears special attention. "At the level of the global economy, the historic link between the growth of wealth of net worth, and the value of economic flows such as GDP [gross domestic product] no longer holds." Economic growth has been sluggish, but net worth has soared. Net worth thus grew much faster than GDP. The total market value of measurable wealth in the ten economies grew from about $150 trillion at the turn of the century or four times GDP to $520 trillion or six times GDP. The ratio of asset prices to national income thus increased 50 percent over its long-run average. Looking at private incomes and wealth (by means of estate tax returns), Piketty also found that this ratio was nearing five to six years and on its way to seven years of national income.[33]

At the consolidated global level, net worth is the price put on real assets, houses, factories, equipment, and intangibles such as patents and intellectual property. Financial assets, such as stocks (equities) owned individually or by endowments or pension funds, fund the production of tangibles and intangibles. Thus, they do not count separately in net worth; moreover, bookkeeping conventions require financial assets to be matched by liabilities so they cancel each other out.[34] Of the tangibles, residential real estate—land and houses—and nonresidential buildings represented half the value; government and corporate buildings and land made up 20 percent, while capital assets—factories, machinery, mineral reserves—amounted to the remainder. To the researchers' surprise, only 4 percent was in intangibles and the result of the digital economy. Of the rise in net worth, 77 percent represented price increases (34 percent in line with inflation, 43 percent beyond inflation) and 28 percent was new net investment while net financial assets had dropped 4 percent of the total. Cumulative net investment was $100 trillion, $180 trillion was new debt and another $180 trillion represented other liabilities. The overall finding of economic observers was that asset prices had become decoupled from income-generating investment.

McKinsey and Piketty both asked why the flow of savings had not yielded higher income instead of rising stock prices and real estate investment. Had the mature capitalist economy entered an era of secular stagnation, an idea that John Maynard Keynes entertained and that has recently been suggested by Laurence Summers and Łukasz Rachel?[35] But when Keynes floated the idea, he envisaged that it would produce not inequality but "the euthanasia of the rentier." In the twenty-first century, it seemed to promise the euphoria of the rentier, that is increasing inequality, as global capitalism increasingly rewarded its wealthiest beneficiaries. As a remedy, the McKinsey economists suggested greater real investment in social needs and decarbonization, while Piketty proposed a progressive tax on capital. Neither the former nor the latter promised political success; indeed, to judge from the century's history covered in this volume, such correctives usually required economic catastrophe to materialize first.

Given the model of collective protagonists that has formed the basis of this book, I would suggest that the historian pay primary attention to the shifting balance of institutional power. Several reasons conjoined. First, as already proposed and as widely credited, the failure of organized labor to insist with more vigor on a redistribution of income shares. This was a trend long in the works intellectually as well as socially. It was certainly explicable: after their being crushed by fascism and Nazism in Central Europe and by military-based dictatorship in Japan, the labor movements in these heavily industrialized countries opted for policies of class collaboration. (They were also under occupation regimes that set limits to their militancy.) Second, the triumph of what four and a half decades ago I labeled the politics of productivity set the stage for decades of fixation on national economic growth rather than on the increase of the wage share. Chapter 5 documented steps in the development of this discourse. The Cold War helped seal the victory of that tendency. By the 1990s, as seen in the preceding chapter, capitalism and neoliberalism exerted an almost hypnotic influence on the telegenic leaders of the center-left parties.

I would further suggest—if only as a speculative hypothesis for discussion that can never be unambiguously resolved—that the fall of a communist alternative in 1990 and the discrediting of the centrally planned economies outside China (which in fact has evolved into a form of state-supervised capitalism currently overinvested in real estate and just as accepting of inequality)— also helped contribute to this exuberant rewarding of the top deciles of society. It was certainly not that the centrally planned economies in Eastern Europe represented a successful alternative model. Almost everyone by the late 1980s recognized that they had proven inadequate. Ideologically, however, they stood for a collectivist regime that despite its deformities and coercion had once appeared a plausible alternative. The existence of the "socialist world" suggested that there was a way to think about running an economy and distributing its fruits that diverged from the capitalist model. As in the

West, the Communist vision of tomorrow stressed "more"—but supposedly a socially equitable "more" even when their creation of a privileged class of party leaders and others belied their propaganda.

The existence of the centrally planned economies had at least intimated that a political determination of primary income distribution, whether as threat or utopia, might be conceivable. Social democracy suggested instead a political intervention into income redistribution through taxation and the welfare state. But as the preceding chapter suggested, social democrats alone could not sustain that ideological commitment, or chose not to, after the demoralization brought by inflation during the 1970s. Concerned about global competition and facing the rise of East Asian industrial competition in particular, Western social democrats joined with neoclassical economists to focus on limiting the national income share claimed by wages in the Western economies. Some of their leaders could yield to the ebullient neoliberal enthusiasm for the magic of markets.

Countervailing power failed in 1989, not in John Kenneth Galbraith's 1950s sense as a protection against monopoly but as a wider default of economic vision. Social democratic coalitions took the lead in stabilizing wage inflation in Scandinavia and West Germany, along with the Netherlands today's "Frugal Four" in the EU. When the left's more militant tendency reappeared—say, in the rhetoric of Greek finance minister Yanis Varoufakis—it seemed intemperate and childish. In that sense, Francis Fukuyama was correct about the fall of state socialism in 1989–1990: at the level of nation-state politics in the global north, there was no serious ideological alternative to liberal democracy left, except perhaps illiberal democracy.

What about the realm of governance? it might be asked. Did the think tanks and the international financial agencies and the vast talky realm of the commentariat not act to deplore this staggering growth of inequality? The number of nongovernmental organizations (NGOs) increased about 20 percent in the decade after 1989—from an estimated 14,333 to 17,364.[36] Certainly, advocacy organizations multiplied. Soros had seeded civil society organizations throughout formerly Communist Eastern Europe; Orbán's hostility testified to their value (as well as to a residual anti-Semitism in the region). Amnesty International and human rights platforms tried to keep up with the abuses of despotism and the wreckage of civil wars, paralleling and encouraging the intergovernmental jurisprudence that was emerging. NGOs and UN agencies oriented toward economic aid had their hands full intervening to keep the most unfortunate from misery. In countries wracked by civil war, whether Sudan or Afghanistan, the UN agencies and foundations—UNESCO, Médecins sans Frontières, CARE, the World Bank, and many others—effectively replaced the welfare functions of governments confined to capital cities.[37] In Asia, the Bangladesh Rural Advancement Committee (BRAC)—little known in the West but distributing the most funds—financed schools, small enterprises, and local medical delivery. NGOs and foundations worked hard to ameliorate the disastrous economic catastrophes of the third world, and this made a difference. Advocacy groups arose on both sides of painful trade-offs. By the mid-1990s, a whole group of NGOs had arisen to challenge the premises of global investment and free trade. Some of the more militant would be in the streets of Seattle in 1999. Environmental activist organizations based in the global north could also push against development programs, such as large dams, that promised to lift communities out of poverty. Savvy corporations formed their own NGOs and, moreover, co-opted the language and, under the pressure of concern about climate change in the late 2010s, hopefully the goals of "sustainable development" and "carbon neutrality" even as they searched for oil. "Far from undermining neo-liberal globalization much of transnational civil society became co-opted by it."[38]

But the purveyors of governance like the politicians of social democracy essentially limited their mission and remit. Their terms of reference accepted the institutional status quo and worked within it. Poverty remained their focus, not inequality per se. As its results began to become visible, many of the foundations and institutions such as Brookings, even private companies (e.g., McKinsey) who maintained research departments began to spotlight this trend, as did academic economists. Global governance organizations did not have the inclination or the toeholds to suggest radical alternatives. Such a move would no doubt have rendered them unwelcome in many of their most desperate arenas. The realm of governance was based on the world as it was—pulled and pushed and tweaked to make it a more humane place and hopefully divested of the prejudices that amplified the necessary human misery it had to accept. Some organizations, such as Oxfam, announced that they were aware of the political conditions that contributed to poverty and hoped to address them, particularly in the question of women's rights. In general, the realm of governance functioned by avoiding distributional issues.

But the problem with the realm of governance was a deeper one. It raised distributional issues of its own. It, too, testified to a dimension of inequality that contributed to the populist reactions. It highlighted education and science as themselves the source of unease, alienation, and reaction. It meant that "meritocracy" was a deeply freighted concept.[39] Members of the governance community did not always grasp the backlash. The American Academy of Arts and Sciences, for example, set up a study committee to examine the skepticism about science in American life, and indeed this author attended its sessions. But skepticism about science arose as much from the claims for scientists as from the content of their teaching. The acolytes of science and sometimes governance more generally could imply despite their best efforts that they were privy to a realm of knowledge that ordinary people did not have the capacity to attain. Yes, this was a newer manifestation of the older problem of anti-intellectualism in a democracy, but it suggested causes deeper than the resentments often attributed by the experts. It was no mere rerun of the Scopes Trial, where the theory of evolution collided with fundamentalist belief. How could equality be reconciled with governance? Spokespersons for the governance community seemed to believe that knowledge should evoke a willing deference on the part of those outside, much as the British gentry or European aristocracy had taken such deference as part of the natural order. The populist movements of the early twenty-first century suggested the limits of this view.

The State as Project: A History of Concepts

It was probably as much the unequal rewards of successful capitalism and the claims of governance as any general failure, therefore, that provided fertile ground for populism. Capitalism and central planning—that is, the state socialism of the Communist bloc—both revealed systemic vulnerabilities in the 1970s and 1980s, but it was socialism as a governing system that collapsed while the mixed economies soldiered on. The term *socialism* itself retained a costly ambiguity: American Republican Party politicians during the campaigns of 2016 and 2020 brandished it to discredit a policy of public provision of social services—the package Europeans labeled social democracy or democratic socialism. As developments of the 1930s and 1940s—the New Deal, the Popular Front, the postwar British Labour government—had demonstrated, states could institute those policies within a framework of private ownership of industry and land and toleration of a vocal opposition, even when the Labour Party declared their intent to nationalize "the commanding heights of the economy" and did so in part after 1945. The states governed by communist parties used the term *socialism* to refer to the collectivization of "the means of production"—generally, large-scale industry and peasant agriculture (though not in Poland)—sometimes by confiscation, sometimes by purchase.

The states that instituted this degree of nationalization had made state socialism their raison d'être. They had been established (between 1917 and 1948 in Europe and from 1945 to 1975 outside Europe), so their political and intellectual leaders proclaimed, to eliminate one economic system and install another. As the economic system they installed after the destruction of capitalism failed to adapt to the diversity of consumer demand in the 1960s and often required continual repression to remain in power, that inadequacy further discredited the political apparatus, which in fact had become primarily motivated by its own survival.[40] In contrast, what Marxists would call the capitalist state developed with diverse objectives. Although protection of property was a major aim for the "liberal" or Lockean state, the "absolutist state" emphasized its political domination over the territorial grandees as just as preeminent a goal. In each case, the successful state created a whole structure of beliefs, justifications, versions of its own history, and rewards of office to those who could dominate. This was a process Antonio Gramsci thought of as achieving hegemony, and Max Weber cast in terms of legitimacy. Through the nineteenth century, both liberal and authoritarian states allowed and often assisted the realm of capital to flourish and expand. This was generally considered a success; GDP growth provided the confirming data. Capitalist growth outpaced that of the Communist states although many of the latter chalked up significant achievements in terms of literacy, medical care, and rapid development from far more retrograde economic origins. When they did not lapse into authoritarianism and fascism—not an insignificant set of deviations—the non-Communist states maintained a far better human-rights record.

Not all regimes or polities need to count as a state. Perhaps the Weberian concept of a state—the community (Gemeinschaft) exercising a monopoly of legitimate violence (Gewalt) in a particular territory (Bezirk) was being fetishized at the beginning of the twenty-first century by historians and social theorists. It reflected the prevailing interpretation of German and Prussian experience as of 1900 but rested on concepts that could be challenged. Territories were continually changing; the monopoly of violence was challenged every day by guerrillas, terrorists, and gun-toting citizens with grievances. Rulers such as the Assads in Syria waged war against their own citizens. Legitimacy often seemed threadbare at best. Weber's classic formulation was more an ideal than an ideal type.

The historian can lose patience with the sociologists' need for classification, but since he has offered a model of his own, the project-state, he cannot dismiss the effort out of hand. To draw to a conclusion, let me review some of the reflections on statehood prompted by the history recounted here. Consider first some earlier alternative models, not the usual British, French, or American schemes but two earlier notions in particular from the German-speaking world, that of the reactionary Swiss political philosopher Karl Ludwig von Haller (1768–1854) and the one expounded by Georg Friedrich Wilhelm von Hegel. Now virtually forgotten, Haller was known for his six-volume tract *The Restoration of State Science* (*Die Restaurierung der Staatswissenschaft*), which allegedly gave its name to the Restoration as a historical period. Like other conservatives from the German-speaking lands during and after the years of Frederick the Great and then the French Revolution, Haller sharply condemned the idea of the state as an abstract concept for centralized rule—a construct derived from Roman law and exemplified by Louis XIV, the Jacobins, and Napoleon. For Haller, life in society was regulated by pacts existing between unequals. If one asked how treaties between unequals might be considered legitimate, Haller responded that it was nature's law that the more powerful commanded the weaker, just as parents ruled children. What was called the state was just the expression of the highest level of all these compacts, the one between subjects and a prince (or the magistrates of a "republic"—he was, after all, a citizen of Bern). The ruler thus stood at the top of a pyramid of unequal treaties with his subjects. Only his independence from a superior differentiated the state from other associations. The polity remained patrimonial, deferential, authoritarian but on an almost personal level. Power, moreover, was not delegated to a ruler by a people, as Lockean liberalism suggested; he inherited it or acquired it from other rulers. Hegel could not contain his scorn with this idea when he published his own *Philosophy of Law* a year later. Yes, Haller was "original," Hegel conceded, but totally unsystematic; he did not recognize that the state had a public essence; it was a higher expression of reason, its laws transcended private contracts and its claim to obedience followed from the fact that its sovereignty transcended interest groups such as composed "civil society" and the economy.[41]

Does this debate make any sense for the modern era? Three-quarters of a century earlier, it certainly would have been foreign to Montesquieu, who wanted to demonstrate how social, religious, and economic institutions conjoined with natural endowments to codetermine historical outcomes. States certainly existed, but they were not transcendent ethical communities as

Hegel was to claim even though kings might enjoy divine sanction. Neither were they merely treaties of private submission but instead, genuinely political societies in which classes and interests contended and in which public offices might be commercialized. In the Anglo-American tradition, they implied a contractual relationship both among citizens and between them and their chosen magistrates or rulers. Reciprocity was at the heart of such contracts, as it had been in continental feudal traditions.[42] If contemporary citizens want to rescue a feasible state, then "political society," the accepted translation of *societas civilis*, might be a less daunting ideal than the Weberian concept. At the least, it might be a more useful way to think about the resultant of forces produced by the ambitious project-state, the irrepressible self-interest of capital, and the high-minded norms of governance.

As Montesquieu and other liberal thinkers, including the American founders, understood, states were delicate communities that were difficult to maintain as liberal and nontyrannical structures. Montesquieu's ideas, like those of John Locke, appealed to the American revolutionaries. He offered a concept that allowed the legal framework of commercial society, private law, to claim as much validity as public law (even if the French monarchy did not), whereas Hegel wished to see the state as making transcendental claims beyond commerce. But Hegel's ideas deeply impacted Marxism, including late Marxist theory a century and a half later when the Frankfurt School exiles attempted to analyze fascism and National Socialism. Before he became a guru for the youth of the 1960s, Herbert Marcuse offered an exposition of Hegel in 1942, *Reason and Revolution*, which attempted to clear the German philosopher of the charge that his reputed statolatry had prepared the way for fascism or Nazism. Properly understood, Marcuse wrote, Nazism was an anti-state, a glorification of the "movement" and the *Volk*. In fact, it represented the triumph of sectoral interests—monopoly capitalism, secret police, and a ruthless party apparatus—that had hijacked democracy, whereas Hegel's state would have kept these ambitious actors in their place. Marcuse's colleague on Morningside Heights, Franz Neumann, published *Behemoth* in 1944, less as a philosophical discussion than as a rich analysis of the Nazi regime such as it was, as a cartel of powerful partial interests—the army, the Junkers and powerful industrialists, and the party with its political police—all held together by Hitler and monstrous ideology. Indeed, this approach informed some of the leading German historical analyses in the 1960s including Martin Broszat's *Hitler-State*, Hans Mommsen's idea of a "weak dictator," and the widespread idea of Nazi polyarchy.[43]

The relevant models have certainly moved beyond Hegel and probably even Weber. Examining a dozen Arab countries, Nazih Ayubi concludes that although they may possess "fierce states," they do not have "strong states": "they are lamentably feeble when it comes to collecting taxes, winning wars or forging a really 'hegemonic' power bloc or an ideology that can carry the state beyond the coercive and 'corporative' level and into the moral and intellectual sphere."[44] In his 2015 account of the Horn of Africa, Alex De Waal, who was active for thirty years in what we might call the effort at African governance, has suggested that regimes or political chief executive officers (CEOs) buy and sell military violence to seize power. "The more that a political entrepreneur can discard humane norms and instead adopt a market-based calculus, the more likely he is to rise to the top and stay there. . . . Over the last decades this auction of loyalties has been liberalized, dollarized and internationalized." Dollars from abroad and territorial mineral resources are the stake and the resource of power although occasionally ideology, whether Marxism or militant Islam, motivate political leaders. "Loyalty is fully commoditized and regularly open for renegotiation. . . . The biggest problem facing a political CEO is that as the political market becomes more perfect, the cost of loyalty rises." The problem for the rest of us is that "violence itself . . . generates emotions including the intoxication and sense of impunity of the immediate victor, bonds of solidarity among those who are fighting, and the impulse to revenge by those who have lost." Perhaps, de Waal suggests, a new generation of leaders who can mobilize the street will replace the entrepreneurs of violence: "It is possible . . . to envisage regular contests between unarmed demonstrators and the police in which unwritten rules determine which side concedes and for what price, or an electoral marketplace in which votes are auctioned."[45] This latter possibility might yield a model for the role of retail violence even in democracies. Milan Vaisnav suggests that the political leader on the local or state level actually benefits by being perceived as a thug in the fragmented Indian political universe, where ascriptive differences—he calls them ethnic and includes caste, language, and religion—run deep. "The fact that voters often perceive candidates associated with breaking the law to be more credible than their counterparts suggested that the emergence of tainted politicians in democracies is not necessarily symptomatic of a breakdown in political and electoral accountability."[46] Americans might still think of the result as a defective regime, using this term to suggest those holding effective power but not necessarily recognized as a state either by the UN or other states.

Of course, India and the regimes in East Africa are recognized as states. So, too, are such sad polities as murderous Syria and hapless Lebanon. Nonetheless, the populist dipole in which demagogue and "the people" call each other into political activity, I would suggest, is not really a state in the sense that Montesquieu, or Alexis de Tocqueville, or John Stuart Mill, or the American founders would have recognized. It looks more in fact like the Haller model of a bundle of contracts between the authoritarian commander and his subjects. On the other hand, after the totalitarian experiences of 1917–1989, there is certainly reason to distrust the claim that a state possesses some inherent rationality, much less Mussolini's claim that the individual is nothing without the state. "Beware the bossy state," warns *The Economist* in early 2022. The American state in particular was constructed on the premise that concentration of power was dangerous, and the state in its then European sense was understood as a concentration of power. American political language stuck with terms such as *government* and *administration* and left the term *state* to describe a territorial component of the federal United States. In terms of this book, applying reason and criteria of the public good to administration came to be the vocation of governance, but governance implies rationality without state power. The exercise of power without taking into account norms or public welfare I would designate as a mere regime.

Post-communist states have provided a special research field and have tested the categories and labels that this book has also hoped if not to supersede at least to recognize as overly simple. In a collection of essays on postcommunist states, Henry Hale has introduced the idea of "patronalism": "a social equilibrium in which individuals organize their political and economic pursuits primarily around the personalized exchange of concrete rewards and punishments, and not primarily around abstract, impersonal principles."[47] Put so generally, however, patronalism would cover Mayor Richard Daley's Chicago as well as post-Communist Romania. The volume's editor, the Hungarian sociologist Bálint Magyar, has made the case most forcefully for a new formation, the post-communist mafia state—as he did in his own earlier study—"arising from the foundations of a communist dictatorship as a product of the debris left by its decay."[48] In comparison with ordinary corruption, "organized criminal groups try methodically to draw the figures of public power into their sphere of influence." Corruption is "elevated from a deviancy to be kept hidden to the rank of state politics, or a general practice overseen centrally.... Under the mafia state private interest takes the rightful place of public interest systemically and permanently, rather than by chance and on occasion. There is virtually no field of activity that is not subject to the concentrated demands of power and wealth accumulation." Fidesz's marching from a set of liberal values to the right-wing value system, as Magyar sketches the history of its evolution during the two post-communist decades, meant "a systematic traversal of the path that led from a political discourse based on rational arguments to one based on populism."[49] The rapid privatization of socialist property meant huge opportunities for enrichment for court favorites, above all in states such as Russia where much wealth was based on mineral extraction. Dissidents to the populist trajectory within Fidesz were bought off with cushy political appointments to the "Goulash Archipelago." In Magyar's chronicle of decay from 1992 through 2010, all developments conduce to political degeneration: "Corruption, oligarchies, state capture—these are perhaps the most often used categories in describing the relationship between politics and economy in the systems that were raised over the ruins of the Soviet Empire." But their corruption is incomplete and almost amateurish; the mafia state comes later: "An undifferentiated use of these terms in the analysis of systemic features of various type and weight obliterates the difference between the alternation of corrupt post-communist regimes and the mafia state. . . . *The mafia state, however, is not just a result of state capture by the oligarchs produced by classical underworld conditions,* but represents rather a case where the head of a political venture disciplines and domesticates the oligarchs in the capacity, as it were, of the godfather settling them into his chain of command."[50] Supportive business enterprises are showered with favors; others are eliminated. Laws of exception become the norm. The 2010 capture of a qualified majority of two-thirds that allowed constitutional changes (even increased in the 2021 election) confirmed the construction of the mafia state, licensed autocracy, and meant that "the institutions of public authority cease to be the sites where real decisions are taken." The organizations of civil society are brought to heel: precarity becomes a norm. *The earlier "little but guaranteed" was replaced by "perhaps more, but no guarantees."*[51] On the other hand, "this is a forgiving, inclusive regime"; "the political family will always be there for them." What Magyar does not stress is that Hungary was combining populism and autocracy with neoliberal policies as well, adopting a flat tax with the highest European value-added tax to secure a regressive fiscal structure. Since Orbán had depended on both securing EU funding and flirting with Putin ideologically, it was not clear how the Ukrainian war would impact the stability of his regime.

Is it unrealistic or perhaps even dangerous to hope for more from a state than what a regime provides? Perhaps the polity of the demagogue and aspiring authoritarian today does not represent what the state as a public legislative association has the potential to become. It remains closer to Haller's vision of patrimonial power: a set of agreements between a Bonaparte and his adoring subjects, between Modi, Erdoğan, Bolsonaro, Trump, Orbán, Putin—or sometimes a collective clique such as the Polish PIS or the Sudanese military—and the assemblage of supporters or bystanders. Some theorists resort to the idea of charisma for such personalist claims to power to be effective. But *pace* Weber, charisma has become a flabby overused concept. What authoritarians require is a feel for articulating and weaponizing grievances (and a good electoral manager). It takes enough collaborators in the project who see their own interest, whether enrichment or reelection, in making it work.

The reader might well ask, is not all this too abstract a level of theorizing? After all, the modern state in many of our countries does operate as a state; it has layers of bureaucracy and specialized offices—a military, an office of homeland security, an internal revenue service to collect taxes, a court system. It is not just a consortium for personal power, not just a market, nor a mere realm of governance; it can enforce rules. These properties alone may add up to a regime, but do they make a state? The current generation of authoritarian-minded leaders care about them only as they can reinforce the bond between themselves and those who will subordinate their autonomy to his will. Many of the countries that the UN credits as states are not really states in the stringent sense.

This is not meant as a plea for some transcendent governing entity, which in the wake of Hegel motivated strands of liberalism in the early twentieth century such as Leonard Hobhouse's in England or Guido de Ruggiero's and Benedetto Croce's in Italy. For the Italian liberals, though not the British ones, such praise of a liberal state was really a way of condemning socialist or labor's goals as unworthy and subversive. Nonetheless, is there not a place for a sense of the "public's matter," the res publica, not just as an oligarchic elitist structure such as Venice preserved until the end of the eighteenth century or British Tories yearned for, but as a forum where voters try to figure out what is best for some posited commonwealth rather than just their respective interests? Admittedly, such a plea has the antique patina of Tory reform. Can it produce a nonpopulist democratic vision? Are we left just mourning Franklin Roosevelt?

No history can predict whether a robust and democratic state—one that is neither Haller's nor Hegel's—can become the force of global history for the rest of this century or beyond. Perhaps it will become one of a confederal structure such as the EU imperfectly embodies. But—and here I depart from the historian's circumscribed role—I would venture to say that tasking the state with projects that transcend mere security or international power—and can grip the public as vividly, say, as space exploration—would help restore government to that role it should occupy between Haller and Hegel, between the strong man and his diminished minions, or the oppressive machine claiming to possess a hold on a higher form of reason. The project-state was at its best a twentieth-century device for advancing what might be called the common good. It was ambitious and, yes, potentially dangerous. Willy Brandt built his Social Democratic Party campaign in 1969 on the slogan "Dare More Democracy." The German coalition government of Social Democrats, Greens, and Free Democrats formed in November 2021 modified it to "Dare More Progress." Today, many political groups are implying "Dare less democracy," also a project and one that requires denying access to the polls and distorting public information.

After the totalitarian experiences of mid-century and the personalized authoritarian ones popular today, dare one write, "Dare more state"?[52] This author would argue with some trepidation, yes. This was the implicit slogan that Theodore Roosevelt ran on in 1904 and after, but his bully-boy imperialism revealed its shadow sides. Teddy's program raises a serious question: can the project-state or the strong state refrain from behaving like an empire? That is, can it refrain from extending its rule over dependent populations who do not have a voice in its running? Teddy's domestic impulses gradually came to guide his cousin Franklin's early New Deal three decades later as well as the aspirations of other leaders and parties across the world. This author, too, would wish for more of a project-state—as against the lobbying of corporate interests, the inflammation of populist impulses or even the earnest recommendations by the advocates of governance. A state will require political argument and recruitment of like-minded partners, thus parties, but parties committed to public projects for expanding membership, fairness, and life chances, even as activists recall that much of life must remain nonpolitical.

We do not know whether such a future or futures is possible. In its analysis of early 2022, *The Economist* declared it was certainly not desirable. The magazine recognized many of the trends that this history has also tracked over a century, but they did so from the viewpoint of capital. "Periods of freer enterprise give way to ones with a more meddlesome state. When change comes, it is after crisis, occasionally exogenous (war, pandemic), at other times provoked by excesses (financial crash, depression, stagflation)....Now the state is again resurgent. Public spending is rising as the welfare state expands. Government is becoming bossier, especially to business."[53] Obviously, this author would weigh the balance differently. Yes, too many states still impose licensing labyrinths that impede economic innovation; it can be debated whether industrial policy ("picking winners") does more harm than good; there are always silly regulations that can be made fun of. And yes, entrepreneurs and inventors have created the economic advances that have transformed the world over two or three centuries, although often for the state as client.

The danger that the state poses is probably different from the one preoccupying *The Economist*. It is the one so cruelly demonstrated by the Ukrainian war—namely, that those acting in the name of the state, whether traditional leaders or populists, will find it easiest to exploit international tension and conflict as the justification for increasing their power. This book has not covered international politics as such. But traditional tension arises from the competitive nature of sovereignty, and it feeds back on politics just as political divisions tempt leaders to use international tension to claim greater authority. Reclaiming state prestige through military action can become a heady project in its own right. No advocate for a robust state should minimize its risk.

This book began by recalling how World War I helped normalize the project-state. It comes to a close as a new war in Ukraine seems to demonstrate that when state needs clash with the web of international capital, the state can at least temporarily subordinate the claims of capital. I would certainly not advocate that the wartime power to place sanctions on commerce and capital be taken as a model for politics in peacetime. Even wartime sanctions designed to strike at foreigners' capital often miss their target and impose a general suffering on an innocent population. And whether they prove successful as a weapon against aggressive regimes remains to be seen. But the experience demonstrates that even the liberal state retains the means to confront the modern economy with instruments of law and regulation. No one wants wartime to become the normal backdrop for politics, but deploying the state to rebalance the relationship with the web of capital is worth considering.[54] In its defense, I would point to the toll taken by the retreat of the state—or more precisely, by the substitution of personal Caesarist government for a sense of a well-regulated state: the growth in inequality and the toll of civil strife and climate catastrophes. Even while the flows of global commerce and migration became denser in the last decades of the twentieth century and the first two of the twenty-first century, so, too, countertendencies increased. Perhaps they could be described as an untethering of civil society, as if some global centrifugal forces gripped our sociopolitical systems and weakened their capacities for institutional cohesion, a failure both of government and of governance. By untethering I mean to suggest a general erosion of societal ligaments—not atomization in the sense of totalitarian shattering, but neither to be measured only in terms of diminishing social capital; rather perhaps to be gauged by random mass shootings broadcast through television coverage, the fracturing of collective audiences such as the cinema, or the dilution of habitual circles of family and friends through the weak connectivity of the internet. These trends were not incompatible with a surge of nationalist sentiment, an emotional bonding often manipulated to disguise the fractures within: the proliferation of great wealth, the quantum jumps in mass communication, and the technological innovations in moving merchandise, people, ideas—and prejudices.

The years around the turn of the nineteenth to the twentieth century as well as those at the beginning of the twenty-first century revealed some similar phenomena. Social observers during the earlier threshold of the twentieth century had a keen eye for the untethering or unraveling, although they sometimes failed in the analytical energy to think it through. Those between 1890 and World War I decried the rise of the masses, sometimes depicted as an unthinking herd, sometimes as the bearer of revolutionary dangers. They praised the rise of the military-social state and the structuring of a hierarchical international society, claiming that higher civilizations had to guide lesser ones. The forces of capital created agents with huge wealth. At the same time, other forces worked to counteract these growing tensions, organizing the masses, using the state to discipline capital, attempting procedures of governance to tame the possibilities for destructive conflict.

At the end of the twentieth century, a similar untethering took place, marked notably by the opportunity for private wealth expressed in orders of magnitude, powers of ten, above the median and the opportunities for the pressure of capital, and a vast explosion of private expression through social media. At the same time, many social observers greeted the disintegration of earlier bonding principles as a form of liberation. Military conscription was abolished with an impact that was probably profound but rarely measured.[55] Family was redefined to embrace all sorts of intimate commitments and not just those that traditionally seemed to affirm collective continuity. Emancipation of the personal realm seemed so beneficial—in the eyes of this author as well—that no one who wanted to be counted as a nonreactionary could resist the trend.

The guardians of governance reaffirmed most of the changes. Some academic and popular prophets of the new untethered society—for instance, the sociologists Anthony Giddens or Ulrich Beck, futurologist Alvin Toeffler, or journalist Thomas Friedman—cheered its opportunities.[56] But they could produce no already existing societal constituency to forge a coherent movement from this epochal flux. The untethered society would hopefully create its guiding party from the computer-savvy, the sensitive, and the enthusiastic. They would rely on governance more than government. The transformational impact of computers, digital technology, and the social media supposedly facilitated it as well. The gathering evidence of climate change unprecedented in the history of *Homo sapiens* and the return of pandemics added to the sense of untethering. We were all swept along by the great winds of change, like ancient sailors scattered by a fierce tempest at sea, reassured—perhaps accurately, perhaps speciously—that it would be a great opportunity for rich and poor alike, for those of the global north with so many choices and even for those of the global south with so many fewer.

Thomas Mann ended *The Magic Mountain*, one of the greatest novels of the long century which this history has tried to make sense of, with a vision of his hero Hans Castorp as a German infantryman, only intermittently visible, charging forward among a mass of soldiers in a nameless battle on the western front in World War I with shells exploding around him, comrades falling ahead of him, and the author claiming not to know whether his protagonist would live or die. Castorp was plunging into a dangerous and incalculable future, certainly unable under fire to put in order all the ideas to which he had been exposed in his Swiss sanatorium, nonetheless, so we must believe, not having been left unchanged by the spiritual and erotic forces that had educated him in his retreat from the world. Reality may have caught up with Mann's evocation of 1914. So, too, the historian leaves his interpreted world, both familiar and transformed, as Mann left his protagonist on the battlefields of World War I—where this history began as well—uncertain of its fate, knowing multitudes might be lost underfoot but still compelled to wager that most would in fact survive, collectively to renew a spirit of the laws that might expand freedom and equity and justice. Today's moment is filled with contradictory possibilities: besides Ukraine, consider the politicized conflict over vaccination and science in the middle of a pandemic; violent clashes resurfacing in Sri Lanka, Latin America, Central Asia, Yemen, the Horn of Africa and the Sahel, climate-afflicted sandboxes for larger regional powers to play out their rivalry; peace precariously preserved in the Middle East by an implicit consensus among some of the same regional powers (supported by their patrons outside the region) to ignore Palestinian grievances; political leaders whether in Africa or in the United States routinely rejecting electoral defeats; natural disasters abetted by human heedlessness; migrants desperately traversing dangerous waters in the belief that they will find economic security and safety from violence and thuggish regimes and police; a giant China ominously overshadowing so many regions; and the United States again, which provided some orientation for the years since World War II, in the grip of severe ideological conflict. The midterm American elections of autumn 2022, held as this book went to press, gave some hope that the spell of the would-be strong man might abate. Still, they testified, as did voting in Brazil, Italy, and elsewhere, to deeply fractured polities. No historian can predict the outcome of events, although his or her account may well be judged in their light. Suppose, then, that authoritarian demagogues continued to arouse enthusiasm; suppose political societies continued to see themselves as divided between the privileged and the disrespected. Social theorists and historians would have to acknowledge that the progressive society they no doubt wished for themselves was not necessarily the end of historical development. We would have to recognize how much of our work remains in the hypothetical.

What conclusions, if any, then remain safe from an uncertain future? I would suggest that we recall how open and crucial political striving remains. Held in check, the state and the capitalist impulse can remain forces for potential human improvement. Warlordism and Mafia, gang, or tribal violence to control turf and trafficking reveal what happens when state authority collapses.[57] Populist enthusiasms short-circuit the institutions needed to govern. But the eternal competition of a state system brings its own perils. I have purposely separated populism from nationalism in this discussion, but modern states do seek to express national identities, which means a new level of contentious collective claims. Mann's Castorp, of course, was fighting for a nation even if it was a state that could compel him to put himself into harm's way. The nation—an emotionally gripping community—raises an entire dimension of claims that states seek to validate. And if we want to restore political society, perhaps the individual project-state should no longer suffice as an aspiration but given the scale of global challenges must ultimately form part of an international society. This, too, had been an aspiration of the twentieth century, cherished by many North and South American, European, African, and Asian intellectuals during the interwar years and after 1945, in some cases influenced by their religious heritages and in others, cherished by secular Enlightenment visions. Many institutions of governance were created to knit together international society.

Possibilities for international confederation exist alongside spectacles of state disintegration—impelled less by ideology than by the requirements posed by environmental degradation: how do we diminish the impact of climate change already upon us? How will we confront the needs of our populations at the edge of rising oceans or those in more arid interiors? Will interstate association work in a world where hierarchies of resources and the legacies of empire continue to exist? Perhaps a reader stumbling on this work decades hence will be able to read this history as an explanation of how and why this evolution managed to take place, or perhaps why it did not succeed. No historian of the contemporary world can predict the outcome; we write while treading the knife's edge between past and future. But neither are they foreclosed.

Notes

Index

Notes

Preface

1. "The political and civil laws of every nation must be consistent with the nature of the people for which they are made; they must be consistent with the government that exists or which one wants to establish; they must relate to the physical attributes of a country . . . to its customs and manners, and finally with each other and with their origin and intention of the legislators, with the order of things on which they're established. . . . This is what I am undertaking in this work: I will examine all these relationships: they constitute what we call THE SPIRIT OF THE LAWS" (Montesquieu, *The Spirit of the Laws*, 1748, Book I, chapter 3).

Introduction

1. *Financial Times*, November 1, 2017, 9.

2. Anna Foa, *La Famiglia F.* (Bari-Roma: Laterza, 2018), 162.

3. David Brooks, "The Century of the Strongman Begins," *New York Times*, February 18, 2022, A23.

4. The sense of democratic triumph was hardly unalloyed during the 1990s. For the mood of democratic disillusion a quarter century ago, see Charles S. Maier, "Democracy and Its Discontents: Moral Crises in Historical Perspective," *Foreign Affairs*, July / August 1994. For recent evocations of contemporary American social atomization, see Robert Putnam, *Bowling Alone: The Collapse and Renewal of American Community* (New York: Simon & Schuster, 2000); George Packer, *The Unwinding: An Inner History of the New America* (New York: Farrar, Straus and Giroux, 2013); J. D. Vance, *Hillbilly Elegy: A Memoir of a Family and Culture in Crisis* (New York: Harper, 2016).

5. For the continuing impact of historical memory, see Tony Judt, *Postwar: A History of Europe since 1945* (New York: Penguin, 2005); for the United States, see Daniel T. Rogers, *Age of Fracture* (Cambridge, MA: Harvard University Press, 2011).

6. Eric Hobsbawm, *The Age of Extremes: A History of the World, 1914–1991* (New York: Random House / Pantheon, 1995); Samuel P. Huntington, *The Third Wave: Democratization in the Late Twentieth Century* (Norman: University of Oklahoma Press, 1991); Francis Fukuyama, *The End of History and the Last Man* (New York: Free Press, 1992); related titles cited below, note 27. An equally massive sociological literature has also focused on these issues. For US authors, see Seymour Martin Lipset, *Political Man: The Social Bases of Politics*, expanded ed. (Baltimore: Johns Hopkins University Press, 1981) to that of Steven Levitsky and Daniel Ziblatt, *How Democracies Die* (Princeton, NJ: Princeton University Press, 2008).

7. Most recently, some social commentators have argued that globalization has run roughshod over communities and that the rise of populism is in effect our penance for cosmopolitan elitism. In the pop sociology of our epoch, they want to redress the distinction between elites and ordinary folk or between those whom David Goodheart has stylized as the "somewheres" and "anywheres." David Goodheart, *The Road to Somewhere: The Populist Revolt and the Future of Politics* (London: Hurst, 2017).

8. "Consigning the Twentieth Century to History: Alternative Narratives for the Modern Era," *American Historical Review* 105, no. 3 (June 2000): 807–831. A roundtable of historians reconsidering the period (and the article) nineteen years later objected that the idea of a "moral narrative" in effect polarized ideological and structural factors. I understand the objection but still believe that the concept is heuristically useful.

9. José Ortega de Gasset, *Invertebrate Spain* (New York: Norton, 1937).

10. See Meredith Wu Cummings, *The Developmental State* (Ithaca, NY: Cornell University Press, 1999). The concept was deployed among others by Chalmers Johnson to describe the Japanese government's active encouragement of industrialization with its key Ministry of Trade and Industry. The project-state, as I conceive it, may strive for economic development but also aspires to profoundly restructure social institutions and sometimes individual mentalities. The concept of modernization during the Cold War—modeled supposedly on American experience—expressed that totalizing ambition and found an expression in the sociology of the era. For other alternative polities to the Weberian state, see Chapter 10.

11. See Samuel E. Finer, *A Primer of Public Administration* (London: Frederick Muller, 1950) and Emmette Redford, *Democracy in the Administrative State* (New York: Oxford University Press, 1969).

12. Charles Tilly, "War Making and State Making as Organized Crime," in *Bringing the State Back In*, ed. Peter Evans, Dietrich Rueschelmeyer, and Theda Skocpol (New York: Cambridge University Press, 1985), 169–191. States made war outside their borders, neutralized rivals within, offered protection to clients within, and mastered "extraction" of resources needed for this. Legitimacy came late in

the game and amounted to little more than finally arriving at acceptance of the transaction.

13. James C. Scott, *Seeing like a State* (New Haven, CT: Yale University Press, 1998); Michel Foucault, *Sécurité, territoire, population: Cours au Collège de France, 1977–1978* (Paris: Gallimard Seuil, 2001), translated by Graham Burchell as *Security, Territory, Population: Lectures at the Collège de France, 1977–78* (Basingstoke, UK: Palgrave Macmillan, 2007); Foucault's *The Birth of Biopolitics: Lectures at the Collège de France*, ed. Michel Senellart, trans. Graham Burchell (Basingstoke, UK: Palgrave Macmillan, 2008) is really on the ideas behind neoliberalism. See also Foucault's essay on governmentality in *The Foucault Effect*, ed. Graham Burchell, Colin Gordon, and Peter Miller (Chicago: University of Chicago Press, 1991).

14. Susan Pedersen's important study of the interwar mandate system, *The Guardians: The League of Nations and the Crisis of Empire* (New York: Oxford University Press, 2015) aptly envisages the league as a "force field." For recent literature, see also Sean Andrew Wempe, "A League to Preserve Empire: Understanding the Mandates System and Avenues for Further Scholarly Inquiry," *American Historical Review* 124, no. 5 (December 2019): 1723–1731.

15. There is now a huge literature on governance that is at last emerging from the naive celebrations of benevolence that characterized earlier statements. For a history of the term's deployment as of a dozen years ago, see Gili S. Drori, "Governed by Governance: The New Prism for Organizational Change," in *Globalization and Organization: World Society and Organizational Change*, ed. Gili S. Drori, John W. Meyer, and Hokyu Hwang (New York: Oxford University Press, 2006), 91–118—a collection that in general celebrates the Weberian rationality of governance and demonstrates its overlap with business organization and education. See also my own contribution, "Governance and Anti-governance," *Parolechiave* 56 (2016)—an issue devoted to governance.

16. This argument is developed in Chapter 3. See also Glenda Sluga and Patricia Clavin, eds., *Internationalisms: A Twentieth-Century History* (Cambridge: Cambridge University Press, 2017) for a programmatic statement with examples; Susan Pedersen, *The Guardians: The League of Nations and the Crisis of Empire* (Oxford: Oxford University Press, 2015) for an outstanding study. For an influential study of international law in this regard, see Martii Koskenniemi, *The Gentle Civilizer of Nations: The Rise and Fall of International Law 1870–1960* (Cambridge: Cambridge University Press, 2002). See Akira Iriye's summary of NGO history, *Global Community: The Role of International Organizations in the Making of the Contemporary World* (Berkeley: University of California Press, 2002). For a study of how "technocratic" schemes for international networks could develop around roads and railroads, see Johan Scott and Vincent Lagendijk, "Technocratic Internationalism in the Interwar Years," *Journal of Modern History* 6, no. 2 (2008): 196–217.

17. See David C. Engerman, "The Anti-politics of Inequality: Reflections on Special Issue," *Journal of Global History* 6, no. 1 (2011): 143–151; see also the editors' introduction, "Editorial—Global Inequality and Development after 1945," *Journal of Global History*, no. 1 (2011): 1–2, http://doi.org/10.1017/S1740022811000015. On NGOs, see Sabine Lang, *NGOs, Civil Society and the Public Sphere* (Cambridge: Cambridge University Press, 2013).

18. Readers may ask how this schema takes account of the international revolutionary and resistance movements determined to undermine the hierarchical stability that the web of governance sought to guarantee. Revolutionary movements played global roles from 1917 to 1924, then again from 1943 through 1947, and from the late 1960s into the 1970s. These movements, however, quickly lost their radical energy and congealed into bureaucratic actors aiming to transform national regimes. When successful, they left their mark with the creation of project-states as described in Chapter 1. So, too, civil-society movements in the 1980s claimed to represent an alternative to traditional state power, but they struggled for liberal and collective political recognition within nation-state structures.

19. David Medvetz, *Think Tanks in America* (Chicago: University of Chicago Press, 2012). Two earlier social theorists are of relevance here: on the right, Vilfredo Pareto's disillusioned critique of elites; on the left, Antonio Gramsci's examination of "organic intellectuals" tied to particular class interests.

20. The literature is immense and cannot be comprehensively listed here. Some recent discussions, collections, and histories of note include Jürgen Kocka and Marcel van der Linden, eds., *Capitalism: The Reemergence of a Historical Concept* (London: Bloomsbury, 2016); Jürgen Kocka, *Capitalism: A Short History* (Princeton, NJ: Princeton University Press, 2016); Jeffrey A. Frieden, *Global Capitalism: Its Fall and Rise in the Twentieth Century and Its Stumbles in the Twenty-First* (New York: Norton, 2020); Sven Beckert is currently writing a historical survey.

21. Karl Polanyi made the operation of the nineteenth-century gold standard the central factor in the capitalist reduction of embedded social relations and ultimately in the success of fascism. See *The Great Transformation: The Political and Economic Origins of Our Time*, c. 1944 (Boston: Beacon, 2001).

22. The analysis of time as a dimension for realizing returns should not be confused with the rationalization of time measurement in labor processes. For the former, the starting point may be Richard Cantillon and the physiocrats. See Joseph A. Schumpeter, *History of Economic Analysis*, ed. Elizabeth Boody Schumpeter (Oxford: Routledge, 1954), 221; also Ronald J. Meek, *The Economics of Physiocracy: Essays and Translations* (Cambridge, MA: Harvard University Press, 1963), 297–312; and for the latter, E. P. Thompson, "Time, Work-Discipline, and Industrial Capitalism," *Past & Present* 38 (December 1967): 56–97 and Vanessa Ogle, "Time, Temporality, and the History of Capitalism," *Past & Present* 243, no. 1 (2019): 312–327.

23. The political scientist Peter Hall refers to the combined economic and political or regulatory framework, embodied respectively in firms and governments, as a "growth regime" but emphasizes that their respective energies are not always synchronized. See. Peter A. Hall, "When and How do Growth Strategies Change?" in *Stato e Mercato*, forthcoming.

24. To take one example, the International Monetary Fund (IMF) has a governance mission of coordinating loans that individual banks might refuse to extend when acting as prudential agents of capital. At the same time, however, the IMF is charged with maintaining the robustness of international capital as a whole. Consider the circumstances of the debt relief programs to Latin America as reviewed in William Cline, *International Debt Reexamined* (Washington, DC: Institute of International Economics, 1995), 206–208.

25. There is a massive sociological and political science literature on the process of institutional change. See, for example, Wolfgang Streeck and Kathleen Thelen, *Beyond Continuity: Institutional Change in Advanced Political Economies* (New York: Oxford University Press, 2005); and James Mahoney and Kathleen Thelen, eds., *Explaining Institutional Change: Ambiguity, Agency, and Power* (New York: Cambridge University Press, 2010). For the debates in economics on the role and limits of institutional analysis, see the essays collected in Volker Caspari, ed., *Schriften des Vereins für Sozialpolitik*, Neue Folge, vol. 115: *Studien zur Entwicklung der Ökonomischen Theorie XXXIII* (Berlin: Duncker & Humblot, 2018); also Harald Bathelt, Patrick Cohendel, Sebastian Henn, and Laurent Simn, eds., *The Elgar Companion to Innovation and Knowledge Creation* (Cheltenham, UK: Edward Elgar, 2017), esp. chap. 1, "Innovation and Knowledge Creation: Challenges to the Field," 1–21.

26. Perhaps the aspirations of 1989 were more ambiguous than we recognized at the time; cf. Paul Betts, "1989 at Thirty: A Recast Legacy," *Past & Present* 244, no. 1 (August 2019): 271–305.

27. Samuel P. Huntington, *Political Order in Changing Societies*, c. 1968 (New Haven, CT: Yale University Press, 1996), 196–197. For more cheerful judgments, see Huntington, *The Third Wave*. Cf. Fukuyama, *The End of History*; also Francis Fukuyama, *The Origins of Political Order: From Prehuman Times to the French Revolution* (New York: Farrar, Straus and Giroux, 2011); and Francis Fukuyama, *Political Order and Political Decay: From the Industrial Revolution to the Globalization of Democracy* (New York: Farrar, Straus and Giroux, 2014).

28. For the difficulties with the concept of order, it is instructive to follow the seminar of leading intellectuals summoned by the Rockefeller Foundation to Bellagio in June 1965 to discuss the issue, including Raymond Aron, Jean Fourastié, Maruyama Masao, and the youthful Henry Kissinger and Stanley Hoffmann. See Stanley Hoffmann, "Report of the Conference on Conditions of World Order: June 12–19, 1965, Villa Serbelloni, Bellagio, Italy," *Daedalus* 124, no. 3 (Summer 1995): 1–26. Aron tried

to win agreement on a descriptive, not normative, definition: "under what conditions would men (divided in so many ways) be able not merely to avoid destruction, but to live together relatively well in one planet?" The discussion of the state was the most concrete—was it a force for order or anarchy? "Discussion of the so-called remedies, or solutions, remained inconclusive." Active optimism asserted itself about the contribution made by scientists and the possibilities for economic planning. Scientific rationality was praised, but "the discussion failed to produce the kind of 'community' some hoped for." As rapporteur, Hoffmann opined that Immanuel Kant's notion of eventual unification of humankind given the costs of war "remains the most likely theory of world order"; but he was thinking of the interstate dimension. Add climate change—and the presence of women who seem to have been notably absent—and the conference could follow the same threads today.

1. Paths to the Project-State

1. On the development of the project, see Katherine Rietzler, "The War as History: Writing the Economic and Social History of the First World War," *Diplomatic History* 38, no. 4 (September 2018): 826–839. James T. Shotwell of Columbia University served as general editor.

2. On the plans for labor, Gerald Feldman, *Army, Industry and Labor in Germany, 1914–1918* (Princeton, NJ: Princeton University Press, 1966); Vejas G. Liulevicius, *War Land on the Eastern Front: Culture, National Identity and German Occupation in World War I* (New York: Cambridge University Press, 2000). On the military imprint in the United States, see William E. Leuchtenberg, "The New Deal and the Analogue of War," in John Braeman et al., eds., *Change and Continuity in Twentieth-Century America* (Columbus: Ohio State University Press, 1964), 81–143.

3. For problems of interpretation, Erik J. Zürcher, *The Young Turk Legacy and Nation Building: From the Ottoman Empire to Atatürk's Turkey* (London: I. B. Tauris, 2010); and for a review of recent literature, Eric Lohr, "The Bolshevik Revolution Is Over," *Journal of Modern History* 92 (September 2020): 635–667.

4. For a comparative treatment of these revolutions, see John Mason Hart, "Global Causation: Iran, China, Russia, and Mexico," in *Revolutionary Mexico: The Coming and Process of the Mexican Revolution* (Berkeley: University of California Press, 1987), 187–234; see also, Charles S. Maier, *Leviathan 2.0: Inventing Modern Statehood* (Cambridge, MA: Harvard University Press, 2012), 221–242.

5. For this result, see Theda Skocpol, *States and Social Revolution: A Comparative Analysis of France, Russia, and China* (Cambridge: Cambridge University Press, 1979).

6. For the racist side of the enterprise, see Paul A. Kramer, *The Blood of Government: Race, Empire, the United States and the Philippines* (Chapel Hill: University of North Carolina Press, 2006).

7. For steps in the argument, see Michel Foucault, *Discipline and Punish: The Birth of the Prison* (New York: Vintage Books, 1979); Graham Burchell, Colin Gordon, and Peter Miller, eds., *The Foucault Effect: Studies in Governmental Rationality* (Chicago: University of Chicago Press, 1991); and James C. Scott, *Seeing like a State: How Certain Schemes to Improve the Human Condition Have Failed* (New Haven, CT: Yale University Press, 1998). For the philosopher Giorgio Agamben, inspired by Carl Schmitt's analysis of the "state of exception" as the essence of sovereign power, there seems to be no firm line between ordinary government and the concentration camp. See Giorgio Agamben, *Homo Sacer: Sovereign Power and Bare Life*, trans. Daniel Heller-Roazen (Stanford, CA: Stanford University Press, 1998). The concentration camp is "the hidden matrix and *nomos* of the space in we are still living" (p. 180).

8. I avoid the term "modernization," which became hopelessly suffused with the self-satisfied defense of partially pluralist capitalist states during the "high" Cold War of the 1950s and 1960s. For the evolving history, see David Eckbladh, *The Great American Mission: Modernization and the Construction of an American World Order* (Princeton, NJ: Princeton University Press, 2010). There has been a decades-long debate on fascism and modernity. A generation ago, Henry A. Turner (along with many other analysts) thought of fascism as the search for a premodern utopia; authors more recently have stressed the kinship of fascism with modernity. See Roger Griffin, *Modernism and Fascism: The Sense of a Beginning under Mussolini and Hitler* (Basingstoke, UK: Palgrave-Macmillan, 2007).

9. For the difficulties of the strong state–weak state distinction, which compares the nineteenth-century United States and France in particular, see Nicolas Barreyre and Claire Lemercier, "The Unexceptional State: Rethinking the State in the Nineteenth Century (France, United States)," *American Historical Review* 126, no. 2 (June 2021): 481–503.

10. See the revealing study of the new Mexican army as a force for stabilizing the revolution in the 1920s by Hans Werner Tobler, "Peasants and the Shaping of the Revolutionary State, 1910–40," in *Riot, Rebellion, and Revolution: Social Conflict in Mexico*, ed. Friedrich Katz (Princeton, NJ: Princeton University Press, 2014), 487–518. Also Hart, *Revolutionary Mexico*; John Womack, *Zapata and the Mexican Revolution* (New York: Vintage, 1970); Friedrich Katz, *The Life and Times of Pancho Villa* (Stanford, CA: Stanford University Press, 1998); David C. Bailey, *Viva Cristo Rey! The Cristero Rebellion and the Church-State Conflict in Mexico* (Austin: University of Texas Press, 1974). For an argument that the *ejido* or communal land institution rested on an illusory and persistent notion of earlier village property relations, see Emilio Kourí, "On the Mexican Ejido," *Humanity: An International Journal of Human Rights, Humanitarianism, and Development* 11, no. 2 (Summer 2020): 222–226; and his wonderful tracing of these ideas in Kourí, "Interpreting the Expropriation of Indian Pueblo Lands in Porfirian Mexico:

The Unexamined Legacies of Andrés Molina Enríquez," *Hispanic American Historical Review*, 82, no. 1 (2002–2002): 69–117.

11. Brian Tsui, *China's Conservative Revolution: The Quest for a New Order, 1927–1949* (Cambridge: Cambridge University Press, 2018), 4. For a narrative of the spectacular multisited collapse of 1911, see Mary Wright, *China in Revolution: The First Phase, 1900–1913* (New Haven, CT: Yale University Press, 1968). New interpretations and special studies are in Joseph W. Esherick and C. X. George Wei, eds., *China: How the Empire Fell* (Abingdon: Routledge, 2014).

12. For a résumé of the controversies, see Joseph Esherick, "Recent Studies of Wartime China," *Journal of Chinese History* 1 (2017): 183–191.

13. Lloyd E. Eastman, *The Abortive Revolution: China under Nationalist Rule, 1927–1937* (Cambridge, MA: Harvard University Press, 1974), 181–226; also Eastman, "New Insights into the Nature of the Nationalist Regime," in *Republican China* 9, no. 2 (February 1984): 8–18, and comments, 19–39. Cf. Joseph W. Esherick, "Reconsidering 1911: Lessons of a Sudden Revolution," *Journal of Modern Chinese History* 6, no. 1 (2012): 1–14.

14. Margherita Zanasi, *Saving the Nation: Economic Modernity in Republican China* (Chicago: University of Chicago Press, 2006); Wang Ching-Wei (Jingwei), *China's Problems and Their Solution* (Shanghai: United Press, 1934). For resistance and collaboration, see also Rana Mitter, *The Manchurian Myth* (Berkeley: University of California Press, 2000). In his combination of talent, leadership potential, and personal ambition, Wang's career can be compared with similar Axis recruits as Suba Chandra Bose or Jacques Doriot. Quisling was more of a convinced racist ideologue. For the fate of Nationalist economic planning into and after World War II, see Chapter 4, **131–137.**

15. Robert Gerwarth. *The Vanquished: Why the First World War Failed to End, 1917–1923* (London: Allen Lane, 2016).

16. On disappointments, Erez Manela, *The Wilsonian Moment: Self-Determination and the International Origins of Anticolonial Nationalism* (New York: Oxford University Press, 2007). On the veterans as an interwar political force, Bruno Cabanes, *La France endeuilée. La sortie de guerre des soldats français (1918–1920)* (Paris: Seuil, 2004); Antoine Prost, *Les anciens combattants et la société française: 1914–1939*, 3 vols. (Paris: Presses de la Fondation nationale des sciences politiques, 1977); John Horne, "Beyond Cultures of Victory and Cultures of Defeat? Interwar Veterans' Internationalism," in *The Great War and Veterans' Internationalism*, ed. Julia Eichenberg and John Paul Newman (London: Palgrave Macmillan, 2013), 207–222.

17. For general accounts, see Adam Tooze, *The Deluge: The Great War and the Remaking of the Global Order, 1916–1931* (New York: Viking, 2014); also Charles S. Maier, *Recasting Bourgeois Europe: Stabilization in France, Germany, and Italy in the Decade after World War I* (Princeton, NJ: Princeton University Press, 1975).

18. For a visual sense, see the catalog of the Montreal Museum of Fine Arts 1991 exhibition, Jean Clair, ed., *The 1920s: Age of the Metropolis*. Also the catalogs for the Centre Pompidou exhibitions: *Paris-Berlin, 1900–1933* (1978) and *Paris-Moscou, 1900–1930* (1979), and for the 1995–1996 exhibits at the Martin-Gropius-Bau in Berlin and the Pushkin Museum in Moscow: *Berlin-Moskau, 1900–1950 = Moskva-Berlin, 1900–1950* (Munich: Prestel, 1995).

19. The significance of prohibition as an ideological product was emphasized by Joseph R. Gusfield, *Symbolic Crusade: Status Politics and the American Temperance Movement* (Urbana: University of Illinois Press, 1963); and most recently as a forerunner of the surveillance state by Lisa McGirr, *The War on Alcohol: Prohibition and the Rise of the American State* (New York: Norton, 2016).

20. For percentages at different dates, see D. B. Grigg, "The World's Agricultural Labour Force 1800–1970," *Geography* 60, no. 3 (July 1975): 194–202. As of 1930, 50 percent of the developed world's labor force and 67 percent of the developing world's labor force still worked in agriculture. Current percentages of employment in agriculture range from 40–75 percent in the poorest African countries to 1–3 percent in the EU and North America. See ILO / World Bank Group, "Employment in Agriculture" https://resourcewatch.org/data.

21. For the economic theory, Alexander Ehrlich, *The Soviet Industrialization Debate, 1924–1928* (Cambridge, MA: Harvard University Press, 1960); Edward Hallett Carr and Robert W. Davies, *Foundations of a Planned Economy: A History of Soviet Russia*, vol. 8 (Harmondsworth, UK: Penguin, 1974). For the loser, Stephen F. Cohen, *Bukharin and the Bolshevik Revolution: A Political Biography, 1888–1938* (Oxford: Oxford University Press, 1980). For the human costs, Anne Applebaum, *Red Famine: Stalin's War on the Ukraine* (New York: Doubleday, 2017).

22. Charles Kindleberger, *A Decade of Depression*, 40th anniversary ed. (Berkeley: University of California Press, 2013); Kenneth Mouré, *Managing the Franc Poincaré: Economic Understanding and Political Constraint in French Monetary Policy, 1928–1936* (Cambridge: Cambridge University Press, 2006); Mark Metzler, *Lever of Empire: The International Gold Standard and the Crisis of Liberalism in Prewar Japan* (Berkeley: University of California Press, 2006); Barry Eichengreen, *Golden Fetters: The Gold Standard and the Great Depression* (New York: Oxford University Press, 1996).

23. For the ongoing controversies over the effectiveness of monetary and fiscal policy, see Nathan Perry and Matias Vernengo, "What Ended the Great Depression? Re-evalutating the Role of Fiscal Policy," *Cambridge Journal of Economics* 38 (2014): 349–367. For the spread of Keynesian ideas, see Peter A. Hall, ed., *The Political Power of Economic Ideas: Keynesianism across Nations* (Princeton, NJ: Princeton University Press, 1989). Keynesian recovery did not strictly speaking require deficit spending; even new government expenditure covered by taxation theoretically produced a rise in gross domestic product equivalent to the budget increase.

24. Franklin Roosevelt, Second Inaugural Address, January 20, 1937. For comparative perspectives, see John Diggins, *Mussolini and Fascism: The View from America* (Princeton, NJ: Princeton University Press, 1972); also Wolfgang Schivelbusch, *Three New Deals: Reflections on Roosevelt's America, Mussolini's Italy, and Hitler's Germany, 1933–1939* (New York: Metropolitan Books, 2006).

25. Yves Cohen, *Le siècle des chefs: Une histoire transnationale du commandement et de l'autorité* (Paris: Éditions Amsterdam, 2013), 419–471.

26. Antonio Costa Pinto, "The New State of Getúlio Vargas," in *Latin American Dictatorships in the Era of Fascism: The Corporatist Wave* (New York: Routledge, 2020), 68–84. Campos citation pp. 72–73.

27. Victoria De Grazia, *The Culture of Consent: Mass Organization of Leisure in Fascist Italy* (Cambridge: Cambridge University Press, 1981); Elena Vigilante, *L'Opera nazionale dopolavoro: Tempo libero dei lavoratori, assistenza e regime fascista, 1935–1943* (Bologna: Il Mulino, 2014); Daniela Liebscher, *Freude und Arbeit: zur internationalen Freizeit- und Sozialpolitik des faschistischen Italien und des NS-Regimes* (Cologne: SH-Verlag, 2009); Sandrine Kott and Kiran Klaus Patel, eds. *Nazism across Borders: The Social Policies of the Third Reich and their Global Appeal* (New York: Oxford University Press, 2018); Jorge Sgrazzutti and Diego Roldan, "Tiempo Libre y Disciplinamiento en las Clases Obreras Italiana y Aleman de Entreguerras. Dopolavoro y Kraft durch Freude: Un Análisis Comparativo," *Historia Social* 52 (2005): 109–127.

28. Cohen, *Le siècle des chefs*; Charles S. Maier, "The Factory as Society," in *In Search of Stability: Explorations in Historical Political Economy* (Cambridge: Cambridge University Press), 19–64, esp. 56–63.

29. On corporatism and Monoilesco, see Philippe Schmitter, "Still the Era of Corporatism?" *Review of Politics* 36, no. 1 (1974): 85–131; for contemporary elaborations of corporatism, see Anna Panicali, ed., *Bottai: Il fascismo come rivoluzione del capitale* (Bologna: Cappelli, 1978) and Louis Rosenstock-Franck, *L'économie corporative fasciste en doctrine et en fait* (Paris: J. Gamber, 1938). Fascist corporatism can be distinguished from (although related to) fascist "syndicalism," a doctrine of labor-union administration of the economy, a tendency that finally had to be curbed in 1928. See David D. Roberts, *The Syndicalist Tradition and Italian Fascism* (Chapel Hill: University of North Carolina Press, 1979).

30. On the facade-like nature, see Gaetano Salvemini, *Under the Axe of Fascism* (New York: Viking Press, 1936); Sabino Cassese, "Corporazione e intervento pubblico nell'economia," in *Il regime fascista*, ed. Alberto Aquarone and Maurizio Vernassa (Bologna: Il Mulino, 1974). But cf. Alessio Gagliardi, *Il corporativismo fascista* (Rome: Laterza, 2010) and for an English-language résumé of the debate, Gagliardi, "The Corporatism of Fascist Italy between Words and Reality," in *Corporativismo Historico no Brasil e na Europa, Estudos Ibero-Americanos* 42, no. 2 (2016): 409–429. See also Bruno Settis, "Fascism and the Economy: Private Powers and Public Intervention

between Development and Crisis," in *Rethinking Fascism: Theory and History*, ed. Giulia Albanese (London: Routledge, 2022), 104–131; and Guido Mellis, *La macchina imperfetta: Immagine e realtà dello stato fascista* (Bologna: Mulino, 2018), 300–320, and on the tensions in the corporativist structures, 412–447. Earlier discussions in Adrian Lyttleton, *The Seizure of Power: Fascism in Italy 1919–1929* (London: Weidenfeld and Nicolson, 1973) and Renzo De Felice, *Mussolini*, vol. 2, pt. 2: *L'organizzazione dello stato fascista, 1925–1929*, vol. 3, *Il duce*, pt. 1 and 2 (Turin: Einaudi, 1970–); Maier, *Recasting Bourgeois Europe*, 545–578.

31. On Vianna, a complex thinker combining elements of eugenics and admiration for the US Progressive era with his corporatism, Melissa Teixera, "Making a Brazilian New Deal: Oliveira Vianna and the Transnational Sources of Brazil's Corporatist Experiment," *Journal of Latin American Studies* 50, no. 3 (2018): 1–29; also Leslie Bethell, "Politics in Brazil under Vargas, 1930–1945," in *The Cambridge History of Latin America*, ed. Leslie Bethell (Cambridge: Cambridge University Press, 2008), 1–86.

32. Rüdiger Hachtman, "Die Krise der nationalsozialistischen Arbeiterver- fassung: Pläne zur Änderung der Tarifgestaltung 1936–1940," *Kritische Justiz* 17 (1984); for more detail, see Charles S. Maier, "Economics of Fascism and Nazism," in *In Search of Stability*, 75–87. Timothy Mason's work remains fundamental to the study of German labor under Nazism although his insistence on the power of their con- tinuing resistance is controversial. See T. W. Mason, *Arbeiterklasse und Volksgemein- schaft: Dokumente und Materialien zur dutschen Arbeiterpolitik 1936–1939* (Opladen: Westdeutscher Verlag, 1975), and the essays in T. W. Mason, *Nazism, Fascism and the Working Class*, ed. Jane Caplan (Cambridge: Cambridge University Press, 1995).

33. E. H. Carr, with R. W. Davies, *A History of Soviet Russia: The Bolshevik Rev- olution, 1917–1923*, vol. I (London: Macmillan, 1951), 233–234; *Foundations of a Planned Economy, 1926–1929*, vol. II (London: Macmillan, 1971, and Pelican, 1976), esp. 309–315, 319, and passim.

34. Dietmar Petzina, *Autarkiepolitik im Dritten Reich* (Stuttgart: Deutsche Verlag- sanstalt, 1968); Adam Tooze, *Statistics and the German State, 1900–1945* (Cambridge: Cambridge University Press, 2001); also Adam Tooze, *The Wages of Destruction: The Making and Breaking of the Nazi Economy* (London: Allen Lane, 2006); F. W. Seidler, "L'Organisation Todt," *Revue de l'histoire de la deuxième guerre mondiale* 34, no. 134 (1984): 33–58.

35. Ian Kershaw, "'Working towards the Führer': Reflections on the Nature of the Hitler Dictatorship," *Contemporary European History* 2, no. 2 (July 1993): 103–118.

36. Martin Broszat, *The Hitler State: The Foundation and Development of the Third Reich* (London: Longman, 1981). See also Chapter 10.

37. Franz Neumann, *Behemoth: The Structure and Practice of National Socialism 1933–1944* (New York: Oxford University Press, 1944); also valuable, Robert A. Brady, *The Spirit and Structure of German Fascism* (New York: Viking, 1937).

38. Arthur M. Schlesinger Jr.'s *The Age of Roosevelt*, vols. 2 and 3, *The Coming of the New Deal* and *The Politics of Upheaval* (Boston: Houghton Mifflin, 1958, 1960) remains a superb narrative. See also David M. Kennedy, *Freedom from Fear: The American People in Depression and War, 1929–1945* (New York: Oxford University Press, 1999) and Ira Katznelson, *Fear Itself: The New Deal and the Origins of Our Time* (New York: Liveright, 2013). On the massive literature surrounding the Supreme Court's turnaround, see Laura Kalman, "The Constitution, the Supreme Court, and the New Deal," *American Historical Review* 110, no. 4 (October 2005): 1052–1079.

39. See Lincoln C. Chen, "China Medical Board: A Century of Rockefeller Health Philanthropy," *The Lancet* 384, no. 9945 (2014): 717–719. On the trope of "eradication" of disease rather than "control," see Nancy Leys Stepan, *Eradication: Ridding the World of Diseases Forever?* (Ithaca, NY: Cornell University Press, 2011). See also Chapter 3.

40. See Thomas Etzemüller, ed., *Die Ordnung der Moderne: Social Engineering im 20. Jahrhundert* (Bielefeld: TrascriptVerlag, 2009).

41. Phoebe Cutler, *The Public Landscape of the New Deal* (New Haven, CT: Yale University Press, 1985); Neil M. Maher, *Nature's New Deal* (Oxford: Oxford University Press, 2008); Sarah T. Phillips, *This Land, This Nation: Conservation, Rural America, and the New Deal* (Cambridge: Cambridge University Press, 2007); Frank Uekötter, *The Green and the Brown: A History of Conservation in Nazi Germany* (Cambridge: Cambridge University Press, 2006).

42. Stephanie Smith, *The Power and Politics of Art in Postrevolutionary Mexico* (Chapel Hill: University of North Carolina Press, 2017); Mary Coffey, *How Revolutionary Art Became Official Culture: Murals, Museums, and the Mexican State* (Durham, NC: Duke University Press, 2012); Alejandro Anreus, Robin Greely, and Leonard Folgarait, eds., *Mexican Muralism: A Critical History* (Berkeley: University of California Press, 2012); Richard D. McKinzie, *The New Deal for Artists* (Princeton, NJ: Princeton University Press, 1973).

43. Patrizia Dogliani, "Environment and Leisure during Fascism," *Modern Italy* 19, no. 3 (2014): 247–259. Quoting L. H. Weir, *Europe at Play, 1937: A Study of Recreation and Leisure Time Activities* (New York: A. S. Barnes, 1937), 10–13. Weir recognized that for all the fascist overlay, Ballila kids enjoyed the sports for their own sake. Nudism had a harder go in Catholic Italy than in Germany where Weimar culture flaunted it even before the Third Reich.

44. Michael K Bess, *Routes of Compromise: Building Roads and Shaping the Nation in Mexico, 1917–1952* (Lincoln: University of Nebraska Press, 2017); Jennifer Jolly, *Creating Patzcuaro, Creating Mexico: Art, Tourism and Nation Building under Lázaro Cárdenas* (Austin: University of Texas Press, 2018).

45. Karl Schlögel, *Moscow, 1937*, trans. Rodney Livingstone (Cambridge: Polity Press, 2012), 276, 278.

46. S. De Martino and A. Wall, eds., *Cities of Childhood: Italian Colonies of the 1930s* (London: Architectural Association, 1988).

47. Akihito Aoi, "Transplanting State Shinto: The Reconfiguration of Existing Built and Natural Environments in Colonized Taiwan," in *Constructing the Colonized Land: Entwined Perspectives of East Asia around WWII*, ed. Izumi Kuroishi (Farnham UK: Ashgate, 2014), 97–121.

48. Chao-Ching Fu, "From Political Governance and Spatial Restructure to Urban Transformation and Architectural Achievements: Discourse on Architecture in the Japanese Colonial Period, 1895–1945," in *Constructing the Colonized Land*, 123–144.

49. For the classic statement, Immanuel Kant, "Perpetual Peace: A Philosophical Sketch," 1795; for the voluminous controversies and bibliography, see the "Democratic Peace Theory," Wikipedia; among other contributions, Michael W. Doyle, *Liberal Peace: Selected Essays* (New York: Routledge, 2011); Bruce Russet, *Grasping the Democratic Peace: Princeiples for a Post-Cold-War World* (Princeton, NJ: Princeton University Press, 1993).

50. For praise of the ordinary business leader in the British war effort, see David Edgerton's revisionist treatment, *Britain's War Machine: Weapons, Resources and Experts in the Second World War* (London: Penguin, 2012), esp. chap. 8. For the American business leaders and the marginalization of labor, see Paul A. Koistinen, "Mobilizing the World War II Economy: Labor and the Industrial-Military Alliance," *Pacific Historical Review* 42 (November 1973): 443–478; Thomas Heinrich, "Fighting Ships That Require Knowledge and Experience: Industrial Mobilization in American Naval Shipbuilding, 1940–1945," *Business History Review* 88 (Summer 2014): 273–301; Robert B. Patterson, *Arming the Nation for War: Mobilization, Supply, and the American War Effort in World War II* (Knoxville: University of Tennessee Press, 2014); Ralph Elberton Smith, *The Army and Economic Mobilization, United States Army in World War II* (Washington, DC: Center of Military History, United States Army); other experiences, Yoshiro Miwa, *Japan's Economic Planning and Mobilization in Wartime, 1930s–1940s: The Competence of the State* (Cambridge: Cambridge University Press, 2014); Ioannis-Dionysios Salavrakos, "A Re-assessment of the Japanese Armaments Production during World War II," *Defence and Peace Economics* 29, no. 7/8 (2018): 871–885.

51. Tooze, *Statistics and the German State*, 254. On economic performance, see also Tooze, *The Wages of Destruction*; also Richard J. Overy, *War and Economy in the Third Reich* (Oxford, 1994); R. D. Müller, "Die Mobilisierung der deutschen Wirtschaft für Hitlers Kriegsführung," in *Das Deutsche Reich und der Zweite Weltkrieg*, ed. B. R. Kroener, R.-D. Müller, and H. Umbreit (Stuttgart: Deutsche Verlags-Anstalt [henceforth DVA], 1988), 5:347–689; G. Janssen, *Das Ministerium Speer: Deutschlands Rüstung im Krieg* (Frankfurt: Ullstein, 1968).

52. Ludolf Herbst, *Der Totale Krieg und die Ordnung der Wirtschaft. Die Krieg-swirtschaft im Spannungsfeld von Politik, Ideologie und Propaganda 1939–1945* (Stuttgart: DVA, 1982).

53. Albert Speer, *Inside the Third Reich: Memoirs by Albert Speer*, trans. Richard Winston and Clara Winston (New York: Macmillan, 1970).

54. D. N. Chester, ed., *Lessons of the British War Economy* (Cambridge: Cambridge University Press and National Institute for Economic and Social Research, 1951); also H. M. D. Parker, *Man Power: A Study of War-time Policy and Administration* (London: HMSO, 1957), 101ff. Germans had a less stringent problem as they dragooned 6 million foreign workers to work in the factories of the Great German Reich. See the discussion of controversies up to the mid-1980s in Charles S. Maier, "The Economics of Fascism and Nazism," in *In Search of Stability: Explorations in Historical Political Economy* (Cambridge: Cambridge University Press, 1987), esp. 104–112..

55. On the debate, see Annette Schlimm, "'Harmonie zu schaffen ist Sinn und Zweck' Der Verkehrsdiskurs und die räumliche Ordnung des Sozialen," in Etzemüller, *Die Ordnung der Moderne)* 67–86.

2. The Promise of Resource Empires

1. Not to be forgotten, countries with overseas empires also ruled over restive national minorities at home: Germany included a significant Polish-speaking population, the formerly French citizens of Alsace and Lorraine, and a small Danish minority—and it called itself a "Reich," an official designation it would retain between the wars, including its years as a republic. Britain still ruled Ireland. The United States had continually expanded over its continent and governed Native American populations. Portugal, which entered the war as an Ally, also possessed colonies, as did Spain and the Netherlands, which remained neutral. Geoffrey Hosking drew the distinction between Britain, which had an empire, and Russia, which was an empire (Geoffrey Hosking, "The Freudian Fronter," *Times Literary Supplement*, March 10, 1995, 27). China was itself an empire, although one in prolonged crisis. For discussion about the varieties of empire, see Charles S. Maier, *Among Empires: American Ascendancy and Its Predecessors* (Cambridge, MA: Harvard University Press, 2006).

2. Jane Burbank and Frederick Cooper, *Empires in World History: Power and the Politics of Difference* (Princeton, NJ: Princeton University Press, 2010); Karen Barkey, *Empire of Difference: The Ottomans in Historical Perspective* (Cambridge: Cambridge University Press, 2008). For a perspective from the viewpoint of those contesting empire as a system of racialized exploitation into the 1970s, see Adom Getachew, *Worldmaking after Empire: The Rise and Fall of Self-Determination* (Princeton, NJ: Princeton University Press, 2019).

3. Robert Delavignette, *Afrique orientale française*, one of the nine commemorative volumes published by the Commissariat général of the Exposition internationale de Paris (Paris: Société d'éditions géographiques, maritimes et coloniales, 1931), 59, 71. ("L'Afrique occidentale française est, en quelque sorte, une fondation de l'armée. Dans chaque poste, au moins, il y a une tombe militaire. . . . Il s'agissit d'abord de transporter rapidement de troupes et de pouvoir réprimer les tentatives d'insurrection. . . . Il s'agissait enfin de lutter contre l'énorme distance . . . , de sonder, une fois pour toutes, la profondeur des terres.")

4. Vladimir Lenin, *Imperialism, the Highest Stage of Capitalism: A Popular Outline* (Moscow: Foreign Languages Publishing, many editions); Joseph A. Schumpeter, *Zur Soziologie der Imperialismen* (Tübingen: J. C. B. Mohr, 1919), translation *Imperialism and Social Classes: Two Essays* (New York: Meridian, 1951). It should be noted that both Lenin and Schumpeter were thinking as much of great power rivalry in Eastern Europe and the Balkans as of colonialisms in Africa.

5. Gian Paolo Calchi Novati, *L'Africa d'Italia: Una storia coloniale e postcoloniale* (Rome: Carocci editore, 2011). For the incoherence of Italian economic policy toward its colonies—broader in coverage than its title—see Matteo Nardozi, "The Economic Policy of the Italian Administration in the Eritrean Colony in the Early 1920s: The Case of the Asmara Chamber of Commerce," *Journal of European Economic History* 50, no. 1 (January 2021): 133–156.

6. Ramon H. Myers, "Creating a Modern Enclave Economy: The Economic Integration of Japan, Manchuria, and North China, 1932–1945," in *The Japanese Wartime Empire, 1931–1945*, ed. Peter Duus, Ramon H. Myers, and Mark R. Peattie (Princeton, NJ: Princeton University Press, 1996), 136–170; Mark R. Peattie, *Ishiwara Kanji and Japan's Confrontation with the West* (Princeton, NJ: Princeton University Press, 1975); see also Louise Young, *Japan's Total Empire: Manchuria and the Culture of Wartime Imperialism* (Berkeley: University of California Press, 1999), 183–240, and Louise Young, "When Fascism Met Empire in Japanese-Occupied Manchuria," *Journal of Global History* 12, no. 2 (July 2017): 274–296, an argument for the particularities of Italian, German, and Japanese fascist empires. The issue followed a conference on the theme of fascist empires, held at the Munich LMU in November 2015. On the changing notions of citizenship and rights for the Japanese who lived in the empire (perhaps 6.5 million by 1945), see the working paper by Andrew M. Levidis, "In the Ruins of Jupiter: Empire, Parliament, and the Reordering of the World," paper presented at Global History and International Law Zoom seminar, Ann-Sophie Schopefel, curator, May 23, 2020; also Emer O'Dwyer's revealing study, "Mantetsu Democracy," *Modern Asian Studies* 47, no. 6 (2013): 1812–1844; and Louise Young, "Imagined Empire: The Cultural Construction of Manchukuo," in Duus et al., eds., *The Japanese Wartime Empire*, 71–97. For German administrative variety in its wartime empire, see Mark Mazower, *Hitler's Empire: How the Nazis Ruled Europe* (New York: Penguin, 2008).

7. Adam Tooze, *The Wages of Destruction: The Making and Breaking of the Nazi Economy* (New York: Penguin, 2008) emphasizes the centrality of US power and resources in Hitler's thinking.

8. See Martha Grzechnick, "Colonialism on the Margins: Polish Colonial Plans in the Interwar Period," research proposal on the Polish Maritime and Colonial League.

9. *Parliamentary Debates: Official Report*, 5th ser., 131 (July 8, 1920): Montagu, 1707–1708; Churchill, 727–733; Spoor, 1742–1743. For a major history of the empire focusing on the recourse to force, see Caroline Elkins, *Legacy of Violence: A History of the British Empire* (New York: Knopf, 2022).

10. Erez Manela, *The Wilsonian Moment: Self-Determination and the International Origins of Anticolonial Nationalism* (New York: Oxford University Press, 2007).

11. Amry Vandenbosch, *The Dutch East Indies, Its Government, Problems and Politics* (Berkeley: University of California Press, 1941), 68. Constitutional and administrative changes, chap. 5, 74–86. Dutch opinion on colonial administration divided between liberals, represented by the faculty of Leiden University and conservatives, dominant in Utrecht and the organized business association. Religious questions also played a large role. For a survey of the Indies between the wars, see M. C. Ricklefs, *A History of Modern Indonesia since c. 1200*, 3rd ed. (Stanford, CA: Stanford University Press, 2001), chaps. 4 and 5.

12. As the Dutch minster of the colonies stated in parliament, "Our work in India [i.e., the Netherlands Indies] will not have been completed within a foreseeable time.... We are in India and will remain there, in the first place in the well-recognized interest of India itself and of the people who inhabit it." Cited in Vandenbosch, *Dutch East Indies*, 70–71.

13. Vandenbosch, *Dutch East Indies*; also *Living Conditions of Plantation Workers and Peasants on Java in 1939–1940. Final Report of the Coolie Budget Commission.* Instituted by decree of the Directors of Justice and Economic Affairs of December 23, 1938. No. E. /82/20/21. December 30, 1941. Translation by Robert van Niel (Ithaca, NY: Southeast Asia Program, Cornell University, 1956).

14. Albert Sarraut, *La mise-en-valeur des colonies françaises* (Paris: Payot et Cie., 1923). For a study of Southeast Asian economic organization that stresses state involvement in systematizing plantation agriculture in the late colonial and postcolonial periods, see Stéphanie Barral, *Capitalismes agraires: Économie politique de la grande plantation en Indonésie et en Malaisie* (Paris: Presses de la FNSP, 2015).

15. For the small costs of the colonies to national budgets, see Elise Huillery, "The Black Man's Burden: The Cost of Colonization in French West Africa," *Journal of Economic History* 74, no. 1 (March 2014): 1–38. See also note 16. On the methodologies involved, cf. Patrick K. O'Brien, "The Costs and Benefits of British Imperialism, 1846–1914," *Past & Present*, no. 120 (August 1988): 164–200. For a general effort to summarize human gains and losses especially during the period

of conquest, see Bouda Etemad, *La possession du monde: Poids et mesures de la colonization (XVIII*ᵉ*–XX*ᵉ *siècles)* (Brussels: Éditions complexe, 2000). See also Patrick K. O'Brien and Leandro Prados de la Escosura's introduction to the articles in *Rivista de historia economica/Journal of Iberian and Latin American History* 16, no. 1 (1998): 29–89, which finds less reward than his *Past & Present* article above.

16. See Ewout Frankem and Frans Buelens, eds., *Colonial Exploitation and Economic Development: The Belgian Congo and the Netherlands Indies Compared* (London: Routledge, 2013). Also Pierre van der Eng, "Exploring Exploitation: The Netherlands and Colonial Indonesia," *Rivista de historia economica/Journal of Iberian and Latin American History* 16, no. 1 (1998): 323–349, which concludes that the colonial enterprises yielded significant interest and dividends although not much greater than the alternative uses of capital would have provided.

17. Lance E. Davis and Robert A. Huttenback, with the assistance of Susan Gray Davis, *Mammon and the Pursuit of Empire: The Economics of British Imperialism*, abridged ed. (Cambridge: Cambridge University Press, 1988). Colonial apologists in the early twentieth century, predominantly but not always on the right of the political spectrum, liked to claim that their proletariats at home received sufficient benefits from the colonies that they should rally to the imperial cause and shun the left parties—a claim socialists and labor advocates usually, but not always, rejected.

18. For the flavor of the celebration, see the lavish commemorative collection published by the Commissariat général of the Exposition internationale de Paris, Delavignette, *Afrique orientale française.*

19. Rosa Luxemburg, *The Accumulation of Capital*, trans. Agnes Schwarzschild (London: Routledge, 2003), 345–346.

20. D. K. Fieldhouse, "The Metropolitan Economics of Empire," in *The Oxford History of the British Empire*, vol. 4, *The Twentieth Century*, ed. Judith M. Brown and Wm. Roger Louis (Oxford: Oxford University Press, 1999), 98; percentages provided on p. 97, taken from Werner Schlote, *British Overseas Trade from 1700 to the 1930s* (Oxford: Blackwell, 1952), appendix, tables 21–22.

21. Paul Bernard, *Nouveaux aspects du problème économique indochinois* (Paris: Fernand Sorlot, 1937), 98

22. Michitake Aso, *Rubber and the Making of Vietnam: An Ecological History, 1897–1975* (Chapel Hill: University of North Carolina Press, 2018); Eric Panthou, *Les plantations Michelin au Viêt Nam: Une histoire sociale (1925–1940)* (Vertaizon, France: La Galipote Editeur, 2013), including also the vivid memoir of labor and rebellion by Tran Tu Binh, *Phu-Riêng: Récit d'une révolte*; for a company-sponsored account, see François Graveline, *Des hévéas et des hommes: L'aventure des plantations Michelin* (Paris: Chaudon, 2006); Corey Ross, *Ecology and Power in the Age of Empire: Europe and the Transformation of the Tropical World* (New York: Oxford University Press, 2017), 99–135; Moritz von Brescius, *A Global History of Assam Rubber* (forthcoming).

23. Jacques Marseille, *Empire colonial et capitalisme français: Histoire d'un divorce* (Paris: Albin Michel, 1984), 154. Elise Huillery's estimates thirty years later suggest both less significant investments and returns. She estimates that for French West Africa (AOF), the contribution from French taxpayers was negligible and provided only 2 percent of the vast region's revenue. Generalizing to French colonies as a whole, she argues that the colonies absorbed 1.6 percent of French annual (public) expenditure. Additionally, some have argued it provided poor or implicitly negative returns for the metropole's investors and payers. Huillery's decomposing of costs and loans contests Marseille's argument that French payments covered colonial trade deficits (which, in any case, could have been deficits of French-owned firms in Africa). See Elise Huillery, "The Black Man's Burden," *Journal of Economic History* 74, no. 1 (2014): 1–38.

24. Ewout Frankema, "Raising Revenue in the British Empire, 1870–1940: How 'Extractive' Were Colonial Taxes?" *Journal of Global History* 5 (2010): 447–477, quote on p. 455. The article contests the model of Daron Acemoglu, Simon Johnson, and James A. Robinson, "The Colonial Origins of Comparative Development: An Empirical Investigation," *American Economic Review* 91, no. 5 (2001): 1369–1401, who argue that tropical climates inhibited the development of settler colonies and the implanting of the legal institutions that allegedly safeguard private property and thus economic development.

25. Babacar Fall, *Le travail forcé en Afrique occidentale française (1900–1945)* (Paris: Karthala, 1993), 154 ("Il faut donc appeler les choses par leur vrai nom: il n'est pas possible de laisser subsister dans la réglementation le principe de la liberté du travail pour l'indigène quand il s'agit du recrutement de main-d'oeuvre dont les particuliers ont besoin"); see also 155–199 on the "second contingent," 201–252 on the *prestations* (essentially shorter terms of corvée), and 253–268, on the debates over the International Labour Organization resolution. For labor conditions, see Catherine Coquery-Vidrovitch, *Le Congo au temps des grandes concessionnaires, 1898–1930* (Paris: Mouton, 1972). On one "exemplary" enterprise, see J. P. Daughton, "The 'Pacha Affair' Reconsidered: Violence and Colonial Rule in Interwar French Equatorial Africa," *Journal of Modern History* 91 (September 2019): 493–524 ("the use of force was closely tied to the remarkable thinness of the French administrative presence on the ground in regions to the north," p. 521); and most recently J. P. Daughton, *In the Forest of No Joy: The Congo-Océan Railroad and the Tragedy of French Colonialism* (New York: Norton, 2021). Cf. Giles Sautter, "Notes sur la construction des chemins de fer Congo-océan (1924–1931)," *Cahiers d'études Africaines* 7, no. 26 (1967): 219–299, which documents the labor conflicts, food shortages, and abuse and mortality when the project was resumed in the 1920s; Ieme Van der Poel, *Congo-océan: Un chemin de fer colonial controverse*, 2 vols. (Paris: Harmattan, 2006) for an anthology of commentaries. On the contradiction between reformist ideologies percolating among the colonial administration in the interwar era

and the resort to violence locally, see Yves Slobodkin, "State of Violence: Administration and Reform in French West Africa," *French Historical Studies* 41, no. 1 (February 2018): 33–61; William B. Cohen, *Rulers of Empire: The French Colonial Service in Africa* (Stanford, CA: Hoover Institution Press, 1971).

26. Marlous van Waijenburg, "Financing the African Colonial State: The Revenue Imperative and Forced Labor," *Journal of Economic History* 78, no. 1 (March 2018): 40–80.

27. Frankema and Buelens, Introduction to *Colonial Exploitation and Economic Development*, 4–6.

28. J. Thomas Lindblad, "Manufacturing and Foreign Investment in Colonial Indonesia," in *Colonial Exploitation and Economic Development*, ed. Frankema and Buelens, 217–219 on investment, 212–213 on industrialization. (There is an apparent confusion on p. 218 concerning the percentage of firms headquartered in the Indies versus the Netherlands.)

29. Ingvar Svennilson, *Growth and Stagnation in the European Economy* (Geneva: Economic Commission for Europe, 1954); Charles Kindleberger, *The World in Depression, 1929–1939* (Berkeley: University of California Press, 1984); Barry J. Eichengreen, *Golden Fetters: The Gold Standard and the Great Depression, 1919–1939* (New York: Oxford University Press, 1992).

30. Marseille, *Empire Colonial*, 370–371. "Au moment où la disaffection de certains milieus d'affaire commence à se manifester, des voix s'élèvent de tous les horizons politiques pour célébrer la grandeur de la France imperiale." See also Vandenbosch, *The Dutch East Indies, Its Government, Problems and Politics*, 68.

31. See Dietmar Rothermund, *The Global Impact of the Great Depression, 1929–1939* (London: Routledge, 1996), esp. chap. 4 for the impact of commodity price declines. On the critical role of labor issues in undermining colonial empire, see Frederick Cooper, *Decolonization and African Society: The Labor Question in French and British Africa* (Cambridge: Cambridge University Press, 1996).

32. Marseille, *Empire colonial*, 44–45. The change was not adverse for the colonial populations. Although the prices of colonial primary products fell during the Depression, so did the price of the goods imported from France (66–76).

33. Marseille, *Empire colonial*, 187–188.

34. Marseille, *Empire colonial*, 189. The "franc germinal" of 1914 had retained the gold value it was given in 1803 and enjoyed a parity of about one-fifth of a dollar and close to one-twentieth of a pound sterling. When revalued in 1926/1928 as the "franc Poincaré," it retained about one-quarter of its prewar parity and would be devalued again during the 1930s, emerging at about 350 to the dollar after World War II.

35. Marseille, *Empire colonial*, 56–57.

36. Bernard, *Nouveaux aspects*, 92–99 (quote from 92: "notre grande possession asiatiatique a franchi le stade de la colonie considerée comme un simple comptoir

susceptible de procurer a la métropole des épices, des fruits exotiques, des articles de bazare d'exposition ou comme un vulgaire marché où l'industrie française peut s'assurer une clientèle aussi abondante que peu éxigeante. Elle doit devoir une véritable métropole-seconde, formant une unité économique plus ou moins distincte"). For an extensive summary, see Marseille, *Empire colonial*, chap. 10.

37. Marseille, *Empire colonial*, 211–219.

38. Marseille, *Empire colonial*, 101, 108.

39. Marseille, *Empire colonial*, 102–103.

40. Marseille, *Empire colonial*, 113.

41. Marseille, *Empire colonial*, 96 for interwar Indochina investment, 105 for postwar colonial investment, 148–149 for anxieties, citing *Cinquième rapport de la Commission des investissements, statistiques et études financières, supplément finances françaises*, no. 17, 61–62.

42. On these trends, see Herrick Chapman, *France's Long Reconstruction: In Search of the Modern Republic* (Cambridge, MA: Harvard University Press, 2018); Andrew Shonfield, *Modern Capitalism* (London: Pickering, 1994). On the almost total American coverage of French war costs in Indochina, see Hugues Tertrais, *La piastre et le fusil: Le coût de la guerre d'indochine 1945–1954* (Paris: Comité pour l'histoire économique et financière de la France, 2002), new edition online by Cambridge University Press, 2005.

43. Fieldhouse, "The Metropolitan Economics of Empire," 96–97, 100, table 4.2, drawing on Davis and Huttenback, *Mammon and the Pursuit of Empire*, table 2.1 (corrected), 40–41.

44. Fieldhouse, "Metropolitan Economics of Empire," 102. These figures excluded unquoted securities and UK company assets held abroad.

45. Fieldhouse, "Metropolitan Economics of Empire," 98–101.

46. For these insights, I am indebted to the ongoing research of Ravindar Knaur, University of Copenhagen.

47. See Fred Cooper, *Colonialism in Question: Theory, Knowledge, History* (Berkeley: University of California Press, 2005).

48. Adom Getachew, *Worldmaking after Empire: The Rise and Fall of Self-Determination* (Princeton, NJ: Princeton University Press, 2019), particularly chap. 5.

49. This is the argument of Christopher R. W. Dietrich's *Oil Revolution: Anticolonial Elites, Sovereign Rights, and the Economic Culture of Decolonization* (New York: Cambridge University Press, 2017). See also Chapter 6.

3. The Realm of Governance and the Web of Capital

1. Nadine Akhund-Lange and Stéphane Tison, "Penser la Grande Guerre au prismes des Balkans: Le témoignage de la Dotation Carnegie pour la paix internationale," *Monde(s)* 1, no. 9 (2016): 95–114.

2. But on the pitfalls of identifying states with territorial units compare John Agnew, "The Territorial Trap: The Geographical Assumptions of International Relations Theory," *Review of International Political Economy* 1, no. 1 (1994): 53–80; and amplified in John Agnew, *Globalization and Sovereignty*, 2nd ed. (London: Rowman & Littlefield, 2018). For a long-term historicization, see Saskia Sasson, *Territory-Authority-Rights: From Medieval to Global Assemblages*, updated ed. (Princeton, NJ: Princeton University Press, 2006).

3. For a brief survey of relevant US actors, Corinna R. Unger, "Present at the Creation: The Role of American Foundations in the International Development Arena, 1950s and 1960s," in *Institutional History Rediscovered: Observing Organizations' Behavior in Times of Change*, ed. Stefanie Middendorf, Ulrike Schulz, and Corinna Unger, theme issue of *Comparativ: Leipziger Beiträge zur Universalgeschichte und vergleichenden Gesellschaftsforschung* 24, no. 1 (2014).

4. Glenda Sluga and Patricia Clavin, eds., *Internationalisms: A Twentieth-Century History* (Cambridge: Cambridge University Press, 2017), 4. See also Glenda Sluga, *Internationalism in the Age of Nationalism* (Philadelphia: University of Pennsylvania Press, 2013). As they recognize, Akira Iriye (a colleague with whom I was privileged to teach together for several years) has been a moving spirit. See his *Cultural Internationalism and World Order* (Baltimore: Johns Hopkins University Press, 2000) and *Global Community: The Role of International Organizations in the Making of the Contemporary World* (Berkeley: University of California Press, 2004). Transnationalism as an overlapping concept suggests the concepts, events, and trends that impact societies across borders, often without formal negotiations.

5. For a Pollyanna-inflected history of the concept since the word began to make its way in the 1970s/1980s—emphasizing, "actorhood," "rationalization," "partnership," "accountability," "transparency," and so forth—see Gili S. Drori, John W. Meyer, and Hokyu Hwang, eds., *Globalization and Organization: World Society and Organizational Change* (New York: Oxford University Press, 2006), esp. the editors' chap. 1, '"World Society and the Proliferation of Formal Organization," and Drori's chap. 4, "Governed by Governance: The New Prism for Organizational Change."

6. Claus Offe, "Governance—an 'Empty Signifier'?" *Constellations* 16, no 4 (2009), https://onlinelibrary-wiley-com.ezp-prod1.hul.harvard.edu/doi/epdf/10.1111/j.1467-8675.2009.00570.x See also Charles S. Maier, "Governance e anti-Governance. Note sulla impasse attuale della politica democratica," in *Parolechiave* 46 (December 2016): 33–44.

7. E. H. Carr argued this point in his revisionist study of interwar international relations, *The Twenty Years' Crisis, 1919–1939: An Introduction to the Study of International Relations* (London: Macmillan, 1939); and Mark Mazower has suggested the same for the impulses behind the establishment of the United Nations: *No Enchanted*

Palace: The End of Empire and the Ideological Origins of the United Nations (Princeton, NJ: Princeton University Press, 2009).

8. For a résumé of critiques and later more positive judgments, see Joseph W. Winn, "Nicholas Murray Butler, the Carnegie Endowment for International Peace, and the Search for Reconciliation in Europe, 1919–1933," *Peace & Change* 31, no. 4 (October 2006): 555–584.

9. According to David Mitrany, membership in the Royal Institute of International Affairs (Chatham House) was by invitation and excluded Labourites and Liberals such as John Hobson. See *The Functional Theory of Politics* (London: Martin Robertson, 1975), 41.

10. See Peter M. Haas, "Introduction: Epistemic Communities and International Policy Coordination," *International Organization* 46, no. 1 (Winter 1992): 1–35.

11. Martei Koskenniemi, *The Gentle Civilizer of Nations: The Rise and Fall of International Law, 1870–1960* (Cambridge: Cambridge University Press, 2002).

12. Steffen Rimner, *Opium's Long Shadow: From Asian Revolt to Global Drug Control* (Cambridge, MA: Harvard University Press, 2018).

13. Winn, "Nicholas Murray Butler," 572.

14. Susan Pedersen, "Empires, States and the League of Nations," in *Internationalisms*, ed. Sluga and Clavin, 116.

15. Oona Anne Hathaway and Scott J. Shapiro, *The Internationalists: How a Radical Plan to Outlaw War Remade the World* (New York: Simon & Schuster, 2017). Since Germany had subscribed, the pact was cited at Nuremberg to support the Allies' charge that planning aggressive war was a violation of international law.

16. For an excellent study of the political impact of international radio transmission, see Heidi J. S. Tworek, *News from Germany: The Competition to Control World Communications, 1900–1945* (Cambridge, MA: Harvard University Press, 2019).

17. As Aden Knapp's ongoing dissertation research emphasizes, the effort to judicialize international dispute resolution through courts and arbitration was well under way before the League was established.

18. F. P. Walters, *A History of the League of Nations* (London: Royal Institute of International Affairs and Oxford University Press, 1952), 169–202 outlines the structure of league bodies; only a couple are mentioned here.

19. See Mira Siegelberg, *Statelessness: A Modern History* (Cambridge, MA: Harvard University Press, 2020).

20. Carole Fink, *Defending the Rights of Others: The Great Powers, the Jews, and International Minority Protection, 1878–1938* (Cambridge: Cambridge University Press, 2004). See also Marc Frey, Sönke Kunkel, and Corinna R. Unger, "Introduction: International Organizations, Global Development, and the Making of the Contemporary World," emphasizing "global governance," in *International Organizations and Development, 1945–1990*, ed. Marc Frey, Sönke Kunkel, and Corinna R. Unger

(Basingstoke, UK: Palgrave Macmillan, 2014), 1–22; Klaas Dykmann, "Only with the Best Intentions: International Organizations as Global Civilizers," *Comparativ* 23, no. 4/5 (2014): 21–46.

21. Natasha Wheatley, "New Subjects in International Law and Order," in *Internationalisms*, ed. Sluga and Clavin, 265–286.

22. See Winn in *Peace & Change*, 562ff., citation, 571; also Nicholas Murray Butler, *The International Mind* (New York: Scribner, 1913).

23. Léon Duguit, *Le droit social et le droit individuel et la transformation de l'état. Conferences faites à l'École des hautes études sociales* (Paris: Alcan 1922). For a summary of the solidarism of Duguit's doctrines, see Stéphane Pinon, "Le positivisme sociologique: L'itinéraire de Léon Dugit," *Revue interdisciplinaire d'études juridiques* 67 (2011–2012): 69–93.

24. See Leonie Holthaus and Jens Steffek, "Experiments in International Administration: The Forgotten Functionalism of James Arthur Salter," *Review of International Studies* 42 (2016): 114–135. I owe the citation to Jamie Martin's, *The Meddlers* (Cambridge, MA: Harvard University Press, 2021).

25. David Mitrany, "The Progress of International Government," in *The Functional Theory of Politics*, 97–98. The version of the lectures included in *The Functional Theory* is an extract from the first chapters of the book with the same title published by Yale University Press in 1935.

26. David Mitrany, "The Making of the Functional Theory of Politics: A Memoir," in *The Functional Theory of Politics*, 60–61 ("In the Romania of my youth popular anti-semitism was endemic.... It was anti-semitism, not Zionism that made Israel. But I also knew that a new 'fatherland' could not be built without the exclusive devotions and emotions that make up the binding power of nationalism. And because I knew this and accepted it as inevitable, I avoided the temptation and invitation to visit Israel and lecture there.")

27. Mitrany, *Functional Theory of Politics*, 13–16. His dismay led to his essay and then book, *Marx against the Peasant: A Study in Social Dogmatism* (London: Weidenfeld & Nicolson, 1951).

28. Mitrany, *Functional Theory of Politics*, 7.

29. For relevant orientations, see Paul Taylor's introduction to Mitrany, *Functional Theory of Politics*; also Hidemi Suganami, *The Domestic Analogy and World Order Proposals* (Cambridge: Cambridge University Press, 1989) on internationalist strategies in general.

30. Mitrany, *Functional Theory of Politics*, 17–18.

31. Mitrany, *Functional Theory of Politics*, 85–90.

32. Mitrany, *Functional Theory of Politics*, 100–101.

33. Mitrany, "Regional Pacts: Their Uses and Dangers," in *Functional Theory of Politics*, 152–153.

34. Mitrany, "The Progress of International Government," in *Functional Theory of Politics*, 99–101.

35. Mitrany, "A Wartime Submission (1941): Territorial, Ideological, or Functional International Organisation?" in *Functional Theory of Politics*, 109–110.

36. Mitrany, "A Wartime Submission," in *Functional Theory of Politics*, 113–122. Quote from 118 and 120–121.

37. See Mitrany, *Functional Theory of Politics*, 23–24 and his 1947 paper, "The Protection of Human Rights," in *Functional Theory of Politics*, 190.

38. "The Protection of Human Rights," 193–194; also *The Road to Security* (London: National Peace Council, 1944), 75–94.

39. Included in "The Protection of Human Rights," 197.

40. Sunil S. Amrith, *Decolonizing International Health: India and Southeast Asia* (Houndsmill, UK: Palgrave Macmillan, 2006); also Sunil S. Amrith, "Internationalising Health in the Twentieth Century," in *Internationalisms*, ed. Sluga and Clavin, 245–264; for nineteenth-century precedents, see Charles Rosenberg, *Explaining Epidemics and Other Studies in the History of Medicine* (Cambridge: Cambridge University Press, 1992); Peter Baldwin, *Contagion and the State in Europe, 1830–1930* (Cambridge: Cambridge University Press, 1999); on the sanitary conferences, see Neville M. Goodman, *International Health Organizations and Their Work* (London: Blakiston, 1952). Addiction was a health and criminality issue. An international convention to control opium traffic had finally been signed in 1912. The League established an advisory committee on traffic in opium and other dangerous drugs, with both the United States and the Soviet Union as members, produced new conventions in 1925 and 1931, and a central board and supervisory board to supervise production and limit exports and imports. Walters, *History of the League*, 183–186.

41. John Farley, *To Cast Out Disease: A History of the International Health Division of the Rockefeller Foundation (1913–1951)* (New York: Oxford University Press, 2004), 5–6. On the idea and practice of eradication, see Nancy Stepan, *Eradication: Ridding the World of Diseases Forever?* (Ithaca, NY: Cornell University Press, 2011), which focuses on Fred Soper and defends the effort: "In my judgement, merely to criticize eradication efforts as such seems wrong—a form of resignation to, or acceptance of, diseases in poor countries that would not be tolerated in rich ones." (16–17).

42. Ligia María Peña Torres and Steven Palmer, "A Rockefeller Foundation Health Primer for US-Occupied Nicaragua, 1914–1928," in *Canadian Bulletin of Medical History* 25, no. 1 (2008): 43–69, quote on 58.

43. The scholarship on public health and social determinants of medicine is imposing and I am not claiming familiarity with it. See Farley, *To Cast Out Disease*, 44–58; also Lion Murard and Patrick Zylberman, "L'autre guerre (1914–1918). La santé publique en France sous l'oeil de l'Amérique," *Revue historique* 276 (1986): 367–398.

44. Cited Farley, *To Cast Out Disease*, 117, who also cites on p. 16, Gladwell's comparison of field officer Fred Soper to Patton in "The Mosquito Killer," *New Yorker*, July 2, 2001, 43–51. See also Darwin H. Stapleton, "Lessons of History? Anti-Malaria Strategies of the International Health Board and the Rockefeller Foundation from the 1920s to the Era of DDT," *Public Health Reports* 119 (March–April 2004): 206–215. On the League's health effort, see I. Borowy, *Coming to Terms with World Health: The League of Nations Health Organsation 1921–1946* (Frankfurt: Peter Lang, 2009); Paul Weindling, ed., *International Health Organizations and Movements, 1919–1939* (Cambridge: Cambridge University Press, 1995); M. A. Balinska, *For the Good of Humanity: Ludwik Rajchman, Medical Statesman*, trans. R. Howell (Budapest: Central European University Press, 1998); also S. G. Solomon, Lion Murard, Patrick Zylberman, eds., *Shifting Boundaries of Public Health: Europe in the Twentieth Century* (Rochester, NY: University of Rochester Press, 2008), 87–113.

45. P. J. Brown, "Failure-as-Success: Multiple Meanings of Eradication in the Rockefeller Foundation Sardinia Project, 1946–1951," *Parassitologia* 40 (1998): 117–130, cited by Farley, *To Cast Out Disease*, 150. On the mosquito campaigns in Egypt, see Nancy Gallagher, *Egypt's Other Wars: Epidemics and the Politics of Public Health* (Syracuse, NY: Syracuse University Press, 1990) and Thomas Michell's encompassing interpretation, *Rule of Experts: Egypt, Techno-Politics, Modernity* (Berkeley: University of California Press, 2002). On eradication, see Stepan, *Eradication*, cited note 41.

46. A. E. Birn, "Backstage: The Relationship between the Rockefeller Foundation and the World Health Organization, Part I: 1940s–1960s," in *Public Health* 128 (2014): 129–140. On the history of the WHO, see Marco Cueto, *The World Health Organization: A History* (Cambridge: Cambridge University Press, 2019) and Amrith's work cited above.

47. Birn, "Backstage," 131–132.

48. See Norman Angell, *Arms and Industry. A Study of the Foundations of International Polity* (New York: Putnam, 1914), esp. Introductory Summary and Lecture III; following on Norman Angell, *The Great Illusion: A Study of the Relation of Military Power in Nations to Their Economic and Social Advantage* (New York: Putnam, 1910).

49. Dirk Hoerder, "Migrations and Belonging," in *A World Connecting, 1870–1945*, ed. Emily S. Rosenberg (Cambridge, MA: Harvard University Press, 2012), 435–589; Adam M. McKeon, "Global Migration, 1840–1940," *Journal of World History* 15, no. 2 (2005): 155–189.

50. Steven C. Topik and Allen Wells, "Commodity Chains in a Global, Economy," in *A World Connecting*, ed. Rosenberg, 594–812; wheat market, p. 699, table 4.8; also on prices, Dietmar Rothermund, *The Global Impact of the Great Depression 1929–1939* (London: Routledge, 1996).

51. For a magisterial history of the role of debt, see Kenneth Dyson, *States, Debt, and Power: "Saints" and "Sinners" in European History and Integration* (Oxford:

Oxford University Press, 2014). On the allied war debts to the United States, see Harold G. Moulton and Leo Pasvolsky, *War Debts and World Prosperity* (Washington, DC: Brookings Institution, 1932), and for the mirage of reparations, Stephen A. Schuker, *American "Reparations" to Germany, 1919–1933: Implications for the Third-World Debt Crisis* (Princeton, NJ: Department of Economics, Princeton University, 1988); and further sources cited in Charles S. Maier, *Recasting Bourgeois Europe: Stabilization in France, Germany, and Italy in the Decade after World War I* (Princeton, NJ: Princeton University Press, 1975), 587–589. Most recently for general context, Jamie Martin, *Meddlers: Sovereignty, Empire, and the Birth of Global Economic Governance* (Cambridge, MA: Harvard University Press, 2022); Adam Tooze, *The Deluge: The Great War, America and the Remaking of Global Order, 1916–1931* (New York: Viking, 2014).

52. Patricia Clavin, "Men and Markets: Global Capital and the International Economy," in *Internationalisms*, ed. Clavin and Sluga, 84–109.

53. Patricia Clavin, *Securing the World Economy: The Reinvention of the League of Nations, 1920–1946* (Oxford: Oxford University Press, 2013). For Salter's experiences as a civil service mandarin, see Martin, *Meddlers*, and Arthur Salter's *Memoirs of Public Servant* (London: Faber and Faber, 1961) and Arthur Salter, *Slave of the Lamp: A Public Servant's Notebook* (London: Weidenfeld & Nicolson, 1967).

54. Patricia Clavin, "The Austrian Hunger Crisis and the Genesis of International Organisation after the First World War," *International Affairs* 90, no. 2 (2014): 265–278; also Clavin "Men and Markets," 97–100. Juan Flores and Yann Decorzant, *Public Borrowing in Harsh Times: The League of Nations Loans Revisited*, University of Geneva Working Paper, WPS 12091 (September 2012); Barbara Susan Warnock, "The First Bailout: The Financial Reconstruction of Austria 1921–1926," PhD diss., Birkbeck University of London, 2015, https://eprints.bbk.ac.uk/id/eprint/40237/, emphasizes the embeddedness of the league's Economic and Financial Organisation with British and other banking elites. Nathan Marcus, *Austrian Reconstruction and the Collapse of Global Finance, 1921–1931* (Cambridge, MA: Harvard University Press, 2018) has a detailed account of the political bargaining; see also Elmus Wicker, "Terminating Hyperinflation in the Dismembered Habsburg Monarchy," *American Economic Review* 76, no. 3 (1986): 350–364; Eduard März, *Austrian Banking and Financial Policy: Creditanstalt at a Turning Point, 1913–23*, trans. Charles Kessler (London: Weidenfeld & Nicolson, 1984), 402–514; the older J. Walré de Bordes, *The Austrian Crown: Its Depreciation and Stabilization* (London: P. S. King, 1924).

55. On the German events, see Carl-Ludwig Holtfrerich, *Die Deutsche Inflation, 1914–1923: Ursachen und Folgen in internationaler Perspektive* (Berlin: Walter de Gruyter, 1980); and Gerald Feldman, *The Great Disorder: Politics, Economics, and Society in the German Inflation, 1914–1924* (New York: Oxford University Press, 1997). On the Dawes Plan, Stephen A. Schuker, *The End of French Predominance in*

Europe: *The Financial Crisis of 1924 and the Adoption of the Dawes Plan* (Chapel Hill: University of North Carolina Press, 1976).

56. See Barry J. Eichengreen, *Golden Fetters: The Gold Standard and the Great Depression, 1919–1939* (Oxford: Oxford University Press, 1992); W. A. Brown Jr., *England and the New Gold Standard, 1919–1926* (New Haven, CT: Yale University Press, 1929), and *The International Gold Standard Reinterpreted, 1914–1934*, 2 vols. (New York: National Bureau of Economic Research, 1940). Marc Flandreau, Jacques Le Cacheux, Frédéric Zumer, Rudi Dornbusch, and Patrick Honohan, "Stability without a Pact? Lessons from the European Gold Standard, 1880–1914," *Economic Policy* 13, no. 26 (1998): 115–162. See also Forrest Capie, "Central Bank Statutes: The Historical Dimension," in *Die Bedeutung der Unabhängigkeit der Notenbank für die Glaubwürdigkeit der europäischen Geldpolitik* (Vienna: Oesterreichische National-bank, 1997), 42–55. See also Beth A. Simmons, "Rulers of the Game: Central Bank Independence during the Interwar Years," *International Organization* 50, no. 3 (1996): 407–443; D. E. Moggridge, *The Return to Gold 1925: The Formulation of Economic Policy and Its Critics* (Cambridge: Cambridge University Press, 1969).

57. On the general conjuncture of inflation and stabilization, see Charles S. Maier, "The Politics of Inflation in the Twentieth Century," originally in *The Political Economy of Inflation*, ed. Fred Hirsch and John H. Goldthorpe (Cambridge, MA: Harvard University Press, 1978), now in Charles S. Maier, *In Search of Stability: Explorations in Historical Political Economy* (Cambridge: Cambridge University Press, 1987), 187–224.

58. E. H. Carr, *A History of Soviet Russia: The Bolshevik Revolution, 1917–1923*, vol. 2 [*The Economic Order*] (New York: Norton, 1985), chaps. 15–20.

59. R. S. Sayres, *The Bank of England, 1891–1944*, 3 vols. (Cambridge: Cambridge University Press, 1976); Stephen V. O. Clarke, *Central Bank Cooperation, 1924–1931* (New York: Federal Reserve Bank of New York, 1967); Kenneth Mouré, *Managing the Franc Poincaré: Economic Understanding and Political Constraint in French Monetary Policy, 1926–1936* (Cambridge: Cambridge University Press, 1931).

60. See Geoffrey Jones, *Multinationals and Global Capitalism: From the Nineteenth to the Twenty-First Century* (Oxford Scholarship Online, April 2005), http://doi.org/10.1093/0199272093.003.0002; also Mira Wilkinson, *The Maturing of Multinational Enterprise: American Business Abroad from 1914 to 1974* (Cambridge, MA: Harvard University Press, 1974).

61. For the International Chambers of Commerce, see Sophia Spiliotis, *Die Zeit der Wirtschaft: Business Statesmanship und die Geschichte der Internationalen Handels-kammer* (Göttingen: Wallstein Verlag, 2019). For the trade treaty and international steel cartel negotiations, see Maier, *Recasting*, 516–545.

62. Anthony M. Endres and Grant. A. Fleming, *International Organizations and the Analysis of Economic Policy, 1919–1950* (Cambridge: Cambridge University Press,

2002), 62–70; Bellerby was praised by Keynes for being part of "the almost revolutionary improvement" in understanding money, credit, and the trade cycle. On the Geneva economists, see also Clavin, *Securing the World Economy*.

63. See Gianni Toniolo and Piet Clement, eds., *Central Bank Cooperation at the Bank for International Settlements, 1930–1973* (Cambridge: Cambridge University Press, 2005); Yago Kazuhiko, *The Financial History of the Bank for International Settlements* (Oxford: Routledge, 2013); Paolo Baffi, *Le origini della cooperazione tra le banchi centrali: l'istituzione della Banca dei regolamenti internazionali* (Bari: Laterza, 2003).

64. Cited Endres and Fleming, *International Organizations*, 72.

65. Kazuhiko, *Financial History*, 48–54.

66. On fascist labor organization, see Italian discussions, cited above, Chapter 1, and in Maier, *Recasting*, 553–572; Gaetano Salvemini, *Under the Axe of Fascism* (New York: Viking, 1936); Adrian Lyttelton, *The Seizure of Power, Fascism in Italy 1919–1929* (London: Weidenfeld & Nicolson, 1973), 217ff.; T. W. Mason, *Nazism, Fascism and the Working Class*, ed. Jane Caplan (Cambridge: Cambridge University Press, 1995).

67. For the Depression, see Eichengreen, *Golden Fetters*; also Charles Kindleberger, *The World in Depression, 1929–1939*, rev. ed. (Berkeley: University of California Press, 1986).

68. See Peter A. Gourevitch, *Politics in Hard Times: Comparative Responses to International Economic Crises* (Ithaca, NY: Cornell University Press, 1986).

69. Mark Metzler, *Lever of Empire: The International Gold Standard and the Crisis of Liberalism in Prewar Japan* (Berkeley: University of California Press, 2006) covers the career of Inoue.

4. Projects for the Postwar

1. Alessandro Pizzorno, "The Individualistic Mobilization of Europe," *Daedalus* 93, no. 1 (Winter 1964): 199–224, quote 202. For the Soviet postwar period in particular, see Elena Zubkova, *Russia after the War: Hopes, Illusions and Disappointments 1945–1957* (New York: M. E. Sharpe, 1998).

2. Cf. Jytte Klausen, *War and Welfare: Europe and the United States, 1945 to the Present* (New York: St. Martin's, Palgrave, 2001). Nationalization and the National Health Services were instituted after Labour won the postponed general elections in 1945.

3. See Steve Fraser, "The 'Labor Question,'" and Nelson Lichtenstein, "From Corporatism to Collective Bargaining: Organized Labor and the Eclipse of Social Democracy in the Postwar Era," both in *The Rise and Fall of the New Deal Order, 1930–1980*, ed. Steve Fraser and Gary Gerstle (Princeton, NJ: Princeton University Press, 1989), 55–84 and 120–152. See also Nelson Lichtenstein, *Labor's War at Home: The*

CIO in World War II (New York: Cambridge University Press, 1982); Paul A. C. Koistinen, "Mobilizing the World War II Economy: Labor and the Industrial-Military Alliance," *Pacific Historical Review* 42 (November 1973): 443–478.

4. For the scenario of premeditated takeover, see Anne Applebaum, *Iron Curtain: The Crushing of Eastern Europe* (New York: Doubleday, 2012); for an earlier reconstruction arguing the defensiveness of Soviet policies, see Joyce Kolko and Gabriel Kolko, *The World and United States Foreign Policy, 1945–1954* (New York: Harper & Row, 1972). For recent scholarship and interpretations, see the essays in Melvyn P. Leffler and Odd Arne Westad, eds., *The Cambridge History of the Cold War*, vol. I: *Origins* (Cambridge: Cambridge University Press, 2010). For a review of the already voluminous literature a half century ago, see Charles S. Maier, "Revisionism and the Interpretation of Cold War Origins," *Perspectives in American History* 4 (1970).

5. Benjamin Martin, *The Nazi-Fascist New Order for European Culture* (Cambridge, MA: Harvard University Press, 2016). A useful comparison for the European postwar starting point is Pieter Lagrou, *The Legacy of Nazi Occupation: Patriotic Memory and National Recovery in Western Europe, 1945–1965* (Cambridge: Cambridge University Pres, 2000).

6. Matthew Hilton and Rana Mitter, "Introduction," *Past & Present*, suppl. 8 (2013): 10, an issue devoted to transnational institutions from the 1930s to the 1960s. The authors perceive a moment of genuine "internationalism" inherited from the interwar years but constrained in stages by geopolitical rivalries from the 1950s through the oil crisis of 1973. More generally, many authors have stressed "continuities" or resumptions of policies across the years of war.

7. For the ambitions of the anti-colonial leadership to go beyond Westphalian statehood, see Adom Getachew, *Worldmaking after Empire: The Rise and Fall of Self-Determination* (Princeton, NJ: Princeton University Press, 2019), chap. 3.

8. Mark Mazower, *No Enchanted Palace: The End of Empire and the Ideological Origins of the United Nations* (Princeton, NJ: Princeton University Press, 2009).

9. For statistics of Germans who came to trial, see Norbert Frei, "Nach der Tat: Die Ahndung deutscher Kriegs- und NS-Verbrechen in Europa—eine Bilanz," in *Transnationale Vergangenheitspolitik: der Umgang mit den deutschen Kriegsverbrechern in Europa nach dem Zweiten Weltkrieg* (Gottingen: Wallstein, 2006). For the Asian figures, see *The Chinese War of Resistance against Japanese Aggression: A Concise History*, a summary volume of *A History of the Chinese War of Resistance against Japanese Aggression*, ed. Bu Ping and Wang Jianlang (Beijing: Social Sciences Academic Press, 2019); see also "How Were the Japanese War Crimes Tried," *Beijing Review*, August 21, 2015, https://www.bjreview.com/special/2015-08/31/content_702186.htm.

10. A. N. Trainin, *Hitlerite Responsibility under Criminal Law* (London: Hutchinson, 1945), the translation of his 1944 Russian original. See Thomas E. Porter, "In Defense of Peace: Aron Trainin's Contribution to International Jurisprudence," *Genocide*

Studies and Prevention: An International Journal 13, no. 1 (2019): 98–112. Porter notes that Trainin, who was Jewish, along with many of the Soviet staff documenting German war crimes, insisted on specifying the anti-Jewish component of the crimes; he also worked with Raphael Lemkin's concept of genocide after the war. His contribution to Soviet law was far less savory; he was Andrei Vishinsky's chief assistant in the Moscow purge trials of 1936–1938. Cf. Arich J. Kochavi, *Prelude to Nuremberg: Allied War Crimes and the Question of Punishment* (Chapel Hill: University of North Carolina Press, 2005); Francine Hirsch, "The Soviets at Nuremberg: International Law, Propaganda, and the Making of the Postwar Order," *American Historical Review* 113, no. 3 (2008): 701–730. Gary Bass is researching the Tokyo war crimes tribunal; for now, see his *Stay the Hand of Vengeance: the Politics of War Crimes Tribunals* (Princeton, NJ: Princeton University Press, 2019).

11. See the case of Vittorio Valetta, the manager of FIAT, in Valerio Castronovo, *Giovanni Agnelli: la FIAT dal 1899 al 1945* (Turin: Einaudi, 1977), 125–155.

12. Among recent studies, István Deak, *Europe on Trial: The Story of Collaboration, Resistance, and Retribution during World War II* (Philadelphia: Perseus/Westview, 2015); István Deak, Jan T. Gross, and Tony Judt, eds., *The Politics of Retribution in Europe: World War II and Aftermath* (Princeton, NJ: Princeton University Press, 2000); Michele Battini, *The Missing Italian Nuremberg: Cultural Amnesia and Postwar Politics* (New York: Palgrave Macmillan, 2007); Benjamin Frommer, *National Cleansing: Retribution against Collaborators in Postwar Czechoslovakia* (Cambridge: Cambridge University Press, 2005); Klaus-Dietmar Henke and Hans Woller, eds., *Politische Säuberung in Europa: Die Abrechnung mit Faschismus und Kollaboration nach dem Zweiten Weltkrieg* (Munich: Deutscher Taschenbuch-Verlag, 1991); Peter Novick, *The Resistance versus Vichy: The Purge of Collaborators in Liberated France* (New York: Columbia University Press, 1968). For a review of the literature about the trials of Germans (and a bit on Japanese trials), see Devin O. Pendas's sobering assessment, "Seeking Justice, Finding Law: Nazi Trials in Postwar Europe," *Journal of Modern History* 81 (June 2000): 347–368. for political context in Germany: Norbert Frei, *Vergangenheitspolitik: Die Anfänge der Bundesrepublik und die NS-Vergangenheit* (Munich: Beck, 1996).

13. For the limitations on the achievements of American labor and institutionalization of the welfare state in the United States, see Steve Fraser and Gary Gerstle, eds., *The Rise and Fall of the New Deal Order, 1930–1980* (Princeton, NJ: Princeton University Press, 1989) especially the essays by Fraser, Alan Brinkley, Nelson Lichtenstein, and Ira Katznelson—also cited below.

14. For the Swedish debates and outcomes and their comparability to Britain's, see Klausen, *War and Welfare*, 129–163. Recent work has rightly emphasized the virtually organic connection between war and welfare. See Theda Skocpol's *Protecting Soldiers and Mothers: The Political Origins of Social Policy in the United States* (Cambridge, MA: Harvard University Press, 1992 (which adds gender analysis to the mix);

David Edgerton, *Warfare State: Britain 1920–1970* (Cambridge: Cambridge University Press, 1993); and for a recent general study of the British experience, Chris Renwick, *Bread for All: The Origins of the Welfare State* (New York: Penguin, 2017).

15. Peter Baldwin, *The Politics of Social Solidarity: Class Bases of the European Welfare State, 1875–1975* (Cambridge: Cambridge University Press, 1990); for Britain and France, Susan Pedersen, *Family, Dependence, and the Origins of the Welfare State: Britain and France, 1914–1945* (Cambridge: Cambridge University Press, 1993); for Italy, see the Banca d'Italia's Collana Storica, *Saggi e ricerche*, vol. VII: Maurizio Ferrera, Valeria Fargion, and Matteo Jessoula, *Alle radici del welfare all'italiana: Origini e futuro di un modello sociale squilibrato* (Venice: Marsilio, 2012). A useful summary of postwar catch-up in Italy (largely in the 1960s and 1970s) emerges from Manfredi Alberti, "Il *welfare* italiano visto dall'osservatorio dell' International Labour Organization (1944–1968)," conference paper at Sissco, Cantieri di Storia, VIII, Viterbo, September 14–16, 2015.

16. T. H. Marshall and Tom Bottomore, eds., *Citizenship and Social Class* (London: Pluto, 1992), 1–52, citation on 40. For fundamental discussions of the conceptual foundation of the welfare state, starting with the French example of the law on industrial accidents in 1898, see François Ewald, *L'État providence* (Paris: Grasset, 1986)—which argued in the face of neoliberal critiques that there could be no crisis of the welfare state, just of options for funding it, furthermore that society exists to overcome social risks—and Ulrich Beck, *Risikogesellschaft: Auf dem Weg in eine andere Moderne* (Frankfurt: Suhrkamp Verlag, 1986), who argues that society itself cannot be divorced from risk.

17. Richard M. Titmuss, *Problems of Social Policy* (London: HMSO, 1950); also *Essays on "The Welfare State,"* 2nd ed. (Boston: Beacon, 1969)

18. Marie Luise-Recker, *Nationalsozialistische Sozialpolitik im Zweiten Weltkrieg* (Munich: Oldenbourg Verlag, 1985), 82–98 on wages, 98–152 on pensions, health, and housing.

19. Recker, *Nationalsozialistische Sozialpolitik*, 300–301; for the postwar, I rely on Hans-Günter Hockerts, *Sozialpolitische Entscheidungen im Nachkriegsdeutschland: Allierte und deutsche Scozialversicherungspolitik 1945–1957* (Stuttgart: Klett-Cotta, 1980), "epochal," p. 11.

20. See Christopher R. Jackson, "Industrial Labor between Revolution and Repression: Labor Law and Society in Germany, 1918–1945," PhD diss., Harvard University, 1993; also T. W. Mason, "The Origins of the Law on the Organization of National Labour of 20 January 1934: An Investigation into the Relationship between 'Archaic' and 'Modern' Elements in Recent German History," now in T. W. Mason, *Nazism, Fascism, and the Working Class* ed. Jane Caplan (Cambridge: Cambridge University Press, 1995). For a valuable older general survey, Friedrich Syrup, *Hundert Jahre Staatliche Sozialpolitik, 1839–1939* (Stuttgart: W. Kohlhammer, 1957).

21. Erich Potthoff, *Der Kampf um die Mitbestimmung* (Cologne: Bund Verlag, 1957).

22. On the factory councils in early–post–World War II Germany, see Michael Fichter, "Aufbau und Neuordnung: Betriebsräte zwischen Klassensolidarität und Betriebsloyalität," in *Von Stalingrad zu Wäherungsreform. Zur Sozialgeschichte des Umbruchs in Deutschland*, ed. Martin Broszat, Klaus-Dietmar Henke, and Hans Woller (Munich: R. Oldenbourg Verlag, 1988), 469–549. The literature on the councils and council movement after World War I is enormous—whether with respect to Weimar Germany's *Betriebsräte*, the councils in Turin, championed by Antonio Gramsci, or the related Guild Socialist movement among British socialists. Important theoretical works included Karl Korsch, *Schriften zur Sozialisierung*, ed. Erich Gerlach (Frankfurt: Europäische Verlagsanstalt, 1969); Antonio Gramsci, *L'Ordine nuovo: Scritti, 1913–1926, Opere di Antonio Gramsci*, vol. IV (Turin: Einaudi, 1987), 135–153; a brief survey in Charles S. Maier, *Recasting Bourgeois Europe*, 133–153.

23. See Stephen Brooke, "Problems of 'Socialist Planning': Evan Durbin and the Labour Government of 1945," *The Historical Journal* 94, no. 3 (1991): 687–702.

24. On the shape of the postwar economy with its mix of private and political industry, which nonetheless produced the "miracle" of the 1950s, see Mariuccia Salvati, *Stato e industria nella ricostruzione: Alle origini del potere democristiano, 1944/1949* (Milan: Feltrinelli, 1982); and the essays in Fabio Levi, Paride Rugafiori, and Salvatore Vento, *Il triangolo industriale tra ricostruzione e lotta di classe 1945–1948* (Milan: Feltrinelli, 1974).

25. For prewar planning, see the survey in Kiran Klaus Patel, *The New Deal: A Global History* (Princeton, NJ: Princeton University Press, 2016), 90–103; French Socialist André Philip, *La crise et l'économie dirigée* (Paris: Éditions de Cluny, 1935), a favorable study of the New Deal; and Ellis Hawley, *The New Deal and the Problem of Monopoly: A Study in Economic Ambivalence* (Princeton, NJ: Princeton University Press, 1966). For the New Deal's flirtation with planning, see also Lewis L. Lorwin and A. Ford Hinrichs, *National Economic and Social Planning* (Washington, DC: Government Printing Office, 1935); Charles F. Roos, *NRA Economic Planning* (Bloomington, IN: Principia, 1937); and Charles Merriam, "The National Resources Planning Board: A Chapter in American Planning Experience," *American Political Science Review* 38 (December 1944): 1075–1088; also Alan Brinkley, "The Idea of the State," in in Fraser and Gerstle, *Rise and Fall of the New Deal Order*, esp. 106–107. For Europeans' planning enthusiasm, Tommaso Milani, *Hendrik de Man and Social Democracy: The Idea of Planning in Western Europe, 1914–1940* (London: Palgrave Macmillan, 2020). De Man's trajectory carried him toward fascism and collaboration.

26. Herrick Chapman, *France's Long Reconstruction: In Search of the Modern Republic* (Cambridge, MA: Harvard University Press, 2018), chap. 5.

27. See Alessandro Persico, *Pasquale Saraceno: un Progetto per l'Italia* (Soveria Mannelli: Rubbettino, 2013); *Pasquale Saraceno e l'unità economica italiana: Convegno tenuto a Milano il 16 e 17 aprile 2012* . . . (Soveria Mannelli: Rubettino, 2013); Roberto Bonuglia, *Tra economia e politica: Pasquale Saraceno* (Rome: Nuova Cultura, 2010). The literature on Monnet tends toward hagiography but see Klaus Schwabe, *Jean Monnet: Frankreich, die Deutschen und die Einigung Europas* (Baden-Baden: Nomos, 2016) and François Duchêne, *Jean Monnet: the First Statesman of Interdependence* (New York: Norton, 1994).

28. For the Thyssen plans, Bundesarchiv Koblenz, Verwaltungsamt für Eisen und Stahl, Z 41/23; on Italian steel planners, F. Bonelli et al., *Accaio per l'industrializzazione: Contribuiti allo studio del problema siderurgico italiano* (Turin: Einaudi, 1982), 335–369, and the documentation in the Archivio Centrale dello Stato, Carte De Gasperi, Busta Sinigaglia.

29. See Brooke, "Problems of 'Socialist Planning,'" 687–702.

30. Alvin H. Hansen, "The Postwar Economy," 10, and Seymour E. Harris, Introduction to *Postwar Economic Problems*, ed. Seymour E. Harris (New York: McGraw Hill, 1943), 3. See in particular the young Richard Bissell's "The State of Capitalism: Capitalism in the Postwar World," 83–110. Bissell coordinated the contributions. Harris became head of the Americans for Democratic Action later in the 1950s: as a prolific editor of timely essay collections, he was introduced once by a colleague, "I am sure Professor Harris needs no introduction; you've all written his books." Notable other contributors included Alvin Hansen, Paul Samuelson, the Marxist Alan Sweezy, and the idiosyncratic Joseph Schumpeter. Always the activist, Bissell went on to serve as a major economist in the headquarters of the Marshall Plan, the ECA, where he gave it a Keynesian emphasis by 1949–1952 and was an advocate of "integration," then to the Ford Foundation and the Central Intelligence Agency, where he helped plan the disastrous Bay of Pigs effort to overthrow Fidel Castro. See his memoir, *From Yalta to the Bay of Pigs: Reflections of a Cold Warrior* (New Haven, CT: Yale University Press), esp. chaps. 4 and 5.

31. Cited from "Manpower," *Socialist Commentary*, April 1949, 6–8, in Brooke, "Problems of 'Socialist Planning,'" 698

32. Robert L. Hardgrave Jr. and Stanley A. Kochanek, *India: Government and Politics in a Developing Nation*, 5th ed. (New York: Harcourt Brace, 1993), 353–359; B.T. Advani, *Influence of Socialism on Policies, Legislation and Administration of India since Independence (1947–62)* (New Delhi: Sterling Publishers, 1972), 35, 97–109, 110; Francine R. Frankel, *India's Political Economy, 1947–1977* (Princeton, NJ: Princeton University Press, 1978).

33. William C. Kirby, "Planning Postwar China: China, the United States, and Postwar Economic Strategies, 1941–1948," communicated by the author, 1–31; also William C. Kirby, "Engineering China: Birth of the Developmental State, 1928–1937,"

in Wen-hsin Ye, ed., *Becoming Chinese: Passages to Modernity and Beyond* (Berkeley: University of California Press, 2000), 137–160. See also Chapter 1.

34. Rana Mitter, *Forgotten Ally: China's World War II, 1937–1945* (Boston: Houghton Mifflin Harcourt, 2013); also Rana Mitter, "Relief and Reconstruction in Wartime China," *European Journal of East Asian Studies* 11, no. 2 (2012): 179–186, and Rana Mitter, "State-Building after Disaster: Jian Tingfu and the Reconstruction of Post–World War II China, 1943–1949," *Comparative Studies in Society and History* 61, no. 1 (January 2019): 176–206; "Imperialism, Transnationalism, and the Recon-struction of Post-War China: UNRRA in China, 1944–7," in *Past & Present*, suppl. 8 (2013): 51–69. Many aspects of post-1949 developed in wartime and postwar refugee policy, 67–69.

35. For a survey of the civil war, Odd Arne Westad, *Decisive Encounters: The Chi-nese Civil War, 1946–1950* (Stanford, CA: Stanford University Press), 2003. For the Communists' initial activity, see Jeremy Brown and Paul G. Pickowicz, eds., *Dilemmas of Victory: The Early Years of the People's Republic of China* (Cambridge, MA: Harvard University Press, 2007), esp. Frederic Wakeman Jr., "'Cleanup': The New Order in Shanghai," 21–58, and Elizabeth Perry "Masters of the Country? Shanghai Workers in the Early People's Republic," 59–79.

36. Christy Thornton, *Revolution in Development: Mexico and the Governance of the Global Economy* (Oakland; University of California Press, 2021); Amy Offner, *Sorting Out the Mixed Economy: The Rise and Fall of Welfare and Developmental States in the Americas* (Princeton, NJ: Princeton University Press, 2019); Albert O. Hirschman, *A Bias for Hope: Essays on Development and Latin America* (Boulder: Westview, 1985); and Albert O. Hirschman, *Journeys toward Progress: Studies in Economic Policy-Making in Latin America* (Garden City, NY: Doubleday, 1965).

37. Cf. Samuel Moyn, *Christian Human Rights* (Philadelphia: University of Penn-sylvania Press, 2015).

38. For a useful survey, Thomas Kselman and Joseph A. Buttigieg, eds., *European Christian Democracy: Historical Legacies and Comparative Perspectives* (Notre Dame, IN: University of Notre Dame Press, 2003). For an earlier comparative perspective, Mario Einaudi and François Goguel, *Christian Democracy in Italy and France* (Notre Dame, IN: University of Notre Dame Press, 1952). Also, Scott Mainwaring and Tim-othy R. Scully, eds., *Christian Democracy in Latin America: Electoral Competition and Regime Conflict* (Stanford, CA: Stanford University Press, 2003); Michael Fleet, *The Rise and Fall of Chilean Christian Democracy* (Princeton, NJ: Princeton Univer-sity Press, 2014).

39. James Chappel, *Catholic Modern: The Challenge of Totalitarianism and the Re-making of the Church* (Cambridge, MA: Harvard University Press, 2018), 200–226. Chappell discusses the impact of the encyclicals on economic issues from Pius XII to John XXIII and emphasizes the role of Austrian Catholics (within the Austrian

Volkspartei or ÖVP) in the evolution of economic ideas. For details on the German pension reform, see Hockerts, *Sozialpolitische Entscheidungen im nachkriegs Deutschland*, 309–319, 357–394, 411–435, and passim.

40. Chappel, *Catholic Modern*, 185–200, citations, 185–187. In France and Austria, the postwar Christian Democrat stress on family and women at home still broke with the emphasis on natalism in the 1930s, and by the 1960s, the clergy was quite upbeat on conjugal sex. For the American counterpart of family reconstitution, see Elaine Tyler May, "Cold War—Warm Hearth: Politics and the Family in Postwar America," in Fraser and Gerstle, *Rise and Fall of the New Deal Order*, 153–181.

41. See Ralf Ptak, "Neoliberalism in Germany: Revisiting the Ordoliberal Foundations of the Social Market Economy," in *The Road from Mont Pèlerin: The Making of the Neoliberal Thought Collective*, ed. Philip Mirowski and Dieter Plehwe (Cambridge, MA: Harvard University Press, 2009), 98–138, with extensive bibliography of ordopolitical writings. On wartime roles, see Ludolf Herbst, *Der totale Krieg und die Ordnung der Wirtschaft: Die Kriegswirtschaft im Spannungsfeld von Politik, Ideologie und Propaganda 1939–1945* (Stuttgart: DVA, 1982). Quinn Slobodian, *Globalists: The End of Empire and the Birth of Neoliberalism* (Cambridge, MA: Harvard University Press, 2018) documents the political implications of the movement. A brief introduction in the context of the emerging West German economic profession provided by Alexander Nützenadel, *Stunde der Ökonomen: Wissenschaft. Politik und Expertenkultur in der Bundesrepublik 1949–1974* (Göttingen: Vandenhoeck & Ruprecht, 2005), 25–51.

42. Pizzorno, 'The Individual Mobilization of Europe."

43. For the reworking of "postcolonial" memory, Todd Shepard, *The Invention of Decolonization: The Algerian War and the Remaking of France* (Ithaca, NY: Cornell University Press, 2006). See also John Darwin, *The End of the British Empire: The Historical Debate* (London: Blackwell, 1991) on British assessments; Els Bogaerts and Remco Raben, eds., *Beyond Empire and Nation: The Decolonization of African and Asian Societies, 1930s–1970s* (Leiden: Brill E-Book, 2012).

44. Wm. Roger Louis, "The Dissolution of the British Empire," in *The Oxford History of the British Empire: The Twentieth Century*, ed. Judith M. Brown and Wm. Roger Louis (Oxford: Oxford University Press, 1999), 329–342. Most recently, Caroline Elkins, *Legacy of Violence: A History of the British Empire* (New York: Knopf, 2022),esp. 480–579 for tactics in Malaya and Kenya.

45. Christopher Bayly and Tim Harper, *Forgotten Wars: The End of Britain's Asian Empire* (London: Penguin, 2008), 158–189.

46. Frances Gouda with Thijs Brocades Zaalberg, *American Visions of the Netherlands: East Indies/Indonesia: United States Policy and Indonesian Nationalism, 1920–1949* (Amsterdam: Amsterdam University Press, 2002).

47. On Yalta, Sergeii Plokhy, *Yalta: The Price of Peace* (New York: Viking, 2010); most recently on the Marshall mission to China, Jeffrey M. Widener, "From General to Diplomat: The Success and Failure of George C. Marshall's Mission to China after World War II," *The Chinese Historical Review* 27, no. 1 (May 2020): 32–49, meticulously researched but without Chinese sources.

48. Philip W. Bonsal to Ambassador Harriman, November 13, 1948; Harriman papers (Abbreviated here as WAH), now in the Library of Congress.

49. See "The Economic Integration of Western Europe," ECA paper PS/AAP (49)3 (Revised, October 15, 1949) and the "Outline of Work Program on Western European Economic Integration"—described as a preliminary summary of the views of (Paul) Nitze, Marin and (Lincoln) Gordon. Both in WAH Files, "Special Representative."

50. *The Collected Writings of John Maynard Keynes* (Cambridge: Cambridge University Press for the Royal Economic Society, 1980), 25:21. Volumes 25–27 provide a wonderful record of Keynes's unfolding ideas. For the Keynes and White Plans and the negotiations at Bretton Woods, see also Benn Steil, *The Battle of Bretton Woods: John Maynard Keynes, Harry Dexter White and the Making of a New World Order* (Princeton, NJ: Princeton University Press, 2013); and Robert Skidelsky's authoritative biography, *John Maynard Keynes*, vol. 3, *Fighting for Freedom, 1937–1946* (New York: Viking, 2000). For British reflections see R. B. C. ("Otto") Clarke's reflections in United Kingdom National Archives, Treasury Papers (henceforth T), T236/2611.

51. R. B. C. ("Otto") Clarke, "Brief for U.S. Negotiations," June (?) 1947 and "The World Dollar Shortage," June 14, 1947, in T236/782/9196.

52. [Baron Thomas] Catto (Governor of the Bank of England, 1944–1949) "Sterling Balances," May 27, 1947, in T236/782/9196.

53. Leslie Rowan in Washington, DC to E. A. Hitchman at the Treasury November 15, 1949, in T232/196/9740 ("Integration1949/50). Supposedly, he reported, the State Department was trying to rein in Hoffman.

54. Robert Hall at the Treasury to the Chancellor of the Exchequer, January 3, 1950 (T232/196/9740). In good civil service fashion, Hall was trying to educate Labour Party chancellor of the exchequer Hugh Dalton on the virtues of Britain's imperial stewardship.

55. T. L. Rowan to "My dear Robert," March 20, 1950, T232/196/9740.

56. Arthur Schlesinger Jr., to Harriman, September 24, 1948 in WAH papers: "France and Italy are currently out of control politically. Both are crucial countries from the viewpoint of the success of ERP; neither has been able to run its own affairs effectively nor contain its internal Communist problem. . . . Britain is the only serious reservoir of political leadership and technical expertise for the tremendous job of uniting Europe."

57. Acheson to Perkins (at OSR) and Ambassador, No. 4013, October 19, 1949. WAH papers, Ambassadors' Meeting, Paris, October 21–22, 1949. For a more de-

tailed narrative of US postwar foreign policy, see Charles S. Maier, "The Making of 'Pax Americana': Constitutive Moments of United States Ascendancy," in *The Quest for Stability: Problems of West European Security, 1918–1957*, ed. R. Ahmann, Adolph Birke, and Michael Howard (London: German Historical Institute and Oxford University Press, 1993), 390–434.

58. See Charles S. Maier, "'Issue Then Is Germany and with It Future of Europe,'" introduction to *The Marshall Plan and Germany*, ed. Charles S. Maier and Günter Bischof (New York: Berg, 1991), 1–39; also Alan S. Milward, "The Marshall Plan and German Foreign Trade," in the same volume, 452–487; Benn Steil, *The Marshall Plan: Dawn of the Cold War* (New York: Simon & Schuster, 2018), 361–362.

59. Alec Cairncross and Barry Eichengreen, *Sterling in Decline* (London: Palgrave Macmillan, 203), 11–155.

60. T237/17, Playfair to Hitchman 9 = T.P. (1)50 34, February 16, 1950. An excellent history of British policy on trade and current issues provided by Martin Daunton, "Britain and Globalisation since 1850: III. Creating the World of Bretton Woods, 1939–1958," *Transactions of the Royal Historical Society* 18 (2008): 1–42.

61. Daunton, "Britain and Globalisation," essential for this; see also Maier, "Pax Americana."

62. For British toughness on policy toward the Soviet Union, see Anne Deighton, "Britain and the Cold War, 1947–1955," in *The Cambridge History of the Cold War*, ed. Leffler and Westad, 1:112–132; also Anne Deighton, *The Impossible Peace: The Division of Germany and the Origins of the Cold War, 1945–1947* (Oxford: Clarendon, 1993).

63. On the NATO Temporary Council Committee of late 1951, see the impressive study by Helmut R. Hammerich, *Jeder fur sich und Amerika gegen alle? Die Lastenteilung der NATO am Beispiel des Temporary Council Committee 1949–1954* (Munich: R. Oldenbourg, 2003); earlier partial treatments in Charles S. Maier, "Finance and Defense: Implications of Military Integration 1950–1952," in *NATO: The Founding of the Atlantic Alliance and the Integration of Europe*, ed. Francis H. Heller and John R. Gillingham (New York: St. Martin's, 1992), 335–351; also Maier, "Pax Americana." For the origins and development of national-income accounting and the role of the OECD in enshrining it, see Matthias Schmelzer, *The Hegemony of Growth: The OECD and the Making of the Economic Growth Paradigm* (Cambridge: Cambridge University Press, 2016), 85–116.

64. On Adenauer and the Federal Republic of Germany, see Hans-Peter Schwarz, *Adenauer*, vol. I: *Der Aufstieg: 1886–1957* (Stuttgart: Deutsche Verlags-Anstalt, 1986).

65. John W. Dower, "Occupied Japan as History and Occupation History as Politics," *Journal of Asian Studies* 34, no. 2 (February 1975): 485–504, citation on 485. See also John W. Dower, *Empire and Aftermath: Yoshida Shigeru and the Japanese Experience, 1878–1954* (Cambridge, MA: Harvard University Press, 1988); and

John W. Dower, "Occupied Japan and the Cold War in Asia," in *The Truman Presidency*, ed. Michael J. Lacy (Cambridge: Woodrow Wilson International Center for Scholars and Cambridge University Press, 1989): 366–409.

66. Geir Lundestad, *The United States and Western Europe since 1945: From Empire by Invitation to Transatlantic Drift* (Oxford: Oxford University Press, 2003) among other essays. Cf. Charles S. Maier, *Among Empires: American Ascendancy and its Predecessors* (Cambridge, MA: Harvard University Press, 2006) for extensive discussion of this issue. Dower himself, the critical analyst of the 1970s, became the mellower historian of Japan's longer postwar development. See John W. Dower, *Embracing Defeat: Japan in the Wake of World War II* (New York: Norton, 1999). His work, often judged as radical in the 1970s, would be rightly celebrated by 2000 for its deep understanding of the country's postwar history and culture.

67. American priorities were debated within the new National Advisory Committee; the assistant secretary of state for international affairs Andrew Overby spoke for the monetary hawks. As discussed Chapter 7, American officials played a strong role in the international "governance" institutions Washington sponsored and funded such as the World Bank.

68. See Mark Mazower, *No Enchanted Palace*; also Mark Mazower, *Governing the World: The History of an Idea, 1815 to the Present* (New York: Penguin, 2012), chap. 8. For examples of prolonging imperial influence through softer measures, see Alexander Keese, 'First Lessons in Neo-colonialism: The Personalisation of Relations between African Politicians and French Officials in Sub-Saharan Africa, 1956–1966," *Journal of Imperial and Commonwealth History* 35, no. 4 (2007): 593–613; William Roger Louis and Ronald Robinson, "The Imperialism of Decolonization," *Journal of Imperial and Commonwealth History* 22, no. 3 (1994): 462–511; Jessica Pearson, *The Colonial Politics of Global Health: France and the United Nations in Postwar Africa, 1945–1960* (Cambridge, MA: Harvard University Press, 2018). I am indebted to Lydia Walker for these references.

69. See the essays devoted to the "technologies of stateness" in *Humanity* 11, no. 1 (Spring 2020) with exemplary articles and bibliography. For peoples aspiring to statehood who did not get the international accreditation that they sought, see Lydia Walker, "States in Waiting: Nationalism, Internationalism, Decolonization" PhD diss., Harvard University, 2018.

70. Eva-Maria Muschik, "Managing the World: The United Nations, Decolonization, and the Strange Triumph of State Sovereignty in the 1950s and 1960s," *Journal of Global History* 13 (2018): 121–144. For the nexus between decolonization and governance, see also Gregory Mann, *From Empires to NGOs in the West African Sahel: The Road to Nongovernmentality* (New York: Cambridge University Press, 2015); David Webster, "Development Advisors in a Time of Cold War and Decolonization: The

United Nations Technical Assistance Administration, 1950–59," *Journal of Global History* 6, no. 2 (2011): 249–272; and Guy Fiti Sinclair, "Forging Modern States with Imperfect Tools: United Nations Technical Assistance for Public Administration in Decolonized States," *Humanity* 11, no. 1 (Spring 2020): 54–83.

71. On the origins of the program, see David Eckbladh, *The Great American Mission: Modernization and the Construction of an American World Order* (Princeton, NJ: Princeton University Press, 2010), 97–111.

72. Harry S. Truman Presidential library, Paul G. Hoffman papers, Box 43: Rowan Gaither to Hoffman, January 2, 1951. The 1949 Gaither report was published with the 1950 Annual Report of the Ford Foundation; it included a statement that democratic systems fulfilled society's needs more than authoritarian ones, but Gaither's "executive summary" for Hoffman, cited here, sharpened the policy conclusions. "More often than not, U.S. philanthropy after 1945 became an arm of American foreign policy," from the introduction (p. 28) to *American Foundations and the Coproduction of World Order in the Twentieth Century*, ed. John Krige and Helke Rausch (Göttingen: Vandenhoeck & Ruprecht, 2012)—a collection of papers fundamental for assessing the role of the Ford, Rockefeller, and Carnegie Foundations and other funders of scientific knowledge. On connections between scientific funding and national security policy (could they ever have been avoided?) as developed in the 1960s, see Krige's chapter, "The Ford Foundation, Physics and the National Security State: A Study in the Transnational Circulation of Knowledge," 190–209. Revealing on the ambiguities of knowledge that was to be both independent yet helpful to American interests is Nicole Sackley's essay in the same volume, "Foundation in the Field: The Ford Foundation's New Delhi Office and the Construction of Development Knowledge, 1951–1970," 231–260, which emphasizes the connections of the local program officer and the Indian elites, a privileged position that eroded with the death of Nehru in 1964. Important also, the many works of Volker R. Berghahn; see in particular, *America and the Intellectual Cold Wars in Europe. Shepard Stone between Philanthropy, Academy, and Diplomacy* (Princeton, NJ: Princeton University Press, 2001). Stone headed the international division of the Foundation.

73. See Nicolas Guilhot's studies, *The Invention of International Relations Theory: Realism, the Rockefeller Foundation, and the 1954 Conference on Theory* (New York: Columbia University Press, 2011), and *After the Enlightenment: Political Realism and International Relation in the Mid-Twentieth Century* (New York: Cambridge University Press, 2017).

74. Tim B. Müller, "Die Macht der Menschenfreunde: Die Rockefeller Foundation, die Sozialwissenschaften und die amerikanische Außenpolitik im Kalten Krieg," in *American Foundations*, ed. Krige and Rausch, 146–172, quote 147. On modernization (which became a crude model for government security agencies) and development ideas, see David C. Engerman's several authored and edited works

including *Staging Growth: Modernization, Development and the Global Cold War* (Amherst: University of Massachusetts Press, 2003), "The Romance of Economic Development and New Histories of the Cold War," *Diplomatic History* 28, no. 1 (2004): 23–54, and with Corinna Unger, "Introduction: Towards a Global History of Modernization, *Diplomatic History* 33, no. 3 (2009): 375–385; also Eckbladh, *The Great American Mission*.

75. Emily Hauptmann, "The Ford Foundation and the Rise of Behavioralism in Political Science," *Journal of the History of the Behavioral Sciences* 82, no. 2 (Spring 2012): 154–173.

76. For pluralism and polyarchy, Robert A. Dahl, *A Preface to Democratic Theory* (Chicago: University of Chicago Press, 1956); Robert A. Dahl, *Who Governs: Democracy and Power in an American City* (New Haven, CT: Yale University Press, 1961); and Robert A. Dahl, *Polyarchy: Participation and Opposition* (New Haven, CT: Yale University Press, 1971). See the generous but critical analysis by Steven Lukes, "Robert Dahl on Power," *Journal of Political Power* 8, no. 2 (2015): 261–270. For the critique of Mills, see Daniel Bell, *The End of Ideology: On the Exhaustion of Political Ideas in the 1950s* (New York: Free Press, 1959).

77. For "pluralism" as devoted to critiques of totalitarian models, see the analyses of Nazi Germany by Martin Broszat and Hans Mommsen; and as applied to the Soviet Union, the work of Jerry Hough whose 1979 revision, *How the Soviet Union Is Governed*, of Merle Fainsod's foundational text, *How Russia Is Ruled* (1953), unleashed indignation. The concept of totalitarianism when it reappeared in the 1980s as a critique of late-communist regimes by dissenters had softer contours. Hannah Arendt's classical analysis of 1950, *The Origins of Totalitarianism*, stressed the role of terrorism; the writers of the 1980s emphasized surveillance, corruption, and self-censorship.

78. Paul Weindling, "From Disease Prevention to Population Control: The Realignment of Rockefeller Foundation Policies in the 1920s to the 1950s," in *American Foundations*, ed. Krige and Rausch, 125–145; on population control in its political context, see Matthew Connelly, *Fatal Misconception: The Struggle to Control World Population* (Cambridge, MA: Harvard University Press, 2008). For the interwar period, see Laurence A. Schneider, "The Rockefeller Foundation, the China Foundation, and the Development of Modern Science in China," *Social Science & Medicine* 16, no. 12 (1982): 1217–1221.

79. Loren R. Graham, *Science, Philosophy, and Human Behavior in the Soviet Union* (New York: Columbia University Press, 1987). Also Andrew V. Sanchez, "Cyber-Nation: The Cold War Context for Cybernetics and Automation in the US the USSR, and Divided Germany," DPhil thesis, Oxford University, 2021.

80. In the summer of 1947, France and Britain had organized the CEEC (Committee on European Economic Cooperation) to interface with the American

proponents of a European Recovery Program. This was transformed formally into the Organization for European Economic Cooperation (OEEC) in April 1948, which continued after the end of the Marshall Plan. French interest waned with the development of the Schuman Plan, but the organization found a new sphere of activity with the run-up to the European Payments Union in 1958 and was reorganized as the OECD in 1959–1960. For the most recent account, with references to the massive earlier scholarship, see Schmelzer, *Hegemony of Growth*, 38–53.

81. Again, see Harris, *Postwar Economic Problems*.

82. For a survey of the ideological mobilization on both sides, see David Engerman, "Ideology and the Origins of the Cold War, 1917–1962," in *The Cambridge History of the Cold War*, ed. Leffler and Westad, 1:20–43, who stresses that the claims for universal validity of the opposed claims made conflict unavoidable. I would emphasize that the conjunction of ideology with the geographical division into coherent territorial blocs was essential.

83. For Myrdal's later activity to mobilize opinion for international economic quality, see Simon Reid-Henry, "From Welfare World to Global Poverty," *Humanity: An International Journal of Human Rights, Humanitarianism, and Development* 8, no. 1 (Spring 2017): 207–226—a reconsideration of Myrdal's 1970 book, *The Challenge to World Poverty: A World Anti-Poverty Program in Outline*.

84. For a notable description of the Western "system" as it functioned through the 1960s, see John Gerard Ruggie, "International Regimes, Transactions, and Change: Embedded Liberalism in the Postwar Economic Order," *International Organization* 36, no. 2 (Spring 1982): 379–415. Cf. Peter A. Hall, ed., *The Political Power of Economic Ideas: Keynesianism across Nations* (Princeton, NJ: Princeton University Press, 1989).

5. Countervailing Power?

1. John Kenneth Galbraith, *American Capitalism* (Boston: Houghton Mifflin, 1952). By the 1950s and 1960s, some social scientists, including one of this author's older colleagues, condemned working with the term *capitalism* as unscientific, presumably because its very use might confirm a Marxist analysis.

2. See Ellis W. Hawley, *The New Deal and the Problem of Monopoly* (Princeton, NJ: Princeton University Press, 1964), 402–419, on the Temporary National Economic Committee or TNEC; also Thurman Arnold, *The Folklore of Capitalism* (New Haven, CT: Yale University Press, 1938) for an earlier influential debunking of the anti-monopoly creed. For the classic analyses of oligopoly, see Edward H. Chamberlin, *The Theory of Monopolistic Competition* (Cambridge, MA: Harvard University Press, 1933) and Joan Robinson, *The Economics of Imperfect Competition* (London: Macmillan, 1933).

3. Galbraith, *American Capitalism*, 110–111, 113. For the major critique of the theory early on, see George J. Stigler, "The Economist Plays with Blocs," *American Economic Review* 44, no. 4 (May 1954): 7–14. The theory was developed subsequentially in terms of producers or suppliers and their "downstream" consumers without reference to labor and employers, and it was increasingly formalized with game theoretic concepts and removed from implications for social conflict. Thomas von Ungern-Sternberg four decades later acknowledged that "mainstream economists" had received the theory badly and that it had little theoretical impact but called for a rethink: "Countervailing Power Revisited," *International Journal of Industrial Organization* 14, no. 4 (1996): 507–519. For a more recent discussion, see Alberto Iozzi and Tommaso Valletti, "Vertical Bargaining and Countervailing Power," *American Economic Journal: Microeconomics* 6, no. 3 (2014): 196–125. Galbraith did at least demonstrate that there was ample countervailing power deployed in the economics profession.

4. For another American example of a countervailing-power remedy in the 1940s and 1950s, see the isometric exercise regime (Dynamic Tension) for young males urged by Charles Atlas's ubiquitous advertisements in *Archie* comic books and elsewhere: Why be a spindly "97-pound weakling" and have sand kicked in your face on the beach by well-built rivals for your girl? 97 pounds! *O corpora, o mores!*

5. See Daniel Immerwahr, "Polanyi in the United States: Peter Drucker, Karl Polanyi, and the Midcentury Critique of Economic Society," *Journal of the History of Ideas* 70, no. 3 (July 2009): 445–466; and among the relevant texts, Peter Drucker, *Concept of the Corporation* (New York: John Day, 1946). Cf. Nils Gilman, "The Prophet of Post-Fordism: Peter Drucker and the Legitimation of the Corporation," in *American Capitalism: Social Thought and Political Economy in the Twentieth Century*, ed. Nelson Lichtenstein (Philadelphia: University of Pennsylvania Press, 2006).

6. Galbraith, *American Capitalism*, 114 on labor market, 136 on the federal government.

7. Karl Marx, *Capital: A Critique of Political Economy*, 3 vols. (New York: International Publishers, 1967), vol. I, chap. 25.

8. Most notably, perhaps, Great Britain and Sweden. For useful accounts, see Andrew Adonis, *Ernest Bevin: Labour's Churchill* (London: Biteback, 2020); Alan Bullock, *The Life and Times of Ernest Bevin*, 3 vols. (London: Heinemann, 1960–1983), esp. vols. 2 (*Minister of Labor, 1940–44*) and 3 (*Foreign Secretary, 1945–51*).

9. Joseph Schumpeter, *Capitalism, Socialism and Democracy* (New York: Harper, 1942). The end of capitalism and the viability of socialism that he foresaw, however, was a sort of entropic managerial evolution, as signaled already in the literature of the 1930s, whether by Adolf A. Berle Jr. and Gardiner C. Means, *The Modern Corporation and Private Property* (New York: Macmillan, 1933), or James Burnham, *The Managerial Revolution; or What Is Happening in the World* (New York: John Day, 1941).

10. Andrew Shonfield, *Modern Capitalism: The Changing Balance of Private and Public Power* (New York: Oxford University Press, 1965). For subsequent work in this vein, see Keith Middlemas, *Politics in Industrial Society: The British Experience since 1911* (London: André Deutsch, 1979); and my own account of the 1920s, *Recasting Bourgeois Europe*; also the essays in John Goldthorpe, ed., *Order and Conflict in Contemporary Capitalism* (Oxford: Clarendon, 1984).

11. See the superbly documented and detailed study by Tim Barker, "Cold War Capitalism: The Political Economy of American Military Spending, 1947–1990," PhD diss., Harvard University, 2022. Barker's key phrase is "military Keynesianism."

12. Charles S. Maier, "The Making of 'Pax Americana': Constitutive Moments of United States Ascendancy," in *The Quest for Stability: Problems of West European Security 1918–1957*, ed. R. Ahman, A. Birke, and M. Howard (Oxford: Oxford University Press, 1993), 390–434.

13. For this development in the United Kingdom, see Ian Kumekawa, "Imperial Schemes: Empire and the Rise of the British Business State," PhD diss., Harvard University, 2020.

14. The contribution of an innovation may be small in terms of a national economy as a whole but will significantly raise the productivity rate within a sector. Economists and historians have puzzled over why total productivity growth seems not to have responded proportionally to digital technology, and Robert P. Gordon has argued that the inventions of the precomputer age have contributed much more to our welfare, *The Rise and Fall of American Growth: The United States Standard of Living since the Civil War* (Princeton, NJ: Princeton University Press, 2016). For a bravura analysis of how hard it is to correlate inventiveness with other factors, see Joel Mokyr, *The Lever of Riches: Technological Creativity and Economic Progress* (New York: Oxford University Press, 1990), 151–192.

15. Centre Historique de Péchinet/Pont-à-Mousson, Direction Générale M. Paul-Cavallier, PAM 70410, Proces-Verbal . . . 5 nov. 1943 of the Conseil Supérieur de l'Économie Industrielle et Commerciale, Commission No. 4; remarks by M. Barbet and M. [Marcel] Paul.

16. Nelson Lichtenstein, "From Corporatism to Collective Bargaining: Organized Labor and the Eclipse of Social Democracy," in *The Rise and Fall of the New Deal Order, 1930–1980*, ed. Gary Gerstle and Steve Fraser (Princeton, NJ: Princeton University Press, 2020), 125–126.

17. Galbraith, *American Capitalism*, 139–142.

18. For a survey of inflation after World War I, see Ragnar Nurske, *The Course and Control of Inflation: A Review of Monetary Experiences in Europe after World War I* (Geneva: League of Nations, 1946). There is a large literature on Germany in particular; see the volumes edited by Gerald Feldman, Carl-Ludwig Holtfrerich, et al., including *The German Inflation Reconsidered: A Preliminary Balance* (Berlin: de Gruyter, 1982);

also Gerald Feldman's *The Great Disorder: Politics, Economics, and Society in the German Inflation, 1914–1924* (New York: Oxford University Press, 1993); and Carl-Ludwig Holtfrerich, *The German Inflation 1914–1923* (Berlin: de Gruyter, 1986). For inflation as a source of taxation, see John Maynard Keynes, *How to Pay for the War* (London: Macmillan, 1940); Phillip Cagan, "The Monetary Dynamics of Hyperinflation," in *Studies in the Quantity Theory of Money*, ed. Milton Friedman (Chicago: University of Chicago Press, 1956). For a survey of theories and literature as of the late 1970s, Charles S. Maier, "The Politics of Inflation in the Twentieth Century," originally in *The Political Economy of Inflation*, ed. Fred Hirsch and John H. Goldthorpe (Cambridge, MA: Harvard University Press, 1978), then reprinted in Charles S. Maier, *In Search of Stability* (New York: Cambridge University Press, 1987), 189–224; also for country studies and theoretical essays, Leon Lindberg and Charles S. Maier, eds., *The Politics of Inflation and Economic Stagnation* (Washington, DC: Brookings Institution, 1985).

19. Alain Bergounieux, *Force ouvrière* (Paris: Seuil, 1975), 55, and Charles S. Maier, "The Two Postwar Eras and the Conditions for Stability in Twentieth-Century Western Europe," in *American Historical Review* 86, no. 2 (April 1981): 327–352, citation on 332. I have drawn on material from that article to construct this chapter, along with archival documentation researched at that time. Secondary material available at that time is cited there. Particularly revealing are the papers collected in *Actes du colloque de l'Université de Lille III, 2–3 novembre 1974: La libération du nord et du pas-de-Calais, 1944–1947*, in *Revue du Nord* 57 (1975). On the Communists, see J.-P. Hirsch, "'La seule voie possible': Remarques sur les communistes du nord et du pas-de-Calais de la libération aux grèves de novembre 1947," 563–78.

20. Milan citation from Febo Guizzi, "La fabbrica italiana Magneti Marelli," in *La ricostruzione nella grande industria: strategia padronale e organismi di fabbrica nel triangolo, 1945–1948*, ed. Luigi Ganapini et al. (Bari: De Donato, 1978), 280. On the pressures at the grassroots, see the AFL's representative (and fervent anti-communist) Irving Brown's recognition that a socialist movement would lose their credibility among French unions if the party accepted to stay on in a cabinet intent on freezing wages. "Brown: Report on Greece, France, and England," July 7, 1947, in State Historical Society of Wisconsin: AFL papers, Florence Thorne Collection, 117/8A, box 17, F.3A. Florence Thorne served as secretary for the International Labor Committee of the AFL; her papers include detailed reports on European trade union activity.

21. John Hickerson to H. Freeman Matthews, June 25, 1947, National Archives, RG 59, box 3. Cited Maier, "The Two Postwar Eras," 346.

22. Anthony Carew, *Labour under the Marshall Plan: The Politics of Productivity and the Making of Management Science* (Manchester, UK: University of Manchester Press, 1987). The AFL and CIO both have voluminous archives—the AFL at the State Historical Society of Wisconsin, the CIO at the Walter Reuther Library of Wayne State University.

23. Wayne State University Labor Archives, Reuther Library, CIO Washington Office, box 64, folder 16, Report of Special CIO Committee to Europe to CIO Committee on International Affairs, March 1, 1951. For the Italian divisions, see Daniel L. Horowitz, *The Italian Labor Movement* (Cambridge, MA: Harvard University Press, 1963).

24. "Declaration of the Schevenels Case by: The International Committee of the A.F. of L.," in State Historical Society of Wisconsin, Madison: A.F. of L. Papers, series 11, file C, William Green Papers, box 11: International Labor Relations. But for a sensitive discussion of the deplorable conditions of French coal miners in Lens and GGT campaigns against the Marshall Plan and "the reluctance of its supporters in the union movement to vigorously defend it," see David Lasser, "Report on French Labor," submitted to the CIO, in Wayne State University, Walter Reuther Library, Archives of Labor History and Urban Affairs: CIO box 122: WFTY ERP. "Vigorous action to tackle France's social problems, must go hand in hand with recovery." CIO observers were horrified by the misery of housing and factory conditions in southern Italy. See among other reports "Gaby's letter" forwarded by Charles Levinson to Walter Reuther, August 14, 1954, Wayne State Library, CIO Archives, Reuther collection, box 457, box 5, folder "Italy 1952–61."

25. Wayne State University, Reuther Library, Archives of Labor History, Collection: CIO Secretary-Treasurer, box 122: WFTUERP: "CIO Notes: World Federation of Trade Unions, Meeting of the Executive Bureau, Paris, 17, 18, 19 January 1949." For the efforts to impart a specifically anti-communist stamp on the new Federation of International Trade Unions, see Irving Brown's report on the National Preparatory Meeting, July 25–29 (letter of July 30, 1949 ("Dear Friends") in Madison: AFL Papers 117A/8A, box 19, F. Irving Brown; also box 19: F. Frank B. Fenton: "Report of Bernard Weisman Submitted upon Request of Mr. Fenton."

26. On the ILO in the Cold War, see Daniel Maul, *Human Rights, Development and Decolonization: The International Labour Organization, 1940–1970* (London: Palgrave Macmillan, 2012).

27. See the long debate, Istituto Gramsci, Torino: Scissione Cristiana, Fondo, Camera Confederale del Lavoro di Torino: A.2/Fasc.1/B.6 dG/Torino Busta 6: Verbali di riunioni 1948–51,1953,1967: "Discussione del Documento Di Vittorio sull'unità e disciplina sindacale," January 25, 1948, a.m. and p.m.

28. For a case study of national labor styles, see Thomas Fetzer, "International Challenges and National Allegiances: British and West German Trade Union Politics at Ford, 1967–1973," *Contemporary European History* 18, no. 1 (2009): 99–122.

29. Renault Archives, "P[ierre] Lefaucheux to M. le Minister," February 12, 1945. For Lefaucheux—a counterpart as an innovative manager of his country's mass-vehicle producer to Vittorio Valletta at FIAT, but a Resistance hero and not a fascist technocrat—see Cyrille Sardais, *Patron de Renault: Pierre Lefaucheux, 1944–1955*

(Paris: Presses de la Fondation nationale des sciences politiques, 2009) and Patrick Fridenson, "L'avenir vu par les patrons: Pierre Lefaucheux," in *Avenirs et avant-gardes en France XIXᵉ–XXᵉ siècles: Hommage à Madeleine Rebérioux*, ed. Patrick Fridenson (Paris: La découverte, 1999), 223–238.

30. Aris Accornero, *La parabola del sindacato: Ascesa e decline di una cultura* (Bologna: Il Mulino, 1992), 29–35. I would modify the insistence on the uniqueness of the Italian situation, which follows from the author's focus on union culture; as Chapter 6 explains, the logic of inflation produced similar effects across many countries, including Argentina and Israel outside Europe.

31. USNA: RG 469, SPE/Labor Information Division/Office of the Economic Adviser, box 5: Joseph Mintzes to Boris Shishkin, Director of the European labor Division, April 11, 1950.

32. US Embassy's Labor Report for November 30, 1950 in RG 469, SPE/Labor Information Division/Office of the Economic Adviser, box 5. In Marshall Plan recipient countries, the economic office of the embassy was integrated with the ECA missions. For general coverage, Carew, *Labour under the Marshall Plan*; and Frederico Romero, *The United States and the European Trade Union Movement, 1944–1951* (Chapel Hill: University of North Carolina Press, 1992).

33. For the best survey and documentation, Bent Boel, *The European Productivity Agency and Transatlantic Relations, 1953–1961* (Copenhagen: Museum Tusculanum Press and University of Copenhagen, 2003); see also Roger Grégoire, "European Productivity Agency," in OEEC, *At Work for Europe*, 5th ed. (Paris: OEEC, 1960), 139–152; also Charles S. Maier, "The Politics of Productivity: Foundations of American International Economic Policy after World War II," *International Organization* (Autumn 1977), reissued as *Between Power and Plenty: Foreign Economic Policies of Advanced Industrial States*, ed. Peter Katzenstein (Madison: University of Wisconsin Press, 1978) and reprinted in Maier, *In Search of Stability*, 121–152. US representatives were not simply against wage increases and in France denied the Patronat's claims that a wage increase would require price increases. See also Nick Tiratsoo and Jim Tomlinson, "Exporting the 'Gospel of Productivity': United States Technical Assistance and British Industry 1945–1960," *Business History Review* 71 (Spring 1997): 41–81; Sergio Chillé, "Il 'Productivity and Technical Assistance Program' per l'economia italiana (1949–1954): Accettazione e resistenza ai progetti statiunitensi di rinnovamento del sistema produttivo nazionale," *Annali della Fondazione Giulio Pastore* 22 (1993): 76–12; and Pier Paolo D'Attorre, *ERP Aid and the Politics of Productivity in Italy during the 1950s*, Working paper no. 85/159 (Florence: European Union Institute, April 1985). D'Attorre deserves remembering as a charismatic, productive labor historian who served also as mayor of Ravenna but was tragically struck down by cancer at age forty-five.

34. Ted Yntema at CED Board of Trustees, October 16, 1947, Paul Hoffman papers box 40, at Harry S. Truman Presidential Library and cited in Maier, "Society

as Factory," in *In Search of Stability*, 64. See also Bruce to Harriman on the wage-price problem in France, September 22, 1948, in NA RG 286 (Agency for International Development records): ECA: Office of Assistant Administrator for Programs, Richard Bissell, Subject Files, 1948- box 17.

35. Philip Armstrong, Andrew Glyn, and John Harrison, *Capitalism since 1945* (Oxford: Blackwell, 1991), 122.

36. Stefan J. Link, *Forging Global Fordism, Nazi Germany, Soviet Russia and the Contest over the Industrial Order* (Princeton, NJ: Princeton University Press, 2020), 207–211; Drucker, *Concept of the Corporation*. Drucker, an Austrian émigré, would enjoy a fabled reputation for two decades, essentially naturalizing in the US ideas that paralleled German concepts of the production community no longer acceptable in their original form but also eclectic influences ranging from the Prussian conservatism of Friedrich Julius Stahl to Kierkegaardian existentialism. See Nils Gilman's acute analysis, "The Prophet of Post-Fordism: Peter Drucker and the Legitimation of the Corporation," in *American Capitalism: Social Thought and Political Economy in the Twentieth Century*, ed. Nelson Lichtenstein (Philadelphia: University of Pennsylvania Press, 2006), 109–131. I am indebted to Bruno Settis for insight into the organization of Ford.

37. Turin: Fondo FIOM, B.102: C. I, 2: "Piano del Lavoro": Convegno sindacale nazionale su l'industria e il Piano del Lavoro: Relazione di Apertura, on DiVittorio, June 22, 1950. "La sola base di sviluppo effectivo dall'industria italiana è e deve essere il mercato interno."

38. Alain Touraine, *L'évolution du travail ouvrier aux usines Renault* (Paris: Centre des études sociologiques, 1955), citations sequentially: 177–178 ("*illusion technocratique*"), 173 ("*dégradation massive*"), 141 ("*encadré . . . subordiné . . . soumis*"), 175 ("*s'intégrer dans un groupe social*"). For a useful survey of industrial sociology in France and Italy, see Daniele Franco, "Dalla Francia all'Italia: Impegno politico, inchiesta e transfers culturali alle origini della sociologia del lavoro in Italia," PhD diss., University of Bologna, 2009.

39. See Link, *Forging Global Fordism*; also Charles S. Maier, "Between Taylorism and Technocracy: European Ideologies and the Vision of Industrial Productivity in the 1920s," *Journal of Contemporary History* 5, no. 2 (April 1970): 27–61, now included in Maier, *In Search of Stability*, 22–53.

40. For a Soviet application, see A. K. Ignatiev, ed., *Organizatsiia u Vnedrenie Vnutrizavodckogo Khozraschet na Zavodakh Mashinostroeniya*, 2nd ed, (Moscow: Mashgiz, 1955). (Self-financing management was an innovation of the mid-1950s, allowing firms to retain profits achieved for production beyond the norms laid down by the planning authorities.) For an explanation of the regulations around norm-setting, including the role that unions played, see Emily Clark Brown, "The Soviet Labor Market," and esp. "Labor Relations in Soviet Factories," *Industrial and*

Labor Relations Review 10, no. 2 (January 1957): 179–200, and 11, no. 2 (January 1958): 183–202; also G. R. Barker, *Incentives and Labour Productivity in Soviet Industry* (Oxford: Blackwell, 1955).

41. Turin, Centro Storico Fiat, "Assemblea generale ordinaria e straordinaria degli azionisti 10 aprile 1951: Relazioni del Consiglio d'Amministrazione e dei Sindaci. FIAT had signaled the previous summer it would emphasize productivity-linked wages: "'Production is the raison d'être of the factory,' management announced and it planned to introduce incentive-based bonuses and 'super' premiums." Verbale, Commissioni Interne del Gruppo Fiat del 20 luglio 1950, Turin, Istituto Gramsci, Fondo FIOM: Commissioni Interni Fiat 1950, IB, Coordinamento C1. Also Maier, "The Making of 'Pax Americana,'" 420.

42. Turin, Centro Storico Fiat, "Assemblea generale ordinaria e straordinaria degli azionisti 10 aprile 1951: Relazioni del Consiglio d'Amministrazione e dei Sindaci.

43. Turin, Istituto Gramsci, Camera del Lavoro di Torino Busta 53 = B.4.1 Fasc. 55. See also Relazione del Segretario Nazionale della FIOM [Federazione italiana dei operai metalmeccanico] al Convegno Nazionale contro il supersfruttamento: Lo sfruttamento dei lavoratori nell' Industri Metallurgica Meccanica in Italia." FIAT, he explained, had raised indexes of production from 100 to 253, the number of workers from 100 to 153, and wages from 100 to138, therefore increasing labor productivity from 100 to 191 from 1948 to 1950. How this figure was derived is unclear: the numbers offered suggested that productivity in terms of labor time had increased by 165 percent and in terms of labor costs by 120 percent. For the conflicts in Turin in the postwar years, see Nicola Tranfaglia, *Storia di Torino*. Vol. IX: *Gli ani della repubblica*; and Emilio Pugno and Sergio Garavini, *Gli anni duri alla FIAT: La resistenza sindacale e la ripresa* (Turin: Einaudi, 1974), who record the years of repression from 1955 to 1962, and the longer-run study by Giuseppe Berta, *Conflitto industriale e struttura d'imprese alla Fiat 1919–1978* (Bologna: Mulino, 1998). On factory culture, Lorenzo Bertucelli, *Nazione operaia: Cultura del lavoro e vita di fabbrica a Milano e Brescia, 1945–1963* (Rome: Ediesse, 1997).

44. Nat Weinberg to Michael Harris, Chief, MSA Special Mission to Germany [and a former union colleague], April 8, 1953, in Reuther Library Archives; CIO-Washington, box 64, folder 20.

45. Housing reports in France, Naples, and Germany in AFL and CIO papers.

46. Andrew Gordon, *The Evolution of Labor Relations in Japan, 1853–1955* (Cambridge, MA: Harvard University Press,1985), 330. I have depended on Gordon's balanced study in this section. See also John W. Dower, *Empire and Aftermath, Yoshida Shigeru and the Japanese Experience, 1878–1954* (Cambridge, MA: Council on East Asian Studies Harvard and Harvard University Press, 1988), chaps. 9–11.

47. Gordon, *Evolution of Labor Relations in Japan,* 338–361, citations 347 and 374.

48. On the "reverse course," see Jerome B. Cohen, *Japan's Economy in War and Reconstruction* (Minneapolis: University of Minnesota Press, 1949); Howard Schonberger, "The Japan Lobby in American Diplomacy, 1947–1952," *Pacific Historical Review* 46, no. 3 (August 1977): 327–360. Also Detroit Public Library, Joseph M. Dodge Papers, esp. box 1, folder: "Budget and Ikeda Interviews," and box 4, F. Finances, Public: Summary of General Financial Problems and Policy, 30 August 1949; and "Japan Assignment 1950," box 3, F. Correspondence Marquat.

49. Gordon, *Evolution of Labor Relations,* 330–334, 374–379, citation 379.

50. Armstrong et al., *Capitalism since 1945,* 129–135. See also Kozo Yamamura, *Economic Policy in Postwar Japan* (Berkeley: University of California Press, 1967); K. Taira, *Economic Development and the Labor Market in Japan* (New York: Columbia University Press, 1970).

51. Gordon, *Evolution of Labor Relations in Japan,* 378–385, citation 382.

52. Renato Perim Colistete, *Labor Relations and Industrial Performance in Brazil: Greater São Paulo, 1945–1960* (Houndmills, UK: Palgrave, 2001), 99–105.

53. Felipe Pereira Loureiro, "Strikes in Brazil during the Government of João Goulart (1961–1964)," *Canadian Journal of Latin American and Caribbean Studies/Revue canadienne des études latino-américaines et caraïbes* 41, no. 1 (2016): 76–94; Renato Perim Colistete, "Productivity, Wages, and Labor Politics in Brazil, 1945–1962," *Journal of Economic History* 67, no. 1 (2007): 93–127. Colistete, *Labor Relations and Industrial Performance in Brazil* emphasizes the importance of shop-floor contestation; Renato Perim Colistete, "Salarios, productividade e lucros na industria brasileira 1945–1978," *Rivista de economia politica* 29, no. 4 (2009): 386–405.

54. For the life of the factory commissions, see Accornero, *Gli anni cinquanta nella fabrica* and *La parabola del sindacato: Ascesa e decline di una cultura.* On forms of protest by workers—informed by the work of James Scott—see Ilaria Favretto, "Toilets and Resistance in Italian Factories in the 1950s," *Labor History* 60, no. 6 (2019): 646–665. On discipline, see Bruno Settis, "Produttori, sabotatori, sorveglianti: I 'tribunali di fabbrica' nella Fiat del 1953," *Italia contemporanea* 282 (2016): 114–140.

55. See Maier, "Society as Factory," in *In Search of Stability,* 19–70, esp. 53–69. For the Roethlisberger quote, see F. J. Roethlisberger and William J. Dickson, *Management and the Worker* (Cambridge, MA: Harvard University Press, 1939), 569, 575.

56. Frank W. Abrams, "Management's Responsibilities in a Complex World," *Harvard Business Review* 29, no. 3 (1951): 33–34, cited in Maier, *In Search of Stability,* 64.

57. Robert N. McMurry, "Man-Hunt for Top Executives," *Harvard Business Review* 32, no. 1 (1954): 61–62, in Maier, *In Search of Stability,* 67. For an interesting survey of the time, see Roy Lewis and Rosemary Stewart, *The Managers: A New Examination of the English, German, and American Executive* (New York: Mentor, 1958), and

the critical fictional account in Sloan Wilson, *The Man in the Gray Flannel Suit* (New York: Simon & Schuster, 1955).

58. See the contributions of Chester J. Barnard, *The Function of the Executive: Wild Ideas about Organization and Administration* (Cambridge, MA: Harvard University Press, 1938), and Chester J. Barnard, "The Nature of Leadership," in *Leadership*, ed. K. Grint (Cambridge, MA: Harvard University Press, 1940), and the suggestive examination of all these currents (including the Soviet system) in Yves Cohen, *Le siècle des chefs: Une histoire transnationale du commandement et de l'autorité* (Paris: Éditions Amsterdam, 2013).

59. Organization for European Economic Cooperation, *Europe: The Way Ahead: Towards Economic Expansion and Dollar Balance*, 4th annual report of the OEEC (Paris: OEEC, 1952), cited in Maier, "The Two Postwar Eras," 345.

60. Charles Kindleberger, *Europe's Postwar Economic Growth: The Role of Labor Supply* (Cambridge, MA: Harvard University Press, 1967); Armstrong et al., *Capitalism since 1945*.

61. This has been suggested by Simon Reich, *The Fruits of Fascism: Postwar Prosperity in Historical Perspective* (Ithaca, NY: Cornell University Press, 2018).

62. For a recent discussion of the history of the concepts of national income (GDP, GNP, national income) and of economic growth, with citation of the massive literature, see Schmelzer, *The Hegemony of Growth*, 1–23; his N-gram (p. 3) shows the explosion of academic articles from 1948–1949 that contain the term *economic growth*. See also Maier, "The Politics of Productivity," also Charles S. Maier, "The World Economy and the Cold War in the Middle of the Twentieth Century," in *The Cambridge History of the Cold War*, ed. Melvyn P. Leffler and Odd Arne Westad (New York: Cambridge University Press, 2010), 1:44–66; and Philipp Lepenies, *The Power of a Single Number: A Political History of GDP* (New York: Columbia University Press, 2016).

63. See Evsey Domar, Roy Harrod, and Robert Solow, cited in Maier, "The Two Postwar Eras," 340n31. Leon Kayserling, "Prospects for American Economic Growth," address in San Francisco, September 18, 1949, Harry Truman Presidential library, President's Secretary's File, 143: "Agencies: Council of Economic Advisers" also cited in Maier, "The Two Postwar Eras," 346. In his very self-preoccupied oral history interview at the Truman Library, Keyserling said that the growth concept had emerged circa 1947. See also Barker, "Cold War Capitalism."

64. On the preoccupation with balance-of-payments viability, see USNA, RG 286; cf. Alan Milward's stress on the European Recovery Program as a response to an interrupted European recovery in *The Reconstruction of Western Europe, 1945–51* (Berkeley: University of California Press, 1987).

65. Daniel Speich Chassé, "Towards a Global History of the Marshall Plan: European Post-war Reconstruction and the Rise of Development Economic Exper-

tise," in *Industrial Policy in Europe after 1945: Wealth, Power and Economic Development in the Cold War*, ed. Christian Grabas and Alexander Nützenadel (Basingstoke, UK: Palgrave Macmillan, 2014), 187–212. On the OECD's importance to growth and development paradigms, Schmelzer, *The Hegemony of Growth*, 217–238. See also Michele Alacevich, *The Political Economy of the World Bank: The Early Years* (Stanford, CA: Stanford University Press and the World Bank, 2009). Also David Ekbladh, *The Great American Mission: Modernization and the Construction of an American World Order* (Princeton, NJ: Princeton University Press, 2010); Heinz W. Arndt, *Economic Development: The History of an Idea* (Chicago: University of Chicago Press, 1987); Albert O. Hirschman, "The Rise and Decline of Development Economics," in *Essays in Trespassing: Economics to Politics and Beyond* (Cambridge: Cambridge University Press, 1981), 1–24.

66. See Jamie Martin, *The Meddlers: Sovereignty, Empire, and the Birth of Global Economic Governance* (Cambridge. MA: Harvard University Press, 2022), chap. 4; Sara Lorenzini, *Global Development: A Cold War History* (Princeton, NJ: Princeton University Press, 2019); see also Mark Mazower, *Governing the World: The History of an Idea, 1815 to the Present* (New York: Penguin, 2012), chap. 10.

67. Stephen Macekura, "The Point Four Program and U.S. International Development Policy," *Political Science Quarterly* 128, no. 1 (2013): 127–160.

68. For Labour's enthusiastic projections for growth—what the author terms "hybristic Keynesianism"—see Samuel H. Beer, *Britain against Itself: The Political Contradictions of Collectivism* (New York: Norton, 1982), 38.

69. Daniel Bell, *The End of Ideology: On the Exhaustion of Political Ideas in the Fifties* (Glencoe, IL: Free Press, 1960).

6. Contesting the Postwar Order

1. The trend shows a significant acceleration during the 1960s. See Evan Schofer and John W. Meyer, "The Worldwide Expansion of Higher Education in the Twentieth Century," *American Sociological Review* 70, no. 6 (December 2005): 898–920. And for statistics on the completion of higher education as a share of age cohorts above fifteen and on enrollment in tertiary education as a proportion of secondary school graduates (both since 1970), see Max Roser and Esteban Ortiz-Ospina, "Tertiary Education," 2013, https://www.ourworldindata.org/tertiary-education.

2. On Kerr's evolution, see Paddy Riley, "Clark Kerr: From the Industrial to the Knowledge Economy," in *American Capitalism: Social Thought and Political Economy in the Twentieth Century*, ed. Nelson Lichtenstein (Philadelphia: University of Pennsylvania Press, 2007), 71–87. Riley suggests Kerr's earlier studies of labor informed his view of the university as a site of pluralist and peaceful negotiation for a postindustrial economy.

3. For the ebullience and disappointments of this postcolonial decade in the Arab-speaking world, see Jeffrey James Byrne, *Mecca of Revolution: Algeria, Decolonization, and the Third World Order* (Oxford: Oxford University Press, 2016). Also Yoav Di-Capua, *No Exit: Arab Existentialism, Jean-Paul Sartre, and Decolonization* (Chicago: University of Chicago Press, 2018).

4. See in particular Charles P. Kindleberger, *Europe's Postwar Economic Growth: The Role of Labor Supply* (Cambridge, MA: Harvard University Press, 1967); Ingvar Svennilson, *Growth and Stagnation in the European Economy* (Geneva: Economic Comission for Europe, 1954) and Ingvar Svennilson, *Prospects of Development in Western Europe, 1955–1975*, trans. Alfred Read (Stockholm: Industriens Utredningsinstitut, 1959); Nicholas Crafts and Gianni Toniolo, *Economic Growth in Europe since 1945* (Cambridge: Cambridge University Press, 1996). I have drawn at several points in this chapter from my essay "Two Sorts of Crisis? The 'Long' 1970s in the West and the East," in *Koordinaten deutscher Geschichte in der Epoche des Ost-West-Konflikts*, ed. Hans Hockerts (Berlin: Oldenbourg Wissenschaftsverlag, Schriften des Historischen Kollegs, 2009).

5. Philip Armstrong, Andrew Glyn, and John Harrison, *Capitalism since 1945* (Oxford: Blackwell, 1991), 117.

6. Herbert Marcuse, *One-Dimensional Man: Studies in the Ideology of Advanced Industrial Society* (Boston: Beacon, 1964). A straw in the wind, Paul Goodman's *Growing Up Absurd: Problems of Youth in the Organized Society* (New York: Vintage Books, 1960), prefigured many of the radical laments about the meaningless of industrial employment.

7. Raymond Aron, *Dix-huit leçons sur la société industrielle* (Paris: Gallimard, 1962) and the translation, *18 Lectures on Industrial Society* (London: Weidenfeld & Nicolson, 1967). Cf. Jutta Kneissel, Andreas Huyssen, and Johanna Moore, "The Convergence Theory: The Debate in the Federal Republic of Germany," *New German Critique*, no. 2 (1974): 16–27. For the role of Talcott Parsons's social theory in the vision of convergence (and of Parsons's reception in Russia in the mid-1960s), see David Engerman, "To Moscow and Back: American Sociologists and the Concept of Convergence," in *American Capitalism*, ed. Lichtenstein, 47–68. Striking in these debates about convergence and managerial capitalism was the absence of reference to themes of gender and race.

8. Ota Šik, *Plan and Market under Socialism* (Prague: Academic, 1967; London: Routledge Revivals, 2018) and similar later publications. Šik called his concept the Third Way—not to be confused with Tony Blair and Anthony Giddens's "third way" during the 1990s. See Chapter 9.

9. For a fundamental critique of the "reform communist" thrust of the state socialist economies from the late 1960s on, as well as a rich evocation of the intellectual world of Hungarian (and Western) economics, see János Kornai, *By Force of*

Thought: Irregular Memoirs of an Intellectual Journey (Cambridge, MA: MIT Press, 2006).

10. John Kenneth Galbraith, *The New Industrial State* (Princeton, NJ: Princeton University Press, 1985), 12. Between *American Capitalism* and *The New Industrial State*, Galbraith published his plea for more generous public spending, *The Affluent Society* (1958), advised the presidential campaign of John F. Kennedy, and served as ambassador to India. For the genesis of Galbraith's ideas, see Kevin Mattson, "John Kenneth Galbraith: Liberalism and the Politics of Cultural Critique," in *American Capitalism*, ed. Lichtenstein, 88–108.

11. See Jacques Doublet and Olivier Passelecq, *Les cadres* (Paris: Presses Universitaires de France, 1973).

12. Martin Broszat, *Der Staat Hitlers* (Munich: Deutscher Taschenbuch Verlag, 1961) with its idea of polyarchy; trans. by Jonathan W. Hiden as *The Hitler State* (New York: Addison Wesley Longman, 1981); Jerry F. Hough, *The Soviet Union and Social Science Theory* (Cambridge, MA: Harvard University Press, 1977). Robert A. Dahl's use of polyarchy as an institutionalization of democracy differed significantly; see *Polyarchy: Participation and Opposition* (New Haven, CT: Yale University Press, 1971), and chap. 4, n77. For the classic analysis of contemporary bureaucracy, see Michel Crozier, *The Bureaucratic Phenomenon* (Chicago: University of Chicago Press, 1964).

13. For a survey of West European national agencies and methods—which in Britain by the 1950s was narrowed to Keynesian demand management—see the PEP (Politics and Economic Planning—a think tank) study by Geoffrey Denton, Murray Forsyth, and Malcolm Maclennan, *Economic Planning and Policies in Britain, France and Germany* (London: Allen & Unwin, 1968). As a large literature on the Soviet government came to emphasize, state planning agencies, like rival branches in the military, fought to establish their respective roles in policy making. Also useful are the contributions to Raymond Vernon, ed., *Big Business and the State: Changing Relations in Western Europe* (Cambridge, MA: Harvard University Press, 1974).

14. Paul Bairoch, *The Economic Development of the Third World since 1900*, trans. Cynthia Postan (Berkeley: University of California Press, 1977), 7–8. After the date of publication, population continued to rise, although the annual rate of increase dropped from its 1962–1963 maximum of 2.2 percent to about half that today. A global population of 1.65 billion in 1900 rose to 3 billion in 1960, 4 billion by 1975, 7 billion by 2011, and 8 billion by late 2022. See *Our World in Data*: Max Roser, Hannah Richter, and Esteban Ortiz-Ospina, *World Population Growth* (rev. 2019). I follow Bairoch in using "less developed," "underdeveloped," "developing" world and "third world," and the more recent "global south" as rough synonyms. Which countries are in this category at any time remains a problematic choice. When Bairoch published, he included Argentina, Chile, China, India, and Thailand among the 170 territories of the third world!

15. See Dirk Hoerder, "Migrations and Belonging, 1870–1945," in *A World Connecting*, ed. Emily Rosenberg (Cambridge, MA: Harvard University Press, 2012), 433–589; Adam M. McKeown, "Global Migration, 1846–1940," *Journal of World History* 15, no. 2 (2005): 155–189.

16. Deborah Cohen, *Braceros: Migrant Citizens and Transnational Subjects in the Postwar United States and Mexico* (Chapel Hill: University of North Carolina Press, 2011); Claudia Bernardi, *Una storia di confine, frontiere e lavoratori: Migranti tra Messico e Stati Uniti (1836–1964)* (Rome: Carrocci, 2018); Jochen Oltmer, Axel Kreienbrink, and Carlos Sanz Díaz, eds., *Das "Gastarbeiter"-System: Arbeitsmigration und ihre Folgen in der Bundesrepublik Deutschland und Westeuropa* (Oldenburg, Germany: Wissenschaftsverlag, 2012); Carolyn Wong, *Lobbying for Inclusion: Rights Politics and the Making of Immigration Policy* (Stanford, CA: Stanford University Press, 2006).

17. For these statistics, see Hania Zlotnik, "International Migration, 1965–96: An Overview," *Population and Development Review* 24, no. 3 (September 1998): 429–468, 435 for the foreign-born statistic, 436 for table 10. For conceptual issues, Ronald Skeldon, *Migration and Development: A Global Perspective* (Harlow, UK: Addison Wesley Longman, 1997).

18. Zlotnik, "International Migration," 436, table 3.

19. Zlotnik, "International Migration," 436, table 3.

20. Zlotnik, "International Migration," 431, table 1.

21. Matthew James Connelly, *Fatal Misconception: The Struggle to Control World Population* (Cambridge, MA: Harvard University Press, 2008). Also Donella H. Meadows, *The Limits to Growth: A Report for the Club of Rome's Project on the Predicament of Mankind* (New York: Universe Books, 1972).

22. For major intellectual argumentation, see Raúl Prebisch, "Commercial Policy in the Underdeveloped Countries," *American Economic Review* 49 (1959): 251–273; Raúl Prebisch, *The Economic Development of Latin America and Its Principal Problems* (New York: United Nations, 1950); Raúl Prebisch, *Change and Development: Latin America's Great Task* (Washington, DC: Inter-American Development Bank, 1970). For Prebisch and the United Nations Conference on Trade and Development's activity, see Chapter 7. For a revealing comparison, Andrés Rivarola Puntigliano and Orjan Appelqvist, "Prebisch and Myrdal: Development Economics in the Core and on the Periphery," *Journal of Global History* 6 (2011): 29–52. Among many theoretical contributions, Samir Amin, *Unequal Development: An Essay on the Social Formations of Peripheral Capitalism* (New York: Monthly Review Press, 1976).

23. Bairoch, *The Economic Development of the Third World*, 198.

24. Cited by both Christopher R. W. Dietrich, *Oil Revolution: Sovereign Rights, and the Economic Culture of Decolonization* (Cambridge: Cambridge University Press, 2017), 26, and Giuliano Garavini, *The Rise and Fall of OPEC in the Twentieth Century* (Oxford: Oxford University Press, 2019), 61.

25. Roger Fouquet, "Historical Energy Transitions: Speed, Prices and System transformation," *Energy Research & Social Science* 22 (2016): 7–12; and B. K. Sovacool, "How Long Will It Take? Conceptualizing the Temporal Dynamics of Energy Transitions," *Energy Research & Social Science* 13 (2016): 202–215; also Vaclav Smil, *Energy Transitions: History, Requirements, Prospects* (Santa Barbara, CA: Praeger, 2010).

26. Sources provide energy data in tonnes for coal (referred to as metric tons in the United States and equal to 1,000 kg or 2,205 lb) and for oil in barrels (bbl). One barrel of oil = 42 US gallons = 159 liters, and its weight varies according to the grade of the fuel, but a barrel of crude is usually assigned an average weight of about 303 lb or 136 kg, so that 1 tonne of oil = 7.35 barrels. Since natural gas and oil are often extracted together, the production units are combined in terms of million-barrels-of-oil equivalent (Mboe), or million tonnes of oil equivalent (Mtoe). When aggregating the consumption of differing energy sources—whether biomass, hydrocarbons, hydropower, nuclear, or renewables—the inherent energy equivalents are usually given in megawatt-hours (1 MWh = 10^6 or 1 million Wh) or terawatt-hours (1 TWh = 10^{12} or 1 trillion Wh). One barrel of crude oil (or 5,800 cubic feet of natural gas) provides according to US definition 1.7 MWh of energy, which means that 1 terawatt-hour equals the energy equivalent of about 588 million barrels of oil equivalent (Mboe) or about 86 million tons of oil equivalent (Mtoe). Conversely 1 Mtoe or 7.35 Mboe = 11.63 TWh. In 2019, global oil production was 52,000 terawatts or 30.6 billion barrels of oil.

27. Statistics from *Our World in Data* and *Statista* websites. Britain of course relied on deep-pit mining; in those places where coal mining continued, viability depended on open-pit mining. This author visited a Ruhr coal mine a half century ago in 1972. Even with advanced equipment, it was clear that the long vertical and horizontal daily treks to and from the coalface, the imperatives of propping up the underground caves, the potential for fire, flooding, or collapse, and the absolute dependence on one's mates thousands of feet underground—not to say the long lineages of mining communities above—created a primeval sense of collectivity. Among the vast literature on coal mining and miners, see for Germany, Ulrich Borsdorf and Hans Mommsen, *Glück auf, Kameraden! die Bergarbeiter und ihre Organisationen in Deutschland* (Cologne: Bund-Verlag, 1979); for France, Rolande Trempé, *Les mineurs de Carmaux* (Paris: Éditions ouvrières, 1971). For a memoir of mining communities in Wales and the United States coupled with a plea for renewables, see Erin Ann Thomas, *Coal in Our Veins: A Personal Journey* (Boulder: University Press of Colorado; Logan: Utah State University Press, 2012). Also Timothy Mitchell, *Carbon Democracy: Political Power in the Age of Oil* (New York: Verso, 2011).

28. For an example of the critical environmental history bound up in this transition, see Matthew Sohm, "Paying for the Post-Industrial," PhD diss., Harvard University, 2022; also Stefan Berger and Peter Alexander, eds., *Making Sense of Mining History: Themes and Agendas* (New York: Routledge, 2020).

29. US Geological Survey report to the Federal Trade Commission, cited Garavini, *The Rise and Fall of OPEC*, 23.

30. Daniel Yergin, *The Prize: The Epic Quest for Oil, Money, and Power* (New York: Free Press, 1991). For the complex changes in oil's corporate structure, see Jeff Desjardins, "Chart: The Evolution of Standard Oil," *Visual Capitalist*, November 21, 2017, https://www.visualcapitalist.com/chart-evolution-standard-oil/.

31. See the Central Intelligence Agency, "Intelligence Memorandum: Algeria: The Importance of the Oil Industry," October 1970; sanitized copy approved for release October 31, 2011. As noted above, the French understood the stakes of Algerian oil during their long effort to suppress the Algerian rebellion. As the hard-line resident minister in Algeria Robert Lacoste noted in his General Directive No. 4 to French military officers, April 3, 1957, "An event of paramount importance, finally, is likely substantially to change the destiny of Algeria and France: the discovery of considerable mineral—especially petroleum deposits in the Sahara. These discoveries ... will justify even further all the efforts of Metropolitan France to restore calm to Algeria, which is the key to the Sahara." Quoted in Charles S. Maier and Dan S. White, *The Thirteenth of May: The Advent of de Gaulle's Republic* (New York: Oxford University Press, 1968), 102.

32. Garavini, *The Rise and Fall of OPEC*, 111; Enrico Mattei, *Scritti e discorsi, 1945–1962* (Milan: Rizzoli, 2012); Valerio Castronovo, "Gianni Agnelli and Enrico Mattei," *The Oxford Handbook of Italian Politics*, ed. Erik Jones and Gianfranco Pasquino (Oxford: Oxford University Press, 2015). For the later effort by privatization advocates to cut Mattei's reputation down to size, see Giuliano Garavini's discussion in "Global ENI: Privatization and the Birth of the Italian 'Investor State,'" (unpublished ms., 1992–1995). For background, see also Leonardo Maugeri, *The Age of Oil: The Mythology, History, and Future of the World's Most Controversial Resource* (Westport, CT: Praeger, 2006), and Leonardo Maugeri, *L'arma del petrolio: Questione petrolifera globale, guerra fredda e politica italiana nella vicenda di Enrico Mattei* (Florence: Loggia de' Lanzi, 1994); also Robert Vale Fisher, "Foreign Policy as Function of Party Politics: Italy, the Atlantic Alliance and the Opening to the Left, 1953–1962," PhD diss., Harvard University, 1994.

33. Garavini, *The Rise and Fall of OPEC*, 54–62. Oil firms also enjoyed an enviable position vis-à-vis their labor force. Although the companies required a workforce to drill wells, lay pipelines, and operate refineries, the labor force was concentrated abroad. The Saudi oil fields employed 15,000, including 3,000 Americans and 12,000 Arabs; even larger was the giant refinery on Iran's Abadan Island offshore, where 40,000 workers toiled for the Anglo Iranian oil company, most of whom lived in squalor, including "houses of empty paper cement bag construction ... without sanitation or no ventilation at all." See the 1949 report of Donald McNeil cited in Touraj Atabaki, "Chronicle of a Calamitous Strike Foretold, Abadan, July 1946," in

On the Road to Global Labour History: A Festschrift for Marcel van der Linden, ed. K. H. Roth (Leiden: Brill, 2017), 93–128; Elwell-Sutton, *Persian Oil*, 75; Garavini, *The Rise and Fall of OPEC*, 78–79; and the remarkable undergraduate honors thesis by Robert Milton Hope III, "The Refinery of Eden: Abadan and the Global Petroleum Order of the Early Cold War, 1940–1954," Harvard University, 2018.

34. See the testimony of a key player, Walter J. Levy, *Oil Strategy and Politics, 1941–1981* (Boulder, CO: Westview, 1982).

35. BP had a 40 percent share of the Iranian consortium, 24 percent of Iraqi and Emirate production, and 50 percent of Kuwaiti output, while Royal Dutch Shell had 14 percent of Iran's and 24 percent of Iraqi and Emirate oil. American firms—Jersey (ESSO), Texaco, Gulf, Mobil, Stancal, and smaller independents—shared 40 percent of Iranian output, ESSO and Mobil split close to a quarter of Quatar's, and Gulf took the other 50 percent of Kuwait's output. ESSO, Texaco, and Socal (aka Chevron) had 30 percent each of their total of Aramco's shares (the rest was Saudi held), while Mobil had the remaining 10 percent. The French Compagnie française des pétroles had to rest content with 6 percent in Iran and 24 percent in Iraq but enjoyed an exclusive presence in Algeria. See Garavini, *The Rise and Fall of OPEC*, 70, table 1. Sources to view, Francesco Petrini, *Imperi del profitto. Multinazionali petrolifieri e governi nel XX secolo* (Rome: Franco Angeli, 2015); David S. Painter, "Oil and the American Century," *Journal of American History* 99, no. 1 (June 2012): 24–39; George Lenczowski, *Oil and the State in the Middle East* (Ithaca, NY: Cornell University Press, 1960).

36. For the perversities and unanticipated results of policy, Irvine H. Anderson, *Aramco, the United States, and Saudi Arabia: A Study of the Dynamics of Foreign Policy, 1933–1950* (Princeton, NJ: Princeton University Press, 1981).

37. Garavini, *The Rise and Fall of OPEC*, 49. See also Dietrich, *Oil Revolution*, 191–262; and David S. Painter, *Oil and the American Century* (Baltimore: Johns Hopkins University Press, 1986); for Iran, see also Lawrence Paul Elwell-Sutton, *Persian Oil: A Study in Power Politics 1955* (Westport, CT: Praeger, 1976).

38. David E. Spiro, *The Hidden Hand of American Hegemony: Petrodollar Recycling and International Markets* (Ithaca, NY: Cornell University Press, 1999), 24. The "Seven Sisters" (Mattei's term) included the Standard Oil offshoots of New York, New Jersey, and California—Mobil, Esso (to become Exxon), Chevron (né Socal)—Texaco, Gulf, Shell, and BP.

39. Garavini, *The Rise and Fall of OPEC*, 101–107, 185–186.

40. Garavini, *The Rise and Fall of OPEC*, 187–203; for American alarm at the trends, see James E. Akins, "The Oil Crisis: This Time the Wolf Is Here," *Foreign Affairs*, April 1973.

41. The concept of "peak oil" originated with K. M. Hubbert's 1956 modeling of US oil reserves. See the persuasive critique by Leonardo Maugeri, "Oil: Never Cry

Wolf—Why the Petroleum Age Is far from Over," *Science* 304, no. 5674 (May 21, 2004): 1114–1115—even before exploitation of shale was under way.

42. Garavini, *The Rise and Fall of OPEC*, 289. See 179–253, and for detailed discussion of the calculations behind the oil price rise, 221–228, 288–289; also Dietrich, *The Oil Revolution*, 263–304. For the impact in the United States, Meg Jacobs, *Panic at the Pump: The Energy Crisis and the Transformation of American Politics in the 1970s* (New York: Hill and Wang, 2016). See also *Foreign Relations of the United States, 1969–1976, Vol. XXXVI: Energy Crisis, 1969–1974* (Washington, DC: US Government Printing Office, 2011) for documents. The prices are provided in Spiro, *The Hidden Hand*, 1. Most recently, see Marino Auffant, "Globalizing Oil, Unleashing Capital: An International History of the 1970s Energy Crisis," PhD diss., Harvard University.

43. See Michael De Groot, "The Soviet Union, CMEA, and the Energy Crisis of the 1970s," *Journal of Cold War Studies* 22, no. 4 (Fall 2020): 4–30. Daniel Park, *Oil and Gas in COMECON Countries* (London: Kogan Page, 1979) covers Soviet production and distribution only to 1970.

44. See Alec Cairncross, *A Country to Play With: Level of Industry Negotiations in Berlin, 1945–46* (Gerards Cross, UK: Smythe, 1987).

45. Reports on "Ruhr Steel," *The Economist*, September 15 and 22, 1945. For the Thyssen concern's petitions and plans to modernize and increase steel capacity, see the material in Bundesarchiv, Verwaltungsamt für Eisen und Stahl, Z 41/23; reports on the Dutch firm Hoogovens NA, in Washington National Archives, RG 469 Mission to the Netherlands, Industry Division, subject files, B2; Italian plans in F. Bonelli et al., *Accaio per lindusrializzazione*, 335–69; also Chapter 4.

46. John Gillingham, *Coal, Steel, and the Rebirth of Europe, 1945–1955: The Germans and French from Ruhr Conflict to Economic Community* (Cambridge: Cambridge University Press, 1991) remains a splendid account.

47. See Charles S. Maier, "The Cold War and the World Economy," in *The Cambridge History of the Cold War*, ed. Melvyn P. Leffler and Odd Arne Westad (Cambridge: Cambridge University Press, 2010), 1:44–66. On the importance of steel to the programs of nationalist development, see Ted Fertik, "Steel and Sovereignty," *Enterprise & Society* 20, no. 4 (2019): 809–825; for a longer version of this essay, which was the introduction to his Yale PhD dissertation (2018), see "Steel and Sovereignty," posted on Academia.edu.

48. Roy Jenkins's address to the European Parliament, February 13, 1980, on introduction of the "Thirteenth General Report on the Activities of the Commission." Cited by Sohm, "Paying for the Post-Industrial," chap. 1.

49. David G. Tarr, "The Steel Crisis in the United States and European Community: Causes and Adjustments," in *Issues in US-EC Trade Relations*, ed. Robert E. Baldwin, Carl B. Hamilton, and Andre Sapir (Chicago: University of Chicago Press,

1988), 175–198. Also useful, Wikipedia, "Steel Crisis," last edited June 7, 2022, https://en.wikipedia.org/wiki/Steel_crisis. Also Yves Mény and Vincent Wright, eds., *The Politics of Steel: Western Europe and the Steel Industry in the Crisis Years (1974–1984)* (Berlin: de Gruyter, 1987), esp. the editors' chapter, "State and Steel in Western Europe," 1–17 for a summary of the contraction, and the chapter by Patrick A. Messelin, "The European Iron and Steel Industry and the World Crisis," 111–136.

50. As of 2019, global production of crude steel amounted to 1.875 billion tons with China producing almost 1 billion or just about half of that sum: 996.3 million tons, India 111.2 million tons, Japan 99.3 million tons, United States 87.9 million tons, Russia 71.6 million tons, and South Korea 71.4 million tons. Germany led Europe's output with 39.7 million tons. See https://en.Wikipedia.org/wiki/List_of_countries _by_steel_production, based on various years of the World Steel Association, *Steel Statistical Yearbook* online. For Europe, see also European Commission, Eurostat, *50 Years of the ECSC Treaty: Coal and Steel Statistics: Data 1951–2000*.

51. Thomas A. Schwartz, *Henry Kissinger and American Power* (New York: Hill and Wang, 2020), 231–261.

52. Average annual rates of GDP growth in the 1960s in leading developed countries included 2.9 percent (United Kingdom), 4.4 percent (United States), 4.6 percent (Federal Republic of Germany), 5.8 percent (Italy), and 11.1 percent (Japan). *World Business Cycles, 1950–80* (London: Economist Newspaper, 1982), 45, 62, 83, 87, 126. For a lucid and brief discussion of the contending theories seeking to account for the growth and then the break in trend, see Gottfried Bombach, *Postwar Economic Growth Revisited* (Amsterdam: North Holland, 1985). He cites, on p. 80, average annual net investment figures for the two periods 1965–1969 and 1975–1969, for the United States 10.9 percent vs. 6.5 percent, a 40 percent drop; for the Federal Republic of Germany 15.5 percent vs. 11.2 percent, a 28 percent drop; and Japan 20.3 percent vs. 22 percent, a 15 percent increase.

53. For an analysis of how in both the United States and the Soviet Union the difficulty of balancing investment in producer goods with final demand for consumer goods resulted in frequent shortages in Russia and stagflation in the United States, see Tim Barker and Yakov Feygin, "Converging on Neoliberalism," forthcoming in *Contemporary European History*.

54. For varying estimates (taking into account the rise in American oil prices along with the OPEC increase), Robert Keohane, "The International Politics of Inflation," in *The Politics of Inflation and Economic Stagnation*, ed. Leon N. Lindberg and Charles S. Maier (Washington, DC: Brookings Institution, 1985), 91.

55. On close examination, these apparently intuitively correlations between inflation rates, high government spending, left parties in power, and the existence of strong labor unions proved far too simplistic. See the following essays in Lindberg

and Maier, *The Politics of Inflation and Economic Stagnation*: Colin Crouch, "Conditions for Trade Union Wage Restraint," 105–139; Rudolf Klein, "Public Expenditure in an Inflationary World," 196–223; and David S. Cameron, "Does Government Cause Inflation? Taxes, Spending, and Deficits," 224–279. For other political-economy approaches, see also Fred Hirsch and John H. Goldthorpe, eds., *The Political Economy of Inflation* (Cambridge, MA: Harvard University Press, 1978), which included my own comparative effort, "The Politics of Inflation in the Twentieth Century" and Colin Crouch, "Inflation and the Political Organization of Economic Interests," 217–239. See also Alessandro Pizzorno, "Political Exchange and Collective Identity in Industrial Conflict," in Colin Crouch and Alessandro Pizzorno, eds., *The Resurgence of Class Conflict in Western Europe since 1968*, vol. 2, *Comparative Analyses* (New York: Holmes & Meier, 1978), 277–298.

56. Gottfried Bombach, ed., *Der Keynesianismus IV: Die Beschäftigungspolitische Diskussion in der Wachstumspoche der Bunderepublik Deutschland. Dokumente und Analysen* (Berlin: Springer Verlag, 1983); Alexander Nützenadel, *Stunde der Ökonomen: Wissenschaft, Politik und Expertenkulture in der Bundesrepublik 1949–1974* (Göttingen: Vandenhoeck & Ruprecht, 2005), 295–306.

57. On the economic controversies around the Phillips curve, see Anthony M. Santomero and John L. Seater, "The Inflation-Unemployment Trade-off: A Critique of the Literature," *Journal of Economic Literature* 16 (June 1978): 499–544. For a careful study of the impact of union activism, see Douglas A. Hibbs Jr., *The Political Economy of Advanced Industrial Societies* (Cambridge, MA: Harvard University Press, 2014).

58. For a detailed study, see Andrew Martin, "Wages, Profits, and Investment in Sweden," in *The Politics of Inflation and Economic Stagnation*, ed. Lindberg and Maier, 404–466. For some economists in the Swedish trade union federation, the LO, and the closely overlapping Swedish Social Democratic Party (SAP), Gösta Rehn in the 1950s, and Rudolf Meidner in the 1970s, the objective was to slowly transfer firms' pretax profits as shares of equity to establish a socialized investment fund (446–452).

59. See Carlo Edoardo Altamura, "The Paradox of the 1970s: The Renaissance of International Banking and the Rise of Public Debt," *Journal of Modern History* 15, no. 4 (2017): 529–553; Joanne Gowa, *Closing the Gold Window: Domestic Politics and the End of Bretton Woods* (Ithaca, NY: Cornell University Press, 1983); Fred Block, *The Origins of International Economic Disorder* (Berkeley: University of California Press, 1977); and Keohane, "The International Politics of Inflation," in *The Politics of Inflation and Economic Stagnation*, ed. Lindberg and Maier, 78–104, esp. 89–97 on the relationship between dollar depreciation and OPEC pricing.

60. Richard Cooper, *The Economics of Interdependence: Economic Policy in the Atlantic Community* (New York: McGraw-Hill, 1968); for discussion of the term,

see also Daniel Sargent, "The United States and Globalization in the 1970s," in *The Shock of the Global: The 1970s Perspective*, ed. Niall Ferguson, Charles S. Maier, Erez Manela, and Daniel J. Sargent (Cambridge, MA: Belknap, 2010), 57–59. In its modern economic use, it had originated at least as early as Norman Angell's discussions of international economics before World War I.

61. Robert A. Mundell, "Capital Mobility and Stabilization Policy under Fixed and Flexible Exchange Rates," *Canadian Journal of Economics and Political Science* 29, no. 4 (1963): 475–485. Reprinted in Robert A. Mundell, *International Economics* (New York: Macmillan, 1968); J. Marcus Fleming, "Domestic Financial Policies under Fixed and Floating Exchange Rates," IMF Staff Papers 9 (1962): 369–379; Maurice Obstfeld, Jay C. Stambaugh, and Alan M. Taylor, "The Trilemma in History: Tradeoffs among Exchange Rates, Monetary Policies, and Capital Mobility," *Review of Economics and Statistics* 87, no. 3 (2005): 423–438. Stressing political trade-offs: Louis W. Pauly, "Capital Mobility, State Autonomy and Political Legitimacy," *Journal of International Affairs* 48, no. 2 (1995): 369–388; Eric Helleiner, *States and the Reemergence of Global Finance: From Bretton Woods to the 1990s* (Ithaca, NY: Cornell University Press, 1994).

62. Phillip Cagan, *Persistent Inflation: Historical and Policy Essays* (New York: Columbia University Press, 1979); cf. Arthur Okun's question, "Who threw the ratchet [of one-way price changes] into the soup?" in *Prices and Quantities: A Macroeconomic Analysis* (Washington, DC: Brookings Institution, 1981), 3; and other literature cited in Charles S. Maier, "Inflation and Stagnation as Politics and History," in *Politics of Global Inflation and Stagnation*, ed. Maier and Lindberg.

63. Garavini, *The Rise and Fall of OPEC*, 289–297.

64. Daniel Yankelovich, "The Noneconomic Side of Inflation," *Proceedings of the Academy of Political Science* 33, no. 3 (1979): 20, cited in Robert J. Samuelson, *The Great Inflation and Its Aftermath: The Past and Future of American Affluence* (New York: Random House, 2008), 19–20.

65. Thomas Sargent, "The End of Four Big Inflations," included in Thomas Sargent, *Rational Expectations and Inflation* (Princeton, NJ: Princeton University Press, 2013). For a discussion of Sargent's work, see Harald Uhlig, "Agents as Empirical Macroeconomists: Thomas J. Sargent's Contribution to Economics," *Scandinavian Journal of Economics* 114, no. 4 (2012): 1055–1081.

7. Deploying Governance

1. See the many works of Charles Tilly and Sydney Tarrow, including *Contentious Politics* (Boulder, CO: Paradigm, 2007), also Doug McAdam, Sydney Tarrow, and Charles Tilly, *Dynamics of Contention* (New York: Cambridge University Press, 2001)

2. N-grams. Other related concepts, "governability," "NGO," and a very American locution, "*think tank*," were part of the same discourse.

3. Otto Gierke, *Das deutsche Genossenschaftsrecht* (Berlin: Weidman, 1869–1913); Heinrich Heffter, *Die deutsche Selbstverwaltung im 19. Jahrhundert: Geschichte der Ideen und Institutionen* (Stuttgart: Koehler, 1950).

4. On the impact of 1848 and the anti-revolutionary context of sociology, Jacques Donzelot, *L'invention du social: Essai sur le déclin des passions politiques* (Paris: Fayard, Éditions du Seuil, 1984); on the 1901 Law of Associations, dissolving many Roman Catholic teaching orders, see, Pierre Sorlin, *Waldeck-Rousseau* (Paris: A Colin, 1966). Pierre Rosanvallon, the contemporary political sociologist who was an activist with the independent trade unions (CFDT) in the 1960s and 1970s, brought out the ambivalence of this tradition: see *Le moment Guizot* (Paris: Gallimard, 1985). For his personal trajectory, pivoted on 1968, see *Notre histoire intellectuelle et politique 1968–2018* (Paris: Éditions du Seuil, 2018).

5. See Serge Audier's exhaustive *La pensée anti-68: Essai sur une restauration intellectuelle* (Paris: La Découverte, 2008), esp. 117–192. The debates of the 1970s and 1980s in both countries revealed anew the ambivalence of the label "liberal." In ordinary American political language, it meant reformist and progressive and thus often, whether in the 1960s or the 2000s, a term of abuse in the mouths of adversaries. Academics who knew its origins in Anglo-American debates often stressed its connection to pluralism as appropriated, for example, by Isaiah Berlin. In Europe it was claimed by politicians hostile to social democratic policies and finally by mandarins such as Raymond Aron, who sought to find an Olympian stance rejecting reaction and collectivism alike.

6. As discussed in Chapter 4, the economic committees were not the only sites for governance: the secretariat had followed a broad mission during the years of decolonization. See Eva-Maria Muschik, "Managing the World: The United Nations, Decolonization, and the Strange Triumph of State Sovereignty in the 1950s and 1960s," *Journal of Global History* 13, no. 1 (2018): 121–144. On the UN's role in global governance, see Daniel Speich Chassé, "Decolonization and Global Governance: Approaches to the History of the UN-System," lecture to the History of International Organizations Network, Geneva, 2013.

7. Philip Mirowski and Dietr Plehwe, eds., *The Road from Mont Pèlerin: The Making of the Neoliberal Thought Collective* (Cambridge, MA: Harvard University Press, 2009); also Richard Cockett, *Thinking the Unthinkable: Think Tanks and the Economic Counter-revolution 1931–1983* (London: Fontana, 1995) on the British milieu. Even John Rawls accepted an invitation from Milton Friedman to join the Mont Pèlerin Society in 1968, according to Avner Offner and Gabriel Söderberg, *The Nobel Factor: The Prize in Economics, Social Democracy, and the Market Turn* (Princeton, NJ: Princeton University Press, 2016), 272; reference in Katrina Forrester, *In the*

Shadow of Justice: Postwar Liberalism and the Remaking of Political Philosophy (Princeton, NJ: Princeton University Press, 2019), 109–110. For an inside memoir of the state of the Washington think tank milieu and its interaction with the Reagan administration, see Howard J. Wiarda, *Conservative Brain Trust: The Rise, Fall, and Rise again of the American Enterprise Institute* (Lanham, MD: Rowman & Littlefield, Lexington Books, 2009).

8. Brian H. Smith, *More than Altruism: The Politics of Private Foreign Aid* (Princeton, NJ: Princeton University Press, 2014), 3–16.

9. For a clear exposition see Thomas A. McCarthy, *The Critical Theory of Jürgen Habermas* (Cambridge, MA: MIT Press, 1978).

10. Union of International Associations, *Yearbook of International Associations 2001* (Brussels: Union of International Associations, 2001), figs. 1.2.1 (a) and (b): approximately 3,500 NGOS in 1970 jumped to over 10,000 in 1980 and 19,000 in 1990. The number of international governmental organizations rose from a few hundred to over 1,000 in 1980 and about 4,000 in 1990. Glenda Sluga, "The Transformation of International Institutions," in *The Shock of the Global: The 1970s in Perspective*, ed. Niall Ferguson, Charles S. Maier, Erez Manella, and Daniel J. Sargent (Cambridge, MA: Harvard University Press, 2010), 223–236.

11. Sabino Cassese, "Sugli usi di *governance*," in *Parolechiave 56: Governance* (2016): 17–18.

12. Gregory Mann refers to the states of the Sahel beginning to mortgage their future from the period of decolonization: "From Empires to NGOs in the West African Sahel: An Introduction," *Humanity* 6, no. 2 (Summer 2015): 287–297 ("mortgaging," 289); also "Interview with Gregory Mann," in the same issue, 299–307. The article is a précis of Gregory Mann, *From Empire to NGOs in the West African Sahel: The Road to Nongovernmentality* (Cambridge: Cambridge University Press, 2015). See also Timothy Nunan's study of NGOs in Afghanistan, *Humanitarian Invasion: Global Development in Cold War Afghanistan* (New York: Cambridge University Press, 2016).

13. It is not clear why the proportional drop in governance did not equal the proportional rise in governability. In any case, the term *governance* was generally used about 100 times more frequently and peaked in 2015; the term *governability* peaked around the year 2000.

14. Since the term was still a rare one—appearing in print only about 1 percent as often as "governance"—the frequency might even have reflected, in the words of one study, "a Foucault effect." For the social theorist Michel Foucault, who deployed the concept in his lectures at the Collège de France during the late 1970s, it denoted a historic transition starting in the late Middle Ages, when states and the church became concerned with the health, size, and moral state of their populations and not just the defense of sovereignty. See Michel Foucault, *Security, Territory, Population: Lectures at the Collège de France, 1977–78*, ed. Michel Senellart, François Ewald, and

Alessandro Fontana (London: Palgrave Macmillan, 2009); Graham Burchell, Colin Gordon, and Peter Miller, eds., *The Foucault Effect: Studies in Governmentality: With Two Lectures by and an Interview with Michel Foucault* (Chicago: University of Chicago Press, 1991). Also, among many discussions, *Parolechiave 56 Governance* (December 2016); Kees van Kersbergen and Frans van Waarden, " 'Governance' as a Bridge between Disciplines: Cross-disciplinary Inspiration regarding Shifts in Governance and Problems of Governability, Accountability and Legitimacy," *European Journal of Political Research* 43 (2004): 143–171; and Grégoire Chamayou, *La société ingouvernable: Une généalogie du libéralisme autoritaire* (Paris: La fabrique éditions, 2018).

15. Trilateral Commission, *Crisis of Democracy*, 7, 11, 68, 112, 161. The editors cited Ronald Inglehart's notable claim of the era that the 1960s generation was pursuing postmaterialist values: *The Silent Revolution: Changing Values and Political Styles among Western Publics* (Princeton, NJ: Princeton University Press, 1977). For a general survey, see Alasdair Roberts, *The Logic of Discipline: Global Capitalism and the Architecture of Government* (Oxford Scholarship Online, 2010), http://doi.org/10.1093/acprof:oso/9780195374988.001.0001.

16. Samuel H. Beer, *Britain against Itself: The Political Contradictions of Collectivism* (New York: W. W. Norton, 1982), 17, on deference and British civic culture, 110–120, and quoting (p. 114) Dennis Kavanagh, "Political Culture in Great Britain: The Decline of the Civic Culture," in *The Civic Culture Revisited*, ed. Gabriel A. Almond and Sidney Verba (Boston: Little Brown, 1980), 170.

17. See Mancur Olsson, *The Logic of Collective Action: Public Goods and the Theory of Groups* (Cambridge, MA: Harvard University Press, 1971); and Mancur Olson, *The Rise and Decline of Nations: Economic Growth, Stagflation, and Social Rigidities* (New Haven, CT: Yale University Press, 1982).

18. Michael Franczak, "Losing the Battle, Winning the War: Neoconservatives versus the New International Economic Order, 1974–82," *Diplomatic History* 43, no. 5 (2019): 867–889, esp. 870. See also Richard N. Gardner, Saburo Okita, and B. J. Udink, *A Turning Point in North-South Economic Relations: A Report of the Trilateral Task Force on Relations with Developing Countries to the Executive Commission of the Trilateral Commission* (New York: New York University Press, 1974).

19. "The New Cold War," *Wall Street Journal*, July 17, 1975, cited in Franczak, "Losing the Battle, Winning the War," 871.

20. Forrester, *In the Shadow of Justice*, chap. 5 follows the debates in the Anglo-American university world, where John Rawls's 1971 *A Theory of Justice* was a key point of reference. I am compressing far more elaborate arguments. Recognition of an obligation to redistribute resources logically entailed recognition of the claimant's right to claim them; but did obligations and rights collectivities extend to states as well as individuals; and what degree of inequality triggered such an obligation, and to what extent?

21. Mark Mazower, *Governing the World: The History of an Idea* (New York: Penguin, 2012), esp. chaps. 9–12.

22. Johanna Bockman, "Socialist Globalization against Capitalist Neocolonialism: The Economic Ideas behind the New International Economic Order," *Humanity: An International Journal of Human Rights, Humanitarianism, and Development* 6, no. 1 (Spring 2015): 109–128. Whether efforts to lower first world tariff barriers to third world exports count as socialist globalization is debatable. UN economists contested OECD free trade orthodoxy. See John Toye and Richard Toye, *The UN and Global Political Economy: Trade, Finance, and Development* (Bloomington: Indiana University Press, 2004) for an intellectual history on which my summary relies.

23. Allen J. Matusow, *Farm Policies and Politics in the Truman Years* (Cambridge, MA: Harvard University Press, 1967).

24. On the European Common Agricultural Policy, see Kiran Klaus Patel, ed., *Fertile Ground for Europe: The History of European Integration and the Common Agricultural Policy since 1945* (Baden-Baden: Nomos, 2009).

25. By the 1980s, this policy path seemed disproved by the "Asian tigers" whose production for export of consumer electronics showed the success of a completely different path.

26. Toye and Toye, *The UN and Global Political Economy*, chap. 5 traces the respective intellectual inputs into the terms-of-trade dispute. Prebisch himself backed away from the prescription by the 1960s. For the debates emerging in development economics—crystallized in part around the World Bank's mission to Colombia in 1949 and the personal and doctrinal conflicts it engendered, see Michele Alacevich, *The Political Economy of the World Bank: The Early Years* (Stanford, CA: Stanford University Press and the World Bank, 2009). Indicative as much probably of the ebullient faith in foreign aid as in his personal merits, Black was distinguished for picking up honorary degrees from Harvard, Yale, and Princeton all in 1960.

27. For careful attempts as of the mid-1960s, see Simon Kuznets, *Postwar Economic Growth: Findings and Questions* (Cambridge, MA: Harvard University Press, 1964).

28. Daniel Ricardo Quiroga-Villamarin, "An Atmosphere of Genuine Solidarity and Brotherhood: Hernan Santa-Cruz and a Forgotten Latin American Contribution to Social Rights," *Journal of the History of International Law* 21 (2019). For Latin American contributions, see also Christy Thornton, "Mexican International Economic Order? Tracing the Hidden Roots of the Charter of Economic Rights and Duties of States," *Humanity* 9, no. 3 (2018): 389–421. Robert L. Rothstein, *Global Bargaining: UNCTAD and the Quest for a NIEO* (Princeton, NJ: Princeton University Press, 1979) focuses on the institutional difficulties revealed by commodity bargaining in the mid-1970s.

29. Cited by Giuliano Garavini, *The Rise and Fall of OPEC in the Twentieth Century* (Oxford: Oxford University Press, 2019), 240. I have drawn on his account, pp. 230–245 for the negotiations of 1973–1975.

30. Based on Marino Auffant, "Globalizing Oil, Unleashing Capital: An International History of the 1970s Energy Crisis," PhD diss., Harvard University. With thanks to the author for letting me draw on this superb piece of research.

31. See Neil Gilman, "The New International Economic Order: A Reintroduction," *Humanity: An International Journal of Human Rights, Humanitarianism, and Development* 6, no. 1 (Spring 2015): 1–16; and in the same issue, Daniel J. Whelan, "'Under the Aegis of Man': The Right to Development and the Origins of the New International Economic Order," 93–108; and Antony Anghie, "Legal Aspects of the New International Economic Order," 145–158; Daniel Sargent, "North/South: The United States Responds to the New International Economic Order," 201–216.

32. Giuliano Garavini, *Dopo gli imperi: L'integrazione europea nello scontro nord-sud* (Milan: Mondadori, 2009), 210–221; also Vanessa Ogle, "States Rights against Private Capital: The 'New International Economic Order' and the Struggle over Aid, Trade, and Foreign Investment, 1962–1981," in *Humanity* 5, no. 2 (Summer 2014): 210–227.

33. Marco Duranti, *The Conservative Human Rights Revolution: European Identity, Transnational Politics, and the Origins of the European Convention* (New York: Oxford University Press, 2017); Samuel Moyn, *Christian Human Rights* (Philadelphia: University of Pennsylvania Press, 2015).

34. See Daniel Sargent, *A Superpower Transformed: The Remaking of American Foreign Relations in the 1970s* (New York: Oxford University Press, 2014).

35. Ian Little, Tibor Scitowsky, and Maurice Scott, *Industry and Trade in Some Developing Countries: A Comparative Study* (London: Oxford University Press 1970); Bela Balassa et al., *The Structure of Protection in Developing Countries* (Baltimore: Johns Hopkins University Press for the World Bank and Inter-American Development Bank, 1971). I have drawn on the clear exposition of the contending arguments in John Rapley, *Understanding Development: Theory and Practice in the Third World* (Boulder, CO: Lynne Rienner, 2002), 51–70. Again, see Forrester, *In the Shadow of Justice*, chap. 5.

36. For a general analysis of the alternative principles at stake, see Stephen D. Krasner, *Structural Conflict: The Third World against Global Liberalism* (Berkeley: University of California Press, 1985); Stephen Haggard and Beth A. Simmons, "Theories of International Regimes," *International Organization* 41, no. 3 (1987); Rothstein, *Global Bargaining*; Antony Anghie, "Inequality, Human Rights, and the New International Economic Order," *Humanity* 10, no. 3 (2019): 429–442.

37. Findings presented to the US House Committee on Foreign Affairs and other American sources, summarized in Robert E. Wood, *From Marshall Plan to Debt*

Crisis: Foreign Aid and Development Choices in the World Economy (Berkeley: University of California Press, 1986), 111–114. Also Wolfgang Benedek, "The Lomé Convention and the International Law of Development: A Concretisation of the New International Economic Order?" *Journal of African Law* 26, no. 1 (Spring 1982): 74–93.

38. Wood, *From Marshall Plan to Debt Crisis*.

39. See Chapter 6. Kissinger proposed the response in December 1973, during the OPEC embargo but before the price hike. The organization was formally launched about a year later.

40. For a general treatment, see Robert Solomon, *Money on the Move: The Revolution in International Finance since 1980* (Princeton, NJ: Princeton University Press, 1999). For an invaluable résumé of the international debt crises of the 1980s and 1990s and the analyses that grew out of them, see William C. Cline, *International Debt Reexamined* (Washington, DC: [Peterson] Institute of International Economics, 1995). Inflations in Austria, Germany, Poland, and Russia after 1918 and in Germany, Greece, Hungary, and China after World War II sent currencies to 10^{-9} to 10^{-12} even to 10^{-15} of their earlier values, ultimately rendering them worthless.

41. James M. Buchanan and Richard E. Wagner, *Democracy in Deficit: The Political Legacy of Lord Keynes* (New York: Academic Review Press, 1977); James M. Buchanan and Gordon Tullock, *The Calculus of Consent: Logical Foundations of Constitutional Democracy* (Ann Arbor: University of Michigan Press, 1962); James M. Buchanan, *The Limits of Liberty: Between Anarchy and Leviathan* (Chicago: University of Chicago Press, 1975); Assar Lindbeck, "Stabilization Policy in Open Economies with Endogenous Politicians," *American Economic Review* 66 (May 1976): 1–19.

42. Again, see Rudolf Klein, "Does Government Cause Inflation?" in *The Politics of Global Inflation and Stagnation*, ed. Leon Lindberg and Charles S. Maier (Washington, D.C.: Brookings Institution, 1985), 224–279.

43. This minimization of psychic costs also marked some of the contributions that Leon Lindberg and I included in our Brookings collection, *The Politics of Inflation.* "Leaving aside the alleged social and political by-products of inflation it is hard to maintain that the consequences of inflation are enormously serious." Brian Barry, "Political Ideas of Some Economists," 283.

44. Buchanan and Wagner, *Democracy in Deficit*, 64–65; cited Barry, "Political Ideas," 284.

45. Forrester, *In the Shadow of Justice*, chap. 4.

46. Brian Barry, "Does Democracy Cause Inflation? Political Ideas of Some Economists," in *The Politics of Inflation*, ed. Lindberg and Maier; also, John H. Goldthorpe, "The Current Inflation: Towards a Sociological Account," in *The Political Economy of Inflation*, ed. Fred Hirsch and John H. Goldthorpe (Cambridge, MA: Harvard University Press, 1978), and for a sample, E. J. Mishan, "The New Inflation in Theory

and Practice," *Encounter* 42 (May 1974). More neutral than Mishan were Samuel Brittan, *The Economic Consequences of Democracy* (London: Temple Smith, 1977), 223–289, and Robert Skidelsky, the biographer of Keynes and later fan of Margaret Thatcher; see his collection, *The End of the Keynesian Era: Essays on the Disintegration of the Keynesian Political Economy* (New York: Holmes and Meier, 1977). For the idea that capitalism tended to undermine the very values needed for its own viability, see Joseph A. Schumpeter, *Capitalism, Socialism and Democracy* (New York: Harper & Brothers, 1942), and then taken up by Daniel Bell, *The Cultural Contradictions of Capitalism* (New York: Basic Books, 1976).

47. Paul W. McCracken, *Towards Full Employment and Price Stability: A Report to the OECD by a Group of Independent Experts* (Paris: OECD, 1977), 14.

48. Robert Wolfe, "From Reconstructing Europe to Constructing Globalization: The OECD in Historical Perspective," in *The OECD and Transnational Governance*, ed. Rianne Mahon and Stephen McBride (Vancouver: University of British Columbia Press, 2008), 25–42.

49. Matthias Schmelzer, *The Hegemony of Growth: The OECD and the Making of the Economic Growth Paradigm* (Cambridge: Cambridge University Press, 2016), 324–325; see also Mahon and McBride, eds., *The OECD and Transnational Governance*; and Richard Woodward, *The Organisation for Economic Co-operation and Development (OECD)* (London: Routledge, 2009).

50. Anne O. Krueger et al., *Trade and Employment in Developing Countries* (Chicago: University of Chicago Press, 1983); summary of findings in Anne O. Krueger, "Trade Strategies and Employment in Developing Countries," *Finance and Development* 21, no. 4 (June 1984): 23–26.

51. For an eloquent French appeal on behalf of Africa contemporary with the Alliance for Progress for Latin America, see René Dumont, *L'Afrique noire est mal partie* (Paris: Éditions du Seuil, 1962). For a sustained critique of development aid, see William Easterly, "Was Development Assistance a Mistake?" *American Economic Review* 97, no. 2 (May 2007): 328–332.

52. Dieter Plehwe, "The Neoliberal Economic Development Discourse," in *The Road from Mont Pèlerin*, ed. Plehve and Mirovski, 238–279; Peter Bauer, *Dissent on Development: Studies and Debates in Development Economics* (London: Weidenfeld & Nicolson, 1971).

53. See "Western Guilt and Third World Poverty," *Commentary*, January 1, 1976, cited in Franczak, "Losing the Battle, Winning the War," 867–889, citation on 875.

54. For a good summary of the controversy, see Daniel Geary, *Beyond Civil Rights: The Moynihan Report and Its Legacy* (Philadelphia: University of Pennsylvania Press, 2015), esp. chap. 4, "The Death of White Sociology."

55. "The United States in Opposition," *Commentary*, March 1975, cited by Franczak, "Losing the Battle, Winning the War," 871. By late 1978, Moynihan would

declare "the breaking of the power of the oil cartel a principal objective of American policy." "How to Cut Off OPEC's Power," *Newsday*, December 27, 1978, cited in Garavini, *Rise and Fall of OPEC*, 278.

56. Minutes of the Secretary of State's Staff Meeting, January 7, 1974, in *FRUS*, 1969–1976, XXXV, National Security Policy, 1973–1975, ed. M. Todd Bennett (Washington, DC: US Department of State, 2014), doc. 29, cited Franczak, "Losing the Battle, Winning the War," 879.

57. Sluga "Transformation of International Institutions," 228–231.

58. Cited Slobodian, *Globalists: The End of Empire and the Birth of Neoliberalism* (Cambridge, MA: Harvard University Press, 2018), 146–181, citation on 159.

59. Krasner, *Structural Conflict*, 314.

60. Wilfried Loth, *Building Europe: A History of European Unification* (Berlin: Walter de Gruyter, 2015), 69–72; Hans Jürgen Küsters, *Die Gründung der Europäischen Wirtschaftsgemeinschaft* (Baden-Baden: Nomos, 1982). Also fundamental, Alan Milward, *The European Rescue of the Nation State* (London: Routledge, 1992); and more highly interpretive, Luuk van Middelaar, *The Passage to Europe: How a Continent Became a Union* (New Haven, CT: Yale University Press, 2013). I follow Loth's summary of institutional negotiations. A European Atomic Community, Euratom, was negotiated in parallel.

61. Loth, *Building Europe*, 118–119; also Morton Rasmussen, "The Origins of a Legal Revolution—The Early History of the European Court of Justice," *Journal of European Integration History* 14 (2008): 77–98.

62. I follow several major accounts in this section: Emmanuel Mourlon-Druol, *A Europe Made of Money: The Emergence of the European Monetary System* (Ithaca, NY: Cornell University Press, 2012); Harold James, *Making the European Monetary Union* (Princeton, NJ: Princeton University Press, 1996), chaps. 4–5, esp. 98–140; and Barry Eichengreen, *Globalizing Capital: A History of the International Monetary System*, 3rd ed. (Princeton, NJ: Princeton University Press, 2019). For institutional development, Loth, *Building Europe*, 199ff.

63. James, *Making the European Monetary Union*, 115.

64. James, *Making the European Monetary Union*, 133; The Kiel Report of December 1974, cited Mourlon-Druol, *A Europe Made of Money*, 35.

65. James, *Making the European Monetary Union*, 136–137; Mourlon-Druol, *A Europe Made of Money*, 47.

66. James, *Making the European Monetary Union*, 139.

67. Mourlon-Druol, *A Europe Made of Money*, 82.

68. Cited in James, *Making the Monetary Union*, 176. Chapter 5 provides the narrative for 1977–1979.

69. Loth, *Building Europe*, 229–240; James, *Making the Monetary Union*, 178–183; Mourlon-Druol, *A Europe Made of Money*.

70. Mourlon-Druol, *A Europe Made of Money*, emphasizes correctly, I believe, that the achievement of EMU was more than an intergovernmental agreement but one dependent on trans-European networks and convictions.

71. Gyan Prakash, *Emergency Chronicles: Indira Gandhi and Democracy's Turning Point* (Princeton, NJ: Princeton University Press, 2019), 303.

72. Prakash, *Emergency Chronicles*, 199.

73. See Nicole Sackley, "Foundation in the Field: The Ford Foundation's New Delhi Office and the Construction of Development Knowledge, 1953–1970," in *American Foundations and the Coproduction of World Order in the Twentieth Century*, ed. John Krige and Helke Rausch (Göttingen: Vandenhoek & Ruprecht, 2012).

74. See Fernando Guirao, *The European Rescue of the Franco Regime, 1950–1975* (Oxford: Oxford University Press, 2021).

75. The best account of these events at the time at least in English was the reporting of Kenneth Maxwell in the *New York Review of Books*. Washington also grew fearful of the rapprochement of Italy's Communist Party—by now independent of Moscow—with the Christian Democrats in part against the Red Brigades. A *compromesso storico* or Christian Democracy–Italian Communist Party government seemed on the verge of formation, but the Communist Party's fortunes crested with the 1976 elections and the compromise was never consummated. Yet Washington remained on edge, and a whole neoconservative subculture with outlets in American magazines of opinion mobilized to sustain an atmosphere of panic.

76. See Garavini, *Rise and Fall of OPEC*, 275–280.

77. See Charles S. Maier, "Malaise," in *The Shock of the Global*, ed. Ferguson et al.

8. Reinventions, 1978–1990s

1. For the ambience, see the essays collected in Niall Ferguson, Charles S. Maier, Erez Manela, and Daniel J. Sargent, eds., *The Shock of the Global: The 1970s in Perspective* (Cambridge, MA: Harvard University Press, 2010).

2. On the diplomacy and impact of the double-track debates, see Georges Soutou, *L'alliance incertaine: Les rapports politico-stratégiques franco-allemands, 1954–1996* (Paris: Fayard, 1996); Werner Link, "Außen- und Sicherheitsplitik in der Ära Schmidt 1974–1982," in *Republik im Wandel 1974–1982, Die Ära Schmidt*, ed. Wolfgang Jäger and Werner Link (Stuttgart/Manheim: Deutsche Verlagsanstalt, 1987), 275–432. France used the crisis and its delay to develop its arsenal; along with Schmidt, Giscard tried to keep the door open with Moscow as would Mitterrand after 1981. When Kohl replaced Schmidt, cooperation intensified.

3. See Ezra Vogel, *Deng Xiaoping and the Transformation of China* (Cambridge, MA: Harvard University Press, 2011). For Gorbachev, see William Taubman, *Gorbachev: His Life and Times* (New York: Norton, 2017).

4. See Konrad Jarausch, ed., *Das Ende der Zuversicht? Die siebziger Jahre als Geschichte* (Göttingen: Vandenhoeck & Ruprecht 2008), including his essay, "Zwischen 'Reformstau' und 'Socialabbau,' Anmerckungen zur Globalisierungs-debatte in Deutschland," 330–352. On the Left's evolution, see Geoff Eley, *Forging Democracy: The History of the Left in Europe, 1800–2000* (Oxford: Oxford University Press, 2002).

5. The formal nomenclature is confusing: When established by the 1957 Treaty of Rome, the European Economic Community (EEC) was considered one of the European Communities, the others being the European Atomic Energy Community (Euratom) and the European Coal and Steel Community (ECSC), established in 1952 as a consequence of the 1950 "Schuman Plan." Both were folded into the EEC in 1967, which in turn would be renamed as the European Community (EC) at the same time members established the European Union (EU) by virtue of the February 1992 Maastricht Treaties, which also set out the phases for European Monetary Union (EMS) to be completed in stages between 1998 and 2002.

6. David E. Spiro, *The Hidden Hand of American Hegemony: Petrodollar Recycling and International Markets* (Ithaca, NY: Cornell University Press, 1999), 1.

7. For the problem of loan supervision and credit crises as they arose in the 1970s, see Alexis Drach, "Supervisors against Regulation? The Basel Committee and Country Risk before the International Debt Crisis (1976–1982)," *Financial History Review* 27, no. 2 (2020): 210–233. For sovereign debt crises as they would arise in the euro crisis a generation later, see Silvia Pepino, *Sovereign Risk and Financial Crisis: The International Political Economy of the Eurozone* (London: Palgrave Macmillan, 2015). For all these questions, consult the magisterial history by Harold James, *International Monetary Cooperation since Bretton Woods* (Washington, DC: IMF and Oxford University Press, 1996).

8. Paul V. Kershaw, "Averting a Global Financial Crisis: the US, the IMF, and the Mexican Debt Crisis of 1976," *International History Review* 40, no. 2 (2018): 291–314.

9. Ethan Kapstein, *Governing the Global Economy: International Finance and the State* (Cambridge, MA: Harvard University Press, 1994), 58–102; also Spiro, *The Hidden Hand of American Hegemony*, 19–126.

10. Cited by Carlo Edoardo Altamura, "A New Dawn for European Banking: The Euromarket, the Oil Crisis and the Rise of International Banking," *Zeitschrift für Unternehmensgeschichte/Journal of Business History* 60 (2015): 29–51, citation on 34. See also Carlo Edoardo Altamura, "The Paradox of the 1970s: The Renaissance of International Banking and the Rise of Public Debt," *Journal of Modern History* 15, no. 4 (2017): 529–553; also Carlo Edoardo Altamura, *European Banks and the Rise of International Finance: The Post–Bretton Woods Era* (London: Routledge, 2017). Jeffrey Frieden, *Banking on the World: The Politics of American International Finance*

(New York: HarperCollins, 1987) emphasizes the freedom of offshore dollars from national controls.

11. For volume of loans, see Bank of International Settlements annual report 1982–1983, cited in Drach, "Supervisors against Regulation?" 215. (To provide some basis for comparison in terms of current levels, the US GDP in 1976 was $1.87 trillion or about 9 percent of 2019's $21.43 trillion. For lending banks' exposure, Drach, "Supervisors against Regulation?" 216–217; also Altamura, *European Banks*, and Harold James, "The Debt Crisis," in *International Monetary Cooperation since Bretton Woods* (Washington, DC: IMF, 1996), 363–408; William C. Cline, *International Debt Reexamined* (Washington, DC: [Peterson] Institute of International Economics, 1995).

12. Robert Solomon, *Money on the Move: The Revolution in International Finance since 1980* (Princeton NJ: Princeton University Press,1999), 7–9.

13. For the narrative on Mexico, I have relied on Solomon, *Money on the Move*, 35–41; George Philip, "Crises and Their Consequences in Latin America: Mexico in 1982 and 1994 and Venezuela in 1994," in *Moments of Truth: The Politics of Financial Crises in Comparative Perspective*, ed. Francisco Panizza and George Philip (New York: Routledge, 2014), 11–26; and James, *International Monetary Cooperation*, chap. 12.

14. Thomas Fleischman, *Communist Pigs: An Animal History of East Germany's Rise and Fall* (Seattle: University of Washington Press, 2020), esp. chap. 7, "The Iron Law of Exports," 162–185. The Warsaw government remembered the clashes of 1970, when the Gomułka government gave way before massive demonstrations over price increases.

15. Jeffrey Frankel and Andrew K. Rose, "Currency Crashes in Emerging Markets: An Empirical Treatment," *Journal of International Economics* 41 (1996): 351–366. See also Carmen M. Reinhart and Kenneth S. Rogoff, "Financial and Sovereign Debt Crises: Some Lessons Learned and Those Forgotten," *IMF Working Paper*, WF/13/266, December 2013.

16. Solomon, *Money on the Move*, 43, but cf. Cline, *International Debt Reexamined*.

17. Jerome Roos, *Why Not Default? The Political Economy of Sovereign Debt* (Princeton, NJ: Princeton Scholarship Online, 2019), chap. 8.

18. Eichengreen and Portes have suggested that countries in default quickly find new lenders; Cline argued that such indulgence would have been unlikely in the 1970s and 1980s. Nonetheless, improvident borrowers, from the sixteenth-century onward have usually found new lenders; ultimately, they need each other.

19. Paul Pierson, *Dismantling the Welfare State? Reagan, Thatcher, and the Politics of Retrenchment* (Cambridge: Cambridge University Press, 1994), 53–73.

20. Pierson, *Dismantling the Welfare State?* 78–87.

21. Jacob S. Hacker, "Policy Drift: The Hidden Politics of US Welfare State Retrenchment," in *Beyond Continuity: Institutional Change in Advanced Political*

Economies, ed. Wolfgang Streeck and Kathleen Thelen (New York: Oxford University Press, 2005), 40–82; also Jacob S. Hacker, *The Divided Welfare State: The Battle over Public and Private Social Benefits in the United States* (New York: Cambridge University Press, 2002). On health insurance, see Theodore R. Marmor, *The Politics of Medicare*, 2nd ed. (London: Routledge & Kegan Paul, 2000).

22. Pierson, *Dismantling the Welfare State?* 105–115; Tony Atkinson and John Micklewright, "Turning the Screw: Benefits for the Unemployed, 1979–1988," in *The Economics of Social Security*, ed. Andrew Dilnot and Alan Walker (Oxford: Oxford University Press,1989).

23. Pierson, *Dismantling the Welfare State?* 115–127, citation on 127.

24. Milan Kundera, *The Unbearable Lightness of Being*, Michael Henry Heim, trans. (New York: Harper & Row, 1984), 257. For Hobsbawm, see Matthew Myers' discussion on the controversy he generated in his "The Forward March of Labour Halted?" DPhil diss., Oxford University, 2020, chap. 3, citing the text published in *Marxism Today* (September 1978): 279–286. I am greatly indebted to the Myers dissertation. Debates on Hobsbawm's address were collected in a volume of the same name published by Verso.

25. Giorgio Ghezzi, *Processo al sindacato: Una svolta nelle relazioni industriali. I 61 licenziamenti FIAT* (Bari: De Donato, 1981); Nicola Tranfaglia and B. Mantelli, "Apogeo e collasso della 'città-fabbrica': Torino dall'autunno caldo alla sconfitta operaia del 1980," in *Storia di Torino*, vol. IX *Gli anni della repubblica*, ed. N. Tranfaglia (Turin: Giulio Einaudi Editore, 1999), 827–859.

26. André Gorz, *Farewell to the Working Class: An Essay on Post-Industrial Socialism*, trans. Michael Sonenscher (Boston: South End Press, 1982); originally *Adieux au prolétariat. Au délà du socialisme* (Paris: Galilée, 1980), 38–39, 44. See the often moving intellectual biography by Willy Gianinazzi, *André Gorz, une vie* (Paris: La Découverte, 2019), esp. 251–276.

27. Aris Accornero, *Era il secolo di lavoro* (Bologna: Il Mulino, 1997), 13, 15. See also Aris Accornero, *La parabola del sindacato: Ascesa e declino di una cultura* (Bologna: Il Mulino Publisher, 1992), cited in chap. 5.

28. See Theo Pirker's bitter denunciation in the foreword to the 1979 reissue of his study *Die blinde Macht: die Gewerkschaftsbewegung in Westdeutschland* (Berlin: Verlag Olle & Wolter, 1979).

29. M. Tracol, "Le gouvernement Mauroy face à la désindustrialisation: De la crise économique à la crise sociale et politique," *20 & 21. Revue d'histoire* 144 (2019): 65–79; A. Daley, ed., *The Mitterrand Era: Policy Alternatives and Political Mobilization in France* (Basingstoke, UK: Macmillan, 1996). On "Fordism," see Stefan Link, *Forging Global Fordism: Nazi Germany, Soviet Russia, and the Contest over the Industrial Order* (Princeton, NJ: Princeton University Press, 2020).

30. S. Musso, *Tra fabbrica e società: Mondi operai nell'Italia del novecento* (Milan: Feltrinelli, 1999); Giuseppe Berta, *Conflitto industriale e struttura d'impresa alla FIAT 1919–1979* (Bologna: Il Mulino, 1998); N. Pizzolato, *Challenging Global Capitalism: Labor Migration, Radical Struggle, and Urban Change in Detroit and Turin* (New York: Palgrave Macmillan, 2013).

31. Myers, "The Forward March of Labour Halted?" chap. 4.

32. Marc Lazar, "La gauche et le défi des changements des années 70–80. Les cas français et italien," *Journal of Modern History* 9, no. 2 (2011): 241–262, 243; F. Descamps and L. Quennouëlle-Corre, "Le tournant de mars 1983 a-t-il été libéral?" *Vingtième siècle. Revue d'histoire* 138, no. 2 (2018): 5–15; Hélène Hatzfeld, "Une révolution culturelle du parti socialiste dans les années 1970?" *Vingtième siècle. Revue d'histoire* 96, no. 4 (2017): 77–90. For a classic account, see P. Favier and M. Martin-Roland, *Le décennie Mitterrand*, 2 vols. (Paris: Seuil, 1990–1991). For further on Italy's 1970s in international and global perspective, see L. Baldissara, ed., *Le radici della crisi. L'Italia tra gli anni sessanta e settanta* (Rome: Carocci, 2001).

33. Cited by Myers, "Forward March of Labour Interrupted." Also among other sources, Ivor Crewe, "The Labour Party and the Electorate," in *The Politics of the Labour Party*, ed. D. Kavanaugh (London: G. Allen & Unwin, 1981); party activists argued that they must win new middle-class voters. Cf. Philip Gould, *The Unfinished Revolution: How the Moderates Saved the Labour Party* (London: Little Brown, 1980).

34. Giorgio Amendola, "Interrogativi sul caso Fiat," *Rinascita* 43 (November 9, 1979), cited by Myers, "Forward March of Labour Interrupted."

35. The conclusion documented by Thomas Piketty, *Capital in the Twenty-First Century*, trans. Arthur Goldhammer (Cambridge, MA: Harvard University Press, 2014), at least for recent decades, if not as a timeless trend.

36. The political philosophers Jean Cohen and Andrew Arato applied the term *civil society*, with its Hegelian and Lockean antecedents, to describe the Eastern European movements, and it was adopted by their own theorists. See Jean Cohen and Andrew Arato, *Civil Society and Political Theory* (Cambridge, MA: MIT Press, 1992); Grzegorz Ekiert, *The State against Society: Political Crises and Their Aftermath in East Central Europe* (Princeton, NJ: Princeton University Press, 1995) for application of the concept.

37. Wilfried Loth, *Building Europe: A History of European Unification* (Berlin: de Gruyter, 2015), 262–265.

38. Andrew Moravcsik, "Negotiating the Single European Act: National Interests and Conventional Statecraft in the European Community," *International Organization* 45 (1991): 19–56—a robust assertion of the role of state diplomacy rather than commission initiatives or interest group pressures in strengthening

the EU. There is a massive literature on the progress of the EC/EU. See also Paul Taylor, "The New Dynamics of EC Integration in the 1980s," in *The European Community and the Challenge of the Future*, ed. Juliet Lodge (London: Pinter, 1999).

39. Kenneth Dyson and Kevin Featherstone, *The Road to Maastricht. Negotiating Economic and Monetary Union* (Oxford: Oxford University Press, 1999), 147. What follows is based on this major study, which focuses on key political leaders, and Harold James, *Making the Monetary Union* (Cambridge, MA: Harvard University Press, 2012), commissioned by the European Central Bank and the Bank of International Settlements and based on the records of the Committee of Governors of the central banks of the member states of the EEC, which met at the Bank of International Settlements in Basel and was later to be succeeded by the EMI in Frankfurt. See also Horst Ungerer, *A Concise History of European Monetary Integration: From EPU to EMU* (Westport, CT: Quorum Books, 1997).

40. Loth, *Building Europe*, 264.

41. Andrew Moravscik, "Negotiating the Single European Act: National Interests and Conventional Statecraft in the European Community," *International Organization* 45 (1991): 19–56; Loth, *Building Europe*, 265–284.

42. Eric Bussiere, "Jacques Delors et l'Europe: Vers la politisation des enjeux économiques (1985–1995)," in *Studi Storici.* 2021,1: 159–187; Helen Drake, *Jacques Delors: Perspectives on a European Leader* (London: Routledge, 2000), 78–112.

43. I owe the point to Matthew Sohm's unpublished analysis of EEC modernization.

44. Loth, *Building Europe*, 297–300: Marie-Thérèse Bitsch, *Le couple franco-allemand et les institutions européennes: une postérité pour le Plan Schuman?* (Brussels: Emile Bruylant, 2001), 487–516; James, *Making the Monetary Union*.

45. On the "economic" versus the "monetarist" approaches, see Dyson and Featherstone, *Road to Maastricht*, 29–30, and on Mitterrand's option to work with Germany, 62–88, 97–98, and esp. 142–151.

46. Loth, *Building Europe*, 289–295; Genscher, *Erinnerungen*, 387.

47. For this appreciation and a careful narrative of the process that led to the euro, see James, *Making the European Monetary Union*, 210–264. On Delors's talents, 212–213; also Alessandra Bitumi, "'An Uplifting Tale of Europe': Jacques Delors and the Extraordinary Quest for a European Social Model in the Age of Reagan," *Journal of Transatlantic Studies* 16, no. 3 (2018): 203–221.

48. Loth, *Building Europe*, 306.

49. Wilfried Loth, *Overcoming the Cold War: A History of Détente,1950–1991* (New York: Palgrave, 2002) 188–204.

50. James, *Making the Monetary Union*, 226–226, Baker citation on 220; C. Randall Henning, *Currencies and Politics in the United States, Germany and Japan* (Washington, DC: Institute for International Economics, 1994), 208.

51. James, *Making the Monetary Union*, 228–236. Among the bank heads besides Pöhl was Jacques de Larosière from France, Wim Duisenberg from the Netherlands, Alexandre Lamfalussy, the manager of the Bank of International Settlements, and Tommaso Padoa Schioppa, as a personal adviser to Delors.

52. James, *Making the Monetary Union*, 259; see his summary of the discussions, 236–264.

53. Defending the correlation, Alberto Alesina and Lawrence Summers, "Central Bank Independence and Macroeconomic Performance," *Quarterly Journal of Economics* 100, no. 4 (1985): 1169–1189; contesting the correlation, Adam Posen, "Why Central Bank Independence Does Not Cause Low Inflation: There Is No Institutional Fix for Politics," in *Finance and the International Economy 7*, ed. Richard O'Brien (Oxford: Oxford University Press, 1993), 40–65, earlier questioning of the robustness of the correlation in John T. Woolley, "Central Banks and Inflation," in *The Politics of Inflation and Economic Stagnation*, ed. Leon Lindberg and Charles S. Maier (Washington: Brookings Institution, 1985), 318–348. For how to determine the correlation, Marco Arnone, Bernard Laurens, and Jean-François Segalotto, *The Measurement of Central Bank Autonomy*, IMF Working Paper no. 06/227 (Washington, DC: IMF, 2006), 8–20. For discussion in the EU, James, *Making the Monetary Union*, 265–273.

54. James, *Making the Italian Monetary Union*, 274–289. On the Italian "divorce," G. A. Epstein and Judith B. Schor, "The Divorce of the Banca d'Italia and the Italian Treasury: A Case Study of Central Bank Independence," in *State, Market and Social Regulation: New Perspectives on Italy*, ed. Peter Lange and Marino Regini (Cambridge: Cambridge University Press, 1989).

55. Tietmeyer cited in James, *Making the European Monetary Union*, 280; Pöhl cited on 286. Pöhl resigned suddenly in early 1989 when Kohl implicitly contradicted his denial that the deutsche mark would be extended to East Germany in the near future.

56. Tommaso Padoa-Schioppa, *The Road to Monetary Union in Europe: The Emperor, the Kings, and the Genies* (Oxford: Oxford University Press, 2000), 186, cited in James, *Making the European Monetary Union*, 322.

57. Dyson and Featherstone, *The Road to Maastricht*, 243–252, citation on 252; also James, *Making the European Monetary Union*, 310–323.

58. James, *Making the Monetary Union*, 324–381.

59. Kenneth Rogoff, *Globalization and Global Disinflation* (Washington, DC: IMF, 2003).

60. Stephen M. Walt, "Keeping the World 'Off-Balance': Self-Restraint and U.S. Foreign Policy," in *America Unrivaled: The Future of the Balance of Power*, ed. G. John

Ikenberry (Ithaca, NY: Cornell University Press, 2002), 121. To be fair, Walt was cautioning against an arrogant policy. For confidence in the military balance, see Barry Posen, "Command of the Commons: The Military Foundation of U.S. Hegemony," *International Security* 28, no. 1 (2003): 5–46.

9. Convergences and Catastrophe

1. See Mary Sarotte, *Not One Inch: America, Russia, and the Making of Post–Cold War Stalemate* (New Haven, CT: Yale University Press, 2021).

2. Susan Strange, *Casino Capitalism* (Oxford: Blackwell, 1986); Olivier Blanchard and John Simon, "The Long and Large Decline in Output Volatility," *Brookings Papers on Economic Activity* 1 (2001): 135–164; see also Ben S. Bernanke, "Remarks by Governor Ben S. Bernanke at the Meetings of the Eastern Economic Association," Washington, DC, February 20, 2004. Blanchard did reconsider his position after the 2008 crisis. See Olivier J. Blanchard, Giovanni Dell'Ariccia, and Paolo Mauro, "Rethinking Macroeconomic Policy," *IMF Staff Position Notes* 2010/003 (Washington, DC: International Monetary Fund, 2010).

3. For valuable defenses of a robust civil society, see among others, László Bruszt, Nauro F. Campos, Jan Fidrmuc, and Gérard Roland, "Civil Society, Institutional Change, and the Politics of Reform: The Great Transition," in *Economies in Transition: The Long-Run View*, ed. Gérard Roland (Houndmills, UK: Palgrave Macmillan and UN University–World Institute for Development Economics Research, 2012), 194–221; Juan Linz and Alfred Stepan, *Problems of Democratic Transition and Consolidation: Southern Europe, South America, and Post-Communist Europe* (Baltimore: Johns Hopkins University Press, 1996); also Guillermo O'Donnell and Philippe Schmitter, *Transitions from Authoritarian Rule; Tentative Conclusions about Uncertain Democracies*, vol. 4 (Baltimore: Johns Hopkins University Press, 1986). To be precise in my critique, it is not the importance of civil society for the transition that I question but its staying power for guiding long-term democratic development.

4. Commission on Preventing Deadly Conflict, *Report on Preventing Deadly Conflict (1997)*, David A. Hamburg and Cyrus R. Vance, co-chairs (New York: Carnegie Corporation of New York), xii.

5. See Misha Glenny, *The Fall of Yugoslavia: The Third Balkan War*, rev. ed. (New York: Penguin, 1994), sharply critical of German and Western policy; Tim Judah, *Kosovo: War and Revenge* (New Haven, CT: Yale University Press, 1995); Noel Malcolm, *Kosovo: A Short History* (New York: Harper Collins, 1999); and Noel Malcolm, *Bosnia: A Short History* (New York: New York University Press, 1998) for long-term histories.

6. Gérard Prunier, *The Rwanda Crisis: History of a Genocide* (New York: Columbia University Press, 1995); Gérard Prunier, *Africa's World War: Congo,*

The Rwandan Genocide, and the Making of a Continental Catastrophe (New York: Oxford University Press, 2009); Georges Nzongola-Ntalaja, *The Congo from Leopold to Kabila: A People's History* (London: Zed, 2002). On intervention, Stanley Hoffmann and Mario Bettati, *Le droit d'ingérence: Mutations de l'ordre international* (Paris: Odile Jacob, 1996).

7. Contrast Samuel P. Huntington, *The Third Wave: Democratization in the Late Twentieth Century* (Norman: University of Oklahoma Press, 1991)—celebratory but with ample caution about the future—with Samuel P. Huntington, *The Clash of Civilizations* (New York: Simon & Schuster, 1996). Francis Fukuyama's "The End of History" appeared as an article in *The National Interest*, no. 16 (1989): 3–18, then in book form as *The End of History and the Last Man* (New York: Free Press, 1992).

8. Commission on Preventing Deadly Conflict, "On Preventing Deadly Violence," xvii.

9. Charles S. Maier, "Territorialisten und Globalisten: Die beiden neuen 'Parteien' in den heutigen Demokratien" (Territorialists and globalists: The two new parties in contemporary democracies), *Transit* 14 (Winter 1997): 5–14 (abridgement in *Frankfurter Rundschau*, February 5, 1998).

10. See Margaret E. Keck and Kathryn Sikkink, eds., *Activists beyond Borders: Advocacy Networks in International Politics* (Ithaca, NY: Cornell University Press, 2018) for a schematic survey; Bernard Kouchner, *Le malheur des autres* (Paris: Odile Jacob, 1991); Samantha Power, *"A Problem from Hell": America and the Age of Genocide* (New York: Perseus–Basic Books, 2002); on restorative justice, Robert I. Rotberg and Dennis Thompson, eds., *Truth v. Justice: The Morality of Truth Commissions* (Princeton, NJ: Princeton University Press, 2000), including my essay, "Doing History, Doing Justice: The Narrative of the Historian and of the Truth Commission," 261–278; Martha Minow, *Between Vengeance and Forgiveness: Facing History after Genocide and Mass Violence* (Boston: Beacon, 1998).

11. Commission on Preventing Deadly Conflict, "On Preventing Deadly Conflict," xiii. I closely paraphrase when not directly quoting.

12. Commission on Preventing Deadly Conflict, "On Preventing Deadly Conflict," xviii.

13. Commission on Preventing Deadly Conflict, "On Preventing Deadly Conflict." But admittedly, donor countries were cutting back on funding through the bank. Increasingly, the bank had to take account of the private sector as a source of funds and of preferences. Private foreign direct investment had climbed from $44 billion in 1990 to $175 billion in 1995 and $230 billion in 1996, whereas World Bank commitments in 1995–1996 were limited to $21.5 billion and overall public lending was by another measure 40 percent of the twenty-four wealthiest OECD nations' investments.

14. John Stremlau and Francisco Sagasti, "Preventing Deadly Conflict: Does the World Bank Have a Role?" See also the *World Development Report 1997: The State in*

a Changing World. Sagasti had headed the bank's strategic planning division created in the mid-1980s. For policies from 1945 to 1952, see Michele Alacevich, *The Political Economy of the World Bank: The Early Years* (Stanford, CA: Stanford University Press and the World Bank, 2009).

15. "A Framework for World Bank Involvement in Post-Conflict Reconstruction" (April 1997)—a report that called for "engagement with civil society, incorporating an approach to development which values . . . the concept of social capital, that is the vision that social organizations matter. . . . Increased focus on governance, . . . accountability, . . . and transparency, . . . a frank exploration of the costs of both random and organized violence in undermining the routine functions of socioeconomic activity."

16. Stremlau and Sagasti, "Does the World Bank Have a Role?"

17. For a vast survey of theories, practices, and societal results from a critical perspective, see Simon Springer, Kean Birch, and Julie MacLeavy, eds., *The Handbook of Neoliberalism* (London: Routledge, 2016). For its fruitful application by a geographer, see David Harvey's work including *A Brief History of Neoliberalism* (New York: Oxford University Press, 2005) and *The Enigma of Capital: And the Crises of Capitalism* (London: Profile, 2010).

18. See Manuel Castells, *The Rise of the Network Society*, rev. ed. (Oxford: Blackwell, 2009). For applications to France, see R. Castel, "De l'indigence à l'exclusion: la désaffiliation," in Jacques Donzelot, *Face à l'exclusion: Le modèle français* (Paris: Le Seuil-Esprit, 1991); Luc Boltanski and Ève Chiapello, *Le nouvel esprit du capitalisme* (Paris: Gallimard, 1999), 376–401, 425–450.

19. Henry Farrell, "Privatization as State Transformation," in *Privatization: NOMOS LX*, ed. Jack Knight and Melissa Schwartzberg (New York: New York University Press, 2018), 171–199. "As privatization has advanced toward the core competences of the state, rather than creating free markets, it makes and reproduces patterns of diffused and complex chains of authority and semi-invisible forms of interchange and mutual advantage between economic and political elites" (175). Farrell cites the now-voluminous literature. See also Colin Crouch, *Post-Democracy* (Cambridge: Polity Press, 2004); Colin Crouch, *The Strange Non-death of Neo-liberalism* (Cambridge: Polity Press, 2011); and for the early theoretical expectations, George J. Stigler, "The Theory of Economic Regulation," *Bell Journal of Economics and Management Science* 2, no. 1 (1971): 3–21, included too in Ram Mudambi, ed., *Privatization and Globalization: The Changing Role of the State in Business* (Cheltenham, UK: Edward Elgar, 2003), a collection of pro-neoliberal arguments.

20. Stephen Driver and Luke Martell, *Blair's Britain* (Cambridge: Polity Press, 2002), 21. For a general account, see Monica Prasad, *The Politics of Free Markets and the Rise of Neoliberalism: Economic Policies in Britain, France, Germany, and the United States* (Chicago: University of Chicago Press, 2006). For a Marxist take, see Leo Panitch and Colin Leys, *The End of Parliamentary Socialism* (London: Verso, 2001).

21. Stephanie Lee Mudge, *Leftism Reinvented: Western Parties from Socialism to Neoliberalism* (Cambridge, MA: Harvard University Press, 2018), 32. Also "What's Left of Leftism? Neoliberal Politics in Western Party Systems, 1945–2004," *Social Science History* 35, no. 3 (Fall 2011): 337–380; and a genealogy of the term and its epistemological conquests in "Neoliberalism, Accomplished and Ongoing," in *The Handbook of Neoliberalism*, ed. Springer et al., 93–104.

22. Peter Hall looks more broadly at the evolving interaction between what he terms "growth regimes" or the goals set by firms for their economic activity as they interact with the regulatory environment set by government and "representation regimes" or the shifting priorities proposed by political leaders as they respond to the electorate's concerns. A growing concern for short-term financial measures of success interacting with a declining emphasis on blue-collar–white-collar class confrontation marked the neoliberal decades, at least until recently. Peter A. Hall, "Growth Regimes," *Business History Review* (2022): 1–25; and Peter Hall, "The Shifting Relationship between Post-war Capitalism and Democracy," *Government & Opposition* 57 (2022): 1–30 (The Leonard Schapiro Lecture, 2021). On the growing role of finance in Western economies, see Greta Krippner, *Capitalizing on Crisis: The Political Origins of the Rise of Finance* (Cambridge, MA: Harvard University Press, 2011), and Thomas J. Palley, *Financialization: The Economics of Finance Capital Domination* (Basingstoke, UK: Palgrave Macmillan, 2013) and the sources in endnote 52.

23. Driver and Martell, *Blair's Britain*, 31.

24. See the special issue of the *Journal of American History* 102, no. 1(June 2015), Kelly Lytle Hernández, Khalil Gibran Muhammad, and Heather Ann Thompson, eds., esp. "Introduction: Constructing the Carceral State," 18–28. Also Elizabeth Hinton, *From the War on Poverty to the War on Crime: The Making of Mass Incarceration in America* (Cambridge, MA: Harvard University Press, 2016).

25. Driver and Martell, *Blair's Britain*, 21, 190–200.

26. See Hinton, *From the War on Poverty to the War on Crime*.

27. Christian Breuer, "Dilemma Hartz IV Geringverdiener entlasten," *Wirtschaftsdienst* 99, no. 2 (2019): 82.

28. "In Merkel's Crisis, Echoes of Weimar," *New York Review Daily: New York Review of Books*, December 4, 2017, http://www.nybooks.com/?post_type=daily&pp=59581&preview=1.

29. Mancur Olson, *The Logic of Collective Action: Public Goods and the Theory of Groups* (Cambridge, MA: Harvard University Press, 1971); see also Mancur Olson, *The Rise and Decline of Nations: Economic Growth, Stagflation, and Social Rigidities* (New Haven, CT: Yale University Press, 1982).

30. On corruption, see Alberto Vannucci, "The Controversial Legacy of 'Mani Pulite': A Critical Analysis of Italian Corruption and Anti-corruption Policies,"

Bulletin of Italian Politics 1, no. 2 (2009): 233–264. For a careful analysis of the electoral strength behind the rise of Berlusconi, see John A. Agnew and Michel E. Shin, *Berlusconi's Italy* (Philadelphia: Temple University Press, 2008), 65–98.

31. Florence Faucher King and Patrick Le Galès, *The New Labour Experiment: Change and Reform under Blair and Brown*, trans. Gregory Elliott (Stanford, CA: Stanford University Press, 2010), 5–10; translation of *Tony Blair, 1997–2007* (Paris: Presses de la Fondation Nationale des Sciences Politiques, 2007); Crouch, *Post-Democracy*, cited 7–10.

32. Anthony Giddens, *The Third Way: The Renewal of Social Democracy* (Cambridge: Polity Press, 1998), 36. Along the same lines, see Oliver Schmidtke, ed., *The Third Way Transformation of Social Democracy: Normative Claims and Policy Initiative in the 21st Century* (Aldershot, UK: Ashgate, 2002). For an analysis of the national conditions behind the trend, see in the Schmidtke volume Peter A. Hall, "The Comparative Political Economy of the 'Third Way,'" 31–58.

33. Ulrich Beck, "Von der Vergänglichkeit der Indusriegesellschaft," *Politik in der Risikogesellschaft: Essays und Analysen* (Frankfurt: Suhrkamp, 1991), 39. Cf. the earlier *Risikogesellschaft. Auf dem Weg in eine andere Moderne* (Frankfurt: Suhrkamp, 1986). The titles had a great resonance; the risks seem to have been the overwhelming of political and social management by technology. Chernobyl provided a metaphor.

34. Anthony Giddens, *Beyond Left and Right: The Future of Radical Politics* (Cambridge: Polity Press, 1994), 193–194.

35. Mark Bevir, *New Labour: A Critique* (London: Routledge, 2005), 121, 102.

36. I visited Prague in the early summer of 1990—the elections had been held. Havel was set to assume the presidency. The woman who rented me a room was a state employee whose job—in these months of expiring state socialism and rising inflation—was to affix new prices for hundreds of common items in stores according to the massive sheaf of lists published by the competent ministry.

37. Philipp Ther, *Europe since 1989* (Princeton NJ: Princeton University Press, 2016), 81.

38. Cited by Barbara Curli, "The 'Vincolo Europeo,' Italian Privatization and the European Commission," *Journal of European Integration History* 22 (2012): 285–302; quote on 295. Giuliano Garavini is working on privatizations, and I have relied on his preliminary paper, "Global ENI: Privatizations and the Birth of the Italian 'Investor State' (1992–1995)." For a general survey, see Stuart Holland, *The State as Entrepreneur: New Dimensions for Public Enterprise. The IRI State* (London: Weidenfeld & Nicolson, 1972).

39. Curli, "Vincolo Europeo," 300. On the complexities of separating public and private, see Sabino Cassese, "Stato e mercato dopo privatizzazione e 'deregulazione,'" *Rivista trimestrale di diritto pubblico* 2 (1991): 378–387. For a critique of the results, see Carlo Brambilla and Fabio Lavista, "Privatizations and Efficiency: Evidences [sic] from the Italian Iron and Steel Industry, 1978–2016," *Industrial and Corporate Change*

29, no. 3 (2020): 757–778, which finds financial gains for the state but no marked production benefits.

40. See R. Gualtieri, "L'Europa come vincolo esterno," in *L'Italia nella costruzione europea. Un bilancio storico (1957–2007)*, ed. P. Craveri and A. Varsori (Milan: Franco Angeli, 2009). The term "external constraint or bond" was coined by Guido Carli, governor of the Bank of Italy and Minister of the Treasury. See also A. Goldstein, *Privatizations in Italy, 1993–2002: Goals, Institutions, Outcomes and Outstanding Issues*, CESifo Working Paper no. 912 (Munich: CESifo, April 2003).

41. See Gur Offer's devastating analysis in "Twenty Years Later and the Socialist Heritage Is Still Kicking," in *Economies in Transition*, ed. Roland, 222–253. For other statistics as of 2008, see Vladimir Popov, "The Long Road to Normality: Where Russia Now Stands," in *Economies in Transition*, ed. Roland, 317–343; and for a more favorable view, Andre Schleifer and Daniel Treisman, "A Normal Country: Russia after Communism," *Journal of Economic Perspectives* 19, no. 1 (2005): 151–174, cf. 253.

42. Wolfram Fischer and Harm Schröter, "Die Entstehung der Treuhandanstalt," in *Treuhandanstalt. Das Unmögliche Wagen*, ed. Wolfram Fischer, Herbert Hax, and Hans Karl Schneider (Berlin: Akademie Verlag, 1993); Peter Christ and Karl Neubauer, *Kolonie im eigenen Land: Die Treuhand, Bonn und die Wirschaftskatastrophe der fünf neuen Länder* (Berlin: Rohwolt, 1991); also the articles in "Transforming the Economies of East Central Europe," a special issue of *East European Politics and Society* 6, no. 1 (Winter 1992); and the discussion at the Harvard Center for European Studies, Program for the Study of Germany and Europe, "Treuhandanstalt: A One-Day Workshop: Rapporteur's Report," Cambridge, Massachusetts, November 16, 1991. For East German efforts at restructuring industry (and not just selling it off), see Harald Barthelt, "Re-bundling and the Development of Hollow Clusters in the East German Chemical Industry," *European Urban and Regional Studies* 16, no. 4 (2009): 363–381; also Charles S. Maier, *Dissolution: The Crisis of Communism and the End of East Germany* (Princeton, NJ: Princeton University Press, 1997), 290–300, and notation, 409–410. For assessments of East European progress twenty years later, see Roland, *Economies in Transition*.

43. Isabella M. Weber, *How China Escaped Shock Therapy: The Market Reform Debate* (London: Routledge, 2021). Cf. Julian Gewirtz, *Unlikely Partners: Chinese Reformers, Western Economists, and the Making of Global China* (Cambridge, MA: Harvard University Press, 2017).

44. Quinn Slobodian, *Globalists, The End of Empire and the Birth of Neoliberalism* (Cambridge, MA: Harvard University Press, 2018), 1.

45. Daniel Immerwahr, *How to Hide an Empire: A History of the Greater United States* (New York: Farrar, Straus and Giroux, 2019).

46. Excellent on Vietnam, Rrederik Logevall, *Embers of War: The Fall of an Empire and the Making of America's Vietnam* (New York: Random House, 2012); on

Africa, Prunier, *Africa's World War*; Nzongola-Ntalaja, *The Congo from Leopold to Kabila*. For an extensive and detailed discussion of Lumumba's career and death with sources see the Wikipedia entry "Patrice Lumumba" (edit of September 20, 2022).

47. Greg Grandin, *Empire's Workshop: Latin America, the United States, and the Making of an Imperial Republic*, rev. ed. (New York: Picador, 2021).

48. For the argument that even as of 1940 the aim of the American foreign-policy elite has become in fact global hegemony, see Stephen Wertheim, *Tomorrow the World* (Cambridge, MA: Harvard University Press, 2020).

49. Among other sources, Daniel Yergin, *Shattered Peace: The Origins of the Cold War and the National Security State* (Boston: Houghton-Mifflin, 1977); Melvyn Leffler, *The Specter of Communism: The United States and the Origins of the Cold War, 1917–1953* (New York: Hill & Wang, 1994).

50. Niall Ferguson and Moritz Scularick, " 'Chimerica' and the Global Asset Market Boom," in *International Finance* 10, no. 3 (2007): 215–239.

51. See Charles S. Maier, *Among Empires: American Ascendancy and Its Predecessors* (Cambridge, MA: Harvard University Press, 2005) for the American transition from an empire of production to an empire of consumption.

52. See Palley, *Financialization*, for an introduction to the problem with extensive economic modeling. Current estimates of the size of the FIRE (finance, insurance, real estate) sector as 10 percent in 1947, 20 percent in 2016, 22.5 percent in 2021 from Christopher Witko, "The Politics of Financialization in the United States 1949–2005," *British Journal of Political Science* 46 (2014): 349–370, fig. 1 on 351, summarized in *Washington Post*, March 20, 2016; and Sean Ross, "Financial Services: Sizing the Sector in the Global Economy," *Investopedia* (accessed September 30, 2021), which cites estimates for financial services at 20–25 percent of the world economy of which insurance premiums amounted to about 6.8 percent. Niall Ferguson spotlighted these trends in *The Ascent of Money: A Financial History of the World* (New York: Penguin, 2008).

53. See Jonathan Haskel and Stian Westlake, *Capitalism without Capital: The Rise of the Intangible Economy* (Princeton, NJ: Princeton University Press, 2018), esp. chaps. 5–8.

54. This theme will return in Chapter 10. For documentation, see the report by the McKinsey Global Institute, *The Rise and Rise of the Global Balance Sheet* (December 2021), www.mckinsey.cim/mgi. Discussed further in Chapter 10.

55. Cf. Palley, *Financialization*, 60: Financialization "should be viewed as the financial arm of the neoliberal policy paradigm that was put in place in the 1980s to counter the challenges faced by capital in the late 1960s and 1970s." Financialization helped fill the hole in demand created by the redistribution (from wages to profits and wage income away from workers to managers/capitalists).

56. Palley, *Financialization*, 28–29, table 2.11.

57. On Minsky, see Palley, *Financialization*, 129–142; also Hyman Minsky, *The Financial Instability Hypothesis*, Working Paper 74, Jerome Levy Economics Institute, Bard College; published in P. Arestis and M. Sawyer, eds., *Handbook of Radical Political Economy* (Aldershot, UK: Edward Elgar, 1993).

58. Palley, *Financialization*, 22, table 2.3.

59. Palley, *Financialization*, 24, tables 2.5, and 2.6. Publicly held federal debt in 2007 was $5,035 of about $53 billion of the US debt outstanding. Since the financial crisis American student debt has become the second largest source of debt, amounting nation-wide to 18 percent of home mortgage debt in 2021, and growing twice as fast as average income. What share of it is equivalent to a productive investment is hard to calculate. The highest real debt-to-income ratio for students was in 2012. See Stacker, "How Student Loan Debt Has Increased over Time," in What's Up News, August 26, 2022; and Melanie Hansen, "Average Student Loan Debt by Year," EducationData.org, January 22, 2022, https://educationdata.org/average-student-loan-debt-by-year.

60. Adan Tooze, *Crashed: How a Decade of Financial Crises Changed the World* (New York: Viking, 2018), 73–74 for debt shares, 206–219 for credits to the Europeans. Beyond specific page references, I am indebted to Tooze's account of the crisis.

61. Palley, *Financialization*, 25, table 2.6, mortgage and household debt; 33, fig. 2.5, equity versus borrowing. Cf. Charles S. Maier, "A History of Profligate Lending," in *Aftershocks: Economic Crisis and Institutional Choice*, ed. Anton Hemerijck, Ben Knapen, and Ellen van Doorne (Amsterdam: Amsterdam University Press, 2009), 67–73.

62. Tooze, *Crashed*, 172; W. Scott Frame, Andreas Fuster, Joseph Tracy, and James Vickery, "The Rescue of Fannie Mae and Freddie Mac," *Journal of Economic Perspectives* 29, no. 2 (Spring 2015): 25–52; originally *Federal Reserve Bank of New York, Staff Reports* 719 (March 2015).

63. Tooze, *Crashed*, 55.

64. For a clear exposition, see Adam Hayes, "Credit Default Swap (CDS)," *Investopedia*.

65. Tooze, *Crashed*, 88.

66. For a definition, Nathan Reiff, "Repurchase Agreement (Repo)," *Investopedia*, updated March 18, 2020. For the mechanisms, G. Gorton and A. Metrick, "Securitized Banking and the Run on Repo," *Journal of Financial Economics* 104, no. 3 (2012): 425–451. On the comparative size of repo contraction versus asset-backed commercial paper, see Arvind Krishnamurthy, Stefan Nagel, and Dmitry Orlov, "Sizing Up Repo," *Journal of Finance* 69, no. 6 (December 2014): 2381–2415. See also "Shadow Banking System," *Investopedia*, July 25, 2020. See Tooze, *Crashed*, 69, 85, and passim for expositions.

67. Was letting Lehman collapse a mistake? Bernanke, Paulson, and Geithner defended the decision saying there was no collateral for lending; Tooze, *Crashed*, 176–177, dissents and claims that the Fed even pushed the firm toward insolvency. Also

critical, Laurence M. Bail, *The Fed and Lehman Brothers: Setting the Record Straight on a Financial Disaster* (New York: Cambridge University Press, 2018), the Introduction and Summary in NBER Working Paper 22410 (2016); also Ben S. Bernanke, Timothy F. Geithner, and Henry M. Paulson Jr., *Firefighting: The Financial Crisis and Its Lessons* (New York: Penguin, 2019).

68. Cited Tooze, *Crashed*, 163; Ben S. Bernanke, *The Courage to Act: A Memoir of a Crisis and its Aftermath* (New York: W. W. Norton, 2015), 386.

69. Cited Palley, *Financialization*, 112.

70. Tooze, *Crashed*, 180–197. Ultimately, share prices recovered sufficiently so that the public made a profit on TARP. This was not the case in Britain where the Royal Bank of Scotland shares had incurred a loss of £27 billion as of 2018. See Federico Mor, *Bank Rescues of 2007–09: Outcomes and Costs*, House of Commons Briefing Paper 5748, October 8, 2018. British and German recapitalizations were more intrusive in bank management than the US Treasury's.

71. Viral V. Acharya and Philipp Schnabl, "Do Global Banks Spread Global Imbalances? Asset-Backed Commercial Paper during the Financial Crisis of 2007–09," *IMF Economic Review* 58, no. 1 (2010): 37–73; estimates of assets in the sector, 42. See also Adrian Tobias, "The Changing Nature of Financial Intermediation and the Financial Crisis of 2007–2009," *Annual Review of Economics* 2 (2010): 603–618. On shadow banking, see Adrian Tobias et al., *Shadow Banking*, Federal Reserve Bank of New York Working Paper (2010); narrative in Tooze, *Crashed*, 73–75, 184–195.

72. For the mechanism, see William A. Allen and Richhild Moessner, "The International Liquidity Crisis of 2008–2009," *World Economics* 12, no. 2 (April–June 2011): 183–193 (originally Bank of International Settlements Working Paper 310). Allen and Moessner estimates that US swaps provided about $700 million at their peak. Tooze, *Crashed*, 202–219, emphasizes their continuing roll-over as the equivalent of $4.5 trillion.

73. See Richhild Moessner and William A. Allen, "Banking Crises and the International Monetary System in the Great Depression and Now," *Financial History Review* 18, no. 1 (2011): 1–20. Originally Bank of International Settlements Working Paper 333.

74. Tooze, *Crashed*, 480–484.

75. Data from Tooze, *Crashed*, 156–163, with chart from Claudio Borio and Piti Diyatat, "Global Imbalances and the Financial Crisis: Link or No Link?" Bank of International Settlements Working Paper 346 (2011). The authors argue, in line with other accounts, that it was less the size of the imbalances than their volatility that made the crisis so acute.

76. See, for this account, William A. Allen and Richhild Moessner, "The Liquidity Consequences of the Euro Area Sovereign Debt Crisis," *World Economics* 14, no. 1

(January–March 2013): 103–125 (110, table 1), originally Bank of International Settlements Working Paper 190.

77. Martin Sandbu, *Europe's Orphan: The Future of the Euro and the Politics of Debt*, new ed. (Princeton, NJ: Princeton University Press, 2015), 85, and for Ireland, chap. 4. Sandbu develops the comparison further; Iceland nationalized the domestic sector and let the foreign sector go bankrupt. But its banks were hardly too big to fail.

78. Sandbu, *Europe's Orphan*, 104.

79. For the Greek crisis, Sandbu, *Europe's Orphan*, chap. 3.

80. Tooze, *Crashed*, 117.

81. Miranda Xafa, "Life after Debt: The Greek PSI [Private Sector Involvement] and Its Aftermath," *World Economics* 14, no. 1 (January–March 2013): 81–102. See also Tooze's dramatic narrative in *Crashed*, 321–446.

82. Xafa, "Life after Debt," 98.

83. Xafa, "Life after Debt," 100.

84. Sandbu, *Europe's Orphan*, 268.

10. The Populist Assertion and the Return of Authoritarianism

1. Extracted from the "Full Text of Victor Órbán's Speech at [25th Bálványos Free Summer University and Youth Camp] Baile Tusnad (Tusnádfürdö) of 26 July 2014," *The Budapest Beacon* (October 13, 2013–April 13, 2018), published by the Real Reporting Foundation. The concept of nonliberal democracy is a venerable one, implicit in Benjamin Constant's 1819 contrast between ancient and modern liberty, developed by Isaiah Berlin's 1958 Oxford inaugural lecture, "Two Concepts of Liberty" and spotlighted by Fareed Zakaria, *The Future of Freedom: Illiberal Democracy at Home and Abroad* (New York: Norton, 2003). See also András Körösényi, Gábor Illés, and Attila Gyulai, *The Orbán Regime: Plebiscitary Leader Democracy in the Making* (New York: Routledge, 2020).

2. Bálint Magyar, *Post-Communist Mafia State: The Case of Hungary* (Budapest: Central European University Press, 2016); Bálint Magyar, ed., *Stubborn Structures: Conceptualizing Post-communist Regimes* (Budapest: Central European University Press, 2019). For a useful summary, see Iván Szelenyi, "Paternal Domination and the Mafia State under Post-communism," *Theory and Society* 48 (2019): 639–644.

3. On Russian populism, James H. Billington, *Mikhailovsky and Russian Populism* (Oxford: Clarendon, 1958); Franco Venturi, *Roots of Revolution: A History of the Populist and Socialist Movements in Nineteenth-Century Russia* (New York: Knopf, 1960); on the Hessian milieu, Dan S. White, *The Splintered Party: National Liberalism in Hessen and the Reich, 1867–1918* (Cambridge, MA: Harvard University Press, 1976). Populism and anti-Semitism were merged in Otto Böckel's Antisemitische Volkspartei in the early 1890s.

4. Most sympathetic, Laurence Goodwyn, *Democratic Promise: The Populist Movement in America* (New York: Oxford University Press, 1976).

5. Richard Hofstadter, *The Age of Reform from Bryan to FDR* (New York: Knopf, 1955). See also Alan Brinkley, *Voices of Protest: Huey Long, Father Coughlin, and the Great Depression* (New York: Vintage Books, 1982).

6. Ezra Pound, *Jefferson and/or Mussolini. L'Idea Statale. Fascism as I Have Seen It* (London: Stanley Nott, 1935, but written 1933), 125. The American one-party system he referred to comprised the period between Jefferson and Martin van Buren, with hostility to the Hamiltonian banking institutions as its unifying thread.

7. Robert S. Jansen, *Revolutionizing Repertoires: The Rise of Populist Mobilization in Peru* (Chicago: Chicago Scholarship Online, 2018). In a full history of peasant mobilization, Catholic counterrevolutionary guerrilla movements such as marked the Vendée in the French Revolution, the San Fedisti of Naples during its French revolutionary occupation, and the Mexican Cristeros of the late 1920s would also merit inclusion.

8. See Federico Finchelstein, *Fascismo, liturgia e imaginario: El mito del General Uriburu y la Argentina nacionalista* (Buenos Aires: Fondo de cultura económico, 2002) and more generally Federico Finchelstein, *From Fascism to Populism in History* (Oakland: University of California Press, 2017).

9. The Argentine experience under Juan Perón led the sociologist Gino Germani to devote considerable effort to distinguish his regime from fascism. See *Authoritarianism, Fascism, and National Populism* (New Brunswick, NJ: Transaction Books, 1978). More recently, see S. Erdem Aytaç and Ziya Öniş, "Varieties of Populism in a Changing Global Context: The Divergent Paths of Erdoğan and Kirchnerismo," *Comparative Politics* 47, no. 1 (October 2014): 41–59.

10. Bolingbroke's term for Richard's tax collectors in Shakespeare's *Richard II*.

11. Pointed out by Cas Mudde and Cristóbal Rovira Kaltwasser, *Populism: A Very Short Introduction* (New York: Oxford University Press, 2017). Among the many recent books, see Jan-Werner Müller, *What Is Populism?* (Philadelphia: University of Pennsylvania Press, 2016); *The Oxford Handbook of Populism* (Oxford: Oxford University Press, 2017); Michael Burleigh, *Populism: Before and after the Pandemic* (London: Hurst, 2021); Benjamin Moffitt, *Populism* (Cambridge: Polity Press, 2020). The new journal *Populism* 3 (2020) provided a special issue on Eastern Europe. Earlier analyses include Robert R. Barr, "Populists, Outsiders and Anti-establishment Politics," in *Party Politics* 15 (January 2009): 29–48, which stresses the instrumental use of populism by political outsiders; Ivan Krastev, "The Populist Moment," *Eurozine*, September 18, 2007, and Pierre André Taguieff, "Le populisme et la science politique: Du mirage conceptuel aux vrais problems," with a rich bibliography, in *Vingtième siècle: Revue d'histoire* 56 (1997): 4–33. For. A survey of sociological and political science explanations, see Jasper Muis and Tim Immerzeel, "Causes and Consequences

of the Rise of Populist Radical Right Parties and Movements in Europe," *Current Sociology Review* 65, no. 6 (2017): 909–930; Rogers Brubaker, "Between Nationalism and Civilizationalism: The European Populist Moment in Comparative Perspective," *Ethnic & Racial Studies* 40, no. 8 (2017): 1191–1226; Rogers Brubaker, "Populism and Nationalism," *Nations and Nationalism* 26, no. 1 (2020): 44–66.

12. Émile Durkheim, *The Elementary Forms of the Religious Life* (Oxford: Oxford University Press, 2001); Victor Turner, *The Ritual Process: Structure and Antistructure* (Ithaca, NY: Cornell University Press, 1966/1969); Aristide Zolberg, "Moments of Madness," *Politics and Society* 2, no. 3 (1972): 183–207; Sidney Tarrow, "Cycles of Collective Action: Between Moments of Madness and the Repertoire of Contention," *Social Science History* 17, no. 2 (Summer 1993): 281–307.

13. The argument is stressed by Serkan Yolaçan, "Iron Fist or Nimble Fingers? An Anatomy of Erdoğan's Strongman Politics," *History and Anthropology*, published online July 20, 2021, http://doi.org/10.1080/02757206.20211946048. My account below draws primarily from this source.

14. Prashant Jha, *How the BJP Wins: Inside India's Greatest Electoral Machine* (New Delhi: Juggernaut Books, 2017). See also Christophe Jaffrelot, *Modi's India: Hindu Nationalism and the Rise of Ethnic Democracy*, trans. Cynthia Schoch (Princeton, NJ: Princeton University Press, 2021) and note 20 below.

15. Jansen, *Revolutionizing Repertoires*; also Robert S. Jansen, "Situated Political Innovation: Explaining the Historical Emergence of New Modes of Political Practice," *Theory and Society* 45 (2016): 319–360. On political repertoires, see Charles Tilly, *Regimes and Repertoires* (Chicago: University of Chicago Press, 2008); on APRA (Alianza popular revolucionaria americana), see Robert J. Alexander, ed., *Aprismo: The Ideas and Doctrines of Victor Raúl Haya de la Torre* (Kent, OH: Kent State University Press, 1973); Alfred Stepan, *The State and Society: Peru in Comparative Perspective* (Princeton, NJ: Princeton University Press, 1978).

16. Omar Acha, "Latin American Populism: Tentative Reflections for a Global Historiographical Perspective," *Nuevo mundo mundos nuevos*, February 10, 2013, http://journals.openedition.org/nuevomundo/64834.

17. Torcuato di Tella, "Populismo y reforma en América Latina," *Desarrollo económico* 4, no. 18 (1965): 391–425; Michael L. Conniff, *Populism in Latin America*, 2nd ed. (Birmingham: University of Alabama Press, 2012); Michael L. Conniff, *Latin American Populism in Comparative Perspective* (Albuquerque: University of New Mexico Press, 1982); Peter F. Klaren, *Formación de las haciendas azucareras y origines del APRA* (Lima: Instituto de estudios peruanos, 1970); Steve Stein, *Populism in Peru: The Emergence of the Masses and the Politics of Social Control* (Madison: University of Wisconsin Press, 1980); Carlos M. Villas, ed., *La democratización fundamental. El populismo en América Latina* (Mexico City: Consejo nacional para la cultura y las artes, 1994); Kurt Weyland, "Clarifying a Contested Concept: Populism in the

Study of Latin American Politics," *Comparative Politics* 34, no. 1 (October 2001): 1–22; Adriano Duarte, "Neighborhood Associations, Social Movements, and Populism in Brazil, 1945–1953," *Hispanic American Historical Review* 89, no. 1 (2009): 111–139 for a defense of autonomous left-wing organizing; Omar Acha, "Sociedad civil y sociedad politica durante el primer peronismo," *Desarrollo económico* 44, no. 174 (2004): 199–230; Acha, "Latin American Populism." For the 1990s and after, see Julio F. Carrión, "Conclusion: The Rise and Fall of Electoral Authoritarianism in Peru," in *The Fujimori Legacy*, ed. Julio F. Carrión (State College: Pennsylvania State University Press, 2006), 294–319; Nicolás Cachanosky and Alexandre Padilla, "Latin American Populism in the Twenty-First Century," *The Independent Review* 24, no. 2 (Fall 2019): 209–226; Steven Levitsky and J. Loxton, "Populism and Competitive Authoritarianism in the Andes," *Democratization* 20, no. 1 (2013): 107–136; also Steven Levitsky and Lucan Ahmad Way, *Competitive Authoritarianism: Hybrid Regimes after the Cold War* (Cambridge: Cambridge University Press, 2010).

18. Phillip Ther, *Europe since 1989* (Princeton, NJ: Princeton University Press, 2016) provides an excellent comparative history of East European political and economic developments.

19. Körösényi et al., *The Orbán Regime*. Orban and Fidesz have held power for four terms since 2002.

20. Suleyman Ozeren, Suat Cubukcu, and Matthew Bastug, "Where Will Erdoğan's Revolution Stop?" *Current Trends in Islamist Ideology* 25 (February 2020): 5–48, 168. AKP's third term after the 2011 general election gave the party "a stranglehold on state institutions" (9). Nikos Christofis, ed., *Erdoğan's "New" Turkey: Attempted Coup d'État and the Acceleration of Political Crisis* (New York: Routledge, 2020); M. Hakan Yavuz, *Erdoğan: The Making of an Autocrat* (Edinburgh: Edinburgh University Press, 2021); Antonino Castaldo, "Populism and Competitive Authoritarianism in Turkey," *Southeast European and Black Sea Studies* 18, no. 4 (2018): 467–487. Also Gaye Ilhan-Demiryol, "Populism in Power: The Case of Turkey," in *Turkey in Transition: Politics, Society and Foreign Policy*, ed. E. Sokullu (Bern: Peter Lang, 2020); Orçnn Selçuk, "Strong Presidents and Weak Institutions: Populism in Turkey, Venezuela, and Ecuador," *Southeast European and Black Sea Studies* 16, no. 4 (2016): 571–589; B. Yabanci, "Populism as the Problem Child of Democracy: The AKP's Enduring Appeal and the Use of Meso-level Actors," in *Southeast European and Black Sea Studies* 16, no. 4 (2016): 591–617 stresses organization of civil society groups rather than economic ills. See below for the economic alliances behind Erdoğan's domination.

21. Jha, *How the BJP Wins*, 219. Cf. Jaffrelot, *Modi's India*, for a detailed and massively documented account of how Modi has delayed and disempowered institutions first in Gujarat and then at the federal level. Both studies focus on the role of Amit Shah, Modi's electoral manager and chief enforcer. Cf. Paul D. Kenny, who

claims that as subnational autonomy increases, populist campaigners gain at the expense of traditional national patronage or programmatic parties: *Populism and Patronage: Why Populists Win Elections in India, Asia, and Beyond* (New York: Oxford Scholarship Online, 2017), 166, http://doi.org.10.1093/oso/9780198807872.001.0001.

22. Jaffrelot, *Modi's India*, 309.

23. See "The Dangers of Hindu Chauvinism," *The Economist*, January 15, 2022.

24. On Modi, BBC News website, November 19, 2021. "Bolsonaro Embraces 'Old Politics,'" *Financial Times*, December 24, 2021, 15.

25. Hannah Arendt, *The Origins of Totalitarianism* (New York: Harcourt Brace, 1951); Carl J. Friedrich and Zbigniew Brzezinski, *Totalitarian Dictatorship and Autocracy* (New York: Praeger, 1965); for a history of the concept, Abbot Gleason, *Totalitarianism: The Inner History of the Cold War* (New York: Oxford University Press, 1995); Juan J. Linz, *Totalitarian and Authoritarian Regimes* (Boulder, CO: Lynne Rienner, 2000).

26. See Barrington Moore Jr., *Injustice: The Social Bases of Obedience and Revolt* (White Plains, NY: M. E. Sharpe, 1978). Moore wanted to explain revolutionary sentiments; but perceived inequity is also critical for understanding populist motivations—often denigrated by the term *ressentiment*. Commentators on the right have ascribed revolutionary feelings to *ressentiment*; writers on the left use it to explain fascism; in both situations, it attributes the politics that the writer finds distasteful and dangerous to a sort of rancor.

27. Dani Rodrick, *The Globalization Paradox: Democracy and the Future of the World Economy* (New York: Norton, 2011).

28. Kurt Weyland, "Neopopulism and Neoliberalism in Latin America: Unexpected Affinities," *Studies in Comparative International Development* 31, no. 3 (Fall 1996): 3–31; Jolie Demmefs, A. E. Fernández Jilberto, B. Hoogenboom, eds., *Miraculous Metamorphoses: The Neoliberalization of Latin American Populism* (London: Zed Books, 2001).

29. Dorottya Szikra, "Democracy and Welfare in Hard Times: The Social Policy of the Orbán Government in Hungary between 2010 and 2014," *Journal of European Social Policy* 24, no. 5 (2014): 486–500. See also Dorothee Bohle and Bela Greskovits, *Capitalist Diversity on Europe's Periphery* (Ithaca, NY: Cornell University Press, 2012) for the agency retained by diverse states; J. Clasen and D. Clegg, eds., *Regulating the Risk of Unemployment: National Adaptations to Post-industrial Labour Markets in Europe* (Oxford: Oxford University Press, 2011); I. Guardiancich, *Pension Reforms in Central, Eastern and Southeastern Europe: From Post-Socialist Transition to the Global Financial Crisis* (Abingdon, UK: Routledge/European University Institute, 2013).

30. See the Marxist-inflected analysis by Yahya M. Madra and Sedat Yilmax, "Turkey's Decline into (Civil) War Economy: From Neoliberal Populism to Corporate Nationalism," *South Atlantic Quarterly* 118, no. 1 (January 2019): 44–59.

31. Thomas Piketty, *Capital in the Twenty-First Century*, trans. Arthur Goldhammer (Cambridge, MA: Harvard University Press, 2014), esp. 24–27. Piketty claims that this growing inequality indicates a general "law" since the Industrial Revolution broken only during the period of the two world wars whose costs reversed the trend. The long-term inevitability has been the most questioned result of the research. Goldhammer suggests some reasons for the avid reception of the book in his contribution to the volume that discussed the original work: Heather Boushey, J. Bradford DeLong, and Marshall Steinbaum, eds., *After Piketty: The Agenda for Economics and Inequality* (Cambridge, MA: Harvard University Press, 2017). As noted above, inequality between nations decreased even as it increased within individual countries; the rise of East Asian economies was a principal reason, but there was some improvement even for the poorest societies. See Christopher Lakner, "Global Inequality," in *After Piketty*, ed. Boushey et al., 259–279; also Paul Collier, *The Bottom Billion: Why the Poorest Countries Are Failing and What Can Be Done about It* (Oxford: Oxford University Press, 2007).

32. See the collection of critiques, Jean-Philippe Delsol, Nicolas Lecaussin, and Emmanuel Martin, eds., *Anti-Piketty: Capital for the 21st Century* (Washington, DC: Cato Institute, 2017) and originally published in France (Nice: Libréchange, 2015). I am not qualified to resolve the issues but found two of the critiques particularly substantive: Phillip W. Magness and Robert P. Murphy, "Challenging the Empirical Contribution of Thomas Piketty's Capital in the 21st Century," 101–140, and Henri Lepage, "A Controversial Assumption," 219–222. See also Paul Schmelzing, "Essays on Long-Run Real Rate and Safe Asset Trends, 1311–2018," PhD diss., Harvard University, 2019; and Paul Schmelzing, "Eight Centuries of Global Real Rates, R-G, and the 'Suprasecular' Decline, 1311–2018," *Bank of England Staff Working Paper* 845 (January 2020), which find a remarkable stability for *r* over seven centuries.

33. McKinsey Global Institute, *The Rise and Rise of the Global Balance Sheet* (November 2021), www.mckinsey.com/mgi. Ninety-five percent of global net worth they find is ultimately held by households.

34. For those like the author who have to think twice about accounting conventions: A bank lends you a million; the note you sign promising to repay with interest is the bank's asset; the million-dollar account it establishes for you to draw against will be its liability as you write checks. That account is your asset, but the promise to repay is your liability. National regulations or international agreements such as the Basel Conventions require the bank to hold a certain fraction of its liabilities in assets that count as money, including cash, gold, treasury bonds, and high-quality commercial paper.

35. Łukasz Rachel and Lawrence H. Summers, *On Secular Stagnation in the Industrialized World*, NBER working paper 26198 (Cambridge, MA: NBER,

August 2019). The Pew Research Center documented similar trends in terms of diverging income.

36. Thomas Davies, *NGOs: A New History of Transnational Civil Society* (New York: Oxford Scholarship Online, 2014), 157–158 for setbacks to NGO work after the financial crisis.

37. Gregory Mann, *From Empires to NGOs in the West African Sahel; The Road to Nongovernmentality* (Cambridge: Cambridge University Press, 2014).

38. Davies, *NGOs*, 163–165. Cf. Thomas Medvetz, *Think Tanks, Free Market Academics, and the Triumph of the Right* (Chicago: University of Chicago Press, 2012).

39. Cf. Michael Sandel, *The Tyranny of Merit: What's Become of the Common Good?* (New York: Farrar, Straus and Giroux, 2020); Daniel Markovits, *The Meritocracy Trap: How America's Foundational Myth Feeds Inquality, Dismantles the Middle Class, and Devours the Elite* (New York: Penguin, 2019).

40. See two approaches twenty years apart: Charles S. Maier, "The Collapse of Communism in 1989: Approaches for a Future History," *History Workshop Journal* 31 (Spring 2009): 34–59; and "What Have We Learned since 1989?" *Contemporary European History* 18, no. 3 (2009): 253–269.

41. See Karl Ludwig von Haller, *Die Restauration der Staatswissenschaft oder Theorie des natürlich-geselligen Zustands der Chimäre des kunstlich-bürgerlichen entgegengesetzt* [The restoration of state science or the theory of the natural and social condition as opposed to the chimera of an artificial civil one], 2nd ed., 6 vols. (Winterthur, 1820–1831). Published online by Google Play. Relevant material from vol. 1 (1820), chaps. 16–22. For Hegel's scorn, see *Hegel's Philosophy of Right*, trans. T. M. Knox (New York: Oxford University Press, 1967), para. 219, pp. 141 and 258, n157–160.

42. But contrast Marc Bloch's notion of feudalism and its institutions, based on contract, in *Feudal Society* (1940) with Otto Brünner's based on military loyalty in *Land und Herrschaft* (1939; translated as *Land and Lordship*, 1982). For a very brief discussion of nineteenth-century state theories, see Charles S. Maier, *Leviathan 2.0: Inventing Modern Statehood* (Cambridge, MA: Harvard University Press, 2012), 155–163.

43. Herbert Marcuse, *Reason and Revolution: Hegel and the Rise of Social Theory* (New York: Oxford University Press, 1941); Franz Neumann, *Behemoth: The Structure and Practice of National Socialism, 1933–1944*, 2nd ed. (New York: Oxford University Press, 1944); Martin Broszat, *The Hitler State: The Foundation and Development of the Internal Structure of the Third Reich* (London: Longman, 1981); Ian Kershaw, *The Nazi Dictatorship: Problems and Perspectives of Interpretation*, 4th ed. (New York: Oxford University Press, 2000). The use of polyarchy to describe the Nazi regime is not to be confused with Robert Dahl's *Polyarchy: Participation and Opposition* (New Haven, CT: Yale University Press, 1971); cf. Michael Mann, "The Autonomous Power of the State: Its Origins, Mechanisms and Results," *Archives européennes de sociologie* 25 (1984): 185–213.

44. Nazih N. Ayubi, *Over-stating the Arab State: Politics and Society in the Middle East* (London: I. B. Tauris, 1995), xi.

45. Alex de Waal, *The Real Politics of the Horn of Africa: Money, War and the Business of Power* (Cambridge: Polity Press, 2015), 3, 214–216. De Waal calls this state of affairs a political marketplace, but it lacks the openness of a market; it is more an arena for gangs. Familiarity with Africa and other examples led Robert Rotberg to identify "failed states" that could not maintain control over their recognized territory, much less deliver public goods such as peace and prosperity. See the introduction to Robert Rotberg, ed., *When States Fail: Causes and Consequences* (Princeton, NJ: Princeton University Press, 2010).

46. Milan Vaishnav, *When Crime Pays: Money and Muscle in Indian Politics* (New Haven, CT: Yale University Press, 2017), 204.

47. Henry E. Hale, "Introduction: Freeing Post-Soviet Regimes from the Procrustean Bed of Democracy Theory," in *Stubborn Structures*, ed. Magyar. See also Henry E. Hale, *Patronal Politics: Eurasian Regime Dynamics in Comparative Perspective* (Cambridge: Cambridge University Press, 2015).

48. Magyar, *Post-Communist Mafia State*, 68. In his own contribution to his later edited volume, *Stubborn Structures*, Magyar explains why "clientelist," "crony," or "kleptocratic" do not serve as well. See "Towards a Terminology for Post-Communist Regimes," 97–176, which fine-tunes the description.

49. Magyar, *Post-Communist Mafia State*, 8, 12, 21. Masha Gessen has adopted the concept in her discussion of Russia under Putin: *The Future Is History: How Totalitarianism Reclaimed Russia* (New York: Penguin, 2017).

50. Magyar, *Post-Communist Mafia State*, 54. See also chap. 5 for elaboration of the relationship of the oligarchs and the "family," also for comparison with premodern society, interwar dictatorship, and Persian Gulf monarchies. "In the mafia state—since the family is sacred, just as in the traditional mafia—the trial by fire is not the sacrifice of family ties as in the Stalinist regimes, but quite the opposite, to gain inclusion into the political family means the acknowledgment and sanctification of loyalty" (112). For an even longer-term perspective—say, the tragedy that precedes the farce—compare Ronald Syme's description of the Augustan state in *The Roman Revolution* (Oxford: Clarendon, 1939), chap. 33, "Pax et Princeps." For differentiation from related terms such as kleptocracy and elaboration of subtypes of the mafia state with special reference to Venezuela, see Anthea McCarthy-Jones and Mark Turner, "What Is a 'Mafia State,' and How Is One Created?" *Policy Studies* (December 2021), http://doi.org.10.1080/01442872.2021.2012141.

51. Magyar, *Post-Communist Mafia State*, 116. Of course, this was the development that Carl Schmitt argued characterized the parliamentary state as well and indeed characterized regime tendencies that I termed corporatist when writing on the 1920s. On precarity, 142. On the new national corporative bodies, 152–154; "forgiving inclusive

regime," 156. On the granting of monopoly privileges to all sorts of enterprises, tobacco shops, gambling, schoolbooks, and so forth, 195–205.

52. See the useful distinctions and the similar plea by Alex Gourevitch, "What Is Politics without the State? A Reply to Hadfield and Weingast," in *Privatization: Nomos LX*, ed. Jack Knight and Melissa Schwartzberg (New York: New York University Press, 2019), 276–298.

53. "Special Report, Business and the State: The New Interventionism," *The Economist*, January 15, 2022.

54. No liberal in any case. For the classic view of politics as inherently conflictual, see Carl Schmidt, *The Concept of the Political*, trans. George Schwab (New Brunswick, NJ: Rutgers University Press, 1976).

55. James Sheehan, *Where Have All the Soldiers Gone? The Transformation of Modern Europe* (Boston: Houghton Mifflin, 2008).

56. On prediction, see Matthew Connelly, "Future Shock: The End of the World as They Knew It," in *The Shock of the Global: The 1970s in Perspective*, ed. Niall Ferguson, Charles S. Maier, Erez Manela, and Daniel J. Sargent (Cambridge, MA: Harvard University Press, 2010), 337–350.

57. See Maier, *Leviathan 2.0*, 294–306 for another statement of alternatives.

Index

Index

Countervailing power, 163, 228; development and, 187–194; growth and, 187–194; isometric exercise (Charles Atlas) and, 436n4; limits of, 168–175; populism in, 376, 377; productivity and, 175–194; wages and, 175–187

COVID-19, 357; populism and, 375, 390; vaccinations for, 6

Craxi, Bettino, 300, 331

Credit default swaps (CDS), 346, 354

The Crisis of Democracy (Brzezinski), 242

Critical race theory, 322

Croatia, 320

Croce, Benedetto, 386

Crosland, Anthony, 135, 191, 282

Crouch, Colin, 331

Crozier, Michel, 242

Cuba, 25, 197, 217, 291; revolution in, 78, 339. *See also* Castro, Fidel

Cultivation system, in Dutch East Indies, 66–67

Cultural revolution, in China, 24, 271

Cultural zones, of EU, 320

Culture, 323

Curaçao, 59

Czechoslovakia, 143, 197, 199, 271, 282, 297, 337; populism in, 367; Prague Spring in, 203, 299, 302; Soviet Union and, 341

DAC. *See* Development Assistance Committee

Daigne, Blaise, 65

Daley, Richard J., 270, 384

Dalmatian Coast, 55

Davignon, Étienne, 223, 305, 306

Dawes, Charles G., 106

Dawes Plan, 59, 106, 110

Dayton Accords, 320

DDT, 99

Deakin, Arthur, 173

Debray, Régis, 196

Debt, 14, 284–297, 343–359; capital and, 100–114; inflation and, 232; populism and, 362; of students, 478n59

Debt-equity conversions, 291

Debt write-downs. *See* Haircuts

Declaration of Human Rights, 249

Decolonization, 64, 74, 78, 154, 208, 339; governance and, 432n70; World War II and, 69

"Deep Throat," 290

Defense budgets, 70

Le défi américain (Servan-Schreiber), 230

De Gasperi, Alcide, 174

De Gaulle, Charles, 60, 78, 133, 143, 169, 175, 193, 199, 229, 230, 277

Delors, Jacques, 239, 267, 283, 305, 306, 308, 310–312

DeMan, Hendrik, 133

Demand management, 134

Democracy, 395n4; John Adams on, 243; governance of, 85; internal friction in, 42–43; of liberals, 360–361; rights in, 250; wars of, 46–47. *See also* Social democracy; *specific countries*

Democratic Convention, in Chicago, 270

Denationalization, 327

Deng Xiaoping, 206, 281–282, 337

Denmark, 245–246, 314

Deutsche Arbeitsfront, 40

Deutscher Gewerkschaftsbund (German Trade Union Confederation, DGB), 130, 172, 182, 222

Devaluation, 150; in France, 413n34; in Great Depression, 36; by US, 218, 263–264

Development, 27; countervailing power and, 187–194; *mise en valeur* and, 60–69; modernization and, 433n74; after resource empires, 77–80; in resource-empires, 396n10; in third world, 189–190

Developmental-state, 5

Development Assistance Committee (DAC), 251

De Waal, Alex, 383

Dexia SA, 354

DGB. *See* Deutscher Gewerkschaftsbund

Díaz, Porfirio, 28

Dictatorships, 1, 3; in Brazil, 268; internal friction in, 42–43; leisure activities and, 38; in Paraguay, 269; in Spain, 33. *See also specific countries and individuals*

Division of Exchange and Education, 91

Di Vittorio, Giuseppe, 173, 178

Divorce, 269

Djilas, Milovan, 158

Dodge Line, 183

Dogliani, Patrizia, 44

Dollar: Bretton Woods and, 229, 231, 262–263; EU and, 309; gold standard and, 229–230; OPEC and, 264, 288

Domain (or web) of capital, 4, 10–18

Domain (or realm) of governance, 4, 10–18

Dopolavoro, 38

Dot-com crisis, 346

Double-track decision, of NATO, 281

Dower, John, 152

Druck, I. G., 300

Drucker, Peter, 163, 178

Dubai, 276

Dubček, Alexander, 203